ARTHURIAN STUDIES XI

KNIGHTHOOD IN THE MORTE DARTHUR

[redacted]

The Round Table at Winchester Castle

The artist has disregarded the long tradition which places Percival, not Arthur, to the right of the Siege Perilous and so created a striking illustration of Malory's typology of knightly ideals: King Arthur himself represents the central, Round Table ideal of Worshipful knighthood; on either side of him Mordred and Galahad (and in his absence, Lancelot) represent Heroic and True knighthood, respectively.

KNIGHTHOOD IN THE MORTE DARTHUR

SECOND EDITION

Beverly Kennedy

D. S. BREWER

First published 1985 by D. S. Brewer, Cambridge
Second edition in hardback and paperback 1992

D. S. Brewer is an imprint of Boydell & Brewer Ltd
PO Box 9, Woodbridge, Suffolk IP12 3DF, UK
and of Boydell & Brewer Inc.
PO Box 41026, Rochester, NY 14604, USA

ISBN 0 85991 354 6 hardback
ISBN 0 85991 355 4 paperback

British Library Cataloguing-in-Publication Data
Kennedy, Beverly
Knighthood in the "Morte d'Arthur". –
2Rev.ed. – (Arthurian Studies Series,
ISSN 0261-9814)
I. Title II. Series
823.2
ISBN 0-85991-354-6
ISBN 0-85991-355-4 pbk

Library of Congress Cataloging-in-Publication Data
Kennedy, Beverly, 1934–
Knighthood in the Morte darthur / Beverly Kennedy. – 2nd ed.
p. cm. – (Arthurian studies, ISSN 0261-9814 ; 11)
Includes bibliographical references and index.
ISBN 0-85991-354-6 (alk. paper) – ISBN 0-85991-355-4
(pbk. : alk. paper)
1. Malory, Thomas, Sir, 15th cent. Morte d'Arthur. 2. Arthurian
romances – History and criticism. 3. Knights and knighthood in
literature. I. Title. II. Series.
PR2047.K46 1992
823'.2–dc20 92-24437

The paper used in this publication meets the minimum requirements
of American National Standard for Information Sciences –
Permanence of Paper for Printed Library Materials, ANSI Z39.48–1984

Printed in Great Britain by
St Edmundsbury Press Ltd, Bury St Edmunds, Suffolk

Contents

Acknowledgements

It is not easy to acknowledge every indebtedness of a book which has been as long in the making as this one. To begin, I must thank Robert M. Lumiansky, in whose graduate seminar I first encountered Malory's work and first attempted to answer the question, 'What does knighthood mean in the *Morte Darthur*?' I tried again to answer that question in my Ph.D. dissertation, 'The Hierarchy of Knighthood in Sir Thomas Malory's *Morte Darthur*' (Duke University, 1969), and for that attempt I must thank Edmund Reiss for his willingness to supervise the final stages of writing. Several years passed before I was able to return to my question. I returned to it, however, with a critical approach much more suitable to the task than the source-study approach I had used in my dissertation. For this new approach I must thank my husband, the cultural anthropologist, A. Norman Klein. I must also thank Marianopolis College for granting me a sabbatical leave for the year, 1978/79, during which I did much of the reading I had to do before I could undertake an historicist interpretation of the meaning of knighthood in Malory's book.

The extent of my indebtedness to the work of other critics, editors and scholars can be gauged by the length of the lists of primary and secondary sources at the end of this book. Over and above the acknowledgements expressed in those lists, however, I want to give special thanks to Robert H. Wilson and P.J.C. Field, whose correspondence over the years has been of inestimable value to me. In this regard I should also mention the helpful letters and conversation of Robert Kelly, Richard Griffith and Victor Haines. Finally, I would like to express a special debt of gratitude to Tomomi Kato for his magnificent *Concordance* to Malory's work. Without that I could not have done the kind of textual analysis which proved necessary in order to answer my question.

For her help with editing, proof-reading and indexing the manuscript I want to thank Suzy Margot Slavin, Acting Head of Reference at the McLennan Library of McGill University. I would also like to thank Grace Prince, Reference Librarian at Marianopolis College, for her help with inter-library loans and Andrea Pitt and Roslyn Yearwood for typing the manuscript.

Finally, I want to thank my children, Anna, Mia, James, Jonathan and Geoffrey Ginter. Without their understanding and support I could not have written this book and therefore I dedicate it to them.

Montreal
November 1984

Note on Sources and Documentation

The style of documentation used in this book is the parenthetical style recently adopted by the Modern Language Association of America. Parenthetical references appear both in the text and in the explanatory notes and are kept as brief as possible, citing page (paragraph or line) numbers only, except when either the last name of the author, or author and brief title, are necessary for complete identification. This system greatly reduces the volume of end-notes. At the same time it simplifies the process of recovering full bibliographical data for any particular reference, since this can be located easily in the bibliography of works cited.

References to Malory's text are to page and line numbers of the revised second edition of the *Works of Sir Thomas Malory*, edited by Eugene Vinaver. Within each parenthetical citation I have also added a reference to the relevant book and chapter division of the Caxton text (e.g. 16.22–23:I.7). It is my hope that such a dual reference system will make this study useful not only to Malory scholars and teachers but also to these students and general readers who are more familiar with Caxton's edition of *Morte Darthur*.

Finally, there are a few parenthetical references for which no entry will be found in the lists of primary and secondary sources. These include the works of Chaucer and Shakespeare, the *Oxford English Dictionary* (*OED*) and the *Middle English Dictionary* (*MED*).

Preface to the Second Edition

If I had written the first edition of this book two or three years later than I did, I might well have called it a 'new-historicist' study, since I had been greatly influenced by the work of new-historicist literary critics and hermeneutic anthropologists.[1] On the one hand, I saw Malory's text as 'an extraordinarily sensitive register of the complex struggles and harmonies' of knightly culture in fifteenth-century England (Greenblatt 5). On the other, I also saw it as a written record of the 'control mechanisms' created by knightly society for 'the governing of behavior' (Geertz 44), and therefore as an interactive part of that knightly culture. In other words, I saw that the *Morte Darthur*, as written by the knight, Sir Thomas Malory, was fundamentally about knighthood.[2] I still see it this way; however, my understanding of the hermeneutic process by which I arrived at this historicist interpretation has been changed by reading the work of Hans Robert Jauss.

Jauss's reception theory offers a way to bridge the gaps which other literary theories have opened up between language and 'reality' on the one hand, and between past and present, on the other.[3] What bridges the gap between texts and the 'real' world is the experience of the reader, who participates in both. And what bridges the gap between past and present is the commonality of the human aesthetic response, even in readers who are responding to the same text from within two different cultures, what Jauss would call two different 'horizons of expectation'. Indeed, Jauss would argue that it is the modern reader's initial aesthetic response to a medieval text which makes historical understanding across the distance in time 'possible . . . in the first place' (*Towards an Aesthetic of Reception*, 146).

According to Jauss the modern critic's next goal as a reader of medieval texts should be to reconstruct, insofar as this is possible, the medieval reader's 'horizon of expectation'. Such a reconstruction will require two sorts of effort: first, paying particular attention to the medieval text's assumptions regarding its readers and second, learning as much as one can of those medieval readers' previous cultural experience. The end of this effort will be 'proper fusion' of the medieval and modern horizons of expectation. The historicist interpretation of the text which the critic then develops within this broader horizon will not be exactly like that of a medieval reader; however, it will avoid the dangers of a reading which is unconsciously distorted by modern prejudices and expectations of meaning.

It seems to me that the *Morte Darthur* makes two major assumptions about its readers. First, it assumes that they will be familiar with every aspect of knighthood and will enjoy extended descriptions of knightly activities like battles and tournaments, much as modern fans enjoy long games of cricket or baseball. Second, it assumes that its readers will be familiar in general terms with the events of Arthur's reign, but will not be intimately acquainted with the French romance versions (or so I infer from Malory's habit of invoking a French source whenever he is being particularly innovative). In other words, Malory's text assumes that its readers will be very English and therefore not only proud of their great king, Arthur, the peer of Caesar and Charlemagne, but anxious to learn why his reign should have ended in catastrophe.

These assumptions suggest that Malory's principal thematic concerns in writing the history of Arthur's reign were knighthood and kingship. What I discovered in the process of reconstructing the medieval reader's horizon of expectation, was that both of these were pervasive concerns in England in the fifteenth century. Late medieval treatises on knighthood and the work of historians of late medieval culture, show that both knighthood and kingship were undergoing profound change during this period. Knighthood was changing, as it become less a matter of noble privilege and more a matter of political and military service to the Crown. And kingship was changing, as late feudal monarchs began the process of arrogating to themselves all forms of coercive power, prerequisite to the formation of a nation-state.

Malory's concern with knighthood in the *Morte Darthur* may be rephrased quite simply in the form of a question: What does it mean to be a *good* knight? Modern critics have almost always responded to this question with a single answer, no doubt because 'chivalry' has survived into the modern world as a single concept, the one implied in that much abused cliché, 'Chivalry is (or is not) dead.' This concept of chivalry as the social practice and ethical code of the noble man is, of course, to be found in the *Morte Darthur*, but only as subsumed under the broader notion of knightly honour, or 'worship'. The primary definition of *chyvalry* in Malory's text is military, referring either to the art of fighting on horseback (*MED* 4b) or to a group of such trained fighters (*MED* 1). However, by a ratio of ten to one Malory himself prefers the term *knyghthode*, whether he is referring to its chief military function, skill in fighting on horseback (*MED* 1d), or to its chief political function as the 'High Order' instituted by God to do the temporal office of governance.[4]

The military and political importance of knighthood in the *Morte Darthur* has been overlooked by modern critics mostly, I think, because of the wide acceptance of Huizinga's thesis that knighthood was 'waning' in the later Middle Ages. We now know that Huizinga was wrong. Indeed, thanks to the recent work of historians like Juliet Barker, J.M.W. Bean, M.G.A. Vale, Maurice Keen and D'Arcy Boulton, we now know that the fifteenth-century may well have been the golden age of chivalry. Certainly it was the golden age of the princely orders of chivalry (Boulton). And their existence may partially explain why, despite the invention of cannon and gunpowder, knighthood did not actually begin to wane in military importance until well into the sixteenth century and continued to be of supreme political importance throughout the Elizabethan period (McCoy).

If it is a mistake to think that late medieval chivalry was primarily a social phenomenon, the code of manners and ethics of the knightly class, it is equally mistaken to think that there was only one code, to which all knights adhered.[5] In fact, there were at least three competing views of knighthood in Malory's fifteenth-century English culture, each with its own code of ethics.

The first of these finds its historical roots in the feudal and military past and is well represented in early medieval epic and *chanson de geste*. This view regards knighthood as the privilege of the aristocracy and judges a knight to be *good* if he is courageous and skilfull in battle and invariably loyal to his lord. The lord of such a knight is likely to be his kinsman, also, and when he is not, a serious conflict of loyalties may occur. Indeed, the family loyalty of such a knight is so great that he commonly pursues the blood feud. He is a Christian, but his God is a tribal God and he himself is a fatalist. In other words, he assumes that his enemies are also God's enemies (and vice-versa) and he believes that God determines his destiny.

The second view of knighthood finds its historical roots in the crusades and is represented in the Grail romances and in religious treatises about knighthood. This view regards knighthood as a 'High Order', ordained by God to govern Christendom, and led by the Holy Roman Emperor. Not surprisingly, therefore, in this view the *good* knight must have more than the feudal virtues of prowess, courage and loyalty. He must also have the religious virtues of piety, chastity and humility. Such a knight believes that he ought to be loyal to God, above all, and that the highest form of knightly service is the religious Crusade. He also believes that God renders the verdict in trial by battle and he knows that a knight must have the grace of God to be fortunate in arms, but he is not a fatalist; rather, he accepts the late-medieval providentialist belief that the future is determined by God and man acting in concert.

The third view of knighthood finds its historical roots in the court culture of the late Middle Ages and is represented both in the French prose romances and in some late medieval treatises on knighthood. This view regards knighthood as an honour bestowed by the king and so judges a knight to be *good* if, in addition to the feudal virtues, he has the virtues and accomplishments expected of a courtier. In order to be successful in a career at court, such a knight must demonstrate courtesy (i.e. good manners but also competence in the courtly pastimes, e.g. dancing, harping, hunting and hawking). And he must demonstrate prudence and justice, both of which are necessary to agents of royal governance.[6] He does not, however, need the religious virtues, and in fact such a knight discounts the likelihood that God will intervene directly in the affairs of men. He trusts rather that his own rationality, strength and courage will enable him to achieve success. This is clearly the most modern of the three views.

Each of these views of knighthood was current and available to Malory and his contemporaries. Which view a particular knight might adopt would have been determined partly by temperament, partly by belief and partly by status or office. Certainly the great knights, or barons, would have been more likely to adopt the feudal view of knighthood than those lesser men who were raised to knighthood by the king and hoped to carve out a career in his service. And either magnate or courtier could have adopted the religious view of his office if he were a very pious man. There must have been a good deal of overlap, for the three views are not mutually exclusive; nevertheless, they do suggest differing social and political orientations and correspondingly different primary loyalties: to family, to God, or to king (and career).

Most of the text of Malory's *Morte Darthur* is devoted to elaborating these three views of knighthood. The courtly and political view of knighthood expressed in King Arthur's pentecostal oath is the most prominent because it is the view of King Arthur himself and most of his knights of the Round Table, Tristram being the greatest of these. But it is not the only view. On the one hand, Gawain and his brethren represent the older, more feudal view that knighthood is the privilege of the aristocratic class and ought to be exercised primarily in the interest of the family. And on the other, Lancelot, Gareth, and the three Grail knights represent the religious view that knighthood was ordained by God to protect and govern Christendom.[7]

These three views produce three distinct types of knight in Malory's text: the Heroic knight, who has only the basic feudal virtues to recommend him; the True knight who combines feudal and religious virtues (and in some cases courtly virtues as well); and the Worshipful knight, who combines feudal and courtly virtues. Depending upon the specific context of time, place and activity, any one of the three types may be perceived as 'good'. The Heroic knight looks best on the field of battle.

The True knight excels in the forest of adventure, and the Worshipful knight shines at court. However, Malory gives his readers the opportunity to judge all of his main characters in each of the three knightly settings: as warriors on the battlefield, as knights-errant in quest of adventure and as courtiers.[8]

These three types — the Heroic, the True and the Worshipful — are supremely embodied in the *Morte Darthur* in the three greatest knights at Arthur's court: Gawain, Lancelot and Tristram, respectively.

I use the word 'type' here in a sense which encompasses both the Weberian notion of 'ideal types' and the Christian exegetical notion of figural types. Malory's types are like Weberian 'ideal types' because they embody a distinct political, religious and therefore ethical point of view within late medieval culture. Indeed, they function within Malory's text in much the same way that George Lukács has shown such types to function in nineteenth-century realist literature.[9] At the same time, Malory's types are also figural types in the modified sense suggested by Warren Ginzberg's phrase, 'literary typology.' In Chrétien's *Yvain*, for example, Ginzberg argues that the adventures of Calogrenant prefigure those of Yvain in a pattern of foreshadowing and fulfillment (195). In Malory's *Morte Darthur*, I would argue that the adventures of every knight foreshadow those of every other knight to come. As a consequence, both the movement and the pattern which results are quite different. The movement is cumulative and the pattern finally produced is made up of three types rather than two (type and anti-type). Thus Malory's typology of knighthood emerges as more of a taxonomy than a set of figural relationships, although the latter pattern is also occasionally to be seen.[10]

Malory's types are not 'characters' in the modern sense developed by novelistic techniques, which is why Jill Mann can say that Malory was not interested in 'character' ('Knightly' 332). Rather, they are characters in the same sense as Chaucer's Canterbury pilgrims are characters, character being defined here as *condicioun* (*MED* 3a–b), the sum of a man's habits, disposition and beliefs.[11] As a consequence, Malory's characters are fairly static; nevertheless, some do change under the influence of strong emotion. For example, in the tale of Tristram, both Lancelot and Palomides are driven to change their 'conducions' by their love for an unattainable woman. Each man becomes more courtly, more like Tristram. Thus, for love of Isode, Palomides gives up the barbarous ways of an Heroic knight (e.g. abducting the lady of his choice) and so achieves moral progress. On the other hand, for love of Guinevere, Lancelot gives up the humility and devotion to chastity which had characterized him earlier as a True knight and so suffers a moral decline.

Lancelot undergoes a similar change and for the same reasons, in the post-Grail narrative. During the Quest for the Holy Grail he heartily repented his sins of pride and lechery, and so redeemed his True knighthood; however, he still loves the queen. In the final, post-Grail narrative, therefore, we see Lancelot struggling to harmonize his love of Guinevere with his love of God and Arthur through the practice of 'vertuouse love'. In the language of late medieval authors like Walter Hilton and Nicholas Love, Lancelot has decided to practice the ideal of the 'mixed life'. That is to say, rather than renounce Arthur's service for the cloistered life of religious contemplation, as Galahad and Percival have done, he will try to achieve Christian perfection in the world by incorporating prayer and meditation (the core of the contemplative life) into an active life of service to his fellow Christians.[12] Lancelot's struggle to love the queen virtuously while living the 'mixed life' at court ends with failure in the 'Knight of the Cart' episode. Immediately following this, however, Malory invents the miraculous 'Healing of Sir Urry' to show that Lancelot has once again repented his sins and been forgiven by God.[13]

Lancelot's changes of *condicioun* are themselves part of what makes him typical of True knighthood, since they take the form of sinful actions followed by repentance. No Christian man can expect to be perfect while living in this world 'unstable' and Lancelot would not be credible as an example of True Knighthood if he never erred. This is not necessarily true of the other two types, however, and in fact they do not change as much. The only dramatic examples other than that of Palomides, cited above, involve Arthur, who sometimes deviates from the ethical standards of Worshipful knighthood when faced with challenges to his royal dignity and power. For example, when faced with the likelihood that his incestuously begotten son will destroy him, he puts all infants born at the same time out to sea in a rudderless boat.

Which brings us to Malory's second major concern, kingship. Insofar as Arthur is a knight first, this concern can also be expressed by the question, What makes a knight/king *good*? But insofar as Arthur is a king first, the important question is, why did his reign end in catastrophe?

The *Morte Darthur* provides two contexts within which to answer these questions, the one practical, or political and the other theoretical, or religious. This division reflects a very real distinction in the way late medieval people actually judged the goodness of their kings. In practical, political terms, the king who could maintain himself in power and give peace and stability to his people was a good king. Machiavelli had not yet written his treatise justifying the cruelty of princes in the name of political stability, but successful late feudal monarchs were already practicing what Machiavelli would later preach. On the other hand, in theory, medieval writers upheld the notion that good governance was a moral matter, that indeed, governance could be no better than the moral quality of the governors. This theory was, of course, informed by the religious view of the king as the highest officer of the Order of Knighthood in the realm and thus the vicar of God in matters of temporal governance. (It is in accordance with this view that Malory shows Arthur being knighted before he is crowned king.) And it was widely believed among pious Christians (sometimes in the teeth of the evidence) that God would punish a bad king by bringing him down.

Is Arthur himself a good knight? A good king? Most modern readers of the *Morte Darthur* would not hesitate to say yes, but then most modern readers have been influenced by more recent Arthurian works like Tennyson's *Idylls of the King* or T. H. White's *Once and Future King*, both of which idealize the British monarch. And English readers in particular, tend to view Arthur with great reverence. However, it is extremely doubtful that any late fifteenth-century reader would have perceived Arthur in this way.

Fifteenth-century Englishmen did not question the historicity of Arthur but they did not idealize him, either. The Tudor glorification of Arthur had not happened yet, as Christopher Dean has recently reminded us. At the same time, the overwhelming popularity of the English chronicle history known as the *Brut* ensured a general climate of 'customary belief' in Arthur, though some chroniclers doubted some of the stories told about him.[14] Even more indicative of late medieval attitudes towards Arthur is the fact that some chroniclers criticized his political judgment (Matheson 'King Arthur' 263). That is to say, even as they acknowledged Arthur's greatness, they showed that they did not regard him as above criticism, any more than Alexander or Charlemagne or any of the other Nine Worthies. To be sure, fifteenth-century English chroniclers liked to make Arthur look as good as possible. Therefore, they usually paid little or no attention to the French romance tradition. Hardyng is quite remarkable for his inclusion of the Quest of the Holy Grail in his chronicle. And Malory is even more remarkable for including in his book everything he could find about Arthur. Richard Barber believes that he must have been 'something of an Arthurian expert' for his time ('Vera Historia' 75). The consequence of this was, however, that Malory had to deal with all of Arthur's alleged faults as a monarch.

One might expect him to have dealt with them in the moralizing spirit of late medieval historical biographies like Lydgate's 'cronycule of Julius Caesar,' better known as *The Serpent of Division*. Lydgate wrote this work at the request of Humphrey, Duke of Gloucester, as a cautionary tale aimed at averting civil strife in England (Matheson, 'Historical Prose' 229). And so, in explaining the downfall of Caesar, Lydgate gives special emphasis to the dangers of pride, willfulness and that special blindness which long prosperity can produce in the great

(56). But Malory never moralizes in this way. Rather he dramatizes Arthur's political faults, leaving his readers free to draw their own conclusions. For example, Malory's first readers must have seen Arthur's nepotism, when the king fails to punish his nephews for the murders of Pellinor, Lamorak and Margawse. And whatever their moral judgment of him for this failure in 'true justyce', they could not deny the political implication that he was either unwilling or unable to control the behaviour of his nephews.[15]

Arthur is even more seriously flawed, of course, if judged by the religious standards of True knighthood, for he is lacking not only in humility, but also in chastity and piety. He indulges in casual sexual liaisons and does not believe that God renders the verdict in trial by battle. And yet, Malory emphasizes that Arthur is maintained as King of England not only by the loyalty and service of his Round Table knights but also by God's special grace, symbolized by the presence of the Grail in Arthur's kingdom. In the post-Grail narrative, Arthur no longer has that special grace, for God has commanded Galahad to remove the Grail, but he still has the loyalty and service of the remnant of his Round Table knights (less than half of whom have survived the Quest). Chief among these are the Heroic knight, Gawain, and the redeemed True knight, Lancelot, both leaders of a large following of knights. There should have been a third group of knights, led by either Pellinor or Lamorak, and exemplifying Worshipful knighthood, but there is not, because Gawain and his brethren have murdered both of these men. Malory's first readers would have noticed this, too, for it means that now Arthur's chief support comes from men who serve him for reasons other than the fact that he is king of England. Gawain serves Arthur because he is his uncle, his mother's brother, and therefore his nearest and dearest kinsmen. And Lancelot serves Arthur because he is the Holy Roman Emperor, the highest officer in the High Order of Knighthood, overlord of the King of France, and the man who made him knight.

Thus, in the post-Grail narrative, Arthur is supported primarily by his kinsmen, on one side, and by Lancelot and his followers on the other. This is exactly his position as depicted on the Winchester Round Table (see frontispiece) by an artist who had no doubt read Malory's work (Field, 'Winchester' 204). The Winchester artist emphasizes the contrast between the two types of knight who support the king, by seating Arthur between Mordred and Galahad. Mordred is the worst of the Heroic knights because he betrays even his own kinsman, while Galahad is the best of the True knights because he is the most devoted to the service of God. However, once Galahad has departed at the end of the Grail Quest, Arthur would be left sitting between his natural son, Mordred, on his right, and, on his left, his son-in-knighthood, Lancelot. Moreover, as the

Winchester artist must have known, in Malory's version of the Death of Arthur, the king has to choose between them.

When Mordred accuses Lancelot of committing adultery with the queen, Arthur is faced with a judicial crisis which he cannot resolve in the usual way. Up to now, the king has always been able to fulfill his promise to stand with 'true justyce' by judging for himself which party is in the right and then ensuring that the stronger knight fight for that side in trial by battle. But when Lancelot is accused of treason, Arthur knows that there is no knight strong enough to 'prove' his guilt by battle, certainly not either of his accusers, Mordred or Aggravayne. Consequently, Arthur resorts to the clansman's tactics for doing justice: he allows Mordred and Aggravayne to set an ambush outside the queen's chamber, with permission to kill the guilty couple on the spot.

By the law of the land in fifteenth-century England, the crime of which Lancelot stands accused is high treason. Modern readers do not take that political fact into consideration, but they should, because it offers the best possible explanation for Malory's radical reinterpretation of the Lancelot-Guinevere love story. Malory knew that his English readers would not respond to the adultery in the same way as the French, for whom Arthur was largely a figure of romance. English readers would see Lancelot's adultery with the wife of their king as high treason. Therefore it is hardly surprising that Malory should have eliminated from his version all but one instance of actual adultery ('The knight of the Cart'). He did this, *not* because he was embarrassed by his hero's sexual sin, but because he was horrified by his treason against Arthur.[16]

The question then arises, how would Malory's first audiences have responded to this radical reinterpretation of the love story? The answer depends upon how familiar one thinks Malory's English readers were with the French romances. What we know of fifteenth-century English readers suggests that their need for translations of French romances increased throughout the century. Before Malory's work there had been translations of the early history of the Grail and of Arthur, and of the Death of Arthur, but Malory himself was the first to render into English the whole story of Lancelot, of Tristram and of the Grail Quest. I still think that the best evidence in this regard is Malory's own text, particularly his habit of pretending that his innovations are authorized by his 'French book'. It seems obvious to me that he does not expect his readers to see through this deception. Modern scholars do, of course, but this only means that their extensive knowledge of Malory's French sources allows them to read Malory's text in a way that few, if any, fifteenth-century English readers could have done.

Most fifteenth-century Englishmen would have been familiar with the general outlines of the story and so would have known that Lancelot was the queen's lover. But they would not have known what his attitude as a lover was, nor how many times he actually committed adultery with the queen. If they had heard of any instance of actual adultery, it would have been the most famous one, that related in 'the Knight of the Cart'. However, their notion of exactly when this incident occurred would have been extremely vague, or so Malory seems to assume when he radically departs from the Vulgate cycle to place it after, rather than before the Quest of the Holy Grail.[17] Therefore, I believe most of Malory's first readers would have accepted without question Malory's characterization of Lancelot as the queen's true lover. As for those who knew the French romances well, I believe that they, too, would have welcomed his version of the love story, for it not only preserves Arthur from the stigma of repeated cuckoldry, it also allows Lancelot to exemplify, however imperfectly, the religious ideal of True knighthood. If this is not the way he was, it is the way he should have been.

Modern readers who wish to have an historical understanding of Malory's text must try to see Lancelot as Malory's first readers would have seen him. And this means that they must overcome the modern tendency to view striving for religious perfection in this world as either impossible or dangerous. For example, Judson Allen argues that Lancelot's goodness throughout the Death of Arthur makes him a 'slandered and disordering outsider whose absent presence explains the chaos of Book Eight.' And he goes on to say that while the ideal of such goodness is 'most desirable', its prolonged 'real presence' in society 'causes either chaos or fascism (251–52). This is a perfectly understandable modern response. But in Malory's time the idea that a lay person might achieve religious perfection while living the 'mixed life' in this world was still very new. Pious men and women went on pilgrimage and wore hair shirts and built private chapels so that they might pray daily and regarded their work in the world as a charitable service to their fellow Christians. They accepted the likelihood of failure but they also believed in the efficacy of repentance, and so there could be no question of not continuing the struggle to achieve reformation in the image of Christ.

In the following six chapters I offer an interpretation of the *Morte Darthur* which is, as nearly as I can make it so, the result of reading his text as I think Malory's first readers would have done, having expanded my own horizon of expectation by experiencing their world through the texts available to me. In the first four chapters I deal primarily with the political point of view and with Malory's elaboration of the three types of knighthood. In the fifth chapter, I turn to the religious point of view and look at Malory's versions of the tale of Balin and the Grail Quest and his use of the *hap* motif. In the sixth chapter I offer an interpretation of the post-Grail narrative as an exploration of 'true justyce' which takes both political and religious points of view into account.

In the revised and expanded conclusions, now the seventh chapter, entitled 'Malory's 'hoole book' and the Death of Arthur', I show how Malory's typology determines not only his handling of the Death of Arthur but also the shape of his 'hoole book'. Medieval readers would have had no difficulty perceiving that it is Malory's elaboration of these three types of knight which structures and unifies his work. If modern readers perceive a lack of unity in the *Morte Darthur* that is because modern notions of what constitutes unity have developed far beyond the late medieval reader's horizon of expectation.

1

The High Order of Knighthood

In the *Morte Darthur* Sir Thomas Malory is clearly concerned with the problems of governance in a late feudal monarchy. His approach to those problems is not that of a man learned in the Latin literature of medieval political theory, however; rather it is that of a man learned in the theory and practice of knighthood.[1] His work assumes that governance is the office of knighthood. Moreover, his representation of knighthood seems to have been informed by those classic treatises which describe the office of the High Order of Knighthood in political terms. Indeed, to speak of knighthood as a 'High Order', as Malory often does, is to take for granted the Christian ideology taught by these treatises, that God himself ordained knighthood to undertake the task of temporal governance. It would be well, therefore, to look briefly at the most popular and influential of these treatises on knighthood before going on to examine the way Malory depicts Arthur's governance and in particular the role his knights have to play in it.

Late Medieval Views of Knighthood

The classic statement of the religious view of knighthood as the governing order of society appears in Ramon Lull's *Libro del orden de caballeria*. Written sometime during the final quarter of the thirteenth century it was soon translated into French to become the standard work on the subject for the next two hundred and fifty years. In Malory's England it was three times translated from the French into English, the best known and most widely distributed translation being that of William Caxton (1484). We know that Caxton was careful to print only those works for which he could be sure of an audience; therefore, the fact that he went to the trouble of translating and printing *The Book of the Ordre of Chyualry* the year before he printed Sir Thomas Malory's *Morte Darthur*, would seem to confirm the continuing popularity and authority of Lull's treatise.

A profoundly religious man, Lull was not concerned with the knight's cultivation of the social graces. Rather he was concerned to define the knight's military and political office as protector of the realm and dispenser of justice. Lull assumes that the use of coercive force will be necessary in order to have justice in this post-lapsarian world. Once 'cruelty, Iniury, desloyalte and falsenes' have entered the hearts of men, justice may be restored only 'by drede' to the 'honour, in which she was wonte to be' (15). That is why, in the beginning, knighthood was established:

> ... And therfore alle the peple was deuyded by thousandes, And of eche thousand was chosen a man moost loyal, most stronge, and of most noble courage, & better enseygned and manerd than al the other (15).

Lull's 'just-so' story makes the institution of knighthood as old as human society itself and it proved enduringly attractive as an origin myth, perhaps partly because he is careful not to specify who made the original choice of one out of a thousand. By the fifteenth century, however, one Frenchman could assert quite confidently that this choice was made by the king 'pour ce qu'il peust le peuple garantir contre les anemis et les mauves justiciers' (E. Kennedy, 'King Arthur' 194), whereas a Scottish knight could assert with equal confidence that 'the peple' made that choice (Hay 11). Their respective choices may well reflect the difference between governance in France and governance in England which Sir John Fortescue was later to characterize as the difference between an absolute monarchy and a monarchy limited by the consent of the people (111–13).

Lull divides his treatise into several sections, in proper scholastic style. After discussing the origin of knighthood, he devotes one chapter to defining the 'office' of knighthood, one to the proper examination of the squire who desires to be admitted into the order, one to the ritual of ordination, and one to the symbolic significance of the knight's arms. He continues with a chapter on the virtues of body and spirit which the true knight must have and concludes with a section in which he argues that since knighthood 'is moche necessary as touchyng the gouernement of the world' (115) it ought to be honoured by all men, high and low, and above all by those who have received the high order.

Lull's treatise makes governance the divinely ordained 'office' of the knight, whether he be emperor, king, duke, baron, or simple knight, and asserts that any knight who preys upon the poor people whom he ought to protect is not a true knight. Lull never says that a man must be of noble birth in order to be admitted into the high order of knighthood. However, his French, Scottish and English translators of the fourteenth and fifteenth centuries more accurately reflect the bias of the hereditary nobility when they say that knights ought to be of noble birth. They cannot deny that it is possible to make knights of commoners ('peple of lytyl lygnage'); however, they assert that it ought not to be done because low born men, like women, will lack that nobility of heart ('noblesse de courage') which is necessary to a knight, and which is natural to a man of high 'parage' (Lull 57, 58; Hay 36–38). At the same time, they fully accept Lull's notion that to be a true knight one must be morally virtuous. Typically, William Caxton manages to have it both ways when he says of his translation, that it 'is not requyste to euery comyn man to haue, but to noble gentylmen that by their vertu entende to come & entre in to the noble ordre of chyualry . . . (121).

Lull's 'lytyl booke' became a classic and spread the Christian ideology of knighthood throughout Europe. According to this ideology all knights, from the Holy Roman Emperor down to the most humble belted knight, were called upon to do justice in God's name by virtue of their office and their order. What is more, by analogy with the priestly hierarchy of the Church (from the Pope on down to the most humble parish priest), the lesser knights were to be obedient to the greater in performing their divinely ordained office.

Lull influenced many writers on the subject, some of whom developed his analogy between knighthood and priesthood even farther than he did. For example, in the mid-fourteenth century, the great French knight Sir Geoffrey de Charny argued that knighthood is a higher order than the order of regular clergy and second only to the order of secular clergy, resting his case on the fact that it is much more difficult to serve God in the world than in the cloister. And though he would not go so far as to make knighthood the highest of God's orders, he would nevertheless conclude from his personal experience that of all orders it is the 'plus doubteux, périlleux et pénibles à faire pour les corps et pour les âmes que nulles autres' (523). One hundred years later, a Scottish knight, Sir Gilbert Hay, took it upon himself to digress from Lull's treatise in order to develop the same argument:

> For and men wald wele knaw and consider the grete chargis and dewiteis that folowis the said ordre, with saule perile, and worschip oft in were, they sald stand grete aw to tak that noble ordre, mare na to be outhir monk, or frere, or othir religiouse of the hardest order that is. . . (39; Lull 62)

Hay's comparison with the orders of friars is of particular interest, since friars were also obliged to fulfill the demands of their order while serving God in the world. Clearly it is the perils which assault a man's body and 'worschip' as well as his 'saule' which make the life of the knight the most difficult.

The Christian ideology of knighthood presumes that a knight's first loyalty is to God rather than to his feudal superior. However, if all knights, from the Holy Roman Emperor down, were to observe the ten commandments and faithfully govern their fellow Christians, protecting them and giving them justice, there should be no conflict between serving one's feudal lord and serving God. Nor does Lull ever broach the possibility of such conflict. However, in his fifteenth-century translation, Sir Gilbert Hay does, by implication:

> . . . all knychtis suld think that there is a lord and syre abone [sic] all knychtis, for the honour of quham thai ar all maid knychtis for to do his will, and serve him fyrst, and syne thair temporale lordis (20).

That Hay should find it necessary to make explicit the knight's obligation to put God first, even before his temporal lord, suggests that the Christian ideology of knighthood had worked so well to transform independent barons into servants of the Crown that by the mid-fifteenth century both kings and knights were overlooking their primary obligation to God.

In fifteenth-century England and France the religious view of knighthood as a great temporal 'order' of Christendom was not the only view put forward in books on the subject.[2] A more rational, pragmatic and humanist view was beginning to find its way into treatises on knighthood like Christine de Pizan's *Epistle of Othea to Hector* (1400) and *The Boke of Noblesse* (c.1461); into chivalric biographies like Antoine de la Sale's *Petit Jehan de Saintré* and Jean de Bueil's *Le Jouvencel*; and into military manuals like the anonymous *Knyghthode and Bataile* (c.1457) and Christine de Pizan's *Livre des fais d'armes et de chevalerie* (c.1410), translated as *The Book of Fayttes of Armes and Chyualrye* by William Caxton in 1489. What all these works have in common is a tendency to stress the practical details of a knight's career, either as a military leader or soldier in the field, or as a local lord or courtier in the king's service. The moral standards they establish are also very high. They exhort the knight to relate to his foes on the battlefield with fairness and compassion, to relate to the ladies of the court with courtesy and respect, and to be loyal to his king and country. However, they assume that both the motives and the rewards for his moral behaviour will be as much, if not more, of this world as of the next. They assume that the knight is a careerist and assure him that if he adheres to this chivalric code of behaviour, he will enjoy a successful and honourable career in the service of the king.

The works of Christine de Pizan may be taken as representative of these fifteenth-century manuals of chivalry. Her *Epistle of Othea to Hector*, first translated into English about 1440 by Stephen Scrope, gives the knight the sort of instruction he will need in order to succeed at court. Indeed, her work may be seen as the culmination of a long tradition growing out of those French romances in which young men were instructed by their aunts or mothers in the behaviour appropriate to a knight before they set off for the court of the King (Bornstein, *Mirrors* 48–49). Christine divides her work into one hundred parts, each consisting of one verse epistle written by Othea the Goddess of Prudence to Hector the great Trojan knight and two separate commentaries upon the epistle. The first commentary, the 'glose', is for the moral edification of the knight and the second, the 'moralité' is for his spiritual instruction. Thus, as Christine observes in her preface, the knight who reads her book will be 'armed with prudent polecye, / In þis present lyff hymselff to auaunce, / & to hys soule gyff gostely sustenaunce' (6). It is significant, I think, that Christine can use the metaphor, 'gostly chiualry' for the knight's struggle to win his soul's salvation and, at the same time, urge him to pursue 'honour and prowess' in the world. Clearly she does not perceive the two goals, the one spiritual and the other worldly, to be inherently contradictory so long as the pursuit of worldly goals does not lead to immoral conduct. In fact, she interprets the very first epistle of Prudence (Othea) to mean that moral conduct is just as 'necessarye to gode polecye' in worldly terms as it is in godly terms to the 'chiualrous spryte' (12–13).

Christine's *Epistle of Othea* has little to say about the knight as a soldier. She makes up for this lack, however, in the *Livre des fais d'armes et de la chevalerie* which Caxton later translated into English. In this work she devotes two chapters to practical information regarding military strategy and tactics, information which she gleaned from classical sources, and two chapters to the *ius militari*, the law of arms. Her book is eminently practical in orientation; nevertheless, an idealized portrait of the knight as soldier emerges: he is prudent, he knows how to 'gouerne his owen peple' and 'to doo right where he ought to doo it'; he is, above all, 'trewe' to his king and loving to God (Bornstein, *Mirrors* 40–44).

Christine's treatises on knighthood differ from that of Ramon Lull in several fundamental ways. First of all, whereas Lull devotes an entire chapter to defining the knight's office, dividing it into parts, or 'items' (such as defence of the Church and one's temporal lord; defence of poor men, women and children; and maintenance of justice), Christine assumes that the knight already knows his office. In the 'gloses' of her *Epistle* she instructs the knight as to the sort of behaviour which will help him get ahead at court, and in the *Fais d'armes* she instructs him as to the sort of behaviour which will help him win wars. She addresses a knight who sees himself as a soldier and a courtier, at least part of the time, whereas Lull addresses a knight who sees himself as a dispenser of justice, a lord who does God's own office. The second and third differences are related to the first. Christine assumes that knighthood is a caste of society, that knights form a social and military elite. On the other hand, Lull describes knighthood as a 'hygh order' established by God and open to any man of virtue. Finally, Christine is often explicitly rationalist. For example, in the thirty-ninth epistle she advises the knight to trust in the science of medicine and 'trew bookes of experience of phesyke' rather than in 'enchauntment & charmez' (66). In the sixty-eighth epistle she advises him not to trust in dreams (104–5) and in the forty-eighth to 'Gyde' himself by 'resoun' (78). Moreover, in the *Fais d'armes* Christine utterly rejects the ancient sacral mode of trial by battle (259). On the other hand, while Lull also advises the knight to have nothing to do with sorcery and superstition, his recommended alternative is not the new science, but the old faith and he specifically endorses trial by battle to settle cases of alleged treason (52, Hay 64).

One can go some way towards explaining these differences simply by taking into account the time difference of one hundred and twenty-five years or so. By the year 1400, late feudal monarchs had to a large extent succeeded in centralizing political power in their realms. As a consequence knights and lesser lords now looked to the royal service as a way of getting ahead in the world, and only the king himself, and perhaps some of his greatest magnates, his 'peers' of the realm, could still think of themselves as dispensers of justice accountable only to God. But elapsed time and changed social and political circumstances alone cannot explain fully the difference in outlook between Christine de Pizan and Ramon Lull, a difference which is apparent in their choice of fictions. Christine's fiction, the series of letters written by Othea, Goddess of Prudence, to Hector, the flower of Trojan chivalry, suggests a classical humanist bias. On the other hand, Lull's fiction, the old knight-hermit who gives a 'lytell booke' to the young squire so that he may learn the 'rule and ordre of Chyualrye', suggests a Christian religious bias. There is a basic polarity here which transcends particularities of time and place.

In his magisterial study of high medieval culture, *Reason and Society in the Middle Ages*, Alexander Murray has labeled these two poles 'Rationalist' and 'Religious', and identified them with the 'Greek' and the 'Hebrew' sources of medieval culture respectively. The two poles remained part of the basic unity which was Christendom simply because 'both parties to the dialectic shared one conceptual language'. Nevertheless there continued to be tension between them throughout the medieval period (5).

Murray's research into French and Italian culture of the twelfth and thirteenth centuries indicates that the Rationalist outlook was characteristic of the rising classes of bourgeois and professional men (the class into which Christine de Pizan was born, her father being a doctor) and that the Religious outlook was characteristic of the established aristocracy (the class into which the Catalan knight, Ramon Lull, was born). Murray points out that it was in the interest of the upwardly mobile bourgeois and professional classes of men to legitimate their claims to political power on the 'rational' basis of their superior education and consequent moral enlightenment. On the other hand, it was in the interest of the established aristocracy, threatened by the increasing wealth and prestige of these aspiring groups, to legitimate their possession of political power on the religious basis of their divine ordination and consequent hereditary right.

Despite the pious and traditionalist arguments of the established aristocracy, however, knighthood remained, in practice as well as in theory, open to commoners. This seems to have been even more true in England than in France where *chevalerie* became virtually synonymous with *noblesse*.[3] As a consequence, knighthood in England was not vulnerable to that vitriolic and class-based criticism characteristic of French social satirists like Philippe de Commynes. Rather it remained free to become symbolic of the governing class as a whole, what A. B. Ferguson has called the 'entire politically active element in the commonwealth' (137–138; 141).

Of course, not all men entrusted with governance in late fifteenth-century England were dubbed knights, but many were. And certainly all those who represented their counties and boroughs in the king's parliament were called knights, whether or not they had ever been dubbed. Moreover, the king himself was always a dubbed knight and so were his greatest magnates, those noble lords who claimed the right to be called his 'peers' and thought of themselves as his natural counsellors in matters concerning the nation's governance. Consequently, a fifteenth-century sermon writer could observe, without any sense of anachronism, 'There be in þis world þre maner of men: clerkes, knyȝthis and commynalte' (Scattergood 265). And another could admonish '. . . knyȝthes and oþur gentils with hem' to 'sett her besines abowte þe good gouernaunce in þe temperalltee . . .' (Scattergood 274). For temporal governance was seen to be the task of 'knyȝtes and oþur gentils' and, as John Lydgate observed, it behooved every man to do the office to which he had been 'ordeynd' by God (Scattergood 272).

William Caxton's decision to translate and print Ramon Lull's treatise rather than that of Christine de Pizan does not necessarily mean that the Religious view of knighthood was more popular in England than the Rationalist. First of all, Christine's *Epistle of Othea* had already been independently translated three times into English,[4] and secondly, Malory's representation of knighthood in the *Morte Darthur* has clearly been influenced by both views.[5] Malory adopts the Religious view of knighthood when he follows his source to portray young king Arthur as God's chosen knight and to define his kingly office as the doing of 'true justyce'. But later he will diverge from his source to show us that Arthur himself does not share this Religious view. That is to say, Arthur does not undertake his governing responsibilities in the spirit of the *rex pius et iustus*, but rather in the rationalist and humanist spirit of a fifteenth-century monarch and forerunner of the Renaissance prince.

The Office of Kingship

In *The Governance of England* (c.1475) Malory's contemporary, Sir John Fortescue, defines the office of kingship as follows:

> . . . a kynges office stondith in ij thynges, on to defende his reaume ayen þair enemyes outwarde bi the swerde; on other that he defende his peple ayenst wronge doers inwarde bi justice . . . (116)

This definition may be seen as a compressed version of Lull's definition of the office of knighthood. Fortescue has eliminated specific mention of the sorts of things which could be subsumed under defence of 'his peple ayenst wronge doers inwarde' (things like defence of Church and clergy and defence of helpless women and children); and he has eliminated specific mention of defence of one's temporal lord, since the king is the greatest lord in his realm. What remains is the essence of the knightly office: the military defense of the realm and the doing of justice (which includes the keeping of the peace). It is highly significant that a great judge and legist of the mid-to-late-fifteenth century should understand the function of governance in terms of the traditional Religious view of the office of knighthood. Fortescue was the second son of a knight of an ancient Devonshire family and he himself was knighted by Henry VI not long after he was made Chief Justice of the King's Bench. He appears also to have been a pious man of indisputable orthodoxy who adopted the providentialist world view characteristic of his age (*Governance* 79–80, 99). If we may assume that Fortescue's understanding of governance represents that of most late fifteenth-century English knights and gentlemen, then it is no wonder that Lull's treatise continued to be regarded as a serviceable book of instruction for royal servants well into the sixteenth century.

The king's office being the office of knighthood, it follows logically that all kings ought to be knights. Lull makes this point most emphatically:

> For and Emperouris kingis and princis had nocht annext to thame the ordre of knychthede, with the vertues and propereteis, and nobiliteis, langand to the said ordre, thai war nocht worthy to be Emperouris, kingis, na princis. (Hay 67; Lull 115)

Lull is making this point by analogy with the priesthood, but whereas the analogy remains implicit in his version, Sir Gilbert Hay goes on to make it explicit:

> For suppose the office be gretare, the ordre is ylyke ane in kingis and in knychtis, as prestehede is ylyke of degree, bathe in pape, cardynale, and patriarche, alsmekle is it in a symple preste. (67)

This explicit analogy between the 'ordre' and 'office' of priesthood and of knighthood suggests that just as reception into the order of clergy is prerequisite to administering the sacraments, so reception into the order of knighthood is prerequisite to administering justice.

Such a notion seems to have been widespread in late medieval England. In both popular romances and in didactic literature knighthood is perceived as a prerequisite of kingship and the king is perceived as the greatest knight in England. For example, Horn refuses both the crown and marriage until he has proved himself as a knight, and Havelok immediately becomes king as soon as he has been knighted (MacCrae 239–40). John Gower uses the terms king and knight interchangeably in *Confessio Amantis* (VII.3529–43) and in a poem dedicated to Henry IV he describes the king as 'fulfilled of grace and of knighthood' (*English Works*, 2:335, 486). In a similar vein, John Lydgate prays that God remember Henry VI, 'thyn oone chose knyght' and, later in the century, an anonymous author assures the new king Edward IV that 'god hathe chose þe to be his knyȝt' (Scattergood 149, 192). Even in the standard treatise on kingship, the *Regement of Princes*, Thomas Hoccleve shifts 'with the utmost ease and unconcern . . . from the word king to the word knight' (Ferguson 193) as though they were one and the same.

Malory clearly shares this view of the king as first and foremost a knight. Not only does he follow his source in having Arthur made knight before he is crowned king, he also inserts a passage much later in his work in which he makes precisely the same point Hay has made in the passage quoted above, and in much the same language. Allowing the specific office to be greater, Hay nevertheless insists that 'the ordre is ylyke ane in kingis and in knychtis'. Malory agrees. When Mador de la Porte comes before Arthur to demand his day of justice, he reminds Arthur 'thoughe ye be oure kynge, in that degré ye ar but a knyght as we ar, and ye ar sworne unto knychthode als welle as we be' (1050.18–20:XVIII.4).

To be 'sworne unto knychthode' in this context means to be sworn to do justice, which is one half of the king's office, according to Sir John Fortescue: 'that he defende his peple ayenst wronge doers inwarde bi justice'. Malory gives particular emphasis to this part of the king's office in his description of Arthur's coronation:

> And so anon was the coronacyon made, and ther was he sworne unto his lordes and the comyns for to be a true kyng, to stand with true justyce fro thens forth the dayes of this lyf.
>
> (16.20–23:I.7)

It is surely significant that Malory's choice of words for this coronation oath should find an echo in Sir George Ashby's *The Active Policy of a Prince*, written for the Lancastrian prince Edward in the year 1471:

> Truste nat oonly in menis multitude,
> Ne in thair myght, ne in Comon clamour,
> But in god & in goode consuetude
> Of *trewe iustice*, without any rigour,
> Otherwise than god woulde, owre Saueour:
> A Kynge, Reulyng al thynges rightfully
> With lawe reigneth with al folk plesantly.
>
> (Scattergood 286, emphasis added)

Young Edward never succeeded his father, Henry VI; however, Henry's Yorkist successor, Edward IV, seems to have benefitted from similar advice, for he did much to strengthen his hold on the Crown of England by devoting time and energy early in his reign to the doing of justice (Ross 399 *passim*). Malory shows us that Arthur, too, understands how important it is to give his people 'true justice' by adding the following paragraph:

> Also thenne he made alle lordes that helde of the croune to come in and to do servyce as they oughte to doo. And many complayntes were made unto sir Arthur of grete wronges that

> were done syn the dethe of kyng Uther, of many londes that were bereved lordes, knyghtes, ladyes, and gentilmen. Wherfor kynge Arthur maade the londes to be yeven ageyne unto them that oughte hem. (16.24–30:I.7)

This is a most remarkable paragraph for many reasons, not the least of which is Malory's reference to the king as 'sir Arthur'. It would seem that when the king does justice, Malory cannot help but perceive him as a knight.

Arthur's promise to 'stand with true justyce' employs the word 'justyce' in the knightly sense. This is the first sense of the word to have been taken over from French into English and it means 'the exercise of authority or power in the maintenance of right, the vindication of right by assignment of reward or punishment, requital or desert' (*OED* 4). It does not mean 'the quality of being fair or just' (*OED* 1). The *Middle English Dictionary* fails to make this distinction: 'the quality of being fair and just, also, the administration of justice' (2a). Yet clearly, if administered 'justyce' always had 'the quality of being fair or just' there would never be a need to qualify the noun further. The adjective 'true' implies that what it modifies may also be 'false'. Both Malory and Sir George Ashby understand this and in the passages cited above use 'justyce' in the knightly sense because they know that 'justyce' may be good or bad, true or false, according to whether it is administered well or ill. Sir Gilbert Hay uses 'justice' in the knightly sense when he observes that knights ought to punish themselves before they presume to punish others, 'for gude justice begynnis at it self, and syne at othir men' (29). And when Sir John Fortescue says it is the king's office to 'defende his peple ayenst wronge doers inwarde bi justice', he, too, means 'justice' in the knightly sense. He means that it is the king's duty to exercise his power and authority to maintain the right.

According to the Religious view of knighthood, the king does justice as the vassal of God. When George Ashby said to young Edward that he must trust 'in god' he was advising him to conform to the medieval ideal of kingship, the *rex pius et iustus*. The great model of this ideal of kingship for the later Middle Ages was the thirteenth-century monarch, Louis IX. Louis had the reputation of being perfectly just in his dealings with other men. Indeed, as a dispenser of justice, he was said to be so impartial that even the members of his own family had to submit to the rule of law. His people loved him for the peace, stability and true justice he gave them and after his death in 1270 the Church canonized him for his piety and crusading zeal. Of course, most medieval kings could not emulate that rare combination of virtues which made Louis a saint as well as a successful monarch. Nevertheless the ideal persisted into the fifteenth century to be praised by men like Alain Chartier and Sir Gilbert Hay. Chartier's *Treatise of Hope* was translated into English not long before Malory sat down to write the *Morte Darthur*. In it the French moralist adopts the feudal analogy implicit in the ideal of the *rex pius et iustus* in order to argue that since kings 'holde of God by parage' [i.e. by right of birth], they therefore 'owe Him both seruice and feithe . . . and to kepe rightwisenes as a commyssioner and a ministour' (54–55). In the same vein Sir Gilbert Hay asserts in his *Buke of the Governaunce of Princis* that the king 'is as depute and mynister to God' and therefore 'suld folow him and be lyke him, and conforme him till him in all his dedis of justice vertue and veritee' (145).

Men like Alain Chartier and Sir Gilbert Hay were perfectly aware, of course, that there was no power on earth strong enough to make an unjust king just. As the highest officer of knighthood in the realm, he was also the highest judge, and from his judgement there was no appeal, except to God. No doubt that is why both men conclude their works with a warning to unjust kings: God will remove them from office if they continue to fail in their duty to Him (Chartier 55; Hay 164). Their warnings are typical of the providentialist world view which characterized the late medieval period. Indeed, it seems to be the case that as medieval men's expectations of receiving 'true justyce' from their kings rose, so did their hopes that God would punish those kings who failed to do their office. The most popular history book in fifteenth-century England was John Lydgate's *Fall of Princis*, largely because Lydgate followed his source, Boccaccio's *De Casibus Illustrium Virorum*, in explaining the downfall of great kings of the past as a divine punishment for their sins. Lydgate does not do this in the case of all kings; significantly, he chooses not to do it in the case of King Arthur, whose downfall he attributes to fortune. But, as H. A. Kelly has observed, this sort of vacillation was typical of fifteenth-century English historians and chroniclers (54). They all tended to attribute the downfall of a great man either to the wrath of God, or to the sudden turning of fortune's wheel, depending upon their political sympathies. Whereas a pious Lancastrian might prefer to interpret Edward's victory at Towton as a reversal of fortune, a pious Yorkist would no doubt interpret it as divine retribution upon Henry VI for his failure to do justice.

The knightly meaning of 'justice' has survived into modern times only in the phrase 'poetic justice'. In this phrase, 'justice' still means the 'exercise of authority or power in the maintenance of right; vindication of right by assignment of reward or punishment, requital or desert'. However, the source of that authority or power is not a king or an armed knight, but an author. Like poetic justice, knightly justice can be good or bad depending upon how well it is administered. And in fact by means of the now common analogy between the author as creator of a fictional world and God as the Author of the universe, we may gain some insight into the providentialist view which underlay late medieval men's hopes for justice in this world. In the first instance they pinned these hopes upon their king. They looked to him to provide a right for every wrong, and insofar as he was able to do this, they praised him as 'lyke to the glorious God almychty' (Hay, *Governaunce* 146).

Medieval kings and knights did not always do justice literally 'bi the swerd'; however, the sword symbolized the power by which they did justice. What is more, the religious form of the knighting ceremony emphasized that they wielded this coercive power by divine ordination. The knight's sword was 'ordanyt to do justice with' (Hay 44; Lull 76) and the new-made knight signified his willingness to use this sword in accordance with God's will by laying it upon the altar. It is significant, I think, that this should be the only detail which Malory has chosen to retain from the description of Arthur's knighting which he found in his French source. Arthur is knighted before he is crowned king, and the only gesture he makes before being dubbed and then crowned is to take 'the swerd' which he had from the stone 'bitwene both his handes' and to offer it 'upon the aulter' (16.18–20:I.7).

Arthur does not need to use his sword in order to enforce the judgments he makes on the first day of his knighthood and kingship. After he has heard the complaints of his subjects, young 'sir Arthur' simply orders 'the londes to be yeven ageyne unto them that ought hem'. Malory tells us nothing about how Arthur 'maade' anyone give back lands which he had wrongfully taken from others. Ultimately, of course, anyone who resisted the king's order could be brought to heel by armed force, but the fact was, and Malory surely knew this from his own experience of royal justice, that the very presence of a crowned king whose legitimacy was unquestioned by the people, was enough to produce acquiescence in his judgments (Bellamy, *Crime* 11). And Arthur's legitimacy has been established first 'by myracle' and then by the assent of both lords and commons before he sits in judgment upon his people.

Arthur's sword plays a much more prominent role in fulfilling the other half of his kingly office: 'to defende his reaume ayen þair enemeyes outwarde bi the swerde.' The good Christian king was never supposed to go to war except in a just cause, for pious men believed that God himself determined the outcome of all battles. Arthur's first war is against the northern kings who refuse to acknowledge his right to rule England, despite the 'myracle' of the sword and the assent of many of the English lords and all the 'comyns'. From the young king's point of view, they are rebels. From their point of view, however, his claim to the throne is unproved. By preparing for war they in effect lay their dispute before God, the supreme judge of nations, according to what H. A. Kelly has called 'a providential code of international justice' (35). In this regard it is significant that in Malory's version some three hundred of the northern kings' knights cross over to Arthur's side as soon as Merlin tells them that Arthur is Uther's legitimate heir (18.34–19.2:I.9). With the addition of this passage Malory makes the remaining northern kings and knights appear to be willfully rebellious and Arthur's victory over them, using the sword which he had 'by myracle', a clear case of divine justice.

By altering the role of Merlin, Malory succeeds in transforming Arthur's first war into an illustration of the workings of divine providence. Malory's Merlin is something like an Old Testament prophet (R. Kelly, 'Arthur' 15–16). In other words, he functions as a go-between in the continuous process of interaction between divine and human wills which constitutes providential history. Malory provides another excellent example of Merlin's functioning when he has the prophet advise Arthur not to chase after the fleeing rebel army at the end of his second battle, the battle at Bedgrayne. Arthur's forces have at last succeeded in pushing the northern kings' forces back across the river and the slaughter has been terrible. As though reading the young king's mind, Merlin rushes up on horseback, before Arthur has actually organized his forces to give chase, and shouts,

> 'Thou hast never done. Hast thou nat done inow? Of three score thousande thys day hast thou leffte on lyve but fyftene thousand! Therefore hit ys tyme to sey "Who!" for God ys wroth with the for thou woll never have done. For yondir a eleven kynges at thys tyme woll nat be overthrowyn, but and thou tary on them ony lenger thy fortune woll turne and they shall encres. And therefore withdraw you unto youre lodgynge and reste you as sone as ye may, and rewarde youre good knyghtes with golde and with sylver, for they have well deserved hit.' (36.26–35:I.17)

In Malory's French source, Merlin also puts a stop to the slaughter, but he does not explain why the killing must stop. He makes no reference to God's 'wroth' nor does he prophesy that 'at thys tyme' the eleven kings may not be vanquished. And he certainly does not imply that if Arthur tries to destroy them completely, his 'fortune woll turne and they shall encres' (*Works* 1294). What is most remarkable about this passage is the clear, almost logical way it assumes a causal connection between God's will and man's fortune. Indeed, Merlin comes close to explaining exactly how providential history works.

The only thing which Merlin does not explain is why God should be 'wroth' with Arthur for wishing to continue the slaughter of his enemies. Any medieval reader could easily have supplied the reason, however, by referring to the orthodox definition of a just war. There were three conditions which had to be met before a war could be regarded as 'just': the man who declared and waged war must be a legitimate ruler; he must have just cause for war; and the belligerents must have the proper intention in mind (Allmand 17–18). Arthur's legitimacy as king of England has been established, so he meets the first qualification easily enough. He also meets the second qualification because the northern kings are both rebels and aggressors and Malory adds a passage to remind his readers of those facts (35.3–8:I.16). The third qualification for a 'just war' — the proper intention in the minds of the belligerents — is, of course, the most difficult to fulfill. Even though war is fought by a legitimate ruler and for a just cause, it may be rendered unjust if his motive for fighting is base, or unjust. Pious medieval knights were advised to pray that God preserve them from succumbing to such motives as personal gain or revenge (Huppé 25). In the Battle of Bedgrayne, we have seen Arthur, Ban and Bors slay 'downeryght on bothe hondis, that hir horses wente in blood up to the fittlockys' in the heat of battle (36.18–20:I.17). So long as the battle formation of the eleven kings held firm, and the issue of the battle remained in doubt, even such slaughter could be justified. However, if Arthur and his men were to pursue and slay their enemies 'downeryght on bothe hondis' as they attempt to flee the field, then they would clearly be killing, not to win the battle, but to have revenge, and the justice of their cause would be destroyed. That is why Merlin tells Arthur that 'God ys wroth with him.' And that is why, if Arthur had not heeded Merlin, but had pursued and killed his enemies regardless, his 'fortune' would have turned.

In his *Book of the Governaunce of Princis*, Sir Gilbert Hay devotes an entire chapter to the 'grete drede' which kings should have 'to scayle and sched mannis blude oure reklesly' and argues that the 'sparing of mannis blude . . . is the thing that plesis maist to God.' What is more, 'God that kennis the secrete thouchtis of mannis hert will reward' the merciful king in his 'grete nede' (102). At the end of this book, in fact, Hay assures all kings that if they follow his advice they will succeed in all their undertakings, but if they do not, they shall suffer 'grevous mischeif and mysfortune' (164). Malory conveys essentially the same message through Merlin's intervention in Arthur's war with the northern kings. Arthur's cause is just and therefore God is on his side and wills him to be victorious; however, should Arthur forget his obligation as God's minister to fight with a true intention, should he attempt to usurp God's office by seeking vengeance (Hay, *Governaunce* 103), then God will make Fortune turn her wheel, and allow Arthur's enemies to overcome him.

King Arthur's Knights

Whether a king is engaged in defending 'his reaume ayen þair enemeyes outwarde bi the swerde' or 'his peple ayenst wronge doers inwarde bi justice' (Fortescue 116), he is 'bot a man allane but [without] his men' (Hay, *Knychthede* 22). The medieval corporate theory of governance illustrated the king's dependency upon his knights with the image of the body politic: the king is the head of this body and his knights are those 'membres' (usually arms and hands) which 'kepe' his realm (Hardyng 133).[6] The image suggests that in order to have effective governance the king must be able to trust his knights as he would trust the 'membres' of his own body. To that end, late medieval English monarchs developed a number of ways to gain and keep the loyalty of the feudal nobility. Malory's King Arthur makes use of all of them. He personally confers the order of knighthood upon most of his knights. He honours the best of them with membership in the elite fellowship of the Round Table, which constitutes the core of his political power, and rewards them further with rich gifts of money and lands. Finally, like both the Lancastrian and the Yorkist kings of England, Arthur makes his knights swear a peace-keeping oath and threatens them with the loss of his 'lordship' and their 'worship' if they should fail to keep it.

The first of these ways of ensuring the loyalty of the king's men depends largely for its effectiveness upon the strength of the Christian ideology of knighthood. Malory never describes in detail a knighting ritual performed by King Arthur; therefore we cannot know whether or not he ever makes use of that solemn ritual which created knights 'of the Bath' in fifteenth-century England. At this time in English history knights 'of the Bath' did not constitute a separate order; however, they did swear a special oath of loyalty to the king. Edward III seems to have been the first English king to make use of this religious ritual, but Henry IV was the first English king to make a regular practice of creating new knights 'of the Bath' on solemn ceremonial occasions such as coronations and weddings.

Henry's innovative practice received a great deal of admiring attention at the time from contemporary chroniclers, and at least one historian has hypothesized that it was a conscious attempt to 'bind an important group of new men to himself personally, upon whose military prowess, local leadership and unflagging personal loyalty he could count in the difficult future which lay ahead' (Winkler 40). The knighting ritual he used emphasized the new knight's obligation to 'love god above all things and be stedfaste in the feythe and sustene the chirche,' but it also emphasized his obligation to 'be trewe un to yowre sovereyne lorde.' In addition, in the version of the ritual which was owned by Sir John Astley, the king's cook steps forward to tell the new-made knight that if he should ever 'be untrewe to yowre sovereyne lorde or doo ayens this hye and worshipfull order that ye have takyn,' then it becomes his office to hack off his spurs. The 'hye and worshipfull ordir' to which the ritual refers is not the 'ordir' of the Bath — that order was not formally established until the eighteenth century — rather it is the 'hye and worshipfull ordir' of knighthood itself, the 'ordir' to which all knights belong by virtue of their ordination.[7] In other words, the knighting ritual 'of the Bath' assumes the Religious view of knighthood as ordained by God. At the same time, however, it places this order at the service of the Crown. After the formal banquet which celebrates the knighting ceremony the new-made knight takes leave of his king by saying, 'moste drede and moste myghty prynce, of my lytyll powre of that that I may I thanke you of all ye worshypes, curtesies, godenesse, which ye have done unto me' (Stowe 113).[8]

What evidence there is suggests that the Lancastrian practice of making knights 'of the Bath' produced a group of men who were exceptionally loyal to their king. And, in fact, the practice was continued by Yorkist and Tudor monarchs (Winkler 40–94; Ross 95; Simons 77, 95, 113). The case of Sir Ralph Grey, knighted by Henry VI and then retained in the service of Edward IV soon after his succession to the throne, sheds a great deal of light upon what Malory's contemporaries expected of a king's knight 'of the Bath'. After having agreed to hold the castles of the North for Edward, Grey reverted to his Lancastrian allegiance and defied Edward at Bamborough Castle. Edward battered down the walls of the castle with his great guns, captured Grey and brought him up for trial before his Constable, Sir John Tiptoft, Earl of Worcester. Reminding the traitor that he who has taken 'the order of knighthood of the Bath . . . ought to keep the faith the which he makes,' the constable ordered Grey's coat of arms to be stripped off and his spurs hacked off, thus degrading him of his 'worship, noblesse and arms, as of the order of knighthood,' before he was executed (Keen, 'Treason Trials' 90–91).

What is most remarkable about this incident is the Constable's assumption that Grey's loyalty as a knight 'of the Bath' should have been to the Crown rather than to the person who had made him knight, Henry VI, still alive and in hiding at this time. Grey himself seems to have felt justified in remaining loyal to Henry, regardless of what he might subsequently have agreed to do for Edward. But Tiptoft was a man who had been exposed to the new humanist learning, having avoided involvement in the civil strife of the 1450s by traveling to Italy where he studied history and politics. At the same time he was a leading member of the Knights of the Order of the Holy Sepulchre and in 1458 had made a pilgrimage to the Holy Land. There, in his capacity as Guardian of the Order, he had knighted some young friends of his companion, Robert Sanseverino, and admitted them into the Order. The solemn religious ceremony entailed the taking of a fivefold oath: to hear Mass daily; to venture one's life and all possessions in defence of the Christian faith; to defend the Church; to avoid all injustice; and to keep peace among Christian peoples, defend widows and orphans, and refrain from homicide and lechery, thus presenting an example of the Christian life (Mitchell 45). Therefore, in the year 1464 Tiptoft was one of the few men in England who could simultaneously and passionately embrace both medieval, religious and early modern, humanist attitudes towards knighthood and governance. A profoundly pious man, he accepted the Religious view of knighthood as a Christian vocation of service in the world. A profoundly learned man, he also accepted the new humanist view of the state. Therefore, in his mind, the High Order of Knighthood had already become what it was destined to become generally in the two succeeding centuries in England: a means of creating deep and abiding loyalty among the male members of the governing class to that abstract entity, the Crown.

Sir Thomas Malory would certainly have known of Sir John Tiptoft, Earl of Worchester. Whatever his own loyalties in the struggle between Lancaster and York, he must also have agreed with Tiptoft that a knight 'ought to keep the faith which he makes.' The way Malory handles the conferring of knighthood in *Le Morte Darthur*, however, suggests that he would have agreed with Sir Ralph Grey rather than Tiptoft in interpreting that obligation. That is to say, he would have expected a knight to 'keep the faith' with the person who made him knight rather than with the institution of the monarchy as such, regardless of who wore the crown. First of all, in *Le Morte Darthur* the king is not the only man who makes knights, although Lancelot is the only man, other than the king, who makes more than one knight.[9] Secondly, both Lancelot and Arthur are sought after as givers of knighthood not so much because of the particular office they hold but because of their reputation as knights. Young men come to Camelot to seek knighthood from the king because he is 'called the moste nobelyst kynge of the worlde' (459.25–26:IX.1) and from Lancelot because he is known as the 'cheff of knyghthode' (316.23:VII.13), the knight who surpasses all others in prowess and noble deeds. In this way Malory gives the impression that young men in King Arthur's days believed it was important to receive the order of knighthood from a particularly good knight.

This is a belief associated with the Religious view of knighthood and it stems from the analogy between knighthood and priesthood. Just as the new-made priest receives a special grace from God by means of the apostolic laying on of hands, so the new-made knight receives a special grace from God by means of the knightly dubbing. But whereas the Church teaches that the grace of Holy Orders is conferred *ex opere operato*, regardless of the moral worth of the priest who administers the sacrament, Roman Lull assumes that an unworthy knight will not be able to confer the 'grace' of knighthood:

> Thenne must the prynce or baron that wyl make thesquyer & adoube hym a knyght haue in hym self the vertue & ordre of chyualry. For yf the knyght that maketh knyghtes is not vertuous, how maye he gyue that whiche he hath not. . . . Suche a knyght is euyl & false that disordynatly wyl multyplye his ordre. For he doth wrong & vylonye to chyualry . . . Thene yf by deffaulte of suche a knyght it happe somtyme that the squyer that receyueth of hym Chyualry is not so moche ayded ne mayntened of the grace of our lord ne of vertue ne of chyualry as he shold be yf he were made of a good & loyal knyght [sic]. And therefor suche a squyer is a foole and al other semblably that of suche a knyght receyueth thordre of chyualry. (72–74)

It is not enough to be a knight, that is, to have received the order; one must also be a 'good and loyal knyght', a 'vertuous knyght', in order to be able to pass on 'the grace of our lorde' to a new-made knight.

Lull was writing in the last quarter of the thirteenth century when the analogy between knighthood and priesthood was still new. Almost two hundred years later, Sir Gilbert Hay tightens the analogy considerably when he argues,

> Rycht as nane may mak preste bot he be preste, sa may nane mak knycht bot first he be maid knycht, sauffand the Pape: for how may he geve that he has nocht? . . . for gif ony lord wald geve the ordre and nocht have it, or unworthily geve it othir

> wayis na the ordre requeris, he dois grete dishonour to the ordre. And thai that takis the said ordre of thame that has na power unworthily, thai have na grace in the ordre to do wele, na prouffit to thame na otheris; and thus is the squyer begylit, and dissavit of his ordre, and all chevalrye sclanderit. (42–43)

Hay says nothing about the giver of knighthood being 'good and loyal' or 'vertuous'; in fact he seems to assume that the 'grace' of the order can be passed on by any lord, so long as he himself has first been made a knight and observes the proper knighting ritual. In other words, Hay assumes that the 'grace' of knighthood, which also comes ultimately from God through his Vicar on earth, the Pope, is conferred precisely like the grace of Holy Orders, *ex opere operato*.

It is significant, I think, that Malory does not adopt this more sacramental view of the knighting ritual. That he does not may be related to his apparent dislike of ritual of any kind. Even though he refers to six knightings by King Arthur and three by Lancelot, Malory never describes the knighting ritual.[10] However, he makes very clear that the giving of knighthood creates an enormous debt of gratitude and loyalty on the part of the new-made knight vis-a-vis the man who made him knight. For example, when Mellyagaunt is about to abduct the queen, she tries to dissuade him from such a dishonourable course of action by reminding him of his obligation to be loyal to 'the noble kyng that made the knyght!' (1122.11–12:XIX.2). Then again, when Neroveus realizes that the knight he has just fought and yielded to is the man who made him knight, he cries out 'Alas! . . . what have I done!' as he falls 'flatlynge to his [Lancelot's] feete and wolde have kyste them, but sir Launcelot wolde nat suffir hym' (468.35–469.1:IX.5). And Lancelot himself believes that because he received the 'hygh Order of Knyghthode' from King Arthur, he 'ought of ryght ever to be in youre [Arthur's] quarell and in my ladyes the quenys quarell to do batayle (1058.21–23:XVIII.7).

The strength of the bond described by these examples suggests an explanation for the curious way in which Malory has handled the knighting of Arthur. Normally kings of England were knighted by their father or by an uncle. Henry V was knighted by his father, Henry IV, and Henry VI was knighted by his uncle the Duke of Bedford. Arthur has neither father nor uncle to make him knight, however. What is more, according to the Religious view of knighthood, the Archbishop of Canterbury (who knights Arthur in Malory's French source) is not qualified to 'gyue that whiche he hath not.' It is essential that the man destined to be king of England receive knighthood from 'a good and loyal knight' if he is to profit maximally from the grace and virtue inherent in the order. At the same time it would be exceedingly awkward to place the young king in the position of owing such gratitude and loyalty to one of his own subjects. Malory makes the best of this delicate situation by passing over the knighting ceremony with a phrase: 'and so was he made knyghte of the best man that was there' (16.19–20:I.7). It is not characteristic of Malory to leave characters anonymous. Quite the contrary, his normal procedure is to invent names even for very minor characters left anonymous by his sources (Wilson, 'Naming'). Therefore, when he invents an important character, as he does in this case — the man who gives knighthood to Arthur — and then refuses to name him, he must have good reason. It was important that the 'best man' be available for this important function of giving the 'hygh Order of Knyghthode' to the king; but it was equally important that no man be able to look upon Arthur as his son-in-chivalry, with all that such a felt obligation might entail.

Malory gives his readers the impression that, except for those who are knighted by Lancelot (and Tristram who is knighted by Mark), all the other knights of the Round Table have been knighted by King Arthur. For example, during the Grail quest, a damsel asks help of Sir Bors 'for kynge Arthures sake, which I suppose made the knyght' (961.10–11:XVI:9). If marginal characters in Malory's world 'suppose' that King Arthur knighted each of his Round Table knights, then surely his readers are entitled to 'suppose' it, too. However, there is less reason to suppose that all Round Table knights will feel as much reverence for the man who made them knight as Lancelot and Gareth do. For these two knights, the giving of knighthood creates a bond of loyalty which is stronger than kinship. Gareth prefers the fellowship of Lancelot to that of his brother, Gawain, and refuses to join his own kinsmen in the plot to destroy Lancelot and the queen. Likewise, Lancelot refuses to do battle with Arthur. Even though Arthur has ravaged his lands and laid seige to his castle at Benwick and even though his own kinsmen urge him to sally forth, for his host outnumbers that of Arthur, Lancelot still refuses to do battle with 'that noble kynge that made me knyght' (1214.10–11:XX.20).[11] Gareth's and Lancelot's near filial piety towards their respective fathers-in-chivalry is probably related to their having adopted the Religious view of knighthood. By contrast, the more worldly and rational among the Round Table knights seem to view knighting by the king in much the same way that Malory's contemporaries, the Pastons, did. The Paston family sought to have young John knighted by King Edward IV as the necessary first step towards a career in the king's household and the political power and patronage which such a career promised (Bennett 12–13). Probably most of the young men knighted by Arthur had similar hopes of a career in the king's service.[12]

Once a young man had succeeded in getting himself knighted by the king, he still had to prove his worthiness to become a fellow of the Round Table. Lancelot's career in Arthur's court may be taken as exemplary in this regard. Like all young and unproved knights, he began as one of the 'Quenys Knyghtes':

> And they were many good knyghtes, and the moste party were yonge men that wolde have worshyp, and they were called the Quenys Knyghtes. And never in no batayle, turnement nother justys they bare none of hem no maner of knowlecchynge of their owne armys but playne whyght shyldis, and thereby they were called the Quenys Knyghtes. And whan hit happed ony of them to be of grete worshyp by hys noble dedis, than at the nexte feste of Pentecoste, gyff there were ony slayne or dede (as there was none yere that there fayled but there were som dede), than was there chosyn in hys stede that was dede the moste men of worshyp that were called the Quenys Knyghtes. And thus they cam up firste or they were renowmed men of worshyp, both sir Launcelot and all the remenaunte of them (1121.16–29:XIX.1).

There is nothing in either of Malory's sources to suggest this practice of beginning one's knightly career in the queen's service, but it could have been suggested to him by Edward IV's decision to create a large number of knights 'of the Bath' on the occasion of his queen's coronation. Edward created even more knights to honour his queen's coronation than he had to honour his own three years earlier: whereas he had been accompanied to the Abbey by twenty-eight new-made knights of the Bath, his queen was accompanied by almost fifty (Shaw I.33–35; Schofield I.376), all garbed in hoods of white silk and blue gowns with a white silk lace on the left shoulder (Schofield I.182). Sir Thomas Malory may actually have seen them escort Elizabeth Wydeville to Westminster Abbey, or he may only have heard about this memorable coronation parade. Either way it is quite possible that the whiteness of the hood and the lace worn by new-made knights of the Bath suggested to Malory the whiteness of the shields borne by Guinevere's knights.

If Malory's 'Quenys Knyghtes' suggest Yorkist knights 'of the Bath', knighted by the king but serving as an escort for the queen, his fellowship of the Round Table suggests the prestigious Order of the Garter. Knights 'of the Bath' and 'Quenys Knyghtes' are new-made knights; however, Garter knights and Round Table knights are well-proved knights who have earned their place at the table by doing great deeds of arms.

The founding of secular orders of chivalry was popular among late feudal monarchs, for they saw in them a means of strengthening their governance as well as promoting their foreign policies. Edward III's Order of the Garter was the most successful and long-lasting among them, probably because he limited the number of Garter knights to a small, elite group of twenty-five, although originally he had planned a fellowship of three hundred knights, twice the size of Arthur's fellowship.[13] Edward seems to have established the Order of the Garter to help further his claim to the French throne and, initially at least, it formed a kind of 'military elite, whom the sovereign was to "prefer" in any warlike expedition' (Barber, *Knight* 305). The verdict of historians is that Edward's innovation was a brilliant success. Garter knights managed to work together as captains of war 'with a remarkable harmony' during the campaigns in France, and, what is perhaps even more important, Edward succeeded in binding 'to himself under an obligation of honour nearly all the greatest names in the land' (Barnie 67).

The role which the Round Table fellowship plays in King Arthur's Roman campaign, both as counsellors of war and as commanders in the field, greatly strengthens the likeness between King Arthur's Round Table fellowship and Edward III's Order of the Garter. Malory never refers to the Round Table fellowship as an 'order', however. What is more, he represents it as much more secular in character than the Order of the Garter. The knights of the Order of the Garter had associated with them an equal number of priests and were committed to the maintenance of twenty-six poor knights. Indeed, the statutes of their order were 'hardly concerned with secular affairs at all' (Barber, *Reign* 166) and emphasized rather their charitable and religious obligations. By contrast, Arthur's Round Table knights have no religious obligations whatsoever, not even the obligation to 'sustene the fayth' and the 'church', or to hear mass once a day. In fact, the scene in which Malory describes the establishment of the Round Table fellowship is almost devoid of the religious sentiment which characterizes both the founding of the Order of the Garter and the founding of the Round Table in other literary versions of the event. John Hardyng's *Chronicle* records that support of the Church was one of the main obligations of the Round Table knights (124–5). Likewise Jacques d'Armagnac reports in his version of the 'serments' that Round Table knights were obliged to hear mass once a day (Sandoz 401–02). What is more, in Malory's immediate source for this scene, the knights of the Round Table are clearly identified as God's knights. Merlin makes much of the mysterious appearance of their names, written in gold letters on the chairs they are destined to occupy, and concludes from this that God is pleased with the fellowship (*Suite du Merlin* 2:68–69). By contrast, Malory allows no religious inference to be drawn from the 'lettirs of golde'. In fact, within his secularized context, the observation that 'Merlin founde in every sege lettirs of golde that tolde the knyghtes namys' seems more likely to mean that Merlin provided the 'lettirs' than that they mysteriously appeared for him to discover (99.5:III.2).

Malory's secularization of the Round Table fellowship makes it easier to perceive yet another similarity between the knights who serve king Arthur and the knights who served fifteenth-century English kings. This similarity is suggested by Arthur's practice of giving retaining fees to his Round Table knights. For example, at the end of the Roman campaign, Arthur offers Lancelot and Bors a magnificent fee, literally a king's ransom, to 'mayntene' their kinsmen 'so that ye and they to the Rounde Table make your repeyre' (245.21–23:V.12). On the same occasion he offers to the newly baptized Priamus the 'fee' of 'fifty thousand quarterly' to 'mayntene' his 'servauntes' on condition that he 'leve not my felyship' (245.30–32:V.12). Arthur is a good and generous lord. He knows how to encourage his men to do deeds of valour and how to win their loyalty with the expectation of generous gifts. And in fact, at the end of the Roman campaign, 'there was none that wolde aske that myghte playne of his parte, for of rychesse and welth they had all at her wylle' (246.1–3:V.12). However, the gifts of money made on condition that the recipients enter his fellowship, suggest that the Round Table knights comprise King Arthur's retinue. That is to say, they are the knights whom King Arthur has chosen to help him with the governance of the realm.

The practice of retaining large numbers of knights in the royal retinue began with the first Lancastrian king, Henry IV, who inherited the retinue of his father, John of Gaunt. In fact, it has been argued that Henry was able to gain and keep the Crown of England largely because of the widespread political support which his father's knights afforded him (Brown 14–19). Throughout the fifteenth century knights who had been retained by the king were known as 'king's knights' (Winkler 34). They performed a number of different military, judicial, diplomatic and political functions. Some of them might have important offices in the royal household. Others might be great magnates who seldom resided in the court. We find both types among Arthur's fellowship. Sir Kay the Seneschal, Sir Lucan the Butler and Sir Dagonet the Fool are household knights. But Sir Lamorak of Wales and Sir Tristram of Cornwall are lords of great lands in their own right and may seldom visit the royal court. Young Sir Gareth, once he has married the lady Lyones, also becomes a lord of great lands. Yet Arthur gives gifts to all of them, whether rich or poor, when they first enter the fellowship, signifying thereby that he is now their 'good lord' and has undertaken to 'mayntene' them.

Maintenance was a serious obligation. It meant not only ensuring that one's retainers had sufficient livelihood to maintain the costs of knighthood, but also supporting them in any quarrel they might have with another lord.[14] The costs of maintaining knighthood were 'grete', as Sir Gilbert Hay observes, including 'expense on hors, harnais, mete and men, and othir necessair thingis.' Indeed, Hay concludes from these economic facts that no man should ever desire to become a knight unless he is either a great lord or has a good and generous 'lord to mynister him all his necessiteis, and halde his honour abufe' (*Knychthede* 39). The Winchester text reports that Arthur gave 'rychesse and londys' to all his Round Table knights. The Caxton text specifies that he gave 'londes' only to 'them that were of londes not ryche' (III.15). Both types of gift — money and lands — are conditional upon the knights' honouring their part of the contractual agreement. Arthur insists that any knight who fails to keep his Round Table oath will forfeit not only his 'worship', that is, his personal honour and status in society, but also Arthur's 'lordship', that is, a significant part of his livelihood, as well. This conditional form of retaining was becoming increasingly common in fifteenth-century England largely because it allowed a lord to have much more control over his retainers than he could possibly have over a knight he had retained in his service for life (Bean, *Decline* 306–7). On every subsequent occasion that Arthur receives new knights into the fellowship and gives them 'grete londis to spende', we should assume that the same conditions obtain, even though they are never again spelled out, if only because each one of these new knights must also swear the Round Table oath annually at the feast of Pentecost.[15]

The Office of the King's Knights

Until now all critics of the *Morte Darthur* seem to have accepted Vinaver's judgment that the oath which Arthur requires his knights to swear each year at Pentecost is an expression of Malory's personal code of chivalry (*Works* 1335). That is, at best, a partial truth. The provisions of the oath do, in fact, have clear ethical implications which delineate one of Malory's knightly types, what I shall call the Worshipful knight (see chapter 4). At the same time, however, the oath is also a peace-keeping oath with clear political and judicial implications which make it crucial to the success of Arthur's governance.

Arthur reflects the practice of both Lancastrian and Yorkist kings when he requires his knights to swear a peace-keeping oath. The historian A. L. Brown thinks that all of Henry IV's knights and squires 'probably . . . had taken part in some form of oath-swearing' while in his service (18). In 1434 Henry VI administered a peace-keeping oath to those of his knights and squires who were suspected of breaking the peace. And in 1461, the newly crowned Edward IV made all the lords in Parliament swear that they would capture evil doers (Bellamy, *Crime* 114–115). There seems to be a kind of progression here from making king's knights swear that they themselves will not break the peace to making all the great knights in parliament swear that they will help capture other men who break the peace. Malory incorporates this progression in his version of Arthur's peace-keeping oath:

> . . . than the kynge stablysshed all the knyghtes and gaff them rychesse and londys; and charged them never to do outerage nothir morthir, and allwayes to fle treson, and to gyff mercy unto hym that askith mercy, uppon payne of forfiture of their worship and lordship of kynge Arthure for evirmore; and allwayes to do ladyes, damesels, and jantilwomen and wydowes socour: strengthe hem in hir ryghtes, and never to enforce them, uppon payne of dethe. Also, that no man take no batayles in a wrongefull quarell for no love ne for no worldis goodis. So unto thys were all knyghtis sworne of the Table Rounde, both olde and younge, and every yere so were they sworne at the hyghe feste of Pentecoste. (120.15–27:III.15)

Arthur's charges may be interpreted as ethical imperatives designed to regulate the behaviour of adventurous knights-errant. At the same time, however, they also refer closely to the doing of justice and, in particular, to the doing of justice by means of trial by battle.

Arthur's first charge is that his own knights never become lawless themselves ('never to do outerage'), and he specifically forbids both murder and treason, the two most serious crimes under English common law, both of which were punishable by death. Arthur's second charge ('to gyff mercy unto hym that askith mercy') can be interpreted either as an ethical imperative applicable to the behaviour of an adventurous knight errant or as a rule applicable to the behaviour of combatants in trial by battle. It sometimes happened that one killed one's opponent in the course of trial by battle, and the common law of England recognized such killing as justifiable homicide. It was no longer justifiable, however, if the defeated opponent had asked for mercy (Squibb 24). Arthur's third charge is a commonplace of the treatises on chivalry but Malory gives it a distinctly judicial colouring when he adds that Round Table knights must undertake to champion the rightful causes of women in trial by battle ('strengthe hem in hir ryghtes'). Women were helpless before the law so long as legal quarrels could be settled only by means of battle and their general helplessness prompts Arthur to add yet another charge, the injunction against rape upon pain of death. This particular injunction is omitted by Caxton, perhaps because he objected to the implication that Round Table knights could be capable of such ungentle behaviour. There is, in fact, no way of avoiding such an implication, which is why its inclusion in the Winchester text points so clearly both to the practical function of the peace-keeping oath and its judicial significance.[16]

Arthur's last charge is that his knights must never defend a guilty party in trial by battle ('take no batayles in a wrongefull quarell'). This charge points to the fact that trial by battle is the only judicial process in King Arthur's realm. Malory has not simply followed his French sources in this regard. On the contrary, he has gone out of his way to add two dramatic examples of trial by battle without any warrant from his source and to eliminate the only example of an alternative judicial process, the judgment of Guinevere by the barons in the *Mort Artu* (93). Malory's decision may have been dictated in part by his historical sense. He may have believed that the only modes of trial in existence in King Arthur's days were the ancient sacral modes. And it is true that prior to the Lateran Council prohibition of 1215 these modes of trial were customary, although even then they were slowly being supplanted by more rational modes, such as trial by jury or inquisitorial examination. On the other hand, trial by battle was not a complete anachronism in Malory's lifetime, and he himself may have favoured it in certain circumstances. For example, in cases of alleged treason, trial by battle had enjoyed a resurgence of popularity during the late fourteenth and early fifteenth centuries under the new guise of the duel of chivalry and J. G. Bellamy has noted that one of the main reasons for its renewed popularity was the 'fear of bribed juries' (*Law* 143). Bellamy has also found evidence indicating that among the gentry and knightly classes in fifteenth-century England 'there was still considerable adherence to the idea that to settle quarrels by the use of arms was to appeal to the judgment of God' (*Crime* 66). Malory himself belonged to this class. Whether he was the Warwickshire knight, the Cambridgeshire knight or the Yorkshire knight, he could have traced his ancestry back to the eleventh century (Field, 'Sir Robert Malory' 257). If indeed he was the Warwickshire knight, it is quite possible that the uncertainty of obtaining justice in the courts is what drove him to seek redress by force of arms. If he was not the Warwickshire knight, he would still have been aware of such propensities among his fellows. To give but one example, as late as 1470 Thomas Talbot challenged William Lord Berkeley to single combat or pitched battle because he despaired of settling their quarrel by legal means. He required Berkeley

> of knighthood and of manhood to appoynt a day to meet me half way, there to try between God and our two hands all our quarrell and title of right, for to eschew the shedding of Christian menns blood. Or els at the same day bringe the uttermost of thy power, and I shall mete thee. An answere of this by writinge, as ye will abide by, according to the honour and order of knighthood. [Signed] Thomas Talbot the Viscount Lisle. (Scattergood 319)

The result was a pitched battle in which one hundred and fifty men lost their lives, including Thomas Talbot.

Of course, this was behaviour which the English Crown could not tolerate. It was not only an affront to 'the fount of honour'; it was an assault upon the sovereignty of the Crown, to bypass the king, the highest judge in the land, and appeal directly to God for a verdict. The anthropologist Julian Pitt-Rivers has observed that 'the change from the period when the law prescribed the judicial combat to that when the duel was made illegal corresponds to an extension of the competence of the state in judicial matters' (30). Rivers is referring to the private duel of chivalry, but the origins of that aristocratic custom can be traced back to the fourteenth century when both Philip the Fair of France and Edward III of England re-introduced trial by battle in chivalric form in order to allow their knights to defend themselves 'as a knight should,' when charged with felony or treason. In this new form, however, trial by battle was strictly under the control of the monarch. Philip established four prerequisites for such a trial: the homicide, treason or other serious crime must be notorious and certain; the crime must be capital; combat must be the only means of obtaining conviction and punishment; and the accused must be notoriously suspected of the deed (Neilson 161). When Edward III established the Court of Chivalry in England he adopted the French model. Clearly both monarchs hoped that by allowing the duel of chivalry, and at the same time controlling it, they could keep their knights content and at the same time strengthen their sovereign claim to supreme judicial power and authority.[17]

Treason duels of chivalry were 'sensational' and popular events (Bellamy, *Crime* 133). Knightly combatants fought on horseback according to the rules contained in 'The Ordenaunce and Fourme of

Fightyng within Listes' made up by Richard II's Constable, Thomas Woodstock, Duke of Gloucester. Either the Constable of England or the king himself sat as judge. The object of the trial was not necessarily to kill one's opponent; however, the combatant who was 'convicte and discomfite', that is, defeated, was to be 'disarmed in the listes by the commandement of the conestable, and a corner of the liste brokyn in the reprove of hym.' Then he was to be 'drawen oute with hors fro the same place, there he is so disarmede, thorugh the listes unto the place of justice' where he would receive a traitor's death ('Ordenaunce' 325). Most appeals for treason never came to trial by battle; however, if there was insufficient evidence to prove the case and if both appellant and appellee were of good repute, then the king might allow the battle. The king could stop the fight at any time, 'take the quarell in his hande and make them accordid withoute more fightyng' ('Ordenaunce' 325). Richard II stopped the battle between the Dukes of Hereford and Norfolk even before it began and banished both young men, instead. Sometimes knights made appeals of treason in order to have personal revenge. In 1384 it was rumoured that Martigo de Vilenos, a Navarrese knight, had appealed John Walsh of treason for such a private motive. When Walsh succeeded in defeating Vilenos, the Constable ruled that the Navarrese knight should pay the penalty for a false accusation of treason. King Richard concurred, and despite the intercession of Queen Joan, Martigo de Vilenos was duly hanged and drawn as a traitor (Neilson 177; Bellamy, *Crime* 143–146).[18]

Trial by battle also survived under the common law in England, despite the prohibition of the Church, because it was useful to the machinery of royal justice. In medieval England the Crown did not have the right to prosecute suspected felons on its own behalf. Rather it had to depend upon local juries to indict or upon individuals to appeal. Well into the fifteenth century an appeal of felony or treason could go to trial by battle if both parties agreed and the judge permitted. For the most part, judges discouraged trial by battle and appellees could usually avoid it by claiming that the appellant was motivated by spite and hatred (Bellamy, *Crime* 126). Nevertheless the appeal of felony or treason was useful to the Crown because sometimes it was the only way to get a conviction, whether the case eventually went to trial by jury or by battle. Frequently the Crown was able to convince 'indicted men of bad record' to appeal their accomplices 'in return for a further lease of life' (Bellamy, *Crime* 127). Such appellants were known as approvers, and there is a 'distinct probability' that considerable pressure was sometimes brought to bear to make them become approvers. In effect an approver 'became the agent of the king in preserving public order' and for his service the 'king would pay him a penny or three halfpence a day' so long as he was in custody (Bellamy, *Crime* 130).[19]

The main difference between the system of royal justice in fifteenth-century England and that which Malory portrays in King Arthur's days is that Lancastrian and Yorkist kings had alternatives to trial by battle, even in cases of alleged treason and felony, whereas Arthur does not. Malory's Arthur has no choice but to do justice 'bi the swerde'. The Yorkist King, Edward IV, could bring a case of alleged treason before his Council which then had the option of resorting to inquisitorial examination, not only of the accuser and accused, but also of anyone else who had knowledge of the facts (Bellamy, *Crime* 136–7). Malory's King Arthur never does this. Not even when his own queen is accused of treason and stands to lose her life for want of a champion does he resort to judgment in council. In both the 'Poisoned Apple' and the 'Knight of the Cart' he personally examines the queen and other witnesses to satisfy himself of her innocence, but he relies upon trial by battle to prove it. He himself can never be her champion because as king he 'muste be a ryghtfull juge', but in the absence of her usual champion, Sir Lancelot du Lac, he is confident that 'somme good knyght shall put hys body in jouparté for my quene rather than she sholde be brente in a wronge quarell' (1050.6, 9–11:XVIII.4).

Once a fifteenth-century king had decided to allow a treason duel of chivalry, he still retained the right to stop the battle at any time and give judgment, condemning the loser to a traitor's death on the scaffold. Malory's Arthur never does this, either. He presides over trials but he never interferes in their process, the operative presumption being that the judgment is made by God through the agency of the combatants themselves. It is for this reason that Arthur makes his Round Table knights swear never to do battle 'in a wrongefull quarell for no love ne for no worldis goodis'. Like most late medieval English kings, Malory's Arthur does not believe that trial by battle invariably yields a true judgment of God. Rather he regards it as a customary mode of settling quarrels which may render 'true justyce' provided it can be regulated to avoid the probability of gross injustice (Van Caenegem 68–70). So long as the best knights in the world always fight for the right, or for what Arthur judges to be the right, then, in all likelihood, 'true justyce' will be done. And indeed the only time Arthur refuses to allow a trial by battle and resorts to summary proceedings instead is when Lancelot himself is accused of treason and Arthur knows of no knight who 'ys able to macch hym' (1163.18:XX.2; see below 314–21).

Arthur's apparent scepticism regarding trial by battle does not mean that he has no faith in God. Rather, it means that he has adopted the

Rationalist attitude toward this essentially irrational mode of doing justice and thus anticipates the orthodoxy of the period after the Fourth Lateran Council (1215). Christine de Pizan summarizes the orthodox position in her *Book of Fayttes of Armes and Chyvalry*.

> We saie that for to aske a thynge ayenst nature or aboue nature is presumpcyon & it displeaseth god, & for to trowe that the feble shalle ouercome the stronge, & and the olde the younge or the sike the hole, by strengthe of goode right, to haue, as haue had & have confidence they that therto putte hemself, suche a thinge is but atemptyng of god & I saye for certeyn that yf it happe them to wynne, it is but an aduenture, & not for the gode ryght that they therto haue. (259)

Christine says it is 'ayenst nature' that a very weak man should vanquish a strong man, that a very old man should vanquish a young man, or that a sick man should vanquish a healthy man. Certainly it is against the odds; and if it should 'happe', Christine is quite certain that the outcome is 'but an aduenture', by which she means something like 'only an accident'.

Not everyone would agree with Christine's rational orthodoxy, however, not even in the fifteenth-century. Both Sir Gilbert Hay and William Caxton translate without demur Ramon Lull's assurance that 'the trewe knyght that fyȝteth for the ryȝt may not be surmounted' (Lull 52). In a world in which men believed God to be immanent, it made sense that He would have a hand in the outcome of trial by battle. And of course the Church never denied this; she only argued that it was sinfully presumptuous to demand that God produce a miracle in order to do justice, particularly when there were more rational modes available to achieve the same end.[20] However, a deeply religious man could easily turn the argument of presumption upon its head. He would not think it presumptuous to believe that God will grant victory to the knight fighting in the right, even if he is weaker and less experienced than his guilty opponent; on the contrary, he would think it presumptuous to believe that a stronger knight can win 'a wrongefull quarell' simply because he is stronger.

A deeply religious man could also explain those occasions when trial by battle appears to result in injustice, as we can see in Sir Gilbert Hay's expanded version of Lull's text:

> . . . never curage of traytour mycht our cum ane noble curage of a trew knycht, bot gif it be throw pride or surquidy, that is callit our presumptuous in him self: the quhilk God tholes quhilom be punyst in bataill place. Bot the curage of a lele knycht, that for a

> lele caus debatis, may nocht be our cummyn, *bot gif it be for sum syn agaynis the order of knychthede.* (31, emphasis added)

If it is presumptuous to think one can win 'a wrongefull quarell' by sheer physical strength, it is equally presumptuous to think one can win 'a rightful quarrell' by sheer physical strength. God sometimes will allow such presumption to be punished by defeat even though the presumptuous knight fights for the right.

Both of these points of view, the Rationalist as well as the Religious, are Christian. Indeed, by Malory's time, the Rationalist point of view had become more orthodox than the Religious point of view. And there is no way of reconciling them. They are two fundamentally different ways of interpreting experience. One of the trials by battle which Malory adds to the *Morte Darthur* is the battle fought by Ywain, the 'yongest and waykest' (163.12–13:IV.20) of three knights who have set out in search of adventures. Ywain fights not one, but two 'perelous' knights who have extorted a barony of lands from the Dame de la Roche. He fights 'for Goddis sake and in the defence of your [the lady's] ryght' (177.15:IV.27) and he wins. Christine de Pizan would interpret this outcome as 'but an aduenture'. Sir Gilbert Hay would interpret it as a judgment of God. And there is no way to determine which one of them would be right.

Malory makes this point with beautiful economy in the first trial by battle to be fought in the *Morte Darthur*, the battle between Arthur and Accolon. In this episode, which occurs not long after the institution of the Round Table, Arthur awakes one morning to find himself in the prison of the notorious Sir Damas. He is told that unless he agrees to fight for his gaoler in a 'wrongefull quarell' he must die of starvation. Malory has altered this episode to make the quarrel between Sir Damas and his brother, Sir Outelake, a clear-cut case of wrong versus right. He also adds that all of Damas' other prisoners have refused to fight for him, eighteen of them having starved to death already as a consequence (138–139:IV.7). In this predicament Arthur decides that he would rather fight than die of starvation, but as a condition of his acceptance he insists that all the other prisoners also be released.

Arthur's willingness to undertake this 'wrongefull quarell' confirms his Rationalist attitude. Clearly he thinks he has a good chance of winning the battle, and we know from the outcome that his intention is to overturn the judgment of God and do 'true justyce' as soon as he has won the field. On the other hand, Accolon's response to Arthur's victory, snatched from what appeared to be certain death, is to assume that a miracle has taken place: 'ye ar the beste knyght that ever I founde, and I se well that God is with you' (145.10–11:IV.10). There is no way of knowing which one of them is right — Arthur who thinks he has won by superior courage and strength, and perhaps a bit of luck, or Accolon, who thinks he has won by miracle.[21]

The Rationalist and the Religious interpretations of the battle between Arthur and Accolon do not exhaust the interpretative possibilities, however. Both men rely on talismans for victory — the same talisman, in fact, for both think they are in possession of Excalibur and its marvelous scabbard which preserves the wearer from loss of blood. The use of magic was explicitly prohibited by the Duke of Gloucester's 'Ordenaunce & Fourme of Fightyng Within Listes'. Gloucester's rules require that appellant and appellee each swear prior to doing battle that he has on his person no 'charme, ne experiment, ne acrocte [talisman], ne othir enchauntement . . . by the which [he] trusteth [him] þe bettir to ovircome' and that he 'trusteth in noon othir thynge, but oonly in god and [his] body . . . [and] on [his] rightfull quarell' (317). It is, of course, ironic that the Rationalist Arthur should put his trust in a talisman, and equally ironic that Accolon, having lost his talisman and consequently the battle, should attribute that double loss to God. The point is that both of them are capable of putting their trust in magic. Arthur can argue, quite pragmatically, that he has already proved the efficacy of Excalibur. But how does he account for the remarkable turn of fortune which allows him to recover Excalibur and save himself from certain death? Malory does not tell us whether or not Arthur is even aware of the Lady of the Lake's presence. But he tells the reader not only that she has come in order to save Arthur's life (142.19–24:IV.9) but also that it was by her 'inchauntemente [that] the swerde Excalibur fell oute of Accalons honde to the erthe' so that Arthur could retrieve it and win the battle (144.24–25:IV.10). Armed with this knowledge, some readers might draw the conclusion that the battle between Arthur and Accolon is really a battle between two witches, one good witch (The Lady of the Lake) and one bad (Morgan le Fay) and that the outcome proves the magic of the good witch to be more powerful than the magic of the bad witch.

I am not seriously advocating such an interpretation of this battle, but it is important, I think, to note that it is just as possible as either the Rationalist or the Religious interpretation. When two men meet in mortal combat, what factors really determine who shall win? If they are fairly evenly matched in terms of position on the field, strength, skill and weaponry, that is to say, if they are fairly evenly matched in physical terms, then we must look either to accident or to metaphysical factors to explain the outcome. Barring accident, the man who believes with his whole being that he will win is very likely to do so, and it does not matter at all whether his belief rests in his own physical strength, in God, or in a magic sword and scabbard.[22] That both participants in late medieval trials by battle were expressly forbidden to employ talismans is, in fact, an explicit acknowledgement of their supposed magical effectiveness. There would be no point in requiring each combatant to swear beforehand that he had no such 'charme' or 'enchauntement' upon his person 'by the which' he trusted 'þe bettir to ovircome' if all those present did not think that such a magical device could make a substantial difference to the outcome of the battle.

There are sixteen trials by battle fought in the *Morte Darthur*. Two of them are primitive *holmganga*, battles fought by single combatants representing entire nations or armies in order to determine which nation shall pay tribute to the other. These are both fought by Tristram, one against Marhalt, Champion of Ireland (380–83:VIII.6–7) and one against Elyas, the leader of the Saxon host (625–26:X.30). In both cases there are witnesses, but no judges. The battles between Arthur and Accolon, Ywain and Sir Edward and Sir Hew of the Red Castle, (177–78:IV.27–28) Gareth and the Red Knight of the Red Lands (325–26:VII.18) and Bors and Prydam le Noyre (957–60:XVI.7–8) are all fought to settle land claims, and once again, although there are witnesses present, there are no judges. Of the eight treason duels of chivalry, however, six are fought in proper lists and before properly appointed judges. Tristram successfully defends the King of Ireland against Blamoure's appeal of treason in the lists of Camelot, with King Carados and the King of Scots sitting as judges (406–407:VIII.21). Again in the lists at Camelot King Mark successfully defends himself against his own knight's charge of treason with King Arthur sitting as judge (592–93:X.15). During the Tournament of Surluse Palomides successfully defends himself twice against charges that he is a 'traytoure' with Galahalt the Haute Prince presiding (658, 664–666:X.43, 47). Back at Camelot after the Quest of the Holy Grail Lancelot successfully defends the queen on two occasions, when she is appealed of treason for the murder of Sir Patryse by Mador de la Porte (1058:XVII.7) and when she is appealed of treason by Mellyagaunt for adultery with one of her ten wounded knights (1138:XIX.9). King Arthur presides over Lancelot's first two trials by battle with Mador de la Porte and Mellyagaunt. He is also present at the siege of Benwick but there he is in no position to assume the authority of judge when Lancelot successfully defends himself against Gawain's appeal of treason (1217–18:XX.21; 1219–21: XX.22). As king of France and lord of Benwick, Lancelot himself should have presided over any treason duel of chivalry fought on his territory. He was under no political necessity to respond to Gawain's appeal, but evidently he felt a strong moral necessity to defend himself against the charge of treason. The only other treason duel of chivalry to be fought without a sovereign judge presiding is Palomides' duel with the murderers of King Harmaunce (717–18:X.63–64) and that is simply because the Red City has no legitimate ruler after the murder of their king.

Whether or not all these trials by battle render 'true justyce' is matter for debate. Sometimes Malory offers corroborating evidence to confirm the justice of the verdict, as when he has the Lady of the Lake come to Camelot to assure everyone of the queen's innocence and to name the knight responsible for the death of Patryse (1059.11–26:XVIII.8). Only once, however, does he present a clear-cut case of trial by battle producing a wrong verdict. That is when King Mark manages to kill Sir Amaunte, even though Amaunte fought 'in the ryghtuous quarell' (592.26–27:X.14). In fact, we already know that Mark is in the wrong, for we have witnessed his crime (578–79:X.7). Yet rather than rationalize this miscarrige of justice, as the *Tristan* does, on the grounds that Mark refused to swear the proper oath beforehand, therefore invalidating the trial, Malory prefers to leave it unexplained except as the inscrutable will of God: 'A, swete Jesu that knowyste all hydde thynges! Why sufferyst Thou so false a traytoure to venqueyshe and sle a trewe knyght that faught in a ryghteuous quarell!' (593.11–13:X.15). On balance, therefore, we have much more reason to believe that trial by battle has resulted in justice than we have to believe the opposite, as we near the end of Malory's long book and the sequence of battles in which Lancelot fulfills his role as the Queen's champion. However we interpret the justice done by means of these battles, we must be aware by the end of Malory's book that there is more than one point of view from which to make our interpretation. In fact, there are three, as I have already suggested in discussing the 'Arthur and Accolon' episode (the only other clear case of a 'wrongefull' judgment of God in the *Morte Darthur*). Malory consistently associates the Religious (what I shall later call the providentialist) point of view with Lancelot and the Grail knights. He just as consistently associates the Rationalist point of view with Arthur and Tristram. And, finally, very near the end of his work, he will associate the magical point of view with Gawain.

Trial by battle is only the most formalized mode of doing justice 'bi the swerd' in the *Morte Darthur*; it is not the only way. Arthur's Round Table knights also function as agents of royal justice whenever they are out upon their adventures. They punish criminals, rescue knights and ladies and pacify rebels to the Crown. In all these activities they may be seen to approximate the judicial and peace-keeping functions of fifteenth-century king's knights. In fact, by the fifteenth century it was possible to define any knight as an 'officer ryale', as Sir Gilbert Hay does in one of his many digressions from his thirteenth-century French source, going on to say that the knight's chief duty is to uphold the 'kingis rychtis' (46). Hay was describing the political situation he could observe in mid-fifteenth-century Scotland and England where most knights had been knighted by the king and many received retaining fees from him, even though they did not reside at court. Now modern historians are turning up evidence to prove that these fifteenth-century king's knights 'did more to uphold the king's authority in his kingdom than the household clerks ever did' and that 'good government' depended in large measure upon them (Keen, *England* 21).

Modern historians use the term 'affinity' to denote the groups of men, not all of them knights, to whom Lancastrian and Yorkist kings gave retaining fees. In some cases, these groups or 'retinues' could be quite large. Henry IV retained several hundred knights and squires, only thirty-five of whom were strictly Household knights (Brown 15–17), whereas Edward IV retained a much smaller number, never more than a hundred (Ross 329). Yet no matter how large his retinue, the king had a personal relationship with each of his men. The word 'affinity', with its lingering connotations of kinship, neatly expresses that personal bond, but it was not available to Malory for that purpose. The meaning of 'affinité' in fifteenth-century England was still overwhelmingly tied to kinship (normally by marriage, but also in some contexts by blood).[23] Therefore Malory uses the word 'fellowship' to refer to the knights whom King Arthur retains in his service. ME *felawship* had a wide array of connotations, all of them, for Malory's purposes, positive: intimate comradeship (*MED* 2a); conviviality (*MED* 3a); charitable fellow-feeling (*MED* 4); a band of fighting men (*MED* 5c) a knightly order (*MED* 6a: 'the knightys of the order and felouship of saint George'); and, one of the heavenly companies of angels or a Christian communion (*MED* 7a, c). In other words, 'fellowship' could not only suggest the personal bond between lord and man, it could also suggest all the functions of King Arthur's knights, from their military duties to their household offices.

King's knights frequently upheld their lord's 'rychtis' and authority by serving as knights of the shire in his parliament, or, if they were great knights (barons or peers), by sitting with other lords in his Council. Therefore, it is significant, I think, that the Caxton text refers to those Round Table knights who are summoned to York to 'holde a parlement' as being of the king's 'retenue' (V.3: 'all that were undir his obeysaunce', 194.16). This is the only time the Middle English term 'retenue' is applied to the Round Table knights in either text. In the late Middle Ages 'retenue' denoted primarily that group of knights who had been retained by their lord to serve him in time of war (*MED* 3). Malory uses it twice in the Winchester manuscript to refer to those men who fight with their lord Priamus (233.14; 238.27). Therefore it is entirely appropriate that it be applied to Arthur's Round Table knights when they gather as a council of war. Whoever made the Caxton revision of this part of the narrative recognized that the Round Table fellowship was functioning both militarily and politically as a royal 'retenue'.[24]

King's knights also served often on royal judicial commissions (Winkler 63). In fact, in fifteenth-century England the 'most powerful instrument' the king possessed for the maintenance of public order throughout his realm was the commission of oyer and terminer. Such a commission would be composed of justices of the king's bench and of common pleas, together with an admixture of noblemen, royal servants and notable gentry. In the fifteenth-century the percentage of noblemen serving on these commissions grew steadily. Commissions of oyer and terminer could be directed to investigate all the crimes committed in a certain district or only a certain category. They could also conduct their own inquests and, although they were not powerful, relying upon the local machinery of justice for punitive measures, they were effective (Bellamy, *Crime* 99). Malory has suggested the activities of these commissions of oyer and terminer, as well as of other royal commissions constituted specially to seek out treasons or to grant pardons to rebels, in the knight-errantry of the Round Table knights.

The only difference between the judicial and peace-keeping activities of Arthur's Round Table knights and those of fifteenth-century royal commissions is that the errant Round Table knights punish the malfactors themselves rather than turn them over to the local sheriff or send them back to King Arthur's court for judgment. In other words, Malory imagines that the Round Table knights function as a kind of itinerant national police force. He may have got this idea from Sir Gilbert Hay, who in his *Buke of Knychthede* comes up with a similar view of the functioning of the 'ordre of knychthede' by comparison with the functioning of judges of the king's bench and justices of the peace:

> Bot thare is nane that all knawis, na all may punyse, bot the Emperoure, the quhilk ordanyt knychthede spirituale, to kepe justice ordinare, be reugle vertuous, in pes and concorde, and justice rigorous, that is, the ordre of knychthede, quhilk suld on force compell evill men, and of wikkit lyf, to desist and cess fra thair wikkitnesse, and punys thame tharfor. (33)

Only God ('the Emperoure') knows all and therefore only He may punish all. Nevertheless, He ordained both the royal judiciary system and the 'ordre of knychthede' to do justice in this world, the former to do justice 'be reugle of justice, to mak gud reugle and gracious concorde and governaunce in the peple,' and the latter to do justice by compelling,

> be fors of armes all tyrannis, traytouris, and all othir mysdoaris, and cruell tormentouris of the haly labouraris, kirk men, merchandis, and travalouris, to cess and desist fra thair wikkitness. (33–34)

Hay's list of criminals covers the gamut, from tyrants, through traitors, down to brigands and thieves. And in his tales of knightly adventure Malory has managed to include examples of every kind, either by wise selection from his sources, alteration of his sources, or invention. What is more, whether he knew Hay's book or not, Malory has responded to the admonishment that 'knychtis of pes' and 'knychtis of the justice rigorous' ought to be 'full of vertues, and gude lyf, to geve otheris ensample' (34). Those knights of the Round Table who are most effective in doing justice and keeping the peace are those who strive to live virtuously.

The best of them all, of course, is Lancelot, the first Round Table knight whose judicial and peace-keeping activities are described at length. In his tale he executes a criminal knight guilty of robbery and rape (269–70:VI.10). He then kills two giants, liberates the ladies who had been imprisoned by them, gives the ladies the giants' treasure as a compensation for their 'grevaunces' and insists that the castle be restored to its rightful owner (272:VI.11). He also rescues the prisoners of the false knight Tarquin, including many knights of the Round Table (268:VI.9), foils a treacherous attempt on his own life, and sends the wife-slayer Sir Pedivere to Arthur's court for his punishment (285–86:VI.17). Even though he has been introduced as the best of the Round Table knights, clearly his activities are meant to be typical of the fellowship as a whole. This is confirmed in the Tale of Gareth when the Lady Lyones, beseiged in her castle, sends to Arthur's court for help. It is confirmed yet again when Gareth finally arrives on the scene and expresses surprise that as yet 'none of the noble knyghtes of my lorde Arthurs have nat dalte with' her oppressor (320.22–23:VII.15). After defeating the felonious Red Knight of the Red Lands, Gareth, like his mentor Lancelot, ensures that justice is done. He might have executed the traitor for his foul murders, but decides instead to spare his life, provided that he will 'make . . . amendys' for all the 'trespasse' that he has done against Dame Lyones and her lands and will give 'assurauns' of his future good behaviour (325–26:VII.18).

Gareth and Lancelot provide the most prominent, but not the only examples in the *Morte* of errant Round Table knights doing justice in the king's name. In the first tale Malory invents an adventure for young Ywain in which he punishes two knights for extorting a barony of lands from the Lady of the Roche (177–78:IV.27) and, in the tale of Tristam, he includes an adventure in which Lancelot helps young La Cote Mal Tayle to subdue the lord of the Castel Pendragon who has long been a 'grete enemy to kynge Arthur'. In fact, when the lord of the castle persists in refusing to become King Arthur's man Lancelot takes it upon himself to deprive him of his lands and give them to La Cote instead (476:IX.9). Even during the adventures of the Holy Grail, Malory keeps before us the social and political consequences of the activities of Arthur's Round Table knights. Bors does battle to preserve the land rights of a great lady (957:XVI.7) and Galahad restores the Castle of Maidens to its rightful owner (887–90:XIII.15). The subsequent symbolic interpretation of these adventures does not alter the fact that through their prowess Arthur's knights have righted great wrongs. Indeed, Malory emphasizes the gravity of the crimes committed by the seven false knights at the Castle of Maidens when he adds to their sexual crimes the following social and political crimes: 'by grete force they helde all the knyghtes of the contrey undir grete servayge and trewayge, robbynge and pyllynge the poure comyn peple' (889.16–19:XIII.15).

The adventures of errant Round Table knights suggest the judicial and peace-keeping activities of king's knights operating from the court as part of the centralized system of royal justice. But in the fifteenth century king's knights could not be everywhere at once and therefore most governance was of necessity a local matter. The King held the most powerful local lords responsible for keeping the peace in their localities, and they, in turn, relied upon their affinities or retinues of knights and squires. Gareth's marriage to the great heiress, the Lady Lyones, and his near kinship to the king make him the greatest lord in his locality. But even before the fortunate event of his marriage, Gareth has acquired an immense retinue simply through the exercise of his knightly prowess. Gareth does not offer to pay them a fee of any kind, but all of the knights he defeats in single combat, including one of baronial rank (Sir Persaunte de l'Inde) and one duke (the Duke de la Rowse), are eager to attach themselves to him by offering 'homage and feaute'. With them they bring their combined retinues of over three hundred knights. Gareth's knightly prowess thus becomes a kind of romance equivalent for the immense political power of a great magnate in fifteenth-century England. And his relationship to his retainers reflects that new type of contractual relationship to be found by Edward IV's time, when peers would agree to be a 'good and favourable lord' to less powerful men who were neither their tenants nor their fee'd retainers.[25] Only at his wedding feast does Gareth reward the three most prominent of his new men by giving each of them a high office in his new household: chamberlain, butler and chief steward, and carver (361–2:VII.36).

These same three knights, Sir Persaunte de l'Inde, Sir Ironsyde, and the Duke de la Rowse, also become knights of the Round Table. In this way Arthur strengthens his position in the area which Gareth has pacified (both Sir Ironsyde and the Duke de la Rowse were once redoubtable enemies of the king), and can look to these men as well as to his nephew to see that the king's justice is upheld in their localities:

> to see that no manner robberies, spoliations, oppressions, or extortions be suffered to be committed amongst any of the king's subjects of those parts, of what estate, degree, or condition soever they be; and in case any happen to be, to see them so offending utterly to be punished according with the king's laws.
>
> (Ferguson 140)

The words come from a letter written by Richard III in 1483, but they could have been written at any time during the fifteenth-century, so well do they describe the essence of the local political and judicial responsibilities of the king's own knights. In fact, Henry VI wrote to Lord Poynings in 1453 to explain that he was giving him a barony of lands in expectation that he would in future do him 'good service', particularly 'in the keping of the rest and pees of our lande, and in letting of all that shode mowe to the contrarye' (Lander, *Crown* 35). Likewise, when Edward IV granted Lord Hastings the forfeited estates of the Earl of Wiltshire, he expected him to keep the peace and do justice in that part of Leicestershire where they lay. Such gifts also increased the political power of the king's men enormously, enabling them to support the king's interests generally in their localities. Edward's grant to Hastings converted a strongly loyal Lancastrian district into a Yorkist sphere of influence (Lander, *Crown* 69). Likewise, Gareth's marriage and the admission of Sir Ironsyde, Sir Persaunte de l'Inde and the Duke de la Rowse into the fellowship of the Round Table convert a district hostile to Arthur into one which will henceforth be governed in his name and in his interest.

In 1945 K. B. McFarlane labeled this method of governance 'Bastard Feudalism', since it resembled the feudal system of governance but had replaced fief and homage with cash fees. More recent historians have questioned his choice of epithet as unnecessarily and inaccurately pejorative. The fact that money or offices rather than feudal land tenure sealed the contractual relationship between lord and man does not seem to have undermined the strength of the personal bond thus created. Indeed, in his essay, 'Bachelor and Retainer', J. H. Bean argues that the nature of the bond between lord and man had not altered much since Anglo-Saxon times. To the Anglo-Saxon household knight, his lord was the 'loaf-giver' (*hlaford*) and he was the 'loaf-eater' (*hlafeotan*); to the fifteenth-century retainer, his lord was his 'good and gracious lord' and he was his 'lover'. In both time periods men looked to their lords for protection, affection and the amenities of life, and quite naturally employed the language of love and kinship to describe their relationship. Maurice Keen comes to a similar conclusion in his study of the three types of relationship most common among aristocratic men in the fifteenth-century: the groups of knights and their lord who comprised the secular orders of chivalry; the groups of knights who swore brotherhood-in-arms during the Hundred Years' War; and the groups of knights who comprised the affinities or retinues of great magnates and of the king. Keen concludes that all three formed relationships tantamount to a 'bond of artificial kinship' ('Brotherhood' 13). All of them were based on the mutual obligation to aid one another in every enterprise, allegience only excepted without dishonour, and all of them involved some sharing of heraldic arms. Thus it is easy to see why historians have chosen the word 'affinity' to denote the groups of men retained by Lancastrian and Yorkist kings. And certainly, whether one thinks of them primarily as a secular order of chivalry, a group of brothers-in-arms, or the retinue of King Arthur, the Round Table fellowship comprises Arthur's 'affinity' his 'family in chivalry'.

Even members of real families quarrel among themselves, and one of the biggest problems which fifteenth-century English kings had was keeping their knights and their greatest magnates from quarreling among themselves and abusing the system of royal justice to achieve their own ends. The administration of a peace-keeping oath was not in itself sufficient to prevent such abuses. The king had to know how to handle his men, how to build as broad a political base as possible throughout his realm by the judicious dispensation of patronage to his knights and how to placate his greatest magnates, his 'peers', by offering them the opportunity to gain glory through war abroad and high political office at home.

Most difficult of all, no doubt, was the task of controlling the behaviour of those closest to him — his household knights and his own kinsmen. In the words of George Asheby, it was essential that none of the king's men

> . . . be their power excedyng,
> Ne mayntenie no people, by youre puissance,
> Ner false quarels take thorough maintenance.
> (Scattergood 318)

Not long after Asheby wrote these words, Edward IV's brother, George, Duke of Clarence, provided a shocking example of such abuse of the royal power when he forced a jury to convict a woman he suspected of having poisoned his wife. Some of the jurors begged the hapless woman's pardon before she was burned at the stake, but they could not stop the proceedings. Perhaps the most sobering conclusion to be drawn from this episode is that the king's brother was able to perpetrate such gross injustice with impunity. Indeed, his crime might never even have been recorded for the historian's notice, if George had not subsequently become involved in a treasonous plot against Edward (Bellamy, *Crime* 57–58).

The fifteenth century was an age of 'change and legal experimentation' which entailed a seeming 'crisis in public order' (Bellamy, *Crime* 160). The old sacral and irrational ways of doing justice had been almost entirely abandoned, but the new rational ways had not yet been fully developed. It was abundantly clear how fallible human judgment could be, even when the intention to do justice had not been stopped by bribery or intimidation, and therefore Englishmen looked above all to their king for redress of grievances. Bellamy has noted that lawlessness fluctuated throughout the late Middle Ages and that there was a positive correlation between a high degree of lawlessness and prolonged absences of the monarch; weak monarchs like Henry VI were almost as bad as absent ones. Therefore, he concludes that historians are warranted in laying great emphasis upon the king's personality and on his will and ability to govern effectively, for without a strong personality and equally strong will to keep the peace and do justice, there 'could be little public order' in a medieval monarchy (Bellamy, *Crime* 11–12).

Fifteenth-century England knew both effective and ineffective governance. The powerful Lancastrian affinity developed by Henry IV served his son Henry V well, both in peace and in war, and did much to offset the weaknesses of Henry VI. In fact, it has been argued that Henry's extraordinarily long reign, despite his incompetence, must be attributed largely to the strength and loyalty of his knights. Edward IV's reign was much shorter, but Edward very early on achieved a reputation for standing with 'true justice'. Bellamy notes that he sat in Westminster for three days on one occasion in an effort to correct some of the lawlessness which had developed during the reign of Henry VI (Bellamy, *Crime* 12).

Malory wrote his *Morte Darthur* during the reign of Edward and it is tempting to speculate that he may have modeled his portrait of Arthur upon the Yorkist monarch. Both Arthur and Edward are commanding figures who generate powerful loyalty in their knights and are successful with the ladies. Both are devoted to doing justice, but have difficulty doing justice upon their relatives (Arthur openly favours his nephews, and Edward was overly generous to his wife's kinsmen) and in both cases their nepotism angers other factions in the court and creates political problems for them. I would not want to push this highly speculative hypothesis any farther; however it is significant that the political dimensions of Malory's history are so clear as to suggest it.[26]

The success of Arthur's governance will depend almost as much upon the ability of his knights as it will upon his own ability as the highest officer of knighthood in the realm. In the next three chapters I will examine the ethical typology of knighthood which Malory develops using Arthur and his knights as examples. If fifteenth-century men were right to view 'the problems of public life, like those of private, in the light of personal morality' and to conclude therefrom that good governance could only be achieved by means of 'a return to virtue on the part of all men, but especially those who have the care of the whole community as their primary responsibility' (Ferguson 138), then the success or failure of Arthur's governance will depend in large measure on the ethical standards achieved by him and his knights of the Round Table.

2

A Typology of Knighthood

Late medieval treatises on knighthood served as ethical handbooks for the governing class of England in addition to providing them with more practical advice. Indeed, one eminent cultural historian of fifteenth-century England has argued that William Caxton published Sir Thomas Malory's *Morte Darthur* for the same reason that he published Ramon Lull's *Book of the Ordre of Chiualry*, because he had 'faith in the efficacy of chivalric literature for the planting of socially desirable virtues' in members of the 'English governing class' (Ferguson 36).

Caxton saw that Malory's book provided many examples of knightly behaviour, both good and bad:

> For herein may be seen noble chyvalrye, curtosye, hymanyté frendlynesse, hardynesse, love, frendshyp, cowardyse, murdre, hate, vertue, and synne.

That presumably is why he advises his readers to 'Doo after the good and leve the evyl' if they wish to come 'to good fame and renommée'. It is quite possible, in fact, that Caxton's awareness of the didactic usefulness of Malory's book helped him to overcome his doubts regarding its historical veracity. He is careful to leave his readers at 'lyberté' to decide for themselves whether or not all that 'is conteyned herin' is 'trewe'; but he insists nevertheless that the *Morte Darthur* contains 'doctryne' which will help them to come not only to 'good fame and renommée in thys lyf' but also to 'everlastyng blysse in heven' (cxlvi.4–16).

Medieval rhetoricians took for granted that writers write for the moral edification of their readers. They were familiar with Aristotle's *Ethics*, if not his *Poetics*, and assumed the existence of an ethical norm for every class of individuals. Therefore, they advised writers to make their characters typical:

> Hence the attributes assigned to the Pope, or Cesar, or the rest, must be understood in such a way that the particular name does not outweigh the relevance of these attributes to other persons of the same condition, age, dignity, office, or sex. The particular designation should be taken to stand for a general designation

according to the nature of the subject and not according to the subject used to exemplify that nature. (Matthew of Vendôme 71)

In this passage Matthew of Vendôme presumes that the main function of the literary character is to be ethically instructive. It is not important, therefore, that the character be fully realized; it is important only that he be typical of his class and that whatever individualizing traits his author gives him should not obscure 'the nature of the subject', that is the particular type or class of human beings which he exemplifies.

In Malory's *Morte Darthur* the subject or class of men to be exemplified is knighthood. However, Malory does not assume that this 'subject' has one unified nature. On the contrary, he presents his readers with three quite different types of knight. Although there is some sharing of qualities among them, each type has its own distinct ethos, determined by its own particular world view and correlative understanding of what it means to be a 'good' knight. Heretofore, critics have tended to fasten on one or the other of these basic types and to argue that it represents either Malory's own personal code of knighthood or the dominant ideal in his book. For example, Eugene Vinaver has concluded that the oath which Arthur requires all his Round Table knights to swear annually at the feast of Pentecost represents 'the most complete and authentic record of M's conception of chivalry' (*Works* 1335; cf. Brewer 105 and Benson 137–39). Michael Stroud has argued that the 'chivalric ethos' portrayed through the actions of Arthur and his knights during the Roman campaign represents Malory's own preference for the values of the fighter, the 'values of the past' (352). And more than one critic has assumed that Malory's preferred ideal of chivalry is the highly religious and ascetic ideal exemplified by the Grail knights (Hynes-Berry 98; Ihle 41). Others have entertained the notion that Malory may have intended to present both worldly and other-worldly types of knighthood as good in themselves. For example, Arthur Ferguson, the intellectual and cultural historian, stresses the practical aspect of Malory's chivalric ethos: knighthood was to him 'a very real institution, its values good and uniquely pertinent to the aristocratic society in which he lived' (46). At the same time, Ferguson acknowledges the importance of the 'religious issue': 'the medieval knight was as concerned as anybody else about his salvation', and it would have been surprising indeed, if Malory had not given 'some thought to the spiritual side of the knightly life' (52). By contrast, as we shall see later in this chapter, C. S. Lewis stresses the religious aspect of Malory's chivalric ethos, and tends to play down the practical, martial or political, aspects. Therefore, although Lewis correctly perceives Malory's admiration for the noble and secular way of the world, he incorrectly identifies Galahad, the mystic and contemplative, as Malory's own choice of the very 'best' knight (239).

As we have seen in the previous chapter, medieval treatises on knighthood were themselves somewhat divided in emphasis. Those written earlier (late thirteenth to mid-fourteenth century) tended to emphasize the religious aspect of knighthood whereas those written during the late-fourteenth and fifteenth centuries tended to give equal or greater emphasis to more practical or worldly considerations. Nevertheless, the treatises with a strong religious bias were translated into English and Scottish in the fifteenth century and continued to be read in England well into the next century, if not longer. At the same time, those treatises which emphasized practical instruction, teaching the knight either the etiquette of the court or the tactics of warfare, also taught him that he could not be regarded as a 'good' or 'noble' knight unless he were virtuous. The problem which Malory addresses in his *Morte Darthur*, and which none of the treatises on chivalry ever confronts, is that not every man will have exactly the same notion of what it means to be a 'good' or 'noble' knight. To some of Malory's characters it means no more than being a good fighter on horseback (cf. *MED* 'chevalerie' 1a: 'A body or host of armoured and mounted warriors or knights serving an overlord'). To many others it means considerably more: it means having the courtly virtues as well, those virtues which make a knight pleasing to his lady and useful to his lord in the social and political context of life at court. And to a few others it means having all the feudal and courtly virtues plus the specifically Christian virtues, as well.

Malory develops his characters through action. His three ethical types emerge gradually through the adventures of many knights, and we cannot say that they are fully defined until they have achieved their most complete and dramatic expression in the three main protagonists of the post-Grail narrative. However, Malory introduces his types very early and outlines them clearly in the repeated pattern of the triple quest which concludes his first narrative unit (Vinaver's Tale of King Arthur and Caxton's Books I–IV). Gawain figures in both quests so that there are only five different knights who undertake these 'stronge' adventures; however, the way they handle the similar situations which confront them suggests that there are only three different ways of understanding what it means to be a good knight. The first set of three adventures Malory found in his source, the *Suite du Merlin*, and he has altered these only in minor details. However, the second set of three adventures is mostly of his own invention, and it is these adventures, with their characteristic Malorian focus upon the social, political and judicial implications of knighthood, which confirm the existence of the three distinct types.

Before commencing a detailed analysis of the adventures of these five knights, it is well to remember that they occur within the context of Malory's providential history of King Arthur. Recently Jill Mann has argued, with regard to these very same adventures, that Malory intended to emphasize the dominance of chance in the lives of his knights (75–79). Mann equates 'adventure' with chance and translates it into Modern English as 'hap' (the more common noun, 'happening' having acquired specific theatrical connotations). She is quite right, of course, to observe that 'adventure' may be interpreted to mean that which happens, or comes to us 'without design' (*OED* 1); however, in the context of Malory's providential history, which makes Arthur king 'by adventure and by grace' (97.2:III.1), one should not discount the possibility that both 'adventure' and 'grace' are part of God's providential design.

According to the late medieval providentialist world view, which is based upon the view described by Boethius in his treatise, *The Consolation of Philosophy*, there is no such thing as sheer 'chance' in this world. Everything must be understood to be part of God's providential design (147). Both 'grace' and 'adventure' come from God. What is more, the final outcome of every 'adventure' will be co-determined by man, specifically by his willingness to make use of God's grace. In this way late-medieval providentialism differs somewhat from the providentialism of the English puritans of the sixteenth and seventeenth century; for, having denounced the efficacy of good works as a means to salvation, the Calvinist Christians of a later period could not exhort men to live virtuously in order to earn God's favour, either here or in heaven. However, late medieval Christians both could and did exhort their fellow Christians to cooperate with God's grace so as to live virtuously and thereby merit God's favour.[1]

The providential context of medieval romance, particularly of secular chivalric romance, is not normally made explicit; rather it is taken for granted, as concepts of such fundamental and pervasive cultural significance usually are. Medieval authors could assume that their readers would understand the inherent ethical and spiritual value of the knight's adventures, because they could assume that their readers shared the providential world view which endowed them with meaning. Adventures often happen without apparent cause in medieval romance, creating a narrative structure with a peculiarly 'episodic' character and generating a profound sense of mystery. Morton Bloomfield has distinguished this type of narrative structure from that which is comprised of a logical sequence of events linked together by cause and effect, by saying that it has 'vertical motivation' rather than 'horizontal motivation'. That is to say, the episodes or 'adventures' come from i.e., are motivated by, a source which transcends the story rather than from a source within the story itself (108). Late medieval readers would have understood that transcendent source to be God, and therefore, as Erich Auerbach has observed, they would have understood that 'trial through adventure is the real meaning of the knight's ideal existence' (135). Every 'adventure' which 'happens' is a test of the knight's relationship to that transcendent source of being.[2]

Malory's technique for developing his ethical typology of knighthood is rather like the French romancer's technique of *entrelacement*. As Rosemond Tuve has observed, French romancers normally make use of a multiplicity of adventures, none of them identical, yet all sufficiently similar to allow them 'to illuminate some difficult conception'. In this way, they gradually lead their readers to 'the significance of events' (363–64). Malory achieves the same effect with his 'unlaced', or, disentangled but parallel, sequences of events. His technique is particularly striking in this first narrative unit because of the repetition of the triple quest pattern within such a brief compass (Caxton's Books III and IV). The very symmetry of the design compels the reader to compare these knights and the way they respond to the adventures which 'happen' to them. Gawain's participation in both sequences not only links them together but confirms their comparability.

Gawain, Tor and Pellinor

In the first occurrence of the triple quest pattern, adventures come to King Arthur's court. They come without warning or explanation. In the midst of the king and queen's wedding feast, a white hart suddenly dashes through the great hall of Camelot, pursued by a white 'brachett'; and these are followed soon after by a lady-huntress, and a 'knyght rydyng all armed on a grete horse'. The hart, wounded by the brachet, runs out again; the dog is taken away by a knight sitting at the 'syde-bourde'; and the lady-huntress, making 'grete dole', is carried off by the armed knight (103:III.5). Bewildered and amazed, the young king allows Merlin to handle the situation, since the prophet assures him that 'thys adventures muste be brought to an ende' (103.14–15: III.5). Merlin decides that Gawain shall go in quest of the white hart, that Tor shall bring back the white 'brachett' and that Pellinor shall rescue the lady. Tor and Gawain are both new-made knights, so this adventure will be the first test of their knighthood. On the other hand, Tor's father, King Pellinor, is already well proved and is Arthur's best knight.

Gawain is the only one of the three who does not set out alone. He takes his brother, Gaheris, with him as his squire. We infer from this that he places very high value upon family ties and this inference is reinforced by his response to two brothers who are fighting. He tells them that brothers should never fight one another and he threatens to fight both of them himself unless they will promise to go to Arthur's court and put themselves in the king's 'grace' (104.17:III.6). Gawain's next encounter is with a single knight holding a *pas d'armes* at a ford. Gawain easily unhorses him and then, after they have dismounted to continue the fight with swords, he smites him 'so harde thorow the helme that hit wente to the brayne' and the knight falls down dead (105.13–15:III.6). Gaheris is impressed by his elder brother's strength and exclaims, 'A, . . . that was a myghty stroke of a yonge knyght' (105.16:III.6). Finally, Gawain spies the white hart and unleashes six of his greyhounds. They pursue the hart into a castle courtyard and there kill it, whereupon the castle knight enters, kills two of them, and then arms himself to face Gawain. Gawain is so infuriated by the killing of his hounds that he refuses to give mercy to his opponent after he has beaten him to the ground. Even though Sir Blamoure of the Maryse offers to 'make amendys' for what he has done, Gawain determines that he must die 'for sleynge of my howndis' (106.15–16:III.7). As he prepares to strike off his head, Sir Blamoure's 'sovereigne lady' (105.28:III.7) rushes in to throw herself 'over' his body and so 'by myssefortune' Gawain strikes off her head instead (106.20–21:III.7).

Gawain's younger brother is just as quick to blame as he was to praise:

> 'Alas,' seyde Gaherys, 'that ys fowle and shamefully done, for that shame shall never frome you. Also ye sholde gyff mercy unto them that aske mercy, for a knyght withoute mercy ys withoute worship'. (106.22–25:III.7).

Indeed, things could not have turned out worse for Gawain. With that one unfortunate stroke he has violated not only the knight's obligation to give mercy to those who ask mercy, but also his obligation to protect and serve women. The sight of the dead lady brings him to his senses and he belatedly offers mercy to Sir Blamoure. In Malory's version, however, Sir Blamoure is so heartsick that he no longer cares whether he lives or dies, and he berates Gawain for having 'slayne with vilony my love and my lady that I loved beste of all earthly thynge' (106.31–32:III.7). Gawain's troubles compound quickly as he and Gaheris are attacked and almost killed by four knights seeking to avenge their lord and lady. They are saved from immediate death only by the intervention of four ladies. Later when one of the ladies discovers that Gawain is King Arthur's nephew, she undertakes to ensure that he 'shall have leve to go unto kynge Arthure for hys love' (108.15–16:III.8). Thanks to the compassion of these ladies and to his near kinship to King Arthur, Gawain is able to survive this first test of his knighthood. However, as a condition of his deliverance, he is made to bear with him the head of the lady, hung about his neck, and the body of the lady draped before him across his horse's neck.

Both King Arthur and Queen Guinevere are 'gretely displeased with sir Gawayne' when he arrives in Camelot. The queen and her ladies insist that he swear 'uppon the four Evaungelystis' that henceforth he will always be 'curteyse' and give 'mercy to hym that askith mercy' (108.30–109.1:III.8). In this, his first adventure, Gawain has proved that he is a knight of great strength and skill in the use of arms, but that he lacks the softer virtues of courtesy and compassion. He has successfully hunted down and killed the white hart which was the object of his quest, but in so doing he has also brought death or desolation to most of the human beings he encountered along the way.

Tor's quest for the white bratchet is narrated next and offers several instructive parallels with Gawain's quest for the white hart. Tor also encounters a major obstacle along his way. Not one, but two knights refuse to let him pass unless he will joust with them. Tor unhorses the first knight easily, but the second offers more resistance. Yet, even though Tor strikes two potentially fatal blows, he does not kill his opponent. Indeed, Malory goes out of his way to assure us that though his spear 'wente thorow the coste of the knyght', the 'stroke slew hym nat'. Then, when they dismount to continue the fight on foot, Tor strikes him 'on the helme a grete stroke' (109.33–35:III.9) but his sword does not go 'thorow the helme' (105.13:III.6) as Gawain's did. His opponent is able to yield and to ask mercy which Tor readily gives. Then, as Tor sends the two knights off to Camelot to become Arthur's prisoners, he bids them 'God spede'. Gawain never employed such pious language, nor did he ever attend mass, as Tor does the next morning. In fact, Tor not only hears mass 'devoutely', he also asks the hermit who has given him shelter 'to pray for hym' as he rides away (111.19–21:III.10). It would appear that by comparison with Gawain, Tor is a very pious man who believes that he must seek the grace of God in order to be successful in his adventures. At the same time his piety makes him humble, willing to 'abyde what adventure that commyth by the grace of God' (111.8–9:III.10).

Tor has dealt with the first part of his first quest very well, overcoming all his opponents without committing manslaughter and carrying away the bratchet alive. The second part of his quest proves to be more problematic, however. An armed knight accosts him and requires him to yield up the bratchet. Tor defends his right to the bratchet in a fierce and bloody battle which concludes with his opponent beaten down to the ground. At this point Tor's situation is precisely that of Gawain once he had succeeded in beating Sir Blamoure of the Maryse to the ground, and the analogous circumstance dramatically points up the contrast in their subsequent behaviour. Gawain's opponent asked for mercy, but Gawain refused to give it. By contrast, Tor offers to give mercy, but his opponent refuses to accept it. Then, just as in Gawain's adventure, a lady comes suddenly upon the scene. However, rather than try to save the life of the felled knight (there is no need, for Tor does not want to kill him), she asks Tor to give her a gift, and that gift turns out to be the 'hede of thys false knyght Abelleus, for he ys the moste outerageous knyght that lyvith, and the grettist murtherer' (112.21–23:III.11). Tor is 'lothe' to keep his rash promise once he realizes what the lady wants, and suggests instead that Abelleus be allowed to 'make amendys in that he hathe trespasced agayne you'. Tor's suggestion should remind the reader of Gawain's refusal to accept 'amendys' for the death of his hounds. And Malory enlarges upon his source to emphasize the point made by this implied contrast. Sometimes making 'amendys' is appropriate (hunting dogs can be replaced), and sometimes it is not. The damsel explains why she 'may nat' accept amends and why Sir Abelleus must be executed:

> '. . . he slew myne owne brothir before myne yghen that was a bettir knyght than he, and he had had grace; and I kneled halfe an owre before hym in the myre for to sauff my brothirs lyff that had done hym no damage, but fought with hym by adventure of armys, and so for all that I coude do he strake of hys hede. Wherefore I requyre the, as thou arte a trew knyght, to gyff me my gyffte, othir ellis I shall shame the in all the courte of kynge Arthure; for he ys the falsyste knyght lyvynge, and a grete destroyer of men, and namely of good knyghtes.'
>
> (112.25–36:III.11)

The circumstances of the case are Malory's invention. In fact this entire passage, beginning with the concrete detail of the damsel's kneeling half an hour in the mire to plead for her brother's life, is not to be found in Malory's source (*Suite* 2:111). Malory is making the same point made by Sir Gilbert Hay in the *Buke of Knychthede*. Knights are supposed to punish evildoers. Any knight who is himself guilty of a crime like rape, theft or murder, is not a 'verray' knight. He is a 'false' knight, 'unworthy for to lyve' and he ought to be taken 'be the prince, or be othir worthy, faithfull and honourable knychtis, and put till dede' (29).

It is not easy to kill a man in cold blood, and Tor does not want to kill Abelleus, even after he has heard of his unamendable crime. Nevertheless, he beheads Abelleus in order not to be 'false of my promyse'. He is referring, of course, to the promise he has made the damsel. However, given the similarities between the damsel's speech and the teaching of the standard work of knighthood, one may safely infer an additional implied reference to his promise to the High Order of Knighthood to do justice as a 'trew knight'. If Tor had promised to give mercy to Abelleus before the damsel appeared, it is not clear how he would have resolved the consequent ethical dilemma, but his last words to Abelleus, reminding him that 'erewhyle' he might have had mercy and 'wolde none aske', suggest that had Abelleus asked and been granted mercy before the damsel appeared to make her request Tor would not have struck off his head, but would rather have referred his case to King Arthur for judgment.

Tor's judgment is subsequently validated in two ways, in Malory's version. First, Abelleus himself betrays his guilt by showing fear and belatedly asking for mercy, whereas in the *Suite du Merlin* he claims the damsel's charge is false, and Tor has no way of knowing which one of them is lying (2:111). Secondly, King Arthur and Queen Guinevere both make 'grete joy' of Tor when they hear how well he has done in his quest, and Malory reinforces this second validation by adding Merlin's praise of his performance and Arthur's reward of 'an erledom of londis' (114.1–8:III.11).

Both Tor and Gawain are new-made knights, but the contrast between their behaviour and achievements in their first adventures is extreme. Gawain takes his brother along with him; Tor goes alone. Gawain refuses to give mercy; Tor offers mercy. Gawain refuses to accept 'amendys' for trespass; Tor suggests that 'amendys' be made. Gawain accidentally kills a lady and spares a knight; Tor deliberately kills a knight and serves a lady. Gawain is proud of the sort of prowess which can kill a man with one blow; Tor is 'lothe' to kill a man, even when he deserves to die for his crimes. Finally, and perhaps most significant of all because it may account for some, if not all, of the above differences, Gawain shows no sign of being a pious man. Tor, on the other hand, hears mass each day, prays for others and asks that they pray for him, and clearly believes not only that all adventures come from God, but that he will need the grace of God to do well as a knight.

The adventures of Pellinor come last and therefore are easily compared with those of Gawain and of his own son, Tor. By comparison with Gawain, Pellinor looks good, for he does not slay a lady. He does, however, refuse to give succour to a lady who cries out to him for help 'for Jesuys sake!' (114.16:III.12), and, as a consequence, her knight-companion dies of his wounds and she kills herself 'for grete sorow and dole' (120.1–2:III.15). To point up the comparison with Gawain's adventure, Malory adds the detail that the dead knight 'was hir love and sholde have wedded hir' (119.31–32:III.15) and has Guinevere, who formerly passed judgment on Gawain, also pass judgment upon Pellinor: 'A, kynge Pellynor,' seyde quene Gwenyver, 'ye were gretly to blame that ye saved nat thys ladyes lyff' (119.22–23: III.15). On the other hand, by comparison with his son, Tor, Pellinor does not look so good, for, although he hears mass once during his quest, he does not hear it 'devoutely'. What is more, he never seeks the grace of God explicitly by means of his own or others' prayers, even though he, too, has occasion to seek out a hermit in order to bury the dead knight (119.5–13:III.14). There is a bit of Tor's piety in him, but it takes a mighty jolt to arouse it. Only when he discovers that the dead damsel was his own daughter and learns what 'penaunce God hath ordayned' him for his failure to give her succour does Pellinor express either repentance or hope in God: 'Me forthynkith hit, . . . that thus shall me betyde, but God may well fordo desteny' (120.9–14: III.15). On the other hand, there is also a bit of Gawain's vengefulness in him, as we see when he threatens the knight who slew his horse: 'Knyght, kepe the well, for thou shalt have a buffette for the sleynge of my horse' (116.7–8:III.12). In short, Pellinor is neither so fierce and vindictive as Gawain, nor so pious and judicious as Tor.

This three-tiered scale of moral worth is confirmed if we judge the knights' performances according to the code of conduct contained in Arthur's pentecostal oath. Indeed, we can hardly avoid doing so, for the oath is sworn by all the knights of the Round Table as soon as the three questing knights have returned:

> Thus whan the queste was done of the whyght herte of whych folowed sir Gawayne, and the queste of the brachet whych folowed sir Torre, kynge Pellynors son, and the queste of the lady that the knyghte toke away, whych at that tyme folowed kynge Pellynor, than the kynge stablysshed all the knyghtes and gaff them rychesse and londys; and charged them never to do outerage nothir mourthir, and allwayes to fle treson, and to gyff mercy unto hym that askith mercy, uppon payne of forfiture of their worship and lordship of kynge Arthure for evirmore; and allwayes to do ladyes, damesels, and jantilwomen and wydowes socour: strengthe hem in hir ryghtes, and never to enforce them, uppon payne of dethe. Also, that no man take no batayles in a wrongefull quarell for no love ne for no worldis goodis. So unto

> thys were all knyghtis sworne of the Table Rounde, both olde and younge, and every yere so were they sworne at the hygh feste of Pentecoste. (120.11–27:III.15)

Gawain has violated nearly every one of Arthur's injunctions. He has committed 'outerage' by failing to give mercy to him that asked mercy. He has failed to help a lady and he has insisted on fighting his opponent to the death simply in order to be revenged for the death of his hunting dogs — a 'wrongefull quarell', certainly. By contrast with Gawain, Tor has violated none of Arthur's injunctions, and has flawlessly balanced the rival claims of justice and mercy in the case of the damsel's charge of murder against Abelleus. In fact, the crime she charged him with is very like the crime Gawain would have committed had Sir Blamoure's lady begged for his life on her knees, rather than throwing her body in the way of Gawain's sword. Had Gawain slain Sir Blamoure he would also have been guilty of 'morthir'; as it is, the worst he can be charged with is 'outerage' since he clearly did not mean to kill the lady who got in the way.

Pellinor's record is not quite so good as Tor's. He has violated one of Arthur's injunctions: 'allwayes to do ladyes, damesels, and jantilwomen and wydowes socour.' It is ironic that he should have failed in this regard since he clearly has great respect for women. After he won the lady-huntress from her abductor, he promised her cousin that he would 'put hir to no shame nother vylony' (116.15–16:III.13), and he kept that promise scrupulously. The irony is not lacking in significance, however. Pellinor failed to help the damsel because he 'was so egir in hys queste' (114.17:III.13). After the queen has chastized him for his failure, he readily admits that he should not have been 'so furyous in my queste that I wolde nat abyde' and repents his misdeed, but he neither explains nor tries to justify his unwillingness to stop for the damsel's sake. Nevertheless, his motive may be inferred. If he had stopped to give her 'socour' he might have lost the damsel Arthur had charged him to bring back to the court, and if he had failed to bring back that damsel, he would have lost much 'worship', and perhaps Arthur's 'lordship' as well. Here is another case of rival claims which must be balanced satisfactorily, the claims of one's lady (or indeed, any lady) and the claims of one's temporal lord. In this case, however, the lady has required Pellinor's help, 'for Jesuys sake!', so we may infer yet another pair of rival claims, the claims of one's God and the claims of one's temporal lord. Whichever way he viewed it, Pellinor chose to serve his temporal lord first, and the consequence was that his own daughter lost her life.

Pellinor has not managed nearly so well as his son the delicate business of balancing the rival claims made upon the medieval knight. Traditionally he was required to acknowledge three loyalties: to God, to his temporal lord, and to his lady (or to all women). Tor is the only one of the three knights who has managed to honour all three: he has served God by observing the sacraments and keeping his promise to do justice as a 'trew' knight of the High Order; he has served the lady who requested that he do justice on her behalf; and he has served his temporal lord, Arthur, not only by succeeding in his quest and returning with the white bratchet, but, more importantly, by doing justice as a king's knight. His father, Pellinor, has served both his temporal lord and the lady who was the object of his quest; but he failed to serve God when he failed to succour the damsel who asked his help 'for Jesuys sake!' Gawain of course, has served only his temporal lord by returning to Camelot with the head of the white hart. He has offended both God and all women by failing to give mercy and killing a lady.

We may sum up briefly by saying that whether we judge these three knights' performances by their ability to adhere to the standards of conduct spelled out in Arthur's pentecostal oath, or by their ability to honour the three traditional knightly loyalties, the same three-tiered scale of moral worth emerges. Gawain is the worst; Tor is the best; and Pellinor falls in between.

It is curious that the knight who best achieves King Arthur's standards for 'worship' should also be the most pious of the three knights, for in the oath which he requires all his knights to swear annually 'at the hygh feste of Pentecoste' Arthur pays no attention at all to their relationship to God. This is a notable omission, and one which would surely have been noticed by those among Malory's readers who were familiar with other versions of the Round Table oath. For example, the 'Lays et ordonnances de l'Ordre des Chevaliers de la Table Ronde', attributed to Jacques d'Armagnac, requires that the knights hear mass once a day, if possible, and at the very least pray daily before a crucifix (Sandoz 401–02); and John Hardyng includes in his version of the Round Table knights' 'rule' the obligation to 'sustene' the 'fayth' and 'ye church' (124–25). Malory may not have known the French work, but he certainly knew Hardyng's *Chronicle* and therefore we must conclude that his omission of the Round Table knights' obligation to sustain the Christian faith and the church was deliberate. In the previous chapter on the office of knighthood, I argued that Arthur's oath had a specific political function, and that it was comparable to those peace-keeping oaths which both Lancastrian and Yorkist kings required their retinues to swear as a means of improving the quality of royal governance. That is certainly true. Nevertheless, it is equally true that every other known version of the Round Table knights' oath makes some reference to the knights' religious duties, and, certainly, the occasion of the oath-taking — the annual feast of Pentecost — rather forcefully calls attention to every man's need of God's grace.

Malory's Arthur seems to assume that his knights will be able to adhere to his ethical code simply by willing to do so. He provides both rewards ('rychesse and londys') and punishments (loss of 'worship' and his 'lordship') to encourage them in this moral endeavour, but it does not occur to him to require that they pray to God for sufficient grace to practice and persevere in virtue. Indeed, Arthur seems to have an almost Pelagian belief in the natural goodness of man. At least, he seems to assume that his well-chosen knights can create a just society without the grace of God. Some scholars have argued that the Pelagian heresy was never completely stamped out in England. And at least one scholar, Helen Adolf, has ventured to suggest that Arthur, the greatest English hero, is also a Pelagian hero, a kind of secular saint (27–28). However, it is not necessary to assume that Malory was thinking in terms of the Pelagian/Augustinian controversy regarding the nature of man and the necessity of grace in order to appreciate that his juxtaposition of Arthur's secular oath with the religious feast of Pentecost creates a paradoxical situation: the oath which Arthur's knights swear tacitly denies the necessity of that very thing which the feast celebrates — the grace of God.

If we look again at the behaviour of Gawain, Tor and Pellinor in the context of this paradoxical situation, we can see that by means of this juxtaposition Malory has raised a question of considerable importance. Can Arthur's knights achieve the standards of behaviour which he requires of them without the grace of God? The record of these three knights would seem to indicate that they cannot. Tor, the most pious, was also the most successful in his quest, more successful even than his more experienced father, King Pellinor. On the other hand, both father and son were more successful than Gawain, who seems to have acted purely upon impulse, giving no thought either to God or to the knightly rules of conduct.

Of the three knights, King Pellinor seems to be the most like King Arthur himself, sharing both his worshipful ideal of knightly conduct and his expectation that it can be achieved by sheer human will power and determination. It is indeed ironic that his only failure should have stemmed from his eagerness to win worship. However, confronted with that failure, Pellinor is able to repent and to hope that the awful 'penaunce' which 'God hath ordayned' for him because of that offense may be avoided. It is significant that his optimism contradicts the fatalism of Malory's French source for this scene. In the *Suite du Merlin*, the prophet assures Pellinor that 'Nus ne puet destorner que la volontés nostre signeur n'aviegne' (2.131). But in Malory's version, Merlin says nothing of the kind so that Pellinor's assertion stands: 'Me forthynkith hit . . . that thus shall me betyde, but God may well fordo desteny' (120.9–10:III.15). Implicit in Pellinor's assertion is the medieval providentialist world view. Pellinor assumes that just as men can earn God's punishment by wrong action, so they can earn God's reward by right action. Though God may be displeased with him now, he may yet hope to earn a better 'desteny' by repentance and amendment. The providentialist assumes that nothing is inalterably decreed and believes that no man's 'desteny' is determined until it has actually happened.

Gawain, Marhalt and Ywain

The three-tiered pattern of moral worth and knightly achievement which we have perceived in the triple quest of Gawain, Tor and Pellinor, is repeated in the triple quest of Gawain, Marhalt and Ywain. This second set of adventures concludes the first narrative unit of the *Morte Darthur* and, like the first, Malory found it in his source, the *Suite du Merlin*. However, he has substantially altered Gawain's adventure with Pelleas and Ettarde and he has invented entirely new adventures for Marhalt and Ywain. His thematic purpose for these massive alterations may be inferred from the sort of adventures he has invented: for Marhalt the pacification of a rebel against Arthur and the execution of a ravaging giant; for Ywain a trial by combat with two 'perelous' knights who have extorted a barony of lands from a helpless woman. The political and judicial implications of such adventures are clear, and, as a consequence, this second triple quest becomes even more significant than the first, in terms of the social, political and judicial obligations of knighthood, even though the first was undertaken in the court and for the king.

As in the first triple quest, the 'motivation' of the knights' adventures is 'vertical' rather than 'horizontal', in Bloomfield's sense. All three knights are actively looking for 'stronge adventures' to test their worth as knights and no other explanation is offered for the sudden appearance of the three damsels at the fountain. Their adventures originate in the romance setting of knight-errantry — the forest — rather than in the political setting of the court. This is important because most of the adventures of Arthur's Round Table knights will be of this type, undertaken not at the king's command but of their own volition, and happening not in the court but in the countryside. Therefore, what this repetition of the triple quest motif makes clear is that the rules of knightly conduct will always be the same, regardless of setting, and that the significance of knightly adventures will likewise be the same. That is to say, how well each Round Table knight 'proves' himself will have not only individual, ethical significance, indicative of his type of knighthood, it will also have social and political significance, indicative of the quality of King Arthur's governance.

Before the second triple quest properly begins, Malory adds two conversations to the scene in which Gawain and Ywain first meet Marhalt. These conversations lay out the rules of conduct which all worshipful knights-errant must obey. The rules cover the knight's relationship to his fellow knights as well as his relationship to ladies, and thus they can also be said to comprise a complete code of behaviour for the man who wishes to be deemed honourable in Arthurian society.

The first rule of conduct to be discussed is whether or not a knight may ever honourably refuse to joust. What emerges from the discussion is two contrary views of this matter. Having watched while Marhalt strikes two knights down 'dede', Gawain expresses a wish to be the next to test his prowess. Ywain argues that they should 'late hym go' since neither of them is a match for him, but Gawain counters, 'hit were shame to us and he were nat assayed, were he never so good a knyght' (160.6–10:IV.18–19). Their difference of opinion reflects one commonly expressed in late medieval discussions of the knightly sports of jousting and tourneying. Both points of view could be regarded as honourable and both found eloquent spokesmen. Because of the risk of serious bodily harm and/or loss of life in jousts and tournaments many men utterly condemned these popular sports. On the other hand, some argued forcefully that jousting and tourneying were the only practical means available to keep older knights fighting fit and to train young knights for battle. Even those who accepted this latter argument, however, usually condemned the practice of private battles, that is, individual combats which took place without the regulating presence of heralds and judges to enforce the rules of fair play and to stop the fighting when knights began to 'wexe wroth' (23.36:I.11; Keen, 'Chivalry' 37).

Private battles seldom took place just for fun in real life whatever the parties to them might have pretended. The fifteenth-century hero of *Le Jouvencel*, a great knight and military commander in the service of the king of France, lectures two young gentlemen on the reasons why they should never participate in such private battles:

Premierement, ceulz qui le font vueillent oster le bien d'autruy, c'est assavoir leur honneur, pour se attribuer une vaine gloire qui est de petite valleur; et, en ce faisant, il ne fait service à nul, il despent son argent, il expose son corps pour tollir la vie ou l'onneur a cellui à qui il a à besongnier, qui lui vient à petit de profit; tant qu'il est occupé ad ce faire, il laisse à exploicter la guerre, le service de son Roy et de la chose publique et nul ne doit exposer son corps, sinon en euvres meritoires.' (2:100)

Le Jouvencel's arguments based on the higher value of service to King and commonweal would be out of place in a typical romance of knight-errantry, but not in *Le Morte Darthur*. As we have seen in the previous chapter on the office of knighthood, Malory regards the knight-errantry of the Round Table fellowship as a form of service to the king. Knights who go out from Arthur's court in search of adventure actually function as a kind of itinerant police force, comparable to the itinerant judicial commissions which were such an integral part of royal justice throughout the fifteenth century. Therefore, Gawain's position, which is that of a very young and very rash man, a hot-head who is further heated by the sight and sound of battle, does not find much reinforcement in Malory's work. The only utterances like it are spoken in time of war (see below 103–6). On the other hand, Ywain's sensible position anticipates that which will be adopted by Dinadan, 'fyne japer' and friend to 'all good knights' in the Tale of Tristram. Dinadan will insist that it is foolish to risk one's life for nothing, and that there is no shame in refusing to joust with a much better knight so long as there is no more than honour at stake (see below 182–3). Ywain is not Dinadan, however. He is not willing, or perhaps he is not able, to endure the scorn of his companion. Therefore, being the 'wayker' of the two, he agrees to meet Marhalt first, so that if he is struck down, Gawain can 'revenge' him. Of course he is easily struck down with the first blow, which hurts him 'on the lefte syde' and so it becomes Gawain's turn.

Gawain's battle with Marhalt illustrates most of the rules governing honourable combat between knights-errant. For example, after Gawain has been unhorsed, he orders Marhalt to 'alyght on foote, or ellis I woll sle thyne horse.' Marhalt thanks him for his 'jantylnesse!' and says, 'Ye teche me curtesy, for hit is nat commendable one knyght to be on horsebak and the other on foote' (160.33–35:IV.18–19). Of course, there is nothing at all 'jantyl' about the threat to kill Marhalt's horse. Such an action was strictly forbidden by the rules of fair play; however, it was also forbidden to fight while one man had the advantage of horseback and the other was on foot. As knights-errant, Gawain and Marhalt fight for no reason but the testing of prowess and the winning of worship, and in such battles, as soon as it becomes clear that the two combatants are evenly matched, good manners requires that one or the other offer to stop fighting since 'oure quarellys ar nat grete'. Malory follows his source, the *Suite du Merlin*, in having these courteous words spoken by Marhalt (2:241). Gawain acknowledges his foe's superior courtesy ('A, . . . jantyll knyght, ye say the worde that I sholde sey'), and then, even though they have been fighting all day and are both severely wounded, they kiss and swear 'eythir to love other as brethirne.' (161.19–23:IV.18–19)

The notion that two men could fight, draw blood, and then kiss and make up, seemed ludicrous to one fifteenth-century Italian diplomat. Amazed to find that the English had 'no idea of the point of honour', he reported home that

> When they do fight it is from some caprice, and after exchanging two or three stabs with a knife, even when they wound each other, they will make peace instantly, and go away and drink together. (Kendall 7)

It would seem that the continental idea of the duel of honour had to be imported into England along with other notions from Italian and French renaissance courts. The English do not seem to have developed it natively. Certainly in Malory's *Morte Darthur* the pattern established by this battle between Gawain and Marhalt will be repeated again and again. The more courteous of the two knights will offer to yield the honour of the combat, prompting the other to yield in turn. They will embrace, express mutual admiration and swear eternal love and brotherhood.

Malory's Gawain may not be so courteous as Marhalt; but he is typically English — if we can believe the Italian observer — in his ability to take no offense for his hurts, but rather to love and honour a worthy opponent for his prowess and his courtesy. It appears he has no difficulty abiding by the rules of fair play so long as his baser emotions are not engaged, but, as we saw in his encounter with Sir Blamoure of the Maryse, he is incapable of abiding by them if he is angry. The death of his beloved greyhounds infuriated him so that he did not care whether or not he lost 'worship' for his lack of mercy. And that, of course, is the heart of the problem, as all writers on the subject of knightly games acknowledge. So long as there are supervising heralds and judges to call a halt to the play when tempers begin to rise, jousts and tournaments may be relatively harmless. But there can be no control exercised over private battles other than the self-control of the combatants themselves. Throughout the *Morte Darthur* Gawain will be a perfect example of the inadequacy of that control. In his relationships to his fellow knights, fear of shame will never be enough to restrain him from committing 'outerage' and even 'morthir' if he is angry enough, or if, by his own standards of right conduct, his action is justified.

The honourable knight's obligation to be courteous also applies to his relationships with women. As Marhalt, Gawain and Ywain are riding back to Marhalt's lodging, Malory adds another brief conversation between Gawain and Marhalt to describe what the honourable knight's attitude towards ladies and damsels should be. Marhalt has just been accused of hating 'all ladyes and jantylwomen', a serious charge for a man of worship. Gawain is amazed by it and asks how it can be possible that 'so valyaunte a man as ye be of prouesse, that ye love no ladyes and damesels'. Marhalt replies,

> '... they name me wrongfully, for hit be the damesels of the turret that so name me and other suche as they be. Now shall I telle you for what cause I hate them: for they be sorsseres and inchaunters many of them, and be a knyght never so good of his body and as full of prouesse as a man may be, they woll make hym a starke cowerde to have the bettir of hym. And this is the pryncipall cause that I hate them. And all good ladyes and jantyllwomen, I owghe them my servyse as a knyght ought to do.' (161.29–161.02:IV.18–19)

The conversation ends abruptly with Marhalt's explanation, so we must presume that Gawain finds it sufficient. Marhalt's distinction between ladies who are 'sorsseres and inchaunters' and 'good ladyes' is another theme which will crop up again, especially in the Tale of Tristram. Malory never bothers to explain exactly how these ladies manage to enchant knights so as to make 'starke cowerdes' of them all, but we may fairly infer that the source of their power is their sexual attractiveness. One rather obvious way to turn a man 'full of prouesse' into a 'cowerde' is to lure him into a courtly life of sensual delight and so to keep him from the knightly pursuit of worship in arms. If this is what Marhalt means, then 'good ladyes' would either not be so sexually attractive, or else, and this is more likely, would not choose to employ their sexual attractions to enslave a man in this way. Good ladies would rather encourage the men who admire them to prove themselves in knightly adventures. Marhalt is willing to acknowledge his duty to serve all such ladies, but clearly he feels no compunction about hating those who would keep a man from his knightly duty. By implication, therefore, this passage also establishes the standards of honourable conduct for ladies; and, as we shall see, these standards will be applied to all ladies in Arthurian society, including Guinevere and Isode (see below 172–3).

After the three knights have been healed of their wounds, they decide to set out together in search of adventures. The second triple quest properly begins, therefore, when they encounter three damsels sitting by 'a fayre fountayne' and decide to accept their offer to show them the way 'unto stronge aventures'. The situation they now face is just as mysterious as the situation in Arthur's court during the wedding feast when the white hart, the white bratchet and the lady-huntress appeared suddenly and for no reason. Like Tor, Pellinor and Gawain on that former occasion, the three knights can no longer remain in fellowship. They must separate in order to undertake their individual quests, each to prove himself as best he can, accompanied by one of the damsels. Caxton acknowledges the importance of the quests as well as the importance of the initial choice each knight must make by beginning a new chapter at the point where the knights agree to accept the damsels' proposal: 'This is well seyde,' seyde sir Marhaus. 'Now shall everyche of us chose a damsell' (163.10–11:IV.20). And, indeed, each knight's choice of a damsel tells us much about his individual character and hints what the quality of his performance as a knight will be. Ywain's humility is suggested when he describes himself as the 'yongyst and waykest' of the three and therefore requests the oldest damsel, 'for she hath sene much and can beste helpe me what I have nede.' Marhalt's courtesy is suggested when he chooses the elder of the two remaining damsels, thus leaving the youngest and most beautiful to Gawain. And, finally, Gawain's sensuality is suggested by his delight with this result: 'hir is me moste levyste' (163.12–20:IV.20).

Like the first set of three quests, this second set also begins with Gawain. Gawain encounters a knight, 'the fayreste' and the 'semelyest' that he has ever seen, but also the most 'dolerous'. He salutes Gawain and prays 'to God to sende hym muche worshyp' (164.4–5:IV.20). Gawain responds in kind. Then he watches in amazement as the knight overthrows ten knights in succession with one spear and then allows himself to be disarmed by them and led away as their prisoner. Gawain's damsel is so disgusted by his failure to help the 'dolerous' knight that she takes the first opportunity that presents itself to leave him. Two knights ride up offering to joust, and while Gawain is fighting with the first one, his damsel leaves with the second. After Gawain and his opponent have 'accorded', Gawain asks him to explain the curious behaviour of the mournful knight. He learns that the knight is named Sir Pelleas, that he is 'the beste knyght I trow in the worlde and the moste man of prouesse' and that he allows himself to be humiliated in this way because he loves a proud damsel, the lady Ettarde. She scorns his love, and so the only way he can ever get a glimpse of her is by allowing her knights to take him prisoner. Gawain decides to help sir Pelleas if he can. The next day he seeks him out and offers 'to do all that lyeth in my powere to get you the love of your lady,' adding, 'and thereto I woll plyghte you my trouthe.' Malory makes much more of this business of trouth-plighting than his French source does. Morever, in his version, Pelleas actually foresees the possibility that Gawain will betray him: 'And, sir knyght, syn ye ar so nye cosyn unto kyng Arthure and ar a kynges son, therefore betray me nat, but help me . . .' (168.1–12:IV.22). There seem to be two points implied by Pelleas' extraordinary prescience. On the one hand, because Gawain is a king's son and the nephew of Arthur, it would be all the more ignoble of him to fail to keep his word. On the other hand, for those very same reasons, he might think he could break his word with impunity, since no man would dare to harm him, given his powerful political connections.

From this point on, Malory's version of the story bears less and less resemblance to his French original. In the French romance, after Gawain has arrived at Ettarde's castle wearing Pelleas' armour and told her that Sir Pelleas is dead, she invites him in, gives him a rich robe, and begins to court him as soon as she discovers that he is King Arthur's nephew. Eventually she forces him to reveal the name of the lady he loves best, and when this turns out to be herself, she offers herself to him 'cuers et corps' (*Works* 1360). Malory's version is quite different. In order to have his will with Ettarde, Gawain employs the old ruse of the rash promise. He induces her to promise that she will do all that she can to 'gete' him the love of his lady. Then he tells her that the lady he loves is herself and that therefore she must 'holde' her 'promyse' or, as she herself admits, 'be forsworne' (169.23–29:IV.23). She agrees 'to fulfylle all his desyre' (169.30:IV.23) and Malory magnifies the degree of Gawain's sensuality by telling us that he lay with her in her pavilion 'two dayes and two nyghtes' (170.02:IV.23). They are still there on the morning of the third day when Pelleas comes to the lady's castle to find out what has happened to his friend and discovers them together: 'Alas, that ever a knyght sholde be founde so false!' (170.16–17:IV.23).

Gawain's counterpart in the French romance also betrays Pelleas, but the degree of his culpability is much reduced by the fact that he truly loves Ettarde, that he is not the aggressor in the affair, that he bitterly repents his 'mesfait' (which does *not* go on for two days and two nights), and that he and Pelleas are reconciled after Gawain has persuaded Ettarde to accept Pelleas as her lover. In Malory's version, on the other hand, Gawain seems to be motivated only by lust and he shows no signs of repentance at all. The only reason he survives his act of treason is that Pelleas cannot bring himself to kill him as he lies there sleeping: 'Though this knyght be never so false, I woll never sle hym slepynge, for I woll never dystroy the hyghe Ordir of Knyghthode' (170.23–25:IV.23). As a friend and as a lover, Pelleas has been a model of truthfulness, and his refusal to commit murder in order to have revenge is consistent with his character. In Malory's French source Pelleas has a second reason for not killing Gawain as he lies there sleeping: he thinks it would be a pity to kill 'si bon chevalier comme il est qui encor poura venir a moult grant chose' ('Abenteuer' 34). Such an estimation of Gawain's character is completely out of keeping with Malory's version of events, however, and so he omits it.

Gawain's shameful behaviour recalls his first quest when he also failed to live up to the honourable code of knightly conduct. On that former occasion he could not control his appetite for vengeance and so failed to give mercy to a fellow knight and accidentally killed his lady. On this occasion he can not control his appetite for sexual satisfaction, and so fails to keep his word to a fellow knight and abuses his lady's integrity. Whatever one thinks of Ettarde's scornful rejection of Pelleas (and Malory makes her appear even more haughty by removing the reason for her rejection of him in the French romance, that is, his 'bas lignage'), one cannot admire the way Gawain has forced her to comply with his desires. He has taken advantage of her aristocratic adherence to 'trouthe' as the 'hyeste thing that man may kepe' in order to 'enforce' her. He has done what no gentleman would ever do. It is as if, in the *Franklin's Tale,* Aurelius were to hold Dorigen to her rash promise instead of allowing her to return to her husband. Of course, Malory gives us no sign that Ettarde is as unwilling to comply with Gawain's 'desyre' as Dorigen is to comply with the desire of Aurelius; but he does let us know exactly how Ettarde feels after she realizes the extent of Gawain's betrayal:

> 'Alas!' she seyde, 'Sir Gawayne, ye have betrayde sir Pelleas and me, for you told me you had slayne hym, and now I know well it is not so: he is on lyve. But had he bene so uncurteyse unto you as ye have bene to hym, ye had bene a dede knyght. But ye have dissayved me, that all ladyes and damesels may beware be you and me.' (171.10–15:IV.23)

Ettarde perceives the situation as an emblem of 'untrouthe', what women have most to fear from men; she feels used, abused, undone. For his part, Gawain cannot even manage the courtesy of a reply and departs 'into the foreste' without a word.

After Gawain has silently left the scene, Malory invents a new ending for the Pelleas and Ettarde story which completes his illustration of how 'good' knights and ladies ought to behave towards one another. Ettarde must be punished because she has violated the worshipful code of conduct for ladies. She has made a 'starke cowerde' of Pelleas, not by seducing him into luxurious idleness, but by scorning his love so that he was willing to do anything, even to act the coward, just to have a glimpse of her rather than die of grief. All the other ladies present at the tournament which Pelleas won for love of Ettarde 'had scorne of hir that she was so prowde', and Malory assures us that there was none of them 'but and sir Pelleas wolde have profyrde hem love they wolde have shewed hym the same for his noble prouesse' (166.34–167.2:IV.22) Indeed, Ettarde is the sort of lady Guinevere had in mind when she said to Sir Kay, 'what lady that ye love and she love you nat agayne, she were gretly to blame' (129.19–20:IV.3).

Malory allows Nyneve, the Damsel of the Lake, to pass judgment upon Ettarde: 'hit is no joy of suche a proude lady that woll nat have no mercy of suche a valyaunte knyght' (171.26–27:IV.23). What is sauce for the goose is sauce for the gander, in Malory's opinion. If a 'knyght withoute mercy ys withoute worship' then a lady without mercy should also be without worship. Or, as Nyneve says to Ettarde, 'ye oughte to be ashamed for to murther suche a knyght' (172.1–2:IV.23). Malory seems to feel very strongly on this subject, and even to take some delight in meting out poetic justice to Ettarde by means of an 'inchauntement' which causes her to love Pelleas 'so sore that wellnyghe she was nere oute of hir mynde' (172.3–4:IV.23). When the bewildered Ettarde asks how it could happen that she now loves 'so sore' the man she has hitherto 'hatyd moste of ony man on lyve', Nyneve pretends that her 'inchauntemente' is 'the ryghteuouse judemente of God' (172.8:IV.23). The reader detects here a rather unlovely tone of self-righteousness. However, it is a tone which Malory must have thought justified since he created it, just as he created the ending of this episode which leaves Ettarde dead 'for sorow' and Pelleas alive and well in the arms of Nyneve, a good lady who knows a good man when she finds him: 'and the Damesel of the Lake rejoysed sir Pelleas, and loved togedyrs duryng their lyfe' (172.29–31:IV.24).

Malory's rehandling of the Gawain, Ettarde and Pelleas episode illustrates by example the remarks made earlier by Marhalt on the proper relationship between worshipful knights and ladies. Thus the thematic focus of Gawain's adventure is social. By contrast the adventures of Marhalt and Ywain emphasize the political and judicial responsibilities of the knight, respectively. These adventures are almost certainly Malory's own invention, for, as Vinaver observes, they have 'little in common with any known French romance' (*Works* 1362).

It would seem that Malory wants us to understand Marhalt's behaviour as characteristic of Round Table knights, for he has Marhalt identify himself to the Duke of the South Marches as a 'knyght of kynge Arthurs and knyght of the Table Rounde' (173.24–25:IV.25), even though he will not be formally received into the fellowship until later, along with Pelleas, at the conclusion of their quests (179.31–32: IV.29). Marhalt is forced to do battle with the Duke and all of his six sons because the Duke seeks revenge for the death of his seventh son, slain by Gawain 'in a recountre'. His youngest son may well have been the knight holding a *pas-d'armes* at a ford in the river whom Gawain struck down during his quest for the white hart, although Malory does not spell out the connection. It is perhaps better this way for, by not making that connection, Malory creates the impression that Gawain does this sort of thing quite often. Knights who go about challenging all comers to a fight, or accepting all such challenges for no good reason, and routinely killing their opponents render their temporal lord no service in this way and may render him great disservice. Ever since Gawain slew his youngest son, the Duke of the South Marches of Wales has been King Arthur's bitter enemy and has persecuted his knights, all those he could get his hands on, and this has been going on a 'longe tyme' (174.8:IV.25). Marhalt's battle the next morning thus has important political consequences. The great prowess, which we have recently seen used to strike down 'dede' the two knights who accompanied the twelve wicked damsels, is now used to subdue the Duke of the South Marches and his six sons. Marhalt forjousts them all but he doesn't kill one of them. He insists, however, that they yield themselves or he will 'do the uttirmust to you all'. Fortunately, the duke is not so foolhardy as to prefer death to honourable defeat, and so all seven men kneel, put the pomels of their swords up to Marhalt and promise 'never to be fooys unto kynge Arthure'. What is more, they promise to be present at the next feast of Pentecost to 'putt them in the kynges grace' (174.36–175.8:IV.26).

Marhalt then takes part in a tournament where he knocks down forty knights and wins 'grete honoure' but Malory passes over this episode in a brief paragraph in order to get on with the next adventure which has important political implications. Marhalt comes into the lands of the Earl Fergus, a young man but 'late com to his londis', whose domain is troubled by the depredations of the giant, Taulurd. Marhalt undertakes to subdue this disturber of the peace, and courteously, too, for when he learns that the giant does not fight on horseback, he agrees to 'fyght with hym on foote' (175.30–31:IV.26).

Marhalt kills the giant by chasing him into a lake and pelting him with stones till he falls down and drowns, then he releases all the prisoners whom the giant held in his castle: 'four-and-twenty knyghtes' and twelve ladyes'. He also helps himself to the giant's treasure, 'grete rychesse oute of numbir, that dayes of his lyff he was nevir poore man' (176.14–17:IV.26). Therefore he can well afford to refuse the Earl Fergus' offer of 'half his londys' as a reward for ridding him of the giant. Marhalt has not only enriched himself considerably, he has won another political ally for King Arthur.

In recounting Ywain's adventures, Malory focuses on the judicial function of knights of the Round Table. Like Marhalt, Ywain participates in a tournament where he wins much worship, smiting down thirty knights, but Malory passes over this exploit, as well as many other 'strange adventures' in order to concentrate on the one adventure which has judicial implications. Ywain's old damsel brings him to the Lady of the Roche, a 'curtayse' lady who has been victimized by two 'perelous knyghtes', Sir Edward and Sir Hew of the Rede Castell who have 'disheryted' her 'of a baronnery of londis by their extorsion.' Ywain's response to her complaint is what we might expect from a humble and pious knight:

> 'Madam,' seyde sir Uwayne, 'they ar to blame, for they do ayenste the hyghe Order of Knyghthode and the oth that they made. And if hit lyke you I woll speke with hem, because I am a knyght of kyng Arthurs, and to entrete them with fayrenesse; and if they woll nat, I shall do batayle with hem for Goddis sake and in the defence of your ryght.
>
> 'Gramercy,' seyde the lady, 'and thereas I may nat acquyte you, God shall.' (177.10–17:IV.27)

Ywain shows the pious knight's awareness of the obligation that every knight has to the 'hyghe Order', but it is 'because' he is a knight of King Arthur's that he presumes to adjudicate this case of alleged 'extorsion'. He would prefer not to take the matter to trial by battle, but rather to persuade them 'with fayrenesse' to give up their ill-gotten lands; however, if they will not be persuaded then he is prepared to fight.

Ywain is prepared to fight 'for Goddis sake' as well as 'in the defence' of the lady's 'ryght'. This I take to mean that he believes not only that God approves of what he will do, but that God also requires him to do it, if necessary, in order to settle the quarrel. This is the attitude towards trial by battle which prevailed throughout Europe before a rising tide of rationalism succeeded in raising sufficient doubts about its validity to cause the Church to withdraw its endorsement (see below 156–8). However, the Lateran Council of 1215 did not immediately change all men's minds on the subject. Many continued to believe, well into the fifteenth century, that the best way to settle a judicial matter was trial by battle, and if more peaceful alternatives failed to produce justice, then it was the only way. Very pious men believed that God would give victory to the knight fighting for the right, even if he were younger, smaller, weaker and less skilled than his opponent. Malory chooses to characterize Ywain as a knight of such extreme piety that he will agree to enter trial by battle with not one, but two knights who are older, bigger, more powerful and more skilled than he is. This is the same Ywain who earlier advised Gawain that neither of them should joust with Marhalt on the grounds that they were no match for such a 'passynge good knyght' (160.7:IV.19). The difference in attitude can only be accounted for by the difference in circumstances. The encounter with Marhalt was pointless, risking one's life for nothing but honour. On the other hand, the encounter with the 'perelous' Sir Edward and Sir Hew will produce a judgment of God, and Ywain appears to have complete confidence that God will render a righteous judgment. He manages to unhorse both knights, and then fights with them on foot, giving and receiving 'grate strokis' and being wounded so 'passyng grevously' that the Lady of the Roche fears for his life. The battle continues for five hours and still Ywain's faith sustains him, until finally he is able to deal Sir Edward a fatal stroke. Then 'sir Hew abated his corrage', yielding to his young adversary. Ywain gives him mercy, as a true knight should, and then commands that he restore the lady's lands to her and come to Arthur's court for the next feast of Pentecost.

When the three knights come together again at the fountain where they initially parted, the youngest damsel who had accompanied Gawain 'coude sey but lytyll worshyp of hym', and the reader can say no more, knowing how he behaved in his relations with Pelleas and Ettarde. Then the three knights are met by messengers from Arthur and brought back to Camelot where 'the kynge made hem to swere uppon a booke to telle hym all their adventures that had befalle them that twelve-monthe before, and so they ded' (179.19–21:IV.29). We must presume that each knight told the truth and was judged accordingly, but this time Malory does not record the reactions of anyone at court: the reader must supply his own judgments, and this is not easy to do, for Malory has altered the order of presentation of his three types. Rather than present them in the order of worst-best-middling (Gawain-Tor-Pellinor), he has presented them in the order of worst-middling-best (Gawain-Marhalt-Ywain). What emerges from a progressive comparison, therefore, is not so much the contrast between the first and the second knights, as the similarities between them, and likewise between the second and third knights.

If one judges them by their ability to abide by Arthur's code, as spelled out in the pentecostal oath, it would be hard to choose between Marhalt and Ywain, the second and third knights. They both obey the rules of fair play (neither of them commits an 'outerage'), and they are both courteous to women (neither of them commits rape, either). What really distinguishes them is Ywain's deep religious faith, which Marhalt shows no sign of sharing. On the other hand, it would also be difficult, but less so, to choose between Gawain and Marhalt, the first and second knights. Gawain does not, in fact, violate Arthur's code, unless one wants to say that he 'enforced' Ettarde when he tricked her into making a rash promise. The worst thing he has done is break his promise to Pelleas, but that is not explicitly forbidden in the oath and, depending upon the sincerity of Gawain's initial intention, it may not, in fact, be dishonourable.[3] What really distinguishes Gawain from Marhalt is the fact that in his quest he has not achieved any solid political advantages for King Arthur. Whereas Marhalt has subdued the rebellious Duke of the South Marches and has made an ally of the Earl Fergus, Gawain has done nothing. Indeed, he has done worse than nothing, for he is, in fact, responsible for the Duke's rebellion, since it was he who killed the Duke's youngest son in a 'recountre'.

Gawain is never chastized by the king for his political failures, and this, too, is a pattern which will recur throughout the *Morte*. Neither will any other knight presume to punish the king's favorite nephew. In the *Suite du Merlin*, Gawain and Pelleas are finally reconciled (*Works* 1362), but Malory assures us that 'Pelleas loved never aftir sir Gawayne but as he spared hym for the love of the kynge' (179.36–180.1:IV.29). Likewise Gawain was spared long imprisonment in Sir Blamoure's dungeon because one of the four ladies who saved his life decided to arrange his release 'to go unto kynge Arthure for hys love' (108.16: III.8). Nevertheless there are covert ways to be safely revenged upon the king's nephew. Malory invents the notion that Sir Pelleas 'oftyntymes at justis and at turnementes . . . quytte sir Gawayne.' Then, in characteristic fashion, he hides his invention by pretending he found it 'in the booke of Frensh' (180.1–3:IV.29).

Judged by the religious standards of Christian charity, it is much easier to distinguish the better from the worse behaviour among the three knights. Gawain is clearly the worst for the way he has exploited and betrayed both Pelleas and Ettarde. And Ywain would seem to be the best, even better than Marhalt, if only because he seeks no reward for his services and is unfailingly humble. Whereas Marhalt takes from the giant's castle 'grete rychesse oute of numbir, that dayes of his lyff he was nevir poore man' (176:15–17:IV.26), Ywain risks his life to get justice for the Lady of the Roche, even though he knows in advance that his only reward will come from God (177.16–17:IV.27). Marhalt's action is not bad, it is simply not so selfless as Ywain's action, and compares unfavourably with the later action of Lancelot, who, in a similar situation, chooses rather to give the giant's treasure to their victims as a recompense for their 'grevaunces' (272.24:VI.11).

It is easiest of all to judge these knights in terms of the three traditional knightly loyalties, to God, to temporal lord and to lady. By this standard, Ywain is clearly the best knight, for he is the only one who not only acknowledges his duty to God, but also serves God, as well as the Lady of the Roche and King Arthur, when he does justice upon the felonious Sir Hew and Sir Edward. Gawain is clearly the worst (again) because his lies and broken promises make him false not only to Ettarde and Pelleas, but also to God. He manages to remain true to King Arthur; however, even the value of this loyalty appears questionable in the political context of the king's governance. And, finally, Marhalt falls neatly in-between these two extremes for, although he has expressed no awareness of his duty to serve God, he has done good service to Arthur, and he has acknowledged his obligation to serve 'all good ladyes and jantyllwomen . . . as a knyght ought to do' (161.36–162.2:IV.18–19). We can begin to see in fact how this third way of judging the three knights is really a short-hand method of expressing the first two. The difference between the knight who acknowledges and observes all three loyalties and the knight who acknowledges and observes only two is a matter of humility and spiritual awareness. It is the difference between the man who takes his Christian belief seriously enough to let it determine his actions and the man who does not. Likewise, the difference between the knight who acknowledges and observes two loyalties and the knight who acknowledges and observes only one is a matter of honour and of political and social awareness. It is the difference between the man who takes the cultured or courtly view of human society seriously enough to let it determine his actions and the man who does not.

The Literary Ancestry of Malory's Three Types

Each of Malory's three basic types has obvious affinities with one or more of the ideal types previously portrayed in medieval epic and romance. In fact, one could argue that his *Morte Darthur* offers a kind of *summa* of medieval chivalry. For it incorporates exemplars of every conceivable type of knightly excellence to be found in the literature of the previous five hundred years, compares them to one another in a lengthy series of knightly adventures and in this way creates a three-tiered typology of knightly types based on the relative ethical, social and political value of each by contemporary standards.

Malory's first type, hitherto represented by Gawain, has the longest literary history, stretching back as far as Beowulf and Roland. We may call it the Heroic type of knighthood because it is the ideal celebrated in heroic poetry from Homer's *Iliad* to the anonymous fourteenth-century English alliterative poem, the *Morte Arthure*, Malory's source for Arthur's Roman campaign. Above all else, heroic poetry in medieval Europe celebrates the loyalty of the fighting man to his lord. During the early period when the clan-based political organization of society was slowly being replaced by the newer feudal organization, a common topic of heroic poetry was the tragic conflict between a man's duty to his kinsmen and his duty to his feudal lord. When the sacred duty of revenge, the *lex talionis*, came into conflict with the equally sacred duty to be loyal to one's feudal lord, there was no way to resolve the conflict. It is surely more than coincidence, therefore, that the greatest culture heroes of this period, both French and English, are preserved from such conflict by the fact that their feudal lords are also their kinsmen. Beowulf is the nephew of Hygelac, Roland is the nephew of Charlemagne, and Gawain is the nephew of Arthur. Moreover, they are their lords' sisters' sons, which we have reason to believe was the nearest and dearest of all kinship ties between men in the patrilineal clan societies of early medieval Europe.[4]

The qualities admired and cultivated by the Heroic type of knight are those of a man who expects to spend most of his life fighting. Along with loyalty to his lord, his most important virtues are courage, or boldness, and prowess, which includes both strength and skill in the handling of weapons. We have seen how Gawain was able to kill his opponent in a casual encounter with one blow of his sword to the head and how his younger brother, Gaheris, admired him for that 'myghty stroke'. Gawain routinely deals blows as hard as he can, and, therefore, when he encounters knights who are less strong and skillful than himself, he routinely kills them. Thus far the only knight he has encountered who is a match for him, even during the hours between nine in the morning and noon when his strength increases threefold, is Marhalt.[5] Therefore his encounter with Marhalt is the only one which has lasted long enough to test Gawain's devotion to courtesy and the rules of fair play. He has proved to be much less courteous than his opponent. When Marhalt enjoyed the advantage at the very beginning of their combat, having unhorsed him, Gawain was quick to point out the unfairness and even threatened to kill Marhalt's horse if he did not dismount immediately. However, while Gawain enjoyed the advantage for three hours, and Marhalt 'had grete wondir how his myght encreced', it never occurred to Gawain to stop the fight, even though their 'quarellys' were 'nat grete'. Rather, he carried on, wounding and being wounded by Marhalt 'passyng sore'. It was left to Marhalt to take pity on his exhausted opponent, who as 'evynsonge' drew near seemed able to 'dure no lenger', and to say the courteous 'worde' which stopped their fight (161.5–20:IV.18–19). Gawain's behaviour indicates that he knows the rules of fair play well enough, but that he abides by them only when it is to his advantage to do so. His behaviour also indicates that he simply loves to fight. Indeed, he seems to take such pleasure in an evenly matched contest that it would never occur to him to stop fighting, no matter how much blood is being shed on either side.

No doubt there were many reasons why Malory chose to make Gawain the chief exemplar of Heroic knighthood. First of all, as a native folk hero, he was already famous — as a warrior, as the leader of a noble Scottish clan, and, above all, as King Arthur's favorite nephew, his sister's son. Secondly, that heroic image had already been brilliantly projected with a strong religious bias in the alliterative epic poem, the *Morte Arthure*.[6] Thirdly, and just as important, Malory found that same heroic image projected in a negative fashion in two of his French sources for the history of King Arthur and his knights of the Round Table.

Malory could not avoid using these French romance sources for they had great authority and in some cases were the only sources available. For example, other than the brief summaries of Arthur's reign to appear in English chronicles, the only sources for the early years of his reign were the *Merlin* branch of the Vulgate cycle and its continuation, the *Suite du Merlin*. The author of the Vulgate *Merlin* sees Gawain in a fairly sympathetic light. On the other hand, the author of the *Suite* goes out of his way to show that by comparison with other knights Gawain is seriously lacking in the refinements proper to a knight of Arthur's court, as he does, for example, in his account of Gawain's quest for the white hart (Bogdanow 179). The Vulgate *Lancelot* again presents Gawain in a relatively favorable light: he is a bit of an adventurer with the ladies, but a paragon of knightly courtesy and a great friend and admirer of Lancelot. However, for reasons which probably had as much to do with his view of Lancelot as with his view of Gawain, Malory chose not to use very much of the *Lancelot* as a source for the middle years of Arthur's reign. He chose rather to rely on the French prose *Tristan*, which represents Gawain as a criminal.

Malory was enough of an historian to realize that he was obliged to make sense of the contradictions in these sources, and his portrait of Gawain offers an exceptional insight into the historian at work, comparing and evaluating his sources. He seems to have found it relatively easy to harmonize the view of Gawain in the post-Vulgate romances with that in the English chronicles. The chronicles present Gawain as a great warrior in the heroic mould. The *Suite du Merlin* and the *Tristan* both present him as a barbarous villain and a murderer. But Malory could explain that apparently stark contrast as a function of social context: in the refined atmosphere of a medieval French court an heroic warrior might well appear to be barbaric; certainly his acts of vengeance as a blood feudist would appear to be savage murders. It was not so easy to deal with the Vulgate view of Gawain as the lover of many ladies and as Lancelot's friend. This courtly view of Gawain contradicts not only the post-Vulgate romances and the English chronicles but the native English romances of Gawain, as well. The English romances also make Gawain a model of courtesy (e.g. *The Carl of Carlisle*), but two of them (*The Wedding of Sir Gawain and Dame Ragnell* and *The Marriage of Gawain*) conclude with his marriage, and one of them (*Sir Gawain and the Green Knight*) offers a unique view of him as a very young knight who is both pious and chaste.

Malory seems to have concluded that this native English romance tradition erred by making Gawain much too good to be true, probably much better than the historical figure really was, and that the Vulgate romances erred by making him over too much in the courtly French image. Thus he resolved the contradictions of his sources by preferring the English chronicles to the English romances and the post-Vulgate French prose romances (the *Suite du Merlin* and the *Tristan*) to the Vulgate romances (the *Merlin* and the *Lancelot*). As a consequence Malory's Gawain remains the epitome of Heroic knighthood, a great warrior who never adapts to the courtly code of knighthood spelled out in his uncle's pentecostal oath.

That oath defines Malory's second type of knight, represented in the triple quests by Pellinor and Marhalt. We may call this type the Worshipful knight, since Arthur's knights abide by his code in order to merit his lordship and win 'worship'. Malory's Worshipful type has obvious affinities with what Sidney Painter points to as the most common type of ideal knight in medieval French literature, the type which combined the virtues of feudal and courtly chivalry (170). Malory encountered this ideal both in the prose *Lancelot* and in the prose *Tristan*, in which knights like Lancelot and Tristan had overcome the conflict between loyalty to kinsmen and loyalty to feudal lord, only to find themselves caught in another potentially painful conflict between loyalty to their feudal lord and loyalty to their special lady. Unlike the conflict between duty to one's kinsmen and duty to one's liege lord, however, this conflict between duty to one's lady and duty to one's liege lord is resolvable. If the lady he loves is the wife of his liege lord, the knight can either stop loving her, or he can at least refrain from having a sexual relationship with her. Either of these resolutions was to be recommended in real life, given the dire penalties for treasonable adultery, although neither had much to recommend it in literature. Renunciation and self-sacrifice never make such good stories as the intrigue and danger of illicit love. Therefore the two most popular exemplars of the feudal-courtly type of knight were precisely those two knights whose ladies were married to their liege lords: Lancelot and Tristan.

The qualities admired and cultivated by Malory's Worshipful knight are those of a man who expects to spend as much time at court, in the company of ladies and in the service of his lord, as he will in joust or tourney or on the field of battle. He has acquired a good many courtly accomplishments: he can sing and dance, write love poems and carry on an elegant conversation with a lady. He has also acquired a keen political sense, tuned to the realities of late medieval 'bastard-feudal' governance: he knows the importance of strong leadership and the doing of 'true justyce' to the maintenance of stability in his lord's realm. He has acquired these social and political skills by means of his education at court, which would have included the reading of such useful books on knighthood as Christine de Pizan's *Epistle of Othea to Hector* or Antoine de la Sale's *Petit Jehan de Saintré*, in addition to more specialized treatises on the arts of warfare and governance (see above 16–18).

The Worshipful knight adds these social and political skills and virtues to his basic skills as a warrior, and to his most fundamental virtue — loyalty to his lord. The new skills and virtues do not eliminate, or even necessarily weaken the old, but they do alter their expression, so to speak. The Worshipful knight exhibits his courage and prowess as much to honour his lady as to serve his feudal lord, for much of his fighting is done in jousts or tournaments where ladies are present. There was still a great deal of opposition to these knightly sports during the twelfth and thirteenth centuries, because of the risk of death and serious injury. By Malory's time, however, they had become so relatively safe, thanks to improved armour, blunted weapons and strict enforcement of the rules of fair play, that they had become a major part of all courtly festivities (Benson 165–69; Barber, *Knight* 159–192). The Worshipful knight always abides by the rules of fair play in joust and in tournament; moreover, he continues to abide by them even when he is not fighting in the presence of ladies. Marhalt carries this part of the Worshipful knight's code to almost ludicrous extremes when he decides to fight Taulurd on foot, since 'there may no horse bere' the giant. The Worshipful knight always treats ladies with respect, even in situations where he might do otherwise with impunity. For example, Pellinor might have taken advantage of Nyneve, the lady-huntress, while he was bringing her back to Arthur's court. Gawain almost certainly would have done so, if the lady had pleased him. But Pellinor does not, because to Pellinor winning 'worship' is even more important than taking sexual satisfaction.

Indeed, the Worshipful knight's most distinguishing trait is his concern to win 'worship'. Nothing is more important to him than this. To win worship he will risk his life and repress his strongest natural desires for revenge or sexual fulfillment, and in these respects he is most admirable. At the same time, however, he will also neglect his Christian duty if he thinks thereby to win great worship. That is not so admirable as Pellinor himself admitted when he repented that he should have been so eager to win worship in his quest for the lady-huntress that he would not 'socour' another lady who begged his help for 'Jesuys sake'.

Malory chooses Tristram rather than Lancelot to be his chief exemplar of Worshipful knighthood, and it is an excellent choice. Tristram's image in England already had a good deal of courtly polish. He was revered as the legendary founder of the rules governing the most popular aristocratic pastimes — hunting and hawking — and he had a reputation as a fine musician. Finally, he was well known as the lover of Queen Isode of Cornwall and as the best knight in the Cornish court. Indeed, he lacked nothing befitting the epitome of worldly goodness and courtly culture. That his liege lord, King Mark, is also his nearest and dearest kinsman (his mother's brother), as well as the man who made him knight, are facts which make him a perfect foil for Gawain. As we have seen in analysing the two triple quests, Malory's most important technique for developing his typology of knighthood is to create a multiplicity of similar situations and events in which the actions and responses of different knights may be compared. Therefore, this precise parallel in the matter of feudal and kinship bonds between his chief exemplar of Heroic knighthood and his chief exemplar of Worshipful knighthood will be extremely important. For their perfect likeness in these ways will make their differences in knightly behaviour all the more obvious to the reader.

Malory's third type is the most recent development in the literary history of knightly ideals. We may call this type of knight the True knight because he is the direct descendant of the thirteenth-century religious-feudal ideal which its formulators designated the 'vrai' or 'veray' knight, to distinguish him from the heroic or purely feudal type and the courtly-feudal type. The religious-feudal knight believed that God Himself had ordained the High Order of Knighthood and that therefore he was obliged to serve God first, even before his temporal lord. This type of knight was not nearly so popular in literature as was the courtly-feudal type, for obvious reasons, but he circulated widely in the first treatises to be written on knighthood, such as those by Ramon Lull and Geoffrey de Charny. Lull defined the 'veray' knight as a man dedicated to God and to his temporal lord, eager to defend women and helpless men and children from harm, and totally committed to the notion that his sword was given him to do justice (77; Hay 44). To do less than justice would be to betray God and the High Order. The portrait of Tor in the *Suite du Merlin* is possibly the earliest literary portrait of such a 'veray' knight, invented, according to one commentator, in order to draw a deliberate contrast with the merciless and vindictive Gawain (Bogdanow, *Romance* 179).[7] As we have already seen, Malory refines this contrast to draw out the political and judicial implications of Tor's actions, and then invents the adventure of Ywain to reinforce the suggestion that the pious knight can be trusted to do justice for God's sake as well as for his king.

One of the ways in which Lull's treatise betrays its ascetic religious bias is by failing to mention that a knight might have a special love relationship with a lady of the court. Lull seems to assume that most knights will be married, for he condemns any knight who tries to seduce another knight's wife (118; Hay 68). At the same time he makes the protection of all women — including fighting for their legal rights in trial by battle — an essential part of the 'office of knighthood' (38–41; Hay 27–28). Both Malory's Tor and his Ywain are exemplary in performing this chaste variety of *frauendienst* and, as we have seen, Malory has altered his source to emphasize the judicial nature of their service. However, their brief adventures do not allow either knight to develop a more personal or intimate relationship with the lady he has chosen to serve in this way. Neither lady appears to be married, so presumably marriage is a possibility in each case, but it would not necessarily matter if she were, for the most famous example of a 'courtly love'[8] relationship in French literature is Chrétien de Troye's *Le Chevalier de la Charette*, where the lady in question is already married. In such a case, of course, there is absolutely no way of harmonizing the courtly ideal of knighthood with the religious ideal by means of Christian marriage.

Sidney Painter assures us that the courtly ideal of knighthood was the invention of women (95) and that Chrétien's Lancelot, or perhaps we should say Lancelot as conceived by Marie of Champagne (since Chrétien asserts that he received both the *sen* and the *matière* of his poem from her), represents its most extreme literary embodiment (130). What distinguishes Chrétien's Lancelot from the courtly-feudal version of his character developed later in the thirteenth-century prose *Lancelot* is his total and uncompromising loyalty to Guinevere. Chrétien's Lancelot will do *anything* for Guinevere, from committing adultery to suffering public humiliation for his presumed cowardice. The author of the Vulgate version sees to it that Lancelot never goes so far as to pretend cowardice. He also makes some attempt to mitigate his treason by making Arthur equally guilty of adultery, by having Lancelot receive the sword of knighthood from the queen rather than from the king, and by making Arthur owe his very kingdom to the prowess of Lancelot (Bogdanow, *Romance* 198–99). But the only way he can imagine to make Lancelot's love affair with the queen appear admirable, in anything like a moral sense, is to insist that Lancelot owes all his gifts of greatness as a knight — his courage, his prowess, his generosity and his courtesy — to the ennobling power of his love for the queen (Bogdanow, 'Treatment' 118).

The idea that to love a lady makes a knight a *better* knight was central to the idealization of heterosexual love expressed in the courtly literature of the late twelfth and thirteenth centuries. The idealization itself may be understood as a kind of rebellion, not only against the asceticism of the Christian Church, but also against the common aristocractic practice of contracting loveless marriages between nobly-born young people for political and economic profit. However, the refined and ennobling passion celebrated in the courts of Marie of Champagne, Alix of Blois, and their mother, Eleanor of Aquitaine, was never looked upon as a basis for marriage and was thought to be quite a different sort of love from the affection which might develop between a man and his wife after they were married. It was, in fact, what we moderns have learned to call 'romantic love'. Andreas Capellanus records one of Marie of Champagne's judgments to the effect that romantic love could not possibly exist between a man and his wife (106–7), and one must allow that there is a good deal of psychological insight in Marie's alleged judgment. Ever since romantic love finally replaced family negotiation as the basis for marriage in the western world, the experience of married couples has been that the romantic passion of courtship does not survive the prolonged intimacy of married life. However, there was very little likelihood of anyone's discovering that truth by means of experience in the late twelfth or early thirteenth centuries. At that time, if a knight loved a woman passionately, with the refined and courtly sentiment of love, and had vowed to be her servant in love as long as he lived, the lady in question was most unlikely to be his wife, or ever to be able to become his wife.[9]

By the fifteenth century, however, the situation with regard to romantic or 'courtly' love and marriage had changed considerably, in literature if not in real life. In both French and English romances marriage was now viewed as the ideal consummation of the love between a knight and his lady (Mathew 134–35). What made this literary synthesis of Christian marriage and 'courtly love' possible was the fact that the two relationships had one principle and one virtue in common. The principle was freedom of choice; the virtue was *trouthe*. It was *true* love, then, which was ideally consummated in Christian marriage, true because it was freely chosen by both lovers and was faithful unto death. As Chaucer's 'turtel' blushingly exclaimed in the *Parlement of Foules*, 'God forbede a lover shulde chaunge!' (1.582). A fourteenth-century Anglo-Norman *Art d'aimer* explains that once the lovers have become 'un char et un saunk', there is nothing more they can possibly desire, since they may now lead forth their lives in bliss, serving God as well as each other in holy matrimony (11.676–83). Thus, the literary synthesis of 'courtly love' and Christian marriage made it possible for a knight to be a True knight according to the religious ideal of Knighthood and yet to be a lover, for he could serve both God and his lady within the bonds of holy wedlock.

Sir Gilbert Hay adds two paragraphs to his mid-fifteenth century adaptation of Lull's treatise to draw out the implication of this synthesis for the ideal of True knighthood:

> Item, lordis na knychtis suld nocht brek the ath of mariage throw misordynate lechery, for that is a poynt that discordis with the poyntis of the ordre; for thare is thre gree of chastitee, the quhilkis all honourable personis ar behaldin till, that is, ane in mariage, ane in widowhede, and ane in maidynhede that is callit virginitee; of quhilk the haly writt biddis thame that may nocht lyve chaste, mary thame, and syne kepe thair maryage. For gif thai do nocht, and thai brek mariage, that brekis thair aithe to godwart, the quhilk is agayn the ordre and office of knychthede; for chastitee is vertu, and misordanyt lechery is vice (32)

Hay's reference to the three degrees of chastity and his allusion to St Paul's reluctant admission that it was better to marry than to burn, inject into his discussion something of the traditionally ascetic Christian attitude towards sex and marriage and, of course, Hay pays no more attention to the purely courtly ideal of knighthood than Lull did. He does not speak of husbands and wives as 'lovers' and his insistence that knights must keep their marriage oath in order to keep their 'aithe to godwart' is couched in the sort of terms which any contemporary preacher might have employed. Nevertheless, his assertion that knights must remain faithful to their wives is suggestive of the literary type of ideal knight which had been developed in late medieval romance, the knight who, like Guy of Warwick, Sir Degrevant and Chaucer's Arveragus, expects to serve his lady in holy wedlock and to live happily ever after.

Many of these romances end with marriage, so the romancer does not have to deal with the conflict between the settled life of a married man and the adventurous life of the knight-errant. Chrétien de Troye's *Erec et Enid* is exceptional, both for its early date and for its sensitive exploration of this conflict. Chaucer's *Franklin's Tale* is also exceptional in the second regard. For most late medieval romances either use the love story as an excuse for the hero's adventures, and bring both the adventures and the romance to a happy ending with the marriage, or else, as in *Guy of Warwick*, have the knight leave his wife in order to pursue a life of adventure, and then bring both romance and adventures to a happy ending with his safe return. Both narrative patterns point to the inescapable fact that, even though marriage provided a resolution to the conflict between the True knight's religious obligation to serve God and his courtly obligation to serve ladies, it created another conflict which the romancers, at least, could not resolve. They could not imagine how a knight could be an adventurous knight and at the same time a good servant to his lady as her husband.

The idea that a knight might successfully remain chaste even without marriage or the prospect of marriage was extremely rare in medieval romance. We find it expressed early in the thirteenth century as part of the purely religious ideal of knighthood exemplified by Galahad and Percival in the Vulgate *Queste del Saint Graal*. However, that ideal was inspired by the great monastic orders of crusading knights, like the Templars and the Hospitallers, and, in fact, young Galahad and Percival do not remain long in Arthur's court. As soon as they have achieved the Grail they depart for the Holy Land and the religious life. By contrast, the ideal knight imagined in the religious-feudal manuals of chivalry must live his entire life in this world in order to perform his office (the military, political and judicial functions of the High Order of Knighthood); and, at the same time he must resist all temptation to become proud, greedy or lecherous. It is easy to understand why Sir Gilbert Hay believed it was more difficult to be a True knight than it was 'to be outhir monk, or frere, or othir religiouse of the hardest order that is' (39). It is also easy to understand why the ideal of True knighthood was not popular with medieval authors of romance.

The only author of romance before Malory to attempt to portray the celibate type of True knight was the anonymous author of *Sir Gawain and the Green Knight*. The Gawain poet seems to have had the idea of making the most famous and well-beloved of Arthur's knights into the best of all possible knights, by adding to his already well-known attributes as a great fighter and a courtly lover of the ladies, those virtues associated with the religious ideal of knighthood. This addition naturally involved some alterations in the first two sets of attributes — as a fighter, Gawain would now have to be both courageous *and* humble; as a lover, he would now have to be both courteous *and* chaste. In order to achieve such a portrait of knightly perfection, the Gawain poet had to do a clever bit of juggling with the elements of Gawain's literary ancestry. However, by dint of presenting his hero as a very young and inexperienced knight, and confining himself to the narrative time and space of one year and a single adventure, the Gawain poet succeeds in transforming his hero into a True knight. We see very little of Gawain as a fighter: one blow to an unarmed opponent in the opening scene and that is all, for the Gawain poet refuses to narrate Gawain's adventures with wild beasts and ogres on his way through the forest in search of the Green Chapel. We also see very little of Gawain as a lover: he appears to be especially devoted either to Queen Guinevere or to the Virgin Mary, or perhaps to both. But in either case his love relationship to his special lady is clearly not of the kind likely to put him in danger of sexual transgression. In fact, when his devotion to chastity is finally tested, it is tested by a relative stranger, and the beauteous lady proves relatively easy to resist.

The author of *Sir Gawain and the Green Knight* is a poet of great genius and this poem is his masterpiece; but it is not the characterisation of Gawain *per se* which makes it so. On the contrary, the characterization of Gawain is the major puzzle of the poem, and readers still disagree on how they ought to respond to him. Of course, we cannot be certain how medieval readers responded, but most modern readers find Gawain much too good to be true until he has finally given in to temptation. What is more, they seem to like him a lot better after he has shown some human frailty. Victor Haines has suggested that reading *Sir Gawain and the Green Knight* is a test of the reader's own moral standards, and that most modern readers fail this test (163). He may be right, for the Gawain poet is certainly clever enough to have intended such a strategem to educate his readers' moral sensibilities. It is a pity that we will never know what was going on in his mind as he created his perfect knight.

Likewise, we will never know what was going on in Sir Thomas Malory's mind when he was deciding which of Arthur's knights should exemplify True knighthood in *Le Morte Darthur* once Tor and Ywain had established the basic outlines. There were several literary precedents for the married type of True knight, but none of them intimately connected with the Arthurian legend except for young Guinglain, son of Gawain, in the *Le Bel Inconnu*. Malory prefers to make Gawain's brother, Gareth, his exemplar of this type; however, he may have adapted an English romance of Gareth which was derived from the same tradition, if he did not invent his own Tale of Gareth on that model (Field, 'Source' 61–5). When it came to choosing an exemplar of the celibate type of True knight, Malory must have experienced much more difficulty. The only literary precedents for the celibate type were the heroes of the *Queste del Saint Graal*, Galahad, Percival and Bors, and the hero of *Sir Gawain and the Green Knight*. For reasons which I have just suggested while discussing Malory's choice of Gawain to exemplify Heroic knighthood, it was not possible for Malory to make Gawain conform to this type. Galahad and Percival would not do, either, because they do not remain long enough in Arthur's service to exemplify the military, political and judicial functioning of the True knight. That leaves Bors, but Bors lives in the shadow of his mighty cousin, Lancelot, and by himself does not have the stature to be the equal of Gawain and Tristram. Therefore, Malory chose Lancelot. Lancelot would be his chief exemplar of True knighthood and complete the array of possible types of True knight along with Gareth and the three Grail knights. All are True knights, but whereas Galahad and Percival place more emphasis upon their religious obligation to serve God (in the religious life), and Gareth places more emphasis upon his courtly obligation to serve his lady (in Christian marriage), Lancelot places more emphasis upon his feudal obligation to serve Arthur.

Malory could not have made a better choice. Lancelot was already known as the best knight in the world in King Arthur's days. And he was already known as one of the world's greatest lovers, devoted to a woman whom he could not possibly marry, even if he had wanted to. Therefore, all that was required to transform him into an examplar of True knighthood was to do for him what the Gawain poet had done for Gawain: to make him the queen's *true* lover, devoted to her, equally devoted to Arthur, and also devoted to chastity 'for drede of God'.[10] The seeds of Malory's transformation of Lancelot were already present in the Vulgate cycle: in the attempt by the author of the prose *Lancelot* to mitigate the adultery by reference to Lancelot's services to the king; in the emphasis which the author of the *Queste del Saint Graal* places upon Lancelot's sincere repentance; and in the picture which the *Mort Artu* draws of Lancelot's last days as a holy man. History, as recorded in the authoritative Vulgate cycle, would not allow Malory to make Lancelot a perfect specimen of True knighthood, but then it is reasonable to believe that Malory would not have chosen to make him perfect even if he had been at liberty to do so. It is one thing to portray a very pious and idealistic young man as a perfect knight over a short period of time, as the Gawain poet does. It is quite another to recount the whole history of a man's career and portray him as never falling beneath the standards of knightly perfection. Malory prefers a hero who is less perfect, but more credible.

Lancelot's relationship to Guinevere is the source of his only imperfections as the epitome of True knighthood, but it is also what humanizes him as a hero. Moreover, it is what invites comparison between him and Tristram as types of knighthood. I have already observed that Malory relies upon the perfect analogy between Gawain's and Tristram's relationship to their liege lord to heighten the contrast between them as types of knighthood. He relies upon the perfect analogy between Tristram's and Lancelot's relationship to their liege lord's wife in precisely the same way. Malory was perfectly aware that in the French romance tradition Tristan and Lancelot were arch-rivals for the title of best knight in the world and truest lover. In the *Morte Darthur* he settles the contest in favour of Lancelot, making him the True lover of his queen and Tristram the Worshipful lover of his queen. Indeed, without the story of Tristram and Isode to serve as a basis of comparison, it would have been much more difficult for Malory to show his readers how Lancelot differs from Tristram as a lover. Tristram justifies his adulterous relationship with Isode on the grounds that his liege lord, King Mark, no longer deserves their loyalty because of his own treason against them. Obviously Lancelot cannot justify an adulterous relationship with Guinevere on such grounds. Therefore, if he is to be the hero of the *Morte Darthur*, and he clearly is the hero of Malory's work, he must be his queen's true, i.e. chaste lover, in intention, whether or not he is able in practice to be perfect.

The apparent inconsistency between Lancelot's sinfulness as the queen's lover and Malory's great admiration for him as the hero of his work has prompted many critics of the *Morte Darthur* to attempt to resolve what they regard as a moral paradox.[11] For example, C. S. Lewis has suggested that Malory did not judge his knights by a simple standard of good and bad. Rather he employed a triple scale of value, 'bad-good-best', a scale which could be read backwards as 'good-bad-worst'. Lewis suggests a forward reading of bad (King Mark), good (Lancelot) and best (Galahad) and a corollary backward reading of good (Galahad), bad (Lancelot), and worst (King Mark). The advantage of this ethical system of judgment, which Lewis attributes to Malory's 'three-storyed mind', is that the middle term can appear 'without any inconsistency' as either 'good' or 'bad', and Lewis insists that Malory is 'equally serious' in making both judgments (239). Lewis does not spell out the personal or cultural points of view to be associated with his forward and backward readings of Malory's triple scale of value, but it seems fairly clear to me that the first one, reading forward, is worldly or secular and that the second one, reading backward, is otherworldly or religious. Now, it is possible to understand how a forward-looking, worldly sort of man might judge Lancelot to be 'good' despite his failure in chastity, whereas a backward-looking, religious sort of man would judge him to be 'bad' because of that same failure; however, once the worldly reader has taken into account the political implications of Lancelot's sexual transgression, there is no way he can judge him to be 'good', for Lancelot's sin of adultery with the queen makes him a traitor to King Arthur.[12]

Lewis cannot resolve the moral paradox posed by Lancelot as the hero of the *Morte Darthur* because it does not exist. Malory does not see anything 'good' in Lancelot's adultery; however, he can forgive Lancelot's failures because he imagines that they were not premeditated, that they were deeply repented, and that they were very few. What is more, Malory is not at all likely to have agreed with Lewis that Galahad is the 'best' of all possible knights. Galahad's type of knightly perfection has its place, but it is not in this world, and Malory is fundamentally concerned with how this world shall be governed. Therefore, for Malory the very 'best' type of True knight must be Lancelot, imperfect though he is, for at the same time as he tries with varying degrees of success to be true to both God and Guinevere, he never fails to serve Arthur by doing justice and pacifying the realm. Indeed, when Arthur banishes him, Lancelot's followers fear for the future of England, now that the man who has done more than any other to ensure the stability of King Arthur's governance will be gone (1203.29–1204.11:XX.17–18).

Lewis is right, however, about Malory's 'three-storyed mind'. If one applies Lewis's triple scale of value to Malory's typology of knighthood, it makes excellent ethical sense, whether one reads it forwards or backwards. Read forwards, from the worldly point of view, the Heroic type of knight, like Gawain, who is loyal to his lord but shows no awareness or appreciation of the courtly virtues or of the political and judicial functions of knighthood, appears to be 'bad'. On the other hand, the Worshipful type of knight, like Tristram and Marhalt, who observe Arthur's code of chivalry, serve all good ladies, and understand the political and judicial functions of knighthood, appears to be 'good'. But the 'best' type of knight, like Lancelot, Gareth and Bors, will add to the feudal and courtly virtues an awareness of his duty to serve God. He will appear to be the 'best' not just because Christian piety is admirable in a Christian society, but because he can be trusted to do justice and to seek no personal reward, for he truly believes that whenever he wields his sword, he acts by the grace of God to do justice, for God's sake as well as for King Arthur.

If one were to read Lewis's scale backwards, from the otherworldly point of view, Malory's typology would still make excellent moral sense. Underlying the otherworldly point of view in the *Morte Darthur* is the providentialist assumption that no man can do well in this world without the grace of God. Therefore the otherworldly point of view does not transcend politics; on the contrary, it subsumes politics, by presuming that the only way to ensure good governance is to put good men in office. It becomes obvious, then, that from this point of view the True knight who serves God as well as his lord and his lady will appear to be 'good'. On the other hand, the Worshipful knight, who serves his lord and his lady but fails to acknowledge his obligation to serve God, will appear 'bad'. He will appear 'bad', not just because of this failure *per se*, but because, having separated himself from the grace of God by his pride of life, he is likely to fall into worse sins, such as lechery, envy and anger. Finally, the Heroic knight who serves only his lord will appear to be the 'worst' of all because he does not even abide by the secular standards of honourable conduct and his rash and brutal behaviour often makes him a casual killer.

However one judges the ethical value of these three types of knight, it is important to realize that they each embody a fundamentally different way of perceiving and understanding the world. They are all Christian, to be sure, but they have quite different ways of understanding their relationship to God. The True knight adopts a mystical, providentialist view according to which God is immanent in His creation and actively intervenes in the affairs of men. This type of knight believes that it is important to remain in a state of grace because God punishes sinful men with misfortune. By contrast, the Worshipful knight adopts a more pragmatic and rationalist view. He is not certain of the extent to which God intervenes in the affairs of men; however, he is certain that men ought to use their God-given reason to solve the problems of everyday life rather than to trust in God for miracles. In the last chapter I referred to these two as the Religious and the Rationalist points of view, respectively, and showed how they corresponded to the two points of view which informed different late medieval treatises on knighthood (18–20). The third point of view, that of the Heroic knight, is also fundamentally relgious; however, it does not find a place in the late medieval treatises on chivalry, for it belongs to an earlier, more primitive age. Like his pagan counterpart in *Beowulf* the Heroic knight is a fatalist. He believes that God determines all things, and, as a consequence, he cannot comprehend either the rationalism of the Worshipful knight or the providentialism of the True knight.

We can locate these three points of view within Malory's text quite easily. The religious, providentialist point of view is to be associated primarily with Corbenic and the Grail, the visible sign of God's grace operating in Malory's Arthurian world. On the other hand, the pragmatic and rationalist point of view is to be associated with King Arthur and his court, Camelot, the seat of temporal governance. The providentialist point of view can also be associated with the trackless wastes and wildernesses through which Arthurian knights-errant journey in search of trial by 'stronge adventures' just as the rationalist point of view can be associated with the well-organised and supervised jousts and tournaments in which they try to win worship. The third point of view is not so immediately visible as the first two, perhaps because it developed initially in the clan-based social organisation which Arthur's more civilized feudal society has replaced. However, as Malory's representation of the relationship between Arthur and his favorite nephew makes clear, Arthur's feudal governance cannot function without the loyalty of the great clans. If the point of view of the Heroic knight can not clearly be associated with either Camelot or Corbenic, with either 'stronge adventures' or jousts and tournaments, it can be associated with the field of battle. In fact it is only there that the Heroic knight's virtues show to advantage and his own values triumph.

In the two chapters which follow I will show how Malory develops the typology of knighthood which he has sketched out in the triple quests of his first narrative unit. Malory devotes the second narrative unit of the Winchester manuscript to an exploration of the virtues, attitudes and behaviours of the True knight, and the third narrative unit (the Tale of Tristram) to a representation of his Worshipful counterpart. Malory never devotes an entire section of his narrative to the Heroic type because he doesn't have to. The typical virtues of the Heroic knight — prowess, bravery and loyalty to his lord — are fundamental to the other two types as well. Therefore, Malory's analysis of the Heroic type of knight runs like a thread throughout both these narrative sections and his portrait emerges fully only by contrast with the other two. Gawain continues to be the chief exemplar of Heroic knighthood and we come to know him better and better as Malory systematically contrasts his behaviour and attitudes, first with those of Lancelot and Gareth in the second narrative unit and then with those of Tristram and Lamorak in the third.

3

True Knighthood

True knighthood is Malory's most complex ethical type because it incorporates elements from all three of the traditional sources for a code of chivalry — feudal, religious and courtly. Malory explores each of these elements in turn, beginning with the most fundamental virtues, those associated with the knight's duty to his feudal overlord, in the tale of Arthur's Roman campaign. Then he examines the religious virtues and beliefs of the True knight in a brief tale devoted to the adventures of Lancelot. And, finally, he explores the courtly virtues and attitudes of the True knight in the tale of young Gareth's quest for love and lordship. Lancelot is prominent in all three tales, and therefore their net effect is not only to define the ideal of True knighthood in its fullness, but to identify that ideal with Lancelot. Thematically these three tales form a unit, and therefore it is probably more than coincidence that the scribe of the Winchester manuscript presents them as the second of its five narrative units (see above 7).

As a type, Malory's True knight derives from the religious-feudal ideal described in Ramon Lull's thirteenth-century treatise. Lull's *Book of the Ordre of Chyualry* was the standard work on knighthood for more than two hundred years and remained popular in England into the sixteenth century largely because his view of knighthood accorded so well with the contemporary English view of governance. According to Lull the knight's office is temporal governance. What is more, that office is divinely ordained: therefore, to be worthy of both order and office the king and his knights must be true to God. By comparison with Lull, later, fifteenth-century treatises on knighthood placed much more emphasis upon practical matters, such as the etiquette of the court or the tactics of the battlefield, and Malory shows that he was aware of these treatises, also. For example, in his version of the Roman campaign he shows that he was familiar with the most up-to-date treatise on military tactics and strategy (Bornstein, 'Military Strategy'). He also shows that he was familiar with recent English romances of chivalry in his Tale of Gareth which concludes in typical fashion with the marriage of the hero. However, there is one fifteenth-century manuscript which could have suggested to Malory all the elements of the composite ideal which emerges from the tales of Arthur and

Lucius, of Lancelot and of Gareth, and that is Sir Gilbert Hay's prose manuscript, composed for William, Earl of Orkney and Chancellor of Scotland, in the year 1456. Hay's manuscript contains an expanded and revised version of Lull's treatise (including an exhortation to knights who may not live chaste to marry and then 'kepe thair maryage'), a translation of the pseudo-Aristotelian *De secretis secretorum*, which he calls 'The Buke of the Governaunce of Princis' and a translation of Honoré de Bonet's treatise on military strategy. Hay's manuscript thus comprises a complete library for the fifteenth-century knight and governor, offering him the latest and best instruction regarding his military, political and judicial responsibilities. It is not impossible that Sir Thomas Malory, whoever he was, knew Sir Gilbert Hay's manuscript; but if Malory had read widely, it is not necessary to postulate such an acquaintance in order to explain the similarity in their ideas on knighthood.[1] Malory and Hay both think of the True knight as a great soldier as well as statesman and as a devout Christian who, if he may not 'kepe' the celibate life, will be a faithful husband.

Not many men could ever achieve this ideal of True knighthood, because most would find it too difficult to resolve the conflicts which could arise between service to God and service to one's lady or between service to one's king and country and service to one's lady. (In theory no conflict could ever arise between service to God and king for they were *ex officio* one and the same.) Nevertheless, history provides several examples of men who came close to realizing this ideal, some of whom would surely have been known to Malory. The first good example from English history is provided by William Marshall, who rose to greatness through his knightly prowess and a fortunate marriage, served his king well and in the year 1219 died a holy death, commending his soul to God whom he addressed as his 'courteous Lord' (Mathew 127). Fourteenth-century France offers the example of Geoffrey de Charny, knight, husband, father and author of two pious treatises on chivalry, who went on crusade to the Holy Land and in 1356 died at Poitiers bearing the standard of France. Fourteenth-century England offers two examples of knights who earned the respect and admiration of their fellows for their piety and zeal to do justice as well as for their more worldly virtues of prowess and courtesy: Sir Henry of Grosmont, first Duke of Lancaster, and Sir John Clanvowe, knight of the Household to Richard II and friend of Chaucer. Both of these men were also authors of works of moral and spiritual instruction.[2] And finally, in Malory's own time we may point to the brother-in-law of Edward IV, Anthony Wydville, Lord Scales. Like Henry of Lancaster and Sir John Clanvowe, Anthony Wydville was a man of letters as well as a champion in the lists. He was a married man, a successful courtier and diplomat, and his piety is attested by his habit of wearing a hair shirt.[3]

Lancelot is Malory's chief exemplar of True knighthood. Malory has anticipated his coming to court in the conclusion of his first narrative unit and he has suggested what type of knight he will be by creating an intimate link between him and Sir Pelleas. Pelleas has already indicated that he is a True knight in his relationship to Gawain during the second triple quest: even though Gawain had betrayed him, Pelleas refused to kill him as he lay sleeping with Ettarde, because he was determined that he would 'never dystroy the Hyghe Ordir of Knyghthode' (170.24–25:1V.23). Pelleas' noble restraint and the reverential way in which he refers to the 'hyghe Ordir of Knyghthode' strongly suggest that he is a True knight.[4] Malory then confirms Pelleas' knightly type by describing him as 'one of the four that encheved the Sankgreal':

> And sir Pelleas was a worshypfull knyght, and was one of the four that encheved the Sankgreal. And the Damesel of the Laake made by her meanes that never he had ado with sir Launcelot de Laake, for where sir Launcelot was at ony justis or at ony turnemente she wolde not suffir hym to be there that day but yf hit were on the syde of sir Launcelot. (180.9–14:IV.29).

Malory may have intended to introduce Pelleas into the Grail quest as the successful fourth knight at the time he wrote this conclusion; however, I think it much more likely that he simply made a 'mistake' — not out of ignorance, as Vinaver would have it — but deliberately. For this 'mistake' has the same thematic usefulness as the one he made earlier when he altered Merlin's prophecy to say that either Lancelot or Galahad would achieve Balin's sword (91.23:II.19; see below 121, 244–50). Both mistakes call attention to the possibility that Lancelot will be the fourth Grail knight.

Any reader familiar with the *Queste del Saint Graal* knows that Lancelot is there regarded as one of the 'four' who 'have no peerys' (941.19–20:XVI.1; *Queste* 148.3–10) because he comes closer than any other knight to achieving it, and that Pelleas does not figure in the quest at all. Therefore, Malory's second 'mistake' forces the knowledgeable reader to correct the error by substituting Lancelot for Pelleas, a substitution which is validated in a curious way by what Malory says next about the relationship between these two knights.

Both Lancelot and Pelleas have an affinity with the Lady of the Lake, or Nyneve, as Malory calls the young woman who accompanied Merlin when he visited Lancelot (*né* Galahad) as a young child (125–26:IV.1).

Although Malory never tells the rest of the story of her relationship to Lancelot, he could assume that most of his readers would be familiar with the legend, and therefore would know that Nyneve, the Lady of the Lake, is Lancelot's foster mother. Malory makes her the wife of Pelleas, as well.[5] Now, Pelleas has just proved himself to be the best knight in the world by winning the prize at Arthur's tournament. Indeed, he is 'so stronge that there myght but few knyghtes stonde hym a buffette with a spere' (179.29–31: IV.29). Therefore, when Malory recounts how Nyneve 'made by her meanes' that her husband 'never' encountered Lancelot at joust or tournament, his readers would quite naturally infer that her intention was to protect her young foster son. Later, of course, after Lancelot has proved 'in all turnementes, justys, and dedys of armys' that he surpasses 'all other knyghtes' (253.8–10: VI.1), her measure will serve rather to protect her husband. Malory has altered his French source to make Nyneve 'unambigously benign' (Holbrook 767): in the 'Arthur and Accolon' episode she has saved Arthur's life; near the end of his work Malory will assure his readers that she has always saved her husband's life (1150.21–23:X1X.11); and at the conclusion of the 'Poisoned Apple', Malory reminds us that 'ever she ded grete goodnes unto kynge Arthure and to all hys knyghtes thorow her sorsery and enchauntementes' (1059.13–15:XVIII.8). By relating Lancelot to her, and to Pelleas, even before he appears at Arthur's court, Malory suggests quite powerfully that the young man will prove to be just like his foster-parents, a force for good in Arthur's court and a True knight.

There are very few individualizing strokes in the portrait of True knighthood which Malory draws in the second narrative unit, using Lancelot as chief exemplar. Lancelot's character emerges by comparison and contrast with other knights for, in this second narrative unit, Malory employs the same technique he employed in the triple quests of the first narrative unit. In the first set of adventures, Malory examines the feudal virtues of the True knight by comparing Lancelot to Gawain during the Roman campaign. In the second set of adventures he examines the religious virtues of the True knight by comparing Lancelot to Galahad. And in the third set of adventures he examines the courtly virtues of the True knight by comparing Lancelot to both Gawain and Gareth. Thus the feudal-religious-courtly pattern of the first triple quest is recapitulated with this difference: in the first triple quest the brief adventures of Gawain, Tor and Pellinor adumbrated all three of Malory's basic types, by focussing on the values most characteristic of each; here, the more extended adventures of Gawain, Lancelot and Gareth

— on the battlefields of France, in the forests of Wales and in the courts and castle yards of England — fully define one type, True knighthood, in each of its three aspects.

Lancelot and Gawain: King Arthur's Warriors

Malory looks at the feudal aspect of True knighthood in its most flattering context — warfare. Indeed, warfare is possibly the only context in which sheer prowess may be idealized to seem more than simple brutality. Yet prowess is absolutely necessary to the knight. Both the circumstances and the actual events of Arthur's Roman campaign demonstrate that the feudal virtues — courage, prowess and loyalty to one's lord — are the *sine qua non* of knighthood. Without them, King Arthur could not protect England from foreign domination. Whatever additional virtues the Church or courtly society might wish to demand of a knight, his king or feudal lord must demand that he be brave, strong and loyal. Chastity and courtesy do not win wars.

In Malory's source for the Roman campaign, the fourteenth-century alliterative poem known as the *Morte Arthure*, King Arthur and his favorite nephew, Gawain, are the central characters. They remain central in Malory's version, but Malory also creates a prominent role for Lancelot so as to compare him to Gawain in the way each knight exemplifies the feudal virtues. Malory still gives Gawain's exploits much more coverage, but he gives Lancelot's much more praise. What is more, Malory's King Arthur gives Lancelot positions of greater trust and responsibility than he gives to his own nephew.

In Malory's version of the Roman campaign, Lancelot is the equal of Sir Cador of Cornwall, Arthur's chief soldier and statesman. Cador speaks first in the council of war and is given the most crucial command, that is, command of the rear guard in the Battle of Sessoynes. Before this battle takes place, however, King Arthur names Lancelot co-captain with Cador of a small group of knights dispatched to escort prisoners to Paris. Their co-captaincy is only implicit in the Winchester text, but is made explicit in the abbreviated Caxton version (212.16:V.6–7). When Lancelot and Cador are faced with an ambush of 60,000 Romans, they confer and agree to fight rather than flee. Then, in the Winchester version the 'two myghty dukis' dub knights on the field of battle (214.13–14:V.7). This particular mark of knightly eminence is lost in the Caxton abbreviation; however, praise for Lancelot's feats of prowess in the ensuing battle remains, not only in

Malory's description of the fighting (216.19–25:V.7), but also in the report which Sir Cador makes to the king:

> 'Sir,' seyde sir Cador, 'there was none of us that fayled othir, but of the knyghthode of sir Launcelot hit were mervayle to telle.' (217.10–12:V.7)

By 'knyghthode' Sir Cador here means strength and skill in horsemanship and the use of arms, as well as sufficient courage and loyalty to spur a man to use his prowess even in the face of death. Lancelot's superlative 'knyghthode' in this feudal and heroic sense of the word later moves Arthur to keep Lancelot by his side in the battle against Lucius rather than let him go with Cador to command the rear guard. Arthur gives Cador permission to take with him whatever knights of the Round Table he likes 'sauff sir Launcelot and sir Bors, with many mo othir'. The first-named Lancelot shall be chief among those who will remain with the king 'in fere' and 'awayte uppon [his] persone' during the battle (219.1–4:V.8).

During the battle, Lancelot performs the greatest feat of arms of any of Arthur's knights: he rides straight into the midst of the Emperor's personal bodyguard, killing one Saracen king and knocking the Emperor from his horse, and then rides away again with the 'baner of Rome' in his possession (220.14–23:V.8). Not even Gawain can equal that exploit, and yet, Malory gives clear evidence that he himself disapproves of such reckless exploits. When Arthur is obliged to come to the rescue of Gawain, Lancelot and Lovell because of a similar daredevil feat, Malory observes,

> . . . oftetymes thorow envy grete hardynesse is shewed that hath bene the deth of many kyd knyghtes; for thoughe they speke fayre many one unto other, yet whan they be in batayle eyther wolde beste be praysed. (223.9–13:V.8)

Malory understands that such foolhardy forays on the part of individual knights are largely motivated by the desire for glory, and that envy of the praise heaped upon others may cause some knights to attempt feats which are beyond their capability. What is worse, their recklessness also endangers the lives of those who feel compelled to rescue them. This is not the way to win battles.

In the Caxton abbreviation all such individual exploits are omitted and the focus of the battle description is on Arthur himself as supreme commander, who

> . . . rode in the bataille exhortynge his knyghtes to doo wel and hym self dyd as nobly with his handes as was possyble a man to doo. (220–221:V.8)

Arthur's slaying of the giant Galapas is singled out for description, as is his single combat with the Emperor Lucius in which Arthur is victorious, killing Lucius and causing the Roman army to scatter in confusion. Other than these, the only feat of arms to be noted in the Caxton text is Gawain's killing of 'thre admyrales' (222:V.8). In the Winchester version that feat occurs as part of the outrageous attack on Lucius made by Gawain, Lancelot and Lovell, the same exploit which obliges Arthur to come to their rescue, for otherwise they 'never were lyke to ascape at that tyme' (223.8–9:V.8), and occasions Malory's disapproving remarks on 'grete hardynesse'. Thus, in the Caxton text, which may well have been revised by Malory himself (*Caxton's* 618), the foolhardy and vainglorious exploits which occasioned his criticism in the Winchester text have been removed, except in the case of Gawain.

In both versions of the Roman campaign. Gawain is clearly Malory's chief representative of the Heroic type of knight if only because he is so much more prominent than any other knight.[6] He is the central figure in the episode of the messengers sent to the Roman camp before the battle of Sessoynes and again, after that battle, he is the central figure in the episode of the foraging party sent out to raid enemy lines during the siege of Metz. In both of these lengthy episodes, Gawain epitomizes the Heroic ideal. He is the superb fighting man who is daunted by nothing and by no one. As a consequence, however, Gawain consistently acts in reckless ways which endanger not only his own life but also the lives of his companions. For example, while he and Bors are still in the tent of the Emperor, having delivered the message from Arthur, Gawain responds to a taunt from one of Lucius' knights by striking off his head. This act, in violation of all the rules of diplomatic decorum, ought to have been suicidal. However, it proves to be so outrageous that Lucius and his knights are stunned into inactivity just long enough to allow Gawain and his companions to escape. They wheel about, gallop out of the camp and manage to reach their own ambush of men-at-arms before the Romans can catch up with them. A furious battle ensues in which the Round Table knights are greatly outnumbered but they fight valiantly and manage to take some valuable prisoners. In Malory's version of this battle, Gawain is sorely wounded and at one particularly low ebb he sends to Arthur for help (210–11:V.6). This alteration of Gawain's behaviour seems to be an invitation to the reader to compare Arthur's nephew with Roland, the nephew of Charlemagne. Roland was also a proud and reckless warrior, the epitome of Heroic knighthood. In fact, his uncle Charlemagne had such confidence in him that he gave him command of the rear guard as the French army returned from Spain. However, when

Roland's small troop of men was overwhelmed by hordes of Saracens, he was too proud to call on his uncle for help until it was too late to save any lives, and so he and his companions died at Roncesvals. By contrast Gawain's behaviour in this episode suggests that he has more sense. At least he is not too proud to send for help when it looks as though he and his companions will die without it. Of course in the end they do not need Arthur's help. They manage to extricate themselves and are returning to camp with their prisoners, just as Arthur is setting out to their rescue. But the point has been made, and in such a way that Gawain appears to be not only more sensible than Roland, but also a more superb warrior.

Gawain's behaviour in the foraging episode continues to invite comparison with Roland. Early on the first morning, while his companions are still sleeping, Gawain slips away in search of adventures. Once again, his foolhardiness is notable: in enemy territory, on a mission of extreme importance which can only be achieved by the utmost stealth, he is willing to risk all for the sake of adventure. He challenges the first knight he sees, who happens to be the mighty pagan knight, Priamus, descended from Alexander and Hector and more than a match for Gawain. Once again, Gawain is almost fatally wounded; once again, he involves his companions in a battle in which they appear to be hopelessly outnumbered; and once again, against all odds, the outcome is fortunate. Gawain attributes his good fortune in defeating Priamus to 'the goodnesse of God' (232.17: V.10). Later he assures his fellow knights that if 'we feyght in fayth the felde is ourys' (238.5:V.11). And in the Caxton text he speaks even more like Roland, the Christian crusader, when he advises his men 'to make vs redy to mete with these sarasyns and mysbyleuyng men and wyth the helpe of god we shal ouerthrowe them' (V.10). Malory eliminates the more courtly sentiments of Gawain's counterpart in the alliterative *Morte Arthure* as out of keeping with his character. His Gawain would never urge men to fight bravely for the love of 'ladyes in dyuerse londes!' (2866). Nor would Roland. Heroic knights do not fight in order to be better loved by their ladies. But if they are Christian knights they do presume that God will be on their side, especially if their enemies are 'sarasyns and mysbyleuyng men'. The only difference between Malory's Gawain and the hero of the *Chanson de Roland* is that Gawain is more fortunate in battle. This may be interpreted as yet another sign of Gawain's superiority to the hero of the French epic poem. Indeed, one could go further and speculate that Malory's hero is more fortunate because he is neither so proud nor so foolhardy as Roland.

Malory was troubled by the vainglory and recklessness which

seemed to be inherent in the Heroic ideal of knighthood embodied by Roland and Gawain. His concern becomes explicit in a scene involving Lancelot and the king. In Malory's source, Arthur is furious with his cousin Cador, who alone commanded the small party of men escorting prisoners to Paris, for having decided to stand and fight when his force was greatly outnumbered. The king accuses him of having 'Kowardely' put his 'best knyghttez' in peril and lost fourteen of them (1923–24). In Malory's version his words are not so cruel, and even though they seem to be directed primarily at Cador, it is Lancelot, Cador's co-captain, who replies to defend their decision:

> Than the kynge wepte and with a keverchoff wyped his iyen and sayde, 'youre corrage and youre hardynesse nerehande had you destroyed, for and ye had turned agayne ye had loste no worshyp, for I calle hit but foly to abyde whan knyghtes bene overmacched.'
>
> 'Not so,' sayde sir Launcelot, 'the shame sholde ever have bene oures.'
>
> 'That is trouthe,' seyde sir Clegis and sir Bors, 'for knyghtes ons shamed recoverys hit never.' (217.23–218.2:V.7)

In the alliterative *Morte Arthure*, Cador defends himself by arguing that he could not allow an enemy ambush to prevent him from carrying out Arthur's orders, and suggests that Arthur should send out larger and better equipped companies if he does not want to lose knights (1928–33). Malory leaves all of this out in order to focus on the different definitions of 'worshyp' and 'shame' which are implied by the disagreement between Lancelot and Arthur. Lancelot and his companions assign enormous value to raw courage, one of the three basic virtues of the Heroic ideal of knighthood. To retreat in the face of danger is always 'shameful'; therefore, a hero never retreats, no matter what the odds against him. On the other hand, Arthur assigns equal value to prudence, one of the more rationally based virtues of the Worshipful ideal of knighthood, and one which is still basic to the ethics of modern soldiering. From Arthur's point of view, there is no shame in acting intelligently, or prudently; in other words, there is no shame in making a strategic withdrawal in order to survive and fight another day.

Arthur's point of view was being explained and defended in fifteenth-century treatises on warfare, most of them based on classical Roman originals, such as Vegetius' *De rei militari*. Authors of books like the anonymous *Knyghthode and Bataile* (1457–1460) and Christine de Pizan's *Livre des Fais d'armes et de chevalerie* (c.1410) were attempting to impose the Roman military values of order, discipline and prudence upon the medieval knight.[7] Their attempts were encouraged and, in some cases, instigated by monarchs looking for ways to increase their military effectiveness. Thus Malory, like his source, the alliterative *Morte Arthure,* quite rightly gives the more modern and rational point of view to Arthur, king and supreme military commander, and gives the more medieval and romantic point of view to his captains of war. However, unlike his source, Malory does not blunt the edge of Arthur's criticism by having him subsequently retract it, praise his men for their courage and reward them for their success with a great feast (1928–48). Malory drops the matter abruptly with Lancelot's fierce rebuttal ('Not so, . . . the shame sholde ever have bene oures') and the concurrence of Clegis and Bors. He does not attempt to resolve or even appear to resolve the disagreement between Arthur and Lancelot. And, in fact, their disagreement cannot be resolved because they are judging knightly behaviour by contradictory standards. Arthur's standard is rational and pragmatic: Lancelot's standard is irrational and impractical. Arthur's rationality is, of course, more sensible, and would have been appreciated as such by Malory's first readers as much as it is by modern readers. However, Lancelot's heroism would have appeared more noble to Malory's first readers, just as it does to us.

The adjective 'noble' is a very elastic word in Modern English, just as it was in Middle English, and can still refer to at least three different kinds of greatness: (1) high birth or exalted rank in society (*OED* 2); outstanding qualities of character or illustrious exploits (*OED* 1); and, finally, moral excellence (*OED* 4, 5). What all these meanings share, nonetheless, is the idea of greatness, the notion of something which rises above the average, the ordinary, and therefore, above the prudent and common-sensical. In the late Middle Ages both the second and third kinds of greatness were thought to be natural to the hereditary nobility. Therefore, it was argued, only men who were born into the nobility should be made knights. Sir Gilbert Hay bases his argument on the heritability of physical prowess and courage (*Knychthede* 36–38). But there was an additional argument to be made based on the nobleman's sense of honour and shame. The anonymous fifteenth-century author of *Knyghthode and Bataile* assures his readers that common men, or *ignobiles,* will prove to be cowards on the battlefield, but that noble men, or *nobiles,* who 'have lond & fee/ With thewys goode' will be mindful of their honour and 'shame wil refreyne hem not to fle' (271–81).[8] Close attention to his words reveals, however, that even he does not presume *all* noblemen born will be brave in battle for fear of shame. Only those 'with thewys goode' can be counted upon. But what constitutes 'thewys goode'? And who decides which 'thewys' are 'goode'?

As we have seen in the previous chapter, different circumstances at different times during the medieval period gave rise to different codes of virtue for the nobleman, codes which may be briefly characterized from their origin as either feudal, courtly, or religious. Not surprisingly, the value subsequently attached to each of these codes also tended to vary with circumstances. In the context of a military campaign the primary feudal virtues — courage, prowess and loyalty to one's lord — will be valued most highly, for these are the virtues which produce an effective fighting force. Arthur's criticism of Lancelot reflects a late medieval courtly modification of the feudal ideal, a modification which produced the modern ideal of the well-disciplined soldier. But even that modern ideal assigns a high value to the exhibition of raw courage in the face of death. In fact, admiration for such courage is to be found in all cultures and in all times (Baroja 94) and therefore we may say that in some respects the Heroic ideal of knighthood has survived into the modern world.

In a broader sense, the heroic virtue which Lancelot defends — and which Malory also clearly values — is what the philosophers termed *magnanimitas*, what the writers on chivalry termed 'noblesse de courage' and what we may call 'greatness of spirit'. According to St Thomas Aquinas, who follows Aristotle in this as in so many things, *magnanimitas* consists in 'imagining and tackling great tasks — tasks whose greatness will test even a great man's capacity'. Therefore, Alexander Murray concludes that perhaps the best modern English translation of this concept would be 'thinking big' (357). In a strictly military context, of course, *magnanimitas* would consist of performing incredibly dangerous feats of arms, as Lancelot and Gawain both do in the Winchester version of the Battle of Sessoynes. However, Aquinas is not so concerned with the military implications of *magnanimitas* as he is with its ethical and religious implications. He agrees with Aristotle that *magnanimitas* is natural to the nobly born and presumptuous in lesser men, but rather than worry about the elitism implied in this premise, Aquinas proceeds to prove as a consequence that noble men ought to undertake the greatest task of all, the imitation of Christ. They ought to give up their freedom and power, their riches and pleasures in this world to live the life of Christian perfection.[9] In other words, the most nobly born ought to aspire to the greatest possible virtue, which is nothing less than holiness, or sanctity. Murray adduces considerable evidence indicating that large numbers of young noblemen were convinced by the Thomist argument (337–48); many more were not, however, and it is for these men that the treatises on knighthood were written.

Although the earliest treatises on knighthood were written from the religious point of view, they assume that their readers have chosen to engage in the active life of a knight in the world (at least until such time as it becomes appropriate to retire from the world to prepare their souls for death). Therefore, these treatises emphasize the importance of cultivating the Christian virtues in order to be a *true* knight. From their point of view the 'thewys goode' which a knight must possess in order to be regarded as *truly* 'noble' are the feudal virtues, plus the Christian virtues. For example, Sir Gilbert Hay, following his late thirteenth-century source fairly closely, assures his readers that the 'worthyast and maist noble man of curage' may be identified by the following 'takenis': 'justice, and temperance, force and prudence, fayth, esperaunce, that is gude hope, and cheritee, and leautee' (35–36; Lull 55–56). In other words, the *truly* 'noble' or 'maist noble' man possesses not only the Heroic virtues — prowess and courage (both of which may be understood as comprised in 'force', or the cardinal virtue of fortitude) and loyalty — but also the Christian virtues, both theological (faith hope and charity) and cardinal (justice, temperance and prudence).

If we compare the actions of Malory's Gawain and his Lancelot during the Roman campaign in light of the above discussion it is easy to see that both knights are 'noble' by the standards of Heroic knighthood. Indeed, in terms of the three basic feudal virtues — prowess, courage and loyalty to their lord — it is not possible to differentiate between them except in one regard, and that is the degree of recklessness which each knight exhibits. Gawain's foolhardy exploits in the messenger episode, and again in the foraging episode, seem to be entirely spontaneous and unthinking actions. He lops off the head of the Emperor's aide because he is angry; and he goes off in search of adventures while his companions sleep in enemy territory presumably because he is bored. One cannot even accuse him of vainglory, so little does he seem to think about what he is doing. However, one can accuse him of imprudence and of needlessly risking the lives of his companions simply because he cannot control his feelings. Lancelot, on the other hand, takes counsel with his co-captain, Cador, and with his men before he decides to stand and fight rather than retreat in face of the enemy's greater numbers. The nobility of his action is not lessened by its premeditation, however. On the contrary, it is heightened. There is something even more 'noble' about acts of bravery which are undertaken with forethought, and to do what Lancelot and his companions did, to take counsel first and then face death, may be as close as it is possible to come to combining the virtues of prudence and courage in the way that Sir Gilbert Hay would have the truly noble knight do. Thus, although Lancelot and Gawain share the three basic virtues of Heroic knighthood, Lancelot shows by the way he exercises those virtues that he is a True knight. At least, this is undoubtedly so in the Caxton revision which, in the account of the Battle of Sessoynes, eliminates all of Lancelot's foolhardy exploits, including his superb geste of snatching the 'banner of Rome' away from the Emperor himself, but retains one reference to Gawain's exploit in which he 'slewe thre admyrales'. The Caxton version thus strenghtens the impression of Lancelot as a courageous but responsible leader of men in battle and, at the same time, leaves unaltered the impression that Gawain is equally courageous, but reckless.[10]

Malory has heightened Gawain's piety in the Roman campaign not only to signal the comparison with Roland, but also to signal another point of contrast with Lancelot, whose piety is not at all like that of the Heroic knight, as we shall see in our discussion of the next tale. Gawain, the Heroic knight, looks to God for victory, particularly when he is fighting against pagans. However, his belief that God will help him and his men to defeat overwhelming numbers of 'sarasyns and mysbylevyng men' (V.10) depends only on his being a Christian, not at all upon his being a morally virtuous man. To merit such 'goodnesse' or 'grace' from God, it is not necessary that he be exceptionally good, it is only necessary that his enemy be God's enemy also. Gawain's piety is not an uncommon sort. On the contrary, it is characteristic of men who have the mentality of a clansman. Such men exist even in this century, as J. H. Campbell shows in his study of Greek shepherd communities, entitled 'Honour and the Devil'. The Greek shepherds are Christian, but their social organization is still based upon patrilineal clans. Therefore, each man tends to divide his world into two camps: *us*, which is his own family; and *them*, which is everyone else, all the other families. His religion is extremely important, for he can only be certain of divine aid in his quarrels and feuds with other families if he observes all the rituals and receives the sacraments. So long as he is observant, however, he can assume that his enemy must have been subverted by the Devil and that God will be on his side.

Malory's Gawain is like these Greek shepherds. His piety is rooted in emotion, fed by ritual observance and has been grafted on to a primitive clansman's mentality. There is nothing wrong with his attitude in the context of Arthur's wars against Lucius, particularly since Lucius has recruited 'sarasyns and mysbylevyng men' in his attempt to subdue Arthur, thus seeming to justify Gawain's natural tendency to regard the enemies of his family as the enemies of God. However, once Gawain returns to Arthur's kingdom and there pursues the blood feud with the House of Pellinor in the same spirit in which he has slain 'sarasyns' abroad, it will no longer be so easy to see him as a 'noble' knight.

Lancelot and Galahad: Potential Grail Knights

In the Tale of Lancelot Malory explores the religious virtues of True knighthood and also gives a good deal of attention to the political and judicial functions of a king's knight. Malory imagines that his hero is committed to the ideal of 'trew' or 'veray' knighthood outlined in Lull's classic treatise and expanded upon in Sir Gilbert Hay's *Buke of Knychthede*. Indeed, he seems quite deliberately to draw attention to this particular definition of the ideal knight by sprinkling four references to Lancelot's 'trew' knighthood in the first ten pages of Vinaver's printed text (the first seven leaves of Winchester, 259.12: VI.4; 264.5, 31:VI.7; 269.6:VI.9). Three of these references are identical assertions, 'as I am trewe knyght', and are spoken by Lancelot himself. So is the one reference to 'verry' knighthood: 'I am sir Launcelot du Lake, kynge Bannys son of Benwyke, and verry knyght of the Table Rounde' (267.5–6:VI.8).

Malory's Lancelot is utterly devoted to the High Order of Knighthood, which means that he sees himself as God's knight as well as King Arthur's knight. What is more, in order to give himself wholly to this religious-feudal ideal of knightly service, he has determined never to marry. Needless to say, Malory had to be radically selective in dealing with his source, the French prose *Lancelot*, in order to derive from it this portrait of an idealistic and ascetically inclined young man. He also had to borrow one rather long episode from the *Perlesvaus* and invent two others in order to illustrate those qualities which are entirely lacking in the hero of his courtly French source. The result is a transformation of Lancelot which is so complete that Vinaver credits Malory with having succeeded 'in concealing from us the essential character' of the French prose *Lancelot* (*Works* 1408).

Even though Malory presents his hero as much more like Galahad, the Grail knight, than his courtly counterpart in the French prose *Lancelot*, Malory cannot entirely overlook Lancelot's fame as the queen's lover. Among his English readers it must have been the single best known fact about the French knight. Even those who had never read the French romances, and therefore would have known little or nothing of the details of the affair, would have thought of Lancelot primarily as Guinevere's lover. Therefore, in the second paragraph of this tale Malory lays the foundation for his own version of the love story:

> So this sir Launcelot encreased so mervaylously in worship and honoure; therefore he is the fyrst knyght that the Freynsh booke makyth mencion of aftir kynge Arthure com frome Rome. Wherefore quene Gwenyvere had hym in grete favoure aboven all other knyghtis, and so he loved the quene agayne aboven all other ladyes dayes of his lyff, and for hir he dud many dedys of armys and saved her frome the fyre thorow his noble chevalry.
> (253.12–19:VI.1)

Young Lancelot loves the queen in the way that any knightly retainer was expected to love his lord, with what John F. Benton, adopting Aquinas' usage, has called 'the love of friendship' (29–31). Likewise, the queen loves and esteems Lancelot for his knightly virtue and loyal service, but holds him in greater 'favoure' than any of her other knights because he surpasses them all in prowess and worship. Such 'love of friendship' was the commonly accepted basis for relationships of political dependency between members of the noble classes during the late Middle Ages. In England noblemen would address letters to a more powerful lord requesting his 'good lordship', i.e. his protection and support, and great lords could sign letters to their social inferiors, 'Your lover' (Kendall 201).

Later, Malory will tell us that Lancelot began his career at King Arthur's court as a Queen's knight, that is, as a young knight who had not yet won great worship in arms, but who received a retaining fee from the queen and rode in her retinue (1121.14–19:XIX.1). Now he has achieved a reputation as the best knight in the world, and, as a consequence, the queen holds him in greater 'favour' than any other knight. But he is still the queen's 'lover' in exactly the same way that all the queen's knights are her 'lovers' and she their good and gracious lady, bounteous of her gifts and favour. Indeed, the queen has an excellent reputation for generosity among those in her service (1054.5–12:XVIII.5). She is also, according to Lancelot himself, 'the treweste lady unto hir lorde lyvynge' (258.5–6:VI.3). In the middle of this tale Malory invents a lengthy speech for Lancelot to show exactly what kind of a 'lover' of the queen he really is. A damsel asks Lancelot why he will love no one but the queen, and reports a rumour that Guinevere has laid an 'enchauntement' upon him so that he may not love any other woman:

> 'Fayre damesell,' seyde sir Launcelot, 'I may nat warne peple to speke of me what hit pleasyth hem. But for to be a weddyd man,

> I thynke hit nat, for then I muste couche with hir and leve armys and turnamentis, batellys and adventures. And as for to sey to take my pleasaunce with peramours, that woll I refuse: in prencipall for drede of God, for knyghtes that bene adventures sholde nat be advoutrers nothir lecherous, for than they be nat happy nother fortunate unto the werrys.' (270.28–36:VI.10)

This speech explains why Lancelot would not carry on an adulterous affair with the queen. Whereas his counterpart in both of Malory's French sources for this tale believes that loving his lady, even in adultery, makes him a better knight, stronger, more skillful, and hence, presumably, more successful in battle (*Lancelot* 52a.109, 85.3; *Perlesvaus* 1:167), Malory's Lancelot believes just the opposite. Therefore, he has determined to remain perfectly chaste, 'for drede of God'.

The importance of this speech can be gauged partially by the fact that Malory's Lancelot is usually so taciturn. This is one of the very few occasions in the entire *Morte Darthur* when he puts more than two or three sentences together. Clearly the rumour mentioned by the damsel is of great concern to him and it is possible that, despite his opening disclaimer, he hopes to put a stop to it by explaining the real reasons for his avoidance of both marriage and love 'peramours'. These reasons might have been lifted out of the pages of Sir Gilbert Hay's *Buke of Knychthede*. There Hay admonishes the knight to serve God first, even before his temporal lord (20), to trust in God for victory rather than in the strength of his own body or weapons (47, 53) and always to be chaste. Hay also reminds the knight of the biblical counsel to marry if he 'may nocht lyve chaste', and in so doing implies that it would be better not to marry (32). Malory's Lancelot has chosen this better and more difficult degree of chastity in order to devote himself wholly to his knightly vocation. At the same time, he is fully aware of what Hay calls 'the sorow and disese that ordanyt is for thame that . . . mysprise his [God's] commandementis' (56), and he clearly agrees with Hay that sin 'grevis God, and castis men of Goddis grace, and gerris thair inymyes oft tymes be maisteris of thame' (64). Therefore he endeavours to live virtuously 'for drede of God'. In short, Lancelot clearly indicates in this speech that he is a deeply pious man who believes that he can do nothing without the grace of God, and not at all the sort of man who would commit adultery with the wife of his liege lord.

Malory does not rely on this speech alone to give his reader the impression that Lancelot is a very devout young man, however. He also attributes to his hero many pious turns of phrase, such as we have seen Tor use in the first triple quest, and, not surprisingly, almost all of them seem to be original with Malory:

(1) 'Damsell, I shall not fayle, by the grace of God.' (259.19:VI.4)

(2) '... I promyse you, by the leve of God, for to rescowe that knyght.' (265.15–17:VI.7)

(3) 'God gyff hym joy that this spere made, for there cam never a bettir in my honde.' (278.4–5:VI.13)

(4) 'Now God sende you bettir comforte.' (279.11:VI.14)

(5) 'Nay, that God me forbede.' (281.6:VI.15)

(6) '... Jesu preserve me frome your subtyle crauftys!' (281.21–22:VI.15)

(7) 'And there, by the grace of God, ye shall fynde me.' (282.8–9:VI.15)

With the exception of the second phrase cited above, not one of these expressions can be found in Malory's sources for this tale, not even the seventh which comes from that part of Malory's text which is based on the Grail romance, *Perlesvaus* (1.349). This is also true of the three instances of reported speech, when Malory tells us that Lancelot 'thanked God that he had escaped' from Sir Phelot (284.13:VI.16), and when he twice records that Lancelot 'betaughte hem all to God' (264.1–2:VI.7 and 272.32–33:VI.11). In fact, this last phrase is of special interest because analysis of its usage in the *Morte Darthur* indicates that, with few exceptions, it is used only by holy men or Grail knights.[11]

Even more than Lancelot's professed chastity 'for drede of God' and his pious turns of phrase, the Chapel Perilous episode and the healing of Sir Melyot, which Malory borrowed from the Grail romance, *Perlesvaus*, give Lancelot the aura of a Grail knight. The damsel who sends him to the Chapel Perilous says,

'... here I shall abyde tyll God sende you agayne. And yf you spede nat I know no knyght lyvynge that may encheve that adventure.' (279.34–36:VI.14)

Her attitude towards Lancelot anticipates of the general attitude towards Galahad throughout the Grail adventures. Lancelot is the only knight living who 'may encheve that adventure' just as Galahad is the only knight living who may achieve the 'adventure' of the shield (877–878) or the 'aventure of the swerde' at Castle Corbenic (1027.27). There is even a faint analogy between Lancelot's healing Sir Melyot with the bloody cloth and sword and Galahad's healing the Maimed King with the blood from the Holy Spear; and Malory strengthens this analogy by altering his source to cast Lancelot more clearly in the role of a blessed deliverer. In the *Perlesvaus* Lancelot and Melyot exchange polite greetings and Melyot inquires after the health of Gawain before the healing takes place (1.348). In Malory's version Lancelot appears to the anguished Melyot as a healing saviour and the wounded knight goes down on his knees to receive him, crying, 'A, lorde, sir Launcelot, helpe me anone!' (281.34:VI.15). These few words eloquently convey the sentiments of the Maimed King when he first sees Galahad: 'Sir Galahad, good knyght, ye be ryght wellcom, for much have y desyred your commyng! For in such payne and in such angwysh as I have no man ellis myght have suffird longe' (1028.22–25:XVII.19).

Malory transforms the Chapel Perilous episode into a test of Lancelot's chastity as well as his piety. In his version the damsel who greets Lancelot after he has emerged from the chapel is a sorceress who has loved him for seven years. She asks him to kiss her 'but onys', and Lancelot refuses: 'Nay, . . . that God me forbede'. Then, when he learns that his chaste refusal has saved his life, he thanks 'Jesu' for having preserved him from her 'subtyle crauftys!' (281.6–22:VI.15). Both these statements suggest that his chastity is a function of his piety, and thus recall his earlier remarks on the importance of chastity 'for drede of God'. At the same time, however, the refusal even to kiss the damsel suggests the excessive prudishness and zeal for virginity of a very young man. Certainly it stands in sharp contrast to his reaction as a much older man when he decides that he may kiss his amorous lady-gaoler without losing any 'worshyp' (1136.24–25:XIX.8). And, in fact, as Benton has observed, 'kisses and embraces . . . were often a part of medieval greetings, for in courtly circles it could be accepted as reasonable and appropriate to kiss a lady . . .' (30). That is why Lancelot's refusal to kiss Hallewes ought not to be interpreted primarily as a proof of his loyalty to Guinevere as it has been hitherto by most critics (Benson 89). Lancelot knew nothing of Hallewes' nature or motives before she asked him to kiss her. For all he knew, his refusal might have had just as disastrous results as his acquiescence. And if he had agreed to kiss her in polite, courtly fashion such a kiss would in no way have compromised his loyalty to the queen, no matter what kind of a lover one thinks he is at this point. Therefore, Lancelot's refusal to kiss the beautiful damsel ought rather to be interpreted as a consequence of his devotion to chastity, a devotion so radical that it may be compared to that which caused some virtuous young people to be burned at the stake as suspected Cathars in the late twelfth century (Benton 34). Lancelot will learn to be less inflexible as he grows older and wiser in the ways of courtly society.

At this stage of his knightly career, however, Lancelot is very much like Galahad, the son he will later beget upon Pelles' daughter. In fact, Malory may well have chosen to borrow the Chapel Perilous episode from the *Perlesvaus* because it is similar in many respects to one of Galahad's first Grail adventures, and therefore reinforces the likeness between father and son. Several features of the Chapel Perilous episode also appear in Galahad's exorcism of a demon from a tomb: (1) the churchyard location, (2) the body of a knight 'all armed' with a sword beside him (882.20–21:VIII.12), (3) the demonic threat (the spirit exorcised by Galahad takes on 'the lykenes of a man' whereas the thirty gigantic knights faced down by Lancelot are clearly demonic), and (4) the steadfast courage of both heroes in the face of supernatural terror. What is more, Malory may also have chosen to use the Castle Tintagel episode from the prose *Lancelot* because it contained features reminiscent of Galahad's next Grail adventure at the Castle of Maidens:

> (1) Each knight is warned to stay away from the castle: Lancelot is told he is 'unhappy to com here!' (271.29:VI.10; the adjective 'unhappy' is not to be found in Malory's source, *Lancelot* 86.7–8), and Galahad is told that the castle and all those in it are 'cursed' (887.18:XIII.15; cf. 'maleoiz', *Queste* 47.6).
>
> (2) Neither knight pays any heed to the warning and subsequently performs an incredible feat of arms: Lancelot defeats and kills two 'grete gyauntis' and Galahad defeats seven knights who attack him simultaneously.
>
> (3) Upon entering the castle, each knight is welcomed by a crowd of people who hail him as a deliverer, and Malory adds two details to heighten the analogy between Lancelot's and Galahad's roles as deliverers. First, whereas the giants' prisoners in the *Lancelot* include both ladies and gentleman, in Malory's version their prisoners are all ladies and damsels, thus creating a closer parallel with the 'many maydyns' which the seven knights defeated by Galahad had 'devoured' (889.30:VIII.15). Secondly, whereas in the French romance, Lancelot accepts for himself the lordship of the castle he has delivered (*Lancelot* 86.10–11), in Malory's version he directs that the castle be returned to its rightful owner, thus creating an almost exact parallel with Galahad's action when he 'made' the knights of the 'contrey . . . do omage and feawté to the dukes doughter . . .' (890.4–5:XIII.15).

These striking analogies between Lancelot's adventure at the Castle of Tintagel and Galahad's adventure at the Castle of Maidens point to yet another and more extraordinary way in which these two young men are alike: neither of them slays his opponents 'lyghtly'. In other words, neither of them commits manslaughter. In Galahad's case this extraordinary fact is attributed to the high degree of his perfection in the Christian life; therefore, it seems logical to assume that the same explanation holds for Lancelot.

The causal connection between sin and manslaughter is a major premise of the *Queste del Saint Graal*. Time and again we are told that sinful men will be killers. Malory accepts this premise, but he then goes farther than his source to accept its corollary with equal seriousness: if sinful knights are killers, then virtuous knights should be able to conquer without killing. In the French romance, after the Castle of Maidens adventure, a hermit assures Gawain,

> 'Et certes, se vos ne fussiez si pechierres come vous estes, ja li set frere ne fussent ocis par vos ne par vostre aide, ainz feissent encore lor penitance de la mauvese costume que il avoient tant maintenue ou Chastel as Puceles, et s'acordassent a Dieu. Et einsi n'esploita mie Galaad, li Bons Chevaliers, cil que vos alez querant: car il les conquist sanz ocirre.' (54.22–28)

The hermit confidently asserts that Gawain's killing was the natural consequence of his sinfulness; however, he does not make explicit the corollary assertion with regard to Galahad's not killing. Rather he leaves us free to assume that Galahad's action was deliberate, that he chose not to kill the seven knights so that they might come to repentance. Malory, on the other hand, makes the corollary assertion explicit when he says 'for sir Galahad hymself alone bete hem all seven the day toforne, but hys lyvyng ys such that he shall sle no man lyghtly' (892.4–6:XIII.16)

The phrase 'to slay lyghtly' seems to refer to manslaughter — killing which is not strictly speaking intentional, but which happens in knightly encounters as a matter of course. The *Middle English Dictionary* isolates a variety of meanings for the adverb 'lyghtly', most of which would make some sense in this context: 'tranquilly' (1e), 'easily' (2), 'quickly' or 'nimbly' (3a), 'cheerfully' or 'gladly' (5), 'causally' or 'carelessly' (6a). However, the meaning which most satisfactorily completes Malory's sentence is, I believe, 'by natural inclination: in accordance with the constitution or disposition of bodily parts or elements; in accordance with the regular course of events; easily, likely' (4b). Galahad is the best knight in the world. One would think, therefore, that he would be *more*, rather than less, 'likely' to kill his opponents 'easily' as a matter or course. And yet Malory insists that this is not so, because of his 'lyvyng'.

Malory does not often use 'lyvyng' as a noun, and then only in the context of the quest of the Holy Grail. For example, he tells us that in order to win worship at the Grail castle a knight must be 'of good lyvynge, and that lovyth God and dredyth God' (799.7–8:XI.4). Then he tells us that the quest of the Holy Grail 'may nat be encheved but by vertuous lyvynge' (886.18–19:XIII.14). And in the passage presently under discussion he has the hermit chastize Gawain for his 'myschevous' living: '. . . whan ye were made first knyght ye sholde have takyn you to knyghtly dedys and vertuous lyvyng. And ye have done the contrary, for ye have lyved myschevously many wyntirs' (891.30–33:XIII.16). When the hermit goes on to explain, 'sertes, had ye nat bene so wycked as ye ar, never had the seven brethirne be slayne by you and youre two felowys' and then to explain that Galahad did not slay them because of 'hys lyvyng', we must conclude that it is an extraordinarily high degree of virtue which makes the 'lyvyng' of the premier Grail knight 'such that he shall sle no man lyghtly'.[12]

Malory does not say that Galahad *will* not slay any man 'lyghtly'. Rather he says that Galahad *shall* not slay any man 'lyghtly'. This 'shall' formulation can express either ability or inevitability in the future; or it can express simply what is likely to happen in the future. But no matter which of these three meanings we choose, the 'shall' formulation does not explain or specify the cause of this future ability, inevitability or likelihood. As a consequences, we are encouraged to look for an explanation or a cause. We may assume of course, that sinful knights are more likely than virtuous knights to *want* to kill their opponents, but that assumption does not explain why sinful knights 'shall sle othir for synne' (946.35:XVI.3) any better than it explains why Galahad 'shall sle no man lyghtly'. Intentions alone never determine the outcome of actions, particularly in a situation like battle between knights, where one tends to be more than usually aware of the operations of chance. As Dame Prudence observes in Chaucer's *Tale of Melibee*, 'the dedes of batailles been aventurouse and nothyng certeyne, for as lightly is oon hurt with a spere as another' (*CT* VII.1667). Dame Prudence is clearly using the adverb 'lightly' in the same sense I have suggested Malory intended in the passage under discussion: 'in accordance with the regular course of events; easily, likely' (*MED* 4b). Therefore, it is of particular significance that she should make this statement within an explicitly providentialist context which explains the uncertainties of warfare as part of God's providential design: God determines the outcome of battle, but 'ther is no man certein if he be worthy that God yeve hym victorie'. Dame Prudence concludes from this that everyman 'sholde greetly drede werres to bigynne' (*CT* VII.1664). Her argument suggests both an explanation and a cause for Malory's two 'shall' formulations: sinful knights 'shall sle othir for synne' and Galahad 'shall sle no man lyghtly'. The cause is God and the explanation is providentialism.

Providentialism is a Christian world view which Malory associates particularly with the Grail knights. We shall have occasion to examine this world view more closely in the fifth chapter; however, it is important to establish now that Malory's Lancelot is also a providentialist. That is to say, he also believes that God rewards virtuous knights with good fortune and punishes sinful knights with misfortune in battle. In the speech in which he explains his refusal to love 'peramours' Lancelot says that sinful knights' misfortunes can take one of two forms: '. . . for other they shall be overcom with a sympler knyght than they be hemself, other ellys they shall sle by unhappe and hir cursedness better men than they be hemself' (270.36–271.2:VI.10). Lancelot calls such knights 'unhappy', a word which acquires rich meaning in the subsequent development of Malory's *hap* motif (see below 230–44). However, this speech already suggests that to be 'unhappy' is to be more than just unlucky: it is also to be wretched because sinful and therefore 'cursed' because lacking God's grace. In order to be 'happy' rather than 'unhappy' Lancelot has determined 'for drede of God' to avoid the sin of lechery. Wanting to be an 'adventures' knight and also to be 'fortunate unto the werrys', he knows that he needs the grace of God and that the only way to be worthy of grace is to live virtuously.

In the Tale of Lancelot, as we have already seen, Malory represents Lancelot as a pious and virtuous man, very like Galahad. It now remains to be seen whether Lancelot also enjoys his son's incredibly good fortune in arms. First of all, we may observe that Lancelot is never defeated. That is not at all extradordinary in one who has been introduced to us as the best knight in the world and Malory did not have to alter his source in order to achieve that record. But then we must observe that Lancelot also never kills his opponents 'lyghtly'. This is not only most extraordinary in a knight of such skill and prowess, but Malory also had to alter his source a good deal in order to achieve such a record.

Lancelot's counterpart in the French prose romance routinely kills his opponents, even in tournaments and jousts, but Malory's Lancelot never kills in these situations, not even in the tournament against the King of North Wales (262–263:VI.6–7; *Lancelot* 78.30), or when, disguised as Sir Kay, he is challenged by three young and inexperienced Queen's knights bearing the tell-tale white shields and hoping to win worship. In the analogous episode in the French romance, Lancelot encounters four brothers at a bridge. After he has struck down the first three (killing one), the fourth knight flees, but

Lancelot chases after him, knocks him to the ground, rides over his body, and then dismounts to rip off his helmet and threaten to kill him if he will not yield (*Lancelot* 99.22). This brutal behaviour is normal for a knight-errant in the French prose romances (Pickford 230–31), but not for Malory's Lancelot. He accepts the young knights' challenge and quite easily knocks the first two off their horses, but when their brother, supposing them to be dead, insists on avenging them, Lancelot refuses to continue the fight:

> 'Now let be,' seyde sir Lancelot, 'I was not far frome the whan thou were made knyght, sir Raynold, and also I know thou arte a good knyght, and lothe I were to sle the.' (276.27–29:VI.12)

In the French romance Lancelot also kills sir Belleus, whereas in Malory's version he binds his wounds (260:VI.5; *Lancelot* 78.17). Likewise, in the French romance, Lancelot welcomes the chance to kill Tarquin, his mortal enemy, whereas in Malory's version, despite Tarquin's crimes against 'good knyghtes', he would prefer to be reconciled with his opponent, so long as Tarquin agrees to release all his prisoners (266–267:VI.8; *Lancelot* 85.42). The only men Lancelot kills in this tale he kills deliberately, either punitively, because of their crimes against knighthood (Sir Perys, the two giants and Sir Phelot), or in self-defense (sir Tarquin and the 'passyng foule carle' who attacks him with a spiked club at the Castle of Tintagel).

This record appears all the more amazing, if not miraculous, when compared with that of other knights in *Le Morte Darthur*. For example Tristram, the second best knight in the world, finds himself in Sir Darras' prison because he has accidently killed three of Sir Darras' sons in the Castle of Maidens tournament. Tristram is sorry for what he has done, but he doesn't see how it could possibly have been avoided: 'And as for the dethe of youre two sunnes, I myght nat do withall. For and they had bene the nexte kyn that I have, I myght have done none othirwyse' (552.20–22:IX.40). Tristram does not see anything essentially wrong in his having accidentally killed 'by fors of knyghthode' some of his opponents in a tournament, and Darras agrees, as he releases him from prison. Their shared attitude is characteristic of the French prose romances and of the feudal-courtly ideal which both Tristan and Lancelot embody there. It is also characteristic of Malory's Worshipful type of knight. Tristram, the supreme exemplar of that type, cannot imagine how such accidental killing might be avoided except, perhaps, by eliminating tournaments altogether, which is unthinkable. The Worshipful knight would dismiss out of hand the notion that one might avoid manslaughter by 'uniting with God in his grace' (the phrase is Rolle's, 'On Grace' 172). Such a notion is inherently mystical and therefore repugnant to a rationalist like Tristram, or like Arthur. They would attribute Lancelot's invincibility to his superior strength and skill and his avoidance of manslaughter simply to chance. But Lancelot himself, like his son Galahad, would attribute both to his virtuous 'lyvyng' and the grace of God.

Malory has prepared his reader for this reinterpretation of young Lancelot as a pious, chaste and hence 'happy' knight by altering Merlin's prophecy regarding the sword of Balin:

> '... there shall never man handyll thys swerde but the beste knyght of the worlde, and that shall be sir Launcelot other ellis Galahad, hys sonne.' (91.21–23:II.19)

In the *Suite du Merlin* the sword of Balin was quite separate from the sword in the stone which only the successful Grail knight, the best knight in the world, might 'handyll'. Malory has conflated these two swords into one, thus creating another powerful link between the story of Balin and the Grail quest, but also creating a new view of Lancelot as the future Grail knight — potentially, at least. If it is not Lancelot, then it will be Galahad, his son, and the implication is clear that if it is not Lancelot it will be because he is *no longer* 'the beste knyght of the worlde' (see below 244–50). In the Tale of Lancelot, however, Malory makes sure that Lancelot is clearly established as the best knyght in the world. What is more, he suggests very strongly that Lancelot *is* the best because, like Galahad in the Tale of the Sankgreal, he is still a virgin, devoted to chastity 'for drede of God', and therefore invincible.

At the same time as he is strikingly like Galahad in his pious devotion to God, Lancelot is also like Gawain in his devotion to King Arthur. Lancelot is a much better king's knight than Gawain is, however. Malory has altered his sources, not only to suggest judicial process through Lancelot's words and actions as a knight-errant, but also to suggest that the behaviour of the knights whom Lancelot condemns and punishes is like Gawain's behaviour.

The first clearly judicial action which Lancelot performs is the killing of Sir Perys de Forest Savage, 'theff' and 'ravyssher of women'. After Lancelot has killed him he exclaims, 'Now haste thou thy paymente that longe thou haste deserved!' (270.7–8:VI.10), thus implying that death is the appropriate punishment for his crimes. And in fact, Arthur has decreed that any Round Table knight who 'enforce(s)' a lady shall suffer 'payne of dethe' (120.23:III.15). Gawain has not yet done anything quite so outrageous as Sir Perys de Foreste Savage — although he will, in Malory's version of the Tale of Tristram (see below 201–2) — but already we have seen that his treatment of Ettarde could be interpreted as a violation of Arthur's code (see above 75–6).

Lancelot's last two adventures in this tale are remarkably well designed to achieve the same dual purpose: to recall Gawain's criminal behaviour and at the same time to demonstrate Lancelot's value as an agent of royal justice. Therefore it is particularly significant that Malory seems to have invented both of them (Vinaver, *Works* 1423). The elaborate plot of sir Phelot to murder Lancelot 'by treson' illustrates for the reader what Malory means when he says that 'all maner of shamefull deth was called treson' in King Arthur's days (1050.3: XVIII.4; 405.5:VIII.20). To kill or attempt to kill a man 'shamefully' or 'by treson' was to take him by surprise, or at a disadvantage, or to employ subterfuge. Such shameful killing was also called 'murthir' and in medieval England the penalty for 'murthir' was death (Bellamy, *Crime* 54). Therefore, Lancelot beheads Phelot:

> '... with falshede ye wolde have had me slayne with treason, and now hit is fallyn on you ...'. (284.5–7:VI.16)

Malory never tells us why Sir Phelot is so determined to kill Lancelot, but, since he troubles to identify him as a 'knyght that longyth unto the kynge of North Galys' (282.28–29:IV.16), we may infer that Phelot is seeking vengeance for the humiliation which Lancelot so recently dealt his lord's party in King Bagdemagus' tournament. Phelot refuses even to allow Lancelot a sword in self defense, saying, 'Nay, ... for I know the better than thou wenyst' (283.23–24:VI.16), so it seems more than likely that he was one of the twenty-eight knights whom Lancelot singlehandedly unhorsed that day (263.20–28:VI.7). And if revenge is Phelot's motive, then the analogy between his behaviour and Gawain's future behaviour is very strong. Gawain will also commit 'murthir' for the sake of vengeance when he knows he is no match for his enemy. Just as Phelot sets a trap for Lancelot so that he may safely kill him while he is unarmed, so Gawain will set an ambush to trap Lamorak into an unequal encounter, four against one (699.20–27:X.58). Malory will strengthen the analogy still more by suggesting that Gawain decided to set the ambush because he was angry that Lamorak should have defeated him and all his brethren in a tournament that day (607–608:X.2l; see below 205–6).

Of all the adventures in the Tale of Lancelot, the one involving Sir Pedivere and his wife is the most suggestive of judicial process. It is also the one in which the behaviour of Lancelot's opponent is most like Gawain's behaviour, in this case his former behaviour in the quest for the white hart. Malory found an analogue to this episode in the French prose *Lancelot*, but he has considerably transformed its elements in order to make it more comparable to the climactic episode of Gawain's quest. Of course, Gawain never intended to kill the 'soveraigne lady' of Sir Blamoure de la Maryse; he killed her 'by myssefortune' and was sorry for it. Nevertheless, it is his killing of the lady which clinches the analogy with Pedivere:

(1) Both knights kill ladies *because* they are 'withoute mercy'. Gaheris uses that phrase to describe his brother (106.24–25:III.7) and Pedivere's wife uses it to describe her husband (285.2:VI.17). And it is worth pointing out that if Gawain had fulfilled his intention, which was to kill the prostrate Sir Blamoure, he would have been just as guilty of 'murthir' as Pedivere is.

(2) Both knights are forced to do the same penance, that is, to go to Arthur's court bearing with them the body and head of the lady they have killed.

(3) both knights are forced to submit to the judgment of ladies for their crime.

Indeed, the only thematically significant difference between them is the consequence of their repentance. Gawain's repentance has no effect on his future behaviour. Even though he has sworn that he will never again be 'ayenste lady ne jantillwoman', the next time we see him he is dishonestly having his way with Ettarde, and, still later, we find him actually abducting a lady in the Tale of Tristram. By contrast, after he has performed his 'penaunce', Pedivere becomes 'an holy man and an hermyte' (286.18:VI.17).

The crimes which infuriate Lancelot the most are crimes against helpless women. He was outraged by Sir Perys de Forest Savage, and he is outraged by Sir Pedivere, even more outraged, perhaps, since Pedivere murders a woman who has sought and been granted his protection. Malory emphasizes the judicial nature of this episode by making the lady in question Sir Pedivere's wife, and by having Sir Pedivere defend his right to kill his wife on the grounds that she 'hath betrayed me'.

> 'Hit is not so,' seyde the lady, 'truly, he seyth wronge on me. And for bycause I love and cherysshe my cousyn jarmayne, he is jolowse betwyxte me and hym; and as I mutte answere to God there was never sene betwyxte us none such thynges. But, sir,' seyde the lady, 'as thou arte called the worshypfullyest knyght of the worlde, I requyre the of trewe knyghthode, kepe me and save me, for whatsomever he sey he woll sle me, for he is withoute mercy.' (284.29–285.2:VI.17)

The lady's passionate and pious self-defense ('as I mutte answere to God') convinces Lancelot to give her his protection, but he is not wily enough himself to suspect Pedivere's 'treson'. When he realizes what Pedivere has done while his back was turned he draws his sword to kill him; but before he can even raise his arm, Pedivere falls to his knees and begs for mercy.

Lancelot is furious and does not want to give this 'traytoure' mercy; therefore, he makes him the same 'large proffir' that he will later make to Mellyagaunt in the midst of a treason trial by battle: he offers to disarm himself except for his sword 'and yf thou can sle me, quyte be thou for ever' (285.26–27:VI.17). In other words, he offers his opponent the chance of acquittal if he can beat him at these odds. We must assume that he does this because he does not want to turn the traitor over to the king for judgment: he wants the immediate satisfaction of a judgment of God. Malory invented both of these 'large proffirs' and they are spectacularly reckless, not only from the point of view of a rationalist like Arthur, but also from the point of view of a providentialist like Lancelot who sincerely believes that God will 'have a stroke' in every battle and is, therefore, 'to be drad' (1133.28–29: XIX.7). Lancelot is not only risking his life on rational grounds, by giving such odds, he is also 'tempting' God by his presumptuous demand for a miracle. His anger must be overwhelming, indeed, thus to override, if only momentarily, both his faith and his reason. However, that only makes his subsequent display of self-control all the more admirable. For Pedivere, unlike Mellyagaunt, refuses to fight, even at these odds. We know that Pedivere will end his life in the same way that Lancelot will, as a 'holy man and an hermyte'; therefore, we are probably right to infer that he refuses to fight because he is a pious man who believes that, being guilty, he could never win, no matter what the odds. In other words, like Lancelot, Pedivere believes that God determines the outcome of every battle and will give victory to the knight fighting for the right.

We may sum up by saying that the Pedivere episode not only reminds the reader of Gawain's vengeful and merciless conduct, it also illustrates Lancelot's ability to control his anger and thus to temper justice with mercy. In fact, a comparison of the Pedivere episode with the white hart episode reveals an elegant structural contrast which points up precisely this difference in the two men's characters. The narrative features common to both episodes are (1) a lady killed by a knight. (2) an angry knight, and (3) a knight who begs for mercy. However, in the white hart episode the lady is killed *because* the angry knight (Gawain) refuses to give mercy to the knight who begs for mercy. By contrast, in the Pedivere episode the angry knight (Lancelot) gives mercy to the knight who begs for it, in spite of the fact that he deserves the death penalty for having killed the lady.

The executions of Sir Perys de Foreste Savage and Sir Phelot and the judgment of Sir Pedivere illustrate Lancelot's fierce commitment to justice and to the moral code of behaviour exacted by King Arthur of all his Round Table knights. At the same time the behaviour of Lancelot's criminal opponents serves to call to the reader's mind the criminal behaviour of Gawain, both past and future. In this way Malory continues the comparison of Lancelot and Gawain as king's knights which he began during his account of Arthur's Roman campaign. In the wartime context Gawain appeared to be almost as noble as Lancelot; however, in the peacetime context he appears much more like Lancelot's criminal opponents. Gawain fails to be a worthy dispenser of justice and keeper of the peace because he lacks the virtues necessary to fulfill that role. Thus far his worst failings can be explained by his inability to control his emotions, either lust or anger. Later, however, we will be able to see that Gawain's very idea of justice is not the same as that which informs Arthur's chivalric code, and that Gawain will prefer his law, the *lex talionis*, to that of King Arthur. By contrast, Lancelot cannot be faulted as an agent of the king's justice. Indeed, he comes close to assuming the duties of a judge on the king's bench when he makes judgments in equity like granting Tarquin's prisoners 'such stuff . . . as they fynde' in his castle, granting the giants' treasure to the ladies held prisoner in the Castle of Tintagel, 'for a rewarde for your grevaunces', and ordering that the castle itself be restored to 'the lorde that is ownere . . . as is his ryght' (268.16:VI.9; 272.22–25:VI.11). Lancelot is a perfect embodiment of both types of judicial knighthood as Sir Gilbert Hay distinguishes them. He is a 'knycht of pes' who makes 'gud reugle' and 'governaunce in the peple' and he is also a 'knycht of the justice rigorous' who compels 'be fors of armes' all criminals 'to cess and desist fra thair wikkitness' (33–34). In other words, he embodies the functions both of the royal judiciary including local justices of the peace (which Hay terms 'knychthede spirituale') and of the 'ordre of knychthede'. What is more, Malory's portrait of young Lancelot seems designed to confirm Hay's belief that only knights who are 'full of vertues, and gude lyf' should do justice, for only they can 'geve otheris ensample' (34).

The last two episodes in the Tale of Lancelot also round off Malory's presentation of Lancelot's courtly virtues. The damsel whom he rescued from Perys de Forest Savage praised him early on as 'the curteyst knyght' and 'mekyste unto all ladyes and jantylwomen that now lyvyth' (270.16–18:VI.10) and he has already illustrated that aspect of his knightly character in his dealings with the daughter of

Bagdemagus and the sister of Sir Melyot de Logres as well as with the ladies and damsels of the Castle Tintagel. But in the Sir Phelot episode we see him perform a service for a 'fayre lady' simply because she knows his name and has required him 'of knyghthode to helpe' and in spite of the fact that he does not really want to do what she has asked of him: 'and yet God knowyth I am an evyll clymber, and the tre is passynge hyghe, and fewe bowys to helpe me withall' (282.32–33: VI.16). The hint of all-too-human reluctance and even petulance in Lancelot's tone looks forward to some of the conversations he will have much later with the queen. In this tale, however, Lancelot's relationship to the queen is still relatively impersonal. That is to say, it is no more personal than the relationship which any other knight who serves the queen would be expected to have with her.

Within a feudal monarchy, all political relationships were personal, in the sense that they were relationships between persons, bound together by 'feudal love', or 'love of friendship' (Benton 29–30). Nevertheless it is rumoured that the queen has enchanted Lancelot. The same damsel who has praised Lancelot for his courtesy and asked him why he would love no lady as his paramour, since he was not a married man, reports,

> 'For I cowde never here sey that ever ye loved ony of no maner of degré, and that is grete pyté. But hit is noysed that ye love quene Gwenyvere, and that she hath ordeyned by enchauntemente that ye shall never love none other but hir, nother none other damesell ne lady shall rejoyce you; wherefore there be many in this londe, of hyghe astate and lowe, that make grete sorow.' (270.20–27:VI.10)

The strength of this rumour of the queen's 'enchauntemente' is further attested by the reaction of the sorceress Hallewes after Lancelot has refused to kiss her and thus evaded her trap: 'I have loved the this seven yere, but there may no woman have thy love but quene Gwenyver' (281.14–15:VI.16). She, too, seems to acknowledge the superior magic of her rival for his love. Malory may have taken the idea for this rumour from one which actually circulated during the early years of the reign of Edward IV. Jacquetta of Luxembourg, the step-mother of Anthony and Elizabeth Wydville, was rumoured to have caused by magic the infatuation of Edward IV for Elizabeth, which ended in their marriage (Kelly, 'English Kings' 233). The damsel who reports the rumour of Guinevere's 'enchauntemente' also reports that she could never 'here sey' that Lancelot ever loved 'ony' woman, and on rational grounds that 'here sey' alone could account for the rumour of the 'enchauntemente'. Since Guinevere was the only woman with whom Lancelot was known to have any sort of relationship at all, it is only too likely that all those ladies 'of hyghe astate and lowe', grieving for unrequited love of the best knight in the world, would conclude that the queen must have enchanted him. Indeed, there is no better remedy for unrequited love and wounded vanity than the comforting belief that one's rival has used sorcery to keep the object of one's affections all to herself. And yet, in this tale Malory offers no evidence at all to suggest that Lancelot loves the queen 'peramours'.[13] Quite the contrary. He has offered a good deal of evidence to suggest that Lancelot is just like Galahad, the Grail knight — a virgin wholly devoted to chastity 'for drede of God'. It is indeed a large and elegant paradox which results from Malory's transformation of Lancelot's character: that his improbable devotion to chastity should occasion the much more probable rumour of his having been 'enchanted' by the queen.

Lancelot and Gareth: The Courtly Option

Malory continues his exploration of the virtues of the True knight in his Tale of Gareth. Here he focusses much more upon the courtly virtues, and, as a consequence, much more of the action actually takes place in courts or in castle yards, rather than in forest or countryside. Indeed, Malory has caught the essence of the difference between Lancelot and Gareth as types of True knighthood in their central adventures: the Chapel Perilous adventure could be achieved only by a knight perfect in faith and chastity; the Castel Perilous adventure may be achieved only by a knight perfect in courtesy. This is not to say that Lancelot is not courteous or that Gareth is not pious and chaste. But it is to say that Lancelot's devotion to chastity is so total that he would refuse even to kiss a damsel, whereas Gareth would never be so discourteous. In fact, Gareth might have been modeled upon Chaucer's Squire, so perfectly does he correspond to the courtly ideal. He is tall, well built and a great fighting man, but he is also handsome, unfailingly courteous, and knows how to please the ladies by singing and dancing. In fact, the Tale of Gareth is the only tale in the *Morte Darthur* in which there is more than one scene involving such courtly pastimes.[14] Last, but definitely not least, Gareth is a passionate lover who, like Chaucer's Squire, loves his lady so 'hoote' that he cannot sleep at night (*CT* I(A).97; cf. 331.26:VII).

The main function of Gareth's tale is to illustrate the more courtly form of True knighthood which is appropriate to 'hoote' lovers like himself and Chaucer's Squire. In the previous tale, Lancelot has illustrated the highest form of True knighthood imaginable to Sir Gilbert Hay, the form which combines the feudal ideal of total commitment to the service of one's liege lord with the religious ideal of celibacy. Hay believed this form of knighthood to be more difficult of achievement than 'to be outhir monk, or frere, or othir religiouse of the hardest order that is' (39). Nevertheless, in the Tale of Lancelot Malory was able to transform Lancelot into a convincing embodiment of the feudal-religious ideal by characterizing him as a very devout young man, whose relationship to the queen had not yet developed beyond feudal love, or the 'love of friendship'. Through Lancelot's protegé, Gareth, Malory will now show that celibacy is not the only acceptable form of sexual morality for the True knight. Sir Gilbert Hay advised those among his readers who might not 'lyve chaste' to marry and be faithful to their wives, for, by observing marital chastity, they also keep 'thair aithe to godwart' (32). Lancelot will never be able to marry the woman he loves. Gareth will be more fortunate because he will love a lady who is free to marry him; however, his success in the quest for love, marriage and social position will remove him from the ranks of Arthurian knights-errant. As a consequence of choosing to marry Lyones, the heiress to great lands, Gareth becomes a governor of men like his uncle and liege lord, Arthur. Thereafter he must 'couche' with his wife, and do what Lancelot has said he is not willing to do — give up 'armys and turnamentis, batellys and adventures'.

Gareth would have appeared especially attractive to Malory as a candidate for the courtly type of True knighthood because as Gawain's younger brother he provides a ready-made means to continue the comparison between Lancelot and Gawain. P. J. C. Field has recently argued that Malory's source for the Tale of Gareth was a now-lost English romance of the Fair Unknown group which was itself based upon a folk tale in which a younger brother proves himself worthy of his established elder brother. The structure of such a folk tale requires that the elder brother be admirable enough to serve as a yardstick for the younger, but Malory's Tale of Gareth violates this structure in two ways: first, every time Gawain does something admirable, Lancelot is said to do it as well or better; and second, at the end of the tale Gareth renounces his brother's 'felyship' in favour of Lancelot's company. Field concludes that such 'inconsistencies . . . must come from a failure to complete the assimilation of the original folktale story to a new context' ('Source' 59). Field may well be right about Malory's having used a now-lost English source for the Tale of Gareth, but I think he is wrong to conclude that the 'inconsistencies' he detects are the result of Malory's 'failure' to assimilate the original folktale structure. Since Malory has already established a pattern of contrast between Lancelot and Gawain in the two preceding tales, it is quite likely that he deliberately altered the thematic structure of the folk tale in order to continue this pattern. At the beginning of the Tale of Gareth both Lancelot and Gawain stand in a potential mentor relationship to Gareth. During the tale Gareth makes a series of crucial choices and, by the end of the tale, we understand why Gareth has chosen Lancelot rather than Gawain to be his mentor and friend.

Gareth comes to Arthur's court at the feast of Pentecost disguised as a poor man and asks only for 'mete and drynke suffyciauntly for this twelve-monthe' (294.15:VII.1). This is enough to convince most people that despite his tall, robust and handsome appearance, he must be 'a vaylayne borne', for no gentleman would ask for food and lodging when he might have asked for horse and armour. Sir Kay mocks the young man unmercifully and makes him eat and sleep with the kitchen boys. Both Lancelot and Gawain offer the Fair Unknown better food and lodging as well as clothes and money but Gareth refuses all gifts and endures his humiliation for twelve months without murmuring. The treatment which Gareth receives is an exaggerated form of what Sir Gilbert Hay recommends for all young men who will some day be great lords:

> . . . for unworthy war he suld be a lord or a maister that knew never quhat it is to be a servand, for he may never wele tak na knawe the suetenes that it is tobe the lord, bot gif he had sum knaulage of the sourness that it is, and payne to a gude hert, to be ane underlout or a servand. (*Buke of Knychthede* 16)

Gareth passes this test of his courtesy with flying colours, never displeasing 'man nother chylde, but allwayes he was meke and mylde' (296.1–2:VII.3). By Hay's reckoning, he will make a 'better' lord for his experience.

Malory contrives to make this episode a test of courtesy for Lancelot and Gawain, as well. They are the only two knights in King Arthur's court who are angered by Kay's great discourtesy to the Fair Unknown and try to befriend the young man. 'But,' Malory explains,

> . . . as towchyng sir Gawayne, he had reson to proffer hym lodgyng, mete, and drynke, for that proffer com of his bloode, for he was nere kyn to hym than he wyste off; but that sir Lancelot ded was of his grete jantylnesse and curtesy. (295.31–35:VII.2)

Malory specifically disallows the possibility that Gawain acts out of 'grete jantylnesse and curtesy' like Lancelot. Rather, he suggests that Gawain acts out of a kind of instinct, blood responding to blood, even without any conscious awareness of the blood kinship. And this he finds reasonable. In fact, he has already suggested a similar explanation for Arthur's initial response to Gareth by having the king say, 'myne herte gyvyth me to the gretly, that thou arte com of men of worshyp' (294.18–20:VII.1); after all, Gareth is also Arthur's sister's son, among the nearest and dearest of his kinsmen. Therefore, we must conclude that Gawain's acts of courtesy and generosity are not motivated by devotion to the ideals of true gentility. On the contrary, here, as everywhere in Malory's *Morte Darthur*, Gawain is motivated primarily by devotion to his kin group.

Unfortunately, the same penchant which makes Gawain behave generously and courteously on this occasion will on other occasions make him a murderer and as soon as Gareth learns this about his brother, he avoids his company:

> For evir aftir sir Gareth had aspyed sir Gawaynes conducions, he wythdrewe hymself fro his brother sir Gawaynes felyshyp, for he was evir vengeable, and where he hated he wolde be avenged with murther: and that hated sir Gareth. (360.32–36:XII.35)

Malory waits until the end of the tale to give us this information, but then he couches his revelation in the pluperfect tense ('had aspyed') to suggest that Gareth had acquired this knowledge of his brother's character ('conducions') some time ago, certainly *before* he left Arthur's court to undertake the quest for Lady Lyones. During the quest Gareth confides in Lynet that he came to Camelot disguised as a poor man in order 'to preve my frendys' (313.8:VII.11). His intention would seem to have been twofold: to discover which knights would be his friends despite the meanness of his apparel; and, to discover which knight(s) he would most admire and like to have as friend(s). No doubt he expected they would be the same knights, and it must have come as a great disapointment to him to learn that the older brother who was so kind to him was also a vengeful murderer. That discovery, however, may well explain why, when it comes time for him to ask for his second and third 'gyfftes' of Arthur, he asks 'that sir Launcelot du Lake shall make me knyght, for of hym I woll be made knyght and ellys of none' (297.16–17:VII.3).

Gareth's request must have created almost as much surprise and stir in the court as his initial appearance the year before. The only other Fair Unknowns to come to Camelot — Lancelot and La Cote Male Tayle — both request knighthood of King Arthur, and Malory has already invited us to compare Gareth with these knights by having Lancelot recall La Cote's arrival on the occasion of Gareth's arrival (295.15–18:VII.2). Both Lancelot and La Cote were able to convince the king to give them knighthood without revealing any more of their identity than their Christian name, omitting both lineage and 'from whens [they] cam' (459.33:IX.1). Gareth cannot do that, of course, for his Christian name alone would reveal his full identity to King Arthur, his mother's brother. However, if the desire to conceal his identity is his only reason for not asking knighthood of the king, Gareth might still have asked his oldest brother to make him knight and keep his identity secret from the king and the rest of the court. Perhaps he thought his oldest brother would not agree to such a plan, or would feel duty-bound to notify his mother of his whereabouts. These are plausible reasons for Gareth's not requesting knighthood either of his uncle, King Arthur, or of his brother. However, they do not suffice to explain the passionate determination with which he insists that Lancelot make him knight, or else no one shall. The explanation for that must come from Ramon Lull's treatise on knighthood. Lull teaches that a special grace is conferred upon the new knight by means of the ritual of ordination, and that those who receive the order from a less worthy knight, will receive correspondingly less of this grace, so necessary in order to do well as a knight:

> . . . by deffaulte of suche a knyght it happe somtyme that the squyer that receyueth of hym Chyualry is not so moche ayded ne mayntened of the grace of our lord ne of vertue ne of chyualry as he shold be yf he were made of a good & loyal knyght. And therfor such a squyer is a foole and al other semblably that of such a knyght receyueth thordre of chyualry.[15] (Lull 73–74)

If Gareth has decided that he wants to be knighted by Lancelot because Lancelot is the best knight at Arthur's court and therefore he will receive correspondingly more of the 'grace' of knighthood from him, he is not the only knight in the *Morte Darthur* to take such care in choosing who shall be 'his fader in knychthede' (the phrase is Sir Gilbert Hay's in *Knychthede,* 69). For example, Melyas, the squire of King Bagdemagus, asks Galahad to make him knight after witnessing the adventure of the Red Cross Shield (881:VIII.11) and Malory tells us that King Arthur himself was knighted by 'the best man that was there' (16.20:I.7; see above 32–33). La Cote Male Tayle requested knighthood of King Arthur because he was called 'the moste nobelyst kynge of the worlde' (459.25–26:IX.1) and we may presume that Lancelot came to Arthur to request knighthood of him for the same reason.

The corollary of this principle that a new-made knight is 'muche the bettir' (350.24:VII.30) for being knighted by a worthy knight is that one should never give the order of knighthood to an unworthy squire (Hay 36; Lull 56–57). Therefore, it is necessary to examine the candidate for knighthood prior to admitting him, to ensure that he will be a worthy knight. If Gareth had openly requested knighthood of his uncle, we may presume that Arthur would have responded exactly as he did when Gawain made the same request: 'I woll do hit with a goode wylle,' seyde kynge Arthure, 'and do unto you all the worship that I may, for I muste be reson ye ar my nevew, my sistirs son' (99.12–14: III.3). Arthur either assumed that Gawain must prove a noble knight because of his noble blood, or else he felt he could not deny his nephew's request, whether or not he were truly worthy of knighthood. But whatever the reason, he did not, in fact, pause to enquire, as he did in the case of the Fair Unknowns, whether or not his nephew 'besemyth well of persone and of countenaunce that he shall preve a good knyght and a myghty' (459.29–31:IX.1). Gareth is not like his oldest brother. He does not want to be made knight simply because he is King Arthur's nephew. Therefore, the first thing Gareth does when Lancelot appears to make him knight, is offer to joust. Lancelot is so impressed by the young man's skill and prowess in arms that he assures him he need have 'no dought of none erthely knyght'; still he will not give him the 'Order of Knyghthod' until Gareth reveals his identity. It is unlikely that Lancelot would have refused the young man knighthood if he had proved to come from a lesser lineage; however, the revelation of Gareth's royal lineage makes Lancelot even 'more gladder' to make him knight than he was before and confirms his long held opinion that the young man was 'of grete bloode' and 'cam nat to the courte nother for mete nother drynke' (299.29–31:VII.5). In other words, like Sir Gilbert Hay, Lancelot does not make noble birth a prerequisite for knighthood in the same way that he makes the knightly virtues a prerequisite; however, again like Hay, he is delighted to find 'nobelesse and gentillesse of curage and gude vertues, . . . and gude thewis' come together (37).[16]

The importance of one's 'fader in knychthede' is one of the *leit motifs* of the Tale of Gareth. When the Lady Lyones first questions the dwarf regarding the identify of her new champion she wants to know three things: his name, his lineage, and 'of whom' he was 'made knyght' (317.19:VIII.14). Like Sir Neroveus, Gareth takes great pride and comfort in the fact that he has been knighted by 'noble sir Launcelot' (301.7–9:VII.5; 468.30–31:IX.5). When Sir Persaunte offers to make him a knight, if it 'please hym to take the Order of Knyghthode of so symple a man', Gareth is happy to say that he is 'bettir spedde', for Lancelot, 'the noble knyght' has already knighted him.

> 'A,' seyde sir Persaunte, 'of a more renomed man myght ye nat be made knyghte of, for all knyghtes he may be called cheff of knyghthode.' (316.21–23:VII.13)

Tristram also agrees that Gareth has benefitted from the fact that Lancelot made him knight. At the Assumption Day tournament he asks the identity of the young knight who fights so well in so many 'dyvers coloures' and is told that he is 'Gareth of Orkeney, brother unto sir Gawayne'. This identification elicits Tristram's praise for the young man's prowess and the remark that 'yf he be yonge, he shall preve a full noble knyght'. He is assured that Gareth is 'but a chylde . . . and of sir Launcelot he was made knyght', whereupon Tristram replies, 'Therefore is he much the bettir' (350.5–24:VII.30).

Sir Persaunte de l'Inde does not know who Gareth is and therefore he cannot know that Gawain is his brother. However, the news that Lancelot, the 'cheff of knyghthode', has made the young man knight inspires Persaunte to list all the most 'noble knyghtes' in the world, and the reader cannot help but notice that the name of Gareth's brother is not among them:

> . . . and so all the worlde seythe that betwyxte three knyghtes is departed clerely knyghthode, that is sir Launcelot du Lake, sir Trystrams de Lyones and sir Lamerok de Galys. Thes bere now the renowne, yet there be many other noble knyghtis, as sir Palomydes the Saresyn and sir Saphir, his brothir, also sir Bleobrys and sir Blamour de Ganys, his brothir; also sir Bors de Ganys, and sir Ector de Marys, and sir Percivale de Galys. Thes and many mo bene noble knyghtes, but there be none that bere the name but thes three abovyn seyde. (316.23–32:VII.13)

Evidently Gawain does not qualify as a 'noble' knight by sir Persaunte's standards. At the same time, however, Gawain has something which makes Sir Ironsyde, the Red Knight of the Red Lands, want to do battle with him. Persaunte explains to Gareth that Ironsyde prolongs the Siege of the Castle Perilous

> '. . . to this entente, for to have Sir Launcelot du Lake to do batayle with hym, or with sir Trystrams, othir sir Lamerok de Galys, othir sir Gawayne, . . .' (316.4–7:VII.13)

These two lists appear side by side in Malory's text and Persaunte speaks them both, first reciting the names of the four knights with whom Ironsyde most wants to do battle and then reciting the names of the ten most noble knights in the world, in his opinion. It is a striking coincidence that the first three names on each list should be the same and therefore all the more striking that Persaunte should not mention Gawain, the fourth knight on Ironsyde's list. The omission has to be deliberate, and therefore we must ask why it is that Ironsyde should long to do battle with a knight whom Persaunte does not deem worthy of inclusion in his list of 'noble knyghtes'.

The reason has something to do with the fact that Malory's Gawain is much more like Sir Ironsyde than he is like Lancelot. Malory stresses the likeness between Gawain and Ironsyde by making both men the possessors of supernatural strength associated with the bright noon day sun, and by letting us know that they are evenly matched in their prodigious strength. When Lynet first came to Arthur's court seeking a champion for her sister, Gawain was readily able to identify her tormentor:

> 'I know hym well, for he is one of the perelest knyghtes of the worlde. Men sey that he hath seven mennys strengthe, and from hym I ascapyd onys full harde with my lyff.' (296.32–35:VII.2)

We may infer from this that Ironsyde seeks a return match with the man who was strong enough to be able to escape from him once. In other words, it is Gawain's extraordinary prowess which has earned him a place on Sir Ironsyde's list. We may also infer that prowess alone is not enough to merit a place on Sir Persaunte's list. At the same time, since Persaunte places Lancelot at the top of his list, we may assume that the qualities he requires of a 'noble' knight are those we have seen exemplified by Lancelot thus far: prowess and courage, certainly, but also loyalty, courtesy,and justice tempered with mercy, not to mention the more specifically religious virtues of chastity and piety. Gawain lacks every one of these virtues except for the first two, prowess and courage. In his dealings with Sir Blamoure and his lady he was neither just nor merciful. In his dealings with Ettarde and Pelleas he was neither loyal nor courteous. And in these failings he is much like Sir Ironsyde. In fact, Lynet's description of Sir Ironsyde quite accurately describes Malory's Gawain, as well:

> '. . . in hym is no curtesy, but all goth to the deth other shamfull mourthur. And that is pyté,' seyde the damesell, 'for he is a full lykly man and a noble knyght of proues, and a lorde of grete londis and of grete possessions.' (320.15–19:VII.15)

Both men are murderers because they are 'withoute mercy'.

Gareth's response to this description of his opponent mirrors his response to his own brother as soon as he discovered Gawain's murderous 'conducions':

> 'Truly,' seyde sir Bewmaynes, 'he may be well a good knyght, but he usyth shamefull customys . . .' (320.20–21:VII.15)

Gareth is using the adjective 'good' here to mean 'good . . . of his hondys', i.e. a 'good' fighting man. The phrase, 'good knight', is used nearly four hundred times in the *Morte Darthur*, making it one of the most commonly used of all phrases, if not the most common, and it is not hard to see why that should be so. Prowess, or strength and skill in the use of arms, is the most basic virtue of the knight, so basic, in fact, that a knight who is not 'good' in this sense may be said to be no knight at all. On the other hand, if he is 'good' in this sense, he need not necessarily possess the additional virtues which would make him honourable, 'worshipful', or, as Persaunte puts it, 'noble' in the opinion of courtly society. Persaunte tells Gareth that if he can 'macche that Rede Knyght' he 'shall be called the fourth of the worlde' (316.33–34:VII.13), an honour which he has deliberately refused to accord Gawain, even though Gawain matched Ironsyde once before. This confirms Persaunte's standards for judging a knight to be 'noble': he must have the courtly virtues. Gareth has already proved to his host that he has them in the way he has conducted himself in single combat and, above all, in the way he has passed the test of courtesy to women by sending his host's virginal daughter out of his bed (315.9–12:VII.12). Therefore, in Persaunte's judgment his young guest is already comparable to Lancelot, Tristram and Lamorak in courtesy and, if he can match the infamous Red Knight of the Red Lands in prowess as well, then he will deserve to be called the fourth best or most 'noble' knight in the world.[17]

Gareth chooses Lancelot rather than Gawain to be his mentor and 'fader in knychthede' partly for the same reason that Persaunte refuses to include Gawain's name on his list of 'noble knyghtes', but also partly because, in addition to the courtly virtues, Lancelot possesses the religious virtues of humility, chastity and piety. Since the first of these religious virtues is best illustrated before Gareth sets out on his quest for the Lady Lyones, I will discuss it now, leaving discussion of the other two virtues till after Gareth has completed his quest.

Lancelot's humility is evident in the way he relates to the Fair Unknown from the very beginning. Apart from Gawain (who is motivated by kinship), Lancelot is the only knight at court to brave the scorn of haughty gentlemen like Sir Kay and attempt to befriend the young lad. Then, he seems to be not at all threatened by the young man's awesome demonstration of prowess when they engage in a friendly battle before Gareth sets out on his quest. Indeed, after they have fought on foot for an hour Lancelot is able to admit 'In Goddys name' and by the 'fayth of [his] body' that he has had as much to do as he could to save himself from defeat (299.11–14:VII.5). Not only is he not too proud to make such an admission, he seems genuinely glad to discover the extraordinary prowess of his young opponent. Throughout the *Morte Darthur* their relationship continues to be exemplary of the way True knights ought to relate to one another, not as rivals who vie for worship but as fellows who give each other support. Lancelot's behaviour vis-a-vis the young man at the Assumption Day tournament provides an excellent example of this. King Arthur asks Lancelot to encounter with the knight who wears many colours and is defeating so many of Arthur's knights. Lancelot refuses to enter the lists, because he can see that the knight is trying very hard to win the prize. Therefore, he suspects that he may be 'beste beloved' of the lady whose hand will be given to the victor, and, he concludes, 'as for me, this day he shall have the honour: thoughe hit lay in my power to put hym frome hit, yet wolde I nat' (349.6–8:VII.29). It is important to note that at this point Lancelot does not even know that the knight in question is Gareth. He does not learn his identity till later, when Gareth rides between Lancelot and two 'perelous' knights of the Castle party who have assailed him and parts 'them in sundir', thus extricating Lancelot from a very 'hote' situation. On the basis of this singular act of courtesy, Lancelot guesses that he must be 'the good knyght sir Gareth' (349.27–28:VII.30).

We may sum up by saying that Lancelot has set his protegé an example of humility and compassion for others and that Gareth is following that example. Their relationship proves that loving fellowship is possible among knights who have true humility. We have seen in the example of King Pellinor — who was so 'egir' in his quest for the lady-huntress that he could not stop to give aid to the damsel who asked his help 'for Jesuys sake!' (114.16:III.12) — that proud knights, 'egir' to win worship are not always able to be compassionate. By contrast, knights who are truly humble are never so concerned to win worship that they cannot stop to help someone in need.

Gareth also follows his mentor's example when acting as a king's knight, an agent of King Arthur's governance. Indeed, since he has so recently matched Lancelot in prowess and also received from him the Order of Knighthood, it is easy to perceive Gareth as a kind of surrogate for Lancelot as he sets off on his quest for Lady Lyones. Certainly, he is every bit as effective as his 'fader in knychthede' when it comes to dealing with injustice. He slays six thieves who have bound and robbed a knight, an exploit somewhat reminiscent of Lancelot's execution of Sir Perys, 'theff' and ravyssher of women. He also slays the Brown Knight Without Pity and liberates his prisoners, thirty ladies, all of whom are widows. This exploit is clearly analogous to Lancelot's liberation of the ladies and damsels held prisoner by two giants at the Castle Tintagel and to Galahad's liberation of the prisoners at the Castle of Maidens. The analogy is strengthened by the fact that Gareth, too, is warned in advance to 'fle' from this most 'perelust knyght that now lyvyth', but pays no more attention to the warning than Lancelot and Galahad do (355.13–15: VII.33).[18]

Gareth's battle with the Red Knight of the Red Lands at the Castle Perilous is the central event in his tale and also his most explicitly judicial act. It is clearly modeled on Lancelot's battle with Sir Tarquin. First, the sites of the two battles are similar: they both take place beside a castle or fortified manor house; there are trees nearby whereon hang the shields of those knights defeated by Tarquin and the shields and bodies of those defeated by Ironsyde; and, finally, there are similar mechanisms for calling Tarquin and Ironsyde to do battle (a bronze basin to be struck for Tarquin and an ivory horn to be blown for Ironsyde). However, the most striking likeness between Tarquin and Ironsyde is that both men are guilty of having killed many good knights in order to be revenged upon either Lancelot or Gawain. Tarquin boasts that he has 'slayne an hondred good knyghtes, and as many . . . maymed all uttirly', and imprisoned still more, all because he wanted vengeance upon Lancelot for the killing of his brother, King Carados (266.25–35:VI.8). Likewise, Ironsyde confesses that he has defeated and then shamefully murdered forty knights, all so that he might have vengeance upon either Lancelot or Gawain, for one of them, he does not know which one, slew his lady's brother (325.1–9: VII.17). It is odd that Ironsyde should not know which one of these two knights actually slew his lady's brother, so odd, in fact, that I am inclined to think his ignorance is designed to draw the reader's attention to the circumstances surrounding the death of King Carados, for Gawain was involved with Lancelot in that killing, also. Indeed, insofar as Lancelot killed Carados in order to rescue Gawain, one could say that Gawain was equally responsible for his death (418–19: VIII.29).

Although Gareth's battle with Ironsyde lasts most of one day, just like Lancelot's battle with Tarquin, its conclusion is much more like the conclusion of Lancelot's encounter with Pedivere, the wife-slayer. Both Ironsyde and Pedivere are characterized as being 'withoute mercy'; therefore in responding to their request for mercy, both Gareth and Lancelot face essentially the same quandary that Tor faced in response to Abelleus in the first triple quest: should a knight give mercy to a man who is guilty of murder and is himself 'without mercy'? It is a difficult ethical question and each one of the three True Knights handles it differently according to his different circumstances. Tor decides to execute Abelleus because his crime (murder) is unamendable; and he has promised the damsel to do her bidding (112–13:III.11). Lancelot tries to avoid giving Pedivere mercy by inducing him to fight for a judgment of God; however, when he cannot persuade Pedivere to fight with him, even by offering to disarm his own left side, he is constrained to give him mercy and send him back to Arthur for judgment. Gareth takes upon himself the role of judge, rather like Tor, but Gareth's judgment is more complex. First he tells Ironsyde that he may not save his life 'for the shamefull dethes that thou haste caused many full good knyghtes to dye'. But then, like a good judge, he agrees to listen to Ironsyde's defense, and to the 'many erlys and barowns and noble knyghtes' who plead on his behalf. Gareth is clearly influenced by the number and quality of the men who plead for Ironsyde. He is also influenced by their very rational argument that to execute him would produce no advantage to anyone. Ironsyde's murders may not be undone, but it is possible for him to make 'amendys' to the Lady Lyones. And finally, Gareth is impressed both by their willingness to let him determine what these 'amendys' shall be and by their offer to become his 'men' and do him 'omage and feauté' (325.16–21:VII.18). To their persuasive arguments Gareth adds his own inclination to blame Ironsyde 'the lesse' inasmuch as he did all his misdeeds at a lady's request. He grants Ironsyde his life on condition that he obtain the pardon of the lady of the castle, that he 'make hir amendys of all the trespasse that he hath done ayenst hir and hir landys,' and that afterwards he go to King Arthur's court and obtain the pardon of Lancelot and Gawain. Ironsyde agrees to all this, offering 'syker assuraunce and borowys' for his future conduct. No other episode in the *Morte Darthur* is so laced with the language of legal settlement and no other knight enacts so fully the role of a royal justice (324.29–325.35:VI.17–18).

In the way he does justice upon Sir Ironsyde, Gareth foreshadows his future role as the husband of Lady Lyones and lord of all her lands. The assumption of lordship distinguishes Gareth from Lancelot as a type of True knight just as surely as his marriage to Lyones. As the younger son of King Lott, Gareth was obliged to make his own way in the world. He did not inherit lordship as Lancelot did, being the elder son of King Ban of Benwick. It is ironic, therefore, that Lancelot should choose to renounce lordship in order to continue serving Arthur as a Round Table knight and that Gareth, who might easily have followed Lancelot's example, chooses not to do so.[19] As we have already seen,

Gareth is not so ascetically inclined by nature or temperament as his mentor and, after he meets the Lady Lyones in the intimate circumstances of her brother's castle, his choice is clear to him. Gareth possesses the same religious virtues of piety and chastity that Lancelot possesses. However, his expression of these virtues can not be the same. His desire for Lyones impels him to express them in Christian marriage and lordship rather than to adopt Lancelot's more ascetic and uncompromising view of the knightly vocation.

Heroes of the earlier medieval romances do not often combine religious with courtly virtues because it is so difficult to harmonize the ascetic bias of the Christian religious virtues with the erotic bias of the courtly idealization of love. The characterization of Lancelot in the thirteenth-century Grail romance, *Perlesvaus,* illustrates the difficulty very well. In this romance Lancelot is a pious man, willing to confess and repent all his sins — except one. That one is his love for Queen Guinevere, and, although he finally confesses it, he absolutely refuses to repent it, not only because it is so 'enracinee el cuer qu'ele ne s'em puet partir', but also because the 'gregnor valor qui est en moi si me vient par la volenté' (3660–61). Like all courtly lovers, Lancelot believes that he owes all his worthiness as a knight to his desire for Guinevere, and therefore, even after the hermit has chided him for his mortal sin, assured him that 'nule valor ne puet venir de tel luxore qui ne li soit vendue molt chiere', and reminded him that his sin makes him a 'traitres a vostre segnor terrien', Lancelot still is not moved to repent. Rather he expresses the hope, as courtly as it is pious, that God will be 'si douz et si plains de deboneretė... qu'il avra merci de nos' (3662–63; 3686–87). It is remarkable, I think, that the hermit does not deny outright that Lancelot could have acquired any 'valor' as a consequence of his love for the queen. All the hermit says is that whatever 'valor' he may have acquired by means of 'tel luxore' must be dearly bought. Thus he tacitly recognizes the value of Lancelot's love at the same time as he condems its illicit expression. Of course, by Christian religious standards, the only legitimate expression of erotic love was within Christian marriage. Therefore, authors of later medieval romance had two choices if they wished to portray heroes who combined courtly and religious virtues. They could create a very young and virginal hero like Gawain, in *Sir Gawain and the Green Knight*, who is able to resist the lure of illicit sexual enjoyment. Or, they could allow their hero to marry the woman he desires. In later medieval romance the second of these two solutions is by far the more common; however, Malory's Gareth rather notably resembles the pious and chaste hero of the English poem, until he meets Lyones.

Gareth's piety is amply illustrated in the early part of his tale. After he has slain the six thieves, he refuses to accept any reward because, as he says, 'this day I was made knyght of noble sir Launcelot, and therefore I woll no rewarde have but God rewarde me' (301.7–9:VII.5). On two subsequent occasions he assures Lynet that he trusts 'to God' or to the 'grace of God' in dealing with his foes (302.20:VII.6; 312.26: VII.11). He also attends mass every day he can (and he has many opportunities since he is normally well lodged in his defeated opponents' castles). However, when his devotion to chastity is tested in Sir Persaunte's castle, we cannot be absolutely sure whether he passes this test because he would not offend God or because he would not offend Sir Persaunte. When Gareth wakens to discover the naked lady in his bed, he first asks her name and then, having learned that she is Sir Persaunt's daughter and has come at her father's 'commaundemente', he asks,

> 'Be ye a pusell or a wyff?'
> 'Sir,' she seyde, I am a clene maydyn.'
> 'God deffende me,' seyde he, 'than that ever I sholde defoyle you to do sir Persaunte suche a shame! Therefore I pray you, fayre damesell, aryse oute of this bedde, other ellys I woll.'
> (315.6–12:VII.12)

The way Malory has worded Gareth's response, ('God deffende me *than* . . .'), one cannot help wondering what he would have replied had she said she was 'a wyff'. It sounds very much as though he would '*than*' have concluded that Sir Persaunte had sent her as a part of his hospitality, which courtesy would have required him to accept. Fortunately, for Gareth as for the chaste hero of *Sir Gawain and the Green Knight*, the laws of hospitality and of Christian morality can be made to coincide and, like Gawain, Gareth avoids offending the young lady by giving her a kiss. His 'God deffende me' recalls Lancelot's response, 'Nay . . . that God me forbede', when Hallewes asked him to kiss her 'but onys', and points up the contrast in the two men's sexual morality: Gareth would never be so discourteous as to refuse a damsell a kiss, which means, of course, that had he been in Lancelot's place at the Chapel Perilous, he would have perished.

By courtly standards, however, Gareth is perfectly chaste, and therefore he is a 'happy' knight, as invincible as Lancelot. Malory draws attention to his 'happiness' by having Lynet continuously accuse him of its opposite. Thinking him to be but a kitchen knave, Lynet cannot understand how he is able to defeat such good and experienced knights except, as she says, 'thorow unhappynesse'. In the space of six pages in Vinaver's edition she uses the words 'unhappy', 'unhappynes' or 'mysehappe' a total of fourteen times, but the climactic passage is surely the following, in which she asks the Black knight to rid her of this 'unhappy knave':

> 'Sir, I can not be delyverde of hym, for with me he rydyth magré my hede. God wolde,' seyde she, 'that ye wolde putte hym from me, other to sle hym and ye may, for he is an *unhappy* knave, and *unhappyly* he hath done this day *thorow myssehappe*; for I saw hym sle two knyghtes at the passage of the watir, and other dedis he ded beforne ryght mervaylouse and *thorow unhappynesse*.'
> (303.18–24:VII.7. Emphasis added.)

When Gareth then defeats the Black Knight handily, the point cannot be lost upon the most inattentive reader. Lynet is wrong about Gareth. He is not an 'unhappy knave'; rather he is a 'happy knight'. However, he is not so perfectly 'happy' as Lancelot has been, for he is not protected against manslaughter.

The only knights in the *Morte Darthur* who are ever explicitly preserved from manslaughter by divine grace are the Grail knights and Lancelot, of whom Nacien will later say, 'sith that he wente into the queste of the Sankgreal he slew never man nother nought shall, tylle that he com to Camelot agayne; for he hath takyn upon hym to forsake synne' (948.21–24:XVI.5). Malory has implicitly given Lancelot the same protection in the Tale of Lancelot by altering his source so that he never in fact commits manslaughter, but he does not give Gareth the same protection. The Black Knight dies of his wounds. Gareth was very angry at the Black Knight, but he did not intend to kill him: he just wanted the right to keep his horse, his armour and his damsel. Later he will excuse the killing as 'knyghtly'. When the Green Knight calls Gareth 'traytoure!' and says, 'thou shalt dye for sleying of my brothir!', Gareth defies him aserting, 'I slew hym knyghtly and nat shamfully' (305.16–20:VII.8). Gareth means that although he may have committed manslaughter he has not committed treason (murder),and therefore he does not deserve to die. The Black Knight's death was simply the unforeseen and, in the event, unavoidable consequence of a fair fight. Tristram will say as much when defending himself for having killed Darras' three sons in a tournament: 'and if I had slayne hem by treson other trechory, I had bene worthy to have dyed.' Fortunately, Darras agrees that since all he did 'was by fors of knyghtode' he cannot be considered guilty of a serious crime (552.20–28:IX.40). And the Green Knight also forgives Gareth his brother's death, but only after Gareth has proved in battle to be 'a bettir knight' (307.28:VII.9) than he is and not an 'unhappy kychyn knave'.

Lacking the sexual purity of a Lancelot or a Galahad, Gareth is denied preservation from manslaughter; however, he is granted protection from defeat so long as he avoids the sin of lechery. Indeed, he confirms the fact that his 'happiness' as a knight is directly related to the degree of his chastity when at the very time he and his lady, Dame Lyones, have agreed to 'abate their lustys secretly' he is severely wounded for the first time in his brief knightly career. His host refers to the wound as an 'unhappy dede' (334.17:VII.22) and later on Gareth himself laments that he has been 'so sore wounded with unhappy-nesse' that he will not be able to perform 'lyke a knyght' at the Assumption Day tournament (342.12–14:VII.27). The supernatural atmosphere of this episode (which is repeated ten days later when Gareth has recovered sufficiently from his first wound to try again) suggests an analogy with the episode in which the chastity of Sir Percival is tested early in his Grail adventures. The similarities are striking: each knight is passionately enamoured; the object of his desire is a very beautiful woman who is also his hostess; each swears an oath of loyalty to her (Gareth plights his troth and Percival promises to be her 'trew servaunte'); and, finally, each is wounded in the thigh as a punishment for his lechery. However, the differences are even more significant than the similarities. Percival, like Lancelot, has chosen to be celibate in order to be worthy of the Grail; he is *not* acquainted with the lady in question (later he learns that she was 'the mayster fyende of helle'); he is saved by the 'grace of God' from going through with his lecherous intent; and, finally, he wounds himself to 'punyssh' his flesh and to offer 'recompensacion' to the Lord (919.12–17:XIV.10). By contrast, Gareth has *not* chosen celibacy; on the contrary, he is betrothed to the lady in question. He is prevented from consummating his marriage in clandestine fashion *not* by the grace of God (who must have blessed their union, given their honest intents), but by the 'craufftes' of Lynet, who thinks it is not 'worshipful' that they should have their 'delytes' before they are publicly wed (333.12–13:VII.22).

The sexual morality which informs the Tale of Gareth is Christian, but it is not ascetic. It is the morality of medieval courtly society which disapproved of clandestine marriages for political and social reasons. This morality was enforced by the Christian Church on the religious grounds that such unions scandalized the Christian community because they left the marriage uncertain and thus opened the way to bigamy (Kelly, *Love* 172–73). Lyones defends herself before her brother by arguing that Gareth is already her 'lorde' and 'muste be' her 'husbonde' (334.10–12:VII.22), and canon law is on her side. Had they been able to consummate their love she and Gareth would have been truly (if not presumptively) married. And while some ecclesiastical judges might have punished them, others would simply have required them to abjure further intercourse until after the public wedding. The lovers' problem is not so much with the Church as with their respective families.

Aristocratic English families were not in the habit of allowing their young people to choose their own partners in marriage. Such freedom of choice would have threatened the entire social order, based as it was upon the system of contracting marriages between families to create or to strengthen economic and political alliances. Before she agreed to come to Gareth's bed, Lyones already knew that her brother approved of the match, as well he might, given Gareth's lineage and near kinship to the king. But evidently her sister Lynet thought it would be shameful if Lyones were to guarantee her marriage in this clandestine way. It would look as though she feared she were not a good enough match for the king's nephew and could never gain his family's approval for a public wedding. At least that is the sort of reasoning we must infer from Malory's observation that Lynet cast the first enchantment 'for savying of hir [sister's] worshyp' (333.9–10:VII.22) and the statement which Lynet herself makes after she has prevented the lovers from consummating their marriage in clandestine fashion for the second time: 'I have nothynge done but I woll avow hit, and all that I have done shall be to your worshyp and to us all' (336.1–3: VII.23).

By late medieval standards, Gareth and Lyones are extremely fortunate. Queen Margawse and King Arthur agree to the marriage when they realize how much the young people love each other, and so they are able to marry with the blessings of society as well as God. But Malory reminds us of the way marriages were normally contracted in courtly society when he tells us that 'kynge Arthure made sir Gaherys to wedde ... dame Lyonet. And sir Aggravayne kynge Arthure made to wedde dame Lyonesseis nees, a fayre lady; hir name was dame Lawrell' (361.8–11:VII.36). This information also suggests that Arthur was willing to bless the marriage of Gareth and Lyones not only because they loved each other, but also because politically it was a good match, one worth cementing with two other unions as well.

Lancelot and Gawain both attend the wedding but since, at the request of Dame Lyones, married knights are not allowed to 'juste at the feste' only Lancelot participates in the tournament. These two knights have stood on either side of Gareth from the beginning of this tale, very often literally side by side at Arthur's court, yet we have never heard them speak a word to one another. Malory has deliberately eliminated the friendship between them which is so prominent a feature of the French prose *Lancelot*. His reason for doing so may be inferred from the reason he has given Gareth for avoiding the 'felyship' of his eldest brother: 'for he was evir vengeable, and where he hated he wolde be avenged with murther: and that hated sir Gareth' (360.34–36:VII.35). Neither Lancelot nor Gareth would choose the 'felyship' of such a man. This is not to say that Gareth does not love and respect Gawain, but it is to say that Gareth much prefers the company of Lancelot. When the two friends are reunited once again on the occasion of Gareth's wedding, Malory exclaims,

> 'Lorde, the grete chere that sir Launcelot made of sir Gareth and he of hym! For there was no knyght that sir Gareth loved so well as he dud sir Launcelot; and ever for the moste party he wolde ever be in sir launcelottis company.' (360.28–31:VII.35)

The contrast between the values of Lancelot, the True knight, and the values of Gawain, the Heroic knight, is beautifully enacted in the battles which each knight fights with young Gareth in this tale. Lancelot's battle with Gareth comes early in the tale and Gawain's battle with Gareth comes at a climactic moment, just before the identity of the Fair Unknown is revealed to the court. The first of the two battles is initiated at Gareth's request. There is no bloodshed and both parties enjoy the game, Gareth perhaps more than Lancelot since the older, more proved knight experiences such unexpected difficulty in matching the younger man. Moreover, this first battle has a rational purpose: Gareth wants to test his prowess against the best so that he can enter upon his quest with confidence. By contrast, the battle with Gawain has no purpose. There is not even a verbal challenge on either side. The two knights encounter one another like two stags in the forest, wordlessly and savagely, simply because their paths have crossed; and it seems fairly certain that if Lynet had not intervened the two brothers would have killed each other just like Balin and Balan. Gareth is horrified to discover that he has fought his bloodiest battle since the encounter with Ironsyde with his own brother. Malory tells us he 'kneled downe to hym and asked hym mercy' and that 'there were many kynde wordys betwene them' (357.18–22:VII.34). Even though he will choose to avoid his companionship in future, Gareth still loves and respects his brother as the head of his clan and as the king's favorite nephew. However, he does not want to be like his brother. He would much rather be like Lancelot, the man he chose to make him knight.

Gareth does not choose to be exactly like Lancelot; in fact, his decision to marry takes him out of the world of knight-errantry. Malory eliminates almost all of Gareth's appearances from the Tale of Tristram which follows because, as a married knight, Gareth must 'couche' with his wife and 'leve armys and turnamentis, batellys and adventures' (270.30–32:VI.10).[20] He will attend only one tournament in the Tale of Tristram, the great tournament at Lonezep, and there he will joust with the younger, unproved knights, indicating that his life as a married lord of great lands has not provided him with much opportunity to keep up his martial skills. He will participate in the Quest, and afterwards he will take part in the Great Tournament, as well (another command performance at court in the presence of the king and queen), but otherwise we will see very little of Gareth in the rest of the *Morte Darthur*.

At first glance the Tale of Gareth appears to endorse the conservative, aristocratic view of gentility, a view which is certainly expressed elsewhere in the *Morte Darthur*. For example, we are told that Balin is worthy to draw out his second sword because he is 'of jantill strene of fadir syde and of modir syde' (62.22–24:II.1). And both Tor's and Galahad's goodness and nobility are attributed to their noble blood (100–101:III.3; 862.5–7:XIII.4). However, Malory's version of the familiar story of the Fair Unknown does not, in fact, support the conservative view that a gentleman born must be full of prowess, virtue and courtesy. On the contrary, the Tale of Gareth undermines that view by means of the comparison between Gareth's two potential mentors, Lancelot and Gawain. If Gareth's extraordinary courtesy were truly the consequence of his 'jantyll bloode', as Lynet thinks it is (312.29–34:VIII.11), then his oldest brother, Gawain, would be just as courteous as he is, and this is patently not the case.

All of Malory's great knights are as well-born as it is possible to be: the sons and nephews of kings. Thus, parodoxically, they may all be said to have been born equal. As a consequence, their varying degrees of virtue as knights must depend on factors other than heredity. Through the example of Gareth Malory suggests what those other factors might be. He is able to do this so clearly in Gareth's case because in his tale we are given a complete history of his brief career as a knight-errant. The first factor is the grace of God, upon which Gareth relies in his quest for love and worship. The second is the exercise of his own free will, for Gareth makes career and life choices which have clear ethical significance. First, he chooses Lancelot rather than Gawain to be his mentor. That choice entails accepting Lancelot's religious view of knighthood as a 'High Order' established by God and rejecting Gawain's view of knighthood as inherited nobility expressed through bodily strength, courage and skill in arms. It also entails accepting Lancelot's belief that only virtuous knights can be 'happy' in the pursuit of their calling and rejecting Gawain's unthinking assumption that God will be on his side simply because he is a Christian, regardless of the moral quality of his 'lyvyng'.

Gareth also chooses to marry his beloved rather than to take her as his 'peramour'. This is the only way in which he may be said to follow his brother's example rather than Lancelot's, for Gawain with his three sons we presume to be a married man, while Lancelot has declared he will never marry. However, Gareth takes his view of marriage from Lancelot rather than from Gawain. We never meet Gawain's wife and therefore have good reason to assume that his attitude towards her and the institution of marriage is like that of every other exemplar of Heroic knighthood: marriage is the means by which a knight produces legitimate heirs and, except for her essential reproductive function, a wife does not play a significant part in his life. By contrast, Lancelot believes a wife is *so* important that a knight must give up battles and adventures for her sake. Lancelot's is the view of the *true* lover for whom marriage, as an alternative to the religious life, merits a man's total dedication. That is clearly the view which Gareth adopts, for not only does he disappear from the Arthurian world of knight-errantry after he has married, he even refrains from jousting at his own wedding feast since his new wife 'desyred of the kynge that none that were wedded sholde juste at that feste' (362.24–26:VII.36).

There is only one knightly career which is compatible with marriage, as Gareth and Lancelot understand marriage, and that is lordship. Therefore Gareth's decision to marry his beloved also entails choosing to settle down with her on her great lands and to accept responsibility for the administration of justice in that part of Arthur's kingdom. He thus exemplifies True knighthood in its most courtly form: he will serve his God and his king as dispenser of justice in his 'contrey' and he will serve his lady as her husband. Gareth has all the noble virtues which his mentor Lancelot has, but he has chosen to express them differently. In particular, he has chosen a lesser degree of chastity, because, having found his true love, he has also found that he may not live chaste. Lancelot has not made all his choices yet, even though he thinks he has, because he has not yet found his true love, nor yet learned that 'love ys a grete maystry'.

The Tale of Gareth is a fitting conclusion to Malory's composite portrait of the True knight, for Gareth is able to honour all three of the traditional knightly loyalties — to his God, to his king, and to his lady — because he has resolved the conflicts among them. He has resolved the conflict between service to God and service to lady by legitimating his sexual desire in holy wedlock. And he has resolved the conflict between service to king and service to lady by choosing to serve his king as a local magnate and occasional courtier, rather than as a knight-errant or captain of war. As a type of True knighthood, Gareth looks forward to the English renaissance ideal of the governor, as expressed in Sir Thomas Elyot's book of that name. He also resembles Malory's

Worshipful type much more than Lancelot does, insofar as he shares the Worshipful knight's appreciation of court life and the society of women. In the next chapter, we will see Lancelot, too, transformed into a much more courtly knight by the power of his developing love for the queen. Unfortunately, Guinevere is a woman Lancelot may never hope to marry. Therefore he will experience much more difficulty than Gareth has experienced in resolving the conflict between his desire to serve his lady and his desire to serve God and Arthur.

4

Worshipful Knighthood

Malory's Worshipful knight represents a kind of middle way between the basic martial ideal of Heroic knighthood and the more lofty religious ideal of True knighthood. In other words, the Worshipful knight exemplifies what R. T. Davies has called the 'noble way of the world' (356). Malory devotes the third and longest of his five narrative units, the Tale of Tristram, to the elaboration of this type and, as we might expect, Tristram is its chief exemplar. He is not the only one, however. Arthur is equally important as an exemplar of Worshipful knighthood and, later on in the tale, Lancelot, Lamorak, Palomides and Dinadan will all have important exemplary roles to play.

As a type, Malory's Worshipful knight was formed in the increasingly civilized and sophisticated milieu of the late medieval court and is clearly reflected in such late fourteenth-century and fifteenth-century courtly works as Christine de Pizan's *Epistle of Othea to Hector* and Antoine de la Sale's *Petit Jehan de Saintré*. These works are both less pious in tone and more practical in outlook than Roman Lull's classic treatise defining the religious deal of True knighthood. They assume basic Christian morality, but they also assume that the knight's primary objective is to rise in the service of his prince, and so they offer him both ethical guidelines and practical advice on how best to achieve this objective.[1]

The Worshipful knight shares with both the Heroic knight and the True Knight the feudal virtues of prowess, courage and loyalty: however, his expression of them is conditioned by values which are unique to his type. The most fundamental of these is the extreme importance which he attaches to his personal honour, or worship. Late medieval treatises on knighthood are unanimous in making the desire for worship the *sine qua non* of a successful knightly career. For example, Christine de Pizan lists the love of 'honneur' as one of the six 'bonnes condicions' which a knight must have (*Livre du Corps* 141). Therefore it is not surprising that Malory's Worshipful knights should be most readily identified by their professed desire to win worship and, of equal importance, by their concern that their worshipful deeds be known. For example, when Palomides is scheduled to do battle with Tristram, he brings with him four knights of King Arthur's court and three sargeants-of-arms so that 'they sholde beare recorde of the batayle betwyxt sir Trystram and hym' (783.16–21:X.88). And Tristram has earlier promised his defeated opponent, Marhalt, that he would bear the captured arms of Ireland 'in all placis where I ryde on myne adventures, and in the syght of kyng Arthure and all the Rounde Table' (383.7–10:VIII.7). His words and subsequent behaviour anticipate those of the Renaissance courtier, whom Castiglione will advise to do his deeds of arms in the presence of many witnesses, 'and, above all, in the presence, or if possible under the very eyes, of the prince he is serving. For it is certainly right to exploit the things one does well' (Barber, *Reign* 184).

This more courtly view of knighthood found concrete expression in the late Middle Ages in secular orders of knighthood, like Edward III's Order of the Garter. It also found expression in the elaborate courtly rituals devised for the conferring of knighthood. In England the most solemn knighting ritual was the religious ritual of the Bath. Knights made by means of this ritual may have been more likely than others to perceive their knighthood as a Christian vocation, but it is doubtful that they would have agreed with Sir Gilbert Hay that their first duty as a knight was to God (*Knychthede* 20). On the contrary, they are much more likely to have assumed that their duty to God and King were one and the same.

The fifteenth-century ritual of the Bath stressed both loyalties: the new knights were to 'love god above all things' and also to 'be trewe un to [their] sovereyne lorde'. However, at the conclusion of the ceremony, they were expected to express their gratitude to the prince: 'Moste drede and moste myghty prynce, of lytyll powre of that that I may I thanke you of all ye worshypes, curtesies, godenesse, whiche ye have done unto me' (Stowe 113). Such a statement clearly anticipates the Renaissance view of the prince as the fount of all honour in his realm.

The prince's claim to be the fount of honour and to arbitrate all matters of honour within his realm rested finally upon his claim to sovereign power. As Julian Pitt-Rivers has observed, 'On the field of honour might is right' (25), and so whom the 'myghty prynce' honours is therefore honourable. Among those late medieval monarchs who successfully laid claim to sovereign power, however, few either cared or could afford to give honours only to men who were morally virtuous and Malory's Arthur will prove, in the end, to be no exception. Nevertheless, at the beginning of his reign he sets high moral standards for the behaviour of those whom he will 'worship' as knights of the Round Table and servants of the Crown. He does not require his knights to observe the religious virtues of piety, humility or chastity — presumably he does not think they are essential to good governance — but he does require that they be loyal, just and courteous — like himself. What is more, should they fail to live up to his ethical code, the king threatens to deprive them of their worship and his lordship 'for evirmore' (120.15–24:III.15).

Malory has anticipated Tristram's exemplary function as the premier Worshipful knight by associating him with Marhalt at the conclusion of the first narrative unit. In the second triple quest Marhalt exemplifies Worshipful knighthood and in the tournament which concludes that quest he takes second prize, after Pelleas. Malory then informs us that 'many dayes aftir' Tristram will fight 'a grete batayle' with sir Marhalt 'in an ilande' and at the last will slay him (180.4–6:IV.29). This suggests most powerfully that Tristram will one day take the place of the knight he has slain both as an exemplary Worshipful knight and as a fellow of the Round Table.[2]

To delineate fully the Worshipful type of knight in the Tale of Tristram, Malory organizes his narrative thematically according to the same pattern he used in the second triple quest. That is to say, he looks first at the feudal virtues of knighthood, then at the courtly virtues, and finally at the religious virtues. Strictly speaking, of course, the Worshipful knight does not possess the specifically religious virtues. Certainly he does not subscribe rigorously to either humility or chastity, and his piety is not of the radical sort which influences actions as well as words. Therefore, it would be more accurate to say that in the third part of the Tale of Tristram, Malory examines the Worshipful type from the religious point of view.[3]

Tristram and Arthur: The Courtier and the Prince

Throughout most of the first part of the Tale of Tristram it is clear that Tristram is striving to win worship, not in order to make himself better beloved of Isode, but to make himself worthy of becoming a knight of the Round Table. Despite the great deeds he has done in the service of the kings of Cornwall and Ireland, when he first comes into Logres he does not think he is 'yet of such dedys of worthynes to be in the companye of such a felyship' (489.30–32:IX.15). It is his greatest desire to become of such 'worthynes' and his desire is fulfilled at last in the conclusion to the 'Round Table' section, in a scene which may be called his apotheosis:

> 'Wellcom,' seyde kynge Arthur, 'for one of the beste knyghtes and the jentyllyst of the worlde and the man of most worship.'
> (571.27–29:X.6)

It is fitting that these words of praise be spoken by Arthur, for he has always been and will continue to be Tristram's model of knighthood:

> 'A!' sayd sir Trystrams, 'ye know nat my lorde kynge Arthure, for all knightes may learne to be a knyght of hym.' (745.28–30:X.73)

Together, Tristram and Arthur fully exemplify what we may call the feudal type of Worshipful knighthood, to distinguish it from the more courtly type later to be exemplified by Lancelot and Palomides.

Malory immediately distinguishes his new hero from those who have gone before by the way in which he becomes a knight and his reasons for doing so. Tristram is not like Gawain, even though he comes to the court of his maternal uncle to be knighted, because he comes to Mark's court as a Fair Unknown. On the other hand, he is not like Lancelot or Gareth because, even though he is knighted by Mark as a Fair Unknown, he does not then prove his worthiness to be a knight before revealing his royal lineage. Tristram deviates from the Fair Unknown pattern because Marhalt, prince of Ireland, refuses to do battle with anyone of lesser nobility and consequently Tristram is forced to reveal his royal lineage in order to establish his right to be champion of Cornwall. There is only one other knight in the *Morte Darthur* who has followed a similar pattern in becoming a knight and that is Arthur.

For both Tristram and Arthur knighthood is a means to an end rather than an end in itself. Tristram has to become a knight before he can be the Champion of Cornwall, and Arthur has to become a knight before he can be crowned King of England (see above 21–22). Both men must also prove to be of royal birth in order to confirm their right to office; however, each is in fact made knight before his royal birth is disclosed.[4] This sequence implies that knighthood is more important than royal birth to the work they are called to do, and, of course, from the religious point of view, knighthood is more important than birth as a prerequisite for wielding temporal power. For it is the knight's religious commitment to the High Order of Knighthood which, in theory at least, curbs the pride and greed which would otherwise be fostered by his family ties and personal ambition. That Arthur and Tristram should both become knights before undertaking their respective offices, and that they should be deemed worthy of those offices even without providing evidence of their royal parentage, is clearly suggestive of the religious view of knighthood. In Arthur's case this suggestion is reinforced by the belief of the commons of England that it is 'Goddes wille' that Arthur should be their king because he has been able to draw the sword from the stone (16.13–14:I.7). In Tristram's case, we are told nothing of the response of the commons of Cornwall to Tristram's offer to be their Champion; however, given their plight and Mark's inability to find a champion among his own knights, this likely-looking young man might well have appeared to be heaven-sent.

This does not mean, however, that either Arthur or Tristram personally regards knighthood as a religious vocation in the same way that Lancelot, Gareth and the Grail knights do. Near the beginning of their respective careers there is some sign that each of them might so regard it: for example, Arthur gives thanks to God for his early military victories (130.4–5:IV.3; 205.11:V.5) and Tristram expresses the wish that God 'may make me as good a knyght as that good knyght sir Launcelot is' (388.34–36:VIII.10). But neither Arthur nor Tristram maintains such a pious attitude towards the vocation of knighthood once he has become thoroughly immersed in the courtly world of late medieval politics. Even though both knights appear initially as heaven-sent protectors of their people, they soon reveal themselves to be practical men, guided principally by reason and occasionally by sheer expediency in the conduct of their affairs. And even though one is a prince and the other a courtier, they share a common goal: the getting and keeping of political power and worship.

Tristram's battle with Marhalt is more fundamentally political in its implications than any of the battles fought by Lancelot and Gareth in the preceding two tales. In fact, in terms of the issue at stake, the battle it most closely resembles is King Arthur's battle with the Emperor Lucius. Tristram defends the sovereignty of Cornwall against the king of Ireland's claim to tribute, just as Arthur defends the sovereignty of England against the Roman Emperor's claim to tribute. To be sure, Tristram's battle is a single combat whereas Arthur's battle involves armies of thousands of men on both sides. However, had Malory decided to follow Geoffrey of Monmouth's account of the Roman campaign, he might have had Arthur fight in single combat also. According to Geoffrey's *Historia*, Arthur and Frollo, the Roman governor of Gaul, fought on an island in the Seine to determine which of them should have the rule of Gaul and Britain (9.11). If Malory knew this account, which was adopted both by Wace and Layamon, he would also have known that reigning monarchs did not usually risk their lives by accepting such challenges. In fact, Layamon reports that Frollo issued the challenge only because he was certain that King Arthur would refuse it (lines 11820–24).[5] Malory avoids putting Arthur in the position of having either to accept or to refuse such a challenge by following the account of the Roman campaign contained in the alliterative *Morte Arthure*. That allows him to demonstrate Arthur's personal courage in the battle with the giant of Mont St Michel.

Equally important, it allows him to make Arthur's prudence appear unequivocally admirable in his capacity as the commander of a great army.

Both Arthur and Tristram value prudence when it comes to military encounters. Before invading the Emperor's territory, Arthur takes counsel with his Round Table knights and receives pledges of their support. Before going to King Mark's court to request the battle with Marhalt, Tristram takes counsel with his father and assures him that once he is knighted he will be a 'matche' for Marhalt (378.4:VIII.5). Such prudent planning ahead with the express aim of winning worship has not been at all characteristic of Gawain, Lancelot or Gareth. None of these knights has ever set out on an adventure, quest, or battle with a plan or with the explicit intention of winning worship. Gawain and Lancelot have both refused to retreat when 'overmacched' in order to avoid 'shame' in battle (213–217:V.7; 235:V.10) and Gareth has refused to withdraw from his quest for the same reason (311.6–7:VII.11), but all three knights have always appeared to regard the winning of worship as the natural consequence of behaving like a knight — the inevitable by-product of knightly deeds, as it were — rather than something which can only be achieved by prudence and forethought.[6] This may at first glance seem to be a rather subtle distinction, but it rests upon a fundamental difference in mentality.

That difference in mentality is no less than the difference between rationality and irrationality. Gawain, Lancelot and Gareth acted quite irrationally when they refused to retreat in the face of impossible odds. They refused because they believed that any knight who retreated from danger would be 'shamed' forever. On the other hand, Arthur has told Lancelot that he and his companions would have 'loste no worshyp' had they retreated when faced with an ambush of thousands of Romans. In Arthur's opinion it is 'but foly to abyde whan knyghtes bene overmacched' (217.26–27:V.7). Tristram's knightly career illustrates the same rational regard for prudence. When the King with the Hundred Knights attacks him with his entire 'felyshyp' and it appears that he must yield or die, Tristram has no qualms about yielding: 'Sir, as for that, I woll rather yelde me to you than dye, for hit is more for the myght of thy men than of thyne handys' (417.1–2: VIII.27). And, on the eve of the tournament of Lonezep, he vetoes Palomides' suggestion that their group of four knights take a stand against all comers:

> 'Nat be my counceyle,' seyde sir Trystram, 'for I se by their pavylouns there woll be four hondred knyghtes. And doute ye nat,' seyde sir Trystram, 'but there woll be many good knyghtes,

and be a man never so valyaunte nother so bygge but he may be overmatched. And so have I seyne knyghtes done many, and whan they wente beste to have wonne worshyp they loste hit; for manhode is nat worthe but yf hit be medled with wysdome. And as for me,' seyde sir Trystram, 'hit may happen I shall kepe myne owne hede as well as another.' (700.13–22:X.59)

The only sentence in this speech which Vinaver could not attribute to Malory's French source is the proverbial 'manhode is nat worthe but yf hit be medled with wysdome.' It is a particularly pithy phrasing of this distinguishing characteristic of Malory's Worshipful knight.

In Tristram's battle with Marhalt there is a great and specific wrong to be righted (from the Cornish point of view, at any rate), and therefore one should not expect him to exhibit as much prudence as he would in a situation where there was no moral or political issue involved. Nevertheless, Tristram's decision to take on the best knight in the world is not so reckless as it might at first appear. He has given the matter much thought, as he makes clear when refusing to give up the battle at Marhalt's request:

> 'And also wete thou well, sir Marhalte, that this ys the gretteste cause that thou coragyst me to have ado with the, for thou arte called one of the moste renomed knyghtes of the worlde. And bycause of that noyse and fame that thou haste thou gevyst me corrayge to have ado with the, for never yett was I proved with good knyght. And sytthen I toke the Order of Knyghthode this day, I am ryght well pleased, and to me moste worshyp, that I may have ado wyth suche a knyght as thou arte. And now wete thou well, syr Marhalte, that I caste me to geete worshyp on thy body.' (381.20–29:VIII.7)

Like Gareth, who challenged Lancelot, Tristram has decided to test his prowess against the best; however, the contrast between these two knights in the same situation is more instructive than the similarity. Gareth challenged Lancelot because he wanted to prove to his mentor that he was worthy of knighthood and he wanted to prove to himself and his damsel, Lynet, that he was worthy to undertake the quest for Lyones. By contrast, Tristram has already proved his worthiness to undertake this battle by his birth and by his knighthood; he accepts Marhalt's challenge because he wants to win as much worship as he can.

As the epitome of Worshipful knighthood, Tristram exemplifies the traditional heroic virtues — courage, prowess and loyalty — modified not only by prudence but also by ambition. Tristram's motives for doing battle are never simple. As he will later explain to the King of Ireland, he decided to undertake this battle with Marhalt 'for the love of myne uncle kynge Marke and for the love of the countrey of Cornwayle, and for to encrece myne honoure' (391.11–13). His opponent, Marhalt, is just like him. Marhalt also agreed to do this battle not only for the sake of his family and his country, but also 'to avaunce my dedis and to encrece my worshyp' (376.25–26:VIII.4). In fact, Marhalt is disappointed to be deprived of the opportunity of winning worship from one of the best knights of the Round Table and proudly assures his young, untried opponent that he will lose no worship 'gyff thou may stonde me three strokys' (382.1–2:VIII.7). Marhalt's subsequent boast — 'For I lat the wete, for my noble dedis proved and seyne kynge Arthure made me knyght of the Table Rounde!' — only whets young Tristram's desire to take that worship from him.

The calculation of worship continues to dominate this battle right down to the very end. Marhalt finds the young man more than a match for him and decides to throw down his weapons and flee for his life. Tristram taunts him with his 'grete shame':

> 'A, sir knyght of the Rounde Table! Why withdrawyst thou the? Thou doest thyself and thy kynne grete shame, for I am but a yonge knyght: or now I was never preved. And rather than I sholde withdraw me frome the, I had rathir be hewyn in pyese-mealys.' (382.36–383.4:VIII.7)

Never before in the *Morte Darthur* has one knight taunted another with the shame of running to save his life, not even during the Roman campaign, although that may be due primarily to the fact that Arthur's knights were too busy chasing and killing the retreating Saracens to waste any words upon them (216–217:V.7; 223–224:V.8). The more civilized Tristram does not pursue his enemy with sword raised to kill; he pursues him rather with words to humiliate him, reminding him that his shame is the greater because he flees from a young, unproved knight. There is nothing very rational about Tristram's accompanying boast that he 'had rathir be hewyn in pyese-mealys' than to have shown cowardice as Marhalt has done, and it is to be doubted whether he would, in fact, have acted so irrationally had he found himself in Marhalt's predicament. However, this boast reminds the reader of the fact that Marhalt has just lost a crucial trial by battle in the only way it could be lost.

Trial by battle was a customary mode of doing justice in some parts of medieval Europe for almost a thousand years (Neilson 5–12, 19–30). We know very little about its earliest form, except what has been preserved in heroic verse and prose sagas. We know, for example, that it was frequently fought on an island location so that the witnesses (and potential interlopers) could be separated from the combatants by a body of water, and this probably explains why the legal term for such a combat in Anglo-Saxon was *holmgang* (Neilson 11). We also know that the combatants continued the fight until one of them had either fled or was dead. However, in the most primitive version of judicial combat, one did not lose by dying. Before the battle, Tristram sends the following message back to his uncle, King Mark:

> '. . . lette hym wete I woll never be yoldyn for cowardyse, and if I be slayne and fle nat, they have loste no trewayge for me. And yf so be that I fle other yelde me as recreaunte, bydde myne eme bury me never in Crystyn buryellys.' (380.32–36:VIII.6)

Tristram knows that even if he should die, so long as he neither flees nor yields himself as 'recreaunte', Ireland can claim no tribute from Cornwall, for the champion of Cornwall will not have been defeated.

This primitive heroic ethic did not survive the Christianization of trial by combat. Christianity transformed the *holmgang* from a test of raw courage into a judgment of God. However, Tristram's request that he be deprived of the rite of 'crystyn buryellys' if he should betray cowardice suggests how this transformation might have come about worked in the minds of the earliest Christians. Pre-Christian warriors must have believed that the death-defying courage necessary to avoid losing a *holmgang* was a gift from the gods. In the case of a judicial combat between the champions of two tribes, each champion would naturally have expected to receive this gift from his own tribal god, and thus their combat would have been perceived as a test of the relative strength of the two tribal gods. After the coming of Christianity, however, there was only one, true God. Consequently, the warrior who betrayed cowardice in trial by battle must have been perceived as less favoured by God than the more courageous victor. From there it followed logically that whoever lost the battle, whether or not he had betrayed cowardice, was also less favoured by God, and one could infer that God had rendered a judgment in favour of the victor. Tristram's message to Mark simply takes the primitive tribal religious attitude and applies it to the Christian God. If God does not give him sufficient courage to win this battle then he is not God's friend and does not deserve to be buried in God's holy ground.[7]

The early Christian church did not approve of this method of doing justice or settling quarrels between Christian nations, but was unable successfully to prohibit it. In the year 501 King Gundobald of the Goths used the Church's own teaching regarding divine providence to justify the practice. Replying to his bishop, he is alleged to have said,

> 'Is it not true that the event both of national wars and of private combats is directed by the judgment of God? And does not Providence award the victory to the juster cause?' (Neilson 6)

For seven centuries this argument prevailed and the Church was forced to tolerate, even to endorse, ritual trial by combat as a common judicial process. Malory never portrays the religious trappings which normally accompanied these trials: the night-long vigil before the altar on the part of both combatants, the prayers and masses said to elicit God's favour. But he does portray the fundamentally irrational, providentialist world view in his portraits of True knights like Ywain, Bors and Lancelot.

These knights take the judgment of God quite literally and believe that God will give not only the courage but also the strength necessary to win a trial by combat in a just cause, even if one's adversary is much bigger, stronger and more experienced. The young and untried Ywain does not hesitate to do battle 'for Goddis sake' and in the defence of the 'ryght' of the Lady of the Roche, even though he will have to fight two 'perelous' knights (177:IV.27). Malory has invented this episode, and he may also have invented or modified Gareth's battle with Ironsyde, reputed to have seven men's strength, in order to represent this radical providentialist view of trial by battle. Not surprisingly, it is also illustrated in the Tale of the Sankgreal in Bors' battle with the redoubtable Prydam le Noire (957–60:XVI.7–8). After the Quest we see it again in the willingness of both Bors and young Lavayne to meet much better knights than themselves in the lists, when Lancelot fails to appear, because they believe the queen to be innocent and are willing therefore to 'jouparté' their lives in her defense (1054:XVIII.6; 1137:XIX.9). Lancelot's own faith in the judgment of God is less easy to perceive because he has the reputation of being the best knight in the world. However, by the terms of his providentialist belief, no amount of strength and skill could protect him against the judgment of God if he were ever to fight in a 'wrongefull quarrel'. It is noteworthy that in Malory's text Lancelot is careful never to offend God in this way. On the other hand, he is twice guilty of 'tempting' God when he tries to induce both Pedivere and Mellygaunt to continue fighting for a judgment of God by disarming his head and his left side (see below 299–301).

The sort of irrational behaviour which Malory's Lancelot exemplifies on these two occasions provided the argument with which the Church finally put an end to its endorsement of judicial combat. The Fourth Lateran Council (1215) argued that to allow such unequal contests 'tempted' God by requiring Him to perform miracles in order that men should have justice (Caenegem 69). This was not only sinfully presumptuous but unnecessary, for by this time the feudal monarchies had devised rational alternative modes of doing justice, either by magisterial inquisition or by jury trial. Nevertheless, the feudal monarchies experienced difficulty in doing without trial by battle altogether and so it survived, despite the Church's prohibition, well into the fifteenth century. In fact, both France and England formally reinstituted a chivalric form of trial by battle in the mid-fourteenth century for certain types of crime and under carefully controlled conditions (see above 39–41).

In terms of the mental attitudes of the combatants and spectators, these late medieval duels of chivalry seem to have had as much, if not more, in common with the primitive *holmgang* than with the ritual trials by battle endorsed by the Church. Of course, the treason duel of chivalry was based upon the premise that God would 'spede the right', but at the same time the 'Ordenaunces' which regulated it forbade the wearing of talismans (317). In other words, the same men who presumed that God would 'spede the right' did not rule out the possibility of effective sorcery. Nor did they suspend their rational faculty. The 'Ordenaunces' also required that the field of battle be policed by sergeants and men-at-arms to ensure that the combatants did not carry concealed and illegal weapons (313) and to prevent their friends from interfering with the combat (321). Indeed, to judge from these 'Ordenaunces' drawn up by Richard II's constable, late medieval men regarded the treason duel of chivalry with a mixture of religious faith, primitive superstition and rational calculation of the odds. And that is precisely the way in which Malory's King Arthur and Tristram regard it.

In Arthur's kingdom trial by battle is the only mode of doing justice, and therefore King Arthur has forbidden his Round Table knights ever to do battle 'in a wrongefull quarrell for no love ne for no worldis goodis' (120.23–24:III.15). Nevertheless, when Arthur awakes one morning to find himself in prison and likely to die of starvation unless he agrees to fight for the 'wronge', he does not hesitate to do it. We must not conclude from this that Arthur has no faith that God will 'spede the ryght' (1051.3:XVIII.4); on the contrary, he may be depending upon it, inasmuch as his intention is to do justice. For, in fact, as soon as he has won the field he assumes his role as rightful judge and reverses the 'wrongefull' judgment of God produced by his victory. Nevertheless, to get that victory, Arthur has depended not only upon divine approval of his just intention; he has also depended upon his considerable strength and skill as a knight and, above all, upon the proven power of his sword, Excalibur, and its magical scabbard which protects him from loss of blood. Arthur is devoted to justice, but he is too much of a rationalist to depend solely upon God regardless of the circumstances. Furthermore, he is accustomed to presiding over trials by combat as 'vicar general undir God' ('Ordenaunce' 305), making sure that the champions are reasonably well matched, that they observe the rules of combat, and that the loser is punished as he deserves if he has not been killed by his opponent. Arthur would not 'tempt' God by allowing a champion to defend the right who was manifestly smaller and weaker than his opponent; but at the same time, he would not scruple to send in a more powerful champion, just as he would not scruple to use magic, in defense of the right.

Like Arthur, Tristram is also devoted to justice and uncertain to what extent God speeds the right in trials by battle. He never doubts the 'ryght' of Cornwall and tells Marhalt, 'I truste to God to be worshypfully proved upon thy body, and to delyver the contrey of Cownwayle for ever fro all maner of trewayge frome Irelonde for ever' (381.30–33: VIII.7). When it comes to defending King Anguishaunce of Ireland against a charge of treason, however, he is more cautious. He wants to be sure that Anguishaunce is in the right before he will fight for him. He makes the king 'swere' that he is in the right and that he was 'never consentynge to the knyghtis deth' (407.24–26). Tristram's concern with the king's innocence is original with Malory and suggests that Tristram shares King Arthur's uncertainty with regard to the role God plays in trial by battle. Tristram knows that he is probably more than a match for Blamoure, since he has already defeated his brother, Bleoberys; however, he is not willing deliberately to perpetrate an injustice, not even to gain the favour of the King of Ireland. He cannot be certain that God does not determine the outcome of trial by battle. (He would not be a medieval man if he could.) Therefore, having assured himself that he will be fighting in the right, he asks King Anguishaunce to give him a reward after he has done the battle, '*yf* God gyff me grace to spede' (407.28:VIII.21; emphasis added). Like Arthur, Tristram would never depend on God to perform a miracle in order to have justice, but he is prepared to accept that in any battle between two evenly matched knights, God will give the 'grace to spede' to the knight fighting in the right.

Even though they are devoted to justice, Tristram and Arthur are equally aware of the political implications of the judicial duel. Historically, the treason duel of chivalry played an important role in the ongoing effort of late medieval monarchs to control feuding among the nobility and, at the same time, to enlarge the sphere of their judicial competence. In the case of Tristram's duel with Blamoure, the defendant is no less a personage than the king of Ireland who has been ordered to appear before King Arthur's court 'uppon payne of forfeture of kyng Arthurs good grace' and the loss of 'his londys' (404.18–21: VIII.20). That Anguishaunce would submit to the judgment of Arthur's court is in itself a testament to his imperial power. No late medieval English monarch was nearly so powerful; in fact, Richard II seems to have had enough difficulty enforcing royal jurisdiction over his own magnates. Richard's last-minute refusal to allow the young Duke of Hereford to do battle with the Duke of Norfolk after appealing him of treason before Parliament in 1398 probably hastened his deposition; for, although both Hereford and Norfolk accepted Richard's sudden change of mind and went into exile, Hereford returned within a year to become Henry IV. It was common knowledge that some appeals of treason were in fact trumped-up charges, mere pretexts which would give the accuser a chance to have personal vengeance. But a king had to be careful. It was one thing to order the execution of a Portugese knight for a false appeal of treason, as Richard II did in 1384 (Neilson 177); it was quite another to presume to pass judgment upon the heir to the greatest dukedom in the land.[8] Malory's King Arthur displays greater political acumen. As we have seen, he does not hesitate to reverse the 'wrongefull' judgment of God which he himself has won against Accolon; but he makes no attempt to reverse the equally 'wrongefull' judgment of God won by King Mark against Mark's own knight, Sir Amaunte (592–93:X.14–15).

King Arthur does not personally preside over the trial of King Anguishaunce of Ireland but his deputies, King Carados and the King of Scots, açquit themselves well in his absence. They are able to do so thanks to the unparalleled courtesy of Ireland's champion, Sir Tristram. According to the rules which actually governed treason duels of chivalry in late medieval England, the king might 'take the quarell in his hande and make them accordid withoute more fightyng' at any time during the battle ('Ordenaunce' 325). In Malory's reconstruction of King Arthur's days this never happens. Even Arthur never presumes to stop a battle to make two parties 'accordid' before one of them has yielded to the other. This makes Tristram's behaviour vis-à-vis his felled opponent all the more remarkable. Although he has clearly lost the battle, Blamoure refuses, heroically, to yield. He is abiding by that primitive code of valour which says that nothing has been lost so long as one does not flee or yield 'recreaunte', and Tristram clearly admires his bravery. In these circumstances the only way Tristram can get a clear judgment of God — and the promised boon from the King of Ireland — is to kill Blamoure. Nevertheless, he chooses not to kill him. Instead he pleads with the judges 'for kynge Arthurs love and for sir Launcelottis sake, that they wolde take this mater in their hondis' (410.5–7:VIII.23) and, at the same time, he appeals to King Anguishaunce to 'have mercy uppon this knyght' (410.14:VIII.23). Anguishaunce is willing to be merciful, but Blamoure's brother Bleoberys, is willing to let his life be spared only so long as it is clearly understood that though Tristram has 'beatyn his body, he hath nat beatyn his harte, and thanke God he is nat shamed this day.' Indeed, Bleoberys is adamant on this point: 'rathir than he be shamed I requyre you,' seyde sir Bleoberys, 'lat sir Trystrames sle hym oute' (410.23–26:VIII.23).

The outcome of the trial by battle between Tristram and Blamoure is a triumph of courtly diplomacy. We do not know whether or not true justice has been done, but we do know that the honour of all parties has been saved. What is more, Blamoure and Tristram kiss and swear everlasting friendship and, Malory tells us, 'for that jantyll batayle all the bloode of sir Launcelott loved sir Trystrames for ever' (411.1–7:VIII.23). Had Tristram decided to kill Blamoure in order to ensure his judgment, the outcome would have been quite different. We know that Lancelot's kinsmen take seriously their duty to avenge the death of one of their family. They appealed the King of Ireland because their cousin had been murdered in his court and they held him responsible for that death. However, their appeal as well as their behaviour on the field of battle shows that they are Worshipful knights who accept the common law distinction between pardonable and unpardonable homicide. Murder is not pardonable. Malory tells us that it was called 'treson' in King Arthur's days (405.2–5:VIII.20) and in his own day it was also regarded as particularly 'heinous' — not so much because it was premeditated as because 'it caught a man off his guard' (Bellamy, *Crime* 53–54). Therefore the brothers feel justified in seeking vengeance upon the man responsible for their cousin's death. However, in seeking this vengeance, they are willing to abide by the Worshipful code of ethics; that is to say, they are willing to abide by the rules of judicial combat and to accept the judgment produced by that combat, even though they might lose. If their cousin had been killed accidentally or even deliberately in the course of a judicial combat, presumably they would not have sought vengeance against his slayer; for, according to the common law, manslaughter is pardonable homicide and killing one's opponent in judicial battle is more than pardonable, it is justifiable homicide (Squibb 24). By the same token, if Tristram had slain Blamoure (and he would have been forced to so if Bleoberys had refused to accept the judges' decision), the rest of Lancelot's kinsmen would not have proceeded against him. They might never have 'loved' Tristram, but neither could they honourably have sought vengeance upon him, for he would have committed no crime.

Not all knights in the *Morte Darthur* are either so honourable or so law-abiding. There are some who care nothing for the common law distinction between pardonable and unpardonable homicide, but demand a life for a life, regardless of the circumstance of the killing. At the end of the Tale of Gareth Malory told us us that Gawain was 'evir vengeable, and where he hated he wolde be avenged with murther' (360.34–35:VII.35). In the Tale of Tristram he shows us why Gawain is like that. Gawain is following a different code of ethics. As an Heroic knight his code is that of the clansman, his law the *lex talionis*. In order to preserve the honour of his family he must take a life for a life and, if necessary, he will not scruple as to means; as we shall see later in this chapter, Gawain is perfectly willing to violate both the Worshipful code of knighthood and the common law of England in order to have vengeance. The Orkney brothers (except for Gareth) are only the most prominent knights in the *Morte Darthur* to abide by this code; they are not the only ones. Balin, the Northumbrian knight, also lives by the code of the blood feud (see below, chapter 5.6ff) and so do many of the knights of Ireland.

Malory takes the opportunity provided by Tristram's first visit to Ireland to illustrate the difference between the Worshipful knight and the Heroic knight when it comes to justice for the death of a kinsman. Tristram goes to Ireland disguised as Tramtryste in order to be healed of the wound he received from the poisoned tip of Marhalt's spear. No one recognizes him as Marhalt's slayer until the queen accidentally discovers his sword with the piece missing, the piece which she recalls having extracted from her brother's 'braynepanne aftir that he was dede' (389.36–37:VIII.11). The reader knows that Tristram killed Marhalt 'knightly' in trial by battle, not 'shamefully' by treachery or stealth; therefore he knows that by the terms of the common law as well as by the Worshipful code of knighthood Tristram has committed no crime. However, by clan law and the standards of Heroic knighthood, Tristram is a 'traytoure' to Marhalt's family because he has killed their most illustrious member, the brother of the queen and the Champion of Ireland. The queen's initial response to the discovery of her brother's killer is typical of clan justice: she immediately tries to murder him with his own sword as he lies helpless in his bath. Fortunately her hand is stopped by Tristram's squire, Hebes, and she is forced to go to her husband to seek justice upon the 'traytoure'.

King Anguishaunce agrees to 'dele with hym', but after Tristram has told him 'all the trouthe' of the matter, the king is bound to agree that 'ye dud as a knyght sholde do and as hit was youre parte to do for your quarell, and to encrece your worshyp as a knyght sholde do' (391.18–20:VIII.12). This response confirms that Anguishaunce is a Worshipful knight. We already had reason to suspect as much when, even before he had heard Tristram's defense, the Irish king offered him safe conduct from his court because 'hit were no worship' to slay a man who had been his guest and a 'full noble knyght' at that (390.18, 28–30:VIII.11). A Worshipful king would do as much even for a man he believed to be guilty of murder, and Tristram is certainly not guilty of murder. Nevertheless, Anguishaunce cannot allow him to remain in Ireland:

> '... I may nat mayntayne you in this contrey with my worship but that I sholde displese many of my barownes and my wyff and my kynne.' (391.20–22:VIII.12)

We may read between the lines of this utterance that the King is not powerful enough to guarantee Tristram's life if he should remain. There are too many barons who, like the queen, would not scruple to murder him in order to avenge the honour of their family.

Before Tristram leaves Ireland, Malory invents a speech for him in which he defines the principles of the Worshipful knight with regard to honour and justice.

> 'Fayre lordys, now hit is so that I muste departe. If there be ony man here that I have offended unto, or that ony man be with me greved, lette hym complayne hym here afore me or that ever I departe, and I shall amende hit unto my power. And yf there be ony man that woll proffir me wronge other sey me wronge, other shame me behynde my backe, sey hit now or ellys never, and here is my body to make hit good, body ayenste body!' (392.21–28:VIII.12)

Tristram is certain that he has intentionally offended no man. However, if he has unintentionally offended any man, he is willing to make amends insofar as he is able. On the other hand, if any man thinks he has done 'wronge' Tristram is prepared to prove the contrary in trial by battle, 'body ayenste body'. He distinguishes between behaviour which may be personally offensive to one man or a group of men and behaviour which is criminally offensive, 'wronge' to society as a whole. The former he will amend if possible (and by implication apologize for); the latter he will defend himself against by means of duly constituted judicial process.

Tristram's categories make little or no sense to the barons of Ireland.

Those 'of sir Marhaltys blood' have a different way of understanding how he has injured them. In their view what he has done is at once greater than a personal affront and less than a crime against society as a whole. Or, perhaps it would be more accurate to say that Marhalt's kinsmen have no clear concept of either personal honour or social justice. Both honour and justice are defined for them by the family. In response to Tristram's speech 'there was not one that wolde sey one worde'. Even those of 'sir Marhaltys blood . . . wolde nat meddyll wyth hym' (392.29–32:VIII.12). No one is willing to accuse him openly of 'treason' presumably because no one is willing to face one of the best knights of the world in judicial combat. At the same time, they know he deserves to die for having killed their most illustrious kinsman. Their response is exactly like that of Gawain and his brethren after Pellinor has killed their father in battle. Pellinor was no more guilty of murder or treason on that occasion than Tristram is now. In fact, Lot was in rebellion against his liege lord, Arthur, when Pellinor killed him (77.8–16:II.10). Nevertheless, Gawain and all his brethren, except for Gareth, believe that Pellinor deserves to die for having killed their father. It is possible that Gawain is not willing to meet Pellinor in single combat; however, if Gawain had tried to accuse Pellinor of 'treson' Arthur could not in justice have allowed the charge. Therefore, Gawain and his brother Gaheris slay Pellinor 'shamefully . . . nat manly, but by treson' (810.11–13:XI.10; cf. 905.24:XIV.1 'thorow outerageousnes'). Later they will deal with his son, Lamorak, the third best knight in the world, in exactly the same way (see below 205–8).

The Worshipful knight differs from the Heroic knight not only in his notions of honour and justice. He has derived these more civilized notions from the experience of governance and social life in the late medieval court and, from that same milieu, he has simultaneously acquired certain courtly refinements and skills, such as the ability to carry on a conversation with a lady or to sing and dance. These social graces also sharply differentiate the Worshipful knight from the Heroic knight; however, in his portrait of Tristram, Malory suggests that they are less important to him than the more manly arts of hunting and hawking. Indeed, during the first part of his tale Tristram gives the impression of being the sort of man who prefers the company of men to the company of women. In one case, even though Tristram is speaking to 'a fayre lady', Malory invents a boasting speech for him which makes him sound very like the hero of a primitive epic:

> 'Wete you well, fayre lady,' seyde sir Trystrames, 'that I slew sir Marhalte and delyverde Cornwayle frome the trewage of

> Irelonde. And I am he that delyverde the kynge of Irelonde from sir Blamoure de Ganys, and I am he that bete sir Palomydes, and wete you welle that I am sir Trystrames de Lyones that by the grace of God shall delyver this wofull Ile of Servage.'
> (442.17–23:VIII.38; cf. 431.13–22:VIII.34)

Not until Tristram goes into exile with Isode at Joyous Garde do we ever see him in the company of ladies in a festive or courtly setting. And even there Tristram manages to go hunting every day (682–83: X.52; cf. 422.3–4:VIII.30). As for his skill in playing the harp and other musical instruments, that too is associated primarily with his legendary role as the founder of the art of venery (375.12–20:VIII.3; cf. 571.29–32: X.6). The only time Malory gives us a picture of Tristram 'as he sate harpynge afore hys lady, La Beall Isode' is when he tells us, much later, how Tristram was slain by King Mark (1149.28–31:XIX.11).

This heroic and manly bias in the representation of Tristram as a Worshipful knight has a considerable effect upon Malory's version of the love story of Tristram and Isode. By highlighting Tristram's feudal virtues and, in particular, his loyalty to his uncle and liege lord, Malory draws attention to a fundamental likeness between Tristram and Gawain, on the one hand, and between Tristram and Lancelot on the other. This likeness then serves to throw into relief the ways in which these three knights differ. Malory compares Tristram and Gawain mainly with regard to their differing notions of honour and justice, as we have just seen. On the other hand, Malory compares Tristram and Lancelot mainly with regard to their differing notions of honour and service to their respective ladies.

During the early part of his knightly career Tristram puts loyalty to his lord and uncle above all other loyalties, even after he has met and grown to love Isode. This represents a significant departure from Malory's source. The hero of the French prose *Tristan* betrays his lord by committing adultery with Isode as soon as he has drunk the love potion on board ship (448). Malory's Tristram does not consummate his love for Isode until after Mark has forfeited his loyalty by committing treason against him.[9] Malory's version of the story thus reinforces the importance of the fundamental political relationship between lord and man. Tristram is King Mark's best knight just as Lancelot is King Arthur's best knight. If a king cannot trust his best knight to be loyal then there can be no good governance. However, the corollary of this principle is equally true, as the story of Mark, Tristram and Isode makes clear: if knights cannot trust their king to be loyal, then good governance is likewise impossible.

In the beginning of the Tale of Tristram, Mark gives no sign of being a false or cowardly king, so Tristram has no reason not to be loyal to his uncle. Moreover, since Mark's first two attempts to do away with his nephew are both covert, the reader is aware of Mark's hatred and treachery long before Tristram is. Even more important, the reader understands what has happened to transform Mark's attitude towards his nephew. In Malory's version Mark's initial love and loyalty are suddenly changed into hatred and treason by sexual jealousy. Mark is passionately enamoured of the wife of one of his courtiers, Sir Seguarides, and he is enraged by her preference for his young nephew. He is so enraged, in fact, that he sets an ambush to kill Tristram on his way to visit the lady one night. Mark's attempt at murder is unsuccessful; however, as Malory assures us in a passage original with him,

> ... as longe as kynge Marke lyved he loved never aftir sir Trystramys. So aftir that, thoughe there were fayre speche, love was there none. (396.8–10:VIII.14)

In Malory's version of what happens next Tristram never does find out who attacked him that night. Therefore, he does not realize that Mark's decision to send him to Ireland to bring back Isode is simply another attempt to do away with him. He is aware of the danger to his life, given the hatred and vengefulness of Marhalt's kinsmen in Ireland; but, whereas his French counterpart cannot refuse to go because Mark has tricked him into making a rash promise before the entire court (*Tristan* 395–398), Tristram will not refuse 'for the pleasure of his uncle' whom he still mistakenly believes to love him (403.21:VIII.19). Nor should Tristram suspect any treachery on Mark's part from the nature of the diplomatic mission itself: to make the princess of Ireland queen of Cornwall, and in this way to make peace between the two kingdoms must appear to be an act of wise and responsible kingship.

Tristram's affair with Seguarides' wife is not simply a major turning point in the relationship between Tristram and his uncle, King Mark. In Malory's handling of the affair it also becomes a crucial indicator of the type of lover Tristram will be. In this respect, as in so many others, Tristram proves to be just like King Arthur. Tristram responds to Seguarides' wife in exactly the same way that Arthur responded to Margawse, the wife of King Lot. What is more, he engages in this illicit union after he has already met and grown to love Isode, just as Arthur bedded Margawse after he had met and grown to love Guinevere. The striking parallel is Malory's invention, created by altering his sources for both affairs, and the inference to be drawn from it is clear. Neither Tristram nor Arthur believes that, simply because he loves another woman whom he hopes to marry, he should not indulge in casual liasions with other willing and beautiful ladies.[10]

The sexual morality of these two Worshipful knights falls, then, somewhere in between that of Gareth, the True knight, and Gawain, the Heroic knight, just as we would expect it to. Gareth has sworn that if he is not allowed to wed his first love, Lyones, 'there shall never lady nother jantyllwoman rejoyse me' (360.3–5:VII.35). On the other hand, Gawain has not scrupled to insist that Ettarde keep her rash promise to help him 'gete' the love of his lady, regardless of her own desires in the matter (169.22–30:IV.23). Neither Arthur nor Tristram would ever 'enforce' a lady, not even in that comparatively gentle fashion; in fact, as we know, Arthur has decreed the death penalty for any knight of his who should commit so foul a deed (120.23:III.15). But just as they avoid that one extreme, sexual aggression towards women, so do they avoid the other extreme, sexual fidelity to one woman. Therefore, we must conclude that neither Tristram nor Arthur has the makings of a 'true' lover. At the same time, we cannot help but notice that they would have been much more fortunate in their lives if they could have been true to Guinevere and Isode, for their casual affairs bring disastrous consequences upon each of them: Tristram begets Mark's undying hatred and Arthur begets Mordred and both prove in the end to be fatal to their progenitors.

As a consequence of Mark's enmity, Tristram is denied the possibility of ever being able to marry his first love, Isode; however, in Malory's version it is not at all clear that he would have wished to marry her himself, at least not so soon. Malory makes a special point of Isode's love for Tristram ('for of all men erthely she loved hym moste' 411.16:VIII.23), but, as Vinaver has observed, he omits the 'corresponding remarks about Tristan' which he found in his source (*Works* 1462). Malory's Tristram has exchanged rings with Isode and agreed that she should marry no one without his permission during the next seven years, and he has also promised to be her knight 'all the dayes of [his] lyff' (392.12–19:VIII.12); but he appears to understand this promise in the same way that Lancelot understands his initial vow 'ever to be [Guinevere's] knyght in ryght othir in wronge' (1058.31–32: XVIII.7). In fact, Tristram first makes his promise to Isode's father, using Lancelot's formula:

> 'I promyse you, as I am trewe knyght, that in all placis I shall be my lady your doughtyrs servaunte and knyght in all ryght and in wronge, and I shall never fayle her to do as muche as a knyght may do.' (391.30–33:VIII.12)

Malory's Tristram is not so much in love with Isode as he is grateful to her (she did, after all, save his life) and determined to be her faithful servant. The sort of service he has in mind is suggested by the formulaic phrase 'in all ryght and in wronge': he is promising to be her champion in trial by battle, regardless of the 'ryght' or the 'wronge' of her case. Considerable irony results from both his and Lancelot's making such a promise for, not only by the religious standards of True knighthood but also by the more secular standards of Worshipful knighthood, a man ought never to make a promise which commits him even to the possibility of fighting against the right. We must interpret their willingness to make such a promise, I think, to the force of their gratitude and respect for their ladies' essential goodness: neither knight anticipates ever having to fight for the 'wronge' on his lady's behalf (see below 290–1).

Once Isode has married King Mark, Tristram's relationship to her becomes perfectly analogous to the relationship between Lancelot and Queen Guinevere. He is the queen's knight and champion and, what is even more significant for the analogy with Lancelot, he is not her paramour. Even though Tristram loves Isode much more passionately after having drunk the love potion intended for the bridal couple, he refrains from consummating their love out of loyalty to his lord and uncle. Malory achieves this perfect analogy between Tristram and Lancelot as lovers by omitting all the references he found in the *Tristan* to his carnal relations with Isode and by adding a passage which shows how much Tristram is like Lancelot in his preference for the adventurous life. Before the wedding of Mark and Isode Malory omits King Anguishaunce's prophetic dream, the consummation scene on board ship (412), and the three months' sojourn in Sir Brunor's castle (416). After the wedding he omits the substitution of Brangwyn for her lady on the wedding night (419) and Isode's part in the plot to murder Brangwyn (since now she has no motive for wishing her dead) as well as the lovers' two day sojourn in Sir Adtherpe's castle (423–26). At the same time Malory adds a passage in which Tristram says clearly, and this after he has drunk the love potion, that he would rather be with Lancelot having adventures than stuck with the task of delivering Isode to Mark:

> 'Alas!,' seyde sir Trystrames, 'and I had nat this messayge in hande with this fayre lady, truly I wolde never stynte or I had founde sir Launcelot.' (419.14–16:VIII.28)

Following this outburst Malory apparently thought he had better remind his readers, on the the occasion of Mark and Isode's wedding, that 'sir Trystrames and La Beale Isode loved ever togedyrs' (419.20–21:VIII.29); however, the only evidence of that love which he offers the reader for the present, is Tristram's rescue of the queen from Palomides.

Tristram's rescue of Isode is analogous to Lancelot's rescue of Guinevere from Mellyagaunt's castle. Indeed, the author of the French prose *Tristan* seems to have modeled the one upon the other, and assumed that Lancelot's rescue took place some two years previously (482). Malory places the 'Knight of the Cart' episode much later; nevertheless the analogy remains, confirmed by several striking similarities of situation and response: (1) both knights are absent when the abduction takes place; (2) both feel they have been 'shamed' by the event and are extremely angry, indeed, 'wrothe oute of mesure' (423.26:VIII.31; 1128.19:XIX.5); (3) both are prevented from fully expressing their anger in battle by the intervention of their queens; (4) finally, and most significantly for Malory's comparison of the two lovers, not long after this episode both knights consummate their love for the first time. Before Tristram and Isode become paramours, however, Isode sends the following message to Guinevere:

> '. . . recommaunde me unto quene Gwenyvere and tell her that I sende her worde that there be within this londe but four lovers, and that is sir Launcelot and dame Gwenyver, and sir Trystrames and quene Isode.' (425.27–31:VIII.3)

In the *Tristan* Isode explains what she means by going on to express the wish that she could 'faire jugement de nos deus biautez et de la bonté et de la valor de nos deus chevaliers' (511). Therefore, her claim 'qu'il n'a ou monde que deus dames et deus chevaliers' clearly means that they are peerless for their beauty and courtesy, and for their prowess and courage. She is not thinking of their loyalty, even to each other, and certainly not of their chastity, since she and Tristan have consummated their love many times before this. In Malory's version of her message, however, Isode gives no clue as to what qualities she is thinking of when she makes the claim that these four lovers are without peer. Therefore, the reader must look for clues in Malory's version of the two love stories thus far and, as soon as he does that, he will realize that the unspecified virtue which these lovers supremely exemplify is their loyal chastity. At this point in Malory's narrative, both pairs of lovers are still chaste and true, not only to each other, but also to God and to their temporal lords, Mark and Arthur. Isode may well be right to judge that there are no other lovers like them 'within this londe'.

Tristram and Isode remain true to Mark until he no longer deserves their loyalty, having tried to murder them both. First, Mark tries to kill Tristram when he finds him conversing privately with Isode 'in a wyndowe'. This is the sort of indiscreet behaviour which, indulged in by Lancelot and Guinevere after the Quest, will set tongues wagging at

Camelot. However, it is scarcely sufficient grounds for killing the best knight of the court as a 'false traytowre'. Mark himself is unable to kill Tristram and his barons refuse to do it for him (426: VIII.32). Peace is restored briefly, but then Mark tries to have his queen and all but four other ladies of his court burned at the stake as adulteresses because they have failed to pass the horn of chastity test devised by Morgan le Fay. Once again Mark's barons intervene. They absolutely refuse to allow the ladies to be 'brente for an horne made by sorsery that cam "frome the false sorseres and wycche moste that is now lyvyng" ... and ... an enemy to all trew lovers' (430.19–23:VIII.34). From then on, however, Tristram and Isode are no longer true to Mark. Malory tells us, 'than sir Trystrames used dayly and nyghtly to go to quene Isode evir whan he myght' (430.30–31:VIII.34).[11]

As soon as Tristram and Isode become paramours, Tristram is no longer just like Lancelot. Rather, the perfect likeness of their situations now points up this new contrast in their behaviour. What is equally important, that contrast is directly, even causally, related to the contrast in their liege lords' characters.[12] Malory's Mark is even less judicious and more vindictive than his French counterpart who has narrowly missed catching Tristan and Isode in his own bed, *in flagrante delicto,* before he first attempts to kill him. Malory's Mark has no such circumstantial evidence pointing to the lovers' guilt and yet he still would have killed them both if the barons had allowed it. By contrast, Malory's Arthur is a model of rationality and judicious behaviour. When Morgan le Fay and King Mark accuse his queen of betraying him with Lancelot, he dismisses their charges because he is aware of their malice and there is no evidence to support them (559:X.1; 617:X.27; see below 193–5).

The difference between Tristram and Lancelot as lovers is made even more apparent when Tristram is forced into exile for a long period of time and succumbs to the charms of Isode of the White Hands. Encouraged by her father and brother, he grows to love this lady 'bothe goode and fayre' until he has 'allmoste forsakyn La Beale Isode' (434.24–29:VIII.36). He remembers 'his olde lady, La Beale Isode' only when it comes time to go to bed on his wedding night, with the consequence that his bride discovers no more of the joys of marriage than 'clyppynge and kyssynge'. When Lancelot hears of this marriage he is furious with his friend for being so untrue to his first lady and love:

> 'Fye uppon hym, untrew knyght to his lady! That so noble a knyght as sir Trystrames is sholde be founde to his fyrst lady and love untrew, that is the quene of Cornwayle!' (435.11–13:VIII.36)

Tristram's letter to Lancelot in which he excuses himself on the grounds that 'as he was a trew knyght, he had never ado fleyshly with Isode le Blaunche Maynys' is Malory's invention (467.29–31:IX.5) and shows that Tristram has missed the point of Lancelot's criticism altogether. From the point of view of the True knight-lover, Tristram's betrayal consists in having loved and agreed to marry the other Isode in the first place. He cannot undo that betrayal by refusing to consummate the marriage he has made. Lancelot's words echo the words of Lyones, when she referred to Gareth as her 'fyrste love' and vowed that he should 'be the laste' (359–60:VII.35). To the True knight, love is a matter of the spirit as well as the body and endures until death; or, as Chaucer's turtle dove puts it, 'God forbede a lovere shulde chaunge!' (*Parlement of Foules* 582).

Tristram's notion of what it means to be faithful to one woman invites comparison once again with King Arthur. Arthur, too, comes very close to betraying Guinevere some time after their marriage. He allows the lady Aunowre to lure him into the Forest Perilous with 'fayre promyses and fayre behestis', but at the last moment, when she desires him 'to ly by her' Arthur remembers 'hys lady' and refuses to grant her desire 'for no crauffte that she cowde do' (490.18–19:IX.16). Like Tristram, Arthur thinks that he is being faithful to his lady so long as he does not actually have sexual intercourse with another woman. And even this degree of fidelity does not become important to either knight until after he has committed himself to a sexual relationship with his lady, either in marriage or in love paramours; for by their standards of sexual morality either of these two types of relationship may be honourable, depending upon the circumstances. Arthur first revealed his own standards when he asked Gareth 'whether he wolde have this lady [Lyones] as peramour, other ellys to have hir to his wyff' (359.25–27:VII.35). The very question itself implies that either choice would have been appropriate in their circumstances as far as he was concerned. Likewise, Tristram revealed his standards when he decided to take Isode 'as peramour' as soon as he could justify his action on the grounds of Mark's treachery. The point is that neither Tristram nor Arthur is chaste 'for drede of God' as Lancelot is; rather, they are chaste only for dread of shame. Where there is no fear of shame, there is no need for chastity. Throughout the realm of Logres King Mark is known to be 'the moste vylaunce knyght of the worlde' (592.13–14: X.14). Therefore, when Tristram and Isode decide to flee from him to live openly together in Arthur's kingdom, they are welcomed by that honourable society with open arms. Lancelot gives them his castle to live in and Arthur concludes that they are 'well besett togydir' (757.17: X.78). Indeed, no one but the saintly Percival seems at all shocked by their behaviour (679.22–28:X.51). However, Percival's refusal to believe that Tristram would 'do hymselff so grete vylany' as to 'holde his unclys wyff' (and Percival is certainly aware of Mark's reputation for villainy), serves to remind the reader that Tristram's conduct must be judged harshly by the religious standards of the True knight.

The Worshipful knight's standards of what constitutes chastity and fidelity in love are more rational than those of the True knight, just as his standards of what constitutes bravery and cowardice are more rational than those of both Heroic and True knights. That is because the Worshipful knight's ethics are consonant with the primary importance he attaches to making a successful political or military career in the world. Just as Arthur cannot afford to risk his life or the lives of his knights in needless acts of derring-do, so he cannot afford to value his queen more highly than those same knights through whom he is able to protect and govern his realm. In fact, Arthur's initial love for Guinevere seems to cool over time until near the end of his reign he can say,

> 'And much more I am soryar for my good knyghtes losse than for the losse of my fayre quene; for quenys I myght have inow, but such a felyship of good knyghtes shall never be togydirs in no company.'[13] (1184.1–4:XX.9)

On the other hand, Tristram's love for Isode seems to increase over time. As a young knight he clearly preferred adventures to being with her. But once they have settled down at Joyous Garde, she has to remind him of his duty to knighthood. When he refuses to attend the feast of Pentecost at Arthur's court (the same feast at which the Grail will appear) because she will not accompany him, Isode exclaims,

> 'God deffende . . . for than shall I be spokyn of shame amonge all quenys and ladyes of astate; for ye that ar called one of the nobelyste knyghtys of the worlde and a knyght of the Rounde Table, how may ye be myssed at the feste? For what shall be sayde of you amonge all knyghtes? "A! se how sir Trystram huntyth and hawkyth, and cowryth wythin a castell wyth hys lady, and forsakyth us" . . . Also, what shall quenys and ladyes say of me? "Hyt ys pyté that I have my lyff, that I wolde holde so noble a knyght as ye ar frome hys worshyp".'
> (839.29–840.5:XII.11)

Tristram responds by thanking her and saying, 'now I well undirstonde that ye love me.' Isode has just reminded him of an important maxim of Worshipful knighthood: in the words of Christine de Pizan, the knight must love his lady 'As resoun requireth, nott owt off mesure.' By this Christine means he should not love his lady so much that he becomes 'feynt' in the exercise of arms, nor so much that he impairs 'hys good name & þe noblenes of hys fame' (*Epistle* 76–77). Isode adds to this that the knight who 'cowryth wythin a castell wyth hys lady' and forsakes arms and knightly fellowship incurs shame not only for himself, but also for his lady.

Tristram incurred such shame in Lancelot's eyes when he preferred to remain in Cornwall with Isode rather than accompany Arthur on the Roman campaign (195.8–10:V.3). In the Tale of Tristram Malory explains why Tristram made that decision: 'all was for the entente to see La Beale Isoud, for without the syghte of her syr Tristram myght not endure' (610.18–20:X.22). However, even though Tristram's love for Isode serves to diminish his usefulness to King Arthur, his presence in Cornwall proves to be extraordinarily useful to King Mark when the Saxons invade under the leadership of Sir Elyas, 'a good man of armys'. Mark is loth to ask for Tristram's help 'for he hated hym dedly' but his barons insist that he send for his best knight. Malory's representation of Tristram's words and actions in this episode beautifully summarizes the ethos of Worshipful knighthood.

Tristram is not present in Mark's court when the Saxons invade, and his absence on this occasion recalls his absence on that former occasion when Mark had need of him because Palomides had abducted Isode. That time he was off hunting (422:VIII.30); this time he has gone off to participate in a joust and tournament. Both occasions suggest that the Worshipful knight's pursuit of pleasure and honour as ends in themselves may diminish his usefulness to his temporal lord. Of course the Worshipful knight would respond to this criticism by arguing that both tournament and hunt are necessary to the maintenance of his horsemanship and skill in arms during peace time. That argument might be sufficient if his occasional absence were all that his lord had to contend with. However, even after Tristram has responded to Mark's call for help, he is unable to do anything for eight days because he must first recover from the wounds he has received in the tournament. While he is recovering, King Mark meets the enemy in a pitched battle which ends in a rout and he and the remnant of his army are forced to take refuge in the Castle of Tintagel. However, Mark's defeat makes Tristram's subsequent victories all the more remarkable. First Tristram proves himself as a leader of men when he takes command of Mark's army as it sallies forth from Tintagel to engage the Saxons. Then, after routing the Saxon army, he once more proves his greatness in single combat when he answers Elyas' challenge to fight for the 'trewayge of Cornwayle'.

When Mark asks Tristram to undertake the judicial combat with Eylas, Malory invents a reply for Tristram which summarizes the Worshipful knight's attitude towards the service of his feudal lord:

> 'Sir,' seyde sir Trystram, 'now I undirstonde ye wolde have my succour, and reson wolde that I sholde do all that lyyth in me to do, savynge my worshyp and my lyff, howbehit that I am sore brused and hurte.' (624.5–8:X.30)

The key word is 'reson'. The Worshipful knight does not act imprudently. He rather thinks first, giving special consideration to the likely effects of his action upon his 'worshyp' and his 'lyff'.

Tristram's judicial battle with Elyas is a re-enactment of his first great judicial battle with one significant exception: when Tristram fought Marhalt for the 'trewayge of Cornwayle' there were no ladies present. There is no mention in Malory's source of ladies being present at Tristan's battle with Elyas either (Löseth 278); therefore, Malory's reference to the effect which Isode's presence has upon Tristram is probably intended to call the reader's attention to a likeness between Tristram and Gareth. When Gareth did battle with Ironsyde, the sight of his lady, Lyones, made his heart 'lyght and joly'; and when it seemed he must surely lose the fight, her tears and shrieks had an even greater effect, causing him to leap to his feet and 'dowble his pace unto the Rede Knyght' (324.18–19:VII.17). Likewise, in Malory's version of Tristram's battle with Elyas, the thought of his lady 'that loked uppon hym, and how he was never lykly to com in hir presence' galvanizes Tristram into action when it looks as though he must lose and causes him to pull up his shield and give Elyas 'many sad strokys, twenty ayenst one' (625.31–32:X.30). In both cases one could argue, on the basis of Malory's description of the battle, that without the presence of their ladies Gareth and Tristram might well have lost. This, then, is the positive side of the coin of courtly service to ladies. If sometimes a knight's devotion to a particular lady can interfere with his service to his temporal lord, it is also true that sometimes a knight's devotion to a particular lady can make the difference between victory and defeat in a battle of crucial importance to his temporal lord.

Tristram is a knight who possesses the basic feudal virtues in superlative fashion; however, he differs from both Gawain and Lancelot in his expression of those virtues. He differs from them in the same way that Arthur does. Even though Arthur is a prince and Tristram is a knight and courtier, they are both Worshipful knights who modify their expression of the basic feudal virtues — courage, prowess and loyalty — to accord with their ambition and their prudence. In other words, they are rational men who avoid taking unnecessary risks that would threaten either life or honour. In brief, they are men of the world. Their primary objective is to make a successful career in the world, the one as a prince, the other as the servant of a prince, and in both cases this means that they may sometimes be disloyal to those to whom they are bound by feudal ties.

Arthur is disloyal to his knights and barons when he commands them to send him their sons born on May Day and then puts all the babes 'in a shyppe to the se'. He does this because Merlin has told him that 'he that sholde destroy hym and all the londe sholde be borne on May-day' and Arthur can think of no other way to save himself and his realm; nevertheless, Malory chooses to heighten the gravity of what Arthur has done by telling us that all the children were killed, except, ironically, for Mordred (55.26–30:I.27). Of course, 'many lordys and borownes of thys realme were displeased' thus to lose their children, but some blamed Merlin more than Arthur, and 'what for drede and for love', they all let it pass. Arthur murdered the children born on May Day for what later political theorists would call 'la raison d'Etat' and Malory diverges from his source to suggest that Arthur's knights and barons were willing to put up with his action for the same reason ('what for drede and for love'). They may not have been aware of Merlin's prophecy, but they were not willing to rebel against Arthur for this singular act of cruelty since in every other way he was such an excellent prince and had become exceedingly powerful as well.

There is nothing in Tristram's career to match this instance of feudal disloyalty on Arthur's part because Tristram never exercises princely power. However, there is another instance of disloyalty in Arthur's career which is perfectly paralleled in that of Tristram: Arthur commits adultery with the wife of one of his vassals and Tristram commits adultery with the wife of his feudal lord. Of course princes were in the habit of pleasing themselves with the wives of their vassals so long as they had sufficient power to get away with it: Arthur owes his very existence to King Uther's desire for the wife of the Duke of Cornwall. And Arthur himself does not hesitate to satisfy his desire for the beautiful wife of King Lott of Orkney (not knowing, of course, that she is his own half-sister). Nevertheless, in terms of feudal law, he thereby commits the same crime committed by Tristram when he consummates his love for Isode, the wife of King Mark. Feudal law was based on the reciprocal obligation of lord and vassal: it was treason to commit adultery with the wife of one's lord, and it was no less treason to commit adultery with the wife of one's vassal (Dessau 194). Neither

Arthur nor Tristram seems to feel that he has committed any crime, however; nor does Arthurian society as a whole condemn them for their actions. This is because in both cases they can justify themselves in terms of that same feudal law. At the time Arthur lay with Margawse, her husband King Lott was in open rebellion against him. And by the time Tristram lay with Isode, her husband King Mark had likewise forfeited his right to feudal loyalty by trying to murder them both.

Arthur and Tristram seem to have reasoned that they had nothing to lose by violating feudal law in these instances and Malory himself never openly criticizes their actions. However, Percival condemns Tristram's 'grete vylany' (679.25:X.51) and Malory shows that Arthur's equally 'grete vylany' is severely punished, not only by the birth and survival of Mordred — which for him was an historical 'fact' — but also by the continued rebellion of King Lott. Malory suggests that in making King Lott a cuckold Arthur was guilty of a grave political error. First, he diverges from his source to praise the bravery and leadership capabilities of the northern king and to suggest that if he and his comrades 'were longyng' to Arthur 'there were no kynge undir hevyn that had suche eleven kyngis nother off suche worship' (35.1–2:I.16). Then he diverges from his source again to explain to his readers why Lott continued in his rebellion against King Arthur, even after the Battle of Bedgrayne:

> And for because that kynge Arthure lay by hys wyff and gate on her sir Mordred, therefore kynge Lott helde ever agaynst Arthure. (77.5–7:II.10)

With this passage Malory not only shows his awareness of the reciprocal nature of the feudal law of treason,[14] he also suggests that King Lott might have accepted the judgment of God in Arthur's favour at the Battle of Bedgrayne if Arthur had not forfeited his right to feudal loyalty by dishonouring his wife. Arthur may justify his slaughter of the innocents born on May Day by 'la raison d'Etat', but he cannot so justify the episode which made that slaughter 'necessary'. Therefore, it is of particular significance that Malory should deviate from his source to make the first crime, the adultery, and not the second, the mass murder, the reason for which King Lott continued to rebel against Arthur.

When it comes to the primary feudal virtue of loyalty to one's lord or vassal, then, the Worshipful knight allows some exceptions on rational grounds. These grounds are limited by the feudal law and by his own code of ethics, but within those limits he feels free to act prudently with regard to his personal well-being. By contrast, both Gawain and

Lancelot are loyal to Arthur beyond the bounds of reason. Gawain remains loyal to Arthur even though Arthur has refused to take his advice against burning the queen at the stake and even though, as a consequence of that decision, Gawain's favorite brothers, Gaheris and Gareth are killed. Lancelot remains loyal to Arthur even though Arthur has refused to give him his day of justice when he was accused of committing adultery with the queen, even though Arthur has sent him into exile after the Pope commanded him to be reconciled, and even though Arthur then brought an army into France to pillage and lay waste his lands and lay seige to his castle at Benwick. This difference in their attitude towards being loyal to their temporal lord may be explained by the fact that for both Gawain and Lancelot loyalty to Arthur is subsumed under a more fundamental loyalty. Gawain's loyalty to Arthur is subsumed under his loyalty to his clan. Lancelot's loyalty to Arthur is subsumed under his loyalty to God and the High Order of Knighthood. On the other hand, Tristram's loyalty to Mark is not subsumed under any more fundamental or sacred loyalty for, when King Mark gives him good reason, Tristram no longer feels obliged to be loyal, even though Mark is his uncle (his mother's brother and therefore his nearest and dearest kinsman) and also the man who made him knight.

Tristram's loyalty to his lady, Isode, is not absolute, either, as we have seen. He is like Arthur in this respect also. And there is yet another way in which these two knights are comparable as lovers: neither has to compete for the love of his lady. Arthur can lay claim to his lady's love as her husband, and Tristram in fact possesses his lady's love as a kind of surrogate husband, having exchanged rings with her and then drunk the love potion intended for Mark. Neither Arthur nor Tristram feels that he must prove his worthiness to be loved in the way that other Worshipful knights do. Therefore, when it comes to the more courtly aspects of Worshipful knighthood, Tristram is not Malory's chief exemplar.

Lovers and Knights-Errant: Lancelot and Palomides

The association of chivalry and love was conventional in late medieval literature, not only in the French romances, but also in the English chronicles. John Hardying follows the line adopted from Geoffrey of Monmouth by both Layamon and Wace when he says of the knights in King Arthur's court,

Ther was no knight accompted of honoure
But if he wer in warre approued thrise,
Nor with ladies beloued as paramoure;
Whiche caused knightes armes to exercyse,
To be vertuous, and cleane of life and wise;
It comforte also ladies and theyr femynitee,
To lyue the more in perfite chastitee. (130)

Hardyng also follows Geoffrey, Layamon and Wace when he assumes that this chivalrous love was virtuous, serving the dual purpose of making the ladies more chaste and the men more keen to 'exercyse' themselves in arms. On the other hand, French romances, including Chrétien's *Erec* as well as the works which celebrated the loves of Lancelot and Tristan, portray the opposite truth: that knights in love are also likely to neglect the exercise of arms in favour of the delights of love. We may suspect more than a touch of chauvinism, therefore, when John Lydgate deviates from his encyclopedic French source to assert that in King Arthur's days knights could love 'paramours' / . . . / Nat but for trouthe and honeste / and hemself to magnyfye' and ladies were 'so feythful & so stable' that 'the knot never was vnknet' once they had decided to love a knight for his 'trouth and worthynesse' (*Reson and Sensuallyte* 3180–3204).

It is Lancelot and not Tristram who exemplifies this chaste ideal of chivalrous love in the *Morte Darthur*, for as soon as Tristram becomes Isode's paramour he disqualifies himself. Tristram degrades himself even further as a chivalrous lover when he allows devotion to Isode to take priority over service to Arthur and chooses to remain in Cornwall 'for the love of La Beale Isode' rather than accompany Arthur on the Roman campaign, making Lancelot 'passyng wrothe' (195.8–10: V.3). This passage is original with Malory and calls dramatic attention to the contrast between Tristram and Lancelot in this regard. Whatever Lancelot's feelings for the queen at this juncture — and Malory tells us nothing about them — they are not such as to keep him away from his lord's war.[15]

Some part of Lancelot's eagerness to accompany Arthur on the Roman campaign may have stemmed from a desire to make himself better loved by the queen. If so, he is successful, for Malory tells us that after the Roman war the queen held Lancelot 'in grete favoure aboven all other knyghtis' because of his great prowess and worship. He also tells us that Lancelot 'loved the quene agayne aboven all other ladyes dayes of his lyff' (253.8–18:VI.1). At the same time, however, his representation of young Lancelot as pious and ascetically inclined, eschewing love 'peramours' for 'drede of God', makes clear that

Lancelot's love for the queen is still chastely in accordance with Lydgate's idealized notion of love in King Arthur's days.

In the Tale of Tristram, Lancelot succumbs to the 'maystry' of love. As a consequence, his desire to win worship in arms for his lady's sake becomes greater than his desire to serve God and he falls from the standards of True knighthood. By those standards he now becomes guilty of *cupiditas*, of loving 'oute of mesure' (i.e. more than God) one of God's creatures. On the other hand, so long as he does not betray his honourable lord by committing adultery, Lancelot's love remains well within the bounds of moderation by the standards of Worshipful knighthood.

Malory portrays Lancelot's transformation from True to Worshipful knight by means of a gradual change in his behaviour as a knight-errant and in tournaments. The pious youth of the Tale of Lancelot never challenged other errant knights to win worship. Rather he went out to seek 'stronge adventures' as a means of testing himself and serving others. He did not participate much in tournaments either. He agreed to help King Bagdemagus in order to gain release from Morgan Le Fay's prison, but he refused to joust at the Assumption Day tournament in the Tale of Gareth, even though Arthur asked him to. In sum, as an exemplar of True knighthood Lancelot did not indulge in knightly games in order to win worship, either as an end in itself or as a means to make himself better loved by the queen.

Early in the Tale of Tristram, there is no sign of any change in Lancelot. He makes a brief appearance in 'Lamerok de Galys' but unlike his French counterpart he refuses to joust when challenged, 'for I have no luste to jape nother juste' (448.26–27:VIII.40; cf. Löseth 64) and later he explains to Lamorak that he is in 'a queste' which he 'muste do . . . alone' (449.8–9:VIII.40). He makes a more extended appearance in 'La Cote Male Tayle' where he becomes the guide and protector of the Fair Unknown. Having heard that the new-made knight has taken upon himself 'the hardyest adventure of the worlde' (467.4:IX.5), Lancelot immediately sets off to help him. The relationship which develops between them is reminiscent of Lancelot's earlier relationsip with Gareth, and the parallel is strengthened when Malory concludes the tale with La Cote's marriage. Throughout 'La Cote Male Tayle' Lancelot continues to exhibit those qualities which characterized him as a True knight. He is pious, merciful and just. He tells the damsel Maledysaunte that he has followed the young man 'for hys sake and pité, that he sholde nat be destroyed' (471.15–15:IX.7). He sends La Cote off to joust first at the castle of Sir Plenoryous, saying 'Jesu be youre spede!' (472.12–13:IX.7). And, near the end of their adventure, he turns out Sir Bryan de les Iles from his castle of Pendragon because he has refused to hold it of Arthur and gives the castle and lands to La Cote Male Tayle instead (476.1–5:IX.9). As a judicial decision this is the obverse of the one made in the Tale of Lancelot when he restored the giants' castle to its rightful owner, and it suggests even more strongly that, on his adventures, Lancelot still acts in the stead of King Arthur himself.

In the next section, 'Tristram's Madness and Exile', Malory gives the reader the first hint that Lancelot's feelings for the queen may have grown stronger than they were in the Tale of Lancelot. When Lancelot and Bleoberis come upon Lamorak and Mellyagaunt fighting in the forest to prove whose lady is 'fayryst', Margawse or Guinevere, Lancelot is furious that any knight of the Round Table should 'disprayse' the 'prynces that thou arte undir obeysaunce and we all.' He alights from his horse and offers to prove upon Lamorak's body that 'quene Guenyver ys the fayryst lady and most of bounté in the world' (487.5–8:IX.14). In Malory's source for this scene Mellyagaunt and Lamorak know that Lancelot is the queen's paramour and therefore do not dare tell him the cause of their fight for fear he will kill Mellyagaunt 'tantost'. Malory's Lancelot pays no attention to Mellyagaunt; rather, he is outraged by Lamorak's behaviour. The point of Malory's alteration seems to be to focus on the political foundation of Lancelot's feelings. Queen Guinevere is renouned for her generosity (her 'bounté') towards her own knights. Indeed, she has been so 'large and fre of hir goodis to all good knyghtes' that she is known as 'the moste bownteuous lady of hir gyfftis and her good grace' now living (1054.9–11:XVIII.5). Nevertheless, Lancelot's anger still seems immoderate if we accept that Lamorak's apparent political disloyalty is its only cause. Certainly Lamorak assumes there is more to it than that when he shifts the grounds of the argument from feudal loyalty to physical beauty as he tries to talk Lancelot out of fighting.

> '. . . and thoughe I prayse the lady that I love moste, ye sholde nat be wrothe. For thoughe my lady quene Gwenyver be fayryst in youre eye, wyte you well quene Morgause of Orkeney ys fayryst in myne eye, and so every knyght thynkith his owne lady fayryste.' (487.11–15:IX.14)

Lamorak was perfectly willing to fight with Mellyagaunt to prove his own lady 'fayryst', but he does not want to fight Lancelot, the best knight in the world and a man he reveres, particularly when he can see how angry he is. Bleoberis agrees with him:

'My lorde, sir Launcelot, I wyste you never so mysseadvysed as ye be at thys tyme, for sir Lamerok seyth to you but reson and knyghtly. For I warne you, I have a lady, and methynkith that she ys the fayryst lady of the worlde. Were thys a grete reson that ye sholde be wrothe with me for such language?' (487.20–25:IX.14)

Bleoberis also speaks 'but reson and knyghtly' and Lancelot is quick to acknowledge his fault and to ask forgiveness for his anger. Nevertheless, the point has been made. Lancelot may not yet be so emotionally involved with Guinevere as to perceive in Mellyagaunt a hateful rival, but he is sufficiently involved to be outraged that any man should deny she is the most beautiful woman in the world. And, as a consequence, he is beginning to act like a Worshipful knight-errant. This is the first time he has ever challenged another knight to do battle without 'grete reson'.

Vinaver assumes that Malory was 'unconscious' of the implications of Lamorak's and Bleoberis' argument, since, if used consistently, it would have 'destroyed the whole fabric of courtly chivalry' (*Works* 1470). But it seems clear to me that Malory was not interested in preserving the fabric of French 'courtly chivalry', — not whole, at any rate. In this scene he appears to have been interested in achieving two ends: to show the very beginnings of the change in Lancelot's attitude toward the queen and to illustrate the sort of rational and honourable conduct which ought to be characteristic of Worshipful knights-errant.

As we have seen in the first chapter, Malory justifies the knight-errantry of the Round Table fellowship by the personal and individual wrongs they are able to right. In so doing he is following the tradition established by fourteenth-century English romances in which the 'knight was conceived as by nature a righter of wrongs, a "justicier" ' (Mathew 120). In the preceding two tales Malory has shown Lancelot and Gareth performing judicial acts which suggest the functioning of fifteenth-century royal commissions, justices of the peace, and sheriffs. Now, in the Tale of Tristram he spells out the rules of conduct appropriate to knights engaged in such activities. In other words, he makes explicit what was implicit in the actions of Lancelot and Gareth. This spelling out of the rules is more necessary for Worshipful knights-errant because, given their great desire to win worship, they are more likely to forget the primary importance of their judicial and peace-keeping functions.

The knight who plays the most important part in spelling out the code for Round Table knights-errant is Dinadan. In the French prose *Tristan*, Dinadan is a great critic of the follies of knight-errantry, so much so, in fact, that his cynicism seems to undermine the enterprise altogether. Not so Malory's Dinadan. Malory has retained only that part of the French Dinadan's 'practical realism' with which he could agree (Ferguson 48). The rest — the lengthy and cynical diatribes and the off-colour jokes — he has omitted. The consequence is that his Dinadan is not a sardonic scoffer. Rather he is a moral humorist, beloved of all good knights, because not only does he wittily censure the follies of others, he also exemplifies in his own conduct the virtues which they lack.

To the ordinary rules of fair play (e.g. fighting only one-on-one, never slaying a horse or hitting a man when he is down), Malory's Dinadan adds two basic rules of conduct for the Worshipful knight-errant. The first is never to challenge or accept a challenge from a vastly superior knight (see above 69–70). This rule also forbids fighting against great odds for trivial reasons, such as whose lady is 'fayryst', as we have seen both Lamorak and Bleoberis argue in the scene just discussed. Dinadan expresses this rule most forcefully in a scene in which King Mark insists on challenging Lamorak to continue their battle on foot after he has already taken a fall on horseback. Afterwards, when Mark tries to imply that Dinadan is a coward for having refused to joust with Lamorak, Dinadan berates him for his folly:

> 'Thynke ye that a shame?' seyde sir Dynadan. 'Nay, sir, hit is ever worshyp to a knyght to refuse that thynge that he may nat attayne. Therefore your worshyp had bene muche more to have refused hym as I ded, for I warne you playnly he is able to beate suche fyve as ye ar and I be.' (581.24–28:X.8)

Dinadan is not advocating cowardice in this passage; rather, like King Arthur, he is arguing that it is never dishonourable to behave with ordinary prudence. In fact, he is going farther than either Arthur or Tristram to argue that it is positively honourable to behave with ordinary prudence.

The reason for his so arguing may be inferred from his own behaviour. Dinadan's actions indicate that if there is 'grete reson' to fight a superior knight, or even more than one knight at a time, then a Worshipful knight should be willing to 'jouparté' his body for that 'reson'. That is why, on the one hand, Dinadan can berate Tristram for his folly in being willing to joust for lodging and, on the other, give him support in taking on thirty knights who have set up an ambush for Lancelot (505–8:IX.23–24). Later, for love of Tristram, Dinadan will offer to fight Palomides, the fourth best knight in the world (532:IX.34); will rescue a lady from Sir Breunys saunz Pité 'bycause of honoure of all women' (553.15–16:IX.41); and, with rather more reluctance, will take on Sir Breunys again in order to save Aggravayne's life (614:X.25). Dinadan's prowess is not nearly so great as that of the four best knights in the world, and yet it is great enough to account for eight of those thirty knights whom he and Tristram encounter together and great enough to defeat the 'perelous' sir Breunys on two separate occasions. We may infer from this list of deeds that the reason for Dinadan's prudent refusals to engage in risky encounters for foolish reasons (or for no reason at all except to win worship) is that he does not want to waste his knightly abilites in that way and so risk not being able to use them when there is need.

The second rule which Malory's Dinadan lays down for the Worshipful knight-errant is never to fight in anger. This rule, too, may be abrogated but only for 'grete reson'. Knights who fight in anger are much more likely to do serious hurt to one another. Therefore, the ordinary sort of knightly encounters which take place in joust or tournament, and occasionally between knights-errant as well, ought to be fought in the spirit of fellowship. It is, after all, only a game to test for prowess. Nevertheless, Dinadan himself seems to be the only one among the lesser Worshipful knights who invariably remembers this and never envies a better knight for his prowess. In fact, in Malory's version, it is well known that Dinadan loves and is loved by 'all good knyghtes' who are 'valyaunte' (614.28–29:X.25). Once, on his way back to Camelot, Dinadan is challenged by a knight and he replies by asking whether the knight wishes to joust 'of love othir of hate?' When the knight responds, 'Wyte you well I aske hit for loove and nat of hate,' Dinadan cannot resist making a joke about the sort of 'harde love' he might proffer with 'an harde speare!' Yet, he offers to joust with him later in the court of Arthur (604.33–605.6:X.20). Again, on his way to the tournament at Lonezep, Dinadan loses a joust to an unknown knight and suggests that they continue the battle on foot. The unknown knight (Gareth) asks 'whether in love other in wrathe?' and Dinadan replies, 'Sir, lat us do batayle in love' (696.5–6: X.57). This time Dinadan does not make a joke about 'hard love' nor does Gareth laugh, for there is nothing inherently funny in the idea that one knight might do battle 'in love' with another, simply to test his prowess. Gareth has done battle like that with Lancelot and enjoyed himself hugely, confiding to his mentor, 'hit doth me good to fele your myght' (299.8–9:VII.4). However, when Gareth and Dinadan discover each other's identity, they prefer to talk rather than fight. They are, after all, both close friends of Lancelot: Gareth is his protegé and Dinadan is his most intimate friend at court.[16]

One of the reasons that Dinadan is able to avoid the hateful rivalries of other Worshipful knights is that he never fights to make himself better loved of a lady. In fact, he pretends to have no use for love at all on the grounds that 'the joy of love is to shorte, and the sorow thereof and what cometh thereof is duras over longe' (693.33–35:X.56). The ensuing dialogue with Isode makes clear that the 'duras' he has in mind is not the sorrow of unrequited love but rather the hardship of constantly having either to 'prove' in battle that your lady is 'fayryst' or to defend your right to love her at all. (Knightly battles fought for such foolish reasons are inherently more likely to be fought in anger, as well, as we have seen above in the confrontation between Lancelot and Lamorak.) Throughout the first half of the Tale of Tristram, Palomides is the main example of a knight who undertakes deeds of arms chiefly to make himself loved of his lady, Isode. His cause is hopeless, for Isode already loves another and better knight; and yet, Palomides can neither stop loving her nor stop trying to make himself worthy of her love by winning greater worship than Tristram already has.

When Lancelot first enters the competition for worship in order to make himself worthy of Guinevere's love, his situation is not unlike that of Palomides in that he loves a queen who already loves another. However, the differences in their situations are much more significant. First, Palomides' lady, Isode, freely chose to love Tristram whereas we have no reason to suppose that Lancelot's lady, Guinevere, freely chose to marry Arthur. Royal princesses were expected to marry according to the aims of their fathers' diplomacy, not according to their own hearts' desire.[17] Therefore, assuming that she did not choose her marriage (any more than Isode chose to marry Mark), Lancelot's lady, Guinevere, is still free to love some other knight for his worthiness, and Lancelot's cause is not so hopeless as that of Palomides. Secondly, Lancelot is not the same sort of knight as Palomides. Lancelot is a True knight, devoted to chastity, when he begins his endeavour to make himself better 'beloved' of the queen. By contrast, Palomides seems to be a Heroic knight. Certainly he behaves very much like Gawain in the means he initially employs to get Isode's love. He manoeuvres her into making a rash promise and then he holds her to it, even in the presence of her husband, King Mark, who lets her go because he knows Tristram will win her back. In Malory's version of the subsequent battle between Tristram and Palomides, Isode intervenes to save Palomides' life saying, 'I wolde be loth that he sholde dye a Sarezen' (425.12–13: VIII.31) and then commands the 'unhappy Sarezen' to leave Cornwall and go to the court of Arthur. Palomides' obedience to his lady's commandment marks the beginning of his education in the noble way of the world. He never again tries to abduct his lady against her will; rather, he tries to persuade her that he is worthy of her love by winning as much worship as he can. Therefore, at the outset we can see that Palomides' quest to win the love of Isode is likely to make him a better knight, whereas Lancelot's quest to win the love of Guinevere is likely to make him a lesser knight than he has been.

Lancelot shows that he has abandoned the humility of True knighthood when he first exercises his prowess simply to win worship. He does this at the Castle of Maidens where, on the eve of the great tournament, we see him issue a challenge to joust for the first time in his knightly career:

> And there com in sir Launcelot de Lake with a shylde of the armys of Cornwayle, and he sente a squyer unto sir Bryaunte and requyred hym to juste with hym. (516.18–20:IX.28)

It is significant that Queen Guinevere is expected to be present at this great tournament. It is equally significant that Lancelot has chosen to disguise himself by bearing the arms of Cornwall. We may infer that he and his kinsmen have done this to honour Tristram, who recently defeated the thirty knights Morgan le Fay had 'ordayned' to kill Lancelot (504–9:IX.23–25). However, bearing the Cornish arms in honour of Tristram also suggests adopting Tristram's standards of behaviour. Tristram entered his first tournament at Isode's request in the expectation that thereby she would become his 'bettir lady' (386.4:VIII.9). We do not know whether or not Guinevere asked Lancelot to enter the Castle of Maidens tournament; it is more than likely, however, that he has chosen to enter this tournament in order to please her, knowing that she will be present.

Lancelot is not able to participate in the tournament on the first day because he has been badly wounded by twelve knights from North Wales. The Welshmen set upon him the night before as he was reposing himself because they wanted to make sure 'that upon the morne at the turnement at the Castell of Maydyns that he sholde nat wyn the victory' (518.9–10:IX.29). Thus, even before the tournament begins, Lancelot experiences for the first time in his career two of the most common consequences of behaving like a Worshipful knight: he is severely wounded and he kills four of the twelve knights who attacked him. More significant than his wounds is the fact that he has committed manslaughter.

This is the first time that Malory's Lancelot has killed an opponent 'lyghtly' — not deliberately or intentionally — but rather as the 'likely' outcome of his disposition and circumstances (*MED* 4a).[18] Chaucer's Parson says, 'he that is proud or envyous is lightly wrooth' (*CT* X(I).534). Malory would add that he that is proud or fights in anger is likely to kill his opponent. During the Quest he will tell us that Galahad's 'lyvyng ys such that he shall sle no man lyghtly' (892.5–6: XIII.16) and, in the tale of Lancelot, he has already shown us that young Lancelot's 'lyvyng' was such that he, too, slew 'no man lyghtly' (see above 117–19). Now, he clearly indicates that Lancelot has fallen from the protective grace of True knighthood. We may infer that the reason for his fall is Lancelot's vainglorious desire to win worship.

On the second day of the tournament Lancelot seeks out Tristram to test his prowess, but when he finds him doing 'so mervaylous dedys of armys' he decides not to challenge him, because if he should 'sette uppon thys knyght now, I ded shame to myselff' (526.7–10:IX.32). On the third day, however, when Lancelot discovers that Tristram has felled twelve of his kinsmen, he challenges him and 'by malefortune' wounds him 'nyghe to the dethe' with his spear (531.33–34:IX.34). Tristram is forced to quit the field. Later, when Lancelot is awarded the prize, he refuses to accept it, 'nother for kynge, quene, nother knyght,' and argues that Tristram better deserves it, since 'he began first, and lengyst hylde on, and so hathe he done the firste day, the secunde, and the thirde day.' The final consequence of this signal act of courtesy, however, is that he wins even more worship:

> 'And all the peple hole for his jantilness, firste the astatis, hyghe and lowe, and after the comynalté, at onys cryed, 'Sir Launcelot hath won the gre, whosoever sayth nay!' (534.8–11)

This great honour does not please Lancelot; on the contrary, he is both 'wrothe and shamed', for he knows he does not deserve it.

Although he has begun to act like a Worshipful knight, Lancelot still judges himself by the standards of True knighthood. He is ashamed of himself for having wounded Tristram so severely, and his use of the phrase 'be mysfortune' (535.26:IX.35; cf. C: 'myshap'), like Malory's use of the phrase 'by malefortune' to describe the event, should remind the reader of Lancelot's youthful conviction that sinful knights shall not be 'happy nother fortunate unto the werrys' (270.35–36: VI.10). Indeed, Lancelot is so ashamed of what he has done that he lies to Arthur about it. He tells Arthur that he would not have 'medled with' Tristram if he 'had seyne hys blacke shylde'; we know, however, that he did see Tristram's shield, for he challenged him with the words, 'Knyght with the blacke shylde, make ye redy to juste with me!' (531.28–29:IX.33). The irony is that Arthur should not have blamed Lancelot if he had told the king the truth, because by the standards of Worshipful knighthood Lancelot has done precisely what he ought to have done. He has avenged the falls of his twelve kinsmen. Arthur himself had promised to avenge his party for the falls they had taken the preceding day (527.35–37:IX.32) and then made good that promise by challenging the 'Knyght with the blacke shylde' (530.17:IX.33). In fact, Lancelot's challenge echoed Arthur's challenge almost word for word, the only difference being that Lancelot's was the more courteous: he addressed Tristram not as 'the' but as 'ye'. Still Lancelot cannot get over the feeling that he must make excuses for what he has done. A little later he will say to Arthur, 'whan men bene hote in dedis of armys, oftyn hit ys seyne they hurte their frendis as well as their foys' (537.17–18:IX.36).

Though Lancelot cannot seem to shake the conviction that he has done something wrong, Arthur regards his 'mysfortune' as commonplace: 'whan two noble men encountir, nedis muste the tone have the worse, lyke as God wyll suffir at that tyme' (535.9–15:IX.35). In other words, Arthur understands Lancelot's having wounded his friend so severely as a matter of chance resulting from simple necessity ('nedis muste the tone have the worse') which has no moral significance at all. This difference between the two men in their response to 'mysfortune' may be explained in terms of their differing conceptions of fortune, or chance. Although Arthur speaks of God, he may as well speak of Dame Fortune, or any other convenient personification of the operations of chance which God, in His providence, allows, or 'suffirs'. Arthur's position is that of the rationalist. It is the position defined by St Thomas Aquinas when he argued that defective acts are sometimes permitted by God 'merely on account of the failure of some [proximate] cause' (34). The most common type of defective act in knightly encounters is what in a more modern context we would call an 'upset'. When Palomides, who is clearly a lesser knight than either Lamorak or Tristram, nevertheless unhorses both of them with one spear, Malory observes,

> Here men may undirstonde that bene men of worshyp that man was never fourmed that all tymes myght attayne, but somtyme he was put to the worse by malefortune and at som tyme the wayker knyght put the byggar knyght to a rebuke.
> (484.18–22:IX.12)

Like all 'men of worshyp', Arthur concludes that Lamorak and Tristram have suffered 'malefortune', and by that he means very much what a modern man means when he says he has suffered 'bad luck'.

The Worshipful knight does not deny God's providence; he would agree with St Thomas that all misfortunes are 'directed by God to some useful purpose' (34). However, he would be sceptical as to the inherent moral significance of such misfortunes and it is here, at this point, that he differs fundamentally from the True knight. The True knight believes that misfortunes are caused by man's sinfulness. Lancelot has already asserted quite clearly that lecherous knights will not be fortunate in battle, for they will either 'be overcom with a sympler knyght than they be hemself, other ellys they shall sle by unhappe and hir cursednesse bettir men than they be hemself' (270.36–271.2:VI.10). In other words, in the past Lancelot has attributed 'upsets' as well as more serious misfortunes, like manslaughter, to men's sinfulness. This position is likewise based on the writings of St Thomas Aquinas. It simply focuses on different aspects of the great Doctor's teaching on Divine Providence. It focuses on the Thomist definition of evil as the absence of good which God tolerates rather than deprive men of free will; for men create evil by freely choosing the finite rather than the infinite good. It then focuses on the belief that God 'orders the sin to the sinner's good' or 'at least to a good which is brought about in him by divine justice when he is punished for his sin' (42). And it concludes from this that misfortunes are God's way of either making the sinner aware of his sinfulness and thus bringing him to repentance or, 'at least', of punishing him for his sin (see below 232–6).

By the moral and religous standards of True knighthood, all Worshipful knights are sinners because they are committed to the competition for worship and the love of women and therefore they are almost by definition both proud and lecherous. However, by the moral standards of Worshipful knighthood, there is nothing wrong with desiring either of these worldly goods, either worship or the love of women, so long as the knight observes the rules of honourable conduct in pursuit of them. If the True knight believes that all misfortune in battle is divine retribution for sin, the Worshipful knight is both more rational and more sceptical regarding man's ability to know God's purposes. We may note that his commonsensical attitude towards misfortune in battle is perfectly consonant with his attitude towards trial by battle. If he is forced to do justice by means of this basically irrational process, he will try to rationalize it by ensuring that the stronger knight always fights on the side of the right. He does not rule out the possibility that God may determine the outcome, but he would argue that it is both foolish and sinfully presumptuous to expect that God will provide a miracle.

The Worshipful knight does not assume that God determines the outcome of all knightly encounters, however, nor does he believe that these encounters have any moral significance. Therefore, when faced with an 'upset' in an ordinary encounter to test for prowess, the Worshipful knight can only shrug his shoulders and say what Dinadan says to Tristram after Palomides has unhorsed him yet again:

> 'Lo, sir Trystram, here may a man preve, be he never so good yet may he have a falle; and he was never so wyse but he myght be oversayne, and he rydyth well that never felle.' (516.3–6:IX.28)

Likewise, when faced with a more serious type of misfortune, such as manslaughter, the Worshipful knight can only say that it could not be helped. At the Castle of Maidens tournament Tristram has inadvertently killed the sons of Sir Darras. Later he excuses himself to the grieving father by arguing that had they 'bene the nexte kyn that I have, I myght have done none othirwyse' (552.21–22:IX.40). The experience of the Worshipful knight has taught him that such misfortunes are an inevitable part of the noble way of the world.

The transformation of Lancelot from True knight to Worshipful knight is completed when Malory gives us dramatic proof that Lancelot has adopted the Worshipful knight's attitude towards misfortune. He provides us with this proof in the 'Round Table' section of the Tale of Tristram in a scene which functions as a kind of apotheosis of Worshipful knighthood: the scene in which the epitome of Worshipful knighthood in princely office, King Arthur, welcomes into his fellowship the man he admires as 'one of the best knyghtes and the jentyllyst of the worlde and the man of most worship,' that is, Tristram himself.

By way of making amends to Arthur for having been the cause of Tristram's sudden disappearance after the Castle of Maidens tournament, Lancelot has sworn to find him and to bring him back to Camelot 'other with fayrenes othir with fowlnes' (537.29–30:IX.36). He begins with 'fayrenes' searching for him in the company of Brangwayne. Then he rides into the country of Surluse with Kay and Gaheris and we hear no more of him. But after Tristram has been released from Darras' prison, he and Palomides encounter a 'stronge knyght' with a covered shield who gives them both a fall. Tristram decides to follow him 'that thus hath shamed us' and learns that the stranger has been speaking 'grete vylony' of King Arthur and especially of Queen Guinevere (566.4–5:X.3). The climactic event of this 'Round Table' section then follows. It is the battle between Tristram and a knight dressed 'all in whyght' with a 'coverde shylde' (568.23–24:X.5) and it takes place where Merlin prophesied that two of the 'beste knyghtes that ever were in kynge Arthurs dayes, and two of the beste lovers' should meet to do battle (568.18–20:X.5). Tristram thinks he is battling Palomides, whom he has agreed to meet here, but his opponent turns out to be none other than the same 'stronge knyght' who 'shamed' him earlier, that is, Lancelot. It would seem that, having failed to find Tristram 'by fayrenes', Lancelot has resorted to 'fowlnes', disguising himself, speaking ill of King Arthur and Queen Guinevere and challenging all comers, on the assumption that Tristram would then soon enough find him, as, indeed, he did.

When this revelation is made at court, Lancelot shows no sign at all of being ashamed or embarrassed by his 'fowle' behaviour; and none of the other Round Table knights are offended by it, either. On the contrary, everyone accepts that his speaking 'no worshyp be youre house' was a satisfactory way of disguising his identity and they are very impressed by the demonstration of his prowess. In fact, Arthur guesses that the stranger must have been Lancelot simply on the basis of the list of knights he has unhorsed: Gawain, Bleoberys, Kay, Palomides and Tristram. In Malory's source the strange knight is never identified, so clearly Malory did not have to identify him as Lancelot. He could have chosen another strong knight, Lamorak, for instance. But Malory must have seen that by identifying Lancelot as the stranger he could prove, in the most dramatic way possible, that his hero has now wholeheartedly adopted the ethical standards of Worshipful knighthood. In his quest for worldly glory, Lancelot has disguised himself in order to beguile his fellow knights into 'having ado' with him so that he might win worship by shaming them. He has even killed one of them, quite unintentionally, the young married knight Sir Galardonne who, had he lived, 'wolde have prevyd a good knyght' (564.28–29:X.3). And if he is 'ashamed' of himself he gives no sign as Arthur turns to welcome Tristram into the Round Table fellowship.

It is fitting that at this moment Arthur should turn from Lancelot to Tristram, for just as Tristram has confirmed his worthiness to be a knight of the Round Table by matching Lancelot in prowess, so Lancelot has proved that he is now a Worshipful knight by adopting Tristram's standards of knightly behaviour. Tristram is no stranger to disguise as a means of winning worship or to manslaughter as an inevitable consequence of the same. He was disguised at the Castle of Maidens tournament when he accidentally slew the sons of Darras. And even though he has defended his behaviour on the grounds that he 'myght have done none othirwyse' (552.22:IX.40), it is easy to see that, had he not chosen to disguise himself, lesser knights could have chosen whether or not to risk their bodies and their lives jousting with such a great knight. Arthur says that this 'is not the fyrste tyme' Lancelot has beguiled the Round Table by disguising himself but, so far as the reader can tell, this is the first time he has ever done so simply in order to win worship.[19] In the Tale of Lancelot he also rode disguised, deliberately so in Malory's version, but only in order to spare sir Kay. Many knights challenged Lancelot in Sir Kay's armour, thinking him to be the lesser knight, but Lancelot himself never issued a challenge. Meanwhile, Sir Kay, wearing Lancelot's armour, rode back to Camelot 'in Goddys pece' since 'no man wold have ado' with him (287.1–3:VI.18). A comparison of these two episodes in which Lancelot 'beguiles' his fellow knights of the Round Table makes clear that his motives were quite different on the former occasion. Then he was not concerned to prove his prowess; now, however, he wants to win worship and, as Kay's experience riding in his armour proves, the only way he can win more worship is by disguising himself. Knights who abide by Sir Tristram's dictum that 'manhode is nat worthe but yf hit be medled with wysdome' (700.19–20:X.59) will not be so foolish as to accept a challenge from a knight whom they can recognize as the best knight in the world.

If Lancelot is already known as the best knight in the world, one may wonder why he should be so eager to win even more worship. Malory suggests that the change in his hero's behaviour is due to a change in the quality of his feelings for Guinevere. Malory first hinted this might be the case in the scene with Lamorak and Mellyagaunt, discussed above (180–1). He has reinforced this hint by telling us that Lancelot was dressed 'all in whyte' when Lamorak encountered him in the forest (448.12–13:VIII.40) and again when he carried the 'covered shield' and fought with sir Tristram at the 'perowne' (568.23–24:X.5). Later, we will learn that Queen's knights always wear 'playne whyte shyldis' while they strive to win worship (1121.16–21:XIX.25). Malory has also let us know that Guinevere was present at the Castle of Maidens tournament (528.5:IX.32), but in his version Lancelot was so ashamed of his behaviour there that he absolutely refused the prize, even though both the king and the queen tried to persuade him to accept it (533.30–32:IX.34). After the 'Round Table' section that does not happen again. On the contrary, Malory goes out of his way, frequently modifying his source material, to create a pattern of increasingly vainglorious behaviour on Lancelot's part in the next two great tournaments. What is more, he attributes that behaviour to Lancelot's relationship with the queen.

Lancelot attends the tournament at Surluse not only in the company of the queen but also at her commandment, and on the first day he enters the lists disguised at her request (653.15–32:X.40). As a consequence, he unhorses Ector 'his owne brother' and later his cousin Bleoberys as well (654.3–7:X.41). He does not joust again in this seven-day tournament, except to rescue Lamorak on the fourth day and to play a joke upon Dinadan the fifth and seventh days. Nevertheless, at the end of the seventh day, in Malory's version, Lancelot accepts the 'pryce' (670.5:X.49).

Lancelot accepts the prize even though Dinadan has twice teased him for the fact that his presence at Surluse deprives lesser knights of worship. On the fifth day of the tournament, while Dinadan was doing 'greate dedis of armys', Galahalt had asked Lancelot to enter the lists and 'stryke hym adowne' and 'Launcelot ded as he was requyred' (665.6–16:X.47). The next day Dinadan railed at Lancelot, 'what devyll do ye in this contrey? For here may no meane knyghtes wynne no worship for the,' and Lancelot railed back, finishing with 'God, forbode that ever we mete but hit be at a dysshe of mete!' whereupon the queen and Galahalt laughed till 'they myght nat sytte at their table' (668.17–27:X.48). It's all very funny and meant to be funny; nevertheless, it reminds the reader that Lancelot used to behave quite differently at tournaments. At the Assumption Day tournament, for example, he refused to enter the lists to knock Gareth down when Arthur asked him to. Lancelot's prank on the seventh day at Surluse must have been the inspiration of either Galahalt or Guinevere, for it is hard to believe that Lancelot himself would have thought of the idea of dressing up as a damsel in the lists. As soon as Dinadan glimpsed 'a maner of a damesell' he suspected it might be 'sir Launcelot disgysed', but he was not quick enough to avoid taking a fall from 'her'. The icing on the cake of this delicious practical joke was to dress the felled Dinadan in the damsel's clothes and, thus apparelled, to bring him before Galahalt and Guinevere. The effect was so devastatingly funny that Guinevere 'fell downe' laughing and 'so dede all that there was'. Dinadan's parting words to Lancelot are original with Malory. 'Well,' seyde sir Dynadan, 'sir Launcelot, thou arte so false that I can never beware of the' (670.1–4:X.49). Their friendship may survive, but one has the impression that it has been sorely tried, and all to please the queen.

Because of illness, Guinevere is not present at the third and last of the great tournaments in the Tale of Tristram, but Malory is able to use that fact to let us know how much farther Lancelot has slipped into the unkind ways of honourable knights set upon winning worship. On the first day at Lonezep, Palomides is exerting himself especially to win worship because he knows that his lady Isode is present in the stands. Everyone is amazed by his feats and Arthur wants to be avenged on this strange knight and his three companions dressed all in green. Lancelot knows who the four are (his protegé Gareth, and his friends Dinadan, Palomides and Tristram). He points out to Arthur that he cannot win 'grete worship' by attacking them, 'for they ar gretly travayled', but Arthur insists, and Lancelot goes along with him. Later, after having rested himself, Lancelot re-enters the field to hear the people saying that the stranger in green has surpassed both Lancelot and Tristram that day, and as soon as he hears that cry, Lancelot rushes upon Palomides 'wyth a grete speare and a longe', thinking 'to have smyttyn hym downe' (738.35–739.1:X.70). This is the first time that Lancelot has ever acted on his own initiative to deprive another knight of the worship he has won, and the complete contrast with his behaviour vis-a-vis Gareth at the Assumption Day tournament is striking. Palomides is so desperate to avoid being unhorsed by Lancelot that he uses his sword to cut through Lancelot's spear and inadvertently kills his horse. Everyone remarks on his unknightly behaviour and, after Ector has avenged his brother's fall by unhorsing Palomides, Lancelot approaches him on foot determined upon revenge. Palomides begs forgiveness and mercy, 'for I have no power nothir myght to wythstonde you' (739.32:X.71) and promises that if Lancelot will spare him on this occasion he will be his knight forever. Lancelot's reply deserves quoting in full, for it is Malory's invention:

> 'Well,' seyde sir Launcelot, 'I se, for to say the sothe, ye have done mervaylously well this day, and I undirstonde a parte for whos love ye do hit, and well I wote that love is a grete maystry. And yf my lady were here, as she is nat, wyte you well, sir Palomydes, ye shulde nat beare away the worship! But beware youre love be nat discoverde, for and sir Trystram may know hit, ye woll repente hit. And sytthyn my quarell is nat here, ye shall have this day the worshyp as for me; consyderynge the greate travayle and payne that ye have had this day, hit were no worship for me to put you frome hit.' (740.6–16:X.71)

Lancelot's feelings for the queen have grown much more intense since the day he interrupted the fight between Mellyagaunt and Lamorak. Were he to come upon them now and discover Mellyagaunt's love for Guinevere, Mellyaguant and not Lamorak would be the one to 'repente' it. Lancelot has learned that 'love is a grete maystry'. And we have seen both at Surluse and now at Lonezep that under the power of love Lancelot is prepared to do what he would never have done before.

Lancelot's moral decline is not swift. His movement downward from True to Worshipful knighthood takes up almost the whole of the long Tale of Tristram. At the same time his decline is balanced by a movement upward from Heroic to Worshipful knighthood on the part of the pagan knight, Palomides. Both men have been transformed by the 'maystry' of love. To please his lady, Lancelot has declined from the humility and compassion of a True knight to the pride and cupidity of a Worshipful knight, avid to win worship. At the same time, to please his lady, Palomides has moved upward from the barbaric behaviour of the Heroic knight to the civilized and honourable behaviour of a Worshipful knight, champion of ladies and damsels. At the tournament of Surluse, while Lancelot was rescuing Lamorak and playing tricks upon Dinadan to amuse Guinevere, Palomides fought three judicial battles in the defense of ladies' rights (655–666:X.41–47). Their paths, both literal and metaphorical, cross again here at Lonezep where Lancelot's discourtesy, committed for love of Guinevere, nearly prevents Palomides from winning worship for love of Isode.

It is ironic that Lancelot's recognition of love as a 'grete maystry', which in one sense makes him a more courtly knight, should at the same time make him less courteous towards other knights. However, that irony is inherent in the Worshipful knight's code: he must win worship in order to be worthy of his lady's love, and he can only win worship at the expense of his fellow knights. In this competitive situation lesser knights are tempted to take advantage of the greater in order to improve their chances of winning worship; but greater knights who disguise themselves also take advantage of the lesser, by tricking them into unequal contests which the more prudent might otherwise avoid. However, the disguises of the great knights like Lancelot and Tristram are acceptable by the ethical standards of the honourable society, whereas the attempts of lesser knights like Palomides to even the odds by desperate measures are regarded as 'unknyghtly'.

Just after the Roman Campaign, Lancelot was prepared to forego love 'peramours' for 'drede of God'; now he has learned that 'love is a grete maystry'. We may infer from this that he has bowed to the power of erotic love or, in other words, that he now loves the queen 'oute of mesure', as he will later confess during the Quest. This does not necessarily mean, however, that he and the queen have become carnal lovers like Tristram and Isode, though some critics have argued that it does (Lumiansky 208); for Lancelot's situation is not at all like that of Tristram. Lancelot's lord, King Arthur, is a Worshipful knight who has done nothing to forfeit the loyalty of his wife and his best knight. Therefore, even though Lancelot's desire for the queen, like his desire to win worship for her sake, must necessarily cause him to decline from the ethical standards of True knighthood, it need not cause him to decline from the ethical standards of Worshipful knighthood.

If Lancelot were to commit adultery with Guinevere, he would violate not only the laws of God but also the laws of man. He would be guilty of the crime of high treason. Tristram can be regarded as innocent of high treason only because by feudal law his lord, King Mark, has forfeited his right to loyalty by first committing treason against him. Lancelot and Guinevere could not justify their adultery in this way and in Malory's version of the Tale of Tristram there is no evidence to indicate that they have become adulterers. Malory has eliminated all those passages from the French prose romance which offer concrete evidence of an adulterous relationship.[20] At the same time, however, he has retained three allegations of adultery, all of which come from enemies of Arthur's court: either from Morgan le Fay, who is known to hate Guinevere (555.1–9:IX.41) or from King Mark. Malory might have eliminated these suspect allegations as well, but clearly he chose not to do so. His reasons may be inferred from the fact that the destructive power of scandal-mongering was not only a common theme in late medieval English sermons (Owst 453), but was also a prominent theme in two important late medieval works about true love: Christine de Pizan's *Livre du duc des vrais amans* and the *Book of the Knight of the Tour Landry*. Christine tells the story of a married lady and an unmarried knight who love one another with true love, which means that they are determined to remain chaste so as not to betray the lady's husband. Nevertheless, they are forced to give up their secret meetings for fear of 'les mauvaises langues' (165). Likewise, the wife of the Knight of the Tour Landry argues against her husband's approval of 'love peramours' in cases where the lovers are good and 'trewe' on the grounds that if 'enuyous folke that haue euylle and cursed tongues' notice any 'semblaunte of loue' they will cause such scandal with their 'fals reports' that the young woman will be blamed as though she were in fact guilty (172).

In the Tale of Tristram we never see Lancelot and the queen engage in private conversations in the court, as they will after the Quest when their love has grown 'more hotter' (1045.18:XVIII.1). This strongly suggests that the allegations which come from Morgan and Mark are 'fals reports' made with malicious intent. To be sure, when Guinevere sees the shield which Morgan has given Tristram to bear at Roche Dure, she is 'sore aferde' (558.20:IX.44); but she has just as good reason to be 'sore aferde' if she is innocent as she would have if she were guilty, for if her husband believes a 'fals report' she will be ruined just as surely as if it were true. The Lady of the Tour Landry offers several examples of innocent women who have been ruined in this way (172). Fortunately for Guinevere, her husband is a Worshipful knight who assumes that other men are as honourable as himself, until he has good evidence to the contrary. And, under the circumstances which Malory has created in his Tale of Tristram, the reader must agree that Arthur is wise to discount the allegations made by Morgan le Fay and King Mark (617.10–16:X.27).

During the second part of the Tale of Tristram, from the end of the Castle of Maidens tournament until the end of the tournament at Lonezep, Lancelot is continuously in residence at court with the exception of the week he spends at the tournament of Surluse in the company of the queen and Galahalt. During this entire time we never once see him speak privately to the queen. Only his behaviour as a knight-errant and at tournaments reveals how his feelings for her have developed. However, we see him constantly in the company of the king. Indeed, Malory gives us good reason to conclude that Lancelot has become Arthur's chief counsellor and courtier.

Already in the Tale of Gareth we have had evidence to indicate that Arthur relied upon Lancelot as one of his chief counsellors. When Margawse comes to court in search of her son, Malory creates a scene in which Lancelot shares with Sir Beaudoin of Bretaygne the role of the king's chief counsellor, much as, in Malory's version of the Roman campaign, he had shared with Sir Cador of Cornwall the role of the king's chief commander in the field. Since no one knows where to find young Gareth, Gawain and his brothers ask leave of Arthur to go seek him. It is Lancelot, however, not Arthur, who initially responds to their request, saying, 'Nay, . . . that shall not nede.' Beaudoin of Bretaygne agrees that it would be better to send for the lady Lyones and Arthur concurs with their 'advyse' (340.29:VII.27). Beaudoin of Bretaygne is the man whom Arthur appointed to be regent of England during his absence on the Roman campaign. Therefore, this little scene suggests rather powerfully that Arthur values Lancelot's advice as much as he does that of the man he deemed worthy to govern his entire realm.

Malory never specifies a particular office for either Lancelot or Beaudoin; however, considering the previous functions they have performed, we may guess that Lancelot is the king's Constable and Beaudoin his Chancellor, the former being the chief military officer of the Crown and the latter the chief judicial officer, although in late medieval England the Constable also played a judicial role as presiding judge of the Court of Chivalry. Indeed, in the Tale of Tristram Malory gives us much clearer evidence that Lancelot is Arthur's Constable when he explains that the treason duel of chivalry fought by Tristram and Blamour is to be judged by King Carados and the King of Scots because neither Arthur nor Lancelot is able to be present (404.22–27: VIII.20). Both King and Constable are present at the duel fought between King Mark and Sir Amaunte, however. The trial results in a miscarriage of justice as the false king wins 'by mysadventure' and then gallops away. Arthur is 'wrothe oute of mesure', Lancelot begs leave to go after King Mark and bring him back to the court, and the king grants his permission (593.25–26:X.15).

Lancelot is not able to amend the injustice of the treason duel of chivalry fought by Mark and Amaunte, although later he will promise 'by the fayth I awghe to God and to the Order of Knyghthode' that if ever Mark should harm Tristram he will 'sle' him with his 'owne hondis!' (160.3–7:X.22). However, there is one occasion, following the Tournament at Lonezep, when Lancelot clearly and successfully functions as an agent of the king's justice. That is when he rescues Palomides from twelve knights who have bound him beneath 'an olde steedis bealy' and are taking him to be hanged at the Castle of Pelownes. Their number suggests a jury, and they assure Lancelot that Palomides 'hath deserved deth, and unto deth he ys jouged' (777.15–17:X.85). However, they have judged him according to the *lex talionis*, the law of the blood feud, not according to the king's justice and the common law of the land. Palomides has accidentally killed their lord at the tournament of Lonezep and the verdict of any duly constituted jury must have been death 'by mysadventure' (Lat. *infortunium*), that is, a death which is pardonable because it was done unintentionally in the course of engaging in a legitimate activity. By Malory's day the royal pardon would have been forthcoming almost automatically (Pollock and Maitland 2:480–484). Since these twelve knights are all retainers of the dead man and Palomides is to receive his 'justyse' from the dead man's father (775.19–25:X.84), it appears to be a clear case of the family taking justice into its own hands. Lancelot's initial response, 'A, Jesu! . . . what mysseadventure ys befallyn hym that he ys thus lad towarde hys dethe?' (777.1–2:X.85) reminds us of this distinction between royal justice and clan justice and suggests very strongly that in liberating Palomides he acts as an agent of the king whose office it was to suppress all private acts of vengeance.

The Constable of England was also responsible for the conduct of tournaments. In fact, Edward IV's Constable, Sir John Tiptoft, Earl of Worcester, drew up a list of rules for conducting and judging the tournaments held at Smithfield in the 1460s. Therefore, although Lancelot's presence at the Castle of Maidens' tournament seems to have been his own idea, and his presence at the tournament of Surluse was clearly the queen's idea, his presence at the last and greatest of the three tournaments in the Tale of Tristram, the tournament of Lonezep, may be explained in terms of his office. This is the only one of the three tourmanents to be called by King Arthur himself. He decides to hold the tournament at the castle of Lonezep because it is near Joyous Garde, where Tristram and Isode are now staying, and he wants to make sure that Tristram will attend. He also decides that the knights of England, Cornwall and North Wales 'shulde juste ayenste' those of all other countries holding of him 'a this halff the se'. Lancelot tries to convince the king that to divide the parties so unequally in this way will 'put us that bene aboute you in grete jouparté' because 'there be many knyghtes that hath envy to us' (682.12–14:X.52), but the king refuses to take his advice. The remarks on envy are original with Malory and indicate that Lancelot has learned a great deal from his recent experience at tournaments.

Arthur's behaviour during the tournament at Lonezep is equally rash when, after the first day's jousting, he decides to ride after Isode and her two knightly companions in order to have a better look at this fair lady. Lancelot points out to him that he is placing himself in 'grete jupardé' but once again Arthur refuses to take his advice, and Lancelot goes along to protect him from the consequences of his rashness. Both Palomides and Tristram take offense at Arthur's intrusion. First Palomides turns and unhorses the king without warning. Lancelot avenges that fall by challenging and unhorsing Palomides, and then Tristram challenges him. Lancelot's response to Tristram shows that he has learned more than prudence as a knight of King Arthur's court. He has also learned the art of diplomacy:

> '... I am lothe to have ado wyth you and I myght chose, for I woll that ye wyte that I muste revenge my speciall lorde and my moste bedrad frynde that was unhorsed unwarely and unknyghtly. And therefore, sir, thoughe I revenge that falle, take ye no displesure, for he is to me suche a frynde that I may nat se hym shamed.' (744.23–9:X.73)

The speech is original with Malory and is a fine specimen of courtly rhetoric, neatly balancing the claims of honour and friendship. Even more importantly, it allows Tristram to recognize his friend and thus turns what might otherwise have been an ugly incident into a triumph of diplomacy. If Tristram had not recognized Lancelot 'by hys persone and by his knyghtly wordis,' however, Lancelot was prepared to risk his life by doing battle with both Palomides and Tristram at once, if necessary, in order to 'revenge' his lord (744.9–13:X.73).

Although Tristram has nothing but praise for both Arthur and Lancelot after this incident, it is clear that Lancelot has demonstrated more wisdom and prudence than the king. Tristram takes particular delight in the fact that Arthur will 'ryde so pryvaly as a poure arraunte knyght' even though he is lord of all Christendom, and asserts that 'all knyghtes may lerne to be a knyght of hym' (745.27–29:X.73). On the other hand, Palomides is simply amazed by the king's foolhardiness and it must be admitted that if Lancelot's diplomatic skills had not prevented the shedding of blood, the outcome of this incident could have been disastrous for the king and his realm.

Lancelot is not openly critical of Arthur on this occasion, but in Malory's version of the Tale of Tristram there are other occasions on which the king's chief counsellor is sharply critical of his judicial or diplomatic decisions. He disagrees violently with Arthur's decision to allow Tristram to return to Cornwall with King Mark, and when Arthur insists that he cannot do more than make 'them at accorde', Lancelot retorts, 'Accorde? . . . Now fye on that accorde!' (609.33:X.22). He is just as critical of Arthur's failure to deal with the felony and 'forecaste treason' committed by his nephew Gaheris when he murdered his mother, Margawse. Lancelot warns Arthur that he will 'lose that good knyght sir Lamerok' and that, moreover, if Tristram should hear of it, 'he wolde never com within your courte' (613.17–18: X.24). Lancelot goes on to inform Arthur of Gawain's plan to slay Lamorak 'by one meane other by another' and Arthur promises to prevent it. It is clear that Lancelot is fulfilling the duty of a king's counsellor by pointing out to Arthur the dangers and risks involved in the decisions he must make; it is not so clear that Arthur is fulfilling the duty of a king when he refuses to take his counsellor's advice.

Whatever his official capacity, Lancelot is clearly regarded as the chief knight of Arthur's court. Sir Ironside tells Gareth that when he and Sir Persaunte and his brethren visited Camelot they undertook 'to holde party agaynste my lorde sir Launcelot and the knyghtes of that court' (343.1–3:VII.27). And when Alexander has just been made knight, Tristram advises him to go to Camelot and 'put hym in the rule and in the hondis of sir Launcelot' (638.10–12:X.35). However, as Arthur's chief courtier, Lancelot is not very 'courtly' in the social sense of the adjective. He is regularly involved in diplomacy, justice, war and tournaments but, unlike Gareth, he never sings, dances or plays games. Equally remarkable is the fact that, unlike Tristram and Arthur, he never goes hunting.[21] These omissions suggest that even as a Worshipful knight, Malory's Lancelot retains the True knight's disapproval of the more frivolous pastimes of the court. Sir Gilbert Hay speaks with contempt of knights who take 'mare plesaunce in haukis and houndis, delicious metis, joly clethingis, fair wommen, gude wynis and spicis, lycht wordis' than in serving 'Goddis pure peple' and keeping 'the lawis of God and man'. As far as Hay is concerned such knights 'ar nocht worthy knychtis, bot erar dispisaris of the ordre, and inymyes to knychthede' (*Knychthede*, 63–64).

Even as a Worshipful knight, then, Lancelot is clearly to be distinguished from Tristram as a type. Although he has become proud and keen to win worship for his lady's sake, he is still a 'trew' lover in the sense that he is true both to Arthur and to Guinevere. And although he has become Arthur's chief counsellor and the most prominent courtier at Camelot, he does not share Tristram's delight in the usual aristocratic pleasures and pastimes.

Rivals for Worship: Lamorak and Gawain

The Worshipful knight who is most like Lancelot in the Tale of Tristram is Lamorak, third best knight of the world. Malory greatly enhances the likeness between these two knights and then uses that likeness to continue the pattern of contrast with Gawain which he began in the Roman Campaign. Just as the pattern of contrast between Gawain and Lancelot sharpened the portrait of True knighthood in the second narrative unit, so now the pattern of contrast between Gawain and Lamorak will sharpen the portrait of Worshipful knighthood in this third narrative unit. What is more, by drawing attention to Gawain's envy of King Pellinor and his son Lamorak, Malory anticipates an important post-Grail theme, Gawain's envy of Lancelot.

Lamorak is known in Arthurian romance only through the French prose *Tristan* and Malory's rendering of it. Yet from the very beginning of his work Malory must have had some idea of the important role Lamorak would later play, for Merlin prophesies that the sons of King Pellinor, Lamorak and Percival, will 'have no felowis of prouesse and of good lyvyng' save 'one in thys world' (51.32–33:I.24). Not long afterwards Merlin further prophesies that the 'one' best knight in the world shall be Lancelot 'other ellis Galahad, hys sonne' (91.23:II.19) and in the Tale of Tristram Lamorak is, in fact, as like to Lancelot 'as for a worldly knyght' as Percival will be to Galahad 'in holy dedis' in the Tale of the Sankgreall (cf. 1149.7–10:XIX.11).

Malory heightens the reader's awareness of a close and loving relationship between Lancelot and Lamorak through several minor alterations of his source. First he eliminates the fact that Tristram made Lamorak knight (Löseth 187). Second, he enhances the degree of Lamorak's admiration and reverence for Lancelot (460.1–3:IX.1; 485.26–28:IX.12). And third, he sees to it that the two knights never encounter one another in battle.[22] One might almost suspect that Lancelot is the man who made Lamorak knight, so close and mutually loving is their relationship (cf. 660.29:X.44; 662.20–22:X.45).

Malory also heightens the likeness between the two men as lovers. Both love queens who become widows and, just as Malory will suggest at the end of his work that Lancelot might have married Guinevere after the death of Arthur (1253.19–22:XXI.9–10), so in the Tale of Tristram Malory suggests that Lamorak might have married Arthur's widowed sister, Margawse. There is a significant difference, however, in that Lancelot himself will express the wish to marry Guinevere, whereas it is Arthur who tells Lamorak that it would have been 'muche fayrer and bettir that ye hadde wedde her, for ye ar a kynges sonne' (664.3–5:X.46). Lamorak is still a young man and therefore it is tempting to think that he has refused marriage for the same reason that young Lancelot gave for refusing it in the Tale of Lancelot: he is not yet willing to 'couche' with a wife and 'leve armys and turnamentis, batellys and adventures' (270.30–31:VI.9). However, young Lamorak's code of ethics as a Worshipful knight does not forbid him to consummate his love for Margawse. She has no husband; therefore, by lying with her he commits no treason.

Finally Malory heightens the likeness between Lamorak and Lancelot as knights of prowess by having Tristram repeatedly compare them favorably in this regard. Before he has encountered either of them, Tristram praises Lamorak by comparing his deeds to those of Lancelot (428.11–12:VIII.33). After he has encountered both of them, he calls Lamorak 'one of the best knyghtes that ever I mette wythall but yf hit were sir Launcelot' (698.25–27:X.58). And in a lengthy passage added by Malory, he first praises Lamorak in terms of courage, strength and endurance by comparing him to Lancelot and concludes, 'there is no knyght in the worlde excepte sir Launcelot that I wolde ded so well as sir Lamerok' (606.8–12:X.20).

Once he has established Lamorak as a kind of surrogate for Lancelot in this way, Malory is able to continue the pattern of contrast with Gawain which he began in his account of the Roman campaign. Malory gives to Lamorak the function of being the exemplary Worshipful knight by contrast with the Heroic knight, Gawain. Then he is able to develop that contrast into an open conflict which foreshadows the conflict which will develop later between Gawain and Lancelot.

To render the contrast between the Heroic knight and the Worshipful knight as stark as possible, Malory takes an episode from the *Tristan* involving the abduction of a lady and completely transforms the actions, attitudes and behaviours of the principal actors. In the French prose *Tristan* Lamorak and Gawain come upon a knight and his lady 'sleeping' by a well. The lady pleases Lamorak and he challenges the knight for possession of her. Gawain watches while Lamorak defeats the knight, but then, before Lamorak can lead her away, he steps forward and claims her for himself. When Lamorak learns that the interloper is Arthur's nephew, he chooses to let him have the damsel rather than fight (*Tristan* 2.625–26). In Malory's version Lamorak is more noble and Gawain more villainous. Gawain abducts the damsel while her knight is sleeping and Lamorak rides after him, crying,

> 'Sir, turne ayen!'
> Than seyde sir Gawayne,

> 'What woll ye do with me? I am nevew unto kynge Arthure.'
> 'Sir, for that cause I woll forbeare you: othir ellys that lady sholde abyde with me, other els ye sholde juste with me.'
> (449.25–31:VIII.41)

Malory's version makes it appear that Lamorak wishes to restore the damsel to her knight, to right the wrong committed by Gawain, but that when he hears that his opponent is Arthur's nephew, he immediately backs down. In other words, Malory's version turns a case of foul play in the knightly game of jousting-for-damsels into a case of *raptus* which goes unpunished because the ravisher is the king's own nephew.

The difference between Gawain in the French prose *Tristan* and Malory's Gawain is that the French knight acknowledges the rules of the courtly game of jousting-for-damsels but chooses not by abide by them, whereas Malory's Gawain appears not to know the rules. Like all Heroic knights, like Palomides (before his transformation for love of Isode) and like Mellyagaunt (whose love of Guinevere seems never to have such a transformative effect), Gawain simply takes what he wants. As far as women are concerned, all that matters to him is whether or not he has sufficient power to take and keep the object of his desire. Palomides could not keep Isode because of the superior power of Tristram. Mellyagaunt will not be able to keep Guinevere because of the superior power of Lancelot. But Gawain is able to keep this damsel, even though his abduction violates the Pentecostal oath he has sworn as a knight of the Round Table ('never to enforce them, uppon payne of dethe') because he is Arthur's favorite nephew and therefore Lamorak dares not try to stop him.

In Malory's version of subsequent events, however, the damsel's knight, Sir Froll, is not daunted by Gawain's parentage. He does what Lamorak feared to do and takes back his damsel 'wyth pure myght', giving Gawain a mighty fall in the process. This only places Lamorak in a further quandary, however, for having been a witness to the fall he feels honour-bound to avenge Gawain, since he is a fellow knight of the Round Table. We have just seen how Lancelot felt similarly obligated to avenge the fall which Palomides inflicted upon Arthur, even though Arthur was in the wrong. Now Lamorak finds himself in precisely the same situation vis-a-vis Gawain. There are significant differences, however. Arthur only attempted to steal a glimpse of Isode, whereas Gawain has stolen the damsel herself. And Lancelot is especially devoted to Arthur since he is the man who made him knight, whereas Lamorak has no special reason to love Gawain. Nevertheless, Lamorak concludes that he must avenge his 'felow' or else 'he woll sey me dishonoure in kynge Arthurs courte' (450.2–3: VIII.41). He issues a challenge, which is instantly accepted, and in the very first joust his lance pierces Sir Froll's body 'thorow bothe sydis' so that he falls 'to the erthe dede' (450.7–8:VIII.41).

This case of manslaughter for honour's sake has disastrous consequences. Having 'lyghtly' killed Sir Froll, Lamorak now finds himself involved in a blood feud with a man whom he does have special reason to love — Sir Bellyaunce le Orgulus. Malory has contrived to make this sequence of events remarkably like the sequence which followed Lancelot's rescue of Gawain from King Carados (418–419:VIII.28). Just as Lamorak slays Sir Froll in the process of avenging Gawain, so Lancelot slew Carados in the process of rescuing Gawain. Then, in Malory's version of what follows, both Lamorak and Lancelot have occasion to do battle with the brothers of the knights they have slain. In Malory's version, also, both knights try to reconcile with their opponents. The brother of Carados, Tarquin, will not give up the blood feud and so Lancelot is forced to fight him to the death (256–57:VI.8–9). On the other hand, Lamorak is at last able to reconcile with Bellyaunce, the brother of Sir Froll (451.20:VIII.41). This reconciliation is of crucial significance, for it represents a victory for the values of Worshipful knighthood over those of Heroic knighthood. In Malory's version, Bellyaunce actually forgives Lamorak for killing his brother: 'But thy jantylnesse is so good and so large that I muste nedys forgyff the myne evyll wyll' (451.19–20:VIII.41).[23] In other words, the force of Lamorak's generosity and compassion proves to be stronger than the force of Bellyaunce's anger and vengefulness.

If we did not know that Bellyaunce was extraordinarily devoted to Lamorak before this episode (so devoted, in fact, that he was willing to sacrifice the life of his own sons in order to save Lamorak's life), we might find his conversion from the ethos of the blood feudist to that of the courteous knight-errant simply incredible. As it is, however, we can accept this transformation in the same way that we accept the transformation of Palomides for love of Isode. To be sure, it is the love of a fellow knight rather than the love of a lady which effects Bellyaunce's change from Heroic to Worshipful knight, but that need not make his transformation any the less credible. In Malory's world of Arthurian knight-errantry the love which binds knights together in fellowship may be as powerful in its effects as the love of a knight for his lady.[24]

In the fifteenth century not all men of the knightly class had adopted the courtly values typical of Malory's Worshipful knights. The older heroic code of values was still honoured by many, particularly in the north of England and in Scotland. Indeed, the society of the Scottish highlands continued to be structured on the basis of patrilineal clans well into the eighteenth century. This may explain why Malory puts so much emphasis on the fact that Gawain and his brethren come from the Orkney Islands, far in the north of Scotland. Gawain is Malory's epitome of Heroic knighthood and he and his brethren (with the exception of Gareth) consistently act in accordance with the values of Scottish clansmen. In the episode which we have just been discussing, Gawain and Lamorak are clearly acting according to different ethical standards of behaviour. Gawain saw nothing wrong with taking the damsel of a knight foolish enough to leave her unprotected by going to sleep. On the other hand, Lamorak saw it as an immoral and unlawful act in violation of his oath as a knight of the Round Table.

The Heroic knight defines honour in relation to his family not in relation to himself as an individual. In fact, it is arguable whether or not he can even understand honour as something belonging to an individual independently of his family. Gawain and Lamorak both regard King Arthur as the source of their honour, but Gawain looks to him as his uncle, the most powerful of all his kinsmen, whereas Lamorak looks to him as his liege lord and the most powerful king in Christendom. Gawain and his brethren expect Arthur to honour them in his court simply because they are his kinsmen. By contrast, Lamorak expects that if he should violate the Worshipful code of honour or fail to keep his Pentecostal oath, Arthur will take away his 'worship' and his lordship 'for evirmore'.

The society of Arthur's kingdom is not organized on the basis of patrilineal clans, but Gawain and his brethren act as though it were just like their native Scottish highlands. The anthropologist Julio Caro Baroja has observed that in a society composed of patrilineal clans, each clan sees itself as engaged in a fierce competition with all other clans to be acknowledged as ' "worth more" than the rest'. Those who are defeated in this competition are automatically 'worth less' and so the 'competition for possession of any existing public honours and offices' is likely to become 'obsessive' (89). Gawain and his brothers see themselves engaged in such a competition with the other two great family groups in Arthur's court: the sons of Pellinor and the sons of Ban and Bors. And from the very beginning of the *Morte Darthur*, Gawain appears to be obsessively concerned with the honours his uncle bestows upon these other knights.

The first knight to be accorded an exceptional honour in King Arthur's court is Pellinor. When the Round Table is instituted, Merlin, Arthur's chief counsellor, gives the seat on the left side of the Siege Perilous to Pellinor, 'for beste are ye worthy to sitte thereinne of ony that her ys.' Malory reports that 'thereat had sir Gawayne grete envy'

(102.8–10:III.4), whereas the author of the *Suite du Merlin* says only that he made 'grant duel' to see the slayer of his father so honoured (2:75). Gawain's 'grete envy' suggests that he expected his uncle to give him the seat of greatest honour at the Round Table, despite the fact that he has only just been knighted and that Pellinor has greatly distinguished himself in Arthur's service. From the familial point of view of the Heroic knight, such political facts do not matter. The elevation of Pellinor makes his family 'worth more' and Lott's family 'worth less' and this should not be allowed to happen to the king's own kinsmen. That Pellinor killed Lott in battle exascerbates the humiliation, no doubt. More importantly, it also allows Gawain to justify killing Pellinor by the law of the blood feud. Nevertheless, Malory's handling of this scene in which Pellinor is honoured by Arthur suggests that envy plays a large part in motivating Gawain and Gaheris to kill Pellinor.

The murder of Lamorak follows the same pattern as the murder of Pellinor.[25] The actual killing is incited and planned as a consequence of what Gawain and his brethren consider to be a humiliation to their family. Shortly after Tristram has praised Lamorak by comparing him favourably to Lancelot (606.7–12:X.20), Arthur calls a tournament at which Lancelot, Tristram and Dinadan refrain from jousting 'for the love of kynge Arthure' so that Gawain and his brethren might be 'suffyrd ... to wynne the degré yf they myght' (606.21–24:X.21). Lamorak enters this tournament in disguise and unhorses twenty knights (including Gawain) so winning the 'pryce ... as a knyght piereles' (607.27–28:X.21) and much attention and praise from the king. Gawain and his brethren are 'wondirly wrothe' with Lamorak 'that he had put hym to such a dishonoure that day' and Gawain calls a counsel:

> 'Fayre bretherne, here may ye see: whom that we hate kynge Arthure lovyth, and whom that we love he hatyth. And wyte you well, my fayre bretherne, that this sir Lamerok woll nevyr love us, because we slew his fadir, kynge Pellynor, for we demed that he slew oure fadir, kynge Lotte of Orkenay; and for the deth of kynge Pellynor sir Lameroke ded us a shame to oure modir. Therefor I woll be revenged.' (608.13–20:X.21)

Gawain's interpretation of Lamorak's liaison with Margawse is completely original with Malory. Gawain seems to think that Lamorak has entered into this 'shameful' affair with their mother for the sole purpose of getting revenge for the death of his father. His interpretation of Lamorak's motives tells us more about his own attitude towards women than it does about Lamorak, however, for we have good evidence that Lamorak is passionately enamoured of Margawse (579.19–25:X.8). At the same time, it is not hard to see that the betrayer of Ettarde and the abductor of Sir Froll's damsel might find it difficult to appreciate Lamorak's feelings, particularly where his own mother is concerned. So, just as Gawain was able to justify the murder of Pellinor, he is able to justify the murder of Lamorak by his own ethical standards. Lamorak has dishonoured his family by dishonouring his mother; 'therefore' Gawain must be revenged. Nevertheless, this conclusion is the last link in a chain of argument which began with his fury that Arthur should have honoured Lamorak, the knight who 'had put hym to such a dishonoure that day.' Gawain cannot endure that his family should appear to be 'worth less' than any other, and particularly not less than the family of Pellinor. Malory's handling of the scene suggests that envy plays a large part in motivating this second murder, as well.

Malory makes much more of the murder of Lamorak than does the author of the *Tristan*. He doubles the number of references to it, includes one long and detailed description of the crime, and records the responses of several individual knights to news of the deed (cf. 688.6–19:X.54, 691.27–34:X.55, 698.28–700.8:X.58, 1149.32–35:XIX.11 and 1190.1–16:XX.11–12). By this means he converts the death of Lamorak into a visible turning point in the Tale of Tristram, the nature of which is made clear in this speech by Dinadan:

> '... sir Gawayne and his bretherne, except you, sir Gareth, hatyth all good knyghtes of the Rounde Table for the moste party. For well I wote, as they myght, prevayly they hate my lorde sir Launcelot and all his kyn, and grete pryvay dispyte they have at hym. And sertaynly that is my lorde sir Launcelot well ware of, and that causyth hym the more to have the good knyghtes of his kynne aboute hym.' (700.1–8:X.58)

Gawain's behaviour is destroying the fellowship of the Round Table. Arthur's best knights all sense their danger and they are responding in one of two ways: either they avoid the court of Arthur, as Tristram now says he will do (698.32–34:X.58) and as Lamorak has done (670.13–27:X.49), or, like Lancelot, they surround themselves with their own kinsmen for protection.

Lancelot now occupies the same seat at the Round Table which Pellinor used to occupy — the seat to the left side of the Siege Perilous. We are never told when Lancelot was given this prestigious seat, but we can assume that he must have been given it sometime after the death of Pellinor. Mid-point in the Tale of Tristram, when Percival takes up his rightful place at the Round Table, Malory departs from his source to specify that his seat is 'to the ryght syde of the Sege Perillous' (611.26–29:X.23) and later, on the eve of the Quest, when Galahad takes up his rightful seat at the Round Table we are told that there 'besyde sate sir Launcelot' (860.9:XIII.4). Therefore, we may infer that Lancelot, like Pellinor before him, sits on the left side of the Siege Perilous because he is 'beste . . . worthy to sitte thereinne.'

This is the last and the most subtle of all the details in Malory's text linking Lancelot to Lamorak. In fact, by not telling us exactly how Lancelot acquires Pellinor's place, Malory leaves open the possibility that Lamorak might have inherited his father's seat at the Round Table for the brief period of time he survived him, had he been willing to risk taking up residence in Arthur's court.[26] Lamorak was not willing to take that risk, however, and after the tournament at Surluse, in a passage which is original with Malory, he explains why he will not accompany Lancelot and the queen back to Camelot:

> 'Sir, I shall undirtake,' seyde sir Launcelot, 'that, and ye woll go wyth us, kynge Arthure shall charge sir Gawayne and his bretherne never to do you hurt.'
>
> 'As for that,' sayde sir Lamerok, 'I woll nat truste to sir Gawayne, nother none of his bretherne.' (670.13–17:X.49)

Lamorak does not say that he will not trust King Arthur, and Lancelot does not promise that Arthur will protect Lamorak from 'hurt' if he comes to his court, only that Arthur will 'charge' his nephews not to harm him. Both men seem to realize, in fact, that Arthur either cannot or will not control the behaviour of his nephews. And so, weeping, Lamorak and Lancelot depart, never to see one another more, and Lancelot rather than Lamorak inherits the seat of Pellinor.

If Gawain experienced 'grete envy' to see Pellinor elevated to the seat on the left side of the Siege Perilous, when he himself was but a new-made knight, we may infer that he experienced even greater envy to see Lancelot so elevated after the death of Pellinor. Gawain is now a proved knight and, upon observing that Tristram was given the seat of the man he had killed (Marhalt), he may well have expected to be accorded Pellinor's seat himself. If so, his disappointment must have been keen and his anger great. From Gawain's point of view, Arthur has made the family of Ban and Bors 'worth more' by so honouring their leader, Lancelot, and at the same time he has necessarily made King Lott's family 'worth less'.

Malory gives us no direct evidence of Gawain's envious feelings towards Lancelot until after he has vowed vengeance upon him for the death of his brothers, Gaheris and Gareth. But then, in a scene largely of his own invention, Malory suggests that just as Gawain envied

Pellinor and Lamorak, so he has long envied Lancelot. At the siege of Joyous Garde, Lancelot observes that if Gawain were not 'so myschevously sett' he 'would nat doute to have the good grace of my lorde kynge Arthur' again, and thus provokes Gawain to retort,

> 'I leve well, false recrayed knyght, for thou haste many longe dayes overlad me and us all, and destroyed many of oure good knyghtes.'
>
> 'Sir, ye say as hit pleasith you,' seyde sir Launcelot, 'yet may hit never be seyde on me and opynly preved that ever I be forecaste of treson slew no goode knyght as ye, my lorde sir Gawayne, have done; and so ded I never but in my deffence, that I was dryven thereto in savyng of my lyff.'
>
> 'A, thou false knyght,' seyde sir Gawayne, 'that thou menyst by sir Lamorak. But wyte thou well, I slew hym!'
>
> 'Sir, ye slew hym nat yourselff,' seyde sir Launcelot, 'for hit had ben overmuch for you, for he was one of the beste knyghtes crystynde of his ayge. And hit was grete pité of hys deth!'
>
> (1189.32–1190.10:XX.11)

The dialogue is entirely Malory's invention and it is a masterpiece of characterization. Lancelot's sorrow for the death of Lamorak does not quite mask his contempt for the treacherous manner in which his friend was slain by Gawain and his three brothers. Nevertheless, Lancelot never allows himself to become so angry as to forget his manners: he always uses 'ye', the more polite form, when addressing Gawain. Gawain, on the other hand, is almost beside himself with anger. He regularly employs the more familiar and insulting form 'thou' when addressing Lancelot and clearly reveals his long-suppressed envy of the greater knight: 'for thou haste many long dayes overlad me and us all.'

After the death of Lamorak, Arthur is caught in a cruel predicament. He once promised Lancelot that he would prevent his nephews from harming Lamorak (613.25:X.24), but he has not kept that promise. Now his favourite nephew is guilty of murder and everyone knows it. Other knights of the Round Table will not punish Gawain and his brothers because of their near kinship to the king but, as Dinadan and Tristram agree, 'yf they were nat the cousyns of my lorde kynge Arthure that slew hym, they sholde dye for hit, all that were concentynge to his [Lamorak's] dethe' (698.29–31:X.58). So, clearly, it is up to Arthur himself to remedy the situation. On the one hand, he loves Gawain, his nearest and dearest kinsman, too much to be able to condemn him to death for committing murder; and yet, on the other hand, if he does not punish his nephew, he makes a mockery of royal justice.

Arthur risks destroying the fellowship as well, if he overlooks Gawain's crime. If Gawain gets away with the murder of Lamorak other knights may be emboldened to imitate his tactics for getting rid of their most envied rivals. At the opening of 'Joyous Garde' Malory alters his source to have Galahalt and Bagdemagus plot to 'destroy' and 'shame' Lancelot because he 'had evermore the hygher degree' (675.5–9:X.50; cf. Löseth 282e, f). And at the conclusion of 'Palomides' Lancelot's own kinsmen plot to destroy Tristram 'bycause of his fame' (785.2–4:X.88). Having suggested in this way what are the likely effects of Arthur's failure in justice, Malory goes on to suggest how the King ought to have dealt with the threat of his nephews' 'treson' by setting Lancelot as an example. When Lancelot hears that his kinsmen are plotting against Tristram, he immediately puts a stop to it with the following speech, which Malory has invented for the occasion:

> 'Wyte you well that and ony of you all be so hardy to wayte my lorde sir Trystram wyth ony hurte, shame, or vylany, as I am trew knyght, I shall sle the beste of you all myne owne hondis. Alas, fye for shame, sholde ye for hys noble dedys awayte to sle hym! Jesu defende,' seyde sir Launcelot, 'that ever ony noble knyght as sir Trystram ys sholde be destroyed wyth treson.'
> (785.7–13:X.88)

We must infer that Lancelot's kinsmen truly believe that he would carry out this threat, for we hear no more of their plotting, and, in the end, it is not they but King Mark who destroys that 'noble knyght ... Trystram ... wyth treson.'

It cannot be easy to punish members of one's own family when they violate the social code of justice; however, that is what is required of a truly just king. King Louis IX of France was canonized in part because of his ability to do justice upon members of his own family, and that tells us a good deal about the importance which medieval man attached to what Malory calls 'true justyce' (16.22:I.7). The medieval ideal of kingship was the *rex pius et justus*, on the presumption that a king would always be just if he were pious. Arthur's failure to punish his nephews' criminal behaviour proves that he falls short of this ideal and Malory's characterization of him allows us to infer that he falls short because he is not a pious man. Malory's King Arthur is a Christian but he is also a rational pragmatist. For him, doing 'true justyce' is a matter of judging rationally and correctly on the basis of the available evidence. As we have already seen, both in this chapter and in the first chapter, the king is an excellent dispenser of justice when his emotions do not interfere with his judgment; however, when his emotions threaten to overpower his judgment, he has no adequate way of controlling them. Certainly, he is not able to transcend the bonds of kinship in the way that Lancelot does in the speech cited above.

Who May See the Grail?: The Testing of Worshipful Knighthood

In 'Launcelot and Elaine' Malory introduces the religious point of view into his narrative once again. Up until this time the atmosphere in the Tale of Tristram has been remarkably secular, as befits a tale devoted to exploring 'the noble way of the world'. However, the murder of Lamorak suggests that this 'noble way of the world' is not sufficient to ensure social stability and justice and therefore we are not surprised that Malory should re-introduce the religious point of view. The narrative of Galahad's begetting and its aftermath serves several thematic functions. It prepares the reader for a Quest of the Holy Grail in which Tristram will take no part. It confirms the 'change of [Lancelot's] name and levynge' (863.25:XIII.5), the change from premier True knight (and potential Grail knight) to premier Worshipful knight. Most important of all, it allows Malory to test each one of his types of knighthood by the religious standards of the Grail.

We will have occasion to examine this testing process in more detail in the next chapter. Here it is only necessary to indicate how Lancelot fares for when he first visits Corbenic Lancelot represents Worshipful knighthood at its best.

In the Tale of Tristram we have seen Lancelot succumb to both of the sins which are typical of the Worshipful knight: pride, or vainglory, and *cupiditas* in the Augustinian sense of loving the goods of this world 'oute of mesure', that is, more than God. However, he has not yet committed adultery with the queen. Therefore, when he first comes into the country of the Grail Castle, his Christian virtue is still sufficient to enable him to save the lady who suffers in scalding water and to slay the serpent in a nearby tomb. Even more significant, in Malory's version, his virtue is still sufficient to enable him to *see* the Grail (793.25–35:XI.2). However, Lancelot's devotion to and 'drede of God' is no longer more powerful than all of his earthly attachments: he may still love God more than his kinsmen, but he no longer loves God more than his lady, Guinevere. When a messenger brings him Guinevere's ring and tells him that she is at a castle five miles away, he is eager to leave Corbenic in order to be with her. That he has seen the Grail and might have seen more of its mysteries if he had passed the night there is not enough to keep him when he believes that his lady desires to see him. Lancelot's response anticipates Tristram's response to the appearance of the Grail at Camelot. Tristram, too, will prefer to be with his lady, Isode, rather than be tested by the 'stronge adventures' of the Sankgreal. Both responses are typical of the Worshipful knight.

The Worshipful knight believes in God and observes the rituals of his religion, but he is a lover of the world. To him the world is a good place which may be made better and is certainly not to be renounced for God's sake. Unlike the True knight he does not regard knighthood as a 'hyghe order' which requires his total dedication but rather as a social elite to which he must belong in order to win the goods of the world: power, honour and love. In fact, one could argue that the Worshipful knight looks upon his religion in much the same light that he looks upon his knighthood — as a social institution which confers honour upon its members and makes them eligible to win even greater honours in this world.

Malory's original conclusion to the Tale of Tristram seems designed to illustrate this attitude of the Worshipful knight towards his religion by telling the story of Palomides' baptism. Malory makes clear that by the time they fight their last battle, Palomides, the 'Sarezen', has become a more courteous knight than Tristram, the Christian. Nevertheless both men speak and act as though Palomides is a lesser man because he is not baptized (cf. 840.24–28:XII.12). That the pagan knight has long had in his 'harte' and in his 'soule' a 'good beleve in Jesu Cryste and hys mylde modir Mary' (842.5–6:XII.13) is not sufficient to earn him the honour of full status in Christian society, and he and Tristram both know that.[27] To deserve this honour Palomides has made a vow to do a certain number of 'batayles' and Tristram is glad to provide the last one. It is the battle itself which proves that Palomides has become a more courteous knight than Tristram. After they have fought for some time Tristram knocks Palomides' sword out of his hand, and Malory tells us that 'yf sir Palomydes had stouped for hys swerde he had bene slayne' (844.10–11:XII.14).[28] Then it is Palomides, not Tristram, who courteously brings the battle to a close by reminding his opponent that their quarrel is not so great 'but that we may be fryendys' (844.22–23:XII.14).[29] When Palomides then begs both forgiveness and baptism from his long-time friend and foe, Tristram responds with gallantry: '. . . as ye sey, so shall hyt be, and all my evyll wyll God forgyff hyt you, and I do' (845.5–7:XII.14). Thereupon he and the wounded knight Galleron stand as 'godfadyrs' while Palomides is received into the society of Christian gentlemen.

Because of his unwavering devotion to 'the noble way of the world' Tristram rather than Lancelot remains the epitome of Worshipful knighthood in the *Morte Darthur*. After sponsoring Palomides' ritual admission into the society of Christian men, Tristram rides with him to Camelot for the feast of Pentecost at which the Grail appears. However, the sight of the Grail will not inspire him with a desire to go in search of the Holy Vessel. Whereas Palomides will follow the Questing Beast (one of the Grail adventures) and Lancelot will choose to leave his lady behind in order to search for the Grail, Tristram will prefer to return to Joyous Garde to be with his lady, Isode (845.25: XII.14).

The main differences between True and Worshipful knights can be related to the fundamental difference in the way they define honour, or worship. The True knight defines honour as equivalent to moral virtue. On the other hand, the Worshipful knight defines honour as social status. Their different definitions are logically consistent with their views of knighthood as such: the True knight believes knighthood to be an order established by God to protect and govern temporal society and therefore tantamount to a religious vocation, whereas the Worshipful knight believes it to be a social and military elite in the service of the feudal monarch and therefore itself a great honour. Pious men like Sir Gilbert Hay may disapprove of men who seek to become knights 'for pryde or covatise, or for to be honourit, or for vane glore, or to wyn richess thareby' (*Knychthede*, 38). But worldly and practical men like Malory's Tristram and Arthur are not convinced that war and politics have anything essentially to do with religion or that being pious, humble and chaste will make one a better soldier, courtier or prince.

In his classic essay, 'Honour and Social Status', the anthropologist Julian Pitt-Rivers has shown that these two different meanings of the word 'honour' or 'worship' — the one moral and religious, the other social and political — actually served a useful function in European society during the late medieval and early modern period, the function of 'social integration'. The more late-feudal monarchies grew in power, the more they successfully arrogated to themselves the exclusive right to bestow honours and to maintain that those whom they honoured were, by definition, honourable. Pious men might privately disagree but they could not openly challenge these ascriptions of honour-as-virtue unless they possessed sufficient honour-as-status-or-power to make good their challenge. Thus, honour was able to do what philosophers say cannot be done, 'derive an *ought* from an *is*' and in the process to ensure 'the legitimation of established power' in late medieval and early modern Europe (Pitt-Rivers 38).

In Malory's *Morte Darthur* most of King Arthur's knights are Worshipful knights who look to the king as the fount of honour and accept without question that whomever he honours is by definition honourable. As a consequence we may say that Arthurian society as a whole functions like a 'shame culture'.[29] However, within this honourable society there are men who do not live by the dominant ethic. On the one hand, we have men like Gawain and his brethren who live by the more primitive code of the patrilineal clans of Scotland and for whom knighthood is no more than the exercise of arms. And, on the other hand, we have men like Lancelot, Gareth and the Grail knights who try to live by the ethical code of the Christian religion and for whom knighthood is a 'hyghe ordir'.

In the next chapter we will look again at these other two types of knight as we examine more closely the religious context of Malory's knightly typology. Both the Heroic knight and the True knight are fundamentally religious types, although in very different ways. The Heroic knight is a fatalist and his god is a tribal God, whereas the True knight is a providentialist and his God is a personal God; but they share one characteristic which sharply differentiates them both from the Worshipful knight. As we have seen in this chapter, the Worshipful knight is a rational pragmatist, his rationalism showing up especially in his approach to trial by battle and his pragmatism in his approach to knighthood as a career, whether as a prince or as a courtier. By contrast, the Heroic knight and the True knight share a profound distrust of reason as a sufficient guide to conduct and choose rather to guide their actions by principles which transcend reason.

5

Happy and Unhappy Knights

Like his contemporary, the chronicler John Hardyng, Sir Thomas Malory accepted the Grail quest as an historical 'fact'. He did not, however, accept the chronicler's interpretation of that 'fact'. Whereas Hardyng presents the achievement of the Grail as a spiritual triumph in which King Arthur and all his knights of the Round Table share fully (133–36), Malory presents it as a partial triumph, at best. In Malory's version most of the Round Table knights, including Arthur himself, do not seem to understand what is demanded of them by the appearance of the Grail at Camelot. Only four are found worthy to enter the Grail castle and more than half 'sle ech othir for synne' in fulfillment of Nacien's prophecy.

Malory's treatment of the Quest of the Holy Grail defines the religious context of his knightly typology just as his treatment of Arthur's governance defines its political context. We have seen in the first chapter how his representation of Arthur's governance conforms to contemporary political theory and practice. Now it is time to consider to what extent his representation of the Grail quest also conforms to contemporary religious belief and practice. What we find is that Malory's understanding of the Grail quest has, indeed, been influenced by both of the tendencies most marked in fifteenth century religion: its mysticism and its this-worldly quality. These two tendencies would seem at first glance to be inherently contradictory and perhaps ultimately they are. But in the fifteenth century mystical notions were being drawn into secular society through popular devotional treatises and, at the same time, the devout lay people who read these treatises were looking for ways to reconcile their religion with the world. They did this in many ways, either individually or in groups, by staging religious dramas and processions, endowing schools, building parish churches, becoming patrons of the arts and giving to the poor. But above all they did it by striving to live virtuously in the world, in imitation of Christ.[1]

Gordon Leff has observed that late medieval popular mysticism shared with the reform movement 'the desire for direct encounter with God' and that for both 'the image of Christ was the focus of activity' (130). Ecclesiastical reformers demanded that the Church conform itself to the life of Christ in the world and pious laymen, influenced by the writings of the fourteenth-century mystics, sought to imitate Christ by living the 'mixed life', that is by combining the active life of good deeds with the contemplative life of prayer and meditation.[2] Richard Rolle feared that it was impossible for ordinary men to imitate Christ in this way (*Fire* 49; *English* 55–56), but Walter Hilton held out the hope that any layman might achieve what he called 'stableness of good living' in the world (*Scale of Perfection* 291) if he would but take care to develop his spiritual life through frequent prayer and meditation.

Malory shows that he has been influenced by the thought of both Hilton and Rolle in his version of the Grail quest. First, he equates 'stableness of good living' with the achievement of the Grail and represents Bors as the sort of pious layman to justify Hilton's optimism regarding the mixed life. The holy man who hears Bors' confession finds in him 'so mervales a lyffe and so stable', despite his one sin of the flesh, that he is fully worthy to be a Grail Knight (956.2:XVI.6). It is important to note here that the choice of adjectives is Malory's: in the *Queste* the holy man finds his life 'si bone' and 'si religieuse' (166.22–23). On the other hand, Malory represents Bors' cousin, Lancelot, as the sort of pious layman to justify Rolle's fears. During the Quest Lancelot tries to make up for his past deficiency by spending a great deal of time in prayer and meditation, especially while he is with his son, Galahad. But it is not enough. Like the religious men and women described by Rolle in his brief prose treatise, 'The Bee and the Stork', Lancelot's 'thoghte' remains fixed on the 'lufes of men and women' and so his effort brings him 'till no stabylnes' (*English* 55–56). The passage in which Malory makes this point through the hermit, Nacien, is perhaps the most well-known of his infrequent additions to his source for the Grail Quest: 'and nere were that he ys nat stable, but by hys thoughte he ys lyckly to turne agayne, he sholde be nexte to encheve hit sauff sir Galahad, hys sonne; but God knowith hys thought and hys unstablenesse' (948.24–27:XVI.5).[3]

Something like Hilton's positive attitude toward the world and the service of one's fellow Christians informs the concept of knighthood as a 'High Order' instituted by God to do justice and to keep the peace in Christendom. John Bossy has argued that in late medieval thinking, certainly at the popular level, peace itself was regarded as 'holy' — the product of the fulfilment of a 'social contract with God'. It was also thought to be 'the condition of the eternal salvation' of Christian men and women in society. Therefore, those who destroyed the peace threatened the eternal damnation of all and, by a corollary extension made explicit by Queen Isabella of Spain, those who kept the peace ought to be regarded as 'a holy brotherhood' (132–33). Malory's understanding of knighthood is certainly along these lines. He commonly refers to knighthood as an 'ordre' or as a 'hyghe ordre' (without any warrant from his sources)[4] and, as we have seen, he also emphasizes the brotherly love and friendship which ought ideally to inform the relations between members of this 'High Order'.

Malory seems to admire the ideal of knightood described in *La Queste de Saint Graal* even though it is extremely ascetic, having been modeled upon the crusading order of Knights Templar whose members were also monks. However, Malory could not accept the Cistercian author's view that there are only two types of knights: ascetic 'veray' knights 'celestiels' who serve God, and lecherous false knights 'terriens' who serve only themselves. Malory knew that a third type had developed in the meanwhile. This is his Worshipful knight who has translated the ascetic religious ideal of knighthood as service to God into the secular political ideal of knighthood as service to the prince. What is more, Malory knew that even though these more courtly Worshipful knights were not very pious, the best of them were nevertheless devoted to the maintenance of peace with justice. Consequently, Malory translates the Cistercian monk's dichotomy of true/false into his own threefold typology: there are True knights who do their knightly deeds for God's sake ('in Goddys workys'); there are Worshipful knights who do knightly deeds for their prince and to increase their honour ('in worldly workis', 886.21–22:XIII.14); and there are Heroic knights who, by either of these standards, do no 'knyghtly dedys' at all (891.30–32: XIII.16).

The specific religious belief which has most clearly affected Malory's interpretation of the Grail quest, as well as his understanding of the knight's relationship to God, is the belief in Divine Providence. This belief seems to have grown very strong during the fifteenth century to judge by the popularity of *de casibus* tragedies like Lydgate's *Fall of Princes* and the common practice of interpreting current events in terms of divine rewards and punishments. Boethius' *Consolation of Philosophy* was also immensely popular and influential in propagating a providentialist view of the relationship between God and man. Boethius' Lady Philosophy teaches that God is immanent in His creation and that every rational creature is responsible to Him for his actions. A man is free to accept or reject the grace of God, but he may not avoid the fact that he lives 'in the sight of a judge who sees all things' and therefore under 'a great necessity to be good' (169). Malory calls attention to this providentialist view through his use of the adjectives 'happy' and 'unhappy' and their derivative forms. As we shall see, their repetition constitutes a *leit motif* which runs throughout his work, beginning in the 'Tale of Balin' and building to a resounding climax in the 'Day of Destiny', by which time the reader understands that to be 'unhappy' is to be unfortunate or 'cursed' because separated from the will and grace of God.

Malory also calls attention to the belief in Divine Providence through the increased use he makes of prophecy. Fifteenth-century Englishmen understood that prophecy was often a 'call to men to involve themselves in the working out of God's purposes in history' (Reeves vii) and Malory reflects this understanding in the way he adapts Merlin's role. In the first two parts of his first narrative unit, the 'Tale of Merlin' and the 'Tale of Balin', Malory transforms the legendary sorcerer into a prophet of God, much like the Old Testament prophets (Kelly, 'Arthur' 15–16). In so doing, Malory is also reflecting Merlin's contemporary status and reputation as a prophet; for, in mid-fifteenth-century England, Merlin had a reputation for prophecy second to none, not even to the holy monk, Joachim of Fiore. Joachim's writings had stimulated a great interest in prophecy throughout Europe during the later Middle Ages. In England, however, they had the added effect of stimulating interest in the prophecies of the legendary Welsh wizard. Manuscripts which combined the prophecies of Merlin and Joachim circulated widely (Reeves 93–95), suggesting that many, if not all, fifteenth-century Englishmen regarded Merlin as a true prophet and one of the few men in the history of the world to whom God had given the gift of illumination so that he might discern His providential order.

As Robert L. Kelly has shown, Malory's *Morte Darthur* clearly embodies 'a providential view of history' ('Arthur' 9–10). I take that to mean that the Quest of the Holy Grail did not have to happen. Certainly, it did not have to happen in the way that it did. According to the late medieval providentialist view of history, the only 'two determined points of the future were the appearance of Antichrist and the Last Day of Judgment. These apart, there was scope for the play of human imagination on the future forms of society and their fate' (Reeves vii). Even more significant, there was scope for the play of human will and action. That is why, in Malory's text, Merlin does not, at the time the Round Table is instituted, prophesy the coming of Galahad (102.2–3:III.4; cf. *Suite* 2:65). And that is why he prophesies that the 'beste knyght of the worlde', the knight who will be able to 'handyll' the sword of Balin and then achieve the Grail, will be 'sir Launcelot other ellis Galahad, hys sonne' (91.22–23:II.19). As an historian, of course, Malory knows who, in fact, achieved the Grail. Nevertheless, within the world created by his text, he maintains the providentialist view of the future. From that point of view the story of the Grail is an historic process whose end is not predetermined. And it begins in the 'Tale of Balin'.

Balin's 'Unhappy Swerd' and the Heroic Code of Vengeance

The story of the Grail begins in the 'Tale of Balin', not only because Balin strikes the 'dolerous stroke' which creates the Wasteland, but also because he provides the first clear portrait of an 'unhappy' knight in the providentialist sense. In Malory's source for this tale, the *Suite du Merlin*, Balain is known as the 'chevalier mescheans', the unfortunate knight who is destined to commit an 'unwitting transgression' which the whole of Logres will have to expiate (Bogdonow, *Romance* 155). The 'dolerous stroke' is explained by his sacrilege in breaking into the Grail chamber and his death at the hands of his own brother is explained as a punishment for the 'dolerous stroke'. Balain himself understands nothing except that God has willed this destiny; he does not understand why. And as he and his brother lie dying, they weep, 'Ha! Dieus, pour coi avés vous souffert que si grant mesqueanche et si grans mesaventure nous avenist?' (*Suite du Merlin* 2:54: 'Oh, God! Why have you suffered such a great mishap and such a great misfortune to come upon us?'). Malory's Balin is quite a different sort of character, and the significance of what happens in his tale differs accordingly.

Malory's Balin epitomizes Heroic knighthood at its best, 'withoute velony other trechory and withoute treson,' and thus, in terms of Malory's typology, he anticipates Gawain. Like Gawain, he is unfailingly loyal to his kin group. Like Gawain, he is an incomparable fighter: 'there lyvith nat a bettir of proues, nother of worthynesse' (75.9–10:II.9). And, again, like Gawain, and also like his counterpart in the French romance, he is a fatalist. That is to say, he believes that the future is determined by the inalterable will of God. His most noticeable characteristic as a Heroic knight, however, is his relentless pursuit of the blood feud.

The blood feud was anathema to late medieval kings because it infringed upon their sovereignty. It was anathema to the Church because it often entailed the shedding of innocent blood. And it was anathema to both Church and State because it was, theoretically, unending. René Girard calls attention to the fact that vengeance always entails the 'risk' that it will 'initiate a chain reaction', the consequences of which would 'quickly prove fatal to any society of modest size, and that is why it is universally proscribed.' Girard goes on to observe that this proscription is actually most strictly enforced 'in the very communities where . . . vengeance seems to hold sway,' that is, in primitive societies; in highly developed societies, on the other hand, a 'sovereign authority specializing in this particular function' exacts what may be called public vengeance (or 'justice') upon those who violate the proscription (15). Malory imagines society in King Arthur's days to fall somewhere in between these two extremes. There is a sovereign authority, embodied in King Arthur, which punishes murderers with death. But that authority is not yet strong enough nor pervasive enough to be able to punish all 'private' acts of vengeance. Therefore, the ultimate danger posed by the blood feud remains.

In Malory's version of the 'Tale of Balin' this danger is embodied in Balin, enacted in the 'dolerous stroke', and symbolized by his 'unhappy swerde' and the Wasteland. What is more, even though Balin and his brother, Balan, take a fatalist view of these events, Malory introduces the providentialist point of view into his narrative by altering the prophecies of Merlin and introducing the *hap* motif.

The damsel who brings Balin's 'unhappy swerde' to Arthur's court describes the knight who 'may draw oute thys swerde' in the following terms:

> '. . . he muste be a passynge good man of hys hondys and of hys dedis, and withoute velony other trechory and withoute treson.' (61.34–62.2:II.1)

This is a complete description of Malory's Heroic type of knight. The damsel even lists the three typical virtues in the usual order: he must have exceptional prowess ('be a passynge good man of hys hondys'); he must have sufficient courage to exercise his prowess ('and of hys dedis'); and he must be loyal. She emphasizes the importance of this last virtue by threefold repetition: 'and withoute velony other trechory and withoute treson.' She does not specify to whom or to what the knight must be loyal, but Balin's first action after achieving the damsel's sword proves that his first loyalty is to his kin group: even though he is in the court of King Arthur he strikes off the head of the Lady of the Lake in order to avenge the death of his mother (66.4–14: II.3). This rash and vengeful action confirms his knightly type.

The Heroic knight lives by the *lex talionis*, the law of retribution which requires an eye for an eye, a life for a life, regardless of cost, motive or circumstances. Gawain and his brethren, except for Gareth, live by the same law. However, the Orkney brothers are the king's nearest and dearest kinsmen; therefore the potential for conflict between the two obligations — loyalty to family and loyalty to feudal lord — is not so readily apparent in their case. In the case of Balin, however, it is apparent from the outset. We know, for example, that Balin has just been released 'by good meanys of the barownes' from six months in Arthur's dungeon 'for sleyng of a knyght which was cosyne unto kynge Arthure' (62.34–36:II.2). Given his behaviour vis-a-vis the Lady of the Lake, we may reasonably infer that he also killed Arthur's 'cosyne' in order to avenge his family's honour. We know that Balin is a 'poore' knight of Northumberland, that he admires King Arthur and would like to be taken into the service of this king so renouned for his 'good grace' and 'bounté'. Nevertheless, Balin is clearly not willing to put loyalty to Arthur before loyalty to his own family.

Malory adds a brief conversation between Balin and his squire which helps to explain his apparently reckless and foolish behaviour:

> 'Alas!' seyde the squyre, 'ye ar gretly to blame for to displease kynge Arthure.'
>
> 'As for that,' seyde Balyne, 'I woll hyghe me in all the haste that I may to mete with kyng Royns and destroy hym, othir ellis to dye therefore. And iff hit may happe me to wynne hym, than woll kynge Arthure be my good frende.' (66.30–35:II.3)

The young king is still beset with enemies and needs good fighting men. Balin knows he can get the lordship of Arthur again if he can destroy his powerful enemy, King Royns. On the other hand, he could not be so certain of having another chance to avenge his mother's death. He had been looking for this Lady of the Lake without success for three years and he was not likely to find her again so easily.

Balin's judgment is validated by Arthur's response. Although the King is infuriated by the beheading of the Lady of the Lake, he says nothing, except that Balin 'sholde have forborne' in his presence, no matter 'what cause' he had (66.15–16:II.3). Then, rather than condemn the murderer to death, the king merely banishes him from the court.

Arthur has put the matter in terms of his honour and that of his court, but much more than honour is involved in Balin's violation of the king's 'sauff conduyghte'. By pursuing his private blood feud in the king's presence, Balin is claiming that the individual's right to do justice takes precedence over that of the king himself. In other words, he is openly challenging the king's sovereignty. That he does not seem to realize this suggests that Balin shares the archaic consciousness of heroes of the Dark Ages. That Arthur in response does no more than banish him from the court suggests that he is aware of his relative weakness as a feudal monarch during this early period of his reign.

Balin killed the Lady of the Lake with the sword he won from the damsel, and Malory's version of why the damsel brought the sword to Arthur's court suggests that it was already cursed and intended to do 'grete harme' as an instrument of vengeance. In Malory's source the damsel had gone to the Lady Lyle for help in getting vengeance upon her own brother and had been promised that the knight who could unsheathe this sword should with it kill her brother (1:223). In Malory's version, she is told that the knight who could unsheathe the sword — and he must be 'one of the beste knyghtes of thys realme' — should with it 'sle *hys* brothir' (68.2–4:II.5, emphasis added). Malory offers no explanation either for the malice of the Lady Lyle or for the damsel's willingness to carry this sword to Arthur's court, even though it will not give her the specific vengeance she desires. And we are left to explain as best we can how the damsel's need for vengeance against her brother could possibly be satisfied by one of Arthur's best knights killing his brother.[5]

Merlin speaks of Balin's second sword in such a way as to call to mind a well-known passage from the scriptures:

> 'And that knyght that hath encheved the swerde shall be destroyed thorow the swerde; for the which woll be grete damage, for there lyvith nat a knyght of more prouesse than he ys.' (68.8–11:II.5)

The passage is original with Malory and the echo of *Matthew* 26:52 is clear: *Qui gladio percutit gladio peribit*: 'He who takes up the sword shall perish by the sword.' Jesus spoke these words in the Garden of Gethsemane to dissuade Peter from taking up arms against the Roman soldiers and they have been cited ever since to justify Christian pacificism. In 1395 they were quoted in a broadside nailed to the door of St Paul's cathedral to protest the granting of indulgences to knights who went abroad on crusades (Jones 245). By that time, however, established Christianity had long since come to terms with the idea of a Christian knighthood. The protesters' use of the quotation would have appeared unorthodox (in fact, they were probably Lollards). The orthodox view was that Christian knights wield the sword of justice with divine sanction, God having ordained knighthood. Therefore, Christ's admonition would apply only to the knight who takes up the sword without divine sanction. Balin already has one sword, which we may presume was consecrated upon the altar when he was ordained a knight just as Arthur's first sword was consecrated (16.18–20:I.7). That first sword may therefore be said to symbolize knight's service which is sanctioned by God. In Balin's case this means service to Arthur, whom God has chosen to be 'rightwys king' of England. The second sword, however, is not only not consecrated, it is cursed. And yet, Balin refuses to give it back after the sword-bearing damsel prophesies what will come of it.

In Malory's version, the sword-bearing damsel appears to be so impressed by Balin's worth that she regrets her initial purpose for bringing the sword to Arthur's court and asks Balin to return it. Balin refuses.

> 'Well,' seyde the damesell, 'ye ar nat wyse to kepe the swerde fro me, for ye shall sle with that swerde the beste frende that ye

have and the man that ye moste love in the worlde, and that swerde shall be youre destruccion.'

'I shall take the aventure,' seyde Balyn, 'that God woll ordayne for me. But the swerde ye shall nat have at thys tyme, by the feythe of my body!' (64.8–14:II.2)

This conversation is also quite original with Malory, in particular Balin's insistence upon taking the 'aventure ... that God woll ordayne.' His meaning is not immediately obvious and has, in fact, been interpreted in two completely different senses by Robert Kelly and Jill Mann. Kelly sees in it an 'Oedipus-like challenge to Providence' suggesting the 'serious flaw of hubris' ('Tale of Balin' 90), whereas Mann sees in it a humble acceptance of 'a destiny laid on him, not created by him' (80). I would like to think that they are both right and that there is, in fact, a curious blend of humility and pride in Balin's response. On the one hand, he bows meekly before the will of God; on the other, he presumes to know better than the damsel what God's will is.

Balin's response is characteristic of the Heroic knight. It is precisely what we would expect of Roland or Beowulf, or Malory's Gawain. Like Roland, Balin places great value upon the virtue of courage and therefore he assumes that this is pleasing to God. To have returned the sword would have been a sign of cowardice. Like Beowulf, there is nothing Balin loves better than a fine weapon and therefore he assumes that God would not wish him to give back such a splendid sword with which to destroy his enemies. Moreover, like all Heroic Knights, Balin does not distinguish between his enemies and God's enemies (see above 110–11).

Malory alters his source to give Balin some evidence for this last assumption in the case of the Lady of the Lake. In the *Suite du Merlin*, Balin accuses her of being responsible for the death of his brother. In Malory's version, however, he accuses her of being

'... the untrwyste lady lyvynge, and by inchauntement and by sorcery she hath bene the destroyer of many good knyghtes, and she was causer that my modir was brente thorow hir falsehode and trechory.' (66.11–14:II.3)

If Balin's charges are true, and we must believe they are since he is a knight 'withoute velony other trechory and withoute treson', then the Lady of the Lake is not only his enemy and God's enemy, but Arthur's enemy, as well.

Malory does not eliminate the possibility that Arthur believes Balin when he says that the Lady of the Lake, the giver of his second sword,

Excalibur, was an evil sorceress and the 'destroyer of many good knyghtes'. Nor does Malory eliminate the possibility that had Balin sought justice from the king, rather than take the law into his own hands, the king would have given him justice. But neither of these possibilities is realized in his text and, consequently, the analogy between Balin's and Arthur's situations is strengthened. Both knights now carry second swords which were given to them by sorceresses in pursuit of vengeance. The boon which the Lady of the Lake asks of Arthur in exchange for the gift of Excalibur is 'the hede of thys knyght that hath wonne the swerde, othir ellis the damesels hede that brought hit. I take no force though I have both theire hedis: for he slew my brothir, a good knyght and a trew; and that jantilwoman was causer of my fadirs deth' (65.21–25:II.3). To save his 'worship' Arthur refuses the Lady of the Lake's request for vengeance. Nevertheless the implication is clear that the Lady of the Lake initially gave him Excalibur in order to have vengeance, just as the damsel brought Lady Lyle's sword to Camelot in order to have vengeance. We may conclude, then, that in Malory's version both 'second swords' — Arthur's Excalibur as well as Balin's 'unhappy swerde' — are strongly associated with vengeance and specifically with the blood feud.

Balin confirms his personal commitment to the blood feud by the first action he takes with his second sword, beheading the Lady of the Lake. Arthur's commitment to vengeance is neither so primitive nor so closely related to the honour of his family — at least not until near the end of his reign when he joins forces with Gawain to pursue the blood feud against Lancelot. As a Worshipful knight and king, Arthur's primary concern is for his personal honour and the honour of his court and, therefore, he seeks vengeance only for affronts to his person or to his knights. The first action he planned to take with his second sword was to 'be avenged' on King Pellinor for the humiliation of defeat (53.23:I.25), but Merlin was able to dissuade him. Now the honour of his court has been affronted by Balin's killing the Lady of the Lake while she was his guest and so Arthur gives permission to sir Launceor of Ireland to avenge 'the despite that he [Balin] hath done unto me and my court' (67.11–17:II.4).

Balin does not want to fight Launceor — by the ethical standards of Heroic knighthood they have no reason to fight — but Lanceor gives him no choice. Balin is sorry when he realizes that he has killed Launceor in their first encounter and sorrier still when Launceor's lady, Columbe, arrives on the scene, making 'grete dole oute of mesure', and threatening to kill herself with her lover's sword. He tries to take the sword away from her but, fearing to hurt her, he lets go, thus allowing her 'suddeynly' to fall upon the blade.

Balin's response to this disaster is very like his response to the sword-bearing damsel's prophecy — a curious blend of opposites: humble, passive acceptance and proud, aggressive action. First, his brother Balan echoes his own former response: '... ye must take the adventure that God woll ordayne you' (70.19–20:II.6) and Balin agrees. At the same time, however, he determines to take vigorous action to win back King Arthur's favour: 'hys love I woll gete othir ellis I woll putte my lyff in adventure.' And Balan agrees to 'ryde with you and put my body in adventure with you, as a brother ought to do' (70.21–30:II.6). The blend of passivity and aggressivity in both brothers is remarkable. Even more remarkable, however, in this conversation which Malory has invented, is the threefold repetition of the word 'adventure'.

The Middle English noun *adventure* does not have a very precise meaning. Or perhaps it would be more accurate to say that it has four different meanings, all of which seem to have developed from the Vulgar Latin (*res*) *adventura* '(a thing) that will happen'. Since a man's attitude towards what 'will happen' in the future is likely to depend on his position regarding the philosophical question of determinism, it is not surprising to find that the first two meanings of the noun 'adventure' listed in the *Middle English Dictionary* reflect the two sides of that philosophical question. The first meaning, 'fate, fortune, chance; one's lot or destiny', reflects the determinist or fatalist position. The second, 'something that happens, an event or occurrence, ... an accident', reflects the belief in free will. For, just as the man who believes that the future is wholly determined must accept whatever happens as his 'fate' or 'destiny', so the man who believes that the future is not wholly determined and that he has freedom of the will must accept the possibility of 'chance' or 'accident'.[6]

A man's attitude toward *adventure* will also depend partially, at least, upon his temperament; therefore, it is not suprising either that the third and fourth meanings of *adventure* listed by the *Middle English Dictionary* should reflect a classic temperamental contrast. The third meaning, 'danger, jeopardy, risk', reflects the attitude of a fearful, passive nature. On the other hand, the fourth meaning, 'a venture, an enterprise; a knightly quest', reflects the attitude of a bold, aggressive nature. A man who believes that the future is wholly determined is more likely to regard it with fear than with optimism, unless he has great trust in a benevolent destining power. On the other hand, a man who believes that the future is not wholly determined is more likely to respond with aggressive enterprise, unless he is naturally of a passive or fearful nature. What characterizes Balin and his brother, Balan, is the relatively rare combination of aggressive enterprise and fatalism.

Even though he knows that the future is determined by the unalterable will of God, Balin nevertheless carries on boldly and aggressively putting his life 'in adventure'. We can only conclude that he believes this heroic course of action to be pleasing to God.

Through Merlin Malory introduces a providentialist view to contrast with Balin's own fatalist perspective upon his adventures. Malory has already established Merlin as a prophet of God in the preceding 'Tale of Arthur' (see above 26–27). Therefore he can now use him to suggest that Balin is wrong: the future is not determined and God is not pleased by his relentless pursuit of vengeance.

When Merlin arrives at the scene of the burial of Launceor and Columbe, he first prophesies the great battle which shall be fought on that site by Lancelot and Tristram. King Mark questions how such a 'boysteous' and 'unlyckyly' man can speak of such 'mervayles' but Merlin refuses to identify himself. Then he turns to Balin:

> 'A, Balyne!' seyde Merlion, 'thou haste done thyselff grete hurte that thou saved nat thys lady that slew herselff, for thou myghtyst have saved hir and thou haddist wold.' (72.19–22:II.8)

The last phrase, with its providentialist emphasis upon the determining effects of Balin's will ('for thou myghtyst have saved hir and thou haddist wold') is Malory's addition to his source (cf. *Suite* 1:231).[7] It foreshadows a very similar scene at the conclusion of the first triple quest when Merlin will chastise Pellinor for failure to save a lady's life because he 'wolde nat abyde and helpe hir' (120.3:III.15). The emphasis upon the determinative effect of Pellinor's will is also original with Malory: in Malory's source Merlin only expresses regret that Pellinor should be 'si mescheans' and comforts him by saying that God sends 'corous et anuis en cest monde' more often to 'preudoumes' than to 'mauvais' (*Suite* 2:128). Malory's Merlin is a different sort of prophet. In the French *Suite du Merlin* Merlin is a fatalist who speaks of the future only in terms so dark that no man can understand. By contrast, Malory's Merlin is a providentialist who reveals his prophetic knowledge of the future as clearly as possible so that men may exercise their free will to cooperate with the will of God.

Merlin's first prophecy regarding Balin was that the 'knyght that hath encheved the swerde shall be destroyed thorow the swerde' (68.8–9:II.5). That prophecy confirmed in general terms what the sword-bearing damsel had augured (and Balin refused to believe) but Balin did not hear it because he had already been banished from the court. Merlin's second prophecy regarding Balin is spoken immediately after he has chastised him for failing to save Columbe's life:

> 'Me repentis hit,' seyde Merlion; 'because of the dethe of that lady thou shalt stryke a stroke most dolerous that ever man stroke, excepte the stroke of oure Lorde Jesu Cryste. For thou shalt hurte the trewyst knyght and the man of moste worship that now lyvith; and thorow that stroke three kyngdomys shall be brought into grete poverté, miseri and wrecchednesse twelve yere.' (72.25–31:II.8)

The causal connection between 'the dethe of that lady' and the 'dolerous stroke' is original with Malory and, since Merlin makes the connection almost immediately after chastising Balin for failing to save the life of Columbe, most critics have assumed that the dead lady in question is she. However, when Merlin was clearly referring to Columbe, whose body lies in the tomb before him, he said 'thys lady that slew herselff'. By contrast, he attributes the 'dolerous stroke' to 'the dethe of that lady'. I think he means the death of that other lady, the Lady of the Lake, whom Balin slew in Arthur's court in order to avenge his mother's death.[8] This is the first time that Merlin has seen Balin since that incident, and therefore the first time that he has had an opportunity to speak to him of it.

As with the sword-bearing damsel, so now with Merlin, Balin defies augury. Indeed, he goes so far as to suggest that Merlin may be a liar:

> 'Nay,' seyde Balyn, 'nat so; for and I wyste thou seyde soth, I wolde do so perleous a dede that I wolde sle myself to make the a lyer.' (73.1–3:II.8)

The comparison between Balin and Pellinor, which Merlin's initial remarks on the death of Columbe suggested, now yields a significant insight. When Merlin tells Pellinor of the punishment God has 'ordayned' for his failure to save the life of a damsel, Pellinor will reply,

> 'Me forthynkith hit . . , that thus shall me betyde, but God may well fordo desteny.' (120.9–11:III.15)

Pellinor is a providentialist. He knows that the future is not wholly determined and that therefore, if he sincerely repents his deed, he may hope for better grace.[9] On the other hand, Balin is a fatalist. He knows that the future is wholly determined by God and therefore he desperately clings to the belief that Merlin is either mistaken about the 'dolerous stroke' or that he is lying.

Balin cannot believe Merlin's prophecy because, as a Heroic knight, he believes that it is his sacred duty to avenge the death of his kinsmen. Even if he could believe that his own free will partially determines the future, Balin could not have avoided 'the dethe of that lady'. He had no choice but to avenge the death of his mother, just as the kinsmen of Launceor and Columbe now have no choice but to avenge their deaths by chasing Balin 'thorow the worlde tylle they have slayne [him]' (71.14–16:II.7). It is not surprising that Balin should refuse to believe that God would allow him to be punished for doing his sacred duty.

In this encounter between Balin and Merlin we can see the conflict between two very different ideas of justice — that of the clan and that of Christendom. To a clansman, vengeance for the death of a kinsman *is* justice, but to a Christian, the only killing which can be justified is killing done by an acknowledged agent of divine justice, an executioner whose sword arm is presumed to do the will of God. That surely is the point of the consecration of the knight's sword upon the altar during the knighting ceremony. Knights who persist in using their swords for acts of private vengeance are not *true* knights. Moreover, they risk the destruction of their society as a consequence of the blood feud. Merlin does not say God has *ordained* that Balin 'shalt' strike the 'dolerous stroke' because of 'the dethe of that lady'. He says, rather, 'because of the dethe of that lady thou shalt stryke a stroke moste dolerous . . .' Since the plot offers absolutely no 'horizontal motivation' (in Bloomfield's sense, see above 59–60) to link the two events and since God has not ordained it so, we are left with Balin's desire for vengeance *per se* as the 'vertical motivation' linking them. This comes close to the Greek tragic notion of character as fate, but Balin's devotion to the *lex talionis* is not, strictly speaking, characterological. It is much more a matter of principle than of individual preference. Balin does not pursue vengeance for his own pleasure but for what he perceives to be his duty. And we may see in his refusal to give back the second sword — the sword borne by the damsel and cursed by the desire for vengeance — a dramatic emblem of his will to vengeance.

It is not just the vengeance of the clansman that is so destructive, however. As a matter of fact, the vengeance which Balin pursues against Garlon and which results in the 'dolerous stroke', is *not* the vengeance of a clansman; rather it is vengeance of the sort which Arthur allowed Launceor to pursue against him — vengeance for an affront to his personal honour. Garlon has slain a knight while the knight was under Balin's safe conduct. His crime is perfectly analogous, therefore, to Balin's crime in killing the Lady of the Lake while she was under Arthur's safe conduct. And Balin responds just as Arthur did.[10]

Malory reinforces the thematic significance of Merlin's second prophecy by making Balin's striking of the 'dolerous stroke' as much like his striking of the stroke which killed the Lady of the Lake as it could be. To begin with, of course, there is the fact that both strokes violate the law of hospitality, thus inviting comparison with the vengeance of Dark Age heroes like Hengest at Finnsburh (*Beowulf* 1066–1159). Secondly, both strokes are struck at enormous personal risk: Balin could not reasonably expect to escape with his life on either occasion. And thirdly, Balin's reason for taking such a risk is the same in both instances: his enemies have supernatural powers and taking this risk seems to offer the only chance of vengeance. Balin had searched three years for the Lady of the Lake before discovering her by chance at Arthur's court. Likewise, he knows that he is not likely to meet Garlon 'agayne at such a stevyn, and muche harme he woll do and he lyve' (83.28–31:II.14). Of course, these three points of resemblance were present in outline in Malory's source, but Malory has heightened them considerably. Even more significant, he has eliminated altogether the suggestion made by his source that Balin committed sacrilege in the Grail chamber and that the 'dolerous stroke' ought therefore to be understood as a divine punishment for this crime. Malory eliminates all the descriptive details, including the mysterious warning voices, which suggest that Balin has entered a holy place and committed sacrilege.[11] His Balin enters a chamber which is clearly a bedroom, containing a bed richly hung with cloth of gold and, on a table, 'a marvaylous spere strangely wrought' (85.7: II.15), a weapon of the same magnificent quality as the sword borne by the damsel, which Balin seizes because he is 'wepynles' and in danger of his life.

Malory's description of the aftermath of the 'dolerous stroke' also draws attention to the theme that vengeance begets vengeance. As Balin makes his way through the Wasteland, the survivors of his stroke curse him:

> 'A, Balyne! Thou hast done and caused grete vengeaunce in thys contreyes! For the dolerous stroke thou gaff unto kynge Pellam thes three contreyes ar destroyed. And doute nat but the vengeaunce woll falle on the at the laste!'[12] (86.3–6:II.16)

This passage suggests what René Girard has analysed as the 'chain reaction' effect of vengeance:

> Vengeance, then, is an interminable, infinitely repetitive process. Every time it turns up in some part of the community, it threatens to involve the whole social body. There is the risk that the act of vengeance will initiate a chain reaction whose consequences will quickly prove fatal to any society of modest size.

> The multiplication of reprisals instantaneously puts the very existence of a society in jeopardy. . . (14–15)

The words 'chain reaction' and 'instantaneously' evoke very powerfully the effect of a 'dolerous stroke' which can destroy a castle instantly and within three days lay waste three 'contreyes'. It is as if Balin's act of vengeance had the destructive force of an atomic bomb.

The *Suite du Merlin* explains the fratricidal death of Balin as God's vengeance upon him for the 'dolerous stroke' (2:47). Malory does not mention this particular 'vertical motivation' until after Galahad has achieved Balin's sword on the eve of the Quest (863.5–9:XIII.5). Consequently, in 'The Tale of Balin' itself the reader is more likely to notice another 'vertical motivation' which links Balin's death with his decision to keep the second sword.

By the terms of the Heroic code of honour, a knight may never retreat from danger, for that is to betray cowardice and incur shame. Earlier I suggested that one of the reasons Balin refused to give back his second sword was that to do so would have appeared cowardly. That motive appears even more clearly in Balin's response to the warning of 'grete daunger' as he approaches the island where he shall encounter his brother Balan:

> '. . . I maye not torne now ageyne for shame, and what aventure shalle falle to me, be it lyf or dethe, I wille take the adventure that shalle come to me.' (89.2–4:II.17)

Balin expressed the same willingness to 'take the adventure . . . that God woll ordayne for me' when he refused to give back the sword cursed by vengeance (64.12–13:II.2), and we can see now that in both cases his 'willingness' is determined by the same necessity. The Heroic code of honour requires that a man never turn back from danger. Therefore Balin could not turn back from the encounter with Balan any more than he could give back the second sword 'for shame'.

The death of Balin foreshadows the death of Gawain. Both knights die as a consequence of adhering to the Heroic ethos at all costs and both knights express the wish that some 'good knyght' might pray for their souls (21.1–2:II.18 and 1231.19–20:XXI.2). But whereas Balin receives the last rites and dies without considering that he might in some way be responsible for this fratricidal encounter, Gawain finally realizes on his death bed that he is to blame for the 'unhappy warre' which is destroying Arthurian society (1230.27: XXI.2).

Balin, too, employs the adjective 'unhappy' before he dies. He speaks of the 'unhappy customme' of the castle (88.21:II.17) and of the 'unhappy knyght in the castle' who 'caused' him to leave his own shield behind (90.12:II.18). In between Malory also describes Balin's sword as 'unhappy' (89.22–23:II.18). The usages are just odd enough and come close enough together to attract notice and to make the reader wonder what it might mean to be 'unhappy'. Can a custom, a person and a thing all be 'unhappy' in the same sense? Balin seems to regard *unhappynesse* as something external to himself, a quality of wretchedness or misfortune which inheres in other people, objects and events, but not in himself. By contrast, Gawain realizes that by pursuing vengeance he has caused his own and his uncle's *unhappynesse*.

Malory's 'Tale of Balin' shows that the pursuit of vengeance brings misfortune not only upon the avenger but also upon his society.[13] And it is within this thematic context that Malory first introduces what I shall call his *hap* motif. Then, at the very end of the tale, Malory links this motif to the Grail Quest through one of his most startling and significant innovations: he makes Balin's 'unhappy swerd' the sword which the premier Grail knight will bear.[14] Merlin gives Balin's sword a new pomel and places it in the stone where it will float miraculously 'many yeres' until 'the beste knyght of the worlde' comes to 'handyll' it (91.15–22:II.19). By this means Malory suggests that the sword cursed by vengeance can be handled without mishap only by a knight filled with God's grace. He suggests further that the wretchedness caused by Balin's relentless pursuit of vengeance can be cured only by a knight whose will is perfectly conformed to the will of God. In short, to employ the language of his *hap* motif, which will be the subject of the next part of this chapter, Malory suggests that *unhappynesse* can be undone only by *happynesse*.

Happynesse and Unhappynesse

Malory's *hap* motif is most noticeable in his account of the Death of Arthur where the usage rate of *hap* and its various cognates nearly quadruples.[15] To my knowledge the only other critic to have noticed it there is Larry Benson, who takes it to be a 'recurring suggestion of accident' which 'clearly implies that Arthur is helplessly and innocently caught in forces beyond his or anyone's control' (240). This is to consider only one possible complex of meanings for *hap*, however, that which centers on the concept of one's 'lot', with special reference to the element of 'chance', understood either as 'luck' or as 'destiny'. But *hap* is a very ancient word whose origins can be traced back to Indo-European *kob*, meaning 'to suit, fit, succeed'. In Old Norse *hap* retains the positive meaning of 'good luck', along with the more neutral meaning of 'chance' and it enters Middle English with this dual connotation. Consequently, the first set of meanings which the *MED* assigns to *hap* ranges from 'lot' or 'luck', whether good or bad (1a–b), through 'good luck, prosperity' (1c), to 'a source of happiness; one of the eight beatitudes' (1d) and 'favour, graciousness' (1e). What is more, the northern dialect of Middle English developed an adjective, *happen*, which clearly means 'blessed' and which turns up in the work of the Gawain poet:

> Aght happes he hem hyght, . . .
> Thay arn happen that han in hert poverté
> For hores is the hevenryche to hold for ever.
> They ar happen also that haunte mekenesse
> For thay schall welde this worlde and alle her wylle have.
> (*Patience* 12–16)

And so he goes on through all the 'happes' or beatitudes to conclude, 'He were happen that hade one, alle were the better' (34). In *Sir Gawain and the Green Knight*, the same poet characterizes the 'fayre folk' of Arthurian society 'in her first age' as 'hapnest under heven' (54–56), and in *Pearl* he uses the noun *happe* three times in contexts in which it means either 'blessing' (16, 713) or 'good fortune' understood as sent by God (1195).[16]

Even if one translates *hap* to mean 'fortune' (*MED* 3a), as in the phrase 'ladi of hap' or Dame Fortune, it must still be understood in the late medieval context which makes God the 'king of hap'. What that phrase meant in the fifteenth century would have varied from individual to individual. To men like Malory's Balin and Gawain it would have meant 'decider of fate' or 'destiny' (*MED* 3b) and reinforced their fatalistic belief in God's unalterable decrees. But fatalism was neither widespread nor orthodox in the fifteenth century. To other men, like Malory's King Arthur and Tristram, it would have meant the equivalent of Dame Fortune's caprice, i.e., 'an unforeseen occurrence' or 'chance event', whose moral significance is unknowable to man, even though, in an ultimate sense, it forms part of the divine plan. To many fifteenth-century men, however, the phrase 'king of hap' would have suggested the providentialist point of view.

Late medieval providentialism differed from the providentialism of the Puritan reformers in its emphasis upon the importance of good works. Indeed, as John Bossy has observed of late medieval popular Christianity, 'the traditional man is also a federal theologian, a man in possession of a covenant; but his *feodus* is more like a covenant of peace than a covenant of grace' and, therefore, the united effort of mankind becomes essential to the 'fulfilment of its part in a social contract with God' (132–33). This kind of 'federal' theologizing was not limited to the members of late medieval religious confraternities, however. It can also be found among the English mystics. According to Richard Rolle,

> We felawchipe with god of hys grace als merchaundes duse to-gedir þat hase chafere in mene: ffor god settis his grace agayne oure werke, to chafere with þame bathe; bot for his dede he will noghte elles, be þe byet neuer sa gret, bot louynge & thankynge, & alle þe prowe he will þat mane haue þat þerof may ryse.
> ('On Grace' 307)

Rolle images the enterprise of life as a business partnership between God and man. God provides the capital — 'his grace' — and man provides the 'werke' in the form of good deeds and prayers. And all the profit ('prowe') goes to man. A very similar notion of a partnership uniting God and man, without the mercantile imagery, can be found in Walter Hilton's short treatise on contemplation, *Eight Chapters on Perfection*. When experiencing a dry period, Hilton advises the contemplative to continue to pray nonetheless so that he might, 'as it were, constreyne God to ȝeue þee feruour and heete of holy de-uocioun'. The reason for this ability to 'constreyne' God, 'as it were', is made plain by what Hilton says next: 'Do þou þat longiþ to þee, and þi loued dere Iesu Crist schal wel do þat perteyneþ to him' (4). If the Christian does his part, then Jesus Christ will surely do His.

The notion that man could somehow 'earn' divine favour because of God's perfect justice was anathema to the Lutheran reformers, though it continued to be orthodox teaching in Roman Catholic countries after the Reformation. Nevertheless, late medieval providentialism was very similar to Lutheran and Calvinist reformed belief in one respect: like seventeenth-century puritans, fifteenth-century providentialists expected God's punishments and rewards on earth as well as in heaven. They also interpreted worldly prosperity as a sign of God's favour (and hence of the prosperous man's virtue) and worldly misfortune as a sign of God's displeasure (and hence, of the un-fortunate man's sinfulness). Not surprisingly, this kind of thinking was particularly apt to be applied to those men least likely to be punished for their misdeeds by any earthly power. It shows up not only in the popular *de casibus* tragedies, like Lydgate's *Fall of Princes*, but also in political commentary on contemporary events, such as the defeat or deposition of kings (H. A. Kelly, *Divine Providence* 35; Lander, *Crown* 58). And in that sixteenth-century compilation of cautionary tales for worldly lords, *The Mirror for Magistrates* (1559), it reaches a kind of apogee of pithy expression in a remark made by the ghost of the Duke of Suffolk: 'Good hap with vices can not long agree' (162.12).

Malory's *hap* motif reinforces the providentialist point of view throughout his work. The first cluster of usages of the adjective 'unhappy' in the 'Tale of Balin' is less clear in its implications because Balin himself is a fatalist and blames his *unhappynesse* upon others. However, the providentialist view is very clear in Gawain's death bed scene when Gawain finally transcends his fatalism and confesses his fault to Arthur:

> 'And all I may wyte myne owne hastynes and my wylfulnesse, for thorow my wylfulnes I was causer of myne owne dethe ... And thorow me and my pryde ye have all thys shame and disease, for had that noble knyght, sir Launcelot, ben with you, as he was and wolde have ben, thys unhappy warre had never ben begunne ...' (1230.19–27:XXI.2)

This speech is original with Malory and makes plain that the 'vertical motivation' of Gawain's tragic end is precisely the same as that of Balin's tragic end: the Heroic code of vengeance. If Gawain had not insisted upon having vengeance for the death of his brothers, Lancelot would never have been banished, he (Gawain) would never have received his death's wound, and 'thys unhappy warre had never be begunne.' Indeed, the emphasis upon Gawain's 'wylfulnesse' suggests that Malory sees Gawain as the hero of a Boethian tragedy, that is to say, the victim of his own wrong choices.

When used of an inanimate thing like Balin's sword, or of a condition, like war, the Middle English adjective *unhappi* means 'associated with, marked by or causing misfortune or mishap; disastrous, miserable or wretched' (*OED* 3 and 4). On the other hand, when used of animals or persons, it can mean either 'causing misfortune or trouble' to oneself or others (*OED* 1) or 'unfortunate, unlucky, ill-fated' (*OED* 2), and the editors note that the first sense to some extent passes into the second. In other words, when used of persons, *unhappi* has both an active and a passive sense, depending upon whether one sees the unhappy person as having caused his misfortune or as suffering it. Malory's Balin and Gawain are 'unhappy' in both senses.

The active sense of 'unhappy' is closely related to the idea of wrong-doing, as we can see from the fifth meaning cited by the *OED*: 'causing or involving trouble or mischief; objectionable, evil, naughty'. This meaning has become obsolete in Modern English, but it was still very much alive in Malory's time and continued to be used in this sense well into the seventeenth century. What is more, the same sense that misfortune is related to evil or wrong-doing inheres in Middle English *unhappynesse*, which can mean either 'misfortune, mishap, ill luck' (*OED* 1), or, 'evil, wrong-doing, mischief' (*OED* 2). As with *unhappi*, this second meaning continued in active use into the seventeenth century.[17] Therefore, we may conclude that throughout the late medieval and early modern period, to be 'unhappy' could mean either to be unfortunate or to be wicked. And once again, we may say that Malory's Balin and his Gawain are 'unhappy' in both senses for, even though they could not see anything wrong initially with pursuing the blood feud, the consequences of their actions prove to be so disastrous both for themselves and for their society that they must be held responsible for their wrong-doing, if not for their wickedness.

A True knight like Lancelot, Bors or Galahad would not have taken so long as Gawain to realize his responsibility. Since True knights typically adopt the providentialist view, they automatically assume that they must have done something wrong whenever they suffer misfortune. This tendency is illustrated with marvelous richness and economy in a scene involving Lancelot and Bors after the tournament at Winchester.

Bors has unwittingly wounded Lancelot at the Winchester tournament because he could not recognize his cousin, who was wearing a plain shield and a damsel's red sleeve (a situation not unlike that which made possible the fratricide of Balin and Balan). When Bors realizes later what he has done, he is overcome with grief and sorrow and, when he next sees his cousin, launches into a lengthy speech which tells us a good deal about the providentialist view of a man's relationship to God:

> 'A, my lorde sir Launcelot, God you blysse and sende you hasty recoveryng! For full hevy am I of my mysfortune and of myne unhappynesse. For now I may calle myselff unhappy, and I drede me that God ys gretely displeasyd with me, that He wolde suffir me to have such a shame for to hurte you that are all oure ledar and all oure worship; and therefore I calle myselff unhappy. Alas, that ever such a caytyff knyght as I am sholde have power by unhappiness to hurte the most noblyst knyght of the worlde! Where I so shamefully sette uppon you and overcharged you,

> and where ye myght have slayne me, ye saved me; and so ded nat I, for I and all oure bloode ded to you their utteraunce. I mervayle,' seyde sir Bors, 'that my herte or my bloode wolde serve me. Wherefore, my lorde sir Launcelot, I aske you mercy.'
> (1083.17–31:XVIII.16)

Bors calls himself 'unhappy' because God has allowed him to hurt his own cousin. He blames himself for his 'mysfortune' and 'unhappynesse' because he knows that he was wrong to have 'overcharged' Lancelot, three against one, in order to have vengeance for the hurts endured by his kinsmen. But he also knows that his 'shameful' action could not have produced such a result if God had not suffered it. And therefore he must conclude that God 'ys gretely displeasyd' with him, which is as much to say as he has fallen from God's grace and therefore has acquired 'power by unhappiness' to hurt others.

Lancelot's response reveals that he, too, is a providentialist:

> 'Fayre cousyn,' seyde sir Launcelot, 'ye be ryght wellcom, and wyte you well, overmuche ye sey for the plesure of me whych pleasith me nothynge, for why I have the same isought; for I wolde with pryde have overcom you all. And there in my pryde I was nere slayne, and that was in myne owne defaughte; for I myght have gyffyn you warnynge of my beynge there, and than had I had no hurte... Therefore, fayre cousyn,' seyde sir Launcelot, 'lat thys langage overpasse, and all shall be wellcom that God sendith.' (1083.32–1084.9:XVIII.16)

Lancelot believes he knows better than Bors whose sin is to blame for this misfortune: it is his own 'pryde' in wishing to prove that he could 'overcom you all'. Therefore, he blames himself for his mishap ('and that was in myne owne defaughte') and concludes that henceforth 'all shall be wellcom that God sendith,' from which we may infer not only that he believes God has sent him this punishment for his pride, but that in future he intends to avoid sin so as to avoid misfortune.

In this conversation Lancelot and Bors are expressing a view of life which is profoundly religious, one might even say, mystical. It is not a view which is common in contemporary Europe or America; however, it is common in all societies which have not developed a highly rationalistic culture and, therefore, it was common in Europe before the seventeeth century. The anthropologist Edward Sapir has defined religion as 'man's never-ceasing attempt to discover a road to spiritual serenity across the perplexities and dangers of daily life.' Every culture must define for itself what constitutes spiritual serenity but, however this is done, the end result is the same. What all religions offer is

> ... the unquestioning and thoroughly irrational conviction of the possibility of gaining mystic security by somehow identifying oneself with what can never be known. (347)

Lancelot and Bors have such an irrational conviction of God's immanence in their world. That is why when they suffer misfortune they conclude that they must, through sin, have alienated themselves from God.

As a young 'adventures' knight Lancelot is 'happy' rather than 'unhappy'. Malory first draws attention to his *happynesse* in an episode which recalls young Arthur's exploit at Mont St Michel. As Arthur approached the giant's lair, an old widow warned him of his danger, saying, 'I holde the unhappy' (200.24–25:V.5; cf. alliterative *Morte Arthure*, 'unblysside' 962). The event proves her to be wrong; however, Arthur later admits that he had 'nere founded, had nat [his] fortune be good' and he asks the people of that country to 'thanke ye God, ... and no man ellys' (205.3, 11:V.5). Malory must have had this event in mind when retelling Lancelot's adventure at the Castle Tintagel. For, as Lancelot approaches the castle occupied by 'two grete gyauntis', the inhabitants shout at him, 'Fayre knyghte, thou arte unhappy to com here!' (271.29:VI.10). The epithet 'unhappy' not only recalls what the old woman said to Arthur as he approached battle with a giant, it also expresses, in shorthand fashion through the *hap* motif, the gist of a much longer conversation which Malory found in his source. In the French prose *Lancelot* a damsel pleads with him not to go into the castle because no man has ever departed from there 'sanz courrouz'. Then, when Lancelot insists on going in anyway, she says, 'Or vos doint Diex... millor eur que li autre n'ont eu' (86.6). Clearly, she does not think it likely that God will give Lancelot better fortune than all those other knights and, in Malory's version, the inhabitants of the castle express precisely the same idea when they call him 'unhappy'. They are wrong to think so. Just like Arthur, Lancelot easily overcomes the two giants. Then he enters the castle hall where sixty ladies and damsels kneel before him to thank 'God and hym of his delyveraunce'. What is more, they go on to praise his exploit in terms which make him appear a divinely appointed saviour: 'blyssed be the tyme, knyght, that ever thou were borne' and 'many tymes have we here wysshed aftir you, and thes two gyauntes dredde never knyght but you' (272.3, 7–9, 17–19:VI.11). None of this is in Malory's source and its effect is to go beyond the comparison with Arthur to invite a comparison with Galahad, the deliverer of the Castle of Maidens (see above 116).

The thematic significance of the Tintagel episode is reinforced by the fact that it follows immediately after Lancelot has just defined what it means to be 'unhappy' — and therefore by implication what it means to be 'happy' — in conversation with a damsel. The damsel asked him why he would not marry or love a woman 'peramours'. Lancelot replied that he would not marry because he did not want to give up the 'adventurous' life of a Round Table knight. As for loving 'peramours' he said,

> 'that woll I refuse: in prencipall for drede of God, for knyghtes that bene adventures sholde nat be advoutrers nothir lecherous, for than they be nat happy nother fortunate unto the werrys; for other they shall be overcom with a sympler knyght than they be hemself, other ellys they shall sle by unhappe and hir cursednesse bettir men than they be hemself. And so who that usyth peramours shall be unhappy, and all thynge unhappy that is aboute them.' (270.33–271.4:VI.10)

This speech is the longest and most significant addition Malory has made to his French source material for this tale. It says quite plainly that Lancelot is a man who lives in pious 'drede of God' because he knows that without the grace of God he can not be 'happy'.

In his little treatise 'On Grace' Richard Rolle also identifies the man who is without God's grace as an 'vnhappy wreche' (308). By this he does not mean that such a man lacks the first degree of grace which God gives to all creatures and which keeps them in life. He lacks rather the second degree of grace (prevenient grace) which is 'more special', which God offers to all men, and without which a man can do nothing good. Rolle imagines this 'more special' grace coming to mankind as to one asleep and saying,

> 'Vmbythynke the, vnhappy wreche, how foule þou arte dounne castyne, & whate perelle þou arte in; for thurgh thi syne þou arte fallene in till thyne enemyes handes, þat ouer all thynge couaytes to wyrke the waa . . .' (308)

Rolle goes on to warn that one should beware receiving the grace of God in vain, for perhaps he 'sall never after þer-till wyne' (309) and concludes, 'For wele es vs in þis lyfe whiles goddis grace vs ledis; ffor whene grace vs leues, we faile of þat wele' (310).

Malory's Lancelot would seem to have taken this orthodox teaching on grace very much to heart and to have applied it directly to his vocation as a knight. If he were to love 'peramours' he would lose the grace of God and with it his 'wele' as a knight. And then he would be liable either to be 'overcom with a sympler knyght' or to 'sle by unhappe and . . . cursednesse bettir men.' In other words he imagines that there would be two major consequences of his loss of grace: defeat and manslaughter. These are such common knightly misfortunes that it seems incredible any knight should expect to be protected from them, and yet there can be no doubt that that is what Lancelot expects, so long as he remains without sin.

The sources of Lancelot's pious optimism are not hard to find. Writing a century before Malory's time, the French knight Sir Geoffrey de Charny repeatedly makes the point that the knight is more subject to 'male meschance' than most men because of the hazardous nature of his vocation. Therefore, he argues, the knight must trust wholly in God. Charny does not go so far as to assert that God will preserve the virtuous knight from misfortune, but he does assert that the presumptuous knight who trusts in himself rather than in God will lose his gifts of strength and skill 'pour deffaute de recognoissance de Celi qui les avoit données' (507). This is very close to the first part of what Lancelot has said about lecherous knights, for the knight who loses his strength and skill because of his failure to acknowledge his dependence upon God will surely be overcome by men he would normally regard as 'sympler'.

Writing about judicial combat a century and a half before Malory's time, Ramon Lull asserts that 'the trewe knyght that fyȝteth for the ryȝt may not be surmounted' (52). Lull does not qualify that assertion, but his fifteenth-century Scots translator and adaptor, Sir Gilbert Hay, does. Significantly, he qualifies it in the covenantal spirit of late medieval providentialism: God will give victory to the knight fighting for the right, provided that he himself is without sin:

> . . . never curage of traytour mycht our cum ane noble curage of a trew knycht, bot gif it be throw pride or surquidy, that is callit our presumptuous in him self: the quhilk God tholes quhilom be punyst in bataill place. Bot the curage of a lele knycht, that for a lele caus debatis, may nocht be our cummyn, bot gif it be for sum syn agaynis the ordre of knychthede. (*Knychthede* 31)

Lancelot's speech simply extends this principal to all knightly encounters and adds a second: that knights who are without sin will also be able to defeat their opponents without committing manslaughter, that is, without killing them unintentionally.

The covenantal spirit of late medieval providentialism also informs Alain Chartier's *Traité de l'Espérance*. The fifteenth-century English translator of this work was Malory's contemporary; therefore it is of particular significance that he consistently uses the adjective 'happy' to mean 'blessed' (*MED* 2a) and 'unhappy' to mean 'causing or involving trouble or mischief, objectionable, evil, naughty' (*OED* 5). He is careful to say that 'the rewardis of happy folkis is not to be gotin in this worlde' (1:42). On the other hand, he is certain that kings who are not 'happy' will be punished by God here on earth. 'Unhappy' kings are those who 'slepe in vayneglorye and make hemselfe dronken in pride' and 'forgette the dreede which [they] shulde by reason owe to Almighty God'. Such kings have the power to bring 'unhappynesse' upon their people, because

> . . . synne is so foule and of so falling a condicion that it drawith vnto hym myserye and seruage and his delyte is always accompenyed with vnhappynesse and pursewid with peyne. And so the diuine iustice, which is rightfull, may nat suffre suche kyngis to reigne ouir the people forasmoche as thei be seruantis vnto synne.' (1:35)

Yet another contemporary of Malory expresses the same providentialist conviction of God's perfect justice. Indeed, in his adaptation of the thirteenth-century pseudo-Aristotelian *Liber de Regimine Principum*, Sir Gilbert Hay goes beyond Chartier to express the positive corollary of this conviction:

> And will thou umbethink the wele of all that I have said and governe the efter my devis and counsale beforesaid, thou salbe haldyn as wys and worthy king, . . . And thou sall cum abone [sic] of all thyne undertakingis and desyris. Quhilkis gif thou faillis to do, thou sall se that thare sall cum grevous mischief and mysfortune, bathe apon the and thy realme and thy governaunce, and it sall nocht be in thy powar to sett remede, . . . Bot here I pray hertfully to the hye and mychty God, makare of hevyn and erde, to geve the grace, as he is gudely gouvernoure of hevin and erde, and of all the warlde, to governe the sa in vertu and in veritee, in justice and leautee, that God and man be payit of the ende. (*Buke of the Governaunce of Princis* 164–65)

Here we see not only the conviction that God will punish sinful kings with misfortune, but also that he will reward virtuous kings with success ('And thou sall cum abone of all thyne undertakingis and desyris'). What is more, Hay makes clear how this covenental system works: God, the 'gudely gouvernoure of hevin and erde', gives His grace; man assents to this grace and uses it to become virtuous, and the result is that both God and man are 'payit'. The image is as much political and judicial as mercantile, and therefore close to Malory's own concern with temporal governance. In fact, one could argue that in Lancelot's speech, Malory has simply taken Hay's (and Chartier's) providentialist convictions regarding kingship and applied them to the entire order of knighthood.

In his adaptation of Lull's treatise on knighthood Sir Gilbert Hay provides an example of a 'happy' knight in the aged knight-hermit who looks back over his life and thanks God for the

> ... grete grace that God has gevin me in this erde to be sa happy till have governyt sa, but [without] lak, the said ordre [of knighthood], that all my grace and gude aventure throw it I had ... (*Buke of Knychthede* 9–10; cf. Lull 11).

This passage is of particular interest for two reasons. First, the old man is clearly a providentialist who credits his ability to be a true knight both to the 'grete grace' of God and to his own efforts to 'govern' himself. And secondly, he uses the terms 'grace', 'happy', and 'gude aventure' (i.e. 'gude hap'), in precisely the way I want to argue that Malory and his True knights use these terms. Hay's knight-hermit uses 'grace' the first time clearly in the sense of 'God's blessing'. The second time he uses the word it could mean what Jill Mann calls 'benign chance' (79), particularly since it is coupled with 'aventure' whose primary meaning in Middle English is 'chance' (understood either as 'luck' or 'fate'). However, in this context it is clear that the old man believes both his 'grace' and his good fortune or 'gude aventure' to have been the result of the combined efforts of God and man. In sum, this passage makes clear that, to a providentialist, to be 'happy' is to be both blessed and virtuous and, therefore, fortunate.

As a concept, then, *happynesse* is the precise opposite of *unhappynesse*. Just as *unhappynesse* can mean either 'misfortune' or 'wrong-doing' so *happynesse* can mean either 'good fortune' or 'God's blessing'.[18] Again, just as in the case of *unhappynesse*, the causation, or 'motivation' of *happynesse* is, to use Bloomfield's terminology for romance narrative, both 'horizontal' and 'vertical'. Put another way, its cause is both immanent and transcendent, in man and from God. In the case of *unhappynesse* much heavier emphasis is placed upon man's activity and responsibility, which is not surprising given the Christian explanation for the origin of evil. As Walter Hilton teaches in *The Scale of Perfection*, original sin (man's fault) is a great 'misfortune' (*mischief*) which the grace of God alone can help (226). To be sure, God remains an active agent in the creation of *unhappynesse* as 'king of hap', but providentialists believe that He permits misfortune only for good reason: either to punish a man for his sins or to recall him to a keener sense of his utter dependence upon God. Likewise *happynesse* is both vertically and horizontally motivated. Without the grace of God a man cannot be 'happy' but a man must choose whether or not he will be 'happy', whether or not he will fully assent to God's grace. God offers His grace freely, but His grace is not irresistible.

Happynesse, then, is the convergence of divine grace and human virtue. Or, to put it another way, it is the convergence of divine will and human will. It is that 'mystic security' of which Sapir speaks, for the 'happy' man is at one with God. On the other hand, *unhappynesse* is the divergence of divine and human wills and is caused by man's wilfull rejection of God's grace. The providentialist accepts that the 'unhappy' acts of 'unhappy' men are part of God's Providence and ultimately turn to good because God is perfectly just and can draw good even from evil. At the same time, of course, he must believe that if all men would assent to God's special grace, then all men could be 'happy'.

The pious optimism of the late medieval providentialist is confirmed in Malory's representation of True knights like Tor and Ywain, young Lancelot and Gareth, and it is quite likely that many of Malory's first readers and listeners would have appreciated this. Cultural historians of the period are generally agreed that fifteenth-century men were looking for ways of 'reconciling their religion with the world,' and that spiritual teachers like Richard Rolle were assuring them that this was possible: 'the world was wide enough and good enough to win heaven in' (Aston 149). The most important conceptual mechanism for achieving this reconciliation was the notion that the layman could imitate Christ (Leff 130). What is more, he need not be a teacher or preacher in order to do so, as we may see from a curious 'vision' recorded by an English monk in the mid-fifteenth century. In his vision the monk sees his friend tempted by three men to leave the monastery. One of these men 'was a sqyere, þe secunde was a clerke, and þe thyrthe was a koke. . .' They invite the monk go with them 'for ȝe myȝt bettyr serue god to lyfe in þe world wyt hem than in ȝoure ordyr' (Colker 105). This notion that a man might serve God 'bettyr' in the world is a clear rejection of the more traditional notion that the cloistered and contemplative life of monks is most pleasing to God. England never developed the lay brotherhoods which characterized the *devotio moderna* movement on the continent, but the English monk's vision suggests that the idea of serving God in the active life was common enough in mid-fifteenth-century England to cause him some anxiety.

The appearance of the 'sqyere' in the monk's 'vision' suggests that the new devotional ideal affected the way fifteenth-century Englishmen viewed knighthood. Of course, knighthood had been viewed as a religious vocation by some men, at least, ever since the Crusades, and this ideal of the knight as the soldier of Christ in the war to win back the Holy Land from the Saracens was not yet dead in the fifteenth century (Keen, 'Chaucer's Knight'; Lander, *Government* 206–7). As late as 1464 there was an unsuccessful attempt to win back Constantinople. Moreover, Sir Thomas Malory may well have felt closer to the crusading ideal than the average fifteenth-century Englishman, since one of his relations, Sir Robert Malory, served as prior of the Hospital of St John of Jerusalem in England from 1432 to 1439/40 (Field, 'Sir Robert'). However, the religious view of knighthood also had a strong association with the office of temporal governance in the many treatises on knighthood written between the late thirteenth and the early sixteenth centuries (Keen, *Chivalry* 16). Indeed, this religious view of knighthood as a universal order of men, established by God to provide mankind with peace and justice, was essential to the late medieval vision of a united Christendom.

Any fifteenth-century English knight or aspirant to knighthood who took this ideal of knighthood seriously would have a ready-made way of reconciling his religion with the world. No matter what his place in the hierarchy of knightly offices, from the Holy Roman Emperor down to the humblest local justice of the peace, he could easily see his temporal office as a Christian vocation of service to his fellow man.[19] In the *Morte Darthur* Malory calls attention not only to the sacred nature of the office of temporal governance but also to the vision of Christendom in his description of Arthur's coronation as Emperor at Rome. Malory probably used Hardyng's *Chronicle* as his authority for this event (E. D. Kennedy, 'Hardyng's'); therefore his deviations from Hardyng's description of the coronation scene are probably significant: Malory tells us that Arthur was crowned 'by the Poopys hondis' and that he was anointed with holy oil (244.20, 245.7–8:V.11). To receive his crown from 'the Poopys hondis' suggests that Arthur's power as Holy Roman Emperor comes from the Pope, and the anointing with holy oil clearly reinforces the notion that this highest temporal office in Christendom is sacred. Taken together, these details suggest that Malory shared the 'theocratic vision of a unified Christendom' (Guillemain 67).

Malory also suggests that knighthood is a sacred office when he has Arthur establish the Round Table at the feast of Pentecost. Pentecost is the feast which celebrates the descent of the Holy Spirit upon Christ's apostles, filling them with divine grace so that they might work miracles of preaching and healing. Therefore, this context implies that Arthur's Round Table knights will also be able to work miracles if they become filled with God's grace. As we have seen, Malory's True knights — Tor, Ywain, Lancelot and Gareth — do work miracles. One thinks particularly of Ywain's victory over the two 'perelous' brothers who had extorted lands from the Lady of the Roche; of Lancelot's victory over the giants of Tintagel and his healing of Sir Melyot; and of Gareth's victory over the six thieves and Sir Ironsyde.

The *happynesse* of Lancelot and Gareth gradually fades from view during the Tale of Tristram, however. Early in this tale young La Cote and Lancelot are still able to perform prodigiously in order to do justice; but, as the narrative progresses, Lancelot's love for the queen grows and eventually he suffers the *unhappynesse* of committing manslaughter for the first time in his career. Other knights also suffer *unhappynesse*. Heroic knights like Gawain and his brethren pursue the blood feud with impunity, murdering both King Pellinor and his son, Lamorak, and Worshipful knights, caught up in the fierce rivalry for honour and the king's favour, stoop to treachery among themselves. By the end of the Tale of Tristram it is clear that Arthur's Round Table knights are not able to fulfill their office. From the providentialist point of view it is equally clear that they are not able because of a lack of grace.

Even though the Round Table was established at Pentecost, the oath which King Arthur requires the fellows to swear each year makes no mention of God or of His grace. Malory's Arthur knows that his knights need 'worship' (in the sense of power and status) and his 'lordship' in order to do justice and keep the peace in his realm, but he does not think they need the grace of God.

Malory's Arthur is a rationalist for whom governance is a practical matter and the Tale of Tristram reflects his more secular point of view. In this tale men do not 'commend' or 'betake' one another to God (see above 114n), nor do they speak of the love of Christ or God. They frequently employ expletives like 'A, Jesu!' and 'So God me helpe!' But they do not really intend a religious meaning. In fact eighty percent (fifty four out of a total of sixty-eight) of the examples of 'So God me helpe!' occur in the Tale of Tristram, and in most contexts it is clear that they bear as little religious significance as their modern counterpart, 'So help me God!'[20] From the providentialist point of view men who speak like this are clearly alienated from the grace of God and that explains why they are not able to protect Arthur's realm from *unhappynesse*.

The providentialist belief that knights who are without sin will be 'happy' in the fulfillment of their office is the 'trouth of the Sankgreall' in Malory's *Morte Darthur*, the 'trouth' of which Merlin said when he established the Round Table,

> 'By them whych sholde be felowys of the Rounde Table the trouth of the Sankgreall sholde be well knowyn.' (906.28–29:XIV.2)

We have already seen the two ways in which this 'trouth' may be made 'well knowyn': the positive way of the True knight who is 'happy' in his vocation because he has fully assented to God's grace and determined to do God's will (e.g. the young Lancelot); and the negative way of the Heroic knight who is 'unhappy' because he has effectively rejected God's grace by preferring to do his own will (e.g. Balin or Gawain). We have also seen in the Tale of Tristram that Worshipful knights, who appeared initially to exemplify the courtly virtues of courtesy and justice, are in fact susceptible to envy because of their pride, and their envy makes them both uncourteous and unjust. Certainly, when men of the calibre of King Bagdemagus and Prince Galahalt plot to destroy Lancelot because in tournaments 'he had evermore the hygher degré' (675.1–9:X.50) and Lancelot's own kinsmen plot to destroy Tristram 'bycause of his fame' (785.1–11:X.88), they appear both unworthy and unable to fulfill their office. Indeed, it is the dark and 'unhappy' context of this last part of the Tale of Tristram which prepares us for the coming of the Grail and the Grail knight to Camelot.

'Lancelot Other Ellis Galahad': The Quest for Happynesse

Malory has profoundly altered the significance of the Grail story by making two alterations in the 'Tale of Balin': first, the premier Grail knight shall bear the 'unhappy swerd' of Balin; and second, this Grail knight shall be *either* Lancelot *or* Galahad. The first alteration strengthens the figural link between Balin and the Grail knight established by the author of the post-Vulgate cycle (Bogdonow, *Romance* 137) and also reinforces Malory's expression of the 'trouth of the Sankgreall', namely, that in order worthily to perform his office, a knight must be filled with the grace of God. The second alteration weakens the figural link between Lancelot and Galahad established by the author of the Vulgate cycle and expresses the providentialist view that Lancelot himself might have been the Grail knight if he could have remained in the world without turning away from God. From a providentialist point of view nothing is determined until it has happened. Therefore, when Merlin says that 'the beste knyght of the worlde' who will achieve Balin's sword 'shall be Lancelot othir ellis Galahad, hys sonne' (91.23:II.19), he is really saying that so long as Galahad has not been conceived, Lancelot may yet fulfill the prophecy, may yet be the one to 'handyll' the sword of Balin, sit in the

Siege Perilous, heal the Maimed King and restore the Wasteland.

During the first part of his work Malory consistently alters his sources to reinforce this notion of Lancelot as 'the beste knyght of the worlde' and the potential Grail knight. First, on the occasion of the founding of the Round Table fellowship, he eliminates Merlin's prophecy that 'li boins chevaliers' will come to fulfill the table and achieve 'les perilleuses aventures del roiame de Logres la u tout li autre faurront' (*Suite* 2:65). Then, in the Tale of Lancelot he depicts young Lancelot as very like Galahad, protected against manslaughter for his perfect chastity, endowed with the gift of healing, and able to bring peace with justice wherever he goes. Finally, even though he allows Lancelot to succumb to the sins of pride and *cupiditas* in the Tale of Tristram as a consequence of growing to love the queen 'oute of mesure', he does not allow him to succumb to the sin of lechery. Despite malicious rumours to the contrary, Lancelot has not yet committed adultery with the queen and is still a virgin at the beginning of 'Launcelot and Elaine'. Therefore, if he can be made aware of his sins and repent them, 'for drede of God', he may yet regain the perfect *happynesse* he enjoyed as a young knight and become worthy once more to 'handyll' the sword of Balin.

Within this narrative context, Lancelot's initial feats after riding 'by adventure' into the country around Corbenic augur well. First of all, he is able to rescue the naked lady who 'boyleth in scaldynge watir' (791.33:XI.1),[21] a feat which Gawain has already attempted in vain. Indeed, Lancelot's success invites comparison with a later feat of Galahad. During the Quest of the Holy Grail Galahad will succeed in cooling the 'welle which boyled with grete wawis' and Malory will deviate from his source to explain that the boiling of the water is 'a sygne of lechory that was that tyme muche used.' This explanation was already implied by the observation of his source that the 'hete' of the well 'myght nat abyde hys pure virginité' (1025.26–32:XVII.18); nevertheless, that Malory troubles to make explicit what was only implicit in his source suggests that this symbolism is of particular importance. We may infer, then, that the boiling of the water which keeps the naked lady in 'payne' has the same symbolic significance as the boiling of the water in Galahad's well. (This inference is also supported by the fact that Morgan le Fay, surely one of the most lecherous ladies in Arthur's kingdom, was responsible for placing the lady there.) By the same token, we may infer that the 'doorys of iron' which locked the fair lady in her 'payne' (and which had earlier remained locked despite all that Gawain could do), 'unloked and unbolted' as soon as Lancelot appeared for the same reason that the 'hete' of Galahad's well 'departed away' — because they 'myght nat abyde hys pure virginité.'

It is worth noting that Lancelot's success in rescuing this lady identifies him explicitly as 'the beste knyght of the worlde' (792.19: XI.1), Merlin's appellation for the knight who should 'handyll' Balin's sword. An even more positive sign of his enduring potential to be the premier Grail knight, however, is Lancelot's ability to see the Grail.

After Lancelot has slain a dragon 'to the plesure of God' and the inhabitants of that country (he does not speak of God in the *Lancelot* 78:46), King Pelles invites him into his castle. The Grail appears and they are fed by it. Afterwards, in response to Lancelot's questioning, Pelles explains:

> '. . . this is the rychyst thynge that ony man hath lyvynge, and whan this thynge gothe abrode the Rounde Table shall be brokyn for a season. And wyte you well,' seyde the kynge, 'this is the Holy Sankgreall that ye have here seyne.' (793.32–35:XI.2)

In Malory's source for this scene, Lancelot also sees the Grail and then explains his good fortune in terms of the graciousness of Our Lord, 'qui tant est debonnaires' that he may not be 'toz jorz courouciez a ses pecheors' (*Lancelot* 78.52). In Malory's version, neither Pelles nor Lancelot say anything of Lancelot's sinfulness; rather, they take for granted that he should be able to see the Grail. Even more important, Malory adds two passages which reinforce the significance of Lancelot's ability to see the Grail now, especially given his inability to see it later because 'he ys unhappy' (895.12–13:XIII.18). The first of these added passages is Nacien's comment that the Grail 'apperith nat to no synners' (948.17:XVI.5). The second is more particular. In the scene in which Percival and Hector are healed by the Grail, Hector is unable to see it, but Malory explains that 'sir Percyvale had a glemerynge of the vessell and of the mayden that bare hit, for he was a parfyte mayden' (816.34–36:XI.14). Clearly Malory associates the ability to see the Grail in particular with the virtue of chastity. Therefore, since Lancelot seems to have more than a mere 'glemerynge' of the vessell during his first visit to Corbenic, we may conclude that he, too, is a 'parfyte mayden' at this time.

That being the case, what happens next is a crucial turning point in Malory's narrative and takes on the nature of a test for Lancelot. King Pelles 'knows' more of the future — or thinks he knows more of the future — in Malory's version than he does in Malory's source. In the *Lancelot* he only knows that either through Lancelot or through 'chose qui de vos istra' his country will be delivered from 'estranges aventures' (78.49). In Malory's text Pelles 'knew well that sir Launcelot shulde gete a pusyll uppon his doughtir, whyche shulde be called sir Galahad, the good knyght by whom all the forayne cuntrey shulde be brought oute of daunger; and by hym the Holy Grayle sholde be encheved' (794.5–8:XI.2). But, on the other hand, Merlin has prophesied that the Grail should be achieved either by Lancelot 'other ellis' by Galahad, 'hys sonne'. Clearly now is the time of determination: which one will it be? In terms of the action, the question is posed by the sudden appearance of a messenger whom Lancelot recognizes as one of the queen's retinue. The messenger gives Lancelot a ring which appears to be Guinevere's and informs him that she is presently at Castle Case 'but fyve myle hens'. It is near nightfall, for Lancelot has spent 'the moste party of that day togydir' with the Grail king. Therefore, he must choose now whether he will stay the night in the Grail castle or whether he will go immediately to Guinevere. If he were to stay the night at Corbenic, he might possibly try the 'stronge adventures' there and learn more of the Grail's mysteries; but Lancelot is 'so fayne' to see his lady that he chooses to set off immediately for Castle Case. In short, he prefers Guinevere to God.

Lancelot's decision is typical of Worshipful knighthood. Guinevere's grace and favour now mean more to him than God's grace and that means, as he will confess later in the Quest, that he loves her 'oute of mesure'. Given the progress of their relationship thus far, it is not at all likely that Lancelot expects to lie with his lady this night (B. Kennedy, 'Malory's Lancelot' 422–28), but that only heightens the dramatic irony of the event. And, indeed, it is fitting that, having preferred his lady to God, Lancelot should in consequence beget his replacement as 'the beste knyght of the worlde'.

Bors' subsequent adventures at Corbenic suggest what Lancelot might have achieved if he had chosen God, instead. Like Lancelot, Bors sees and is fed by the Grail, but then, unlike Lancelot, he asks about the 'stronge adventures' known to be at Corbenic. King Pelles tries to dissuade him, but Bors persists and, in the end, proves that he 'lovyth God and dredyth God' more than any of God's creatures when he is able to win great 'worshyp' there (799.8–9:XI.4).

Bors' adventures at Corbenic may be seen as a divine parody of Lancelot's adventures at Castle Case. First, like Lancelot, Bors is led into a bedchamber and thence into bed, but whereas Lancelot was deprived of his rational and moral powers of judgment by a 'kuppe of wyne' which made him 'so asoted and madde that he myght make no delay but wythoute ony let he wente to bedde' (795.8–10:XI.2),[22] Bors lays himself down on the bed fully conscious and clothed in full armour. Secondly, whereas Lancelot experienced physical pleasure, Bors experiences physical torment and psychic terror. And, finally, whereas Lancelot knew that he had done 'amysse' and was 'shamed' (795.23–25:XI.3) as soon as he rose to open the bedroom window, thus breaking the enchantment, Bors leaves the chamber with the assurance that he has 'full worshypfully . . . encheved this' (801.13–15:XI.5). Then, in case one has missed these parodic elements, Malory calls attention to them in his version of the old man's farewell speech:

> 'Now . . . go ye to youre cousyn sir Launcelot and telle hym this adventure had be moste convenyent for hym of all earthely knyghtes . . .' (801.25–27:XI.6)

Knowing that Lancelot did not undertake this 'adventure' because he preferred to be with Guinevere, we realize that it is his sin of loving her 'oute of mesure' which the old man finds 'so foule in hym' and which accounts for the fact that 'in this spyrytuall maters he shall have many hys bettyrs' (801.27–33:XI.6; cf. *Lancelot* 98.42). Still the old man's phrasing leaves open the possibility that, even though he will have 'many hys bettyrs', Lancelot may yet prove capable of some 'holy dedys'.

Lancelot's decline in the Tale of Tristram from 'happy' knight to 'unhappy' knight is completed by his madness. Before that affliction, Lancelot had not known misfortune; and as Walter Hilton warns, such extreme good fortune can be perilous for the soul, making 'a man blind, unless he be ware through God's grace' (*Goad of Love* 120). Lancelot's unwary turning away from God was also helped along by his growing love for the queen; therefore, it is fitting that his affliction should come upon him as a consequence of committing adultery with her in thought, if not in deed. Actually, he betrays her, as well as God and Arthur, by lying with Elaine of Corbenic a second time. The awareness of his triple disloyalty drives him mad, and he remains out of his mind for two years, wandering in the forest, until 'by . . . adventure' he comes to the 'cité of Corbyn' where Elaine finds him and brings him into the presence of the Grail to be healed (817–23:XII.1–3).

Lancelot seems to assume that his madness was caused by his sin, and this should not surprise us, given what we know of medieval attitudes towards madness. Penelope Doob has shown that insanity was regarded as 'more horrible' than other diseases by medieval men because it deprived them of reason, 'the image of God'. Moreover, medieval men recognized an 'especially close resemblance between sin and madness' since sin also typically involved the overthrow or perversion of the reason by the will and passions. Therefore they perceived madness to be 'the most appropriate punishment for sin.' Doob concludes that in medieval literature generally, no matter what 'the immediate cause of madness, the ultimate moral causes are always implicit' (10–11). Certainly they are implicit in Malory's text in

Lancelot's words and behaviour after he has been healed by the Grail. When he first regains consciousness he begs Elaine 'for Crystes love' not to tell anyone what has happened to him, 'for I am sore ashamed that I have be myssefortuned' (825.14–15:XII.5). Then he takes upon himself the name 'Le Shyvalere Ill Mafeete, that ys to sey "the knyght that hath trespassed" ' (826.22–24:XII.6).[23] Finally, when he returns to the court he speaks cryptically of the 'foly' that he has done and deserved (833.1–2:XII.10) in a way which suggests that he regards his madness ('foly' *MED* 3) as a punishment for his sexual sin ('foly' *MED* 2).

The spiritual utility of misfortune is a common Boethian theme (cf. *Consolation of Philosophy* 142–44) which turns up frequently in the work of the fourteenth-century mystics. Rolle's gloss of Psalm 56 interprets suffering and misfortune as God's merciful punishments which have the effect of driving the soul away from the world towards God (*English Writings* 14). Likewise, Hilton argues that afflictions are 'profitable' because they 'open our inner eye to knowing of our wretchedness and so afterward to the knowing of God' (*Goad of Love* 120). This seems to be the effect which Lancelot's affliction has upon him. The first indication we have that Lancelot's affliction has in fact opened his 'inner eye' to the knowing of his 'wretchedness' is his response to the maiden who appears after Galahad has 'handylled' the sword of Balin. The maiden informs Lancelot that he is no longer 'the best knyght of the worlde':

> 'As towchyng unto that,' seyde sir Launcelot, 'I know well I was never none of the beste.'
>
> 'Yes,' seyde the damesell, 'that were ye, and ar yet, of ony synfull man of the worlde.' (863.28–31:XIII.5)

This dialogue, which appears to be wholly Malory's invention, suggests that Lancelot is 'yet' the 'best' of 'ony synfull man of the worlde' precisely because of his humility.

According to Richard Rolle, humility is the foundation of 'al gastly strengh' ('Form of Living' 10.104). Therefore, this scene suggests that Lancelot may yet redeem himself in the Quest for the Holy Grail, especially if, like Bors at Castle Corbenic, he is first willing to be 'clene confessed' of his sin. Lancelot and Bors are very much alike. In fact, Malory has gone out of his way to call attention to the likeness between them in the matter of their sexual transgression: almost immediately after Lancelot had begotten Galahad upon Elaine, Malory told us that Bors had begot a child upon king Braundegorys' daughter and 'that sauff for her sir Bors was a clene mayden' (799.21–24:XI.4). Then Malory has handled subsequent events to make it appear that

Lancelot too is a 'clene mayden' except for Elaine (whatever one thinks they were doing while they lived together on Joyous Ile). Therefore, it is reasonable to hope that Lancelot, like Bors, may be 'one of the four' who achieve the Sankgreal (180.9–10:IV.29).

In Malory's *Morte Darthur* the Grail 'is at once a symbol of grace, the vessel of transubstantiation and the vehicle of mystical union with the divine' (Whitaker, 'Christian' 13). Moreover its appearance at Camelot during the Feast of Pentecost is analogous to the biblical event which this feast celebrates — the descent of the Holy Ghost upon the apostles of Christ. Therefore it would appear to be both an extraordinary visitation of God's grace upon Arthur and his knights and also a call to them to assent fully to that grace. If they will 'felawchipe with god of hys grace', to use Rolle's words, they will surely profit by it ('On Grace' 307). For once they have become filled with God's grace, that is, become 'happy' knights, then they will be able to fulfill their office of bringing peace and justice to Arthur's kingdom.

If we take Lancelot as representative of all the sinful knights of the fellowship (all the black bulls of Gawain's vision), we see that the appearance of the Grail at Camelot is an exact reversal of the appearance of Guinevere's ring at Corbenic. Both objects stand for the grace and favour of the persons associated with them and in both cases they appear at the castle which stands for their opposite: Guinevere's ring appears at the castle which houses the Grail and the Grail appears at the castle which houses Guinevere. Moreover, in both cases their appearance precipitates a choice: at the sight of her ring, Lancelot had to choose whether to go to Guinevere or to remain with God and the Grail at Corbenic. Now, at the sight of the Grail, all of the Round Table knights will have to choose whether to go in search of God's grace or to remain at Camelot, loving the goods of this world 'oute of mesure'.

In Malory's version, when the Grail first appears at Camelot, the 'grace of the Holy goste' actually illumines each knight from within so that each seems to the other 'fayrer than ever they were before' (865.21–23:XIII.7). This phrase suggests the transformative effects which Walter Hilton attributes to God's grace in the *Scale of Perfection*, particularly in the first chapters of Book Two where he sketches the Christian scheme of redemption and explains how grace operates to restore men to bliss by reforming them in the image of their Maker. God's grace is not irresistible, however; therefore the transformation which takes place for the brief period of the Grail's presence at Camelot cannot be sustained without the full and freely willed assent of each knight.

What is expected of a man who has willed to be transformed in God's image by His grace? Because both Galahad and Percival choose to forsake the world for the contemplative life after achieving the Grail, it may be thought that the appearance of the Grail at Camelot is a call to all the Round Table knights to follow their example. This is not so, however; nor are any of Malory's first readers likely to have understood it to be so, if they were at all familiar with the thought of Walter Hilton. In the second book of the *Scale of Perfection*, which he seems to have written with a general public in view, Hilton asserts that every man must do the work that his 'degre' and his 'state' oblige him to do, provided that it does not hinder his desire to love God (114). And in the 'Epistle on Mixed Life' he develops a lengthy argument designed to convince a lay lord who had a desire for the contemplative life that he would not do 'wel' to abandon his worldly obligations. Hilton assures this lord that it is just as important to show his love of God by washing the feet of Christ, that is by caring for his fellow Christians in the world, as to show his love by adorning Christ's head, that is by engaging in contemplative prayer (273). On the other hand, if the lord has received from God the 'ȝift' of 'grace of deuocion' and the 'sauour of gostli ocupacion', he would not do 'wel' either to devote himself 'holliche to bisynes of þe world' (267). In this way Hilton leads his reader to the conclusion that he must choose to live the mixed life in imitation of Christ who did good works and also prayed to the Father, so that some men might follow his 'ensaumple' (269). Hilton was convinced that the mixed life 'longeþ speciali' not only to prelates of the Church but also to 'worldly lords þat rule oþer men' (268). He was convinced of this because it seemed to him that to abandon the care of one's fellows was to abandon charity, the greatest of the theological virtues and the only commandment of Christ.

The appearance of the Grail at Camelot, then, would probably have been interpreted by both Malory and his readers as a call to the Round Table knights to live the mixed life in imitation of Christ. The knights are not to abandon their worldly obligation to serve Arthur and Christendom by doing justice and keeping the peace, but neither are they to continue to give themselves 'holliche to bisynes of þe world'. Rather, they must learn to strengthen their spiritual lives through prayer and meditation. Malory would have understood the appearance of the Grail at Camelot and the illumination of the Holy Ghost to be a very 'special grace', more 'speciall' even than the vision of Gawain which God granted Arthur the night before his battle on Salisbury plain (1234.13:XXI.3). And if Malory was familiar with the thought of Richard Rolle he would have known that Rolle believed such 'special graces' were given by God to some men to make them 'better þan oþer, noght anely for þamself, bot alswa for þam þat wil do wele after þaire ensawmpell' ('Form of Living' 6.141–44). What is more, Malory would have known that Rolle warns men against failing to take advantage of the grace which God sends, for perhaps they 'sall neuer after þer-till wyne ('On Grace' 309). This is certainly true of the appearance of the Grail at Camelot, as Malory must have known even before he began writing his own version of the story. If the Round Table knights fail to respond properly to the appearance of the Grail at Camelot, this 'special grace' which God has sent them will not come again. If they fail to learn how to pray so that they may live the mixed life and thereby achieve 'stableness of good living' in this world (Hilton, *Scale of Perfection* 291–92), they will 'faile of þat wele' which they might have had if they had agreed to be led by God's grace ('On Grace' 310).

Let us turn now to examine the responses of the Round Table knights to the appearance of the Grail at Camelot to see how they understood its significance. Only three knights respond verbally: Arthur, Gawain and Lancelot, the same three knights who will dominate Malory's post-Grail narrative. The three Grail knights say nothing. We may guess that they are already living the mixed life and therefore know enough to respond with silent prayers of thanksgiving, even after the vessel has departed and all have 'breth to speke'. The king speaks first, as is proper, expressing the thought that they all 'ought to thanke oure Lorde Jesu Cryste gretly that he hath shewed us thys day at the reverence of thys hyghe feste of Pentecoste' (865.37–866.2:XIII.7). Arthur is clearly aware that God has done him and his court a great honour but his words give no hint as to what he thinks might be the significance of what God 'hath shewed us thys day'. Gawain, the most impulsive of the three men, is the first of the Round Table knights to swear to go in quest of the Holy Vessel. And Lancelot, like the Grail knights, says nothing until Arthur's sorrow over the departure of his knights prompts him to comfort the king. Each of these responses not only characterizes the man but also identifies him with one of Malory's three knightly types.

Gawain responds to the Grail as though it were a talismanic object:

> 'Now,' seyde sir Gawayne, 'we have bene servyd thys day of what metys and drynkes we thought on. But one thyng begyled us, that we myght nat se the Holy Grayle: Hit was so preciously coverde. Wherefore I woll make here a vow that to-morne, withoute longer abydynge, I shall laboure in the queste of the Sankgreall, and that I shall holde me oute a twelve-month and a day or more if nede be, and never shall I returne unto the courte agayne tylle I have sene hit more opynly than hit hath bene shewed here. And iff I may nat spede I shall returne agayne as he that may nat be ayenst the wylle of God.' (866.3–13:XIII.7)

Gawain describes the Grail as though it were a cornucopia having the magical capacity to serve whatever 'metys and drynkes' one might think of, and he is willing to undergo great hardship in order to see it 'more opynly'. He seems to understand that this marvellous object comes from God, but he betrays the fatalism typical of the Heroic knight when he concludes, 'And iff I may nat spede I shall returne agayne as he that may nat be ayenst the wylle of God.' Like Balin, it never occurs to him that he might fail to achieve his objective because of some lack in himself.

After Gawain has sworn his oath and most of the Round Table knights have followed his example, Arthur becomes 'gretly dysplesed'. He is more than displeased, he is disconsolate. For, unlike his counterpart in the *Queste del Saint Graal*, he continues to bemoan the loss of his knights right up to the moment of their departure when he is unable to 'speke for wepyng' (872.2–21:XIII.8). In Hardyng's *Chronicle* Arthur also laments the departure of his knights, but for specific political reasons:

> 'O God, yt deth wold brest myne hert on twayne,
> Who shall maynteyne my crowne & my ryghtes,
> I trowe nomore to see you eft agayne
> Thus hole together, and so goodly knightes;
> Would God I might make myne auowe & hightes,
> To passe with you in what land so ye go,
> And take my parte with you both in well and wo.' (134)

Malory's Arthur is neither so pious nor so politically aware as Hardying's king. Even though he depends utterly upon his knights for the governance of England, he never once alludes to this fact while lamenting their departure; nor does he ever express the pious wish that he might accompany them on their quest. He simply regrets that his knights should leave him, some of them never to return. Why is he so unconsolable?

Malory first suggests an answer to this question in Arthur's speech asking his knights to joust in the meadow by Camelot:

> 'Now,' seyde the kynge, 'I am sure at this quest of the Sankegreall shall all ye of the Rownde Table departe, and nevyr shall I se you agayne holé togydirs, therefore ones shall I se you togydir in the medow, all holé togydir in the medow of Camelot, to juste and to turney, that aftir youre dethe men may speke of hit that such good knyghtes were here, such a day, holé togydirs.' (864.5–12:XIII.6; cf. *Queste* 13.19–26)

In this passage Malory makes particularly good use, through repetition, of a phrase he probably borrowed from Hardyng — 'holé togydirs' (in fact, Malory's use is much more lyrical than Hardyng's) — to suggest that Arthur's emotional attachment to his knights is very strong. Arthur's speech berating Gawain for the 'avow' he has made again emphasizes the strength of his attachment:

> '... for thorow you ye have berauffte me the fayryst and the trewyst of knyghthode that ever was sene togydir in ony realme of the worlde. For whan they departe frome hense I am sure they all shall never mete more togydir in thys worlde, for they shall dye many in the queste. And so hit forthynkith nat me a litill, for I have loved them as well as my lyff.' (866.20–867.1:XIII.8)

Arthur loves his knights. And he is proud of them. They are the 'fayryst and the trewyst' in the world and as dear to him as his own life. In the religious context of the appearance of the Grail, however, this response points to what Hilton could call an 'unordinate affection' (*Goad of Love* 146). Arthur is a 'lover of the world' and its goods rather than a lover of God. And in this way he is exactly like Tristram. Tristram loves his lady, Isode, so much that he chooses to return to her at Joyous Garde rather than follow Gawain's example.[24] Arthur loves his knights so much that he would, if he could, choose to keep them at Camelot rather than let them seek the grace of God. By Grail standards, both loves are 'oute of mesure'.

Lancelot's response to the appearance of the Grail is exactly the opposite of Arthur's. He tries to console the king by reminding him that this quest shall 'be unto us a great honoure, and much more than we dyed in other placis, for of dethe we be syker' (867.11–12:XIII.8). And he tries to console the queen by assuring her that he will 'com agayne as sone as I may with my worship' (872.12–13:XIII.8). But clearly his love for her is no longer 'oute of mesure' if he has determined to leave her in order to 'se the mysteryes of oure Lorde Jesu Cryste' (869.1–4:XIII.8). In short, Lancelot has reversed the decision he made earlier at Corbenic.

The way to follow in order to see these 'mysteryes' is marked out by Galahad, whom Malory presents as a Christ-figure. He found this figural significance already in his source, but he has actually enhanced it by telling us that Galahad is 'full blyssed' (890.28:XIII.16; cf. 'Chevaliers tiex come il doit estre', *Queste* 52.4) and that he 'worchith all by myracle' (906.13:XIV.1). The imitation-of-Christ theme was the central focus of late medieval devotional literature and spirituality, and, as we have seen, it formed the basis of Walter Hilton's argument in favour of a worldly lord's adopting the mixed life. Therefore, it is not likely that Malory viewed Galahad's example as beyond the capabilities of all Round Table knights. On the contrary, the earlier examples of Tor, Ywain, young Lancelot and Gareth suggest that the sort of miracles which Galahad works are not beyond the capacity of any knight who lives in dread of God. And given the way each knight is illumined by the 'grace of the Holy Goste' when the Grail appears at Camelot, we are surely right to infer that they may all be as 'full blyssed' as Galahad, if they will choose to follow him. In the literal terms of Malory's narrative, this means following the path which Galahad has taken after leaving Camelot. In terms of the spiritual significance of his narrative, however, it means first cleansing one's soul and then assenting fully to be united with God in His grace.

This spiritual significance is reinforced by the way in which Malory handles the adventure of Melyas, the man who chooses to follow Galahad as his squire. Although he is not a knight of the Round Table, Melyas may be taken as emblematic of Worshipful knighthood because his behaviour recalls that of its greatest exemplar, Tristram. Melyas is the squire of King Bagdemagus (himself a Worshipful knight) until he witnesses Galahad's feat in winning the Red Cross shield. Then he begs Galahad to allow him to remain in his company 'tyll he had made hym knyght'. His assurance that 'that Order, by the grace of God, shall be well besette in me' (881.29:XIII.11) recalls Tristram's youthful assurance that God might make him 'as good a knyght' as Lancelot (388.34–36: VIII.10). And his implied motive for seeking knighthood of Galahad also suggests Tristram's motive: to win worship. As soon as Galahad has knighted him, admonishing him 'to be a myrroure unto all chevilry' since he is 'com of kynges and quenys' (883.7–9:XIII.12), Melyas requests the privilege of accompanying Galahad 'in thys queste of the Sankgreall'. We suspect that he makes this request because he knows from the episode of the Red Cross shield that Galahad will surely achieve the Grail and he wants to share that honour. This suspicion is borne out by his behaviour when he and Galahad come to a crossroads.

> 'NOW YE KNYGHTES ARRAUNTE WHICH GOTH TO SEKE KNYGHTES ADVENTURYS, SE HERE TWO WAYES: THAT ONE WAY DEFENDITH THE THAT THOU NE GO THAT WAY, FOR HE SHALL NAT GO OUTE OF THE WAY AGAYNE BUT IF HE BE A GOOD MAN AND A WORTHY KNYGHT. AND IF THOU GO ON THE LYFFTE HONDE THOU SHALL NAT THERE LYGHTLY WYNNE PROUESSE, FOR THOU SHALT IN THYS WAY BE SONE ASSAYDE.' (883.24–30:XIII.12)

Melyas' decision to take this more difficult way, even though Galahad advises against it, reminds us of Tristram's eager desire to test himself against Marhalt. For a Worshipful knight, the stronger his opponent, the greater the worship he can win by defeating him.

Malory follows his source faithfully in recounting Melyas' subsequent adventures: after two days' riding Melyas comes into a clearing where he finds a crown of gold set upon a chair within a lodge and 'many delycious metis' set out upon cloths. He is not hungry, but the gold crown appeals to him and so he rides off with it. Soon he is challenged by a knight who accuses him of taking what is not his and unhorses him. Galahad comes along 'by fortune' and, after defeating this knight, as well as his companion, he takes Melyas to a nearby abbey where a 'good man' interprets the spiritual significance of their adventure. At this point Malory diverges considerably from his source to express his own providentialist understanding, not only of this adventure but of the Quest as a whole.

First, rather than interpret the two ways at the cross-roads to mean the worldly life of a knight ('la chevalerie terrienne') and the spiritual life of a knight ('la chevalerie celestielle'),[25] Malory interprets them as two different ways of living in the world: the 'way of synnars and of myssebelevers' on the left hand and 'the way of a good trew lyver' on the right. Secondly, Malory does not turn this episode into an allegory of Melyas' past sins of pride and greed. Rather, he interprets this 'real' adventure in providentialist terms. Melyas was defeated and near-fatally wounded because he became guilty of 'covetyse' and 'theffte' when he took the gold crown. At the same time, Galahad was able to defeat both of Melyas' opponents because he was 'withoute dedly synne' (886.25–30: XIII.14). In other words, Malory's good man interprets Melyas' defeat and rescue as examples of *unhappynesse* and *happynesse*.

Melyas' sins — pride and cupiditas — are emblematic of Worshipful knighthood and he has revealed them in ways which are typical of the Worshipful knight. First, he presumed that he did not have to seek the grace of God in order to do well as a knight and so he failed to repent, confess and do penance for his sins before setting out. Second, the same desire for worship which seems to have motivated his decision to seek knighthood from Galahad probably also motivated his decision at the cross-roads to take the more difficult way in which he would be 'sone assayed'. Third, his theft of the crown of gold suggests that he is as eager to win worship in the sense of status, power and riches, as he is to win fame as a knight, and that his ethical code in this endeavour is sheer expediency. But, as the good man points out, even though such expedient action might bring success in the world, in the quest of the Sankgreall Melyas may not succeed 'but by vertuous lyvynge' (886.18–19:XIII.14).

Malory's version of the good man's speech to Melyas spells out the differences between the standards of True knighthood and those of Worshipful knighthood and recalls by its choice of terms a very similar speech made by King Pelles to Bors at Corbenic. Since Pelles' speech provides the clearer exposition I quote it in full:

> '... for well may thys place be called the adventures place. For there com but feaw knyghtes here that goth away wyth ony worshyppe; be he never so stronge, here he may be preved. And but late ago sir Gawayne, the good knyght, gate lytyll worshyp here. For I lat you wyte,' seyde kynge Pelles, 'here shall no knyght wynne worshyp but yf he be of worshyp hymselff and of good lyvynge, and that lovyth God and dredyth God. And ellys he getyth no worshyp here, be he never so hardy a man.'
>
> (799.1–9:XI.4)

King Pelles' vocabulary shows him to be more knowledgeable in the 'noble way of the world' than the good man who interprets Melyas' adventure. Pelles understands that all knights want to win worship: it is simply a question of what standards shall be required for the winning of worship. Sheer power is not enough, as Gawain's example is used to prove.[26] Neither is 'worshyp', as defined by purely worldly concerns, enough. In order to win worship by Grail standards a man must also be 'of good lyvynge' and 'lovyth and dredyth God'.

These two speeches — the speech of the good man to Melyas and the speech of King Pelles to Bors — reflect upon one another to clarify the distinction between two ways of living in the world as a knight. The good man's admonition that the Grail 'may nat be encheved but by vertuous lyvynge' reinforces Pelles' insistence upon 'good lyvynge' in order to win worship at Corbenic. And the good man's amazement that Melyas 'durste' take upon himself 'so rych a thynge as the hyghe Order of Knyghthode ... withoute clene confession' recalls Pelles' insistence upon loving and dreading God. Both men view knighthood as a Christian vocation which should not be pursued for worldly and selfish motives of pride and greed. Rather it must be pursued for the Godly motive of charity. This is what the good man means by contrasting 'knyghtes dedys in worldly workis' on the one hand and 'hevynly dedys, and ... knyghtly dedys in Goddys workys' on the other (886.21–22:XIII.14). In some cases the actual 'knyghtes dedys' will be the same and then it is the intention with which they are done which will matter, as we shall see when comparing Lancelot and Galahad (see below 264–5). The Worshipful knight typically does his deeds in order to further his career in the world; the True knight typically does his deeds in order to help his fellow Christians and to serve God.

Melyas' mistake was to apply the ethical standards of the Worshipful knight when in quest of the Grail. He did not understand that what was to be tested in this quest was not his physical prowess, but his spiritual prowess, for in order to achieve 'stableness of good living' in the world a great deal of spiritual prowess is required. The active life of good works and ritual observance is not enough. The True knight must live the mixed life, gaining God's grace through contemplative prayer so that he may perceive the spiritual significance of his adventures.

The next knight to follow Galahad is Gawain, who concludes, 'I am nat happy that I toke nat the way that he wente' (890.21–22:XIII.16). Gawain seems to mean by this only that he is unfortunate. However, one of the monks who overhears him expands the meaning of his *unhappynesse* by explaining that Galahad 'woll nat of youre felyship' because 'ye be wycked and synfull, and he ys full blyssed' (890.25–29: XIII.16). Somewhat later, after Gawain and his two companions, Ywain and Gareth, have killed the seven knights from the Castle of Maidens, the good man who explains the spiritual significance of that adventure reinforces the contrast between Gawain's *unhappynesse* and Galahad's *happynesse*:

> '. . . whan ye were made first knyght ye sholde have takyn you to knyghtly dedys and vertuous lyvying. And ye have done the contrary, for ye have lyved myschevously many wyntirs. And sir Galahad ys a mayde and synned never, and that ys the cause he shall enchyve where he goth that ye nor none suche shall never attayne, nother none in your felyship, for ye have used the moste untrewyst lyff that ever I herd knyght lyve. For sertes, had ye nat bene so wycked as ye ar, never had the seven brethirne be slayne by you and youre two felowys: for sir Galahad hymself alone bete hem all seven the day toforne, but hys lyvyng ys such that he shall sle no man lyghtly.' (891.30–892.6:XIII.16)

The good man begins by defining the *happynesse* of True knighthood in one phrase, 'knyghtly dedys and vertuous lyvyng'. This phrase recalls both Pelles' insistence upon 'good lyvyng' as a requisite for winning worship at Corbenic and the other good man's description of the 'ryght' way at the crossroads as the way of a 'good trew lyver'. Then he goes on to define its opposite, *unhappynesse,* even more briefly as living 'myschevously'. *Mischief* is of course one of the synonyms for *unhap,* along with *mishap, mischaunce, misfortune* and *misadventure;* however, it retains even closer connection than they do with the notion of man's wrong-doing. For example, *mischief* is the word which Walter

Hilton chooses to denote Original Sin (*Scale of Perfection* 226). The connection with man's wrong-doing is particularly close in the adverbial form, as we might expect, given the providentialist conviction that it is primarily man's activity which causes earthly misfortune.[27] Therefore, we may say that this speech, too, reinforces Malory's *hap* motif, by explaining the difference between *happynesse* and *unhappynesse* as the difference between living 'vertuously' and living 'myschevously'.

The good man goes on to deal with some of the consequences of living 'myschevously'. The first is lack of success in knightly endeavours: Gawain and all those like him 'shall never attayne' what Galahad is able to achieve, and this should remind us of what Lancelot has said about sinful knights being 'nat happy nother fortunate unto the werrys.' The second consequence is manslaughter, which we discussed in looking at Lancelot's speech on *hap* and to which we shall return. The third is the 'unhappy' effect which a knight like Gawain has upon his companions. Lancelot concluded his remarks on *hap* by saying that 'unhappy' knights should cause 'all thynge ... that is aboute them' to be 'unhappy', too (271.3–4:VI.10). We have seen his maxim illustrated in Balin, Malory's first 'unhappy' knight, and now we see it again in Gawain. In the 'Tale of Balin' the notion that *unhappynesse* was somehow contagious was expressed primarily through Balin's cursed 'unhappy swerd'. Here it is expressed through Gawain's simple presence. The good man assures him that had he 'nat bene so wycked ..., never had the seven brethirne be slayne by you and youre two felowys.' Gawain's 'two felowys' in this case are Ywain and Gareth, both of whom Malory has portrayed as True knights in the past. We do not know the present state of their 'lyvyng' but the fact that they have entered the Quest suggests that it is still 'good' and 'vertuous'. In any case, the good man lays the blame for these killings squarely upon Gawain, not upon them. What is more, when the good man said earlier that Gawain should never be able to 'enchyve' what Galahad can achieve, he added, 'nother none in youre felyship', thus implying that anyone in his company would automatically become just as 'unhappy' as he is, would be somehow infected by his *unhappynesse*. If this is so, then it casts additional light upon Galahad's alleged unwillingness to be of Gawain's 'felyship' (890.26:XIII.16).

So long as he remains separated from God by his sinfulness, Gawain will continue to be an 'unhappy' knight who kills 'lyghtly' and makes 'all thynge' near him 'unhappy', too. Therefore, he ought to repent his sins. When the hermit tells him that he must 'do penaunce' for his sin, however, Gawain refuses, and the reason he gives for his refusal reveals his lack of understanding. He does not refuse, like his counterpart in the *Queste*, because he believes he could not endure 'la peine' (55.24). He refuses because he already endures a great deal of pain: 'we knyghtes adventures many tymes suffir grete woo and payne' (892.19–20). Of course, that is to miss the point of penance altogether. As a fatalist, Gawain has no concept of a covenantal relationship with God, no notion that his present choices and actions may in any way determine his future. The idea that by confessing, repenting and doing penance he might deserve the grace of God and become as 'full blyssed' as Galahad makes no sense to him because he believes that everything is determined. Both he and Galahad are as they are because God has willed it so, and that is that.

By contrast, Lancelot is a providentialist. He, too, makes a point of riding 'aftir sir Galahad' (905.1–2:XIV.1; cf. 893.23–25:XIII.17), 'for he knows that he is 'a verry wrecch and moste unhappy of all knyghtes' (895.36–37:XIII.19.) and he also knows why (895.32–33:XIII.19). At first he understands only that his 'olde synne' interferes with his achieving worship in the seeking 'of holy thynges' (896.2–9:XIII.19), but he soon learns better from the hermit who hears his confession. The hermit reminds him that he 'ought to thanke God more than ony knyght lyvynge, for He hath caused you to have more worldly worship than ony knyght that ys now lyvynge.' He reminds him also that he ought 'more ... than ony other man to love Hym and drede Hym, for youre strengthe and your manhode woll litill avayle you and God be agaynste you' (896.29–897.4–7:XIII.19). Weeping, Lancelot acknowledges the truth of what the hermit has said and admits that he has not confessed his sins in fourteen years. This last statement is Malory's invention. It dates Lancelot's last confession sometime after the birth of Galahad (who is now fifteen years old) and before the onset of his madness (which lasted more that two years) and implies that, up until the time he slept with Elaine the second time, Lancelot was going reqularly to confession. In the *Queste*, by contrast, he says that he has been a mortal sinner ever since he was 'primes chevaliers' (62.1–7) and says nothing about previous confessions. Malory's uncharacteristic concern with chronology, then, not only points to a fundamental difference in his conception of Lancelot's spirituality, but also to a corresponding difference in his conception of the love affair.

In the French romance, Lancelot and the queen consummate their love quite early in their relationship. Malory on the other hand imagines that Lancelot's love of the queen has grown slowly over time, from an initial feudal 'love of friendship', appropriate to their political relationship, to the chivalrous or 'courtly' love we saw illustrated in the Tale of Tristram when, for the first time in his career, Lancelot sought out adventures and entered tournaments simply in order to win worship. Lancelot proved that his love for Guinevere had grown 'oute of mesure' when he chose to go to her at Castle Case rather than remain at Corbenic with the Grail, but he has never committed adultery with her, not 'in dede', at any rate. And therefore he does not confess to the sin of adultery.[28] Rather he confesses that he has 'loved a quene unmesurabely and oute of mesure longe':

> '. . . all my grete dedis of armys that I have done for the moste party was for the quenys sake, and for hir sake wolde I do batayle were hit ryght other wronge. And never dud I batayle all only for Goddis sake, but for to wynne worship and to cause me the bettir to be beloved, and litill or nought I thanked never God of hit.' (897.17–22:XIII.20)

He confesses to the sins of pride and *cupiditas*, understood in its Augustinian sense of desiring the goods of this world more than God.

That Lancelot has entered the Quest of the Holy Grail aware of his sinfulness and able to make this confession indicates that he no longer loves the queen 'oute of mesure', and the hermit responds accordingly. He advises him to avoid the 'quenys felyship as much as ye may forbere' in the future and assures him that if he can keep that promise, he 'shall have the more worship than ever ye had' (897.25–31: XIII.20). In Malory's version there is no question of Lancelot's giving up knighthood (cf. *Queste* 71.1–3). The hermit assumes that he will remain in Arthur's service as a knight of the Round Table and that therefore he will not be able to avoid the queen's 'felyship' altogether. However, he must not let his love for her grow 'oute of mesure' again, for, as the hermit warns him,

> '. . . now oure Lorde wolde suffir the no lenger but that thou shalt know Hym whether thou wolt other nylt.' (898.15–16:XIII.20)

This warning is not in Malory's source and it points clearly to Malory's providentialist understanding of the Quest, that is, to the 'trouth' of the Sankgreall: God wills all men to be saved and, in the past, he has given Lancelot the grace to have 'more worldly worship' than any man, even after he became a sinner. But now God will 'suffir' him no longer unless Lancelot fully acknowledges Him. Lancelot understands and assents:

> 'Sertes,' seyde sir Launcelot, 'all that ye have seyde ys trew, and frome hensforewarde I caste me, by the grace of God, never to be so wycked as I have bene but as to sew knyghthode and to do fetys of armys.' (898.36–899.3:XIII.20)

Lancelot's understanding of this providentialist doctrine is credible, given his explicit beliefs as a young man. He knew then what was required if a man were to be 'happy' in arms, and he is willing to acknowledge that truth once again. Henceforth, he will trust in the grace of God.

The same warning which the hermit gives explicitly to Lancelot in this scene has already been given implicitly to all the Round Table knights with the appearance of the Grail at Camelot. Just as the obligations which bind Arthur and his knights are reciprocal, so the obligations which bind Arthur and his knights to God are reciprocal. Arthur rewards his knights with riches and worldly worship on condition that they do his bidding and the providential view of man's relationship to God presumes the same reciprocity. God will reward His knights with grace and worship, both on earth and in heaven, if they will do His bidding. Richard Rolle and Walter Hilton tend to express this reciprocity in the mercantile terms of a partnership, but Sir Gilbert Hay expresses it in terms of a reciprocal obligation of honour:

> for rycht as knycht, be his ordre, takis bathe of God and man honoure, worschip, and warldly prouffit, rycht sa he is behaldyn till governe, kepe, and manetene his ordre in all honour, worschip, and reverence undefoulit. (*Knychthede* 10)

God may freely choose to favour those who are not true to Him, but He is not honour bound to do so.

Malory continues to draw our attention to the contrast between Lancelot and Gawain in the rest of their Grail adventures. Both men begin their quest as black bulls, black with the sins of pride, greed and lechery, and Malory calls attention to their comparability in a cryptic passage he has invented for Gawain. When Hector complains that he 'can nat hyre' of Lancelot nor of Galahad, Percival and Bors, Gawain replies,

> 'Lette hem be, . . . for they four have no peerys. And if one thynge were nat sir Launcelot he had none felow of an erthely man; but he ys as we be but if he take the more payne uppon hym. But and thes four be mette togydyrs they woll be lothe that ony man mete with hem; for and they fayle of Sankgreall, hit ys in waste of all the remenaunte to recover hit.' (941.19–25:XVI.1)

In an effort to make sense of this passage, Vinaver has emended the second sentence in his second edition to read, 'And if one thynge were nat [in] sir Launcelot he had none felow of an erthely man.' However, it actually makes better sense the way I have quoted it above. For that 'one thynge' is Galahad, or the begetting of Galahad, or the choice which led to the begetting to Galahad. It does not matter how far back one goes in the chain of causation. The fact is that in Malory's version

Lancelot himself might have been the Grail knight, might have 'had none felow of an erthely man,' if he had been able to remain as he was in the Tale of Lancelot. He was not able to do so and therefore he has become just like all the other sinful knights of the Round Table. Nevertheless, Gawain recognizes that Lancelot still has some quality which merits ranking him among the Grail knights as one of the 'four' who have 'no peerys'. That quality, as we have seen, is his humility and his consequent willingness to 'take the more payne uppon hym' to become at one again with God.

Gawain is unwilling to take any 'payne' upon himself, not because he is afraid of it, but because he does not understand the function of the sacrament of 'penaunce'. He does not understand that it is necessary to repent, confess and make satisfaction to God for one's sins in order to deserve God's favour in future. After he is told a second time that he is 'an untrew knyght and a grete murtherar' because of his sinfulness (having accidentally slain his cousin, Ywain), Gawain still does not draw the inference that a providentialist would draw from 'thys mysadventure' (945.5, 20:XVI.3). Rather, he draws the inference of a fatalist: 'Sir,' seyde sir Gawayne, 'hit semyth me by youre wordis that for oure synnes hit woll nat avayle us to travayle in thys quest' (948.30–32:XVI.5). Nacien agrees that in his present state he cannot prevail, but then he asks Gawain to consider changing his life. Even though he has never yet served God as a knight, he might still 'yelde to oure Lorde' what is left. Gawain's counterpart in the *Queste* says he would like very much to speak to Nacien privately and will return as soon as he can (*Queste* 161.24–28). Malory's Gawain simply says he has no 'leyser' to talk. Evidently he does not see the point of such talk, and there would be no point, of course, to a fatalist.

Not long after this conversation with Nacien, Gawain gives up his quest to see 'more' of the Holy Vessel. He gives up as a consequence of being badly wounded by a 'grete' stroke of Galahad's sword (981–82:XVII.1). As we know, Galahad's sword is the sword of Balin, the 'unhappy swerd' of vengeance, which in the hands of the premier Grail knight has become the sword of divine justice. And it is just that Gawain should fail in his quest. He has learned nothing from his 'mysadventures' and nothing from the good men who have interpreted their spiritual significance and tried to persuade him to amend his life. Gawain remains, in fact, just like Balin — a proud, Heroic knight and a fatalist. He is brave, strong and loyal, but from the providentialist point of view of the True knight and in the language of Malory's *hap* motif, he is one of those 'unhappy' knights who make 'all thynge unhappy that is aboute' him. The final proof of Gawain's *unhappynesse* is provided by Lancelot's discovery of the tomb of King Bagdemagus. The tombstone records that the king's nephew, Gawain, slew him and Lancelot laments his loss: 'A, lorde God! Thys ys a grete hurte unto kynge Arthurs courte, the losse of suche a man!' (1020.7–14:XVII.17). In Malory's text we never learn how many knights Gawain has killed in his quest,[29] but we may be sure that he interprets most of these killings — certainly the accidental killing of his cousin, Ywain — as 'mysadventure[s]' which 'befelle' him (945.5–6:XVI.3) In other words, just like Balin, he accepts them as the fate which God has ordained for him.

Lancelot's Grail adventures provide a perfect contrast to those of Gawain. Not only does he begin by confessing his sins and vowing to 'sew knyghthode', he also learns from his misfortunes. When he decides to enter a tournament to help the castle party, who are arrayed in black and being 'putt to the wars', he suffers a humiliating defeat, but he immediately recognizes this as a sign of God's displeasure: 'now I am shamed, and am sure that I am more synfuller than ever I was' (932.17–18:XV.5). The recluse who interprets the spiritual significance of his 'mysseaventure' confirms this. Her interpretation is Malory's invention and illustrates the providentialist viewpoint. Lancelot went to help the black knights with the intention of 'incresyng . . . his shevalry', and that, according to the recluse, 'caused thy mysseaventure, that thou sholde know God frome vayneglory of the worlde; hit ys nat worth a peare' (933.32–934.12:XV.6). His punishing defeat should teach him to know better in the future.

Malory underlines the importance of doing good works with the proper intention through the perfect parallel between Lancelot's action in this episode and Galahad's action later on. Both knights come upon tournaments in progress in which the castle party is being put to the worse. Galahad 'thought to helpe them' (981.11–12:XVII.1). But Lancelot 'thought . . . for to helpe there the wayker party in incresyng of his shevalry' (931.24–25:XV.5). The only thing which distinguishes their actions, other than the colour of armour worn by the knights they help (a feature of the French allegory which is not of central importance to Malory), is their intention. Galahad is motivated by perfect faith and charity. He wants only 'to helpe them' and he trusts wholly in God for the necessary strength and skill. By contrast, Lancelot is motivated by imperfect faith and charity. He wants to help them, but he also wants to help himself by improving his fighting skills.[30] His concern recalls the worldliness of those knights who fight with Palamon and Arcite in Chaucer's *Knight's Tale*, 'For love and for encrees of chivalrye' (*CT* I(A).2183). It also suggests that he has not yet cast off completely the attitudes characteristic of Malory's Worshipful knights. The recluse reminds him that 'all that muste be leffte in that queste' and remonstrates with him for being 'so feble of evyll truste and good beleve' (934.1–3:XV.6).

Lancelot makes a good deal of progress after this setback. He is able to cross the river Mortays without fear or hesitation 'in the name of God' and when a black knight kills his horse, he does not complain but rather thanks 'God of hys adventure' (934–35:XV.6). However, when he has his first experience of contemplative prayer, he shows that he is not accustomed to such spiritual exercise, for he tires of it relatively quickly. Lancelot arrives at the ship which bears the body of Sir Percival's sister in response to a vision which comes to him because he was willing to take 'the adventure that God wolde sende'. As soon as he enters the ship he experiences 'the moste swettnes that ever he felte,' and is 'fulfylled with all thynge that he thought on other desyred.' This description suggests the sweetness of contemplative prayer as described by Richard Rolle and Lancelot's initial response to it is delight and gratitude: 'Swete Fadir, Jesu Cryste! I wote natt what joy I am in, for thys passith all erthely joyes that ever I was in.' He remains on the ship some time, praying daily, and Malory tells us that when he has 'seyde hys prayers', he is 'susteyned with the grace of the Holy Goste.' Nevertheless, after he has been in the ship 'a moneth and more' there comes a night when he goes 'to play hym by the watirs syde' because he has become 'somewhat wery of the shippe' (1011.26–1012.1:XVIII.13). Lancelot's weariness is Malory's invention and suggests that he is a beginner in the spiritual life. By contrast, while Bors and Percival wait on board ship for Galahad to join them, 'ever they were in theyre prayers' (975.17:XVI.17), an observation which is likewise Malory's invention. It would seem that Malory wished his readers to know that by comparison with the Grail knights, Lancelot has had very little experience of contemplative prayer.

Lancelot's relative inexperience makes him less 'stable' as a lover of God. In the best known passage relating to Lancelot in Malory's version of the Quest, the hermit Nacien praises him for his humility, his repentance and his determination to 'forsake synne', but goes on to say,

> 'And nere were that he ys nat stable, but by hys thoughte he ys lyckly to turn agayne, he sholde be next to encheve hit sauff sir Galahad, hys sonne; but God knowith hys thought and hys unstablenesse.' (948.24–27:XVI.5)

In this passage Nacien is using the language adopted by the fourteenth-century mystics, Richard Rolle and Walter Hilton, for whom the adjective 'stable' describes the true lover of God. According to Rolle, a true lover of God is so 'stable' that nothing can turn his thoughts away from God. Such stability is not to be achieved either easily or quickly, however. Even among those who have devoted themselves wholly to 'Godes servys' in the contemplative life there are some who are yet so taken up with 'othire thoghtes þat are in thaym, þat it brynges thaym till no stabylnes.' Rolle compares such men to storks who may not fly 'for charge of body' (*English Writings* 55–56). Because 'stableness' refers to love of God Rolle lists 'unstabylnes of thoght' as one of the 'synnes of þe hert' ('Form of Living' 6.25); and in Nacien's speech quoted above Malory tells us that this is the sin which troubles Lancelot. Before the Quest, Lancelot led an active life in the world, which meant that he was necessarily in greater danger of falling away from true love of God than are men who have chosen the contemplative life. After the Quest he will go back to the world. Therefore, during this Quest it is crucial that he learn how to pray so that he may achieve what Hilton calls 'stableness of good living' (*Scale of Perfection* 291).

Malory's Nacien does not say that Lancelot shall fail in the Quest, only that he is not 'lyckly' to be second only to Galahad in achieving it. The two knights who are 'nexte to encheve hit sauff sir Galahad' are Bors and Percival. Therefore, in their adventures we can see what Lancelot has yet to achieve.

Bors' love of God is so 'stable' that he has only once succumbed to a sin of the flesh (956.2–3:XVI.6) and a holy abbot marvels that one so young should be 'so stronge in the grace of oure Lorde Jesu Cryste' (966.29–31:XII.12). This suggests that Bors has lived the 'mixed life' even before the Quest, developing his spirituality and hence his ability to resist worldly temptations by means of prayer and meditation. He gives a particularly striking demonstration of his faith and charity, and also of his habit of resorting to prayer, in the episode involving his brother Lionel. Bors' love of God is such that he experiences little difficulty choosing to help a maiden who is threatened by the loss of her virginity rather than help his brother who, naked and bound to a horse, is being beaten by three knights. As a consequence of this choice, however, his brother accuses him of being a traitor and vows to kill him (969.29–32:XVI.14). Malory has already characterized Lionel as a 'murtherer' who 'doth contrary to the Order off Knyghthode' (968.12–13:XVI.13), thus suggesting that he is like Gawain. And certainly, his response to Bors suggests that he shares Gawain's belief that a knight must be loyal first and foremost to his family. Initially Bors is paralyzed by this conflict: he cannot take up arms against his brother and he cannot run away because he is too badly wounded. Therefore, he must watch as his brother kills first an old priest and then sir Collgrevaunce. At last Bors realizes that he must take up his sword; however, at the same time he also resorts to prayer:

> 'Well,' seyde sir Bors, and drew hys swerde, all wepyng, and seyde, 'fayre brother, God knowith myne entente, for ye have done full evyll thys day to sle an holy pryste which never trespasced. Also ye have slayne a jantill knyght, and one of oure felowis. And well wote ye that I am nat aferde of you gretely, but I drede the wratthe of God; and thys ys an unkyndely werre. Therefore God shew His myracle uppon us bothe, and God have mercy uppon me, thoughe I defende my lyff ayenst my brothir.'
> (973.23–31:XVI.16; cf. *Queste* 193)

At the same time as he raises his sword, he prays to God for a 'myracle' so that he shall not have to use it. And God answers his prayer, thus acknowledging his perfect faith. The first thought which comes to Bors' mind as the fiery cloud descends is that 'God had takyn vengeaunce uppon hym' but he soon realizes that it is in fact a merciful response to his 'entente' to do good. Malory then adds the scene of reconciliation with his elder brother to complete Bors' *happynesse* (974.14–17:XVI.17).

Percival benefits from an equally dramatic manifestation of divine favour as a consequence of prayer. As he is about to give up his virginity to a beautiful lady whom he has sworn as a 'trew knight' to serve, Malory tells us,

> '. . . by adventure and grace he saw hys swerde ly on the erthe naked, where in the pomell was a rede crosse and the sygne of the crucifixe therin, and bethought hym on hys knyghthode and hys promyse made unto the good man tofornehande, and than he made a sygne in the forehed of hys. (918.29–34:XIV.9)

Instantly the pavilion where they lie goes up in smoke. Like Bors, Percival's first thought is that God is punishing him, so he prays, 'Fayre swete Lorde Jesu Cryste, ne lette me nat be shamed, which was nyghe loste had nat Thy good grace bene!' (919.3–4:XIV.10). At that the 'lady' appears again to scream, 'Syr Percivale, ye have betrayde me', before she exits 'with the wynde, roryinge and yellynge, that hit semed all the water brente after her' (919.8–9:XIV.10).

As with the 'myracle' which saved Bors from fratricide, so with this 'myracle' which saves Percival from the loss of his virginity, the initial intentions and prayers of the men involved are presented as crucial to the outcome. Particularly significant is Malory's choice of phrase to explain how it was that Percival 'happened' to catch sight of his sword hilt just at the critical moment — 'by adventure and grace'. Malory has added the 'and grace' to the 'par aventure' of his source (*Queste* 110.3) to point to a providentialist interpretation of the event. If it was by chance that Percival glimpsed his sword hilt, it was by the grace of God that the sight of the cross brought him to remembrance of his 'knyghthode' (cf. 'se souvint de soi' *Queste* 110.7). Moreover, that grace can be seen as an answer to Percival's prayer earlier that 'oure Lorde Jesu' would not suffer any 'temptacion sholde brynge hym oute of Goddys servys' (913.10–13:XIV.6).

These adventures of Bors and Percival not only illustrate their perfect faith and charity (and consequent *happynesse*), but also point to the way the True knight resolves the potential conflicts among his three knightly loyalties. In the case of conflict between his obligation to serve God and his obligation to serve his kinsmen, the True knight does not hesitate to serve God first. Bors made the correct choice of 'a verry knyght and the servaunte of Jesu Cryste' (968.21–22:XVI.13) when he rescued the maiden who 'conjoured hym, by the faythe that he ought unto Hym "in whose servyse thou arte entred" ' rather than rescue his own brother. His decision invites comparison with the decision of Pellinor who chose not to help a maiden who begged his help 'for Jesuys sake!' Malory strengthens the point of the comparison by having the maiden who asks for Bors help ask it 'for kynge Arthures sake', also (961.7–10:XVI.9). Thus he implies that the knight's duty to succour the helpless is as much a duty to his temporal lord as it is a duty to God, for his temporal lord is, after all, God's minister of justice.

On the other hand, Percival's conflict is not so inherently political, although the conflict between a knight's obligation to serve ladies and his obligation to serve God could develop political implications if his special lady were married either to his lord or his vassal. In Percival's adventure the lady in question is an incarnation of Satan whose only object is to lure him into mortal sin. However, had she been a mortal woman who loved him, Percival's response as 'a trew knyght' must have been the same, unless he were not committed to celibacy and could marry her.

When Percival and Bors finally join Galahad on the Ship of Faith, Bors expresses the hope that his cousin, Lancelot, will be of their company, for 'than mesemed we fayled nothynge'. In Malory's source, Galahad replies, 'il n'i puet estre, puis qu'il ne plest a Nostre Seignor' (*Queste* 200.22–23). However, in Malory's version the issue is still in doubt: 'That may not be . . . but if [i.e. unless] hit pleased our Lorde' (984.17–18:XVII.2). After this, Galahad joins his father for six months aboard the ship bearing the body of Percival's sister. It is significant, I think, that Galahad arrives just as Lancelot is growing weary of his spiritual exercise. He needs guidance if he is to develop in the spiritual life and presumably that is what Galahad gives him during the months they spend together, serving God 'dayly and nyghtly with all their power' (1013.3–5:XVII.13). When Galahad is called away, Lancelot prays that the 'hyghe Fadir conserve me and you both' and Galahad pays his father the enormous tribute of replying, 'Sir, ... no prayer avaylith so much as youres' (1014.1–2:XVII.14). By contrast, in the *Queste*, Galahad's words are spoken in response to Lancelot's request that his son pray for him and are intended as a mild rebuke (252.22–27). It is hard therefore to avoid the conclusion that Malory invented this tribute to call our attention to Lancelot's spiritual progress under the tutelage of his son.

In Malory's version, it is still possible that Lancelot may become sufficiently 'stable' to be one of the four who achieve the Grail up until the time he enters the Grail castle. However, there, as once before (see above 246–8), his reactions to events show why he cannot be a Grail knight. First, his reaction to the lions who guard the entrance proves that he has not achieved perfect faith. Second, his reaction to the sight of the old man struggling with his burden in the Grail chapel proves that he has not achieved perfect obedience to the will of God. This second reaction is more problematic than the first, however. Clearly Lancelot has learned to pray, for it is in response to his fervant prayer that the door to the chapel opens before him. However, when he tries to enter, a voice forbids him. Obedient to the voice, he watches from outside as the priest receives the body of a man between his hands, put there by two older men — a clear symbol of the Trinity and the doctrine of transubstantiation. But then, when it appears that the priest 'sholde falle to the erth' with the burden of this body and when Lancelot sees that there is no one 'aboute hym that wolde helpe hym,' he comes forward, praying, 'Fayre Fadir, Jesu Cryste, ne take hit for no synne if I helpe the good man whych hath grete nede of helpe' (1016.5–6:XVII.15). The reason this response is problematic is that, on the one hand, it suggests that Lancelot has become perfect in charity, insofar as charity or love of God is defined as service to one's fellow Christians. On the other hand, insofar as charity may be defined as perfect conformity to the will of God, this response suggests that he is far from perfect. His sin is a sin of disobedience, more admirable perhaps than that of Adam and Eve because he disobeyed only in order to help his fellow, but a sin nevertheless, and he is instantly struck down by the fiery breath of the Holy Ghost.

Lancelot's fault, which prevents him from becoming one of the four who achieve the Sankgreal, shows that his will is not yet perfectly conformed to the will of God. Lancelot has always been a man of action. The hardest thing to ask him to do is nothing, especially when he can see with his own eyes that someone needs his help. He presumed to know better than God what needed to be done and his presumption reflects the chief danger, from the religious point of view, of the active life in the world — the danger that one will think he knows better than God what is best to do. The Worshipful code of Arthurian society is the product of such presumption, and Lancelot shows that despite the months spent in contemplative prayer he is still affected by it.

After he has awakened from his trance and learns that it has endured four and twenty days he immediately concludes that this number signifies the four and twenty years he has been a sinner.[31] However, his description of the visions he received during those four and twenty days invites us to consider his experience as a reward rather than a punishment:

> 'Why have ye awaked me? For I was more at ease than I am now. A, Jesu Cryste, who myght be so blyssed that myght se opynly Thy grete mervayles of secretnesse there where no synner may be?
>
> 'What have ye sene? seyde they aboute hym.
>
> 'I have sene,' seyde he, 'grete mervayles that no tunge may telle, and more than ony herte can thynke. And had nat my synne bene beforetyme, ellis I had sene muche more.'
>
> (1017.6–13:XVII.16)

This echo of St Paul's *First Epistle to the Corinthians* (2.9) is also to be found in the corresponding place in the *Queste* (258.6–13); however, Malory models Lancelot's description of his experience even more closely on the French Galahad's description of his experience during the Eucharistic feast at Corbenic, where Galahad saw the 'respostes choses qui ne sont pas descovertes a chascun, fors solement aus menistres Jhesucrits' and which 'cuers de terrien home ne porroit penser ne langue descrire' (274.13–14). Then Malory drastically condenses Galahad's speech at the corresponding place in his own text and completely removes the allusion to *First Corinthians* (1032.1922: XVII.21) so that in his version of the Grail quest, Lancelot becomes the only knight to describe his experience of the Grail in terms which suggest that it is a reward for his love of God.[32]

Before putting on his courtly robes to be entertained by King Pelles, Lancelot places a hair shirt next to his skin and presumably he is still wearing this garment when he returns to Camelot. This wearing of a hair shirt was evidently not an uncommon practice among pious men who had adopted worldly careers in the late fifteenth and early sixteenth centuries. Sir Anthony Wydeville, Lord Rivers, is known to have worn one. And so did Sir Thomas More, that most eminent example of a man who deliberately chose not to become a monk but to live the mixed life instead. Cardinal Wolsey actually owned three hair shirts, although there is no evidence that he ever wore any of them (Greenblatt 51). The wearing of a hair shirt was not so much an act of mortification as it was an act of remembrance, so that one should not be led astray by the beauty and brilliance of the court and the secular values of the honourable society. And Lancelot needs to remember the 'promyse and the perfeccion that he made in the queste' (1045.11–12:XVIII.1).

Like his cousin Bors, Lancelot has chosen the mixed life. Bors' stableness indicates that he was already living the mixed life before the Quest. By the same token, Lancelot's 'unstablenesse' indicates that he was living the active life only. That is to say, before the Quest Lancelot was doing good works and assisting at the sacraments but he was not engaging in contemplative prayer. Therefore, in terms of Walter Hilton's striking image, he was a man living continuously on the brink of the pit of mortal sin and it is scarcely surprising that he should have fallen in. Malory's unaccustomed care with chronology where Lancelot's life as a sinner is concerned allows us to infer that even after he first fell into the mortal sins of pride and *cupiditas* he was able to climb back up again, for we know that he continued to go to confession until fourteen years before the Quest even though he counts his years as a sinner at twenty-four. However, as Hilton points out, a man living the active life will always be falling in and scrambling up out of the pit again, so long as he does not take time to advance in the spiritual life (*Scale of Perfection* 291). During the Quest Lancelot has learned the sweetness and, it is to be hoped, some of the discipline of the contemplative life. Therefore he may now be able to imitate Christ by living the mixed life as his more 'stable' cousin has long been doing.

There is another quality which these two knights will share as a consequence of their achievements in the Quest: so long as they remain without sin, they will be protected from *unhappynesse*, including the misfortune of manslaughter.

During the Quest the hermit Nacien assured us that Lancelot 'slew never man nother nought shall, tylle that he com to Camelot agayne; for he hath takyn upon hym to forsake synne' (948.22–24:XVI.5). Nacien's comment is made in the context of his speech on Lancelot's 'unstablenesse' and presumes that Lancelot will 'turne agayne' from God and thus lose his protection from manslaughter. However, it is not impossible to enjoy such protection in the world, as Lancelot's early career indicated. The adventures of the three Grail knights also illustrate this truth, since for Malory the Grail adventures are 'real' adventures, which happen in the 'real' world. He calls attention to the this-worldly quality of the Grail adventures by adding such concretizing details as the crimes of the seven knights of the Castle of Maidens against the poor ('robbyng and pyllynge the poure comyn peple', 889.18–19.XIII.15), and the political and judicial actions of the Grail knights ('and than he made hem to do omage and feawté to the dukes doughter', 890.4–5:XIII.15). Such details also recall Sir Gilbert Hay's definition of the 'office' of true knighthood: 'to help the wayke agayne the stark, and the pure agayn the riche; for ofttymes sik folk ar, be mare stark na thai, pelit and derobbit, and thair gudis tane, and put to destructioun and povertie, for fault of power and defense' (*Knychthede* 27; cf. Lull 38–39). What is remarkable about the three Grail knights is that, while performing their 'office', they wield their swords at one with God in perfect *happynesse*.

When the three Grail knights realise that they have slain a 'grete multitude' of people at Castle Carteloyse, they at first conclude that they must be 'grete synners'. Bors tries to comfort Galahad with the observation that if God had 'loved' their opponents, 'we sholde nat have had power to have slayne hem thus', but Galahad counters, 'if they mysseded ayenst God, the vengeaunce ys nat owris, but to Hym which hath power theroff' (997.4–11:XVII.8). Bors' argument will be adopted later on by Lancelot when he kills thirteen of Arthur's knights while escaping from the ambush they have set for him outside the queen's chamber (1197.21–27:XX.15). But Galahad's counter-argument is ultimately unanswerable, except by God himself. Therefore it is surely significant that in Malory's text it *is* answered by God himself. First, a priest assures the Grail knights that their foes were great sinners, and not christened either. Then Lord Hernox expresses joy at having been delivered from his enemies. And finally, a loud, unexplained voice says, 'that all folke harde, Sir Galahad, well hast thou ben avenged on Goddis enemyes' (998.21–23:XVII.9). In the *Queste*, Lord Hernox speaks these words on behalf of the 'Hauz Mestres' (233.28–31). By contrast, Malory never explains the source of the voice, so that, in this deeply religious context, the reader readily assumes a supernatural source. Moreover, after this experience the Grail knights become conscious of their divinely guaranteed invincibility. When sixty knights issue from a castle to attempt to force them to give up Percival's sister, the three knights plead with the sixty to turn back:

> 'Now, fayre lordis,' seyde thes three knyghtes, 'have mercy on yourselff, and have nat ado with us.' (1001.11–12:XVII.10)

In the *Queste*, these words are spoken by an old man and addressed to the three Grail knights, which makes very good sense (238.4–6). Any man seeing three knights about to be attacked by sixty would surely plead with the three to save themselves. But Malory's Grail knights know now that they have become agents of divine retribution. They have become what Shakespeare's Hamlet would willingly believe himself to be, heaven's 'scourge and minister' (III.iv.175). Moreover, their 'lyvyng' is such that they 'shall sle no man lyghtly' (892.5–6: XII.16) because God himself guides their sword arm, sparing his friends and slaying only his enemies.

Malory's handling of these adventures of the three Grail knights illuminates the moral and spiritual significance of Gawain's 'mysadventure'. The term 'misadventure' is still the term used in English law for killing unintentionally while in the performance of a legitimate action. Malory's Heroic knights regard such misfortunes as 'ordayned' by the will of God. His Worshipful knights regard them as unavoidable accidents. But his True knights regard them as divine punishments for sin, and Malory's version of the Grail quest suggests that the True knights are correct.

Nacien had prophesied that the sinful knights of the Round Table should 'everych of them . . . sle othir for synne' (946.35:XVI.3) and in Malory's version we discover that 'more than halff' have in fact been slain during the Quest (1020.21:XVII.17). Malory's calculation more than doubles the number reported missing by the *Mort Artu* (2.16) and, taken together with the announcement that God will withdraw the Grail from Arthur's kingdom, bodes ill for the future. This great number of slain knights should also remind us of the warning which the hermit gave to Lancelot, and by extension to all those sinful knights who entered (or who chose not to enter) the quest for the Holy Vessel:

> 'And now oure Lorde wolde suffir the no lenger but that thou shalt know Hym whether thou wolt other nylt.' (898.15–16:XIII.20)

Before the Quest God had heaped graces upon Lancelot and upon Arthurian society as a whole, and yet they would not leave their 'synne for no goodness that God hath sente.' The Grail symbolizes that divine grace and that goodness and favour which allowed Arthur and his knights to have the better wherever they came regardless of their sins. Now they will no longer be so protected:

> 'For he ys nat served nother worshiped to hys ryght by hem of thys londe, for they be turned to evyll lyvyng, and therefore I shall disherite them of the honoure whych I have done them.'
> (1030.26–29:XVII.20)

Those knights who do return from the Quest will have to acknowledge their dependence upon God's grace or else suffer the *unhappynesse* which, according to the providentialist view, is the inevitable consequence of man's sinfulness.

Among those knights who do return, the most prominent, largely because of the attention given to their adventures during the Quest, are Lancelot, Bors and Gawain. Malory has woven a pattern of contrast between Lancelot and Gawain into his narrative ever since these two knights served together in Arthur's Roman Campaign, and that pattern has continued in the Tale of the Sankgreal with respect to their spiritual achievements. Lancelot has repented, confessed and done penance and experienced the joys of contemplative prayer. If he has not actually achieved the Grail, he has redeemed himself as a True knight. By contrast, Gawain has done none of these things, has suffered a series of 'mysadventures' and, despite the teaching of holy men, has learned nothing from them because he has remained a fatalist. Nevertheless, unlike Tristram, Gawain did choose to enter the Quest. His choice points to a likeness between Lancelot and Gawain which we first glimpsed during the Roman Campaign: they are both pious men. Unlike the rationalists, Tristram and Arthur, Lancelot and Gawain both have great respect for spiritual power, power which transcends the material world of cause and effect and which cannot be explained rationally. They desire to possess this power and know that it comes from God, but they have very different notions of how a man achieves it. Gawain, the fatalist, puts his faith in ritual and talismanic objects, which is what he understands the Grail to be. By contrast, Lancelot and his cousin Bors, both providentialists, put their trust in contemplative prayer and the grace of God, which is what the Grail means to them.

The scene in which Lancelot and Bors pledge mutual love, service and companionship is Malory's invention to conclude his Tale of the Sankgreal. It reminds us of the warm and loving relationship which Lancelot established with his saintly son during the Quest, because Bors brings back with him a message from Galahad to his father, bidding him 'remembir of thys unsyker worlde, as ye behyght hym whan ye were togydirs' (1036.28–29:XVII.23). Galahad's warning was commonly deemed necessary by orthodox teachers of spirituality, for late medieval mystics were inclined sometimes to believe that once they had experienced the most powerful raptures of mystical union with God, they were incapable of ever sinning again. In the *Goad of Love* Hilton adds some passages to his continental source to warn against precisely this danger: 'So by this mayst thou understand that there is no rest properly in this life, neither is no sikerness, but aye doubt and dread . . .' (154). Lancelot has even more need of such warning than men who have chosen the contemplative life for he has chosen to live the mixed life in the world, subject to all its temptations. Therefore, it is encouraging to think that in his endeavour to remain true to God, to Arthur and to Guinevere, Lancelot will be able to rely not only on the prayers of his son but also on the prayers, counsel and companionship of Bors. Their pledge of mutual support and loving embrace suggest not only that Bors acknowledges Lancelot's leadership, as Benson has observed (222), but also that Lancelot can depend upon the steadfast Grail knight's help in dealing with 'thys unsyker worlde'.

6

Standing With 'True Justyce'

The court setting of Malory's post-Grail narrative is inherently more political than the fields and forests which have hitherto provided most of the settings for knightly adventure. Consequently, in the final narrative unit of the *Morte Darthur* Malory is able to return to his initial concern with governance. In the first narrative unit he defines the office of kingship in the same way that his contemporary, Sir John Fortescue, defines it in *The Governance of England*: to defend his people against 'þair enemeyes outwarde bi the swerde' and to 'defende his peple ayenst wronge doers inwarde bi justice' (116). Arthur swears at his coronation 'to stand with true justyce fro thens forth the dayes of this lyf' and his first act as king is to sit in judgment upon his people as 'sir Arthur' to right the many 'grete wronges' that have been 'done syn the dethe of kyng Uther', his father (16.22–27:I.7). Nevertheless, during the early years of his reign, the military aspect of the king's office is Arthur's primary concern, as he subdues rebel kings and lords and establishes stable governance throughout England and the Holy Roman Empire. That goal achieved, however, the judicial aspect of the king's office may once again become Arthur's primary concern.

Until now Arthur has managed to fulfill his coronation oath to do 'true justyce' with two exceptions: he did not punish his nephews for their murders of Pellinor and Lamorak and he did not try to reverse the judgment of God which King Mark won 'by mysadventure' (592.22–27: X.14). These exceptions suggest that there are two ways in which Arthur's kingly powers of doing justice are limited. He either cannot or will not do justice upon his own kinsmen. And, in a case where he has allowed an appeal to the judgment of God in trial by battle, he will not interfere with that judgment. Arthur's function when presiding over such trials is simply to ensure that the opponents are more or less evenly matched and that they obey the rules of fair play. As a Worshipful knight, he takes the rationalist attitude towards trial by battle and accepts the argument of the Lateran Council that it is a sin to 'tempt' God by allowing trials which would require a miracle to produce 'true justyce'. However, once a trial of well-matched combatants has commenced, the king would not presume to interfere. In Malory's day the king or his constable could stop a trial by battle at any time and render judgment, but Malory does not allow Arthur such latitude. Consequently the most that Arthur can do to manipulate the outcome of these trials is to see that the stronger knight fights on the side which he judges to be in the right. To that end he has insisted that his Round Table Knights swear annually at Pentecost that they will never 'take no batayles in a wrongefull quarell for no love ne for no worldis goodis' (120.23–24:III.15).

Not all of Arthur's Round Table Knights share his rationalist point of view on the doing of 'true justyce', however. On the one hand, an Heroic knight like Gawain believes that 'true justyce' consists in doing whatever is necessary to maintain the honour and well-being of his clan. Gawain's law is the *lex talionis*. In fulfillment of that law he has ruthlessly pursued the blood feud against the house of Pellinor and, in fact, we never see him engage in a formal trial by battle until he accuses Lancelot of treason in order to avenge his brothers. On the other hand, a True knight like Lancelot believes that 'true justyce' is the judgment of God and is convinced that God actually determines the outcome of every trial by battle, regardless of how evenly matched the combatants may be. Lancelot is well known as the willing champion of ladies and damsels and in the final narrative unit he fights three great treason trials by battle on behalf of the queen.

Although Eugene Vinaver has divided Malory's post-Grail narrative into two tales (The Book of Sir Launcelot and Queen Guinevere and The Most Piteous Tale of the Morte Arthur Saunz Guerdon) and William Caxton has divided it into four books (XVIII–XXI), it is really a unit thematically structured by three allegations of treason and the battles which follow. Each allegation creates a judicial crisis more difficult to resolve than the last. In fact, we may view this post-Grail narrative unit, with its thematic emphasis upon the king's governance, as a political test of the three knightly types which is comparable to the religious test posed by the Grail quest. In the first two cases of alleged treason Arthur is able to stand by his coronation oath to do 'true justyce' because he is able to field a stronger champion on the side he has judged to be in the right. And in both of these cases the judgment of God which Lancelot elicits by battle as the queen's champion tallies with Arthur's own judgment. However, the third and last allegation produces a judicial crisis which Arthur cannot resolve in his accustomed manner because Lancelot stands accused with the queen. In the drama which follows, Malory's typology of knighthood endows each of the princpals with the thematic weight and significance of characters in a political morality play. Gawain, Arthur and Lancelot all act according to their most deeply held convictions and the result is tragedy of the highest order.

Lancelot Versus Mador De La Porte

In the first case of alleged treason to come before Arthur all three of Malory's chief protagonists are involved. Lancelot, the True knight, is the queen's champion. Arthur, the Worshipful knight, presides over her trial as 'a ryghtfull juge'. And Gawain, the Heroic knight, is the cause of the queen's misfortune.

Gawain's role in the affair is quite original with Malory. In both the *Mort Artu* and the stanzaic *Morte Arthur*, Gawain is present at the fateful banquet and in the stanzaic poem he is later revealed to have been the intended victim (1648–55). However, only Malory develops an explicit link between the murder of Patryse and the ongoing blood feud between Gawain's family and the house of Pellinor. In his list of the twenty-four knights whom the queen invites to her 'pryvy dynere' Malory names 'sir Pynell le Saveayge' last and takes care to mention that he 'was cosyne to sir Lameroke de Galis, the good knyght that sir Gawayne and hys brethirn slew by treson' (1048.24–26:XVIII.3). Therefore the reader is not at all surprised to learn that 'Pyonell hated sir Gawayne' and 'for pure envy and hate ... enpoysonde sertayn appylls for to enpoysen sir Gawayne' (1049.3–5:XVIII.3). Even Gawain is not surprised and understands immediately after the unfortunate sir Patryse has died from eating an apple, that the poison was meant for him:

> 'My lady the quene!' seyde sir Gawayne. 'Madam, wyte you that thys dyner was made for me and my felowis, for all folkes that knowith my condicion undirstonde that I love well fruyte. And now I se well I had nere be slayne. Therefore, madam, I drede me leste ye woll be shamed.' (1049.17–21:XVIII.3)

It is possible that Gawain also suspects why (and, therefore, by whom) he was marked for death, for he does not accuse the queen. At the same time, however, he knows that she will be held responsible for Sir Patryse's death because she 'lette purvey' the fruit at the banquet and there are twenty-three witnesses to that fact.

The killing of Patryse is all the more shocking because it takes place amidst revelry and feasting in the civilized setting of a private dinner party given by the queen. It should remind the reader of the killing of the Lady of the Lake whom Balin beheaded in the court of the king. There is something especially horrifying in the juxtaposition of the savagery of the blood feud with the civility of the court; and both killings are particularly messy, even the poisoning, for Malory tells us that the unfortunate Patryse swelled up with the poison 'tylle he braste' and 'felle downe suddeynly dede amonge hem' (1049.11–12:

XVIII.3). Both killings are also clear cases of murder, like the Orkneys' killing of Lamorak, because they combine the elements of stealth and surprise. Like Lamorak, who was ambushed in the forest and finally stabbed in the back, Sir Patryse and the Lady of the Lake had no chance to defend themselves, and the manner of their deaths leaves no doubt as to the malicious intent of their killers.

None of these killings is perceived to be a crime by its perpetrator, however. Each one of the killers is a Heroic knight who killed in order to fulfill his sacred duty to avenge the death of a kinsman. Significantly, five of the six men involved are from the north, where social organization in the fifteenth century was still based to a greater or lesser extent upon the patrilineal clans: Balin comes from Northumberland and Gawain and his brethren are from the Orkney Islands. Malory does not identify Pynell by geographical region; however, he does give him the same epithet as Balin — 'Le Saveage'. This identification is original with Malory, for in the *Mort Artu* the killer is named Avarlan and in the stanzaic *Morte* he remains an anonymous squire; therefore we are probably justified in inferring some kind of kinship between Pynell and Balin. It may not be blood kinship, for Balin's own brother, Balan, is never called 'Le Saveage', but it is surely typological kinship. Both men are exemplars of that type of knight for whom family bonds are sacred; therefore, in order to avenge the death of a kinsman, both are willing to behave like a 'saveage' in the civilized setting of the court.

According to the law of England at the time Malory was writing, murder was an unpardonable crime which demanded the death penalty. It was not a common crime, to judge by extant records, and it was regarded as particularly 'heinous . . . because it caught a man off his guard' (Bellamy, *Crime* 54). The sense of horror engendered by this crime has never been better expressed than in the words of the ghost of Hamlet's father, who complains of having been

> 'Cut off even in the blossoms of my sin,
> Unhouseled, disappointed, unaneled,
> No reck'ning made, but sent to my account
> With all my imperfections on my head.
> O horrible! O, horrible! most horrible!
>
> (I.5.76–80)

Malory imagines that both the law and the attitude of horror engendered by murder were the same in King Arthur's days. Therefore, when Mador de la Porte stands up and 'opynly' holds the queen responsible for his cousin's death, the queen is in a desperate situation. King Arthur enters the hall and Mador repeats his charge of 'treson'. This prompts Malory to explain, parenthetically, that 'the custom was such at that tyme that all maner of shamefull deth was called treson' (1050.2–3:XVIII.4). Indeed, the customary use of the word 'treason' to refer to 'murthir', when otherwise it referred to the killing or betrayal of one's feudal lord or vassall, confirms the horrific nature of the crime in King Arthur's days.

The Queen's situation, and Malory's parenthetical observation, should remind the reader of the time when Blamour de Ganys and his brother Bleoberis 'appeled the kynge of Irelond of treson', accusing him of having 'slayne a cosyn of thers in his corte in Irelonde by treson' (404.29–32:VIII.20). That appeal was also made before King Arthur and elicited the following explanation from Malory:

> For the custom was suche tho dayes that and ony man were appealed of ony treson othir of murthure he sholde fyght body for body, other ellys to fynde another knyght for hym. And alle maner of murthers in thos dayes were called treson.
>
> (405.2–5:VIII.20)

Malory's extension of the word 'treson' to cover the crime of 'murther' or 'shamefull death' reflects French feudal law of the twelfth century (York, 'Legal Punishment') but his assertion that trial by battle was the customary way to deal with such cases partially reflects late medieval English practice, as well. Trial by battle was not encouraged as a means of making judgments in fifteenth-century England, but in cases where there was insufficient evidence upon which to base a jury trial, men did resort to trial by battle, both under common law and under the law of chivalry (Bellamy, *Crime* 133–34; *Law* 143–46). The cases involving King Anguishaunce of Ireland and Queen Guinevere are precisely parallel. Both royal personnages are held responsible for a crime committed in their court, and perhaps in their presence (we are never given the details of the murder committed in the court of Ireland), but both deny that they are guilty. Anguishaunce swears that he was never 'consentynge to the knyghtis deth' (407.25:VIII.21), and Guinevere swears that she

> 'made thys dyner for a good entente and never for none evyll, so Allmyghty Jesu helpe me in my ryght, as I was never purposed to do such evyll dedes, and that I reporte me unto God.'
>
> (1050.28–32:XVIII.4)

In other words, both swear that they are intentionally innocent of the crime.

The normal English judicial process of the late medieval period could not deal with cases like this. Judges and juries could not know a man's intentions. As one judge on the bench of Edward IV declared, 'The thought of man shall not be tried, for the devil himself knoweth not the thought of man' (Pollock & Maitland 2:475). Of course, modern judges and juries cannot be certain that they are able to determine liability only for harm that is both done and intended, either, but rather than resort to the judgment of God to determine the intention of the accused, they depend upon the more rationally based evidence of psychiatric specialists and lie detectors. In Malory's time, however, men were still willing to depend upon the judgment of God, particularly in those cases where it seemed obvious that the more rational procedures available to them would not be adequate. For example, in the stanzaic *Morte Arthur* Guinevere could have chosen trial by jury rather than trial by battle, but does not because she knows that any jury of her peers must find her guilty:

> For welle she wiste to deth she yede
> Yif she were on a queste of knightis
> (918–19; cf. 1320–23)

They can judge only on the basis of circumstantial evidence and many knights of the court actually saw her give the poisoned apple to the knight who died. Malory never brings up the possibility of trial by jury, but his Guinevere also knows that only God can help her in this case, as her references to 'Allmyghty Jesu' and to 'God' indicate. Like her counterpart in the French romance, she realizes that only 'Dex en soit au droit si veraiement comme ge n'i pensai desloiauté ne traison' (*Mort Artu* 84.12–13) and therefore only trial by battle can prove her innocence.

In order for the judgment of God to work, however, two men who are trained in the martial arts must be willing to 'jouparté' their bodies. A knight's attitude towards the taking of this risk tells us a good deal about what type of knight he is. The religious-feudal treatises on chivalry assert that it is the knight's duty to take part in trials by battle, not only as a means of punishing traitors, but also as a means of protecting his lord (Hay, *Knychthede* 22, 30–31; cf. Lull 29, 32). They assume that the 'trewe knyȝt' will trust in God and that God will give him the victory if he fights in the right. However, Hay allows for the possibility that God may sometimes cause a knight to be vanquished, even when his cause is just, if he himself is guilty of some sin, the sin of pride being the only one Hay mentions in this context (31). Consequently, any knight who agrees to take part in a trial by battle has to face the possibility that, even if he believes his cause to be just, God may choose this occasion to punish him with defeat for his own sin. And, of course, if he should enter such a trial trusting in his own strength and skill or in the magic powers of a talisman rather than trusting only in God, then he is already guilty of a serious sin (either pride or superstition) which 'grevis God, and castis men of Goddis grace, and gerris thair inymyes oft tymes be maisteris of thame' (Hay, *Knychthede* 64). It is hard to imagine any late medieval Christian facing trial by battle without giving careful thought to the part God will play.

None of the twenty-three knights who were present at the queen's dinner and who saw Sir Patryse die of the poisoned apple are willing to 'jouparté' their lives for the queen's sake; in fact, they 'all had grete suspeccion unto the quene bycause she lete make that dyner' (1049.30–32:XVIII.3). Even Gawain, who in Malory's version realizes immediately that the poison was meant for him (and therefore must realize that the queen is not likely to have put it there) will not fight for her. Malory spares us the sight of Arthur pleading with Gawain 'por Dieu et por l'amor de moi' to fight for his queen, just as he spares us the sight of Guinevere throwing herself down upon her knees, pleading for 'mercy' and begging him to help her 'in thys nede'. In this way Malory preserves his image of Gawain as an Heroic knight. The Gawain portrayed both in the *Mort Artu* and in the stanzaic *Morte* is an honourable man and a worthy companion to Lancelot. He refuses both requests with tears in his eyes. Nevertheless he refuses because, as a witness to the queen's guilt, he can not defend her 'loiaument' (*Mort Artu* 79). Or, as he puts it in the English poem, 'A-gayne the Ryght wille I not Ryde' (1356–70). Malory's Gawain cannot say so much, primarily because loyalty to his kin is such an overriding priority with him. Therefore, had Arthur asked him to defend his queen, he could not have refused. Later we will learn that Gawain has fought many trials by battle in his lifetime, relying upon his supernatural gift of increasing strength to give him the victory, and that there are 'but feaw knyghtes lyvynge' who know of that gift, which implies that 'feaw' of Gawain's opponents have survived these trials. Moreover, King Arthur has made an ordinance that all trials by battle should begin at the hour of nine in the morning so that 'by lyklyhode if sir Gawayne were on the tone parté, he shulde have the bettir in batayle whyle hys strengthe endured three owrys' (1217.1–9:XX.21). Obviously Malory's Gawain would have no reason at all to refuse to act as the queen's champion if he were asked, and therefore Malory could not allow either Guinevere or Arthur to ask him.

Arthur, the Worshipful knight, would be more than willing to fight as his queen's champion, if he could:

> 'Fayre lordys,' seyde kynge Arthure, 'me repentith of thys trouble, but the case ys so I may nat have ado in thys mater, for I

> muste be a ryghtfull juge. And that repentith me that I may nat do batayle for my wyff, for, as I deme, thys dede com never by her. And therefor I suppose she shall nat be all distayned, but that somme good knyght shall put hys body in jouperté for my quene rather than she sholde be brente in a wronge quarell.'
>
> (1050.4–11:XVIII.4 cf. stanzaic *Morte* 912ff and *Mort Artu* 67)

Arthur's regret that he may not be his queen's champion because he must be her 'ryghtfull juge' is original with Malory and serves to remind us not only that the king is a knight, but that 'Sir Arthur' has had experience as a champion in the battle with Accolon.[1] His willingness to be her champion is at least partly due to his conviction of her innocence, just as Tristram's willingness to act as champion for Anguishaunce of Ireland was due partly to the Irish king's assurance that he was never 'consentynge to the knyghtis deth' (407.24–25: VIII.21). However, that is probably not the whole reason, since we know from the example of his battle with Accolon that Arthur is willing to fight in a 'wrongefull quarrell' for sufficiently good reason. He agreed to be Damas' champion in order to save his own life and that of the other knights who were starving to death in Damas' prison, so it is conceivable that he would agree to be his queen's champion, even if he thought her guilty, in order to save her life. Tristram likewise was willing to fight for Anguishaunce, even before learning of his innocence, because he badly needed 'to wynne the love of the kynge of Irelonde' (406.18:VIII.21). And just as Tristram knew that he was more than a match for Blamoure de Ganys, so Arthur knows that he is more than a match for any knight in his kingdom so long as he bears Excalibur (even though he has now lost the magical scabbard). However, Arthur does not need to take the extraordinary step of defending his queen's innocence himself, so long as he can find some other good knight to do it.[2] Ordinarily he would rely on Lancelot, but since Lancelot is not presently at court and may not even be 'within thys realme', he counsels the queen to ask Bors to be her champion 'for sir Launcelottis sake, and uppon my lyff he woll nat refuse you' (1051.9–20:XVIII.4).

Arthur has great confidence in Bors as a champion because he thinks him 'one of the nobelyst knyghtes of the worlde, and moste perfitist man' (1055.2–3:XVIII.6). The reference to Bors' superlative 'perfeccion' reminds us that he is a Grail knight, stable in love of God and virtuous living because he lives the mixed life of good deeds and contemplative prayer. As a True knight Bors believes that God determines the outcome of all battles and, in fact, during the Grail quest he fought a trial by battle for a lady who had been disinherited of her lands and he won 'by the grace of God' (959.4:XVI.8). Bors is not a knight of great physical prowess but he is a knight of great spiritual prowess and he would not be afraid to do battle, no matter who his opponent, so long as he knew he was fighting for the right. Therefore, among all those knights present at the queen's banquet, Bors is the one most likely to be willing to defend the queen, provided he can be convinced of her innocence.

Bors is reluctant to take up the queen's quarrel at first, not so much because he thinks she is guilty, but because he is angry with her for having banished Lancelot from the court and also because he knows that his fellow Round Table Knights will disapprove.[3] Nevertheless he promises both king and queen that he will be her champion 'onles that there com by adventures a better knyght than I am to do batayle for her.' Then, as soon as he can slip away from the court, he goes to Windsor forest where Lancelot is staying with the hermit, Brastias, to tell his cousin 'of all thys adventure'. Lancelot is overjoyed. Before leaving the court as a consequence of the queen's displeasure, he had asked Bors, 'in that ye can, gete me the love of my lady quene Gwenyvere' (1047.36:XVIII.2). Therefore, as he now observes, 'thys ys com happely as I wolde have hit' (1053.16–17: XVIII.5). Nothing is more likely to dissolve the queen's jealous rage than the gratitude which she must feel after he has saved her life.

Lancelot, the True knight, was not present at the queen's 'pryvy dynere' because she had banished him from the court in an excess of jealousy and vindictiveness. In fact, if she had not quarreled with Lancelot she probably would never have thought of arranging to have twenty-four other knights of the Round Table dine with her 'in a prevy place by themselff'. She did it, according to Malory, to cover up her distress over Lancelot's departure and to 'shew outwarde that she had as grete joy in all other knyghtes of the Rounde Table as she had in sir Launcelot' (1048.13–15:XVIII.3). In other words, she did it to make him jealous, too (assuming that he had not taken himself so far away from the court that he would not hear of it), and to even the score for all those 'damesels and maydyns' who had been resorting to Lancelot as their champion.

It is ironic that Lancelot's activity as the champion of 'damesels and maydyns' should make the queen jealous, for Lancelot has undertaken that activity in order to keep the promise he made during the Quest of the Sankgreal: 'frome hensforewarde I caste me, by the grace of God, never to be so wycked as I have bene but as to sew knyghthode and to do fetys of armys' (899.1–3:XIII.20). Malory makes sure that the reader will remember this promise by opening his account of the 'Poisoned Apple' with a reference to Lancelot's return from the 'queste of the

Sankgreall' and by specifying that Lancelot does battle for these damsels 'in all such maters of ryght... for the plesure of oure Lorde Jesu Cryst' (1045.24–26:XVIII.1). With these references Malory also reminds the reader that Lancelot is doing what a True knight ought to do, using his sword arm to defend the rights of helpless women, in other words, performing the 'office' of knighthood.

It is not just this zealous doing of his knightly duty which has prompted the queen to become jealous, however. At the same time as he applied himself 'dayly' to do battle for various 'ladyes and damesels' who 'dayly resorted unto hym', Lancelot also, 'ever as much as he myght', began to withdraw himself 'fro the company of quene Gwenyvere for to eschew the sclawndir and noyse' (1045.26–28: XVIII.1). In this way he tried belatedly to keep that other promise he made during the Quest, to 'no more com in that quenys felyship as much as ye may forbere' (897.25–26:XIII.20), a promise which he 'forgate' upon first returning to the court:

> Than, as the booke seyth, sir Launcelot began to resorte unto quene Gwenivere agayne and forgate the promyse and the perfeccion that he made in the queste; for, as the booke seyth, had nat sir Launcelot bene in his prevy thoughtes and in hys myndis so sette inwardly to the quene as he was in semynge outewarde to God, there had no knyght passed hym in the queste of the Sankgreall. (1045.10–16:XVIII.1)

Malory is not repeating here what Nacien has already said, namely that Lancelot would have been second only to Galahad in achieving the Grail if he had been more 'stable' in his 'thoughte' (948.24–27:XVI.5). Malory is saying that Lancelot would have been the premier Grail knight if his 'prevy thoughtes' had not been 'sette inwardly to the quene'. Therefore, this statement can not refer to Lancelot's 'myndis ... sette' during the Quest, after Galahad was born; rather it must refer to his 'myndis ... sette' before the Quest and before Galahad was conceived. Then, indeed, Lancelot seemed to have his thoughts set upon God when he expressed his determination to remain a virgin 'for drede of God'. Now, however, Malory implies that if Lancelot had really been so devoted to God as he then appeared to be, Galahad would never have been conceived. Lancelot would have been worthy of his own baptismal name and would never have chosen to go to Guinevere at Castle Case rather than remain at Corbenic to try the Grail adventures. The truth of the matter is that Lancelot has always loved the queen and has never been able completely to suppress his feelings of love for her. Even during the Grail quest, 'ever his thoughtes prevyly were on the quene' and so, Malory adds, after

Lancelot returned to Camelot he and the queen 'loved togydirs more hotter than they dud toforehonde, and had many such prevy draughtis togydir that many in the courte spake of hit.' (1045.16–20:XVIII.1)

I have argued elsewhere that this passage should not be interpreted to mean that Lancelot and the queen are committing adultery ('Malory's Lancelot' 433–34). To 'haven a draught' in Middle English means simply to take a walk. It is a common idiomatic expression which should never have been misinterpreted except that readers and critics were looking for evidence in Malory's text of what they knew was going on in the French version of the love story. Of course, frequent arm-in-arm and tête-à-tête strolls by Lancelot and the queen, in full sight of the court, are more than enough evidence to set tongues wagging, malicious tongues especially. At the same time, however, except for their frequency, they offer no more proof of a guilty relationship than the conversations between Lancelot and all those ladies and damsels who daily beseech him to be their champion. Malory in fact calls attention to the similar nature of these meetings by using the same word to describe them: Lancelot 'began to resorte unto quene Gwenivere agayn' and Lancelot also had 'many resortis of ladyes and damesels which dayly resorted unto him . . .' (1045.22–24: XVIII.1). It is pitifully ironic that Lancelot's efforts to help these ladies should make the queen jealous. However, it is at the same time completely understandable. She is no longer young and she knows that on at least two occasions Lancelot has slept with a younger and more beautiful woman — Elaine, the daughter of King Pelles. Therefore she suffers as any middle-aged woman would suffer if she had reason to suspect that her husband or lover now prefers more youthful beauty.

The queen calls Lancelot to her chamber and accuses him of betraying her. This situation is Malory's invention and it elicits a response from Lancelot which confirms that he has not entirely forgotten 'the promyse and the perfeccion' he made in the Quest.

> 'A, madame,' seyde sir Launcelot, 'in thys ye must holde me excused for dyvers causis: one ys, I was but late in the quest of the Sankgreall, and I thanke God of Hys grete mercy, and never of my deservynge, that I saw in that my queste as much as ever saw ony synfull man lyvynge, and so was hit tolde me. And if that I had nat had my prevy thoughtis to returne to youre love agayne as I do, I had sene as grete mysteryes as ever saw my sonne sir Galahad, Percivale, other sir Bors. And therefore, madam, I was but late in that queste, and wyte you well, madam, hit may nat be yet lyghtly forgotyn, the hyghe servyse in whom I dud my dyligente laboure.' (1046.3–14:XVIII.1)

His concluding phrase ('hit may nat be yet lyghtly forgotyn') does not bode well for the future, but for now, at least, Lancelot wants to try to keep his 'promyse' and some degree of the 'perfeccion' he achieved in the Quest.

Perfection was a relative term to the medieval Christian; 'it was understood that some would be more perfect than others' (Howard 90). Moreover, Arthur's description of Bors as the 'moste perfitist man' shows that fifteenth-century men no longer believed Christian perfection to be attainable only in the religious or contemplative life. The orthodox definition of perfection was 'the love of God and love of our neighbour' or *caritas* (Flew 236). The first level of this perfection was thought to be obedience to the ten commandments, avoidance of the seven deadly sins and love of God and neighbour (Rolle, *English Writings* 63–64). The second level of this perfection required that one 'forsake al þe worlde, þi fader and þi moder, and al þi kyn, and folow Criste in poverte' (64) and, in the fourteenth century, Richard Rolle interpreted this to mean literally forsaking the world to live the contemplative life of a monk or recluse. In the early fifteenth century, however, theologians began to contest this traditional interpretation of Christ's counsel to those who would be 'perfect', arguing that monastic vows were 'only one form of virtuous life and provided a disposition rather than a way to perfection' (Aston 156).[4] Indeed, the example offered by the Brethren of the Common Life and the great increase in manifestations of lay piety in the fifteenth century may be seen as a movement to achieve this higher level of perfection while remaining in the world. The movement was encouraged in England by Walter Hilton, who recommended to lay lords who desired the higher degree of perfection that they live the mixed life; that is, that they combine the active life of good works with the contemplative life of prayer and meditation, in imitation of Christ ('Epistle on Mixed Life').

By returning to Camelot rather than adopt the contemplative life chosen by Galahad and Percival, Lancelot and Bors are both observing the 'ordre of charite' in accordance with Hilton's strictures in his 'Epistle on Mixed Life' (267–69). Both men return in order to 'sew knyghthode' in the world, that is, in order to serve Arthur as agents of his governance, for that is the 'office' of True knighthood. Lancelot has also desired to see the queen again; however, that need not mean that he lose the 'perfeccion' he achieved during the Quest, if he can keep the promise he made to avoid the 'quenys felyship' as much as he 'may forbere' (897.25–26:XIII.20). In this speech he tries to persuade the queen that this is the best course to follow, not only for the sake of the 'hygh servyse' in which he was so lately engaged, but also because they are in real danger from the malice of Aggravayne and Mordred.

He dreads what these two knights may do more for her sake than for his own, and he would be 'lothe' to see her 'dishonoured' (1046.15–31: XVIII.1).

Lancelot's speech is clearly pleading in tone; however, the queen is so caught up in her own feelings of jealousy and rage that she literally cannot hear him. In her pain, she lashes out, accusing him of being a 'common lechourere' and banishing him from the court. There is nothing Lancelot can do or say to allay her suspicions without incurring shame and disaster for them both; therefore, he leaves the court, convinced that 'she woll never be my good lady as she hath bene,' and determined to return to France.

At this point Bors steps in to play the role anticipated for him in the final scene of Malory's Tale of the Sankgreal. He advises his cousin against taking such a drastic course of action, reminding him that he has 'many grete maters . . . in honde' at the court and that the queen has been angry with him 'many tymys' before and soon repented her anger. He suggests instead that Lancelot go to the forest of Windsor to stay with the hermit Brastias until he can send 'bettir tydynges' (1047.15–24:XVIII.2). Bors' speech neatly summarizes Lancelot's predicament: as a True knight Lancelot has important political and judicial functions to fulfill at the king's court, but he cannot fulfill them unless he retains the grace and favour of the queen, that is, unless she is willing to be his 'good lady' in the most fundamental, political sense of that collocation (see above 112, 180). By being so unreasonably jealous, Guinevere makes it impossible for Lancelot to remain at Camelot and still maintain the degree of 'perfeccion' he achieved in the Quest. However, it is possible that she can be made to change her mind and heart. Bors promises Lancelot to do what he can to 'get . . . the love' of the queen again while his cousin goes into retreat with a holy man, where he may gain spiritual strength and some much needed perspective.[5]

Through the good offices of Bors, Lancelot is able to defend his queen against Mador de la Porte's charge of treason. Malory's version of this trial by battle is much more dramatic than that of either of his sources. One critic has in fact accused him of melodrama for calling attention to the 'grete fyre made aboute an iron stake' that awaits the queen, should Mador de la Porte have 'the bettir' (Donaldson 465). However, Malory's purpose for doing this seems to be to emphasize his theme of justice. Indeed, he goes out of his way to call attention to Arthur's admirable and extraordinary dedication to 'true justyce' even where his own queen is concerned: 'for such custom was used in tho dayes: for favoure, love, nother affinité there sholde be none other but ryghtuous jugemente, as well uppon a kynge as uppon a knyght, and as well uppon a quene as uppon another poure lady' (1055.11–15:XVIII.6). Arthur is fairly certain that Bors will win this battle because he is 'in sertayne that his queen ys untruly defamed' (1052.26–27:XVIII.5) and he knows that Bors is 'one of the nobelyst knyghtes of the worlde, and moste perfitist man'; but he would be much more confident of the outcome if he knew that Lancelot were going to be the queen's champion.

During the late medieval period it is probable that most men felt about trial by battle as Arthur does. Certainly many men were unwilling to accept the judgment of God if it did not accord with their own judgment. For example, in the stanzaic *Morte*, Mador de la Porte does not accept the judgment of God, as such. Rather, he is so delighted to discover that he has 'foughten with launcelot du lake' and survived in honourable defeat, that he offers to forgive his brother's dethe 'to the quene for thy [Lancelot's] sake' (1621). But King Arthur does not let the matter rest there. Clearly he does not think that this judgment of God is sufficient 'proof' of the queen's innocence either. Therefore he arrests all the squires who had served at the queen's banquet and puts them 'in harde payne' until one of them confesses to the crime (1648–1655). Then, and only then, is Mador fully convinced 'That no gylte hadde the lady shene' (1657) and, after begging her forgiveness, he attends the execution of the traitor:

The squyer than was done to shende
As it was bothe lawe and Ryght,
Drawen and hongyd and for-brende
Be-fore syr mador, the noble knyghte.
(1664–67)

It does not seem to bother anyone that the squire's confession was exacted by torture, least of all Mador de la Porte, who has the satisfaction of watching the enemy of his house die a traitor's death.

By contrast, in Malory's version everyone seems to accept the judgment of God, even Mador himself. One might argue that Mador's willingness to release 'the quene of hys quarell' indicates no more than a desire to save his life and, indeed, Lancelot seems to suspect as much for he replies that he will not grant Modor his life unless he 'frely reales the quene for ever, and that no mencion be made uppon sir Patryseys tombe that ever quene Gwenyver consented to that treson' (1058.1–3:XVIII.7). However, once Mador has agreed to these conditions and everyone in the court has rejoiced at the outcome, the case is closed. Arthur does not try to prove the verdict by any other means. Malory is then able to confirm the queen's innocence, without throwing into question the generally accepted validity of the judgment of God in King Arthur's days, through Nyneve, the Damsel of the Lake. She comes to court to reveal the name of the murderer, thus confirming that the queen 'was never gylty' (1059.17:XVIII.8).

This first case of alleged treason serves to 'place' each of Malory's three types in the judicial setting of King Arthur's court. Only Arthur, the Worshipful knight, is fully at home here. Gawain, the Heroic knight, is as out of place as the barbarism of the blood feud; and Lancelot and Bors, the True knights, are as out of place as the asceticism required for Christian 'perfeccion'. However, one could easily argue that there is more need for men like Lancelot and Bors at the court than there is for men like Gawain. As this episode shows, Gawain plays no constructive role at Camelot. His kinship with the king ensures him a place at court, but the values he brings with him are inimical to the honourable society. In fact,in the passage describing the flight of sir Pynell, Malory takes care to remind his readers that Gawain's pursuit of the blood feud is ultimately responsible for the death of sir Patryse:

> And thys knyght sir Pynell fledde unto hys contrey, and was opynly knowyn that he enpoysynde the appyls at that feste to that entente to have destroyed sir Gawayne, bycause sir Gawayne and hys brethirne destroyed sir Lamerok de Galys which sir Pynell was cosyn unto. (1059.20–25:XVIII.8)

Gawain's pursuit of the blood feud has also endangered the life of the queen, for had there been no knights at court willing to 'jouparté' their lives for a judgment of God, she would have been burned at the stake.

So long as trial by battle is the only way to do justice, Arthur has great need of knights like Lancelot and Bors who are willing to risk their lives fighting for the right. However, as a True knight and champion of the 'ryght' Lancelot is less perfect than Bors because of his attachment to the queen. At the end of the battle with Mador, we learn that long ago Lancelot promised the queen that he would 'ever' be her knight 'in ryght othir in wronge':

> 'My lord,' seyde sir Launcelot, 'wytte you well y ought of ryght ever to be in youre quarell and in my ladyes the quenys quarell to do batayle, for ye ar the man that gaff me the hygh Order of Knyghthode, and that day my lady, youre quene, ded me worshyp. And ellis had I bene shamed, for that same day that ye made me knyght, thorow my hastynes I loste my swerde, and my lady, youre quene, founde hit, and lapped hit in her trayne, and gave me my swerde whan I had nede thereto; and ells had I bene

> shamed amonge all knyghtes. And therefore, my lorde Arthure, I promysed her at that day ever to be her knyght in ryght othir in wronge.' (1058.21–32:XVIII.7)

Lancelot made that unconditional promise when he was very young and overwhelmed by gratitude, but he would never renege on a promise once made; nor is there any reason to think that he would now wish that promise unmade. No matter how his personal feelings for the queen have developed in the meanwhile, he still regards his political relationship to her as primary and definitive: she is his 'good lady' in the same way that her husband, Arthur, is his 'good lord' (1047.25–28:XVIII.2) and as their man, he ought 'of ryght' to support them in their 'quarells'.

Such support was the primary service expected of their men by fifteenth-century 'good lords'. Moreover, retainers of the king always pledged their loyalty and service without exception, other than the commonly understood qualification preserving honour and conscience.[6] If Lancelot is to be a True knight, however, he can not support the queen in a 'wrongefull quarell', for that would constitute disloyalty both to God and to Arthur. This time there has been no problem, for even though Guinevere appeared to be guilty, she was, in fact, innocent. The next time Guinevere is acused of treason, however, Lancelot's situation as her champion will be more problematic.

Lancelot Versus Mellyagaunt

In the second case of alleged treason to come before Arthur the three knightly types are once again represented. Gawain's role as Heroic knight and instigator of the judicial crisis is here played by Mellyagaunt. Arthur continues to represent Worshipful knighthood as 'ryghtful judge'. And Lancelot ultimately faces Mellyagaunt in battle as a True knight, although initially he responds to Mellyagaunt's appeal of treason as a Worshipful knight would respond. Therefore, we must first of all look at what has happened since the last judicial crisis to make Lancelot respond in this way. What has happened to cause him to recapitulate the moral decline from True to Worshipful knighthood which we first witnessed in the Tale of Tristram? As in the Tale of Tristram we will find that the decline can be attributed to his relationship with the queen and that it manifests itself primarily through his behaviour in three tournaments.

Lancelot disguises himself at the first of these, the tournament at Winchester, thus recalling his behaviour in the first tournament in the Tale of Tristram at the Castle of Maidens (see above 185). This time we can be sure that he does not enter the lists to please the queen — quite the contrary — but he does go to Winchester because of her. Lancelot had already decided not to participate in the Winchester tournament and had excused himself on the grounds that he was not yet fully recovered from the wounds he received in battle with Mador de la Porte. However, when Guinevere then decided not to accompany the king to Winchester, she put Lancelot in a very delicate situation. She, in effect, forced him to go to Winchester in order to avoid the appearance of remaining behind at Camelot to have his 'plesure' with her. The hint of sarcasm in Lancelot's response after the queen has pointed this out to him suggests that he sees through her manoeuvre:

> 'Have ye no doute, madame,' seyde sir Launcelot, 'I alow youre witte. Hit ys of late com syn ye were woxen so wyse!'
>
> (1066.5–6:XVIII.9)

Nevertheless he has no choice but to go. He decides to disguise himself and to fight against the king's party, evidently not so much to win worship as to vex the queen since she has advised against it; but his parting observation, 'Madame, ... I shall take the adventure that God woll gyff me' (1066.17–18:XVIII.9) is ominous, foreshadowing the 'mysseaventure' which will befall him there for his pride.

No part of this conversation is traceable to either of Malory's sources. It appears to be entirely his own invention, designed to show how and why his hero begins this second moral decline. Lancelot is finding it exceedingly difficult to act like a True knight while resident in the court. This manoeuvre of the queen has irritated him and provoked him to do something he would not otherwise have done; but he does not immediately decline so far from the spiritual awareness of a True knight as to be unable to recognize the significance of his 'mysseaventure'. He confesses to his cousin Bors that he 'wolde with pryde have overcom you all. And there in my pryde I was nere slayne, and that was in myne owne defaughte' (1084.1–3:XVIII.16).

It is not long before he relapses, however. When he hears of the Allhallowmass tournament at which the queen is to be present, he is so eager to be there that he foolishly tries on his armour and mounts his horse before the wound he received at Winchester has fully healed (1086.30–34:XVIII.17). The effort re-opens his wound and he is unable to go to the tournament, but Bors reports to the queen that his cousin wished to be there 'for the love of you' (1087.21–22:XVIII.18).

Finally, just as Malory has invented the conversations cited above, so he seems to have invented in its entirety the third tournament to complete the pattern of Lancelot's moral decline. The 'Great Tournament' demonstrates that Lancelot is now as wholly committed to the vainglorious competition for worship as he was at the tournament of Lonezep, and for the same reason — to please his lady the queen. He goes to this tournament explicitly to please her and agrees, for her sake, to 'force' himself there 'that men may speke you worshyp' (1103.19–20:XVIII.21). What is more, he, who before the tournament at Winchester had never worn the favour of any woman, not even of the queen, now wears the queen's golden sleeve.[7] Finally, we can be certain that Lancelot has lost the humility and spiritual awareness of a True knight when not even the 'myssefortune' of being wounded in the buttocks just before the tournament is sufficient to shock him into an awareness of his pride. On the contrary, he seems determined to persist in his vainglory, despite his 'unhappynesse':

> 'A, mercy Jesu!' seyde sir Launcelot, 'I may calle myselff the moste unhappy man that lyvyth, for ever whan I wolde have faynyst worshyp there befallyth me ever som unhappy thynge. Now, so Jesu me helpe,' seyde sir Launcelot, 'and if no man wolde but God, I shall be in the fylde on Candilmas day at the justys, whatsomever falle of hit.' (1106.4–9:XVIII.22)

Lancelot uses the word 'unhappy' to describe both the event and himself, but he does not draw from his misfortune the inference which a True knight would draw. Indeed, rather than attribute his misfortune to the wrath of God, he actually calls upon 'Jesu' to help him in his vainglorious pursuit of worship for the queen's sake. He has adopted both the language and the way of thinking of a Worshipful knight. 'So God me helpe' is a phrase commonly used by knights who think that the desire for worship is a good thing because it motivates men to do great deeds (see above 243).

Lancelot's pride cuts him off from the grace of God so that when he is faced with strong sexual temptation, as he was in 'Launcelot and Elaine' the second time he lay with Elaine (thinking her to be the queen), he is not able to resist. I have argued elsewhere against the popular hypotheses that Malory tried either to cover up Lancelot's adultery with the queen or to excuse it ('Malory's Lancelot' 436–40). It is my conviction that Malory regarded Lancelot's adultery with horror, not just because it was an offense against God and the 'hygh Order of knyghthode', but also because it was 'hyghe treson' against the most noble king in the world. That is why Malory has altered the love story to make the 'Knight of the Cart' the only instance of actual adultery and then done everything he might to make it possible for his readers (and God) to forgive that one offense: first, he places the event in the 'lusty' month of May; second, he reminds us beforehand how these two have loved each other many years without giving in to 'lycouris lustis'; third, he makes it plain that their intention is not to commit adultery, but only to speak to one another through a window barred with iron; finally, he suggests the overwhelming force of the desire which moves Lancelot when, 'for love' of the queen he is able to rip the bars of iron 'clene oute of the stone wallys' (1131.19–20:XIX.6). As one might expect, after such long restraint and in the grip of such passion,

> sir Launcelot wente to bedde with the quene and toke no force of hys hurte honde, but toke hys pleasaunce and hys lykynge untyll hit was the dawnyng of the day; for wyte you well he slept nat, but wacched. (1131:28–32:XIX.6)

Nor is he able to sleep much before the noise and confusion caused by the discovery of the queen's blood-stained sheets brings him back to her chamber to answer Mellyagaunt's charge of treason.

Lancelot responds to Mellyagaunt's accusation of treason against the queen as a Worshipful knight would respond. He thinks only of saving his lady's life and honour. He knows that she is both actually and intentionally guilty of treason; therefore, when reminded that 'God woll have a stroke in every batayle,' he is careful to swear only that she is innocent as charged, as indeed she is. She did not sleep that night with one of her ten wounded knights, and no one but the queen herself knows this better than Lancelot, so he can say that he fights, technically, in the right. But he is also furious with Mellyagaunt for his treacherous behaviour and longs for the chance to kill him. As he said to the queen upon first arriving at Mellyagaunt's castle, there was no one else on earth, except the king, who could have stopped him from killing Mellyagaunt there and then (1129.15–17:XIX.5). Mellyagaunt has only confirmed his barbarism by 'unworshypfully and shamefully' drawing open the curtains of the queen's bed while she still lay in it. Not even the king would have dared so much unless 'hit had pleased hym' to exercise his conjugal rights. In brief, there is no doubt in Lancelot's mind that a man who has abducted his queen, killed his horse and invaded the privacy of his lady's bed is a traitor who deserves to die.

Lancelot's willingness to undertake this 'wrongefull quarrel' may usefully be compared with Arthur's willingness to take up Damas' 'wrongefull quarrel'. Both men are willing to violate the Pentecostal oath in order to save the lives of their loved ones — Guinevere the queen, in Lancelot's case, and in Arthur's case the Round Table knights who are dying of starvation in Damas' prison. However, both men intend by means of this violation to do justice. After winning his case as Damas' champion Arthur assumes his rightful role as judge and proceeds to punish the felon. Likewise, Lancelot wants to punish Mellyagaunt. He is convinced that Mellyagaunt deserves to die as a traitor and he fears that his treachery may never be punished if he is allowed 'to hyde hys owne treson' by means of this technically false appeal of the queen (1133.4:XIX.6).

Throughout this episode Mellyagaunt represents Heroic knighthood. Both his motives and his actions are characteristic of the type of knight who refuses to be bound by the Worshipful code of conduct in his relations with ladies and fellow knights. His crime, *raptus*, matches in severity the crime of Sir Pynell and likewise deserves the death penalty, since the abduction of the queen is a clear case of 'hyghe treson'.[8] Malory linked Sir Pynell's crime to one of Gawain's former crimes by explaining it as an attempt to be avenged for Gawain's murder of Lamorak. He also links Mellyagaunt's crime to one of Gawain's former crimes, not explicitly but implicitly, by means of a strong analogy. One of Gawain's former crimes is the only other case of *raptus* in the *Morte Darthur* and Malory is responsible for attributing it to him: in Malory's version of an episode he found in the *Tristan*, Gawain abducts the damsel of a sleeping knight, despite Lamorak's protestations, because he knows Lamorak will not fight with him for fear of displeasing King Arthur (see above 201–2). Likewise, Mellyagaunt takes care to ensure his immunity. He has loved the queen 'passyngly well' for 'many yerys' but he forbears taking any action until he knows she will be away from the court and unprotected by Lancelot. This version of the abduction is quite original with Malory and its forest setting both heightens and confirms the analogy with Gawain's abduction of the damsel. Thus we may conclude that while Gawain himself has no role to play in Malory's version of the 'Knight of the Cart', his type is portrayed by Mellyagaunt.[9]

Bors has no role to play in the 'Knight of the Cart', either, but his type is not altogether absent from the action for, after he has suffered a great misfortune, Lancelot repents his sin to become a True knight once more. Mellyagaunt is certain that he is in the right, but he is not at all certain that he can prove this in trial by battle with Lancelot. Therefore, he arranges to have Lancelot fall through a trap door 'more than ten fadom into a cave full off strawe' where Lancelot endures 'grete payne' (1134.34–1135.26:XIX.7–8). This version of Lancelot's imprisonment is quite original with Malory. In the French romances Lancelot is imprisoned twice in castles where he is treated well. By contrast, Malory's Lancelot is imprisoned only once in a dungeon where he endures not only physical pain but mental anguish, as well. For in Malory's version, unlike the French romance, Lancelot knows that if he does not escape from this prison within eight days, his lady will be burnt at the stake in default of her champion.

This makes it all the more remarkable, of course, that Lancelot should refuse to take the opportunity of escape which presents itself in the form of his amorous lady-gaoler. Nevertheless he does refuse to lie with her. Day after day he refuses, despite her reminders that Guinevere 'shall be brente in [his] defaute' unless he accepts her offer to help him escape. Lancelot's reponse to this situation appears to be that of a man who is certain that God is displeased with him and punishing him for his sin, and who is therefore determined to repent, to amend his life, and to place himself wholly in God's hands:

> 'God deffende,' seyde sir Launcelot, 'that she should be brente in my defaught! And if hit be so,' seyde sir Launcelot, 'that I may nat be there, hit shall be well undirstonde, bothe at the kynge and the quene and with all men of worship, that I am dede, syke othir in preson. For all men that know me woll say for me that I am in som evyll case and I be nat that day there. And thus well I undirstonde that there ys som good knyght, othir of my blood other som other that lovys me, that woll take my quarell in honde. And therefore,' seyde sir Launcelot, 'wyte you well, ye shall nat feare me, and if there were no mo women in all thys londe but ye, yet shall nat I have ado with you.' (1136.1–13:XIX.8)

The lady is stunned by the magnitude of his folly. She cannot believe that any man would refuse her request knowing that as a result he must be 'shamed' and 'destroyed for ever'. However, she is thinking only of 'worldis shame', whereas Lancelot is also thinking, once again, of what would be shameful by Grail standards:

> 'As for worldis shame, now Jesu deffende me! And as for my distresse, hit ys welcom, whatsomever hit be that God sendys me.' (1136.15–17:XIX.8)

In Boethius' *Consolation of Philosophy* Dame Philosophy suggests that God sometimes allows evil men to make others suffer so that they may reform and become virtuous (140). It would seem that this is what has happened to Malory's Lancelot, for now, rather than commit another sin against chastity, he is willing to accept whatever misfortune God may send, even the death of the queen. His ability to take such 'aduersitee in gree' proves that 'he is happy', according to the English translator of Alain Chartier's *Quadriloque Invectif* (*Fifteenth-Century English Translations* 2:48). According to Richard Rolle he is 'blessed'

('Form of Living' 6.180), for his will is perfectly conformed to the will of God.

From a rational and worldly point of view, of course, Lancelot is being uttterly foolish. A Worshipful knight would not hesitate to give the lady what she wanted in order to get out of prison and save his own lady's life. But Lancelot says that he would not have 'ado' with this lady even if she were the last woman on earth! That sounds like the extremely ascetic young man we first encountered in the Tale of Lancelot, who was vowed to chastity 'for drede of God' and would not even kiss a damsel who asked him for a kiss. Lancelot has clearly turned to God again. His repentance may have been prompted initially by the enormity of his present misfortune, but it is quite likely that it has been fostered by reflection upon the enormity of the sin he has just committed. Whatever the cause of his repentance, however, whether fear or love of God, Lancelot is determined not to commit another sin against chastity, not even to save his lady's life. He hopes it is God's will that she be saved from the fire, but he will not commit a sin in order to save her. Fortunately, Lancelot has learned enough of the ways of courtly society to know that even a True knight may kiss a lady and 'lese no worshyp'. Therefore, when his amorous goaler returns on the day appointed for the battle and asks him to kiss her 'but onys', he does so gladly and then sets off for Camelot, pell-mell, having 'commaunded the lady unto God' (1137.2:XIX.8).[10]

Meanwhile back at Camelot the appointed day has come and Lancelot has failed to appear at the appointed hour. The queen is 'brought tyll a fyre to be brente' (1137.6–7:XIX.9) and Mellyagaunt, who is sure that Lancelot will never appear, keeps crying 'uppon sir Arthur to do hym justyse othir ellys brynge forth sir Launcelot' (1137.9–10:XIX.9–10). Arthur is convinced of his queen's innocence because he has taken it upon himself to question all ten of the wounded knights and discovered that there is not one of them who, if he were healed of his wounds, would not gladly do battle with Mellyagaunt to prove that what he has charged the queen with 'ys wronge'. Arthur has done what any late fifteenth-century English monarch might have done, he has conducted an inquisitorial examination of both principals and witnesses prior to the trial (Bellamy, *Crime* 136–37). He can not use this evidence during the trial, of course, because it will be conducted by battle rather than by jury. However, his belief in the innocence of the accused clearly affects the way he handles himself as presiding judge. First, he is willing to allow Lavayne to fight for the queen in Lancelot's stead and then, as soon as Lancelot appears on the scene, he allows him to tell 'opynly' before all those present

> how that sir Mellyagaunce had served hym first and laste. And whan the kynge and quene and all the lordis knew off the treson of sir Mellyagaunte, they were all ashamed on hys behalffe. Than was the quene sente fore and sette by the kynge in the grete truste of hir champion. (1138.7–12:XIX.9)

With this paragraph, Malory comes as close as he can to converting the trial of Guinevere into the trial of Mellyagaunt. As far as Arthur is concerned, at least, it does become a trial to prove Mellyaguant's treason, for he is now just as convinced of Mellyaguant's guilt as he was before of Guinevere's innocence. Therefore he allows the queen to leave the stake to be seated by his side. He did not do this when Lavayne was to be the queen's champion, presumably because he could not be so certain of the outcome. However, with Lancelot fighting for the queen, Arthur is sure of her acquittal. 'Sir' Arthur's attitude towards trial by battle is still that of a Worshipful knight.

Lancelot faces Mellyagaunt in trial by battle as a True knight. Moreover, the fact that he has repented his own sin and placed himself in the hands of God also tends to convert the trial into a trial of Mellyagaunt, for it makes Lancelot's role in the trial analogous to that of an approver. Approvers played a key role in the English system of royal justice long after trial by battle had been condemned by the Church because under the common law the Crown lacked the right to prosecute alleged criminals on its own behalf. It had to depend upon the private appeals of individual citizens and therefore it became customary to induce men who had already confessed their guilt to appeal their confederates in crime and offer to do battle to back up the appeal. In practice, the system of relying upon approvers was open to much abuse (Bellamy, *Crime* 127–31). In theory, however, by doing battle the approver 'proved' not only the truth of his appeal but also 'the sincerity of his own repentance' (Neilson 43).

Lancelot's first trial by battle, the battle against Mador de la Porte, suggested that only God could do 'true justyce' because only God could try the thought of man. His second battle with Mellyagaunt suggests that only God can do 'true justyce' because only He can pardon certain crimes. If Lancelot had confessed his guilt to Arthur and requested his forgiveness, it would not have mattered whether or not Arthur were humanly capable of forgiving him; the king would still have had to condemn him to death as a traitor. In the fifteenth century it was customary to be pardoned by the king for some crimes, like accidental killing or killing in self-defense, but Lancelot's crime is such that, even if the king had wanted to pardon him, he could not have done so without losing his worship and risking his crown. By the ethical standards of the honourable society which Arthur governs, a man may be a secret cuckold and lose no worship, but if he is known to be a cuckold he loses all worship unless he is powerful enough to exact vengeance. From Lancelot's point of view it is fortunate, therefore, that he may appeal directly to the judgment of God. God will choose which one of the two combatants, both traitors to Arthur, deserves to die for his treason and which one may be pardoned.

No matter how complete and sincere his repentance, Lancelot must still dread God's judgment. That may partially explain his willingness that some other 'good' knight should do battle for the queen in his stead. However, having been allowed by Providence to escape without shame from his prison, he does not try to avoid this battle and, after beating Mellyagaunt to the ground, he has good reason to believe that God will decide in his favour. Therefore, when Mellyagaunt refuses to continue the battle 'to the utteraunce' and insists that Lancelot save his life, Lancelot is furious. Mellyaguant tries to induce the king to intervene by crying out that he yields 'as overcomyn' and puts his life 'in the kynges honde and youres' (1138.21–26:XIX.9); however, the king may not take this matter in his hand unless Lancelot, the apparent victor, makes the same request. Malory tells us that Lancelot 'had lever than all the good in the worlde that he myght be revenged uppon' Mellyagaunt, and that he looks to the queen to see what she would have him do. She makes a sign that he should 'sle hym' but, as a True knight, Lancelot cannot slay a man who is on his knees and has asked for mercy. Therefore, he has only two choices: to turn Mellyagaunt over to Arthur and a traitor's death (hanging, drawing and quartering) or to induce him to fight 'to the utteraunce!' so that he can, if it be God's will, kill him in battle. Lancelot would much prefer the latter, and so he offers Mellyagaunt the same 'large proffir' he offered once before to Pedivere in the Tale of Lancelot: he will 'unarme' his head and the left side of his body, allow his left hand to be tied behind him, and in that guise continue the battle (see above 124). Unlike Pedivere, Mellyagaunt leaps at the chance to get Lancelot at such a disadvantage and he asks the king to see that Lancelot abides by his word. Arthur allows this extraordinary 'proffir' to stand, but, Malory tells us, 'Wyte you well there was many a lady and many a knyght mervayled of sir Launcelot that wolde jouparté hymselff in such wyse' (1139.27–29: XIX.9).

Malory may have got the idea of Lancelot's 'large proffir' from reading Christine de Pizan's *Epistle of Othea to Ector*. In her ninety-fourth epistle Othea warns Ector against using arms 'folyly' and she cites the example of Ajax whose left 'arme was vnarmed continuelly', and who thought thereby to win 'synguler wurschyp'. She notes that

Ajax was slain nevertheless, despite 'all hys myght of meyne', and she concludes from this that 'þer is no wurschyp' in such displays of bravado, but only 'grett foly & perell'. However, in 'moralizing' this particular epistle, Christine applies Ajax's behaviour to 'ghostly chiualry', that is, to the struggle of man's soul for his salvation and, on that spiritual level, his behaviour is to be commended. He becomes like the man who follows the advice of St Augustine and does not 'truste in hys owne freelnes' but rather in God when he faces temptation. Christine also cites *Second Corinthians* 3:4–5: 'Such is the assurance I have through Christ towards God. Not that we are sufficient of ourselves to think anything, as from ourselves, but our sufficiency is from God' (138). Of course, the religious-feudal treatises on chivalry had always advised the knight not to put his trust 'in his armoure na wapnis, bot in his awin vertu, and in Him that maid him, and in His merci' (Hay, *Knychthede* 47; cf. Lull 81). Indeed, insofar as the knight did not trust in God but rather trusted in himself, his weapons and his own strength, he was guilty of the sin of overweening pride (Hay, *Knychthede* 31; cf. Lull 52). However, no knight in the *Morte Darthur* except Galahad has ever pushed this article of the True knight's faith quite so far as Lancelot does in his encounters with Pedivere and Mellyagaunt.

What the reader makes of Lancelot's 'large proffir' will depend partly upon his judgment of Lancelot's character and partly upon his own point of view on such matters. If he is a rationalist like Christine de Pizan or Malory's Arthur, he will have difficulty imagining that Lancelot could truly believe that Jesus will be his shield and his armour, and will probably conclude that Lancelot is a fool to make such a 'large proffir'. Of course, after Lancelot has defeated Mellyagaunt, that same reader would have to conclude from the evidence that Lancelot is so great a knight that he can beat any man with one arm tied behind his back. Such a conclusion is much easier to come to after the event, however. Whatever Lancelot's abilities as a knight, with or without armour, Mellyagaunt thought he had a good chance of killing him at those odds and so did many of those present at the trial. On the other hand, if the reader is a providentialist like Ramon Lull or Malory's Bors, then he will have no difficulty imagining that Lancelot really hopes that Jesus Christ will be his shield and his armour. And he will remember that Galahad did very much the same thing when he fought in Arthur's tournament before the Quest of the Sankgreal and insisted upon entering the lists without a shield (864.21–34:XIII.6). At the same time, however, the pious providentialist might be horrified by Lancelot's presumption, regardless of the example of Galahad (who succeeded in defeating all his opponents, except for Percival and

Lancelot), for, by disarming himself in such fashion, Lancelot is doing precisely what the Fourth Lateran Council condemned most explicitly when it forbade trial by battle. He is demanding that God perform a miracle so that justice can be done upon this traitor, Mellyagaunt. He is 'tempting' God, which is a shorthand way of saying that he is taking a terrible chance that God may be so angered by his presumption that He will allow Mellyagaunt to kill him instead.

Both types of reader must be satisfied with the outcome of this trial, however, just as all those present at Arthur's court are satisfied. Those who think that Lancelot has won simply because of his incredible strength are pleased because the more worshipful knight has prevailed and because once the full extent of Mellyagaunt's treason was 'opynly' revealed, they could dismiss his appeal of the queen on rational grounds as a trumped-up charge invented to 'hyde his owne treson'. On the other hand, those who think that God has determined the outcome must be relieved that He has punished Mellyagaunt and spared Lancelot, despite the temptation of Lancelot's 'large proffir'. As for Lancelot himself, he proves the sincerity of his repentance and his gratitude to God for this victory by scrupulously keeping the promise he made during the Quest to 'forbere' the 'quenys felyship' as much as possible. According to Malory, for the next twelve months Lancelot goes about his adventures 'caryed in a charyotte' and does 'more than forty batayles' (1154.7–11:XIX.13). As a consequence, he is not at court when Sir Urry of Hungary arrives seeking to be healed by the best knight of the world.

The 'Healing of Sir Urry' completes the pattern of recapitulation which has informed Malory's post-Grail narrative thus far. Lancelot has repeated the moral decline from True to Worshipful knighthood which we first witnessed in the Tale of Tristram and, as a consequence, he has also succumbed to the temptation of lechery. His sin of actual adultery with the queen in the 'Knight of the Cart' parallels his sin of mental adultery in 'Launcelot and Elaine' when he lay with Elaine the second time believing her to be the queen. His subsequent misfortune and repentance parallels his madness and his repentance during the Quest of the Holy Grail. And, finally, his ability to achieve the miraculous cure of Sir Urry parallels not only his healing of Sir Melyot in the Tale of Lancelot, but also the ecstatic trance he experienced at the end of his quest in the Grail castle. This second parallel is less obvious, perhaps, but ultimately of more significance to an understanding of Lancelot's spirituality. Both his twenty-four day trance and his second healing experience, which causes him to weep like a 'chylde that had bene beatyn!' (1152.35–36:

XIX.12), could be (and have been) regarded as forms of punishment for his presumption, but both could also (and should) be regarded as signs of God's special grace.[11]

Before each visitation of the Holy Ghost Lancelot has prayed to God. At Corbenic he prayed,

> 'Fayre Fadir, Jesu Cryste, ne take hit for no synne if I helpe the good man whych hath grete nede of helpe.' (1016.5–6:XVII.15)

And at Camelot he prays,

> 'Now, Blyssed Fadir and Son and Holy Goste, I beseche The of Thy mercy that my symple worshyp and honesté be saved, and Thou Blyssed Trynyté, Thou mayste yeff me power to hele thys syke knyght by the grete vertu and grace of The, but, Good Lorde, never of myselff.' (1152.20–25:XIX.12)

A comparison of these two prayers suggests that Lancelot has developed considerably in his spiritual life. In the first prayer he asked God's permission to do something which he had been told he was unworthy to do, whereas in the second he asks for God's help to do something which he already knows he is unable 'in worthynes to do'. This indicates that he has advanced both in obedience to God and in humility. Again, in the first prayer Lancelot prayed only to the Father and the Son, whereas in the second he also prays to the Holy Ghost and explicitly invokes the Blessed Trinity. This indicates that he has advanced in understanding the great mysteries of the faith and, in particular, of the operations of the Holy Ghost. In short, this second prayer characterizes Lancelot as a man of deep spirituality. How are we to account for such a development?

It is quite possible that Lancelot's experience in the 'Knight of the Cart' episode has taught him a deeper and truer humility than he has ever known before, if only because, in Malory's version of the love story, he had never before sinned so grievously. After the Quest Lancelot presumed to know better than the holy man who heard his confession when he decided to remain at court to enjoy the 'felyshyp' of the queen. He thought he could resist sexual temptation but he was wrong and the experience may well have had a profoundly humbling effect upon him.

Walter Hilton teaches that only a man who has 'true humility' may be reformed in his soul to the image of God and by 'true humility' he means complete awareness of the fact that one can do nothing of himself but 'allow Jesus to work in him as He pleases' (*Scale of Perfection*, 190–1). Lancelot's prayer ('but, Good Lorde, never of myselff') suggests that he has learned such humility. Moreover, his invocation of the Holy Ghost suggests that he is particularly concerned to avoid the sin of presumption. Late medieval confessors were advised that pride is not only the first sin that assails a man, it is also the last that 'leueþ hym bihynde whan hee haþ ouercome all oþere vices, for þan pride assaileþ hym alþer most' (*Book of Vices* 12). What is more, presumption, the third branch of pride, whereby 'a man weneþ or tristeþ more to hymself þan he scholde' (13) is one of the sins which is 'specially aȝens þe Holy Gost' (24). Lancelot's success in healing Urry indicates that he has been able to avoid this sin of presumption because his humility is sufficient to provide a resting place for the Holy Ghost (Rolle, 'Form of Living' 10.103–4).

The tears which Lancelot sheds afterwards, then, ought to be regarded as the tears of a holy man, for in order to achieve this miraculous healing by the laying on of hands he has been filled with the Holy Ghost. In the *Book of Vices and Virtues* the Dominican Friar Lorens classifies the tears of holy men into six categories, the first of which is tears for their own sins and the last of which is tears caused by the feeling of excessive joy which accompanies the indwelling of the Holy Ghost:

> Þe sixte comeþ of deuocion and of grete plente of ioye & of plentee of Ihesu Crist and of þe felyng of þe Holi Gost, and þilke ben y-blessed ariȝt þat so wepen, for þe schulle be conforted, as holy writ seiþ, as þe norise conforte þe childe þat wepe ...
> (160–161)

It is significant, I think, that these are the only tears which Lorens compares to the sobbing of a child. He does not specify that the child weeps because he has been beaten, as Malory does; nevertheless, I think we may fairly infer, knowing that children do not ordinarily weep and need to be comforted unless they have been hurt in some way, that he chooses this analogy for the same reason that Malory does — to describe that kind of weeping which is characteristic of children, the kind which convulses the entire body with wracking sobs. For such convulsive sobbing is also characteristic of holy men who have been overwhelmed by the 'felyng of þe Holi Gost'.

The 'Healing of Sir Urry' re-establishes Lancelot as the 'beste knyght of the worlde', not only 'as for a worldly knyght' but also 'in holy dedis'. Throughout the *Morte Darthur* the phrase, 'beste knyght of the worlde', has consistently been associated with Grail standards of worship: Merlin so described the knight who would draw Balin's 'unhappy swerd' from the floating stone (91.22:II.19) and during the Quest a good man so described the knight who should achieve the Grail (955.12:XVI.6). What is more, this supernatural feat of healing by the laying on of hands is clearly analogous to the healings performed by his son, Galahad, during the Quest of the Holy Grail and, like them, is also in imitation of Christ as the Divine Physician (R. L. Kelly, 'Wounds' 176–7). It is all the more significant, therefore, that Malory should refuse to narrate the rest of 'the very mater of Shevalere de Charyot' — the year-long period during which Lancelot did more than forty battles — in order to proceed directly to the Death of Arthur (Spisak 229). For, as a consequence, this image of Lancelot as healer and holy man is still fresh in the reader's mind when Mordred and Aggravayne decide to accuse him openly of adultery with the queen.

Lancleot Versus Gawain

The logic of alliteration requires that Lancelot's third opponent in trial by combat be Mordred rather than Gawain. However, when Lancelot is trapped inside the queen's chamber by Mordred and Aggravayne and then pleads his innocence, despite the incriminating circumstances, Arthur refuses to allow a trial. The king believes that Lancelot and the queen are guilty but he also believes that there is no knight who could prove their guilt in trial by battle against Lancelot. Therefore, this third allegation of treason creates the most grave judicial crisis the king has yet faced because it appears to him to make the customary mode of doing justice impossible.

Each of the three main protagonists embodies one of Malory's three knightly types. Lancelot, who so recently healed Sir Urry, represents True knighthood. Arthur the 'ryghtfull juge' represents Worshipful knighthood. And Gawain and his brethren (excluding Gareth) represent Heroic knighthood. As before, it is the Heroic knights (Aggravayne and Mordred) who instigate the crisis. If the reader has noticed that the first two instigative acts were both crimes (murder and rape, respectively) he will expect the third instigative act to be a crime also, to complete this pattern. Malory responds to this expectation in the way he handles the episode, strongly suggesting that it is a crime, the crime of slander, with the malicious intent of destroying Lancelot.

In the opening paragraph of 'Slander and Strife' Malory calls Aggravayne and Mordred 'unhappy knightis' and credits them with a motive for destroying Lancelot and the queen which is in keeping with their past behaviour. He tells us that 'thys sir Aggravayne and sir Mordred had ever a prevy hate unto the quene, dame Gwenyver, and to sir Launcelot' (1161.11–13:XX.1) and thus reminds us of what we learned earlier in the Tale of Tristram from a speech made by Dinadan:

> 'For sir Gawayne and his bretherne, except you, sir Gareth, hatyth all good knyghtis of the Rounde Table for the moste party. For well I wote, as they myght, prevayly they hate my lorde sir Launcelot and all his kyn, and grete pryvay dispyte they have at hym.' (700.1–6:X.58)

Dinadan's speech implies that the 'prevy hate' of Aggravayne and Mordred is a family affair, since it is also felt by Gawain and his brethren (except for Gareth) and not only for Lancelot but for 'all his kyn' as well. Therefore we may infer that it stems from a rivalry for honour and status in Arthur's court and that inference is borne out by Dinadan's phrase, 'grete pryvay dispyte'. According to the *Book of Vices and Virtues*, 'despyt' is the second branch of pride and consists on the one hand of refusing to 'honoure and worschipe' those whom one 'scholde', and on the other of despising those who are 'betere' than oneself. Moreover, it is a particularly pernicious form of pride, for it commonly gives rise to two other deadly sins, anger and envy (15).

Envy formed a substantial part of the Orkneys' motive for murdering Pellinor and Lamorak. Pellinor was the best knight in Arthur's court at the time of the establishment of the Round Table and later his son was called the third best knight in the world, after Lancelot and Tristram. Arthur honoured Pellinor for his greatness by seating him on the left side of the Siege Perilous, and sometime after the death of Lamorak he honoured Lancelot in the same way (see above 205–7). Gawain and his brethren expect, by right of kinship, to be the knights most honoured at Camelot and when their uncle honours the leaders of other family groups they respond with envy. In their view the three great family groups at Arthur's court are all engaged in a fierce competition for honour. Therefore, if the king honours another clan, he makes it ' "worth more" than the rest' and the other family groups automatically become ' "worth less" ' (Baroja 89). This is intolerable to them. Indeed, it is so intolerable that they have virtually destroyed the family of King Pellinor; therefore, by the logic which governs their actions, they should proceed next to destroy the family of Kings Ban and Bors and in the same way, by destroying its leader, Lancelot.

The *Book of Vices and Virtues* likens envy to the adder, because it is the sin which makes a man 'most like to þe deuel'. The devil hates nothing more than another's good, and loves nothing more than another's harm, '& so doþ þe enuyous man or womman' (22). Envy is also like the 'addre þat al enuenime' because first it poisons a man's heart, then it poisons his mouth, and lastly it poisons his deeds:

> 'For þe kynde of þe enuyous is to distreyne and destroie wiþ al his myȝt al good, be it little good or more god or riȝt moche good,

> and þerfore he is like to þe basiliske, a worm þat suffreþ no grene þing aboute hym . . . (23)

Malory has been illustrating the destructive effects of envy ever since the beginning of *Le Morte Darthur*. When Balin achieved his second sword, Malory remarked that 'many knyghtes had grete despite at hym' (63.33–34:II.2). In particular that proud knight from Ireland, sir Launceor, had 'grete despite at Balyne' that he should 'be accompted more hardy or more of prouesse' (67.9–12:II.4) Even more like the Devil himself is Arthur's sister, Morgan le Fay, who, in Malory's version tried to destroy her brother simply because he was good, the 'moste of worship and of prouesse of ony of hir bloode' (145.33–35:IV.II). During the Roman campaign Malory observed, 'oftetymes thorow envy grete hardynesse is shewed that hath bene the deth of many kyd knyghtes' (223.9–11:V.8), and throughout the Tale of Tristram envy played a large part in motivating men to harm one another.[12] Therefore, when he introduces Aggravayne and Mordred as two 'unhappy knightis' who harbor a 'prevy hate' for Lancelot, Malory is suggesting that they are like the 'worm' of envy, the 'basiliske' who 'suffreþ no grene þing aboute hym'. Indeed, the cadence suggests Lancelot's observation regarding 'unhappy knights' who make 'all thynge unhappy that is aboute them' (271.3–4:VI.10).

Aggravayne and Mordred are clearly worse than their two older brothers because, in addition to participating in the family feud with the house of Pellinor, they have acted independently to kill Dinadan during the Quest of the Holy Grail, 'cowardly and felonsly' and for no reason other than their hatred.

> Whan they undirstode that hit was sir Dynadan they were more wrothe than they were before, for they hated hym oute of mesure bycause of sir Lameroke. For sir Dynadan had suche a custom that he loved all good knyghtes that were valyaunte, and he hated all tho that were destroyers of good knyghtes. And there was none that hated sir Dynadan but tho that ever were called murtherers. (614.25–31:X.25; cf. 615.5–8:X.25)

Aggravayne and Mordred are the only knights, other than caricatures of evil like Sir Breunys sanz Pitié, who ever kill a man for no reason other than his goodness and their hatred of that goodness.

More common than murder as a consequence of envy is slander. Since he has already likened envy to the 'basiliske', a kind of snake, or 'addir', Friar Lorens likens slander to the adder's bite. Slander slays the spirit rather than the body, and, like presumption, is a sin directed especially against the Holy Ghost. Spiritually, it has the power of slaying three 'at o stroke: þat is, hym þat mysseiþ & hym þat here þit, and hym þat he mysseiþ of' (59). It is such a great sin, in fact, that 'who-so mysseiþ his neiȝebore, he is mysseid and cursed of God' (64). Friar Lorens is not alone in condeming slander. It is a frequent target of fourteenth and fifteenth-century English sermons. Indeed, the author of the *Hereford Homilies* declares that defaming one another is one of the particular characteristics of the English people (Owst, *Literature* 453–54).

The preachers of England inveighed against slander largely because of the social ills which resulted from quarrels between great lords, and this, of course, is the context in which Malory illustrates the evils of slander. When the queen and Lancelot indulged in their private strolls just after Lancelot had returned from the Quest, 'many in the court spake of hit' but 'in especiall' sir Aggravayne spoke of it, for 'he was ever opynne-mowthed' (1045.19–21:XVIII.1). The malice behind his gossiping may be inferred from his envy of Lancelot and his 'prevy hate' of both Lancelot and the queen. Indeed, Malory's image of him as 'opynne-mowthed' may well have been suggested by Lorens' analogy between the mouth of an envious man and a barrel of ale. The mouth of an envious man is 'ful of cursednesse and bitternesse and of tresoun' which has welled up from a heart full of 'enuyous þouȝtes & fals jugementes', so that when his mouth opens, 'nedes suche licour as is in þe tunne mote nedes come out at þe faucetes hoole' (*Book of Vices* 22–23).

In both of Malory's sources for the Death of Arthur there is no doubt of Lancelot's and the queen's guilt. Not only do the narrators confirm Aggravayne's suspicions for the reader but in the *Mort Artu* Aggravayne does a bit of detective work to assure himself that 'Lancelos amoit la reine de fole amour et la reine lui autresi' (4.17–18). What is more, in both of Malory's sources Aggravayne is more or less unwilling to reveal what he knows to the king: Arthur has to wrest the information from him. Aggravayne is rather more willing in the stanzaic *Morte* (1714ff) than he is in the *Mort Artu*, where Arthur has to threaten to kill him before he will tell (86); but only in Malory's version are both Aggravayne and Mordred determined, despite the opposition of their older brothers, to inform Arthur 'how sir Launcelot lyeth dayly and nyghtly by the quene.' Gawain, Gaheris and Gareth neither affirm nor deny their younger brothers' allegation; however, the nature of that allegation is such that no one, not even the alleged lovers themselves, could prove it false. That is what makes Aggravayne's slander — if it is that — so pernicious. If what he says is true, one wonders why he has not troubled to catch the pair *in flagrante delicto*, for we know that Aggravayne, at least, has been spying on them for some time now (1153.32–24:XIX.13; cf. 1046.17:XVIII.1). On the other hand, if it is merely a suspicion, only his malice could explain why he voices it 'thus opynly, ... that many knyghtis myght here' (1161.17–20:XX.1). Gawain implies as much when he says to Mordred, 'ever unto all unhappynes, sir, ye woll graunte' (1161.31–32:XX.1).

In both of Malory's sources, King Arthur already knows that what Aggravayne reveals so reluctantly is true. By contrast, in Malory's version Arthur is not at all sure:

> 'Gyff hit be so,' seyde the kynge, 'wyte you well, he ys non othir [but a traitor]. But I wolde be lothe to begyn such a thynge but I myght have prevys of hit, for sir Launcelot ys an hardy knyght, and all ye know that he ys the beste knyght among us all, and but if he be takyn with the dede he woll fyght with hym that bryngith up the noyse, and I know no knyght that ys able to macch hym. Therefore, and hit be sothe as ye say, I wolde that he were takyn with the dede.' (1163.12–19:XX.2 cf. stanzaic *Morte*: 'But sythe it is so, withouten fayle', 1744)

Malory disguises this remarkable departure from his sources by claiming the following authority:

> For, as the Freynshe booke seyth, the kynge was full lothe that such a noyse shulde be uppon sir Launcelot and his quene; for the kynge had a demyng of hit, but he wold nat here thereoff, for sir Launcelot had done so much for hym and for the quene so many tymes that wyte you well the kynge loved hym passyngly well. (1163.20–25:XX.2)

It is hardly surprising that Arthur should have had a 'demyng' of an illicit affair, given the rumours ('noyse') circulating in the court. Indeed, Malory tells us that the king has been most unhappy about them because he loves Lancelot so well. (The reader will notice that even at this early stage of events, Arthur's thoughts are not for his queen but for his knight.)

Malory could not alter his history so radically as to have Arthur dismiss his nephews' allegations the way he earlier dismissed those of Morgan le Fay and King Mark, even though Arthur is aware of his nephews' 'evyll wyll' towards Lancelot (cf. 1184.8–11:XX.9). But he makes it perfectly clear that Arthur is not convinced that they are right about Lancelot and the queen. The king may hope that his insistence that they take the lovers 'with the dede' will satisfy them that he is just as concerned for the honour of the family as they pretend to be ('and we be your syster sunnes, we may suffir hit no lenger'). At the same time, he may also hope to hear no more of it, either because Lancelot will be too smart to allow himself to be caught or because what his nephews allege is not true. If it is true, Arthur can only hope that they are able to take Lancelot and the queen 'wyth the dede'. In that case his nephews would undoubtedly kill them on the spot, just as Gaheris killed their mother, Margawse, when he caught her with Lamorak. But even if his nephews should spare their lives to bring them before the king, Arthur would not have to worry about customary judicial procedure. Their treason would be so manifest that he could legally condemn them to death without a trial.

In Malory's handling of this episode the malice of Aggravayne and Mordred and the doubts of Arthur point to the possibility of Lancelot's innocence. The recent portrait of Lancelot as a holy man in the 'Healing of Sir Urry' plus certain other details in Malory's narration then raise that possibility to a strong probability. First of all, we have the ostensibly small detail of Mordred's and Aggravayne's certainty that Lancelot will not go hunting with the king the next day (1163.27–28:XX.2). The success of their plot hinges upon this and yet they offer no explanation for their certainty. In the *Mort Artu* Lancelot normally goes hunting with the king, so the king has to exclude him from the invitation in order to ensure that he remain at court (88.32–35). In the stanzaic *Morte* Lancelot has stayed behind before in order to visit the queen and is expected to repeat this behaviour (728–35, 1752ff). In Malory's text, however, Lancelot has never stayed behind from one of the king's hunting expeditions in order to visit the queen. In fact, in Malory's text Lancelot has never gone hunting at all. Therefore, another hypothesis suggests itself to explain Mordred and Aggravayne's certainty: they know that Lancelot will not go hunting with the king because they know that he never goes hunting.

We have seen that Malory never portrays Lancelot as a hunter in the Tale of Tristram, even after he has become a courtier and a Worshipful knight. This is one of the things which differentiates him from Tristram as an exemplar of Worshipful knighthood. Malory's Tristram is the author of 'all the termys of huntynge and hawkynge' and 'of all mesures of blowynge' and hunting is his chief diversion (571.29–31: X.6). By contrast, the only time that we ever see Lancelot take up arms against an animal he is, quite literally, out of his mind (821.7–20:XII.3). Hunting was a favourite pastime among the gentry and aristocracy of fifteenth-century England and Malory himself seems to revere Tristram for his legendary contributions to the art (682.26–683.4:X.52). In the opinion of Sir Gilbert Hay, however, it was a pastime which had limited value. It might serve as a means of teaching a knight to be 'wele ryddin' (*Knychthede* 23; Lull 30), but it was much more likely to serve as a means of diverting him from his duty to the 'ordre' of knighthood (63–64). Hay leaves little doubt that he would expect a 'veray' knight never to indulge in such frivolity. Indeed, the notion that hunters could not be 'holy' men seems to have been proverbial in the late Middle Ages, to judge from the stout denial of the truth of that 'texte' by Chaucer's worldly Monk (I(L).177–78). Therefore, it seems fair to conclude that Malory reinforces the image of Lancelot as a True knight, and as a holy man, by never representing him as a hunter. At the same time, he transforms what in the stanzaic *Morte* serves as an indication of Lancelot's guilt — the certitude that he 'woll nat go' hunting with the king — into an indication of his probable innocence.

Then we have the larger, much more obvious detail that Malory specifically refuses to say whether the queen and Lancelot went to bed that night or were 'at other maner of disportis' (1165.12:XX.3). In this way Malory forces his readers to decide for themselves whether or not the lovers were 'abed'. At the same time he strongly suggests that the lovers were not in bed. He does this in several ways. First of all, in the consultation scene which precedes Lancelot's going to the queen, he shows that the former Grail knight, Bors, does not disapprove of Lancelot's going to see the queen, only of his going to see her when he knows that Aggravayne is determined to 'do you shame and us all' (1164.24:XX.2). Bors has had such fears before, but never so strongly as on this occasion, when the king is away from the court and therefore it is to be feared that he himself is involved in laying 'som wacche for you and the quene' (1164.24–29:XX.2). Secondly, we have Lancelot's assurance that he will 'go and com agayne and make no taryynge', an assurance which he also gives in the stanzaic *Morte* (1790–91), and his surprise that Bors, of all people, should advise him to disobey the queen and act like 'a cowarde' (1165.1–2:XX.2). His choice of words suggests that Lancelot refuses to take Bors' counsel for two reasons. The first is one which Gawain would appreciate for it is equally part of the Heroic knight's code of ethics: to disobey the queen for fear of Aggravayne would be to show cowardice and he 'woll nat' ever be a 'cowarde'. The second is one which Tristram, the Worshipful knight, is more likely to appreciate. Lancelot has promised 'ever' to be Guinevere's knight 'in ryght othir in wronge' (1058.30–32:XVIII.7) and to renege on that promise would be shameful.

Lancelot does not fear 'worldis shame' in this case but rather the shame of failing to be true in some more absolute sense; for if he were to disobey the queen, the world would never know it. Worshipful knights are concerned only for their reputation. Later on Bors will have occasion to assert that 'there was never yet man that ever coude preve kynge Arthure untrew of hys promyse' (1173.24–25:XX.6). He does not say that Arthur never *was* 'untrew of hys promyse', only that no one was ever able to 'preve' that he was. Now, surely, if Lancelot were to be 'untrew' to the queen on this occasion, no one could ever 'preve' it, for who would tell? Certainly not Bors or Guinevere! We must conclude therefore that Lancelot's refusal to be 'untrew of hys promyse' is not prompted by the fear of 'worldis shame'. Rather Lancelot keeps his promise to Guinevere for the same reason that Arveragus in the *Franklin's Tale* insists that Dorigen keep her promise to Aurelius: 'Trouthe is the hyeste thyng that man may kepe' (*CT* V(f). 1479). 'Trouthe', like justice, is an attribute of God. Therefore the True knight must be absolutely true to every man and woman.

In Chaucer's romance, Arveragus is rewarded for keeping 'trouthe' by the safe return of his wife. In Malory's history Lancelot may not be so rewarded for keeping 'trouthe' because Aggravayne and Mordred are not like Aurelius. They do not respond with generosity and compassion to Lancelot's assurance that he and the queen are innocent. Standing armed outside the queen's chamber door, Aggravayne and Mordred and their entire cohort have no doubt of Lancelot's guilt, but Malory prods his reader to consider the possibility that they may be wrong when he explains his refusal to say what has really been going on behind that door: 'me lyste nat thereof make no mencion, for love that tyme was nat as love ys nowadayes' (1165.12–13:XX.3). It is not at all self-evident what his reluctance to speak has to do with the way love was in King Arthur's days; therefore the reader is virtually compelled to go back and re-read Malory's essay on 'vertuouse love' in order to grasp his meaning here. This essay precedes his narration of the 'Knight of the Cart' and includes the following comparison of 'love that tyme' and love . . . nowadayes':

> But nowadayes men can nat love sevennyght but they muste have all their desyres. That love may nat endure by reson, for where they bethe sone accorded and hasty, heet sone keelyth. And ryght so faryth the love nowadayes, sone hote sone colde. Thys ys no stabylyté. But the olde love was nat so. For men and women coulde love togydirs seven yerys, and no lycoures lustis was betwyxte them, and than was love trouthe and faythefulnes. And so in lyke wyse was used such love in kynge Arthurs dayes.
> (1119.31–1120.6:XVIII.25)

Elsewhere I have argued that the function of this passage is to remind Malory's readers that Lancelot and the queen had loved each other virtuously a long time ('and no lycoures lustis was betwyxte them') before they finally succumbed to the power of 'kyndely' love in 'The Knight of the Cart' ('Malory's Lancelot' 436–38). Now Malory seems to be asking his readers to keep this passage in mind as they decide for themselves (and he does insist that they decide for themselves) whether or not the lovers have been 'abed' on this occasion.

Different readers will decide differently according to their opinion of the possibilities of human nature and their judgment of Lancelot's character. The month of May has come around again, that 'lusty' season 'whan every harte floryshyth and burgenyth' (1161.1–2:XX.1) and so they must ask themselves if they think Lancelot could have resisted the temptation of 'kyndely' but illicit love this time. To put the question in Malory's terms, they must decide if they think that Lancelot is now any better able to 'florysh hys herte in thys worlde: firste unto God, and nexte unto the joy of them that he promysed hys feyth unto' than he was in the 'Knight of the Cart' (1119.24–26:XIX.25).

Malory's handling of the scene inside the queen's chamber suggests very strongly that Lancelot is much better able now to resist sexual temptation than he was in the 'Knight of the Cart'. Indeed, he appears to be the same holy man who was able to heal Sir Urry. First of all, he both speaks and acts like a man wrongfully accused, not just when he is addressing his accusers but also when he is addressing the queen and her ladies, with whom he need not pretend innocence if he were in fact guilty. He asks for armour so that he might 'sone stynte their malice, by the grace of God!' (1165.26–27:XX.3). Then he asks the queen to pray for his soul if he should be killed (1166.17:XX.3). And ultimately he faces his accusers, armed only with a sword, praying, 'Jeus Cryste, be Thou my shylde and myne armoure!' (1167.5–6:XX.3). None of these pious expressions is to be found in Malory's sources (*Mort Artu* 90; stanzaic *Morte*, 1808ff). But the most striking addition which Malory makes to this scene is the speech in which Lancelot affirms his innocence and offers to defend it 'as a knyght shulde', in trial by battle:

> 'Sires, leve youre noyse,' seyde sir Launcelot, 'for wyte you well, sir Aggravayne, ye shall nat preson me thys nyght! And therefore, and ye do be my counceyle, go ye all frome thys chambir dore and make you no suche cryyng and such maner of sclaundir as ye do. For I promyse you be my knyghthode, and ye woll departe and make no more noyse, I shall as to-morne appyere afore you all and before the kynge, and than lat hit be sene whych of you all, other ellis ye all, that woll depreve me of treson. And there shall I answere you, as a knyght shulde, that hydir I cam to the quene for no maner of male engyne, and that woll I preve and make hit good uppon you wyth my hondys.'
>
> (1167.33–1168.10:XX.4)

Malory found the first sentence of this speech in the stanzaic *Morte*, but the rest is his own invention. It is an affirmation of innocence which would be unthinkable in either of Malory's sources but which in Malory's version of events could well be true.

Mordred and Aggravayne never doubt that Lancelot is lying and let him know that they have permission from the king to slay him or save him as they like (1168.11–14:XX.4). Therefore if he is to save his life and that of the queen, Lancelot has no choice but to attempt to defeat his accusers. Later, he will look back on this battle, thank God that he 'ascaped their daungere' (1169.18–19:XX.5) and assert that their defeat was a judgment of God upon them:

> 'For they that tolde you tho talys were lyars, and so hit felle uppon them: for by lyklyhode, had nat the myght of God bene with me, I myght never have endured with fourtene knyghtes, and they armed and afore purposed, and I unarmed and nat purposed ... in their quarell they preved nat hemselff the best, nother in the ryght.' (1197.20–31:XX.15)

Once again Malory has taken the first line of this speech from the stanzaic *Morte* and expanded upon it to suggest that Lancelot is not lying, as he is in Malory's source, but rather telling the truth as he perceives the truth. What is more, Malory has given us enough evidence to be able to believe Lancelot if we wish.

Aggravayne's and Mordred's failure to take Lancelot and the queen 'with the dede', Lancelot's subsequent affirmation of his and the queen's innocence and his miraculous escape from their ambush create for Arthur the very situation he had hoped to avoid. Although the circumstantial evidence is sufficient to convict the lovers in Arthur's judgment, they have not been caught *in flagrante delicto*. What is more, Lancelot is requesting his right to a trial by battle, just as Arthur feared he would. Now Arthur has only two choices. One is to let Lancelot have his trial and to accept the judgment of God which results, even if Lancelot should win. The other is to judge him and the queen guilty on the basis of the circumstantial evidence alone.

Gawain tries very hard to convince his uncle to let Lancelot have a trial. This is the first time since Malory's account of the Roman campaign that we have seen Gawain act in the capacity of the king's counsellor, and it is the longest speech he ever makes in the *Morte Darthur*:

> 'My lorde Arthure, I wolde counceyle you nat to be over hasty, but that ye wolde put hit in respite, thys jougemente of my lady the quene, for many causis. One is thys, thoughe hyt were so that sir Launcelot were founde in the quenys chambir, yet hit

> myght be so that he cam thydir for none evyll. For ye know, my lorde,' seyde sir Gawayne, 'that my lady the quene hath oftyntymes ben gretely beholdyn unto sir Launcelot, more than to ony othir knyght; for oftyntymes he hath saved her lyff and done batayle for her whan all the courte refused the quene. And peradventure she sente for hym for goodness and for none evyll, to rewarde hym for his good dedys that he had done to her in tymes past. And peraventure my lady the quene sente for hym to that entente, that sir Launcelot sholde a com prevaly to her, wenyng that hyt had be beste in eschewyng and dredyng of slaundir; for oftyntymys we do many thynges that we wene for the beste be, and yet peradventure hit turnyth to the warste. For I dare sey,' seyde sir Gawayne, 'my lady, your quene, ys to you both good and trew. And as for sir Launcelot, I dare say he woll make hit good uppon ony knyght that woll put uppon hym vylany or shame, and in lyke wyse he woll make good for my lady the quene.' (1174.31–1175.18:XX.7)

The reader will have to decide for himself whether Gawain really believes what he is saying here, or whether he is only saying it to dissuade Arthur from taking a course of action which he knows will be politically ruinous. Gawain's hypothetical reconstruction of events is actually plausible, given Malory's characterizations of Lancelot and Aggravayne and his handling of events, but even if Gawain is not certain of Lancelot's innocence, he is certain that Arthur's 'hasty' judgment is wrong.

Gawain's argument in favour of trial by battle reminds us that even in the later Middle Ages kingship was not so far removed from kinship as it was to become in the modern state. Early medieval kings were of course little more than patriarchs of large and powerful clans, as the derivation of Anglo-Saxon *cyning* from *cynn* tells us. These patriarch-kings endorsed ritual trial by combat because it represented a distinct improvement over the clansman's blood feud. Once the battle had been fought and one man had killed the other the case was closed. No man could openly question the judgment of God and so, in theory at least, the blood feud could not continue. That is the premise underlying Gawain's impassioned plea to allow Lancelot to fight to prove his innocence. Gawain's primary concern is to protect his uncle's hold on the Crown, to keep his clan in power. To that end, much to Arthur's amazement, he is willing to forego revenge for the deaths of his brother and two of his three sons (1176.9–11:XX.7). Evidently, Gawain does not baulk at the prospect of Lancelot's killing Mordred (his only remaining accuser) in trial by battle, either. Presumably, from Gawain's point of view the loss of one more brother would be preferable to the loss of Arthur's kingship. And if Arthur insists on summarily condemning the queen to the fire, he will force Lancelot to rescue her and thus risk a civil war in which Lancelot's forces are very likely to be greater than the king's.

Gawain's position is uncharacteristically rational and exhibits an awareness of political realities which we are not accustomed to seeing in him. However, we can explain these apparent developments in his consciousness in terms of his primary loyalty to the kin group: Arthur is the most powerful man in Gawain's family and Gawain is willing to do whatever is necessary, even to sacrifice some of his own kinsmen, in order to keep Arthur in power. On the other hand, Arthur's uncharacteristic irrationality is harder to explain. By condemning the queen to death without a trial, Arthur risks everything — his life, his fellowship and his crown — when it would appear that he could save all these if he would only allow Lancelot his right to defend himself 'as a knyght shulde'. This is the first time Arthur has ever refused to allow one of his knights that right and so we must give some consideration to his reasons for refusing.

First of all, it is well to point out that, unlike Gawain, Arthur has no doubt of Lancelot's guilt. As an honourable man of the world, his own experience of what goes on when a gentleman visits a lady in her chamber by night is enough to convince him that Lancelot and the queen must have been 'abed'. Therefore, only a verdict of 'guilty' would render 'true justyce' in this case. If Gawain were as sure of Lancelot's guilt as the king is, and if he were also willing to appeal Lancelot of treason and fight with him to prove his guilt, I think it is fair to assume that Arthur would have allowed the trial, for Arthur knows about Gawain's supernatural gift of increasing strength between the hours of nine and noon. In fact, he has established the rules governing trial by battle so that 'by lyklyhode' Gawain can always win (1217.1–9:XX.21). Gawain is not convinced of Lancelot's guilt, however; so in any trial by battle the appellant would have to be Mordred, the only one of Lancelot's accusers left alive after the melée outside the queen's chamber.

If Arthur thought that either Aggravayne or Mordred had a chance of beating Lancelot in a fair fight he might have insisted from the beginning that they make their appeal before the entire court and back it up in trial by battle. But Lancelot is the strongest knight of the fellowship and, in Arthur's opinion, 'trustyth so much uppon hys hondis and hys myght that he doutyth no man' (1175.19–21:XX.7); so Arthur chose instead to let his nephews resort to the tactics of the blood feud and lay an ambush for Lancelot outside the queen's chamber. Arthur's assumption that Lancelot trusts in 'hys hondis and hys myght' rather than in God tells us much more about his own rationalist attitude towards trial by battle than it does about Lancelot's providentialist faith. However, it is the king's judgment which is determinative here, and the king does not think that Mordred would have a chance against Lancelot in trial by battle, despite Lancelot's guilt.

A determination to do 'true justice' upon Lancelot for his treason is not the only reason for Arthur's refusal, however. There are three other reasons why Arthur will not allow a trial by battle to take place. One has to do with his emotional attachment to his knights; the second has to do with the importance he attaches to his personal honour, or worship; and the third has to do with his love of Mordred and his concern for the succession to the throne.

When Mordred, 'sore wounded and all forbled', first came to Arthur to tell him what had happened outside the queen's chamber, Arthur was 'sore amoved'. In describing this scene Malory refers to 'this ire', but he does not directly attribute the emotion of anger to the king (1174.12–19:XX.7). However, Lancelot fully expects the king to be furious when he hears of the death of his knights. What is more, he fears that in 'thys hete and malice' Arthur may condemn the queen without a trial (1171.9–20:XX.5). Bors and the rest of those with whom Lancelot takes counsel are not so sure the king would do such a thing, but Malory gives us reason to believe that Lancelot knows the king better than they do when he tells us,

> And ryght so was hit ordayned for quene Gwenyver: bycause sir Mordred was ascaped sore wounded, and the dethe of thirtene knyghtes of the Round Table, thes previs and experyenses caused kynge Arthure to commaunde the quene to the fyre and there to be brente. (1174.25–29:XX.7)

The wounding of Mordred and the death of thirteen knights do not constitute 'previs' of the queen's infidelity; on the contrary, as we have seen, they may be construed by a providentialist as a judgement of God which 'previs' her innocence. But the queen's presumed infidelity is not what is uppermost in Arthur's mind when he makes the decision to condemn her. Later he will say explicitly that he cares more for his knights than he does for his queen, because 'quenys I myght have inow, but such a felyship of good knyghtes shall never be togydirs in no company' (1184.1–5:XX.9). Therefore, it is not surprising that Malory should imply in this passage that it was the wounding of Mordred and the death of his knights which 'caused' Arthur to condemn Guinevere. In effect, Malory implies that the king condemns his queen in order to be avenged upon Lancelot.[13]

Another reason for Arthur's refusal to allow a trial by battle is suggested by his initial response to Mordred's news of Lancelot's escape: 'now hit ys fallen so, . . . that I may nat with my worshyp but my quene muste suffir dethe' (1174.16–18:XX.7). Arthur's honour as a husband is now publicly impugned and must be recovered. According to the honourable code of the gentleman, there are two ways a man can recover his honour when his wife is suspected of having made him a cuckold. First, he can surprise his wife and her lover *in flagrante delicto* and kill them. Arthur has already tried this tactic and failed. But there is another way. That is to engage in a duel of honour with the man he suspects of having made him a cuckold. As King of England Arthur could not personally engage in such a duel, but he could preside over a treason duel of chivalry which would recover his honour just as effectively, no matter how it turned out. If the appellant were to defeat Lancelot, Arthur's honour would be saved because the guilty man (and woman) could then be executed as traitors. On the other hand, if Lancelot were to win, Arthur's honour would still be saved because the charge of treason would have publicly been proved false (no matter what some men might think privately to themselves). One cannot help wondering, then, why Arthur does not adopt this expedient to save his 'worshyp'.

The reason he does not, I think, is because this expedient would in Arthur's opinion put the life of the appellant in great jeopardy. The appellant would have to be Mordred, because Mordred is the only one of Lancelot's accusers left alive, and Malory gives us excellent reason to suppose that Arthur is immoderately attached to this sister's son who is also his own son.

All the great and legendary kings of western Europe had an especially close relationship with the heroes who were their sister's sons. Charlemagne loved Roland best of all his knights. Mark wished to make his sister's son, Tristan, his heir. And Hygelac did pass on his kingdom to his sister's son, Beowulf. Arthur has more than one sister's son. Indeed, the number of his sisters and sister's sons varies considerably from one version of the legend to another. The English chronicles give him only two: Gawain and Mordred, both sons of King Lott. The French romances give him six: Ywain, son of Morgan le Fay, and the five sons of Margawse, wife of King Lott, that is, Gawain, Aggravayne, Gaheris, Gareth, and Mordred. The German epics and the romance of *Lanzelet* also add Lancelot to the number of Arthur's sister's sons (Bell 150, 152, 156), no doubt to explain the close and loving relationship between them, since among the German tribes this blood tie was regarded as particularly close and sacred. Among the patrilineal clans of Scotland and the north country of England this blood tie was also regarded as the 'nearest and dearest' between men. In their literature one may find numerous instances of sister's sons taking the place which ordinarily a son would take, and in the border ballads which recount tragedies of love and kinship, we find the sister's son offered as the ultimate, highest sacrifice, after both property and progeny (Gummere 141–5).

As we might expect, Malory makes much more of the relationship between Arthur and his sister's sons than his French sources do and, what is more surprising, he makes more of it than his English sources do, as well.[14] More surprising, still, is that Malory should also make more of Arthur's paternal relationship to Mordred than either of his sources for the Death of Arthur. The authors of the Vulgate cycle seem to have invented the notion of Mordred's incestuous birth, perhaps on the model of the legend of Charlemagne's incestuous begetting of Roland, perhaps on the more general, 'almost unversal tradition of heroes born in incest', simply 'to heighten the horror of the final tragedy' (Bogdanow, *Romance* 144). But to Malory it must have seemed odd that they paid so little attention to the possibility this relationship raised for the succession to Arthur's throne. Of course Malory knew from the English chronicles that Arthur was actually succeeded by Constantine, the son of Cador of Cornwall, Arthur's half-brother and the grandson of Igrayne and her first husband, the Duke of Cornwall. However, with his fifteenth-century Englishman's sensitivity to the arguments for and against succession in the female line, Malory must have realized that this particular act of succession, through Arthur's mother, placed on the throne a man who was in no way related to Arthur's royal father, Uther Pendragon.[15] Malory never suggests that Mordred ought to be Arthur's successor, but he does suggest that Arthur might have thought along those lines:

> And there kynge Arthur made sir Mordred chyeff ruler of all Ingelonde, and also he put the quene undir hys governaunce: bycause sir Mordred was kynge Arthurs son, he gaff hym the rule off hys londe and off hys wyff. (1211.8–11:XX.19)

In the *Mort Artu* Mordred puts himself forward and asks to be made the queen's guardian and Arthur agrees even though this displeases the queen (129). In the stanzaic *Morte Arthur* Arthur's knights choose Mordred to be the 'steward' (2508–23). The *Mort Artu* does not specify why Arthur is willing to let Mordred be regent, but the stanzaic *Morte* does specify that Arthur's knights chose Mordred to be regent because they knew he was Arthur's son (2957). In rejecting both of these versions Malory may have been influenced by Hardyng who, true to the English chronicle tradition, makes Mordred only a nephew but stresses how much Arthur loved and trusted this nephew (149). It is only a short step from there to the idea that Arthur loved and trusted Mordred more than any other knight 'bycause' he was his son.

Malory does not give us enough information to be able to conclude with certainty that Arthur refused to risk Mordred's life in trial by battle against Lancelot because Mordred was his son and possible successor. However, he certainly allows for the possibility that it constituted part of Arthur's motivation. Therefore we must ask what has happened to change the king's mind since the time he tried to murder his incestuously begotten son by seizing all the infants born on May day and putting them 'in a shyppe to the se'. At that time presumably Arthur believed Merlin's prophecy that, if he lived, Mordred 'sholde destroy hym and all the londe' (55.21–22:I.27); however, at that time, Arthur must also have hoped to have legitimate offspring by his fair young queen, Guinevere. Now, his marriage is still, and probably forever will be, childless, but Mordred is alive and well. He alone of all the infants survived 'by fortune'. When the ship crashed against the rocks, he

> was cast up, and a good man founde hym, and fostird hym tylle he was fourtene yere of age, and than brought hym to the courte, as hit rehersith aftirward and towarde the ende of the MORTE ARTHURE. (55.30–33:I.27)

Malory never gives us the scene anticipated here, so we never find out how Arthur discovered that Mordred was the son he had tried to kill. And we can only imagine how the king's feelings for the child must have changed from fear and mistrust because of the prophecy to love and trust because he is his own son. In any case, Arthur's pragmatism and rationalism would encourage him to give more credence to the evidence of his own eyes, and perhaps even to the good 'fortune' of his son's survival, than to the prophecy of Merlin, which may or may not prove true. It would seem, indeed, that Arthur's judgment of his son is somewhat clouded by his love and need. Gawain knows that his youngest brother has a penchant for mischief (1161.31–32:XX.1) and Lancelot sees clearly that he is 'passyng envyous and applyeth hym muche to trouble' (1204.10–11:XX.18). Evidently Arthur sees nothing of the sort, given his willingness to make his son regent.[16]

If Arthur were an heroic tribal chieftan, he would have led his nephews in the ambush to trap and kill Lancelot and the queen in her chamber. If he were an ideal feudal monarch, a true *rex pius et justus*, he would not hesitate to allow Lancelot an appeal to the judgment of God. And if he were an ideal Machiavellian prince, he would act wholly rationally in the way best calculated to save his crown, even if that meant sacrificing 'true justyce' and the lives of his knights and kinsmen. As it is, however, Arthur is none of these; or, perhaps it would be more accurate to say that he is a little bit like all of them. He is a rational and pragmatic prince whose first priority has always been the stability of his governance. He is an honourable late feudal monarch who loves his knights and has sworn to stand with 'true justyce'. And he is a loyal kinsman who has never punished his nephews for their crimes against the honourable society. For many reasons, then — to do 'true justyce', to save his worship as a husband, to avenge the deaths of his kinsmen and knights, and to protect the life of Mordred — Arthur invokes the law which allows him to condemn the queen to be burnt at the stake without a trial:

> And the law was such in tho dayes that whatsomever they were, of what astate or degré, if they were founden gylty of treson there shuld be none other remedy but deth, and othir the menour other the takynge wyth the dede shulde be causer of their hasty jougement. (1174.20–25:XX.7)

Under the common law in England it was possible for certain royal officers, or for the king himself, to condemn criminals without a trial if they were manifestly guilty; however, by the fourteenth century the practice was 'confined to the crime of treason' (Bellamy, *Crime* 134–35) and even so it was not popular. When Edward IV's Constable, John Tiptoft, Earl of Worcester, summarily condemned traitors to death without a trial, he was nicknamed 'the butcher of England', even though his summary powers came directly from the king (Squibb 26–7). Arthur's decision is not popular, either.[17] No one dares accuse him of butchery, but his own nephews refuse to have anything to do with the queen's execution. Gawain refuses to be present and, although Arthur succeeds in forcing Gaheris and Gareth to be there, he cannot force them to bear arms in defense of his 'hasty jougement'. In fact, Malory tells us there were many who stood by 'wepyng and waylynge and wryngyng of hondis' and 'but feaw in comparison that wolde beare ony armoure for to strengthe the dethe of the quene' (1177.11–14:XX.8).

Arthur has resolved his judicial crisis. He has acted summarily and in anger, but probably not without giving the matter a great deal of thought. Nevertheless, his decision has disastrous consequences. Lancelot has no choice now but to rescue the queen, or die in the attempt, as Gawain well understands. Indeed, Gawain's initial response to the news of Lancelot's rescue is to applaud it: 'he hath done but knyghtly, and as I wolde have done myselff and I had stonde in lyke case' (1184.22–24:XX.9). However, when Gawain hears that his brothers, Gaheris and Gareth have been slain, unwittingly, by Lancelot, then it is his turn to discover that he has no choice.

The worst thing that can happen to a Heroic knight is to learn that one of his kinsman is responsible for the death of another kinsman, because in that case vengeance is impossible. In Malory's version of events this is what happens to Gawain when he learns of the deaths of Gareth and Gaheris, for the man he must hold responsible for their deaths is not Lancelot, the unwitting instrument, but Arthur, who ordered the queen's execution despite Gawain's advice and then ordered his nephews to be present even though they refused to bear arms. In a scene which Malory has invented, Arthur asks Gawain to 'suffir' his younger brothers to be present at the execution site and Gawain refuses to give his permission, although he allows Arthur's power to compel their presence (1176.25–28:XX.8). Then Gaheris and Gareth likewise place all responsibility upon their uncle:

> 'Sir ye may well commande us to be there, but wyte you well hit shall be sore ayenste oure wyll. But and we be there by youre strayte commaundement, ye shall playnly holde us there excused: we woll be there in pesyble wyse, and beare none harneyse of warre uppon us.' (1176.31–1177.2:XX.8)

What is more, Arthur accepts responsibility for their well-being and on their terms, when he responds, 'In the name of God, . . . than make you redy, for she shall have sone her jugemente' (1177.3–4:XX.8). Gawain departs, weeping, and when he hears of the deaths of his brothers cries out 'Alas, . . . now ys my joy gone!' before falling down in a swoon (1185.10–12:XX.10).

Gawain cannot say of Gaheris and Gareth as he did of Aggravayne and his sons that they 'ar the causars of their owne dethe' (1176.9: XX.7) for having failed to take his advice, but he can say it of Arthur. However, if he blames Arthur as, rationally, he ought to do, then he must forego vengeance yet again. He was willing to forego vengeance for the deaths of Aggravayne and his two sons in order to protect his uncle's hold on the Crown, but now it appears that there must be civil war in any case. Therefore Gawain unleashes his pent-up desire for vengeance and swears to take Lancelot's life for the life of his kinsmen. Gawain has long envied Lancelot his superior prowess and his favour with the king (700.1–6:X.58), but it is not until he finally confronts Lancelot during the siege of Joyous Garde that we learn what has rankled most of all:

> 'Now, fy on thy proude wordis!' seyde sir Gawayne. 'As for my lady the quene, wyte thou well, I woll never say of her shame. But thou, false and recrayde knyght,' seyde sir Gawayne, 'what cause haddist thou to sle my good brother sir Gareth that loved the more than me and all my kynne? And alas, thou madist hym knyght thyne owne hondis! Why slewest thou hym that loved the so well?
>
> 'For to excuse me,' seyde sir Launcelot, 'hit boteneth me nat, but by Jesu, and by the feyth that I owghe unto the hyghe Order of Knyghthode, I wolde with as a good a wyll have slayne my nevew, sir Bors de Ganys, at that tyme. And alas, that ever I was so unhappy,' seyde sir Launcelot, 'that I had nat seyne sir Gareth and sir Gaherys!'
>
> 'Thou lyest, recrayed knyght,' seyde sir Gawayne, 'thou slewyste hem in the despite of me. And therefore wyte thou well, sir Launcelot, I shall make warre uppon the, and all the whyle that I may lyve be thyne enemy!' (1189.9–25:XX.11)

This is not only one of the most moving scenes in Malory's Death of Arthur, it is also one of the most crucial for his characterisation of these two knights. Gawain, the Heroic knight, for whom kinship is the ultimate value in this world, cannot forgive Lancelot for having won greater love and respect from his brother Gareth than he himself could win (see above 128–44). That Lancelot should then have killed this brother is unbearable. Gawain cannot understand that Lancelot could have loved Gareth as much as, or even better than, his dearest kinsman, Bors, because Gawain cannot see that for Lancelot kinship is not the ultimate value, nor is the kin group the only meaningful fellowship. For Lancelot, as a True knight, the ultimate value is service to God in the High Order of Knighthood and the most meaningful fellowship is that of all good Christian knights. Gareth was such a knight and, therefore, just as Bors called himself 'unhappy' after he had almost killed Lancelot at the Winchester tournament because he did not recognize him in his disguise, so Lancelot calls himself 'unhappy' after he has unwittingly killed Gareth and Gaheris at the execution site because they did not bear their arms and so he did not 'see' them (1189.20–21:XX.11).[18] Gawain cannot accept that the killing was accidental. And in passing judgment upon Lancelot he reveals much about himself. To kill a beloved brother 'in the despite of' a bitter enemy is something Gawain would do, not Lancelot.

Gawain's decision to seek vengeance upon Lancelot converts the civil war which follows into a blood feud. Even before Gawain appears, Arthur anticipates what will happen next:

> 'I shall never have reste of hym tyll I have destroyed sir Launcelottys kynne and hymselff both, othir ellis he to destroy me.' (1183.29–31:XX.9)

His words show that Arthur possesses a clear and complete understanding of the blood feud, which allows of no end until all parties — on one side, at least — are dead. Yet, in conversation with Gawain, the king makes no attempt to dissuade his nephew. On the contrary, he urges him on, being the first to speak of shaping a 'remedy for to revenge their dethys' (1185.34–35:XX.10), and seems to accept his complicity in the feud by virtue of his kinship. He never tries to make Gawain see the conflict as a civil war between feudal factions which might result in a negotiated peace settlement. Rather he encourages his nephew to hope for total victory: 'and as I suppose I shall be bygge inowghe to dryve hym oute of the bygyst toure of hys castell' (1186.20–22:XX.10). Arthur, the most worshipful king in Christendom, now appears as the heroic leader of his clan, determined to have vengeance.

Arthur's leadership is temporary, however, lasting only so long as his own desire for vengeance lasts, which is to say, only so long as his interests and those of his nephew coincide. As soon as Arthur has made a show of force against Lancelot and drawn blood at the siege of Joyous Garde, the king becomes willing to negotiate a peace settlement. The principle upon which Arthur is now acting appears to be that of the duel of honour. Lancelot has offended Arthur by (1) killing his knights and (2) taking away his queen — and Arthur lists his offenses in that order (1187.28–34:XX.11). To cleanse these affronts to the king's honour it is not necessary that either party to the duel be killed (although Arthur has tried very hard to kill Lancelot), it is only necessary that each party's courage and strength be demonstrated (Pitt-Rivers 29). To be sure, Arthur is applying these honourable principles not to a duel between two men but to a pitched battle involving thousands of men. However, as king of England Arthur could not himself challenge Lancelot to a private duel of honour and, as we have seen, for various reasons he was unwilling that his son, Mordred, should openly appeal Lancelot of adultery and fight him in a treason duel of chivalry. On the other hand, it was not uncommon in Malory's day to interpret the outcomes of great battles such as this as though they rendered judgments of God (H. A. Kelly, *Divine Providence*), so why not also interpret them as vindications of honour? Certainly it would seem that this is the way the king chooses to interpret the outcome of their battle at Joyous Garde. For, as soon as the victorious Lancelot has explained his behaviour as a matter of right, in his own self defense and that of the queen (1188.1–36:XX.11), Arthur is prepared to take his queen back 'and to have bene accorded with sir Launcelot' (1190:17–20:XX.12).

If Arthur thought Gawain would go along with this honourable solution to the conflict, he should have known better. Arthur, the Worshipful king and knight, may be satisfied with the appeal to the test of courage, but Gawain the Heroic warrior is not. And now he forces his uncle to choose between him and Lancelot. After Lancelot's speech at Carlisle, in which he once again affirms his innocence, reminding the king of his past service and offering to do extraordinary penance for the death of Gareth (1197.4–1200.9:XX.15–16), the king is moved to tears. Nevertheless, he sits in silence as Gawain tells Lancelot, 'And if myne uncle, kynge Arthur, wyll accorde wyth the, he shall loose my servys' (1200.17–18:XX.16). Forced to choose between Lancelot and Gawain, Arthur chooses Gawain and the continuation of the blood feud.

Arthur is Lancelot's 'good lord' not only because he made him knight and then retained him for life in his service as a knight of the Round Table, but also because, as the Holy Roman Emperor, he is the feudal overlord of the King of France.[19] When he decides to invade Lancelot's kingdom to pillage and burn 'thorow the vengeaunce of Sir Gawayne, all that they myght overrenne', he commits treason against his vassal. Consequently, the third and last trial by battle to be fought in the *Morte Darthur* is the most complex of the three, in terms of the issues it may be said to settle.

In the first trial between Lancelot and Mador de la Porte the moral and legal issues to be settled were one and the same — whether or not the queen was guilty of murder. In the second trial, between Lancelot and Mellyagaunt, the moral and legal issues were separable. In a moral sense, both Lancelot and Mellyagaunt were guilty of treason against Arthur. However, the legal question to be settled was straightforward — whether or not the queen had committed adultery with one of her ten wounded knights. Now, in this third trial, neither the moral nor the legal issue to be settled is straightforward. Gawain accuses Lancelot of treason, but it is not clear whether he means treason against Arthur, by adultery with the queen, or treason against his clan, by the killing of his three brothers.[20] On the other hand, Lancelot feels compelled to defend himself against Gawain's appeal of 'treson' because by his standards of justice that word can apply only to the alleged adultery with the queen. Lancelot has never ceased to proclaim his innocence of this charge (cf. 1171.1–5:XX.5, 1188.1016:XX.11, 1195.7–20:XX.14, 1197.20–31:XX.15, 1202.6–21:XX.17) and therefore he could hardly refuse an opportunity to prove it in trial by battle. Indeed, Gawain, who has always claimed to believe Lancelot and the queen innocent of adultery, probably realized that to call him 'traytour' was the only way to induce Lancelot to do battle. Therefore, in this trial it is not even clear which legal or moral issue is to be settled, for each of the combatants seems to have a different reason for fighting.

To add to the complexity, the battle between Gawain and Lancelot may be seen in yet another way which puts Arthur on trial as well. Lancelot never presumes to accuse his 'good lord' of treason, but there can be no doubt that that is what he has committed by ravaging Lancelot's lands and beseiging his castle. Therefore the battle between Lancelot and Gawain may also be seen as a battle between the champions of two opposing armies to determine the 'ryght' of this war in terms of feudal law.[21]

Both Gawain and Arthur expect Gawain to win because of his gift of increasing strength. Indeed, Malory now reveals that Arthur initially ordained the nine a.m. to noon scheduling of trials by battle so that his nephew should 'by lyklyhode' have 'the bettir in batayle whyle hys strengthe endured three owrys' (1217.5–7:XX.21). This passage makes clear that Arthur's devotion to honour and justice as the most worshipful king in Christendom has always overlaid a kinsman's heart. Therefore, in retrospect, his decision to pursue the blood feud with Gawain rather than to accord with Lancelot, as the Pope commanded him, is not to be wondered at. The passage also confirms that Arthur's rationality ('by lyklyhode') overlays a more primitive belief in magic. Malory has altered his French source to make Gawain's supernatural strength appear less like a 'grace' of God and more like a magical 'gyffte', comparable to Excalibur, the Lady of the Lake's gift to Arthur (1216.31–32:XX.21).[22] Unlike Arthur's second sword, however, Gawain's 'gyffte' was given him by 'an holy man', and therefore presumably comes from God. Nevertheless, neither Gawain nor Arthur appears troubled that this gift should be used to achieve vengeance for their dead kinsmen. Such vengeance has always been 'true justyce' from the Heroic knight's point of view.

On the other side, Lancelot is reluctant to take up this battle for fear of killing yet another of Arthur's kinsmen; but he feels compelled to fight, 'dryvyn thereto as beste tylle a bay' (1216.5–6:XX.20), in order to defend himself and the queen against Gawain's charge of treason. In Malory's English source, Lancelot knows of Gawain's gift and plans his battle strategy accordingly, saving his strength at first (2806–09). In Malory's version, however, there are 'but feaw knyghtes lyvynge that knewe thys advauntayge that sir Gawayne had' and Lancelot is not one of them. He is taken completely by surprise when he feels Gawain's strength double and thinks he must be 'a fyende and none earthely man' (1217.7–15:XX.21). Nevertheless, Lancelot is able to cover himself and keep his might and his breath during those three hours. Then, as soon as he feels Gawain's strength return to normal, he is able to beat him down to the ground with one mighty blow of the sword. Gawain refuses to yield and insists that Lancelot will have to kill him in order to settle their quarrel, but Lancelot will never 'smyte a felde knyght' and Gawain is unable to rise on his feet. This situation is exactly analogous to the situation in which Tristram found himself in the battle he fought against Blamoure, Lancelot's cousin. In order to avoid killing Blamoure, Tristram asked the judges who presided over the trial, King Carados and the King of Scots, to take the matter in hand. In Malory's French source for this battle, Lancelot also asks Arthur what to do, thus casting the king in the role of presiding judge (*Mort Artu* 157); but Malory's Lancelot does not look upon Arthur as a rightful judge. From his point of view, Arthur has failed to stand with 'true justyce'. Therefore Lancelot decides for himself that his ability to 'endure' Gawain 'be Goddis grace!' is sufficient and he leaves the field. The phrase 'be goddis grace' is Malory's addition to this scene and suggests very strongly that Lancelot sees here the judgment of God.

From Lancelot's point of view, then, Gawain's defeat in this first battle proves that he and the queen were not quilty of committing adultery the night that Aggravayne and Mordred trapped them inside her chamber. It also proves that Arthur, his feudal lord, has wrongfully invaded his lands. From Gawain's point of view, on the other hand, it proves nothing because Lancelot has refused to slay him and the feud must go on until one of them is dead.

It is a little more difficult to judge how Arthur views the outcome of this battle. There is some slight evidence to indicate that he accepts it as a judgment against him, for afterwards his party keeps the siege 'with lytyll warre wythouteforthe' (1218.22–25:XX.22). He does not, however, try to dissuade his nephew from the second vain attempt, or even from a third attempt to be revenged upon Lancelot. Just as Arthur refused initially to be accorded with Lancelot, despite the counsel of Lucan the Butler and all the other knights 'aboute the kynge' except for Gawain (1213.3–7:XX.19), so now the king continues to let his nephew govern him. In effect, Arthur is no longer either King of England or Holy Roman Emperor, for Mordred rules England as his regent and Gawain rules his knights in France.

That middle way, between the primitive code of the Heroic knight and the religous code of the True knight, that 'noble way of the world' which Arthur as the most worshipful king of Christendom has long represented, effectively disappears from Malory's narrative when Arthur, forced at Carlisle to choose between Gawain and Lancelot, chooses Gawain. At the Siege of Benwick he seems to regret that choice but to be powerless to alter the course of events. Indeed, the scene which concludes the first judicial battle between Lancelot and Gawain creates a powerful visual emblem of his plight, torn between the two knights he has loved most in this world (cf. 1230.11–17:XXI.2). The wounded Gawain has been carried back to his tent and Lancelot has entered the gates of Benwick, leaving Arthur alone on the field of combat. Then Lancelot reappears on the walls to salute the king:

> 'Now have good day, my lorde the kynge! For wyte you welle ye wynne no worshyp at thes wallis, for and I wolde my knyghtes outebrynge, there shulde many a douty man dye. And therefore, my lorde Arthur, remembir you of olde kyndenes, and howsomever I fare, Jesu be your gyde in all placis.'
>
> (1218.12–17:XX.21)

Caxton ends a chapter with this tableau and this speech and begins the next with Arthur's response: 'Now, alas,' seyde the kynge, 'that ever thys unhappy warre began!'

In this way, whether or not it was his intention to do so, Caxton calls the reader's attention to Malory's *hap* motif. On his death bed Gawain will repeat Arthur's phrase, 'thys unhappy warre', but he will be referring not to the war between him and Lancelot but to the war between Mordred and Arthur which his pursuit of vengeance against Lancelot has made possible. And, as the story of the Death of Arthur continues, Malory's *hap* motif will continue to be noticeable, ringing like a death knell, as it calls the reader's attention to the providentalist view which informs Malory's Arthurian history and suggests that there are religious as well as political reasons for the fall of King Arthur and his knights of the Round Table.

7

Malory's 'Hoole Book' and the Death of Arthur

Caxton entitled Malory's book *le morte Darthur*, 'Notwythstondyng' the fact that it is about much more than the death of Arthur. He may well have done this because he realized that the Death of Arthur is integral to the 'hoole book', to 'the byrth lyf and actes of the sayd kyng' as well as to the adventures of his Round Table knights. It is so in two ways. First, everything in the 'hoole book' is there to help the reader come to an understanding of the Death of Arthur. And we should remember that in his farewell explicit, Malory assumes that his 'jentyl' readers will have read his book 'from the begynnyng to the endyng'. Second, the typology of knighthood which informs Malory's 'hoole book' also informs his account of the Death of Arthur. Indeed, the Death of Arthur proper is only the final part of a long and complex structure of interdependent parts.

The parts of the *Morte Darthur* are interdependent both chronologically, insofar as they recount the beginning, middle and end of Arthur's life and reign, and thematically, insofar as they elaborate the three types of knighthood. Malory's chronology is exact only in the very beginning of his book and in the post-Grail narrative. The vast middle portion in which he elaborates the three types of knighthood is generally suggestive of time passing, but as Ellen Olefsky has argued, it is impossible to establish a detailed and unified chronology for it by selecting certain parts to be read as retrospective narrative (cf. Moorman 'Internal Chronology'). According to the *Brut*, Arthur reigned for twenty-six years, most of them years of peace and prosperity. Malory himself must have found it impossible to establish a chronology for those years based on the French romance sources at his disposal. Therefore, my own feeling is that in this middle section of his book, Malory attempted to achieve two things. The first was to provide his readers with enough stories about Arthur's Round Table knights to suggest the long duration of his reign. The second, equally if not more important, was to develop through these stories a complete typology of knighthood.

In the first narrative unit of the Winchester manuscript (Caxton's Books I–IV and Vinaver's Tale I) all three knightly types are introduced. Heroic knighthood is established in Arthur's wars against the barons and also in the behaviour of Balin, who is both a feudist and a Christian fatalist. Worshipful knighthood is established next in the founding of the Round Table fellowship. And True knighthood is also adumbrated in the two sets of triple quests which follow. Thus, by the end of the first narrative unit, the reader already knows that there are three different codes of ethical behaviour operative among Arthur's knights. For an Heroic knight like Balin (or Gawain) it is ethical to commit murder in order to avenge a kinsman (or a hound). For a Worshipful knight like Pellinor or Marhalt, murder is never ethical, nor is it ethical to abduct a lady or take unfair advantage of a knightly opponent in battle. But for a True knight like Tor or Yvain, not only are murder and rape unethical, any sort of behaviour which breaks God's law is unethical.

In the second narrative unit (Caxton's Books V–VII and Vinaver's Tales II–IV) Malory presents Lancelot, his chief exemplar of True knighthood, in each one of the three knightly settings: on the battlefield, where he proves to be just as good a warrior as Gawain, and better insofar as he is less bloodthirsty and rash; in the forest of adventure, where he proves that he is pious and humble and firmly committed to chastity 'for drede of God'; and in Arthur's court, where he appears as one of Arthur's two chief counsellors (the other being Bedwer) and mentors young Gareth. Gareth not only loves and admires Lancelot but also adopts his knightly code of conduct, the only difference between them being that Gareth chooses to observe a different degree of chastity in marriage. On the other hand, Gareth disapproves of Gawain's heroic code of conduct and avoids his brother's fellowship because of his vengeful and murderous 'conducions' (360.32–36:VII.35).

In the third narrative unit (Caxton's Books VIII–XII and Vinaver's Tale V) Malory presents Tristram as the epitome of Worshipful knighthood and as the Round Table knight most like Arthur. Tristram shares not only the king's sexual ethics, prudence and courtesy, but also his concern for personal honour. Indeed, as Malory tells the story, Tristram's concern for his honour is *so* powerful as to restrain him from consummating his love for Isode until *after* he can do so with honour. He does not go to Isode's bed until after Mark has betrayed them both, and so broken the contracts which bind them to him as vassal and wife. Consequently, Arthur can fully approve of Tristram's behaviour, including his decision to leave Mark's service and bring Isode with him to live in Logres. For as the most worshipful king in Christendom, Arthur shares Tristram's conviction that a 'worshipful' knight need not be loyal to a traitor.

In the fourth narrative unit (Caxton's Books XIII–XVII and Vinaver's Tale VI) Malory completes the ideal of True knighthood in his rehandling of the Quest for the Holy Grail. This is the only part of Malory's book to be told entirely from the religious point of view and the importance of this switch from worldly to otherworldly values is marked in the

Winchester manuscript by leaving two folios blank, and then beginning the text of the Grail story with an elabaorately decorated three-line initial, blue with red, and a decorated first line. By the simple expedient of choosing the Vulgate rather than the *Tristan* version of the Quest story, Malory keeps Tristram out of it and so underscores once again his similarity to King Arthur. Having witnessed the mysterious appearance of the Grail at Camelot, neither Tristram nor Arthur feels the need to go in quest of it. Their rationalist and pragmatic approach to the pursuit of knighthood makes it impossible for them to see that God's grace might be essential to their worldly success.

Most of Arthur's Round Table knights fail in the Quest. Gawain, the Heroic knight, not only kills his kinsmen, Ywain, but is seriously wounded by Galahad, and so fatalistically gives up the quest, as one who 'may nat be ayenst the wylle of God' (866.7–13:XIIII.7). On the other hand, Lancelot redeems his True knighthood by repenting and confessing his sins and then doing penance. Indeed, his relative success in Malory's version of the Quest is so great that he is regarded as one of the 'four' knights who 'have no peerys' (942.19–20:XVI.1). Taken together, these four knights represent two different versions of the ideal of True knighthood, distinguished in pairs by the life choices they make once the Grail has been achieved. We have already seen that Gareth represents a more courtly version of True knighthood because of his decision to choose marriage and lordship. Now we can see that Galahad and Percival represent a more religious version because of their decision to renounce the world altogether for the religious life of prayer and contemplation. And that leaves Lancelot and Bors who, because of their decision to return to the world to serve Arthur, represent a more feudal version of True knighthood, the most difficult, according to Sir Gilbert Hay, because it requires them to maintain chastity without benefit of either marriage or the religious life. They will attempt to do this by living the 'mixed life', a popular fifteenth-century lay Christian ideal, which advocates combining an active life of service to one's fellow Christians with a spiritual life of prayer and meditation.

The final narrative unit (Caxton's Books XVIII–XXI and Vinaver's Tales VII and VIII) returns to focus on Arthur and his court with an emphasis on power politics which we have not seen since Arthur was crowned Holy Roman Emperor. Now, however, Malory portrays court life in the spirit of Alain Chartier's *Curial*, as a place where virtuous men are made wretched by the envy and slander of ambitious courtiers. Indeed, in Malory's post-Grail narrative, envy and slander pale by comparison with the more foul crimes of murder, rape, and treason, suggesting that the failure of most Round Table knights to redeem themselves in the Grail quest is already producing evil consequences. Lancelot struggles to live virtuously in this setting, but once again, largely because of his love for the queen, succumbs to the sins of pride and lechery. What is truly remarkable about Malory's handling of this part of the story, however, is Lancelot's subsequent redemption. Malory achieves this innovation by postponing the 'Knight of the Cart' episode, the only instance of actual adultery in his text, until this time and then following it immediately with an episode of his own invention, the 'Healing of Sir Urry'. Lancelot's ability to heal Sir Urry by the laying on of hands proves that he has once again repented his sin and been forgiven by God. Thus, when the curtain goes up on the Death of Arthur, the reader knows that Lancelot is now a holy man.

The Death of Arthur proper comprises the second half of this final unit, and it is here that Malory's ethical typology of knighthood comes most fully into play. Indeed, it informs the actions of the three chief protagonists, Gawain, Arthur and Lancelot, to such an extent that their dramatic interaction takes on some of the weight of a morality play. Each man acts strictly in accordance with his own knightly code of ethics, and the consequences are nevertheless disastrous.

Gawain represents Heroic knighthood at its best by comparison with his younger brothers, Aggravayne and Mordred. He is a better man than they because he adheres strictly to his code of ethics, which means that he acts consistently to ensure the safety and honour of his family. In contrast, Aggravayne and Mordred only pretend that the honour of the family is their motive for accusing Lancelot and the queen. Malory tells us that actually they are motivated by 'prevy hate' and rancorous envy. Gawain, too, has long envied Lancelot's pre-eminence in his uncle's court, but he loves Arthur too much to attempt to destroy the man who is most responsible for the stability of his reign. The only time Gawain betrays his Heroic code of ethics is when he fails to exact vengeance for the death of Aggravayne and his two sons, and this apparent failure is in fact part of his attempt to save Arthur.

Likewise, Arthur adheres strictly to the Worshipful knight's code of ethics as events unfold, and in particular to his coronation promise to stand with 'true justyce'. Ironically, it is his determination to do justice upon Guinevere (since he cannot get his hands on Lancelot) which precipitates civil war. Had Arthur been more prudent, he would have taken Gawain's advice to allow Lancelot to defend himself in trial by battle, even if that meant losing Mordred. Certainly, Arthur knew that the summary execution of the queen would not be popular. He also knew that Gawain would not support it and that Lancelot would do all in his considerable power to prevent it. Nevertheless, impulsively and in anger, Arthur condemned the queen to be burned at the stake. In *The Prince,* Machiavelli observes that some circumstances require a prince to be impetuous while others require that he be circumspect (133). In the early part of his reign, Arthur's impulsiveness and even his anger served him well in overcoming his enemies and extending his dominion. Now, however, in the dispensing of justice, these same qualities prove to be his undoing. In the event he does not command sufficient power to enforce his judgment at the execution site and the consequence is civil war.

Lancelot is also perfectly true to his own code of ethics throughout the Death of Arthur. From a strictly rationalist and pragmatic point of view, of course, Lancelot's unconditional adherence to 'trouth' makes him appear a fool, not only when he insists upon obeying Guinevere's commandment to visit her despite Bors' warning, but also when he repeatedly refuses to kill Arthur, even after the king has done all in his power to kill him. But if he is a fool, he is a holy fool, his loyalty to both Guinevere and Arthur having been subsumed under his loyalty to God and being, therefore, absolute. Certainly it has always taken precedence over loyalty to his own family and nation. Having chosen to love and serve Guinevere, Lancelot has steadfastly refused to marry another woman, despite the wishes of his kinsmen and the need to provide an heir to the throne of France (Kennedy, 'Malory's Lancelot' 445–52). And having chosen to love and serve Arthur, Lancelot has not only threatened to kill his dearest kinsman, Bors, if he should harm Arthur at the seige of Joyous Garde (1192.16–19:XX.13) he has also, at the seige of Benwick, refused to sally forth to engage Arthur's host even though the English forces were ravaging his lands (1212.18–26:XX.19). In sum, Malory's Lancelot has accepted the Christian definition of vassalage which makes it his duty to remain loyal unto death, no matter what his lord's (or his lady's) deserving. In the eleventh century the Bishop of Limoges rebuked a man who had killed his lord, even though the man had been provoked by his lord's threats, saying, 'Thou shouldst have accepted death for his sake, thy fidelity would have made thee a martyr of God' (Bloch 232). Lancelot is never brought to the pass of literal martyrdom, but one could argue that figuratively speaking he has sacrificed his own life for the well-being of his lord and lady. In order to serve them wholly, he has even renounced lordship, leaving his own lands in France in the governance of regents.

It is apparent that throughout the Death of Arthur, Malory represents Lancelot as fulfilling the kingly ideal which Arthur could not fulfill — that of the *rex pius et justus*. As we have seen, Malory's Arthur failed to fulfill that ideal when he failed to do justice upon his own kinsmen for the murders of Pellinor, Margawse and Lamorak, whereas Lancelot has twice threatened to do justice upon his own kinsmen, once as a group when they were set to harm Tristram and again when Bors wanted to kill Arthur at the siege of Joyous Garde. Even more striking is the difference between them in the matter of their eagerness to shed Christian blood. It was a commonplace of medieval treatises on kingship that God would eventually punish those kings who failed to 'be of grete drede to scayle and sched mannis blude oure reklesly' (Hay, *Governaunce* 102). Obviously, this responsibility was taken more or less lightly by medieval kings, according to their position on the field. Until victory was assured, one could not afford to be too careful about the shedding of Christian men's blood, as Arthur himself has shown in the Battle of Bedgrayne. Moreover, it was easy to get carried away by the killing and correspondingly difficult to tell when victory was assured. At the Battle of Bedgrayne Merlin stopped Arthur from pursuing his defeated enemies and slaying them all (36.28–32:1.17). When Merlin was not around, however, as in the battle with the five kings or the battle against the Emperor Lucius, there was no one to stop Arthur from slaughtering his enemies to the last man (130.1–2:IV.3, and 224.15–23:V.8).[1] In contrast, when Lancelot is in command of an army, he proves extremely reluctant to shed the blood of Christian men. At Joyous Garde, when he saw that so many men had been slain 'their horsis wente in blood paste the fyttelokkes', then 'for verray pité' he withdrew his forces (1193.28–1194.3:XX.13). And later, at the seige of Benwick, he absolutely refused to sally forth 'for shedynge of Crysten blood' (1212.18–49:XX.19).

The ethical typology of knighthood also functions in the Death of Arthur to provide the reader with two fundamentally different points of view from which to explain why Arthur's reign ends in disaster. The first, and more modern viewpoint, is the rationalist and pragmatic one associated with Worshipful knighthood and embodied in the king himself. Modern readers have no trouble seeing from this point of view. On the other hand, they do have difficulty seeing from the religious viewpoint associated with True knighthood and embodied in Lancelot. Indeed, for many this point of view does not exist, since their horizon of expectation has contracted so far as to eclipse the possibility that God might intervene in the affairs of men.[2] Modern readers therefore often fail to see the dual perspective on the Death of Arthur which Malory's text offers to them. Malory's first readers would not have done so. No matter what ethical code in fact governed their behaviour in their daily lives, all of them would have been able to see both the political drama of cause and effect and its larger context of providential history, in which God also has a part to play.

From the rationalist and pragmatic point of view what the reader sees is the political drama chronicling causes and effects. As this drama plays itself out, each of the three major protagonists makes serious errors of political judgment. Lancelot should not have kept 'trouth' with the queen when he knew that the king had probably set a trap for him.

Arthur should not have refused Lancelot's request for a trial by battle after his nephews' ambush had failed to catch the alleged lovers *in flagrante delicto*. And Gawain should not have continued to pursue vengeance upon Lancelot after the Pope had commanded Arthur to accord with him and Arthur was willing to do so. However, as we have already seen in the last chapter, each of these judgments was made strictly in accordance with the knight's own code of ethics. This realization leads to the conclusion that nothing could have been done to prevent the fall of Arthur and, in fact, one of the most common modern responses to the Death of Arthur is to perceive it as inevitable, perhaps even fated (cf. Wilson 'Fate and Choice').

Fifteenth-century readers, however, were looking for political lessons to learn and late medieval authors commonly wrote their histories with explicitly didactic intentions of a political nature. We know, for example, that John Lydgate wrote his chronicle of Julius Caesar in hopes of teaching his contemporaries how to avoid the evils of civil war. We cannot know whether Malory shared Lydgate's politically didactic intention, but we can assume that his readers would have looked to his account for some useful lessons in governance.

The first political lesson they would have learned is that a king must always take counsel before making critical decisions. This was in fact a commonplace of medieval treatises on kingship, all of which stressed the evil which results from failure to take counsel or from taking evil counsel. Above all they warned the king against making decisions 'reklesly' touching 'grete mater . . ., for that is reprovable in a prince, bot do all thing be rype counsaile' (Hay, *Governaunce* 151). This is precisely the error Arthur makes when he condemns the queen to be burnt at the stake without a trial. He consults none of his knights except Gawain, and then he rejects Gawain's advice. In contrast, Lancelot never undertakes a course of action which risks the lives and honour of his men without first taking counsel with them in a parliament which gives every man a voice. Malory adds the long scene in which Lancelot takes counsel with Bors and his other followers before deciding what to do after he has fought his way out of the queen's chamber (1169.16–1173.31:XX.5–6) and he adds another shorter scene in which Lancelot takes counsel with his followers before returning into France (1202.32–1204.16:XX.17–18).

The second political lesson they would have learned is that late feudal monarchs cannot afford to fail in 'true justyce' where their mightiest magnates are concerned. At the time Malory wrote the *Morte Darthur*, the ideology of the modern state had not yet been developed nor were there many men in England who had been exposed to the new Renaissance notions of statecraft. Nevertheless, the most successful of fifteenth-century English monarchs knew well enough that they should not proceed against a magnate who was potentially more powerful than they. When Arthur condemns his queen to the stake without a trial, he fails to do true 'justyce' in the eyes of both Gawain and Lancelot — his two greatest knights — and, from the purely political point of view, that proves to be a disastrous mistake. He invokes the law of treason as though he he were the head of a modern state commanding a monopoly of armed force, when in fact he is a late feudal monarch who depends utterly upon the support of his great knights.

The third lesson they would have learned is that royal nepotism can be politically dangerous. They would have seen that Gawain has always served Arthur, not because he is king of England, and certainly not because he is Holy Roman Emperor, but because he is his mother's brother, and therefore his nearest and dearest kinsman. They would have seen, too, that the greatest among those Worshipful knights who used to serve Arthur simply because he was 'rightwys kynge borne of all Englond' were no longer there to support him, because Gawain and his brethren had killed them in pursuit of the blood feud. Both Pellinor and Lamorak are dead, and the knights who used to follow them now follow Lancelot. Tristram is also dead, victim of Mark's treachery, and those knights who used to follow him now follow Lancelot, as well. Consequently, when Arthur allows Gawain to banish Lancelot, he loses two-thirds of the Round Table fellowship.

There are three different views of political society operative in the Death of Arthur. We may diagram them as a series of concentric circles, representative of the clan, the feudal nation and Christendom, respectively. Gawain would inhabit the smallest circle representing the clan, the basic political unit of society in his native Scotland. As King of England, Arthur would inhabit the next larger circle representing the feudal nation, but as Holy Roman Emperor, highest officer of the High Order of Knighthood, his figure would grow to inhabit the largest circle, representative of Christendom. Lancelot would inhabit this largest circle, too, because even though he is heir to the kingdom of France, he has always preferred to serve Arthur.

The dramatic functioning of these three views is best seen in the episode of the Pope's attempt to make peace between Arthur and Lancelot. Representing Christendom, the Pope's messenger goes to Carlisle, where Arthur is holding court, and 'uppon payne of entirdytynge of all Inglonde' he commands Arthur to take back his queen and also to reconcile with Lancelot (1194.17–19:XX.13). Lancelot thanks God that the Pope has reconciled his queen to her husband and swears that he will be 'a thousandefolde more gladder to brynge her agayne than ever [he] was of her takyng away' (1195.7–15:XX.14). He had the option of behaving like a clansman in this situation, for, as he has demonstrated at the siege of

Joyous Garde, he has sufficient power to keep the queen for himself. He does not keep her because he knows he has no 'ryght' to her (cf.1197.6:XX.15); he chooses rather to return her to Arthur and clearly hopes that he, too, may be reconciled with his lord. At Carlisle, Lancelot makes a moving plea in his defense, insisting once again that he and the queen have been victims of the malice of 'lyars' and offering to do extraordinary penance for the unintentional killing of Gareth and Gaheris. Arthur's tears suggest that Lancelot has convinced him of his innocence, and evidently Gawain fears as much, for he says, 'if myne uncle, kynge Arthur, wyll accorde wyth the, he shall loose my servys' (1199.5, 1200.17–18:XX.16). Forced in this way to choose between his nephew, the chief of the Orkney clan, and his vassal, the King of France, Arthur silently chooses his nephew. He says nothing in response to Lancelot and allows Gawain to pronounce upon him the sentence of exile.

The political and military consequences of this decision are disastrous. One hundred knights of the Round Table choose to go into exile with Lancelot rather than remain with him. They foresee that 'in thys realme woll be no quyett, but ever debate and stryff, now the felyshyp of the Rounde Table ys brokyn' and Lancelot himself foresees that Arthur's youngest nephew, Mordred, 'woll make trouble' (1203.30–1204.11:XX.17–18). Ironically, the king will soon give Mordred the maximum opportunity to make trouble by appointing him regent while he and Gawain invade France in pursuit of vengeance upon Lancelot. Thus within our political model of concentric circles, Arthur shrinks in stature. From being the Holy Roman Emperor, who commands all of Christendom with the support of Lancelot and the Pope, he is reduced to being Gawain's kinsman. And he cannot even command his kinsman.

The rationalist and pragmatic point of view is not the only point of view the reader may take when looking for the causes of the Death of Arthur, however. Largely by means of his *hap* motif, Malory also invites the reader to assume the religious point of view of the Christian providentialist. This point of view, associated with the Grail knights, and especially with Lancelot and Bors, suggests a very different explanation for Arthur's downfall. For throughout the *Morte Darthur*, these pious men have expressed their belief that misfortune is the consequence of sin.

Malory may have been inspired to develop his *hap* motif by Hardyng's *Chronicle*. At the end of his account of the Death of Arthur Hardyng addresses the following rhetorical question to the spirit of Mordred.

> What vnhappe thy manly ghost hath moued
> Vnto so foule a cruell hardynesse,
> So many to be slayne through thyn vnhappynes? (149)

How is it possible for one man to create so much misery for others? And why does the 'good Lorde God' suffer 'suche treason & vnrightes, / That myght haue lett that cursed violence . . .?'(148). Such questions profoundly disturbed late medieval men. Hardyng offers no answer to his own question, but Richard Rolle suggests an answer in one of his treatises:

> Gyf all men treuly lyfed, withouten doute in pes & tranquillite, withouten debate & battell we suld duell; bot sen emonge few gude ar many ill, many disesys cum, þat ill may be chastissyd; & þis euyll þingis to gude men happyns for þai with ill ar mengyd vnto þere dede. (*The Fire of Love* I.9)

Rolle goes beyond the strict providentialist line which held that every misfortune is either deserved punishment or else necessary to bring men to an awareness of their sins. He states simply that sometimes 'euyll þingis' happen to 'gude men' because 'þai with ill ar mengyd.'

Malory's Lancelot said something very like this as a young man when he asserted that sinful, 'unhappy' knights make 'all thynge unhappy that is aboute them' (271.2–4:VI.10). What is more, Malory's use of the *hap* motif in the Death of Arthur suggests that Lancelot was right.

The *hap* motif rings like a death knell throughout Malory's Death of Arthur. In the first thirty lines of 'Slander and Strife' it occurs three times (1161.7–32:XX.1). First Malory announces the 'grete angur and unhappe' which shall destroy Arthurian society. Then he blames this misfortune upon two 'unhappy knyghtis whych were named sir Aggravayne and sir Mordred.' And finally he has Gawain give the name of 'unhappynes' to Aggravayne's decision to allege the adultery openly before Arthur. The progression from 'unhappe' to 'unhappy' to 'unhappynes' suggests the ripple effect which a stone causes when dropped into a pond, each added syllable representing an enlargement of the circle of misfortune. If we were to superimpose this religious image of an ever widening circle of sin and misfortune upon our previous political image of concentric circles representing the clan, the feudal nation and Christendom, its movement would suggest that the envy and vengeance originating in the family circle have enough destructive power to engulf all of Christendom in *unhappynesse*.

Like his contemporaries, Alain Chartier and Sir Gilbert Hay, Malory consistently uses both *hap* and *unhap* in that doubly active sense which assumes a covenantal relationship between man and God. Men are 'happy' in the sense of fortunate when they are also 'happy' in the sense of blessed (i.e. virtuous and hence filled with the grace of God). Likewise men are 'unhappy' in the sense of unfortunate when they are also 'unhappy' in the sense of wretched or cursed (i.e. vicious and hence cut off from the grace of God).

Malory first introduced his *hap* motif in the Tale of Balin to suggest that Balin's tragic end 'happened' because of his wilfull pursuit of the blood feud and his proud adherence to the Heroic code of ethics. In the Death of Arthur Malory uses the *hap* motif to suggest that the fall of the Round Table 'happens' because of those same human passions: the pride, envy, anger and vengefulness which motivate the blood feud and also cut men off from the grace of God. Viewed in this way, the 'great angur and unhappe' caused by those 'unhappy' knights, Mordred and Aggravayne, becomes analogous to the Wasteland caused by Balin's 'dolerous stroke.' The chain-reaction effect which follows their attack upon Lancelot is slower than that which follows Balin's stroke, but in the end it damages not just three 'contreyes' but all of Christendom. And in both cases good men suffer for the evil which other men do. In Rolle's terms, 'euyll þingis to gude men happyns for þai with ill ar mengyd' (1.9) and in the terms of Malory's Lancelot, 'unhappy' knights have slain 'by unhappe and hir cursednesse bettir men than they be hemself,' and so made 'all thynge unhappy that is aboute them' (271.1–4:VI.10).

If *unhappynesse* is somehow contagious, if it can spread throughout a population affecting the 'gude' as well as the 'ill' as Rolle says, then *happynesse* ought also to be capable of producing a chain-reaction effect. We in fact see this corollary principle illustrated in Chaucer's *Franklin's Tale* when the *unhappynesse* threatened by Aurelius' self-seeking is reversed and transformed into *happynesse* by Arveragus' selfless devotion to 'trouthe.' The *Franklin's Tale* is, of course, a romance and when writing romance, medieval authors were not constrained by historical 'fact'. They were free to idealize human nature and society and so free to give narrative expression to the power of 'trouthe.' On the other hand, when re-telling old stories found in old books that were thought to be historically true, medieval authors were not so free. When retelling the story of *Troilus and Criseyde*, for example, Chaucer was not free to reward Troilus for his 'trouthe' to Criseyde. Just so, when retelling the Death of Arthur, Malory was not free to reward Lancelot for his 'trouthe' to Guinevere and Arthur. There was no getting around the 'fact' that, despite his 'trouthe' the *unhappynesse* of Arthur's kinsmen was powerful enough to cause a catastrophe. From a rationalist perspective, this catastrophe may be explained as the consequence of mistakes in political judgment, but from a religious perspective, it must be explained as the consequence of *unhappynesse*.

Arthur was chosen by God to be rightwise king of England, but as soon as he breaks the sword he had 'by myracle' while seeking vengeance against King Pellinor, the reader knows that he will not be a *rex pius et justus.* Arthur has always understood that to be the most worshipful king in Christendom, he must have the best possible fellowship of knights in his service. However, he has never understood that he (and they) also need the grace of God. He is too much of a rationalist to accept the mystical belief that a knight may be 'happy' in adventure if he is at one with God through His grace and so he does not understand the providentialist meaning of the quest for the Holy Grail. When the Grail appeared at Camelot, the king regarded it as an honour bestowed upon him by God and was grateful for it. However, he did not understand what the Grail's appearance required of him and his knights and so he has done nothing to develop his spiritual life. Indeed, so far as we know, Arthur has never repented his sins.

Arthur's *unhappynesse* begins when he allows his 'unhappy' nephews to lay an ambush for Lancelot outside the queen's chamber rather than require them to make a formal appeal of treason, which would give Lancelot his knightly right to the judgment of God in trial by battle. His *unhappynesse* then spreads to Lancelot, when the king determines to burn the queen at the stake, without a trial. Lancelot has no choice but to rescue her and is 'so unhappy' as not to recognize Gaheris and his beloved Gareth at the execution site without their armour, and so 'unhappely' he kills them by his own hand that 'unhappy day!' (1189.20:XX.11;1183.25:XX.9;1199.28: XX.16). Arthur's *unhappynesse* then engulfs Gawain who has no choice but to swear vengeance upon Lancelot for the deaths of his brothers since he cannot take vengeance upon his uncle for commanding their unarmed presence at the execution site. Throughout this sequence of events Arthur never suspects that he might in any way be responsible for the widening gyre of *unhappynesse*. Rather, like Balin, he attributes his misfortunes to others, as when he blames the 'evyll wyll' of Mordred and Aggravayne 'unto sir Launcelot' (1184.8–11:XX.9), or simply regrets 'that ever sir Launcelot was ayenst me!' (1216.16:XX.20). At other times, he projects his *unhappynesse* into the environment, as when he regrets 'that ever thys unhappy warre began!'(1218.18–19:XX.22).

It is common to speak of Arthur's downfall as 'tragic', and of the *Morte Darthur* as a tragedy (cf. Moorman), even though the medieval concept of tragedy, insofar as it can be traced through the period, was quite different from the modern concept, based upon classical and renaissance drama.[3] There can be no doubt that Malory's method of telling the post-Grail narrative is extremely dramatiç. In scene after scene, he disappears to let his characters do their own talking, and this is particularly true of the death scenes of Gawain, Arthur and Lancelot, where, as each man faces death, he reveals once again the values which have governed his life as a knight.[4]

On his deathbed Gawain realizes that by pursuing the blood feud against Lancelot, he has hurt Arthur. He has not only provided Mordred the opportunity to seize the throne, he has also deprived his uncle of the one military force which might have crushed the usurper, since one hundred knights of the Round Table went with Lancelot into exile in France. Gawain confesses his fault to his uncle in an emotionally charged scene, during which he also writes a letter to Lancelot begging him to return to England to rescue Arthur. Then, with his final breath, he charges Arthur to cherish Lancelot above all other knights.

We have here all the ingredients necessary to a moralized *de casibus* tragedy such as Chaucer's Monk might have told, or such as Boccaccio and Lydgate might have included in their collections of stories of the fall of great men. Moreover, Malory seems to suggest such an interpretation to his audience by having Gawain refer specifically to his sins of 'wylfulnesse' and 'pryde' (1230.18–24:XXI.2). Gawain himself, however, lacks the spiritual awareness of a providentialist. Gawain is still an Heroic knight and a fatalist. He takes care to satisfy the ritual requirements for the salvation of his soul by requesting confession and extreme unction, but these Christian rituals do not provide the dramatic focus of this scene. We do not hear Gawain confess to a priest and seek forgiveness from God; rather we hear him confess to Arthur and seek forgiveness from Lancelot. His final act — the letter to Lancelot — is yet another attempt to save Arthur.

It is therefore highly ironic that after his death Gawain should become an agent of God's providence. Just before dawn on the day that King Arthur's army is to engage Mordred's army on Salisbury Plain, God 'of Hys speciall grace' allows Gawain to appear to Arthur in an 'avisioun':

> 'Thus much hath gyvyn me leve God for to warne you of youre dethe: for and ye fyght as to-morne with sir Mordred, as ye bothe have assygned, doute ye nat ye shall be slayne, and the moste party of youre people on bothe partyes. And for the grete grace and goodnes that Allmyghty Jesu hath unto you, and for pyté of you and many mo other good men there shall be slayne, God hath sente me to you of Hys speciall grace to gyff you warnyng that in no wyse ye do batayle as to-morne, but that ye take a tretyse for a moneth-day. And proffir you largely, so that to-morn ye put in a delay. For within a moneth shall com sir Launcelot with all hys noble knyghtes, and rescow you worshypfully, and sle sir Mordred and all that ever wyll holde wyth hym.' (1234.6–19:XXI.3)

This is an expanded version of the visions recorded by the *Mort Artu*, in which Gawain simply tells Arthur not to fight but rather to send for Lancelot (176) and the stanzaic *Morte*, in which Gawain tells him to take a month's truce and assures him that Lancelot will come by then (3216–23). Most of the expansion is devoted to explaining God's will: His 'grete grace and goodnes' towards Arthur and His plan that Lancelot should come to rescue Arthur and kill Mordred. In other words, most of the expansion is devoted to reinforcing the notion that God wills Arthur to be saved from Mordred's treachery.

Late medieval Christian providentialism accommodates both free will and chance as part of God's providential design and on the field of Salisbury plain both play a part in bringing about the battle despite God's 'speciall grace.' First, Arthur and Mordred both choose to direct their knights to attack should they see a sword raised during the parlay, because neither trusts the other. Arthur 'in no wyse truste[s]' Mordred, and Mordred 'know[s] well [his] fadir woll be avenged uppon [him]' (1235.13–17:XXI.4). Then an adder comes out of a bush and stings one of the knights at the parlay, causing him to raise his sword 'to sle the addir' thinking 'none othir harme' (1235.20–24:XXI.4). The sting of the addir is a genuine accident, a matter of chance. And Malory uses it to make this scene a dramatic emblem of his *hap* motif.[5]

In the popular *Book of Vices and Virtues*, the adder is symbolic of envy (23) and the adder's bite symbolic of slander (59), the most common result of envy. Therefore, in this scene its appearance and its action of biting may be taken to symbolize the envy which motivated Mordred's and Aggravayne's 'sclaundir' of Lancelot and the queen. Envy is a human emotion and the slander which it motivates is a freely willed human action. On the other hand, taken literally, the adder's bite is a chance occurrence in Nature, which is without malice. By symbolically linking the two Malory suggests that *unhappynesse* may originate either from human choice or from accident. Nevertheless, such widespread *unhappynesse* as results from Mordred's and Aggravayne's slander (choice) and the adder's bite (chance) is not inevitable. In both cases most of the 'unhappy' (in the sense of unfortunate) effects of the initial act might have been avoided if the human participants had been more 'happy' (in the sense of blessed or virtuous). If Arthur had refused to allow his nephews to set an ambush for Lancelot and had insisted rather that they appeal him openly of treason, thus allowing him to answer the appeal in battle 'as a knyght shulde,' their malice would not have been so deadly. If Arthur and Mordred had not each anticipated the treachery of the other in the same way, the adder's bite would not have been so deadly, either. As it 'happens', however, both adder's bite and malicious 'sclaundir' produce a chain reaction of *unhappynesse* which ends only with the carnage on Salisbury plain.

According to Gawain's prophecy, Arthur should have died in the course of the battle of Salisbury plain, but late medieval Christian providentialism holds that no event in human history is determined until it has 'happened.' As King Pellinor once observed, 'God may wol foredo desteny' (120.10:III.15). Gawain has told us that it is God's will that Arthur be preserved from Mordred's treachery and that Mordred be punished by Lancelot. A mixture of chance (the adder's bite) and free will (Mordred's and Arthur's treacherous intentions vis-a-vis one another) might have 'foredone' God's will in this regard, but, as Lucan the Butler observes to Arthur, God 'of Hys grete goodnes' has decided to preserve Arthur's life, anyway. That being the case, Lucan pleads with Arthur to accept the will of God and to leave Mordred alone:

> 'Sir, latte hym be,' seyde sir Lucan, 'for he ys unhappy. And yf ye passe this unhappy day ye shall be ryght well revenged. And, good lorde, remembre ye of your nyghtes dreme and what the spyryte of sir Gawayne tolde you to-nyght, and yet God of Hys grete goodnes hath preserved you hyddirto. And for Goddes sake, my lorde, leve of thys, for, blyssed by God, ye have won the fylde: for yet we ben here three on lyve, and with sir Mordred ys nat one on lyve. And therefore if ye leve of now, thys wycked day of Desteny ys paste!'
> (1236.28–1237.4:XXI.4)

Arthur has a choice. If he will assent to the will of God, he may live to be 'ryght well revenged' by Lancelot. On the other hand, if he will not assent to the will of God, he must fulfill the prophecy. Arthur chooses his own will. He wants vengeance. Indeed, he is so angry that he does not care whether he lives or dies, so long as he may be avenged upon this 'traytoure,' Mordred.

Malory's description of their battle to the death is his own invention (cf. *Mort Artu* 190–91 and stanzaic *Morte* 3384ff) and suggests that father and son re-enact the scene of the adder's bite. Like the adder, Arthur deals the first blow 'with a foyne of hys speare,' and then, like the mortally wounded knight, Mordred retaliates as soon as he feels that he has 'hys dethys wounde,' even though that retaliation cannot help him. With one grim movement, he thrusts himself with all his might 'upp to the burre of kyng Arthurs speare,' so that he can kill his father with his sword (1237.14–19:XXI.4). If the sting of the adder and its aftermath was a fitting emblem of the destructive power of envy and slander, this deadly embrace of father and son is a fitting emblem of the destructive power of vengeance. The Lot-Pellinor feud has already demonstrated that vengeance in the form of the blood feud threatens to destroy the larger human society. But in the Heroic tradition, vengeance within the circle of kinsmen has always been taboo. Arthur's killing of Mordred breaks that taboo in a manner even more chilling than the accidental fratricide of Balin and Balan, because his act is deliberate. That is why this scene conveys such a powerful and immediate sense of desolation.

When the bond of kinship is breached by the power of vengeance, men may well fear that chaos is come again.

In all the events leading up to Arthur's death, Malory's redaction has reinforced the operations of God's providence. However, Arthur's own response to these events has been like that of a hero of classical humanist tragedy, such as Shakespeare might have written. Arthur does not take nearly so long to believe his ghost as Hamlet to believe his, but that fact merely points to a difference in the basic temperament of the two princes. Hamlet is a prince who tends by nature to be circumspect, whereas Arthur is a prince who tends by nature to be impetuous. And, as Machiavelli observed, princes prosper only so long as circumstances require the sort of behaviour they are prone to by virtue of their character (133). From this classical humanist point of view, then, Arthur's tragedy is a tragedy of character, his propensity to act impetuously in anger being the cause of his downfall from first to last. Nevertheless, in the scene where Arthur is borne away to Avalon, the king himself exhibits no awareness of having made mistakes. Nor does he express any awareness of sin, for, unlike Gawain, he does not ask to receive the sacraments. Arthur confronts death with very much the same attitude as Hamlet. Indeed, the undertones of Celtic mystery, the barge and the four queens who accompany Arthur to Avalon, dramatically confirm Hamlet's conviction that death is the ultimate unknown, in Arthur's case literally a journey to an 'undiscovered country, from whose bourne / No traveller returns' (*Hamlet* 3.1.79–80).

The pious reader may moralize Arthur's fall as a *de casibus* tragedy; however, this is clearly not the way Arthur himself understands his fall. He neither fears damnation nor hopes for heaven, and his parting request for prayers seems almost like an afterthought. What most troubles Arthur at the moment of his departure from this world is that he must say to his one remaining knight of the Round Table, 'Comforte thyselff, . . . and do as well as thou mayste, for in me ys no truste for to truste in' (1240.31–32:XXI.5). To the end, then, Arthur's primary loyalty is to his knights and his primary concern is his kingly power. He has lost that power, and, what is even worse from the point of view of such a man, he has failed to ensure the succession. His only son is dead, a traitor, and he has no way of knowing whether or not his more distant kinsman, Constantine of Cornwall, will be able to restore his kingdom.

The deaths of Arthur and Gawain are both tragic, in the sense that both men leave this world having lost everything they held most dear. The death of Lancelot is a much different matter. In fact, it is questionable whether Lancelot's death is at all tragic, since in Malory's version he dies literally in the odour of sanctity, with a smile on his face. Nevertheless, in the succession of dramatic scenes leading up to his death, Malory makes clear that Lancelot's saintly acceptance of God's will was hard won. More than once he has been overwhelmed by a sense of undeserved misfortune and intolerable loss.

The first of these misfortunes was the edict of banishment pronounced upon him by Gawain. Lancelot had hoped to be reconciled to his lord, Arthur, by the Pope's commandment and to continue to serve him in this 'moste nobelyst Crysten realme' of England. He has always insisted that he and the queen were innocent of any wrongdoing on the night Mordred and Aggravayne trapped them in the queen's chamber. And now he is overwhelmed by the injustice of being thus 'shamefully banysshyd, undeserved and causeles!' Rather surprisingly, he blames his misfortune on the mutability of Fortune: 'But fortune ys so varyaunte, and the wheele so mutable, that there ys no constaunte abydynge' (1201.9–15:XX.7). Since Malory has eliminated Arthur's dream of Fortune's wheel, this reference to Dame Fortune is the only one to be found in the *Morte Darthur*. It is striking for that reason alone, but it is even more striking because uttered by Lancelot, who has always adopted the providentialist view that misfortune is punishment for sin. It would appear that Lancelot is having difficulty coping with totally undeserved misfortune. He cannot blame God, and he will not blame Arthur, and yet he clearly feels the need to blame *someone*.

Lancelot's second great misfortune is Mordred's treachery in usurping Arthur's throne. This time his initial response is to ring all the changes on the knell of *unhappynesse*:

> 'Alas! that double traytoure, sir Mordred, now me repentith that ever he ascaped my hondys, for much shame hath he done unto my lorde Arthure . . . And in an unhappy owre was I born that ever I shulde have that myssehappe to sle firste sir Gawayne, sir Gaherys, the good knyght, and myne owne frynde sir Gareth that was a full noble knyght. Now, alas, I may sey I am unhappy that ever I shulde do thus. And yet, alas, myght I never have hap to sle that traytoure, sir Mordred!' (1249.12–29:XXI.8)

If only he had managed to kill that 'double traytoure' (i.e. traytoure to Lancelot and Arthur) outside the queen's chamber that night, this newest misfortune could not have happened. This time, Lancelot himself was the instrument of a number of mishaps which ensued from that treacherous ambush, but the problem of blame still remains, because he did not *intend* any of them. Desperate for an explanation, he falls back on astrology, a form of fatalism which was particularly popular during the late medieval period, and attributes his misfortune to the influence of the planets at the hour of his birth. Coming from a providentialist, this is even more surprising than his earlier reference to Dame Fortune and her wheel. Certainly, it heavily underscores two things: first, Lancelot's continuing conviction of his own innocence and second, his great need to understand why that traitor, Mordred, should have been so successful. He clearly cannot believe that it is the will of God.

His cousin, Bors, rebukes Lancelot for his 'complayntes', and urges him to hasten his return to England to save Arthur. But there, Lancelot must face and learn to accept not just misfortune, but irreparable loss. He learns that he has come too late to save Arthur's life. And when he goes in search of his lady, Guinevere, he discovers that she, too, is lost to him. She has taken the veil and is therefore not 'dysposed' to return with him to France as his queen. This loss he accepts with even more difficulty, but he does accept it. Since he would have forsaken the world for the religious life after the Quest, had he not been bound by his love to continue to serve her and Arthur, he finds it 'ryght' to forsake it now, since that is her choice (1253.10–19:XXI.9). As a consequence, Lancelot ends his days, not as a knight, but as a priest and a hermit.

Lancelot's decision to become a priest and to live the life of a hermit should not be interpreted as a complete rejection of the goods of this world. On the contrary, when he is called upon to celebrate the requiem mass for his lady and then to bury her by the side of her husband at Glastonbury, we are allowed to perceive that he has never stopped loving them, and has not yet completely accepted their loss. When he first saw the corpse of his lady, he 'wepte not gretelye, but syghed'; however, after placing her in Arthur's tomb, he 'swouned, and laye longe stylle,' grieving for them both. The Glastonbury hermit chides him, saying that his 'sorow- makyng' is displeasing to God, but Lancelot does not accept this:

> 'Truly, . . . I trust I do not dysplese God, for he knoweth myn entente: for my sorow was not, nor is not, for ony rejoysyng of synne, but my sorow may never have ende. For whan I remember of hir beaulté and of hir noblesse, that was bothe wyth hyr kyng and wyth hyr, so whan I sawe his corps and hir corps so lye togyders, truly myn herte wolde nat serve to susteyne my careful body. Also whan I remembre me how by my defaute and myn orgule and my pryde that they were bothe layed ful lowe, that were pereles that ever was lyvyng of Christen people, wyt you wel,' sayd syr Launcelot, 'this remembred, of their kyndenes and myn unkyndnes, sanke so to myn herte that I myght not susteyne myself.' (1256.26–39:XXI.11)

At last Lancelot is able to blame himself. He blames himself for his 'pryde' and also for his 'defaute', his failure. He does not specify the nature of that failure, but if we remember his providentialist belief that *unhappynesse* is caused by sin and *happynesse* by virtue and willing cooperation with the grace of God, we may infer it. Lancelot's 'defaute' was his failure to be virtuous enough and to cooperate fully enough with God's grace, so that these two 'Christen people' need not have been 'layed ful lowe.'

Such extreme humility and readiness to blame himself entirely for the fall of Arthur suggest that during his years as a hermit and priest Lancelot has achieved sanctity, a suggestion which is borne out by the manner of his death. After a long period of mourning, he asks the Bishop for his last rites as a Christian and dies that night. His companions find him lying in his bed with a smile on his face, 'and the swettest savour aboute hym that ever they felte' (1258.15–17:XXI.13). Yet neither the Bishp's joyful laughter as he dreams that Lancelot's soul is borne into heaven by flights of angels, nor Lancelot's own smiling face, can stop the tears of those he leaves behind. Lancelot's death is not tragic for him, because he has finally been able to accept all his worldly losses as the will of God. And, according to Richard Rolle such perfect acceptance is the mark of a man full blessed and a true lover of God ('Form of Living' 6.176–181). However, Lancelot's personal transcendence cannot compensate for his loss to Christendom. As Lancelot wept for Arthur and Guinevere, so Sir Bedwer and Sir Bors weep for him.

The succession of dramatic scenes which makes up the Death of Arthur proper reiterates each one of the three ethical points of view — Heroic, Worshipful and True — but validates only the last of them. Gawain's pursuit of the blood feud has been shown to be destructive of Arthurian society and his fatalism is canceled when he becomes a posthumous agent of God's providence. Arthur's concern for his personal honour and trust in his own rational judgment have led him to make disastrous political mistakes, moreover, from the religious point of view these mistakes appear to be the result of a consistent refusal to put his trust in God. If Arthur had not refused Lancelot's request for a judgement of God, Mordred would have had to face Lancelot in trial by battle and probably would not have survived; and if Arthur had not refused Lucan the Butler's plea to do the will of God by letting Mordred live to be punished by Lancelot, Arthur would certainly have survived the battle of Salisbury plain. No matter how admirable Gawain and Arthur have proved to be in some ways, Malory has handled the narrative of the Death of Arthur so as to reveal the inadequacies of their knightly codes. It is not enough to trust in the bond of kinship. And it is not enough to trust in oneself.

There is good evidence that Malory's first readers saw in Lancelot the highest ideal of knighthood and the model for all men to follow. In his 1498 edition of the *Morte Darthur* following the death of Lancelot, Wynkyn de Worde praises the didactic value of Malory's book in the following terms:

> Therfor me thynketh this present boke called La mort dathur [sic] is ryght necessary often to be radde. For in it shall ye fynde the gracious knyghtly and vertuous werre of moost noble knyghtes of the worlde, wherby they gate praysyng contynuell. Also me semyth by the oft redyng therof. Ye shal gretly desyre tacustome yourself in folowynge those gracyous knyghtly dedes. That is to seye, to drede god, and love ryghtwisnes, faythfully & courageously to serve your soverayne prynce. And the more that god hath geven you the tryumfall honour, the meeker ye oughte to be, ever feryng the unstablynesse of this dysceyvable worlde. (Cited in Life 22–23)

This is an enormous tribute to the power of the ideal represented by Lancelot: 'to drede God', to serve one's 'soverayne prynce' faithfully, and to beware of this unstable world, remembering always that God is the ultimate source of all worldly 'honour'.

But Malory's 'hoole book' of Arthur and his knights does not end here, with the death of Lancelot. Malory adds a brief and totally original ending which emphasizes the continuity of the Arthurian past with his readers' present. First he tells them that Constantine did reign after Arthur, and that he was 'a ful noble knyght, and worshypfuly he rulyd this royame' (1259.27–29:XXI.13). And then he tells them that Lancelot's final companions returned to their own countries where they lived 'as holy men' until they had 'stablysshed theyr londes' and then traveled to the Holy Land, where they battled the Turks and at last 'dyed upon a Good Fryday for Goddes sake' (1260.4–15:XXI.13). Thus Malory confirms the continuation of Arthur's world, England as well as Christendom, into his present. In so doing he also demonstrates his awareness of two very important and contemporary concerns. Ever since the conflict between the houses of Lancaster and York began, fifteenth-century Englishmen had had good reason to be concerned for the orderly and safe succession to the throne of England. And ever since the Turks occupied Constantinople in 1453, they had had good reason to be concerned for the safety of Christendom. The last crusade to relieve the city had failed in 1464, when the Pope died at Ancona, and many, including the English king Edward IV, were talking of taking up the crusade again.

So what kind of a book is it that Sir Thomas Malory has written? Modern readers and critics have difficulty answering this question. They disagree as to what literary genre it represents, for it is drawn from both chronicle and romance and embraces both tragedy and divine comedy. And they also disagree as to whether or not it is a unified work of literature.[6] I believe that much of this disagreement is due to insufficient historical understanding. We have only just begun to write the history of the reception of Malory's work (Parins), but it is possible to anticipate what that history will teach us. Major changes (what Jauss would call 'horizon shifts') have occurred in English society and culture over the past five hundred years and their effect has been to obscure important aspects of the *Morte Darthur* from the view of modern readers. Within a hundred and fifty years of Malory's writing, the Tudor Reformation and the development of the English nation-state had already obscured Malory's representation of the ideal of Christendom. Then the Victorian romanticisation and idealisation of Arthur completed the process begun by the Tudors, to obscure Malory's representation of him as a great but fallible monarch. The consequence of these two horizon shifts has been to eclipse from the modern reader's view not only Malory's dual perspective (political and religious) on the Death of Arthur, but also his three different types of knighthood (along with their differing ethical points of view). In other words, the consequence of these two horizon shifts has been to prevent the modern reader from perceiving the very stuff of which his literary structure is made.

For a long time after the publication of Eugene Vinaver's edition of Malory's *Works*, critics were concerned to demonstrate that he was wrong to think Malory's book lacked unity. But recently, perhaps under the influence of post-structuralist literary theory, it has become more common to focus on the discontinuities in Malory's work. For example, both Felicity Riddy and Robert Merrill have recently argued that Malory's work is deeply divided, reflecting fundamental differences within Malory's society and culture. I believe that argument needs to be turned on its head. What Malory has done is to take these social and cultural differences and weave them into a complex literary structure. In this way, through his work, he can be said to have performed the most fundamental task of culture itself, which is to create harmony from disharmony and significance from randomness, in short, to create patterns of meaning.

The only generic label which to me seems appropriate for a work of such scope, is epic. Among previous critics of Malory's work, Vida Scudder alone has perceived that Malory's work is 'the epic of a civilization' (216). Literary historians of the epic genre have overlooked the *Morte Darthur* because it is not written in verse (cf. Tillyard). However, cultural historians have long recognized its profound similarities to the *Chanson de Roland* and the works of Homer. For like them, the *Morte Darthur* has drawn into itself 'many levels of cultural experience: mythical, legendary, often historical, and also contemporary, with fictional details supplied by its final creator' (Levy 13).

As far as I know the only literary theory of genre which would classify Malory's work as an epic is the theory of Northrop Frye. Frye begins by reminding us that epics need not be written in verse. Even though verse may be the most common form, it does not constitute a distinguishing characteristic of the genre. According to Frye there are four criteria which define the epic genre. The first and most fundamental is that epic is always composed for oral recitation. When epics come to be written down, they retain that oral quality in their style, whether verse or prose, and until a culture attains a very high degree of literacy, most people will encounter them as listeners rather than readers. Malory's work certainly fits this description. Almost all critics have noticed the orality of his prose style, and I find it highly probable that most of his first audience was composed of listeners rather than readers. R. F. Green has shown that the reading of very long texts in installments over an extended period of time, was a popular form of entertainment in late medieval courts (99–100). And I have calculated that one could read the *Morte Darthur* aloud, at the speed necessary for effective recitation, in approximately sixty hours. Therefore, if divided into daily two-hour installments, the recitation could have been accomplished within one month.

The second distinguishing feature of epic is its episodic and encyclopedic nature. That is to say, short pieces of epic composition tend to accrete to form larger, encyclopedic works. The most common reason for such epic accretion is the desire to gather together everything that may be known of a great hero of the past. This is particularly true of historical figures who are believed to have played an important role in the founding of nations. All sorts of stories may be told of such men, stories which are not necessarily accurate in the sense of being historically factual, but nevertheless 'true' in the sense of expressing a people's values and ideals. Malory's *Morte Darthur* is obviously a work of this kind. Indeed, what distinguishes Malory's work from his sources is this explicit aim of writing a 'complete story', a 'hoole book', which not only chronicles the reign of a great national hero and king but also recounts the acts of the knights who served him. One could go further and argue that it is more than a national epic, it is an epic of Christendom, insofar as its national hero, King Arthur, was also crowned Holy Roman Emperor. In both these respects, in fact, Malory's work is much like *Charles the Great*, the French prose epic of Charlemagne, which William Caxton published in the same year he published Malory's text (Goodman 269).

In choosing which stories to include in his 'hoole book' of Arthur, Malory was more discriminating than modern critics have been willing to allow. Malory seems to have regarded all his sources as historical, the French romances as well as the English chronicles. This may seem naive to a modern historian, but we must remember that medieval writers of history had neither 'explicit criteria' nor any 'practical method of proceeding' to determine the accuracy of any particular account of the past (Levine 21). The most learned of late medieval Latin chroniclers accepted the historicity of Arthur, even if they doubted the truth of some of the stories told about him (Matheson). And Malory's attitude seems to have been much the same.[7] For example, he tells us that he could find very little about the actual circumstances of Arthur's death 'wrytten in bokis that bene auctorysed.' He accepted as accurate the story of Arthur's interment by the Archbishop, because 'thys tale sir Bedwere, a knyght of the Table Rounde, made hit to be wrytten.' On the other hand, he dismissed the oral tradition that 'som men sey in many partys of Inglonde that kynge Arthure ys nat ded . . . and shall com agayne . . .'. Malory refuses to 'saye that hit shall be so' (1242.3–26:XXI.7). The very improbability of such a story would have weighed against its credibility, but the fact that it had not been written down in 'bokis that bene auctorysed' made it easier to dismiss. Malory showed the same kind of discrimination when choosing between two accounts of the same event, as, for example, when he had to choose between the Vulgate or the *Tristan* version of the Grail Quest. He chose the one which made better sense of the history of Arthur's reign as he understood it.[8]

The third distinguishing feature of epic, according to Frye, is that both the arrangement of epic stories and the motive for collecting them into larger wholes, is always 'thematic', by which he means to say 'educational in the broadest sense' (*Anatomy* 54). In fact, he would argue that such encyclopedic works function like a secular equivalent to sacred scripture, insofar as they take root in a specific culture and 'tell that culture what it is and how it came to be' (*Secular Scripture* 9). Again, we recognize Malory's work in this description. Malory was too much of an historian to alter the basic facts as 'given' in order to idealize the figure of Arthur (cf. Pickering 3). However, he makes them 'educational in the broadest sense' in the way he arranges the parts of his history. By adding the Tale of Tristram, Malory clarifies Arthur's own Worshipful code of ethics since Malory portrays Tristram as the Round Table knight most like the king. Then by elaborating the ethical ideal of True knighthood through Lancelot, transformed as the queen's 'true' lover, Malory achieves several important 'educational' effects. First, he makes Arthur look more noble, by eliminating most of the shame of cuckoldry. Second, he makes Lancelot a credible (because fallible) exemplar of True knighthood. And last, he is able to draw a comparison between Lancelot's religious ideal and Arthur's secular ideal of knighthood. Finally, by transforming Gawain into an Heroic knight, admirable for his loyalty to Arthur, but as a feudist clearly destructive of Arthurian society, Malory is able to draw another set of comparisons, between Gawain's primitive style of exacting vengeance for the sake of family honour and Arthur's (and Tristram's) more civilized style of exacting vengeance for the sake of personal honour. Thus, Malory succeeds in 'placing' Arthur in the middle of a spectrum of ethical positions, all of which co-existed within his own culture.

Indeed, Malory's prose epic sums up almost a thousand years of European cultural history, from the first Christian warriors of the Dark Ages to the first humanist princes of the early Renaissance, at the same time as it reflects the diverse views of knighthood still extant in late-fifteenth century England. Even the early feudal ideal of the knight as warrior in the service of his kinsmen or his feudal lord survived in the English border counties and in Scotland, which explains why Malory chose Gawain and his brethren, and the Northumbrian knights, Balin and Balan, to embody this type of knighthood. The late feudal ideal of the knight as servant of the Crown was dominant in Malory's day and had been developing ever since the mid-fourteenth century when Edward III founded the Order of the Garter, which explains why Malory chose to embody this view in King Arthur and his knights of the Round Table, and especially in Tristram, whose greatest ambition, like that of many young noblemen in Malory's day, was to win a place among the elite fellowship of the king's knights.

The religious ideal of knighthood still survived in Malory's day, but was no longer a majority view (if, indeed, it ever had been, even during the height of the Crusades). Yet, it was still the preferred view of some of the greatest knights of late medieval England: Sir John Clanvowe, for example, who ended his life on crusade (Catto); and, in Malory's own time, Sir John Tiptoft, Edward IV's Constable and Earl of Worcester, who made the pilgrimage to the Holy Land, belonged to a religious order of knighthood, and when condemned to death by the Lancastrians, asked the executioner to dispatch him with three strokes of the axe, in honour of the holy Trinity. Malory chose mostly French knights, Galahad and Percival, Lancelot and his cousin Bors, to represent this ideal of knighthood in his book, perhaps because of the fame of the saintly French king and crusader, Louis IX. But there can be no doubt that Lancelot was greatly admired by Malory's English audiences as the passage from Wynkyn de Worde, cited above, shows.

From the modern point of view, Malory's three types of knight can be seen as basic psychological and ethical types still common in western culture. Certainly, there is good evidence that they survived as ethical types into the sixteenth-century. For one can see them reflected in Tudor dress in the persons of King Henry VIII, his mightiest magnate, the Duke of Norfolk, and his most loyal sevant, excepting only God, Sir Thomas More.

The last distinguishing characteristic of epic, according to Frye, is patterns of recurrence. Such patterning, whether temporal or spatial, is a structural principle of all art; but it is particularly noteworthy in the epic.

In verse epics, temporal rhythms of recurrence take the form of a regular meter. In Malory's prose epic, however, they are neither so regular nor so pervasive as metre; rather they take the form of the repetition of key words, phrases and ideas throughout his text, words like 'worshipful', 'noble' and 'unhappy'. Jill Mann has observed that such repetitions can be seen to form the 'skeletal structure of his work' ('Knightly' 332). But even more important than these are the spatial patterns of recurrence in his text.

Spatial patterns of recurrence can be found at every narrative level of the *Morte Darthur*, and they are all created by his three-fold typology: (1) the Heroic knight, (2) the Worshipful knight and (3) the True knight. Malory always presents these types (and/or exemplifies their distinguishing (1) feudal, (2) courtly and (3) religious virtues) in only two of the six possible patterns: 1–2–3, and 1–3–2. The recurrence of these two patterns describes, if indeed it does not determine, the order of narrative units in the *Morte Darthur* from the most limited to the most extended in scope. In the first narrative unit, the quests of Gawain, Tor and Pellinor, are ordered according to the 1–3–2 pattern, whereas the quests of Gawain, Marhalt and Ywain, are ordered according to the 1–2–3 pattern. On a much larger scale, the second, third and fourth parts of the second narrative unit, which focus successively on the feudal, religious and courtly virtues of True knighthood, are ordered according to the 1–3–2 pattern. In contrast, the three parts of the tale of Tristram, which focus on the feudal and courtly virtues of Worshipful knighthood and then test the Worshipful knight for his religious virtues, are ordered according to the 1–2–3 pattern. Finally, on a scale which encompasses the 'hoole book' we can see that Malory introduces the three great knightly types into his narrative in the 1–3–2 pattern (Gawain, Lancelot and Tristram) but has them exit in the 1–2–3 pattern (the death scenes of Gawain, Arthur and Lancelot).

One of the major consequences of the broad ethical scope of Malory's work is that his readers enjoy a great deal of interpretive freedom. And with this freedom comes much of the responsibility for establishing the meaning of his text. Someone concerned for the didactic value of the book, as Caxton was, might well be anxious, as Caxton seems to have been, regarding the interpretive choices readers would make. He urges readers to make the right choices ('Doo after the good and leve the evyl') and he reminds them that the whole point of reading should be to learn how 't'exersyse and folowe vertue'. But his prefatory exhortations cannot alter the fact that Malory has left the didactic worth of his book 'to the creative action of the reader' (Kirk 288).

In this book I have argued that medieval readers would have seen in Malory's book an epic of their own culture, with its different and sometimes conflicting ideologies of knighthood. They would have sympathized with the major protagonists according to their own ethical principles. But whatever their sympathies, they would have recognized, and learned from, the political errors made by Arthur, Gawain and Lancelot. Moreoever, within the Christian providentialist context of their culture and Malory's book, they would have realized that the Fall of Arthur was not inevitable. They would have realized that if all three protagonists, Arthur and Gawain as well as Lancelot, had been *happy* knights, at one with God through His grace, their *happyness* could have turned back the tide of *unhappynesse* caused by the malice of lesser men.

Notes

Preface to the Second Edition

1 'New-historicist' has since become something of an umbrella term; as Lee Petterson shows in his 'Critical Historicism and Medieval Studies' there are many disagreements among new-historicist critics as to both theory and method.
2 Internal evidence yields these facts about the author of *Le Morte Darthur:* his name was Sir Thomas Malory, therefore he was a knight; he was sometime in prison; and he completed his work in the ninth year of the reign of Edward IV, that is, sometime between 3 March 1469 and 4 March 1470. Three candidates have been proposed as author: Thomas Malory of Newbold Revell, Warwickshire (Field, 'Sir Thomas' and 'Thomas Malory' and 'Last Years'): Thomas Malory of Hutton and Studley, Yorkshire (Matthew, *Ill-Framed*; cf. Field 'Hutton Documents'); and Thomas Malory of Papworth St. Agnes, Cambridgeshire (Griffith, 'Authorship'). There are good reasons for thinking any one of these three men might have been the author, but the most persuasive arguments have been put forward by Field, who also shows that the Malorys had been of knightly rank for over three hunded and fifty years (Field, 'Sir Robert' 257).
3 Lee Patterson reviews the problem of recovering past meanings from medieval literature in his *Negotiating the Past*. And in *Aims of Representation*, Murray Krieger introduces a variety of essays grappling with the theoretical problem of relating subjects, texts and history.
4 The *MED* does not acknowledge this as a separable meaning; nevertheless, it does not seem to me to be adequately covered by any of their rubrics: 'the rank or status of a knight' (2a), 'a particular knightly order' (2b) or 'the knights as a class, the aristocracy' (2c).
5 Although Benson grants the possibility of more than one view of knightly ethics, he believes that the *Morte Darthur* exhibits one 'rigid code', which he calls the code of the 'High Order of Knighthood'. Moreover, he equates this code 'in its simplest aspect' with the oath which King Arthur's knights must swear each year at Pentecost (148–49; cf. Moorman, *Kings* 163–64).
6 Governance was a relatively new word at the time Malory was writing, at least in the sense of political rule, and Malory uses it only twice in this sense (246.18:V.12, 446.20:VIII.39). However, 'governance' was the word which Malory's contemporary, Sir John Fortescue, chose to denote what we would now call the government of England and, since the more modern word 'government' implies governing functions which did not enter into fifteenth-century political consciousness, I have chosen to use the earlier word to refer to Arthur's system of political rule.
7 Wendy Clein, who has more recently, and quite independently, undertaken a study of late medieval texts on chivalry in order to illuminate its meaning in *Sir Gawain and the Green Knight*, has also concluded that there were three different traditions or views of chivalry in the late medieval period. She identifies them

by the sources in which they are primarily to be found, i.e. the 'romance tradition', the 'heraldic' tradition and 'moralist views'.

8 In *Arthur's Kingdom of Adventure*, an admirable book which appeared too late for me to use in writing this study, Muriel Whitaker examines Malory's use of visual imagery with the iconographic expertise of an art historian, paying particular attention to two of these three settings: the 'perilous forest', the setting of the adventures of knight-errantry, and the castle, the setting of aristocratic social and political life.

9 Insofar as Malory's types also exist in his culture, they might be called distinct 'mentalités' in the tradition of the French annales school of medieval historians. The usefulness of this term has recently been questioned by the new French historians of culture who find it too 'unfocussed'. They find it better to focus upon discursive practice and upon textual 'representations of the social world', which they see also as 'constituents of social reality' (Hunt, 6, 7, 10).

10 Robert Kelly perceives a figural relationship between Arthur and Galahad and Deborah Signer has concluded that figuralism is a major structuring principle in the *Morte Darthur*.

11 In his *Ethical Poetic of the Later Middle Ages*, Judson Allen traces this ethical and normative concept of character back to Averroes' who, in translating Aristotle's *Poetics*, summed up *consuetudo*, 'actions in material reality' and *credulitas*, 'acts of mind of which the Truth is the measure and judge', (26) to produce *conditio*, or, in Middle English, *condicioun* (*MED* 3a–b). Chaucer employs the singular form 'condicioun' when speaking of his Canterbury pilgrims (*GP* I.38), but Malory prefers the plural form, 'conducyons'.

12 In his admirable book *Pastors and Visionaries: Religion and Secular Life in Late Medieval Yorkshire*, Jonathan Hughes shows that by the mid-fifteenth century the 'mixed life' was a popular notion among pious laymen (256). He has found a 'growing respect for practioners of the mixed life' in writings of the time, although he has to admit that the only evidence for its actual practice comes from literary texts, the Thornton manuscript being his best example. This finding must be of particular interest to Malory scholars. We can be fairly certain that Malory knew this manuscript, since he seems to have borrowed from it the Latin phrase, HIC IACET ARTHURUS, REX QUONDAM REXQUE FUTURUS (Lumiansky, 'Arthur's Final' 9–10). Therefore, Hughes' description of it as a book 'which would have served as a rule on the mixed life for the Thornton family and their neighbours' (296) suggests a possible source for Malory's characterization of Lancelot.

13 Lancelot's convulsive weeping afterwards is a sign that he has been overwhelmed by the indwelling of the Holy Spirit. Therefore his experience may be seen as a sign of God's forgiveness, for, according to Richard Rolle, mystical ecstasy is "the only secure sign of God's forgiveness" (*Judica Me Deus*, cited in Hughes 262).

14 The phrase is Lister Matheson's. Only the most educated of readers, most likely monks, would have known that William of Newburgh's twelfth-century chronicle expresses doubt regarding Arthur's existence because he is not mentioned in Bede. Other chroniclers doubted the truth of some of the wilder tales told about Arthur, but none doubted his existence. In this contxt, Matheson finds Caxton's little story concerning his doubts of Arthur's existence both 'unexpected and surprising' and theorizes that Caxton might have inserted it in his preface to the *Morte Darthur* in order to justify a rebuttal (264). Levine also finds Caxton's story 'unexpected and peculiar' (41).

15 To date only American critics have been willing to make much of Arthur's shortcomings as a king. In addition to myself, there are Robert Kelly and, most recently, Ginger Thornton. Stephen Knight recognizes that the *Morte Darthur* is about 'power in the real world' (xiv) but in his discussion of Malory he does not dwell on Arthur's political mistakes.

16 Most modern critics assume that Malory played down the adultery because he was embarrassed by Lancelot's sexual relationship with the queen. This is to assume that Malory was a prude, which he definitely was not; as Terence McCarthy has observed, his attitude towards sex is quite 'down-to-earth' (59). Like all critics, McCarthy nevertheless assumes that Lancelot and Guinevere's adultery goes on for some time behind the scenes, if not in the Tale of Lancelot, then in the Tale of Tristram, since he reads the Grail book to mean that 'the lovers are guilty' (46). In her study of Malory's Grail romance, Dhira Mahoney has observed that most critics of Malory's text are so 'obsessed with the theme of adultery' that they 'do not seem to notice that neither in the French nor in the English [Malory's] Quests is adultery the main issue' (118).

17 It is possible that some of Malory's readers, and even Malory himself, could have encountered the episode in a form separate from the chronology of the Vulgate cycle, the short prose romance entitled *Le Conte de la charrette*. According to Fanni Bogdanow, both the Charrette episode of the Vulgate *Lancelot* and this short romance are prose renderings of Chrétien de Troyes' verse romance (*Romance* 6).

Chapter 1

1 In her analysis of Malory's political *sen* Elizabeth Pochoda overlooks the treatises on chivalry and makes use of the Latin legists, Bracton and Glanvill, instead. At the same time, she does not see any reason 'to try to prove that Malory was capable of or interested in working out the intricate legal theory which accompanied the political writing of his time' (32).

2 Lull's treatise was not the only one to put forward the religious view of knighthood, either. It was simply the most comprehensive and influential among a number of late medieval works which perceived the knight as a *miles christi* ordained by God to do justice on earth. The most interesting and important of them are *Le chevaler Dé*, an Anglo-Norman poem of the late thirteenth century; *Le songe du Vieil Pélerin*, by Phillipe de Mézières, who dreamed of a chivalric order which would not only inject new vigour into the crusades but would also establish order in the countryside by suppressing *routiers*; and two fifteenth-century works, Alain Chartier's *Le breviaire des nobles*, which is based on Lull, and Olivier de la Marche's *Le chevalier délibéré* (1486) which was translated into English in the sixteenth century as *The Resolved Gentleman* by Lewis Lewkanor (1594). Two other fifteenth-century works also seem to fit in this category. They have not yet been edited and published but they are summarized in recent scholarly articles: Jean de Courcy's *Chemin de vaillance*, summarized by Wenzel; and Richard Ullerston's *De officio militari*, summarized by Bornstein ('Reflections').

3 Maurice Keen points out that the French words *chevalier* and *chevalerie* became very ambiguous in the later Middle Ages. *Chevalier* could refer either to the (inherited) noble rank of the knight or to his (chosen) vocation in the government and/or military service and *chevalerie* could bear virtually the same meaning as *noblesse* (*Chivalry* 145). Of course knighthood as such was never inheritable on the continent, but, as Keen observes, both Bartolus of Sassoferrato and Oliver de la Marche assume that knighthood 'automatically' confers nobility upon a man and his heirs (150).

4 There is no reason to suppose that Caxton knew any of these translations of Christine's *Epistle*; however, he most probably knew her work in French since it seems to have been widely available, having survived in forty-six different manuscripts. Indeed, in one manuscript compiled for Edward IV (B.M. MS Royal 14 E ii) it exists in company with a French translation of Lull's treatise, as though the compiler of the manuscript (or Edward himself) regarded the two works as complementary. However, the decision to translate and print Lull's treatise rather than Christine's was probably not Caxton's decision at all but that of his anonymous patron, 'a gentyl and noble Esquyer', very probably of the Woodville faction at court (Blake 94). Indeed, it is quite possible that this same anonymous patron was one of those 'many noble and dyvers gentylmen' who urged Caxton to publish Malory's *Morte Darthur* the next year.

5 It is not possible to determine which treatises on chivalry Malory actually read. Like his contemporary, John Paston, he may have owned both

Ramon Lull's 'Book of Knighthood' and Christine de Pizan's 'de Othea' (Bennett 261). But whatever the state of his personal library, it is hard to believe that a man so widely read in Arthurian literature would not have read the standard treatises on knighthood, as well.

6 Pochoda provides a useful summary of this theory in her second chapter, 'Medieval Political Theory and the Arthurian Legend'.

7 Shaw lists all the knights 'of the Bath' of whom there is a record (1:109ff), and also offers a useful history of the Order (1:x–xxi).

8 There is a very similar description of the ritual of the Bath in Viscount Dillon's study of the ordinances of chivalry belonging to Lord Hastings (67–69), also reproduced as Appendix VI in Winkler (324–29).

9 According to Winkler (118), the making of knights had not yet become a royal prerogative in Lancastrian England. This is confirmed by the fact that Shaw lists many 'knights Bachelors' dubbed by great lords, usually on the field of battle, during the third quarter of the fifteenth-century (2:12–23).

10 These references are as follows: King Arthur knights his nephew Gawain and Tor (101.33–34:III.4), La Cote Male Tayle (460.29:IX.1), Percival (611.12:X.23), Lancelot (1058.23–24:XVIII.7) and Mellyagaunt (1122.11–12: XIX.2); Lancelot knights Galahad (854.28:XIII.1). Equally significant in this regard is that when Malory finds a more complete description of a religious ritual of knighting, as he does in the French prose *Tristan*, he omits it (379.11:VIII.5; cf. *Tristan* 1.149).

11 Lancelot gives the same reason for his reluctance to take up arms against Arthur on two other occasions (1187.27:XX.11; 1192.18:XX.13). Gawain also refers to this special bond between them in his letter begging Lancelot to come to Arthur's rescue (1231.27:XXI.2) and so does Lancelot, in response to Gawain's letter (1249.18:XXI.8).

12 For a discussion of Lancelot's and Gareth's religious attitudes towards the vocation of knighthood see Chapter 3, pp. 111–21, 139–44, and for a discussion of the more secular and careerist attitudes of a knight like Tristram, see Chapter 4, pp. 150–2, 175–7.

13 The orders founded by John the Good and Philip the Good were in fact much larger. John's Order of the Star consisted of two hundred knights and Philip's Order of the Golden Fleece, initially modelled upon the Order of the Garter and consisting of twenty four knights, was soon increased to fifty (Barber, *Knight* 303–07).

14 Maintenance in this sense could, and frequently did, produce serious abuses of the royal system of justice in the fifteenth-century (Lander, *Conflict* 175–80). Indeed, Malory points to the possibility of such abuse in his handling of an episode in the tale of Tristram (777:X.85). See Chapter 4, pp. 200–1.

15 Arthur receives new knights into the Round Table fellowship at the end of the Tale of Gareth (362–63:VII.36), at the end of 'La Cote Male Tayle' (476.11–13:IX.8) and at the end of 'The Healing of Sir Urry' (1153.20–24: XIX.13). Each of these occasions is probably Malory's own invention, although one cannot be certain about the Tale of Gareth.

16 Since 1285 the penalty for rape in England had in fact been 'a judgment of

life and member', even if the woman herself was content not to sue (Pollock & Maitland 2:491). What is more, one of the manuscripts of the fifteenth-century 'seremons et ordonnances' of the knights of the Round Table also adds the injunction that no knight should 'prandre ne toucher nulle Dame ne damoiselle proposant quilz leussent conquise de force darmes si elle ny prenoit plaisir et que elle y fut consentante' (Sandoz 402).

17 Squibb points out that in England the High Court of Chivalry was necessary in order to be able to try cases of alleged treason which had been committed abroad and hence did not come under the common law; 'however it tended to encroach upon civil jurisdiction of common law courts and attempted to obtain jurisdiction over appeals of treason and homicide committed within the realm' (25).

18 The last treason duel of chivalry to be fought in England took place in the year 1447 (Neilson 201). In Scotland the treason duel of chivalry endured much longer: Neilson cites cases from the years 1532, 1537, and 1548 (291–97).

19 The last recorded battle to be fought between an approver and his appellee took place in London in 1456 (Bellamy, *Crime* 132); however, the common law right to trial by battle endured until 1819 when it was finally removed by statute (Neilson 328–31).

20 Honoré de Bonet gives a brief summary of the arguments against 'wager of battle' according to 'divine law, the law of nations, the law of decretals, and civil law' (195–96) before he goes on to discuss those cases in which it is permissible, nevertheless, according to 'certain laws which are extraordinary'. He lists sixteen of these exceptional cases, including what we would now call both grand and petty treason, murder, adultery and perjury (196–98).

21 Given both men's intentions, Arthur's to do justice and Accolon's to commit treason by murdering his liege lord, a devout providentialist would certainly conclude that God had rendered a true judgement that day, using Arthur as his instrument. On the providentialist view, see Chapter 5, pp. 216–7, 231–3.

22 In the second chapter of his ground-breaking work, *Religion and the Decline of Magic*, Keith Thomas has applied the usual anthropological distinction between magic and religion to popular Christian belief and practice during the late Middle Ages and concluded that late medieval religion had a strong admixture of magic ('The Magic of the Medieval Church').

23 The only time Malory uses 'affinité' it seems to mean 'kinship of any kind' (1055.13:XVIII.6; *MED* 1b).

24 William Matthews has argued persuasively that only the author, Malory himself, could have made the Caxton revision of the narrative of the Roman campaign (*Caxton's Malory* 618). A particularly good and comprehensive over-view of the functioning of the royal retinue under Edward IV is provided by Morgan who remarks in passing that the *Morte Darthur* is a work 'apposite to the politics of affinity' (23).

25 A lively account of the 'scramble' for 'good lordship' in this sense is provided by Kendall (185ff).

26 In the course of disputing the Lancastrian bias usually attributed to the *Morte Darthur*, Richard Griffith ('Political') has argued that Malory makes Arthur resemble Edward IV.

Chapter 2

1 See Chapter 5 for a more extended discussion of providentialism in the *Morte Darthur*. For a concise summary of Puritan providentialism, which is much more predestinarian because of the Puritans' denial of the efficacy of good works, see chapter 4 of Thomas.

2 Morton Bloomfield likens the meaning of knightly adventure in medieval romance to the meaning of medieval sacral ordeals: 'It is the victory of grace over reason, Augustinianism over Pelagianism, of the supernatural over the natural' (107). In this regard it is noteworthy that he rates the *Morte Darthur* as 'a great and enduring masterpiece' of romance literature 'which generates the powerful sense of mystery characteristic of romance' (110).

3 Julian Pitt-Rivers has shown that 'a man commits his honour only through his sincere intentions' (32). Therefore, if Gawain did not mean initially to keep his promise to Pelleas, then he is not dishonoured by his subsequent betrayal. However, if he did mean to keep his promise, and Malory has given us absolutely no reason to suspect any mental reservations on Gawain's part — he had not yet seen the fair Ettarde, after all — then Gawain is not only dishonoured by the secular standards of the honourable society, he is also dishonoured by the religious standards of the High Order of Knighthood and is not 'worthy to be in thordre of Chyualry' (Lull 54; Hay 32).

4 Anthropologists are still unsure of the reason for the unusual closeness between mother's brother and sister's son in patrilineal societies. It may be the vestige of an earlier matrilineal social organization, or it may simply be the recognition of a blood bond which can never be questioned (as it can in the case of a father and son). The only studies of this nearest and dearest of male kinship relationships in European literature are both quite old (Gummere and Bell), and the subject would seem to deserve another look in view of more recent anthropological theory and research.

5 Malory has deviated from his French source in order to give Gawain such a decided edge for such a long period of time. According to the *Suite du Merlin*, Gawain's strength merely 'doubloit . . . entour heure de miedi' (2:239); however, this was sufficient to ensure that he overcame all the opponents he ever faced in his life, except for six. Malory's alteration, not only emphasizes the superiority of those knights who are able to beat Gawain, but also stresses the extent to which King Arthur favours his nephew. The late fourteenth-century 'Ordenaunce and Fourme of Fightyng Within Listes' assumes that all trials by battle to be fought before the King or his Constable will begin at nine o'clock in the morning, and

that if the appellant fails to appear by noon, he will lose his appeal (311–313). Near the end of his long work Malory will explain that King Arthur made 'an ordynaunce' that all trials by battle to be fought before him should begin 'at undern', i.e. at 9 a.m., so that 'by lyklyhode if sir Gawayne were on the tone parte, he shulde have the bettir in batayle whyle hys strengthe endured three owrys' (1217.2–7:XX.21). See Chapter 6 pp. 325–6.

6 In his interpretation of the alliterative *Morte Arthur* William Matthews sees the heroic figure of Gawain as a type of Christ, sacrificing his life for his people (*Tragedy* 148–50).

7 Linda Paterson has argued that the earliest evidence in French literature of 'the Church attempting to sublimate the violence of the professional soldiers into the ideal of the Peace' (34) occurs in the Occitan epic, *Girart de Roussillon* (c.1150).

8 Since the phrase 'courtly love' has become so controversial among historians and critics I place it within inverted commas; however, until some other phrase finds general acceptance as denoting the idealisation of heterosexual love which originated in the courts of the late twelfth century, I shall continue to use it. For a summary of the controversy, see Boase.

9 In *Love and Marriage in the Age of Chaucer* H. A. Kelly has argued forcefully against the idea that 'courtly love' was from the beginning essentially immoral and antimatrimonial (31–99); however, his argument is for the most part theoretical, not practical, based on literature and law rather than life.

10 In 'Malory's Lancelot: "Trewest Lover, of a Synful Man" ' I have argued at length that this is precisely what Malory did.

11 For a review of other critical solutions to this moral paradox see my 'Malory's Lancelot' (454–55).

12 Adultery with the wife of one's liege Lord had always been regarded as treason by feudal law. However, Edward III's statue of 1352 distinguished adultery with the sovereign's wife as 'high' treason (Bellamy, *Treason* 87).

Chapter 3

1 A Sir Thomas Malory served with the Yorkist forces in the north of England in the autumn of 1462, but he is not likely to have made any friendly contact with a Scottish nobleman. It is much more likely that a Sir Thomas Malory had occasion to meet the Scottish ambassadors who came to London in early October, 1463. William, Earl of Orkney, was among them and they remained at Edward's court some time (Schofield 1:207, 214).

2 Henry of Lancaster wrote *Le Livre des Seynts Medicenes*, a confessional treatise organized around the seven deadly sins. Sir John Clanvowe wrote 'The Two Ways' a homily on the contrast between the sinful way of the world and the way of the true Christian.

3 In a letter dated 9 March 1983, R. W. Griffith has suggested to me that Malory modeled his characterization of Lancelot upon Anthony Wydville, his friend and patron.

4 The concept of knighthood as a 'hyghe Ordir' is religous in origin (see chapter 1 pp. 13–16). Those who refer to knighthood in this way in the *Morte Darthur* are either True or Worshipful knights (never Heroic knights), women or holy men. Consultation of Kato's *Concordance* and Vinaver's critical apparatus to the *Works* reveals that thirteen of the total sixteen usages seem to be original with Malory (including two from the Tale of Gareth); the three which are not come from the *Queste del Saint Graal*.

5 Malory refers briefly to the legend in recounting the begetting of Galahad (796.32–33:XI.3). As Holbrook notes in her fine article this is the only reference to the 'Lady of the Lake' which cannot be linked certainly either to the lady who gave Arthur his sword or to Nyneve. However, Holbrook argues persuasively that it must refer to Nyneve, since Malory portrays her elsewhere as the protector of Lancelot (765).

6 In order to achieve this prominence, Malory has eliminated several episodes featuring other knights such as King Lott and the Earl of Antele. Vinaver attributes these omissions to Malory's wish for 'a more direct narrative' (*Works* 1369).

7 For a useful summary of the content of these military manuals, see Bornstein, *Mirrors* 23–45.

8 This idea is expressed in the alliterative *Morte* by Gawain's son, Florent (2743–44) and in the Winchester text by the pagan knight, Priamus (235.26–28:V.10), but it is completely eliminated from the Caxton revision. It is interesting to speculate that Malory himself may have eliminated it, not only because it is so at odds with the Christian definition of 'true nobility' as virtue, but also because it denies the upward mobility of bourgeois aspirants to knighthood.

9 The Thomist argument reached a wide audience through the Dominican Friar Laurent's popular treatise, *Somme des vices et vertus*, commonly known as *Somme le roi* (1279). This treatise was translated several times into Middle English, the most popular translation being *The Book of Vices and Virtues* in which the Thomist argument appears in the section devoted to the virtue of magnanimity (164–165).

10 In this regard, it is noteworthy that William Matthews based part of his argument for Malory's authorship of the Caxton revision of this tale upon characterization. Since some of the revisions affect the characterization of Arthur and Lancelot, Matthews concluded that only the author of the entire *Morte Darthur* is likely to have made them. Spisak summarizes Matthews' argument in his Introduction to their edition of *Caxton's Malory* (618).

11 The phrase 'betaughte (betoke, bytaught) unto God (Jesu Christ)' is used seven times in the *Morte*. Lancelot, Bors (974.28:XVI.17), Galahad (886.31:XIII.14) and a hermit (111.21:III.10) account for five of these. The other two are attributed to Pellinor, as he bids farewell to a knight he has

wounded (48.10:I.23) and Gawain, as he bids farewell to a hermit (892.23:XIII.16). Even more remarkable is the usage pattern of the phrase 'commaunde(d), commende(d) . . . to God'. This phrase is used sixteen time in the *Morte* and again all but two of the usages are spoken either by Lancelot (928.13:XV.2; 934.25:XV.6; 1019.33–34:XVII.17; 1137.1–2:XIX.8), or by the three Grail knights: Galahad (879.10:XIII.10; 890.11:XIII.15; 983.6:XVII.1; 1026.32–33:XVII.19; 1035.7–8,9:XVII.22); Percival (934.25–26: XV.6); Bors (962.24:XVI.10; 1004.32–33:XVII.11); or all three speaking at once (1000.11:XVII.9). It may be significant that Galahad is the only one of the Grail knights to use the phrase more frequently than Lancelot (six times to Lancelot's four). The other two usages are attributed to King Arthur, as he bids farewell to queen and courtiers on his way to France to meet the army of the Emperor Lucius (195.14: omitted in Caxton revision) and Gawain and Ector, as they bid farewell to a hermit (949.1:XVI.5).

12 In every other instance Malory qualifies the noun 'lyvyng' with an adjective denoting good or bad. In addition to the three passages already cited in this paragraph there are three more, two in which 'lyvyng' is qualified as 'good' (51.33:I.20 and 872.25:XIII.8) and one in which the removal of the Grail from Logres is explained by the 'evyll lyvyng' of the inhabitants (1030.28:XVII.20)

13 Kato's *Concordance* lists twenty-eight usages of the word 'paramour' ('peramour') and an analysis of these usages indicates that it always refers either to to a carnal relationship or to a relationship in which the lover(s) experience(s) strong sexual desire, as, for example, in the case of Palomides' unrequited and therefore unsatisfied love 'peramoures' for Isode (684.3:X.53).

In light of this conversation between Lancelot and the damsel, it is ironic that Guinevere should later comfort Isode for Tristram's infidelity in marrying Isode of the White Hands, by saying that Tristram 'was so noble a knyght called that by craftes of sorsery ladyes wolde make suche noble men to wedde them' (436.4–6:VIII.37).

14 There are five scenes in the Tale of Gareth involving such courtly pastimes as singing and dancing (320:VII.15, 331:VII.21, 335:VII.22, 346:VII.28, 362:VII.36). There is also one scene in the 'Tale of Balin' involving 'daunsynge and mynstralsye and alle maner of joye' (88.16:II.17) and one in the Tale of Tristram at the court of King Mark where Elyas the harper sings at the 'grete feste' celebrating the defeat of the Saxons (626.19–20: X.31).

15 Sir Gilbert Hay's version of this passage does not make this point so clearly. In fact, Hay strengthens the analogy between knighthood and priesthood by presuming the only way a squire can be deceived 'of his ordre' is to be dubbed by a lord who is not himself a knight (42–43; see also Chapter 1 pp. 30–32). In other words, Hay presumes that the 'grace' of knighthood passes from one knight to another *ex opere operato*, regardless of the moral virtue of the donor, just as it does in the priesthood. However, Hay's interpretation is not shared by his Scottish successor, Adam Loutfut, who bases his text on Caxton's printed translation of Lull.

Byles prints Loutfut's text beneath Caxton's and includes this note in the margin: 'þat he suld be a knycht of gud lif & without repruf þat suld gif thordre of cheualry or mak a knycht' (Lull 73). The example of Gareth suggests that Hay's interpretation is not shared by Malory, either.

16 In view of Lancelot's behaviour at the knighting of Gareth, it may at first appear surprising that later he does not insist on knowing the identity of the Fair Unknown (Galahad) whom twelve nuns ask him to knight. One cannot explain his reticence as a consequence of Malory's following his source in every detail, for, in fact, Malory omits Bors' part in the knighting ceremony and adds Lancelot's question, 'Commyth thys desyre of hymselff?' whereupon Galahad and 'all they seyde "Yes" ' (854.10–23: XII.1). Malory must assume that Lancelot recognizes his son, just as he does when Galahad sits in the Siege Perilous (861.13–14:XIII.4; cf. *Queste* 9), and therefore does not need to ask his identity. But he does need to know whether or not Galahad himself desires to be knighted by his father. That he does in Malory's version and that Bors has no part in the knighting ceremony (in Malory's version) greatly strengthen the similarity between these two knighting scenes.

17 The phrase 'noble knight' is more elastic of meaning than the phrase 'good knight', but it is less commonly used in the *Morte Darthur* (almost 250 usages). It is frequently used in the sense which Sir Persaunte intends; however, in some contexts it seems to mean no more than 'good' in the sense of a 'good fighter', whereas in others it seems to refer primarily to birth and social status. For example, in the passage under discussion Lynet calls Ironside a 'noble knyght' but immediately qualifies the meaning of 'noble' by adding the phrase 'of proues' (320.18:VII.15). When she goes on to describe him as 'a lorde of grete londis and of grete possessions' she suggests the other way in which he might be considered 'noble' but which also has nothing necessarily to do with the courtly virtues.

On the other hand, the phrase 'good knight' always refers to a man's prowess, even when it is used of Galahad, for it calls attention to his invincibility. Malory may well have adopted this style of usage from the French romancers who typically use 'bonté' to refer to the sum of a knight's fighting abilities; e.g. in the *Tristan* Gauvain seeks the conqueror of Dolorous Garde 'por la bonte de li' and admires the prowess ('bonte de chevalerie') that he has seen Tristan exercise (338). Gervase Mathew cites Chandos Herald to the effect that it is the possession of prowess which merits the appelation 'bon chevalier' (118), and Malory's own usage is unambiguous on that score. For example, every time Lancelot is called a 'good knight' the context makes clear that the reference is not to his moral and religious virtues but to his fighting ability. The most telling example, because it is completely original with Malory, comes from the conversation between Lancelot and a damsel in search of protection. The damsel says to Lancelot, '. . . thou semyst well to be a good knyght, and yf thou dare mete with a good knyght I shall brynge the where is the beste knyght and the myghtyeste that ever thou founde' (264.17–20:VI.7). The other 'good knyght' in question is the giant Sir Tarquin. For other examples, see

276.20:VI.12, 396.17–19:VIII.15, 407.13–19:VIII.21, 427.9–13:VIII.32, 509.28–32:IX.25.

18 Unlike the other two knights, Gareth does not perform any further judicial acts. He does not, for example, offer recompense to the widows for their grievances or restore the castle to its rightful owner; however, there has been no indication that the Brown Knight does not hold his castle 'of right', and there can be no full recompense for widowhood. It is tempting to speculate that Malory gave Gareth widows to rescue, rather than ladies and damsels, or virgins, because it was more appropriate to the type of True knighthood he exemplifies, he being the only one of the three who becomes a wedded man.

19 Malory leaves unanswered the question of who rules Benwick in Lancelot's absence after the death of King Ban; he also leaves unspecified the time of King Ban's death. However, we may infer that at some time Lancelot deliberately renounces lordship (appointing regents, if necessary) for, even after Arthur has exiled him from England and he is forced to return to France, he still chooses not to rule his lands. Malory tells us at this point that Lancelot 'was lorde of all Fraunce and of all the londis that longed unto Fraunce', a fact which Malory attributes to Lancelot's 'noble proues'. However, rather than take up this lordship, Lancelot shares it among Bors, Lyonell and Ector, making Ector 'prynce of them all' and leaving nothing for himself. Although Malory does not remark upon it, Lancelot is here acting like a man who has determined to renounce the world altogether (1204–1205:XX.18), apparently because he can no longer serve Arthur.

20 For example, in the *Tristan* Gareth (Gaheriet) accompanies Marhalt to Cornwall (1:147) and it is he rather than Gaheris (Gueherres) who kills Margawse (Löseth, par. 256).

Chapter 4

1 No chivalric literature of the late medieval period could be perfectly 'realistic' regarding the politics and business of court life. As Richard Firth Green has observed of Antoine de la Sale's biography of Jehan de Saintré, it is 'at best, a fictional oversimplification' (45) although it 'remains one of the most vivid, realistic, and entertaining pictures of court life in the late middle ages' (39).

2 In the French prose *Tristan* this competitive aspect of the feudal and courtly ideal of knighthood is incorporated into the customs of the Round Table fellowship. Löseth reports that it was the custom never to admit a new 'compagnon' unless his name appeared on the seat destined for him and unless he was 'meilleur chevalier que son prédécesseur' (206).

3 This structure is not precisely the same as the tri-partite structure identified by Lewis and Nancy Owen. Their part one, 'Tristram the young hero and lover', and mine correspond precisely, concluding with 'The

Round Table'. However, the Owens' second part, 'Mark's villainy', includes only 'King Mark', 'Alexander the Orphan' and the 'The Tournament at Surluse', whereas I find that Malory continues to focus upon the courtly virtues of Worshipful knighthood right through 'Joyous Garde', the 'Tournament at Lonezep' and 'Sir Palomides' and that he does not adopt the religious point of view until 'Launcelot and Elaine'.

4 Merlin tells the northern rebels that Arthur is the legitimate son of Uther just before the Battle of Bedgrayne (17–18:I.8), but Arthur's royal parentage is not publicly revealed, not even to himself, until much later (43–45:I.20–21).

5 According to Pollock and Maitland, battle by champions was customary in a Writ of Right, whereas in an appeal of felony battle had to be offered by the appellant's own body (2:632). That may explain why the King of Ireland does not come in his own person to defend his right to tribute from Cornwall and why it never occurs to King Mark to answer in his own person. However, that solution would never have done for Arthur, since it allows the suspicion of personal cowardice.

6 As the most courtly knight of the three, however, Gareth seems to be just as aware of the positive value of winning worship as he is of the negative value of acting shamefully (cf. 321.2–7:VII.15).

7 In Malory's source for this episode, Tristan prays for victory in a night-long vigil preceding the combat (Löseth 28). By eliminating this particularly Christian trapping of ritual trial by combat, Malory succeeds in highlighting his Tristram's primitive and tribal attitude towards the impending trial.

8 By comparison with Richard II, his grandfather Edward III was an exceptionally strong monarch, especially after the Battle of Crécy, and his reputation as an 'arbiter of chivalry' was such that in 1350 Thomas de la Marche, the Bastard of France, and John Visconti presented themselves at his court and demanded to settle their quarrel before him. Needless to say, the Bastard's half-brother, King John, was incensed that Thomas should have taken his quarrel for judgment before the English king (Barnie 85).

9 The argument which follows is a considerably expanded version of the argument I first made in 'Malory's Lancelot' (419–22).

10 Arthur's meeting with Guinevere during his visit to Camylarde ('and ever afftir he loved hir') is Malory's invention (39.16–18:I.18) according to Vinaver, who cites R. H. Wilson's research (*Works* 1296), and so is the conditional betrothal which precedes Tristram's first departure from Ireland (392.13–16:VIII.12; cf. *Tristan* 2:352–3).

11 Malory has altered his source considerably to achieve this effect. The talking-in-a-window scene 'voiant toz' is also in his source — in fact, the lovers are talking about Lancelot and Guinevere (*Tristan* 2:513) — but it is not this minor indiscretion which provokes the king's anger. It is the following scene, which Malory omits, in which Tristan and the queen are surprised in the king's bedroom and, thanks to Governal's warning, Tristan 'se trest ensus de la roin' before Mark rushes in, sword in hand

(2:514). Malory also omits the two other failed attempts to trap Tristan and Iseult *in flagrante delicto* (*Tristan* 2:531–33)

12 For a systematic study of the way Malory has handled the characterization of these two kings, by comparison with his sources, see E. D. Kennedy, 'Malory's King Mark and King Arthur'.

13 In 'The Arthur-Guenevere Relationship in Malory's *Morte Darthur*,' E. D. Kennedy has shown how Malory systematically altered several of his sources in order to portray this cooling off of Arthur's love for Guinevere.

14 Malory would have been sensitive to the reciprocal nature of the feudal law of treason, not only because it is so clearly illustrated in his thirteenth-century French sources, but also because it still informed the fifteenth-century English constitution through the concept of the limited monarchy. In *The Law of Treason*, J. G. Bellamy contends that the Roman law concept of 'lese majesty' never supplanted the feudal concept of treason in England (11).

15 It is not at all clear when this juncture is. Malory's remarks regarding Tristram's absence on the Roman campaign suggest that this tale as well as the tales of Lancelot and Gareth and some part of the Tale of Tristram ought to be read as retrospective narrative, but then in the opening passages of the Tale of Tristram he clearly dates Tristram's birth after Arthur has gained overlordship 'unto Roome' (371.19:VIII.1). Both of these passages are original with Malory, but the first occurs in a tale which we know was revised, either by Malory himself or by Caxton. Therefore it seems reasonable to me to give it greater authority, in thematic terms at least, since Ellyn Olefsky has shown that it is not possible to develop a perfectly consistent chronology for the *Morte Darthur* on the basis of the text(s) which have come down to us.

16 We have already seen how close is the relationship between Gareth and Lancelot. In the Tale of Tristram Malory suggests that Dinadan's friendship with Lancelot is even more intimate. Dinadan is the only knight in whom Lancelot confides that King Mark has sent a letter to Arthur alleging that Lancelot and the queen are adulterers. Dinadan suggests to his friend that he ought to revenge himself for Mark's villany by sending a harper into Cornwall and he himself offers to compose the song to be sung before the Cornish court (617.34–618.12:X.26–27).

17 Malory's account of the marriage negotiations makes fairly clear that Guinevere's wishes were not consulted in the matter (97–98:III.1), just as his account of the negotiations between Tristram and Anguishaunce suggests that Isode's wishes were never considered when making the decision to give her to King Mark (411.19–37:VIII.24). However, Malory's version of the conversation between Merlin and Arthur preceding the negotiations shows that Arthur knew beforehand that Guinevere and Lancelot were destined to love each other, and that this knowledge did not alter his purpose to make her his wife (97.29–31:III.1; cf. B. Kennedy, 'Malory's Lancelot' 444–45).

18 For a discussion of Lancelot's killings in the Tale of Lancelot, including a detailed comparison of his behaviour in the French prose romance and in

Malory, see Chapter 3 pp. 116–21. The only passage in the early part of the Tale of Tristram which casts doubt upon Lancelot's former protection against manslaughter is a statement by Mordred to the effect that as a young knight Lancelot was often 'put to the worse on horsebacke, but ever uppon foote he recoverde his renowne and slew and defowled many knyghtes of the Rounde Table' (466.24–26:IX.4). Since this passage seems to be original with Malory, it is especially important to understand what it means. First, it is just as likely that 'slew' means 'struck down' as that it means 'killed'. In the Roman campaign Malory describes how the Round Table knights 'slew hem downe' (209.11–12:V.6), and in the Quest, he refers to a man recently killed as having been 'dedly slayne' (909.9–10: XIV.4). Second, Malory frequently uses 'defoyled' in its literal sense of 'covered with mud' as a consequence of being struck down in battle (29.5:I.14) or tournament (349.17:VII.30; cf. 539.9:IX.37 and 864.31:XIII.6), or, as in the case of Marhalt's shield, of having had 'mire' thrown upon it (159.32:IV.17). The metaphorical usages ('defoyled with shame', 62.20:II.1; 'defoyled with falsehed', 528.30:IX.32; and, 'defoyled in dedly synne', 947.26:XVI.4) as well as the use of 'defoyle' to denote defloration (315.10:VII.12 and 968.16:XVI.13) derive from this literal sense. And finally, one must note that the only other time Malory uses 'slew' in a collocation, it clearly means 'struck (or hewed) down': 'a grete ost . . . brent and slewe and distroyed clene byfore hem bothe the citeis and castels, that hit was pité to here' (126.35–36:IV.2). Thus, we may conclude that the collocation 'slew and defowled' could very well mean 'struck down and mired in mud'.

The alternative reading, 'killed and shamed', is possible only if one understands that some of the knights were 'killed' and others were 'shamed' by being defeated. However, Malory doesen't normally use 'and' when he means 'either/or', and the only way in which 'slew and defowled' could mean 'killed *and* shamed' is if one pictures Lancelot first killing and then defiling the bodies of his victims. This is so far from the behaviour one would expect of Lancelot that one's first impulse is to discredit the statement and question its source. Mordred is, after all, Lancelot's mortal enemy. His hatred will not become widely known until later, after the murder of Lamorak; however, there is no reason to believe that he is kindly disposed towards Lancelot now. In fact, Malory encourages us to suspect that he is not, by having Mordred leave the company of the damsel Maledysaunte as soon as Lancelot appears, which is something he does not do in Malory's source (467.22–23:IX.5). Of course, had Mordred remained, and had Lancelot overheard and taken exception to his words, Mordred could always say that he did not mean that Lancelot killed and defiled the bodies of his opponents, only that he knocked them down in the mud.

19 Maureen Fries has observed that Lancelot's quest for Tristram is a parody of his quest in the Tale of Lancelot ('Tragic Patterns' 88). In her analysis of Tristram as a 'counter-hero' created by Malory to contrast with Lancelot, she emphasizes Tristram's 'sexual immoderation and uncurbed force' (612)

as the two qualities which especially mark that contrast, although she also notes his betrayals of ' "trew love" ' by contrast with the 'virtuous love' which characterizes Lancelot in the third tale (608).

20 He eliminates the picture of a knight and lady 'qui s'entrebaisoient' on the shield meant for Lancelot which Sir Bruynys sanz Pité intercepts (405:VIII.20–21); he eliminates the ring which Guinevere gave Lancelot 'par druerie' and which Morgan steals and sends to the king as proof of his wife's infidelity (*Tristan* 2:467); and he eliminates the description of the room in Morgan's castle where Tristram has occasion to sleep one night (553:IX.41) and which contains the murals which Lancelot painted in captivity, detailing the history of his love affair with the queen (Löseth 190). Since, in his version, the 'Knight of the Cart' episode occurs after the Grail quest rather than before, Malory also omits the *Tristan*'s reference to it and replaces it with a reference to Lancelot's rescue of Gawain, instead (418–19:VIII.28).

21 The only exception to this rule occurs during the 'Launcelot and Elaine' section when Lancelot picks up a spear and kills a wild boar, but on this occasion he is, quite literally, out of his mind (821.10:XII.3). See also Chapter 6, pp. 309–10.

22 They come close to doing battle when Lancelot denounces Lamorak for being disloyal to Guinevere (487:IX.14), but otherwise, even when they meet as knights-errant, neither challenges the other (499.1–10:VIII.40; 485.30–33:IX.13). In the *Tristan*, however, they joust after Lancelot has unhorsed sir Froll (Löseth 64).

23 In order to achieve this parallelism, Malory has had to alter two sources. In the *Lancelot* Lancelot does not attempt to reconcile with Tarquin (85.42), and in the *Tristan* Lamorak neither asks for nor receives forgiveness. Rather, he asks either for life or death, according to Belinant's will, for he knows he deserves death and yet hopes for life (*Tristan* 2:632).

24 Muriel Bradbrook has observed that Malory's 'very strong sense' of the fellowship of knights is what 'enables him to rise to the heights of the last two books' (23) and, while discussing the final tragedy under the rubric, 'All the Love That Ever Was Betwixt Us', Mark Lambert has observed that the love between lover and mistress in Malory's world is not 'radically different from love of brother and brother or lord and knight' (211).

25 Although Gawain and Gaheris would not call it murder, we know that, judged by the standards of Worshipful knighthood, they did not kill Pellinor 'knyghtly' but rather 'shamefully', two against one. Gaheris boasts of this to Lamorak (612.26–27:X.24) and later, during the Quest, Percival's aunt and mother confirm that Pellinor was 'thorow outerageousnes slayne' (905.24:XIV.1), 'nat manly, but by treson' (810.11–13:XI.10).

26 Lamorak learns of the death of his father from Gaheris who, after killing Margawse boasts that he and his brother Gawain have also slain Pellinor (611.26–27:X.23). Lamorak does not long survive his father and his lover. When Gawain learns that Gaheris has slain their mother but let Lamorak go free, he is furious (613.9–11:X.24) and therefore we may presume that the brethren seize the next opportunity which presents itself to kill him.

We never see Lamorak again after the tournament of Surluse, so we may assume that it was either 'at his departynge' from this tournament or one which occurred soon after that Gawain and his brothers 'mette hym ... and wyth grete payne ... slewe hym felounsly' (688.8–10:X.54).

27 At the tournament of Surluse Galahalt urges Palomides to be baptized, assuring him that then 'all knyghtes woll sette the more be you' (666.23–24). His meaning is made even more clear in the Caxton text in which he adds, 'and say more worship by yow' (X.47).

28 This has been the pattern for the conduct of great battles between Worshipful knights throughout the Tale of Tristram. It requires that the more courteous of the two combatants be the first to suggest that they stop fighting if their 'quarellys ar nat grete'. The pattern is first established in the battle between Marhalt and Gawain (161.16–17:IV.18–19; see Chapter 2 pp. 70–71), and is then repeated exactly in the battles between Lancelot and Gareth (299:VII.4), Tristram and Lamorak (483:IX.11), and Lancelot and Tristram (569:X.5), and in modified form in the battle between Palomides and Lamorak (602–3:X.5).

29 Brewer has observed that honour 'may be said to be the strongest single motivationg force in the society which Malory creates' (*Morte* 25) and Lambert attributes a 'shame-orientation' to Malory himself (198).

Chapter 5

1 In his introduction to the collection of essays entitled *The Pursuit of Holiness in Late Medieval and Renaissance Religion*, Charles Trinkhaus asserts that there is an 'underlying unity' in this period 'characterized by a fervent piety and a merging of the sacred and profane' particularly in the North of Europe and in Italy (xi). John Bossy's review article on this volume is particularly suggestive and enlightening as to what the practice of religion probably meant to the common man during the pre-reformation period. On the manifestations of lay piety in late medieval England see the last two chapters in DuBoulay's *Age of Ambition* and J. R. Lander's survey, 'Religious Life', which takes the most recent scolarship into account in *Government and Community* (105–51).

2 On the widespread influence of Rolle and Hilton see Knowles's *English Mystical Tradition*, Allen's preface to her edition of Rolle's *English Writings*, and Helen Gardner's essay on Hilton. Hilton's 'Epistle on Mixed Life' was widely read in the fifteenth-century along with his *Scale of Perfection* which, by the time of its first printing in 1494, had become a 'devotional classic' (Knowles 118). G. W. Owst argues that the 'extraordinary extent' of Rolle's influence is 'better realized' in the sermon literature of the fifteenth-century: 'hardly an English homily of the new century lacked some affinity' with the work of Rolle and his followers (*Preaching* 116).

3 In this regard it is interesting to note that both Hilton's 'Epistle on Mixed Life' and two of Rolle's brief treatises, 'Desyre and Delit' and the 'Bee and

the Stork' (in both of which Rolle stresses the difficulty of achieving 'stableness') are in the Thornton manuscript (*English Writings* 38 and Milosh 35). This manuscript also contains the sole surviving copy of the alliterative *Morte Arthure* and William Matthews has argued that it is the copy which Malory actually used while writing his Tale of Arthur and Lucius (*Ill-Framed* 89–99.) If Malory did read the entire Thornton manuscript, then he must have been aware of both possible explanations for Lancelot's decision not to forsake 'the vanytees of the worlde' in the Quest of the Holy Grail: that, like Bors, Lancelot could not abandon his temporal obligation to serve Arthur in the world (Hilton's advice), or that he simply could not give up all thoughts of his lady, Guinevere (Rolle's fear). Both explanations have survived textually, the former in Caxton ('had not youre lord ben' XXI.9) and the latter in the Winchester manuscript ('had nat youre love bene' 1253.14).

4 According to Kato's *Concordance* Malory used the phrase 'hygh ordre of knighthode' sixteen times. A check of Vinaver's critical apparatus reveals that eleven of the sixteen (not counting the two from the Tale of Gareth) are original with Malory. It is worth noting that the last two — the only instances after the Quest — are both spoken by Lancelot (1058.24:XVIII.7 and 1189.18:XX.II). Malory also uses the phrase 'ordre of knyghthode' fifteen times: one each in the tales of Arthur and Lancelot, both without warrant from his sources, three in the Tale of Gareth, four in the Quest, and six in the Tale of Tristram, 'most' of which, Vinaver assures us, are not to be found in his source (*Works* 1435).

5 The Caxton text has been 'corrected' to read 'her brother', even though it would appear that the Winchester text must be correct since, as Vinaver observes, Malory later specifies that Balin actually kills his brother 'with that unhappy swerd', i.e. with the sword he had from the damsel (*Works* 1321). However, as one of my students, Ian Sirota, has observed, both Caxton and Winchester could be correct if the sword-bearing damsel is Balin's and Balan's sister. This hypothesis cannot be proved from Malory's text, but it neatly resolves not only the textual difficulty but also the enigma regarding the motivations of the damsel and the Lady Lyle. What is more, it adds yet another parallel to the long list of parallels which invite comparison between Balin and Arthur: both knights suffer great misfortune because of an encounter with a sister whom they fail to recognize.

6 The argument of St Thomas Aquinas against the determinists was the same for both chance and free will: since both are limited to the space-time continuum in which man has his being, neither is annulled by God's providence, His 'seeing-forth' from the vantage point of eternity. Simultaneously, of course, the effects of both chance and free will remain part of God's providential design (*Providence and Predestination*). It was this Thomist argument which made possible that form of providentialism which is peculiar to the late Middle Ages and which John Bossy has described as 'federal' (see below pp. 231–2).

7 In the *Suite du Merlin* Merlin only asks Balin why he allowed 'que ceste

damoisele s'ochist?' and suggests afterwards that he was perhaps a bit slow ('lens') in responding, certainly much slower than he will be when he will strike 'le dolereus cop' (*Suite* 1:231).

8 Vinaver assumes that Merlin means 'that lady', too, although, as Kelly points out, he is mistaken in identifying her as the sword-bearing damsel (*Works* 1277; Kelly, 'Malory's "Tale of Balin" ' 91–2). Wright also accepts that 'the Dolorous Stroke punishes Balin for killing the lady who claims his head at Arthur's court' (45), that is, the Lady of the Lake. However, both Jill Mann (81) and Robert Kelly (93) believe that Merlin's prophecy refers to the death of Columbe, partly because the two events are related, albeit not causally, in Malory's source, and partly because, as Mann notes, the prophecy follows immediately upon Balin's protest, 'I myght nat save hir, for she slewe hirselff suddenly' (72.23–24:II.8). These reasons would be more persuasive if one could make some sense of this causal connection which Kelly and Mann believe Malory to have invented. Mann's thesis, of course, is to deny the possibility of making sense of Balin's adventures in this way, but Kelly goes on to draw a line of 'causation backward through the deathe of Columbé' and to conclude that Merlin's prophecy does refer ultimately to the beheading of the Lady of the Lake, since Balin 'is culpable to a degree for Columbé's death' only because 'his rash beheading of the Lady of the Lake, has provided Launceor with a reason for revenge (94).

9 Pellinor's response completely contradicts the fatalistic tenor of the *Suite du Merlin* (2:125–30; cf. Chapter 2 pp. 67–8). However, it is the more orthodox of the two possible responses. In fact, one of the examples cited by John of Salisbury to attack the fatalism of the astrologers was the story of King Hezekiah (*Kings* 20.1) which proved that God could alter His own prophecies (*Policraticus*, 2.24, cited in Wedel 39).

10 Balin swears to pursue vengeance against Garlon in terms which foreshadow the vengeance of Gawain against Lancelot: 'That shall I do,' seyde Balyn, 'and that I make avow to God and knyghthode' (80.17–18: II.12). The oath is original with Malory and anticipates almost word for word Gawain's vow to kill Lancelot 'by the faythe that I owghe to God and to knyghthode' (1213.29–30:XX.20). These two oaths are practically unmatched in the entire *Morte Darthur*. The only other knights to swear anything like such a solemn vow of vengence are Alexander the Orphan and Lionel. Alexander, charged by his mother upon her blessing and the 'hyghe Order of Knyghthode', promises 'to God' and to her that he will be revenged upon King Mark for the death of his father (636–37:X.34–35). Lionel makes his 'avow to God' to be revenged upon his own brother, Bors, during the Quest of the Grail (969.25:XVI.14). Lionel's oath, like Balin's, is Malory's invention and in the context of the Grail Quest is a clear condemnation of the religious mentality of the Heroic knight.

11 In the French romance, Balin runs wildly through room after room before finally arriving at the Grail chamber. A mysterious voice forbids him to enter [the chamber] but he enters anyway to find a magnificent altar upon which rests a silver vessel in which a lance balances itself miraculously, point down. The voice forbids him to touch the lance but again he

disobeys and so strikes the 'dolerous stroke'. The episode, which is missing from the Huth Manuscript is reproduced from the Cambridge manuscript by Bogdanow, *Romance* 241–49.

12 In the *Suite du Merlin* the survivors in the Wasteland express the conviction that 'Dieus nous en vengera, qui est si sourains vengieres' (2:31. Moreover, a damsel sent by Merlin confirms this, 2:47). However, they do not speak of the 'vengeaunce' which Balin has done. Rather they speak of the damage or evil ('tant demal') which he has done.

13 Jill Mann has concluded that the 'Tale of Balin' offers a miniature version of the 'final cataclysmic adventure, in which the whole of the Round Table is destroyed' (91) and although I disagree with her interpretation of the tale's thematic significance, I must applaud this insight. There are many points of resemblance between the death of Balin and the Death of Arthur, not the least of which is that both Knights With Two Swords meet tragic ends because they either cannot, or will not, overcome their desire for vengeance.

14 In Malory's source, the *Suite du Merlin*, there are two swords: the sword of Balin with which Lancelot is destined to kill Gawain, the knight 'qu'il avra plus amé' (thus re-enacting Balin's tragic slaying of his brother); and another sword destined for Galahad, which Merlin places in the floating stone (2:58–59). By conflating these two swords into one and then retaining the prophecy that 'with thys swerde' Lancelot will slay 'the man in the worlde that he lovith beste', i.e. Gawain, Malory creates two difficulties. The first stems from the fact that everyone (certainly *most* of his readers) knows that Lancelot will never achieve 'thys swerde'. That is only an apparent difficulty, however, which should operate to make the reader aware of the providentialist point of view. Granting the providentialist point, there remains yet a second difficulty: it is not Gawain whom Lancelot will love best in Malory's version of the text, but Gareth. Moverover, it is Gareth whom he will, in the end, unwittingly slay. I cannot resist the speculation that the present reading, 'Gawayne' is a scribal 'correction' of 'Gareth', which must have appeared an egregious error to any copyist familiar with Malory's French sources but not yet with Malory's own version of the story.

15 There are a total of sixty-one usages of *hap* and its various cognates in the *Morte Darthur*. Fifteen of these, almost exactly one quarter of the total, occur in Malory's eighth and last tale, the Death of Arthur, which represents only one-twelfth of the book.

16 John Gardner's translation of these three passages is unaccountably idiosyncratic, given the explicitly religious context of the poem: 'And heuen my happe and al my hele' becomes 'And raised my fortune and all my estate' (16); 'For happe and hele þat fro hym [Jesus] ȝede' becomes 'For blessing and the healing works He did' (713): and 'Bot ay wolde man of happe more hent' becomes 'But always man longs for some luckier chance' (1195). Even in more secular contexts, however, modern readers should be aware of the medieval Christian assumption that all fortune comes from God and particularly good fortune. This assumption is clearly reflected in

the set of meanings for *grace* and *blessyd*. *Grace* means primarily 'God's gift or favour' (*MED* 1a–c), but in more secular medieval contexts it appears to modern readers and editors to mean no more than a stroke of good luck (*MED* 3c). Likewise, *blessyd* means primarily 'filled with God's grace' (*MED* 1), but in secular contexts it, too, appears to mean no more than 'lucky' (*MED* 4).

17 The primary modern meanings of 'unhappy' and 'unhappiness' as referring to an internal mental or emotional state do not appear until the early eighteenth century.

18 The *MED* offers no evidence that the word *happynesse* was ever used during the Middle Ages. It turns up in Palsgrave's dictionary in 1530 as a translation of Fr. *prosperité* (*OED* 1) which suggests that it may have been current during Malory's lifetime; however, even if Palsgrave coined the noun from the adjective *happi* he was certainly not creating a new concept. *Happynesse* continued to be used both in the sense of prosperity and in the sense of blessedness well into the seventeenth century. In *Paradise Lost* John Milton has the Archangel Raphael explain to Adam: 'Let it suffice thee that thou know'st / Us happie, and without Love no happiness' (8.620–21).

19 Other than the literary evidence provided by Malory himself in his representation of True knighthood, there are a few indications that late fifteenth-century Englishmen might have begun to see knighthood in this light. First there is the precedent established by the Ricardian and Lancastrian Lollard knights who, despite successful political careers, remained susceptible to the 'new devotion of the mystics' (Medcalf 101). Second, there is a slight indication that among French knights of the fifteenth-century, English knights had a reputation for being pious: the fifteenth-century French version of the Round Table 'seremens' explains the large number of crosses in England in terms of the piety of English knights (Sandoz 402). Third, there is the fact that either William Caxton or his patron chose to translate and print Ramon Lull's religious-feudal treatise on the 'Ordre' of knighthood rather than Christine de Pizan's more secular view of knighthood in the *Epistle of Othea*. And, finally, there is good evidence that the religious view of knighthood was held at least by some knights in the late fifteenth and early sixteenth-century. Sir Anthony Wydeville and Sir Thomas More both wore hair shirts and the life of More, at least, offers abundant evidence of his effort to serve both God and Henry (Greenblatt 51). Even more suggestive, in relation to Malory's typology, is Ruth Kelso's discovery of three distinctly different sixteenth-century points of view on the duty of a gentleman: that of the country gentleman; that of the legally-trained servant of the prince; and that of the churchman who stresses the 'Christian duty of the gentleman' (312–13).

20 For examples of such usage on the part of Tristram and Arthur see 721.28:X.65; 728.14:X.66; 733.27, 734.6:X.68; 735.4:X.69. As a very young knight Tristram once says, 'But in God is all: He may make me as good a knyght as that good knyght sir Launcelot is' (388.33–35:VIII.10). But he says this in Ireland just after Isode has healed him of the wound he

received in the battle with Marhalt and before returning to Cornwall to the affair with Sir Seguarides' wife and the 'noble way of the world'.

21 Stephen C. B. Atkinson's assumption that the naked lady is Elaine, daughter of King Pelles (342), is extremely puzzling. There is nothing in the French romance to support it, nor in Lumiansky's discussion of the event (which Atkinson cites from *Malory's Originality* 231), nor in Lancelot's response to Elaine the morning after he has begotten Galahad (796.4–24:XI.3). Atkinson may have been influenced by Malory's description of this lady as 'the fayryst' Lancelot had ever seen while she was 'naked as a nedyll' (792.13–14:XI.1) and later in 'her clothis' as the fayryst 'lady that ever he saw *but yf hit were quene Gwenyver*' (792.22–23: XI.1, emphasis added). It is true that Malory describes Lancelot's appraisal of Elaine's beauty in very similar terms; however, when he sees Elaine in her clothes, he *still* thinks she is 'the fayrest woman that ever he sye in his lyeff dayes' (803.17–18:XI.7). It seems to me there are two inferences to be drawn here: (1) Lancelot has difficulty comparing other ladies' beauty to Guinevere's beauty unless they are clothed, presumably because he has never seen his own lady naked; and (2) the lady he rescued from the boiling water cannot be Elaine, since he appraises Elaine's beauty, when she is clothed, as much greater, greater even than that of Guinevere.

22 In a letter dated 9 March 1983, R. W. Griffith observed to me that Malory's phrasing here suggests that if Lancelot had not been drugged some 'let' would have impeded, if not stopped altogether, his progress into Elaine's bed. In Malory's source for this scene the 'let' is Lancelot's concern for the etiquette of the bedroom (*Lancelot* 78.56). I would argue that in Malory's version the 'let' would have been his reluctance to lose his virginity.

23 In Malory's source Lancelot feels shame only on account of his trespass to the queen, as evidenced by the shield he devises for himself while in exile (*Lancelot* 107.46). In Malory's version, the evidence of this shield depicting a knight kneeling before a lady is sharply undercut by the observation that Lancelot looks once every day 'towarde the realme of Logrys, where kynge Arthure and quene Gwenyver' are, and weeps (827.12–13:XII.6).

24 See Chapter 4, p. 212. Malory achieves this effect primarily by the simple means of changing sources when he gets to the Grail story, using the Vulgate version rather than the version contained in the French prose *Tristan*. The effect is not accidental, however, for Malory has altered his version of the Queste to accord with his view that some Worshipful knights, like Tristram and Arthur, were so devoted to the goods of this world as to be unwilling to leave them, even temporarily, in order to seek the Grail. Whereas the *Queste* asserts that 'tuit' of the knights present when the Grail appeared swore the oath with Gawain (16.26–28), Malory says that only 'the moste party' of those present swore the oath (866.15–16: XIII.7)

25 Vinaver notes that in the *Queste* 'la chevalerie celestielle' sometimes seems to refer to the religious life of contemplation, as it did frequently among the Cistercian monks of the thirteenth century (*Works* 1563). But this is not what Malory means by 'hevynly dedys' and 'knyghtly dedys in Goddys

workys', either. He means the mixed life which achieves 'stability' in virtuous living through prayer and contemplation, in contrast to the active life which so easily degenerates into a worldliness governed by pride and greed.

26 Gawain is a 'good' knight in the sense of being a good fighter (see Chapter 3 pp. 134–5), but he is without any of the other virtues which would win for him the epithet 'worshipful', even by the standards of the honourable society. In fact, Gawain is never said to be 'worshipful' in the *Morte Darthur*. Malory consistently eliminates the epithet, even in his version of the Roman campaign, when he would have found it frequently used in his source, the alliterative *Morte Arthure* (cf. 'Wardayne fulle wyrchipfulle', 2494 and also lines 2513, 2678, 2739 and 3021.) The only exceptions to this are Ywain's assurance that 'of a much more worshipfuller mannes hande myght I nat dye' (945.8–9:XVI.3), a rather ambiguous compliment under the circumstances, and Malory's observation near the end of the *Morte Darthur* that Gawain's gift of increasing strength caused him 'to wynne grete honour' (1216.34–1217.1:XX.21).

27 The *MED* offers three definitions of *mischevousli*: (1) miserably, wretchedly; cruelly, painfully; (2) unfortunately, regrettably; and (3) wickedly, sinfully; wrongfully, illegally, treacherously; also, in error, misguidedly. Only the second and the last part of the third of these definitions could be regarded as morally neutral. For the second, the editors offer only one example from Mannyng's *Chronicle*, and for the last part of the third again only one, from the English translation of Chartier's *Treatise of Hope*, and I would contend that their reading of this text is 'in error'. When Chartier says that 'thei shall fynde that they live myschevously' he means that they shall find that they are living 'wickedly, sinfully'.

28 In another uncharacteristic confirmation of chronology, Malory lets us know that Lancelot does not return to Camelot after his madness until the same year that Galahad becomes fifteen. As Lancelot is about to depart from Joyous Ile, Elaine reminds him that at 'thys same feste of Pentecoste shall your sonne and myne, Galahad, be made knyght, for he ys now fully fyftene wynter olde' (832.8–10:XII.9). Therefore, Malory's Lancelot had little opportunity, even if he had the inclination, to commit adultery with the queen before setting out on the Quest. For a more detailed analysis of Lancelot's confession, see my 'Lancelot' 430–32.

29 In the *Mort Artu* Arthur forces his nephew to confess that during the Quest he killed eighteen knights with his own hands, but Gauvain is sorry and ashamed of this fact. He explains that it was not because of his superior prowess but rather because 'la mescheance se torna plus vers moi que vers nul de mes compaignons. Et si sachiez bien que ce n'a pas esté par ma chevalerie, mes par mon pechié; si m'avez fet dire ma honte' (3.19–25). Malory omits this scene since it attributes to Gawain a spiritual awareness which is totally out of character for a Heroic knight.

30 Vinaver glosses 'shevalry' to mean 'reputation' in this passage but this meaning finds no support at all either in the *MED* or in Malory's own usage. According to Kato's *Concordance*, Malory uses the noun 'chyvalry'

eleven times compared with approximately one hundred uses of the noun 'knyghthode'. A check of the contexts in which 'chyvalry' appears in his text reveals that he uses it normally to mean either a group of armed knights (e.g. 20.8:I.9; cf. *MED* 1a) or martial skill and prowess (e.g. 972.15:XVI.15; cf. *MED* 4b) and more commonly the latter. In order to convey a desire to increase his 'reputation' as a knight, Malory would have had to make 'shevalry' plural in the sense of 'a feat of arms; an exploit:' (*MED* 4c).

31 Since Lancelot has already said it is fourteen years since his last confession (897.12:XIII.20), we must infer that during the ten years prior to his madness he was both a sinner and a man who went to confession, at least occasionally. Presumably this ten year period would coincide with the period after he began to seek worship for the queen's sake and before the 'foly' which caused his madness.

32 Lancelot's remark that he would have seen 'muche more' had not 'my synne bene beforetyme' has been changed in the Caxton text to read 'had not my sone ben', a reading which Vinaver finds obviously absurd, but which may well have been an attempt to clarify which 'synne' Lancelot was referring to, since Malory's Lancelot is not guilty of such 'grans pechiés' as his French counterpart. On the other hand it is not at all likely (but possible) that he is referring to the sin of disobedience which brought on his trance in the first place. Caxton's wording would seem to be an attempt to make clear to the reader which sin Lancelot is referring to — the sin which led to the begetting of Galahad.

Chapter 6

1 In the three and a half page description of the battle between Arthur and Accolon Malory refers to the king as 'Sir Arthure' a total of twelve times.

2 It would be extraordinary for Arthur to 'jouparté' his life in trial by battle but it would not be unprecedented. Geoffrey of Monmouth (followed by Wace and Layamon) records that Arthur fought a trial by battle with Frollo, the Roman governor of Gaul (9.11). Of course this was a battle to determine the sovereignty of Gaul, but even so it was thought remarkable that Arthur should risk his life by accepting Frollo's challenge (Layamon 11820–24).

3 Later Bors manages to convince 'some' of his fellows that the queen is innocent, in thought if not in deed; that is, she invited them all to dinner 'for good love . . . and nat for no male engyne' (1054.18–19:XVIII.5).

4 Malory appears to use the noun 'perfeccion' conservatively to refer to the religious life *per se* (1253.18, 19:XXI.10). However, these three usages also imply the higher degree of perfection, or love of God, which Lancelot and Guinevere actually achieve in the religious life. On the other hand, the only usage which does not seem to refer to the religious life, the reference to the 'perfeccion' which Lancelot 'made in the queste' (1045.12:XVIII.1)

could also be interpreted to refer to the means of his achieving it: the six or more months he devoted to the contemplative life with his son, Galahad.

The highest level of perfection was perfect union with God, and medieval mystical theologians disagreed on whether this was possible in this life or only in the afterlife. They also disagreed on how many levels of perfection there were, three or four. Rolle teaches that the third or highest degree of perfection is attainable in this life but that scarcely any men are able to achieve it ('Form of Living' 8.85).

5 This retreat with a holy man is also Malory's invention. There is nothing like it in either of his sources for this tale, although Lancelot does stay briefly with a nameless hermit who heals the wounds inflicted by the lady-huntress both in the stanzaic *Morte* (953) and also in the *Mort Artu* (64).

6 The retainers of lesser lords could also except their liegeance to the king without loss of honour (Keen, 'Brotherhood' 13–14).

7 In both of Malory's sources, it is well known that Lancelot would wear only the queen's token (*Mort Artu* 28–29; 31–32; stanzaic *Morte* 296); therefore, to make sure that his readers understand that this is not really 'true', Malory adds five passages in which first Lancelot himself asserts that he has never worn any woman's token (1068.3–5:XVIII.9) and then a series of other characters corroborate his assertion: Gawain (1071.16–17: XVIII.11, 1079.10–14:XVIII.14), Arthur (1080.9–12:XVIII.14), and, finally, those who should know best, Bors and his other kinsmen (1081.1–6: XVIII.15). That it is totally uncharacteristic behaviour is what makes wearing the Fair Maid's red sleeve such a good disguise (and also makes it analogous to Lancelot's equally uncharacteristic exploit in the Tale of Tristram, when he rode disguised and spoke 'villainy' of King Arthur and his court). Finally, of course, it makes his willingness to accept the queen's golden sleeve all the more noticeable as a sign of his increasing worldliness and vainglory.

8 The Treason Statute of 1352 made it high treason 'to defile the king's wife' (Pollock & Maitland 2:502) and it is hard to believe that any court in fifteenth-century England would have considered that a man deserved less than a traitor's death for abducting the queen, whether or not he actually got round to assaulting her sexually. His intention would have been clear enough.

9 Gawain's absence from the 'Knight of the Cart' is best explained in terms of Malory's knightly typology. In both Chrétien's poem and the French prose *Lancelot*, Gawain appears as Lancelot's friend and companion. Malory replaces him with Lavayne in order to preserve Gawain's consistency of character. Gawain has never before appeared as the friend and companion of Lancelot in the *Morte Darthur* and it would appear both startling and inappropriate for him to take up that role now, the more so that Malory has gone out of his way in the Tale of Tristram to suggest that Gawain is envious of Lancelot's greatness as a knight and of his favour with the king (see Chapter 4 pp. 206–8).

10 Lancelot used this phrase in the Tale of Lancelot (264.1–2:VI.7, 272.32–33: VI.11), and again during the Quest of the Sankgreal after he had repented

and confessed his sins (928.13:XV.3, 934.25:XV.6, 1019.34:XVII.17). A check of Kato's *Concordance* reveals that with very few exceptions it is a phrase which is used in the *Morte Darthur* only by holy men, Grail knights and Lancelot. The exceptions are four out of a total of twenty-four and I include in this total those phrases using the verb 'betoke' ('bytaught', 'betaught') as well. This verbal pattern would seem to reinforce the interpretation I have suggested for Lancelot's response to his imprisonment.

11 Most critics interpret Lancelot's tears as a sign of his own sense of unworthiness (Lewis, 'English Prose *Morte*' 20; Tucker 99; Lumiansky 231; Benson 229; Lambert 65; Atkinson 349). Only Vinaver interprets his tears as tears of 'joy and gratitude' ('On Art' 38) and only Edmund Reiss emphasizes the miraculous nature of the cure, relating it to the task of exorcism and concluding that Lancelot's tears must be tears of relief that he has been allowed to perform the healing and yet live (171–72).

12 In Malory's version it affects not only the relationship between Tristram and Palomides, but is also responsible for Mark's initial attempt to destroy Tristram (396.7–10:VIII.14) and for the attempt on Branguine's life by two Cornish ladies-in-waiting (419.26–28:VIII.29). It is also frequently a cause of harm at tournaments. Lancelot advises Arthur to counterbalance the effects of the envy of their opponents by making the two parties of the tournament at Lonezep more even in numbers (682.1415:X.52) and Galahalt and Bagdemagus call a tournament for the specific 'entent to sle syr Launcelot other ellys uttirly to destroy hym and shame hym, bycause sir Launcelot had evermore the hygher degré' (675.5–7:X.50) It is highly significant, I think, that none of these passages is found in Malory's source. Guinevere's observation that 'all men of worshyp hate an envyous man' (764.29:X.81) is likewise his invention.

Even more significant, with regard to the motivation which Malory attributes to Mordred and Aggravayne for their allegation of treason against Lancelot and the queen, is the parallel which it creates with the Tristram story. In Malory's Tale of Tristram Andred plays the Mordred role, being envious of Tristram and hoping to profit from his destruction. Moreoever, after spying on them for some time, he accuses Tristram and Isode of treason on the basis of no more evidence than a conversation 'in a wyndowe' (426.13:VIII.32). Caxton adds that his intention was to 'take hem and *sklaundre* hem' (emphasis added) and, in Vinaver's opinion, this particular reading is one of those which is 'either clearly preferable to W' or 'likely to throw some light on it' (*Works* cxxiii).

13 E. D. Kennedy has also observed that Arthur's 'sentence appears to be based upon this "treason" [Lancelot's killing of fellow Round Table knights] and not upon her infidelity' ('Arthur-Guenevere' 35).

14 This is particularly evident in Malory's version of the Death of Arthur where Mordred and Aggravayne appeal to this kinship bond when they accuse Lancelot and the queen (1163.8:XX.2); Arthur addresses Gawain as his 'syster son' as Gawain lies dying (1230.11:XXI.2) and again when Gawain appears to him in a vision (1233.31:XXI.3); and Gawain refers to

himself as 'systirs sonne unto the noble kynge Arthur' in his letter to Lancelot (1231.10:XXI.2). None of these usages is to be found in either of Malory's sources for this tale.

15 In their article, 'Right to Rule in England, 1327–1485', William H. Dunham and Charles T. Wood survey the arguments put forward to justify five different depositions of English monarchs. The topic of rightful succession was particularly alive during the early Yorkist years, given Edward's questionable hereditary claim to the throne.

16 If the above hypothesis is true, then Mordred's treachery must have been particularly painful for Malory's Arthur, and this inference is supported by the way Malory deals with the scene in which news of Mordred's treachery reaches the king. The stanzaic *Morte* reports that the king 'Full moche mornyd . . . in hys mode / That suche treson in ynglond shulde be wroght' (2949–50). Malory displays his dramatic genius by not even attempting to describe Arthur's reaction — he relegates the scene off stage.

17 The vocabulary of the law which Malory cites points to the crime of theft since 'menour' (*MED* 'meinoure') means 'stolen goods'. It is difficult to see how the concept of stolen goods can be applied literally to the crime alleged against Lancelot and the queen and yet, since they were not taken 'wyth the dede', the 'menour' must denote the proof of their guilt, whatever it is that justifies their summary conviction. When citing this passage the *MED* suggests that perhaps the term refers to the armour which Lancelot stole from Collgrevaunce, but surely, even if that were so, it is hard to see how Lancelot's theft could prove the queen's guilt and thus justify burning her at the stake. Malory must be using 'menour' here metaphorically to refer to the circumstances (bed chamber, closed door) in which the queen and Lancelot were caught, for they certainly were not caught literally 'with the goods', i.e. *in flagrante delicto*.

18 This explanation of why Lancelot did not recognize Gareth and Gaheris at the execution site is suggested by his words at Carlisle, 'God wolde they had ben armed, . . . for than had they ben on lyve' (1199.11–12:XX.16), which have to mean one of two things: either that (1) had they been armed they would have defended themselves successfully; or that (2) had they been armed, Lancelot would have recognized and avoided them in the mélée.

19 Malory never specifies at what point in time Lancelot and his kinsmen become 'lorde of all Fraunce and of all the londis that longed unto Fraunce . . . throrow sir Launcelottis noble proues' (1204.20–22:XX.18). Probably it was after the wars against Claudas, which Malory dates after the begetting of Galahad (802.22–27:XI.6). Lancelot also refers to these wars during the siege of Benwick and speaks of his father and uncle as though they were alive at that time (1212.20–24:XX.19); therefore, we may infer that Lancelot and his kinsmen must have inherited their lordships sometime after the begetting of Galahad.

20 The word 'treson' can also be used to denote shameful killing or murder in the *Morte Darthur*. Lancelot has not murdered any of Gawain's brothers, but then clan justice does not recognize the common law distinction

between pardonable and unpardonable homicide; therefore, it is probable that when Gawain calls Lancelot a 'false traytour knyght' he means no more than 'killer' of 'my three brethirne' (1215.11–14:XX.20).

21 This view of the battle is reinforced by the fact that in Malory's version Arthur does not preside over the trial as he does in the *Mort Artu*; he is simply a spectator. In the *Mort Artu* Lancelot asks Arthur what to do when Gawain refuses to yield and Arthur gives him permission to leave the field if he likes 'car ja est eure passée' (157.42–44). The stanzaic *Morte* represents the battle more as Malory does; at least there is no suggestion that Arthur presides over the trial.

22 Malory also makes the gift much more formidable. In the *Mort Artu* Gawain has been blessed since his baptism by means of the holy man's prayer to 'Jhesucrist', so that he may never be vanquished about the hour of noon, for at that hour of the day, no matter how badly wounded and exhausted he may be, he will experience a sudden renewal of energy (154.35–36; cf. stanzaic *Morte*, 2802–03). In Malory's version, Gawain's gift is that his strength will increase for three hours, from nine in the morning until noon, and can reach 'as much as thryse hys [normal] strength' (1216.31–34:XX.21).

Chapter 7

1 Neither of these passages is in Malory's source (*Suite* 2:167–68; allit. *Morte* 226ff.) and the second passage has been omitted from the revised version of the Roman campaign in Caxton. If Malory himself made that revision, he may have decided that he had initially gone too far, farther even than his alliterative source, in suggesting that Arthur was a proud and bloodthirsty conqueror like Alexander.

2 In *Medieval Narrative and Modern Ontology* Evelyn Vitz observes that modern structuralist theories of narrative are totally inappropriate to medieval narratives because they find 'unthinkable' medieval views regarding the existence and omnipotence of God (8–9), views which frequently determine not only why a medieval story is told but also how it is told.

3 H. A. Kelly has argued that modern critics are wrong to attribute a conscious Chaucerian theory of tragedy to the author of the alliterative *Morte*. Malory, however, could have been influenced by Lydgate's account of Arthur in his *Fall of Princes*. As Kelly notes, Lydgate is the only Arthurian historian who 'considered his account a tragedy' ('The Non-Tragedy of Arthur' 96).

4 The following discussion of the deaths of Gawain, Arthur and Lancelot is a slightly altered version of an argument I have made at greater length in 'Re-emergence' (270ff).

5 Phillip McCaffrey has also argued that Malory uses the adder emblematically as well as dramatically and notes that the image of a snake in the grass is a common emblem of domestic or political betrayal.

6 Except for recent books by Riddy and Merrill, there seems to be a concensus among critics that Malory's work is unified. There is still no agreement as to what makes it unified, however. Recently, Judson Allen suggested that the unity of the *Morte Darthur* is grounded in medieval rhetorical principle, specifically in the eight-part *distinctio* thought to be appropriate for works of history (*Ethical Poetic* 156–66). Murray Evans has argued that the wholeness of Malory's book is created by the many narrative links between the five parts of the Winchester manuscript ('*Ordinatio* and Narrative Links').

7 Malory's characters twice refer to old 'cronycles' (188.6:V.1; 1201.16:XX.17) but Malory himself always refers to his sources as either 'bookes' or 'tales' and gives much more authority to the former than to the latter. Even when tales are written down, Malory speaks of them as being 'told', 'spoken' or 'said' and sometimes questions their truth (cf. 1162.25:XX.02 and 1197.20:XX.15).

8 Historiographers have only recently begun to explore the extent to which writing history is like writing exegesis or fiction. Nancy Partner compares history to exegesis, an analogy which she does not intend as a derogation but rather an explanation of 'the kind of truth it is' (110), a 'hermeneutic striving for truth' (113). Hayden White argues that the only meaning history can ever have is that produced by a narrative imagination. The same historical sequence of events can be 'emplotted in a number of different ways so as to provide different interpretations of those events and to endow them with different meanings' ('Historical Text' 282).

Bibliography

I. PRIMARY WORKS CITED

'Die Abenteuer Gawains: Ywains und le Morholts mit den drei Jungfrauen. . . .' Ed. H. O. Sommer. *Beihefte zur Zeitschrift für Romanische Philologie* 47 (1913).

Andreas Capellanus. *The Art of Courtly Love*. Trans. John Jay Parry. New York: Ungar, 1959.

'Un art d'aimer anglo-normand.' Ed. O. Södergard. *Romania* 77 (1956):289–330.

Boethius. *The Consolation of Philosophy*. Trans. V.E. Watts. Harmondsworth: Penguin, 1969.

The Boke of Noblesse. Ed. J.G. Nichols. London: Roxburgh Club, 1860.

Bonet, Honoré. *The Tree of Battles*. Trans. G.W. Coopland. Liverpool: Liverpool University Press, 1949.

The Book of Vices and Virtues: A Fourteenth-Century English Translation of the 'Somme le Roi' of Lorens d'Orléans. Ed. W. Nelson Francis. Early English Text Society o.s. 217. London, 1942.

Bueil, Jean de. *Le Jouvencel*. Ed. Léon Lecestre. 2 vols. Paris: Renouard, 1887.

Caxton's Malory; a New Edition of Sir Thomas Malory's 'Le Morte Darthur'. Ed. James W. Spisak and William Matthews. 2 vols. Berkeley: University of California Press, 1983.

Charny, Geoffroi de. *Le Livre de chevalerie*. In *Oeuvres de Froissart*. Ed. Kervyn de Lettenhove. vol. 1. 2. Brussels: Academie Royale de Belgique, 1863, 463–533.

Chartier, Alain. *Le breviaire des nobles*. In 'Deux poèmes sur la chevalerie.' Ed. W.H. Rice. *Romania* 75 (1954):54–97.

———. *The Curial*. Trans. William Caxton (1484). Ed. Frederick J. Furnivall. Early English Text Society e.s. 54. 1888. rpt. London, 1965.

———. *Fifteenth-Century English Translations of 'Le Traité de l'Esperance' and 'Le Quadrilogue Invectif.'* Ed. Margaret Blayney. 2 vols. Early English Text Society o.s. 270, 281. London, 1980.

Le chevaler Dé. Ed. K. Urwin. *Revue des langues romanes* 68 (1937):136–61.

Clanvowe, Sir John. 'The Two Ways.' In *Works*. Ed. V.J. Scattergood. Cambridge: Brewer, 1975.

Fortescue, Sir John. *The Governance of England: the Difference between an Absolute and Limited Monarchy*. Ed. Charles Plummer. Oxford: Clarendon, 1885.

Geoffrey of Monmouth. *History of the Kings of Britain*. Trans. Sebastian Evans. Rev. Charles W. Dunn. New York: Dutton, 1958.

Hardyng, John. *Chronicle*. Ed. Henry Ellis. London: Rivington, 1812.

Hay, Sir Gilbert. *Prose Manuscript (A.D. 1456)*. Vol. 2: *The Buke of Knychthede and the Buke of the Governaunce of Princis*. Ed. J.H. Stevenson. Scottish Text Society 62. Edinburgh: Blackwood, 1914.

Hilton, Walter. *Eight Chapters on Perfection*. Ed. Fumio Kuriyagawa. Tokyo: Keio Institute of Cultural and Linguistic Studies, 1967.

———. 'Epistle on Mixed Life.' In *Yorkshire Writers*. Ed. C. Horstmann. London: Sonnenschein, 1895–96, 1:264–92.

———. *The Goad of Love: an Unpublished Translation of the 'Stimulus Amoris' Formerly Attributed to Bonaventura*. Ed. Clare Kirchberger. London: Faber and Faber, 1952.

———. *The Scale of Perfection*. Ed. E. Underhill. 1923. rpt. London: J.M. Watkins, 1948.

Knyghthode and Bataile. Ed. R. Dyboski and A.M. Arend. Early English Text Society o.s. 201. London, 1935.

La Marche, Olivier de. *Le Chevalier délibéré*. Ed. E. Morgan. Washington D.C.: Library of Congress, 1946.

Lancaster, Henry Grosmont, Duke of. *Le Livre de seyntz medicines*. Ed. E.J. Arnould. Anglo-Norman Text Society 2. Oxford, 1940.

Lancelot; roman en prose du xiii siècle. Ed. Alexandre Micha. 9 vols. Gèneve: Droz, 1978–83.

———. *Le roman en prose de Lancelot du lac: le conte de la charrette*. Ed. Gweneth Hutchings. Paris: E. Droz, 1938.

La Sale, Antoine de. *Le Petit Jehan de Saintré*. Ed. Jean Misrahi and Charles A. Knudson. Gèneve: Droz, 1965.

La Tour Landry, chevalier de. *The Book of the Knight of the Tower*. Trans. William Caxton. Ed. M.Y. Offord. Early English Text Society s.s. 2. Oxford: Oxford University Press, 1971.

Layamon. *Brut*. Ed. G.L. Brook and R.F. Leslie. Early English Text Society o.s. 250, 277. London, 1963.

Löseth, E. *Le roman en prose de Tristan: analyse critique d'après les manuscrits de Paris*. 1891. rpt. New York: Burt Franklin, 1976.

Love, Nicholas. *The Mirror of the Blessed Lyf of Jesu Christ*. Ed. L. F. Powell. London: H. Frowde, 1908.

Lull, Ramon. *The Book of the Ordre of Chyualry*. Trans. William Caxton. Ed. A.T.P. Byles. Early English Text Society o.s. 168. London, 1926.

Lydgate, John. *Reson and Sensuallyté*. Ed. E. Sieper. Early English Text Society e.s. 84. London, 1901.

———. *The Serpent of Division*. Ed. Henry Noble McCracken. London: Oxford University Press, 1911.

Macchiavelli, Niccolò. *The Prince*. Trans. George Bull. Rev. ed. Harmondsworth, Eng.: Penguin, 1975.

Matthew of Vendôme. 'Introductory Treatise on the Art of Poetry.' Trans. Ernest Gallo. *Proceedings of the American Philosophical Society* 118 (1974): 51–92.

Mézières, Phillipe de. *Le Songe du vieil pèlerin*. Ed. G.W. Coopland. 2 vols. London: Cambridge University Press, 1969.

The Mirror for Magistrates. Ed. Lily B. Campbell. 1938. rpt. New York: Barnes & Noble, 1960.

La Mort le roi Artu: roman du xiiie siècle. Ed. Jean Frappier. 3rd ed. Genève: Droz, 1964.

Le Morte Arthur: A Romance in Stanzas of Eight Lines. Ed. J.D. Bruce. Early English Text Society e.s. 88. London, 1959.

Morte Arthure [alliterative]. Ed. Edmund Brock. Early English Text Society o.s. 8. 2nd ed. 1871. rpt. London, 1961.

'The Ordenaunce and Fourme of Fightyng Within Listes.' In *The Blacke Booke of the Admiralty*. Ed. Sir Travers Twiss. 4 vols. London: Longmans, 1871–76, 1:300–329.

Perlesvaus: le haute livre du graal. Ed. W.A. Nitze and T.A. Jenkins. 2 vols. Chicago: University of Chicago Press, 1932.

Pizan, Christine de. *The Book of Fayttes of Armes and Chyualrye*. Trans. William Caxton. Ed. A.T.P. Byles. Early English Text Society o.s. 189. London, 1932.

———. *Le livre du corps de policie*. Ed. Robert H. Lucas. Genève: Droz, 1967.
———. *Le Livre du duc des vrais amans*. In *Oeuvres poétiques*. Ed. Maurice Roy. Vol. 3. Paris: Société des anciens textes français, 1896.
———. *Epistle of Othea to Hector: a 'Lytil Bibell of Knyghthode.'* Ed. James D. Gordon, Philadelphia: University of Pennsylvania, 1942.
Rolle, Richard. *English Writings*. Ed. H.E. Allen. 1931. rpt. Oxford: Clarendon, 1963.
———.*The Fire of Love and the Mendyng of Life*. Trans. Richard Misyn. Ed. R. Harvey. Early English Text Society o.s. 106. London, 1896.
———. 'The Form of Living.' In *English Writings*. Ed. H.E. Allen. 1931. rpt. Oxford: Clarendon, 1963.
———. 'On Grace.' In *Yorkshire Writers*. Ed. C. Horstmann. 2 vols. London: Sonnenschein, 1895–96, 1:305–10.
Stowe, J. *Memoranda*. In *Three Fifteenth Century Chronicles*. Ed. James Gairdner. London: Camden Society, 1880, 94–147.
Suite du Merlin. Merlin, roman en prose du xiiie siècle. Ed. Gaston Paris and Jacob Ulrich. 2 vols. Paris: Société des anciens text français, 1886.
Thomas Aquinas. *Providence and Predestination: Truth, Questions 5 & 6*. Trans. Robert W. Mulligan. Chicago: H. Regnery, 1961.
Tristan. Le roman de Tristan en prose. Ed. Renée L. Curtis. vol. 1. München: Hueber, 1963; vol. 2. Leiden: Brill, 1976.
The Works of Sir Thomas Malory. Ed. Eugene Vinaver. 2nd ed. rev. 3 vols. Oxford: Clarendon, 1973.

II. SECONDARY WORKS CITED

Adolf, Helen. 'The Concept of Original Sin as Reflected in Arthurian Romance.' In *Studies in Language and Literature in Honor of Margaret Schlauch*. Warsaw: Polish Scientific Publishers, 1966, 21–30.
Allen, Judson B. *The Ethical Poetic of the Later Middle Ages*. Toronto, University of Toronto Press, 1982.
———. 'Malory's Diptych Distinctio: the Closing Books of His Work.' In *Studies in Malory*. Ed. James W. Spisak. Kalamazoo, Mich.: Medieval Institute, Western Michigan University, 1985, 237–55.
Allmand, C.T., ed. *Society at War: the Experience of England and France During the Hundred Years' War*. Manchester: Manchester University Press, 1973.
Aston, Margaret. *The Fifteenth Century: The Prospect of Europe*. London: Thames and Hudson, 1968.
Atkinson, Stephen C.B. 'Malory's "Healing of Sir Urry."' *Studies in Philosophy* 79 (1981):341–52.
Auerbach, Erich. *Mimesis: The Representation of Reality in Western Literature*. Trans. Willard R. Trask. Princeton: Princeton University Press, 1953.
Barber, Richard. *The Knight and Chivalry*. 1970. rpt. London: Sphere Books, 1974.
———. *The Reign of Chivalry*. New York: St. Martin's Press, 1979.
———. 'The *Vera Historia de Morte Arthuri* and Its Place in Arthurian Tradition'. *Arthurian Literature* 1 (1981):62–77.
Barker, Juliet R. V. *The Tournament in England*. Woodbridge, Suffolk: Boydell and Brewer, 1986.
Barnie, John. *War in Medieval English Society: Social Values and the Hundred Years' War*. London: Weidenfeld & Nicolson, 1974.

Baroja, Julio Caro. 'Honour and Shame: An Historical Account of Several Conflicts.' In *Honour and Shame: The Values of Mediterranean Society*. Ed. J.G. Peristiany. London: Weidenfeld & Nicolson, 1965, 79–138.

Bean, J.M.W. 'Bachelor and Retainer.' *Medievalia et humanistica* 3 (1972):117–31.

———. *The Decline of English Feudalism, 1215–1540*. Manchester: Manchester University Press, 1968.

———. *From Lord to Patron: Lordship in Late Medieval England*. Manchester: Manchester University Press, 1989.

Bell, C.H. *The Sister's Son in the Medieval German Epic: A Study in the Survival of Matriliny*. Berkeley: University of California Press, 1922.

Bellamy, J.G. *Crime and Public Order in England in the Later Middle Ages*. London: Routledge & Kegan Paul, 1973.

———. *The Law of Treason in England in the Later Middle Ages*. Cambridge: Cambridge University Press, 1970.

Bennett, H.S. *The Pastons and Their England: Studies in an Age of Transition*. 2nd ed. 1932. rpt. Cambridge: Cambridge University Press, 1977.

Benson, Larry D. *Malory's Morte Darthur*. Cambridge, Mass.: Harvard University Press, 1976.

——— and John Leyerle, eds. *Chivalric Literature: Essays on Relations between Literature and Life in the Later Middle Ages*. Kalamazoo: Medieval Institute, Western Michigan University, 1980.

Benton, John F. 'Clio and Venus: An Historical View of Medieval Love.' In *The Meaning of Courtly Love*. Ed. F.X. Newman. Albany: State University of New York Press, 1968, 19–42.

Blake, Norman F. *Caxton and His World*. London: House & Maxwell, 1969.

Bloch, Marc. *Feudal Society*. Trans. L.A. Manyon. London: Routledge & Kegan Paul, 1961.

Bloomfield, Morton W. 'Episodic Motivation and Marvels in Epic and Romance.' In *Essays and Explorations*. Cambridge, Mass.: Harvard University Press, 1979, 97–128.

Boase, Roger. *The Origin and Meaning of Courtly Love: A Critical Study of European Scholarship*. Manchester: Manchester University Press, 1977.

Bogdonow, Fanni. *The Romance of the Grail: A Study of the Structure and Genesis of a Thirteenth-Century Arthurian Prose Romance*. Manchester: Manchester University Press, 1966.

———. 'The Treatment of the Lancelot-Guenevere Theme in the Prose *Lancelot*.' *Medium Aevum* 41 (1972):110–20.

Bornstein, Diane. 'Military Strategy in Malory and Vegetius' *De re militari*.' *Comparative Literature Studies* 9 (1972):123–29.

———. *Mirrors of Courtesy*. Hamden, Conn.: Shoestring Press, 1975.

———. 'Reflections of Political Theory and Political Fact in Fifteenth-Century Mirrors for the Prince.' In *Medieval Studies in Honor of Lillian Herlands Hornstein*. Ed. J.B. Bessinger and Robert R. Raymo. New York: New York University Press, 1976, 77–85.

Borst, Arno. 'Knighthood in the High Middle Ages: Ideal and Reality.' In *Lordship and Community in Medieval Europe*. Ed. Frederic L. Cheyette. New York: Holt, 1968, 180–91.

Bossy, John. 'Holiness and Society.' *Past and Present* 75 (1977):119–37.

Boulton, D'Arcy J. D. *The Knights of the Crown: the Monarchical Orders of Knighthood in Later Medieval Europe, 1325–1520*. Woodbridge: Boydell and Brewer, 1987.

Bradbrook, Muriel C. *Sir Thomas Malory*. London: Longmans, Green, 1958 (Writers and their Works, no. 95).

Brewer, Derek. 'Malory: The Traditional Writer and the Archaic Mind.' *Arthurian Literature* 1 (1981):94–120.

———. 'Malory's "Proving" of Sir Lancelot.' In *The Changing Face of Arthurian Romance: Essays in Memory of E. Pickford*. Ed. A. Adams *et al*. Woodbridge: Brewer and Boydell, 1986, 123–36.

———, ed. *The Morte Darthur: Parts Seven and Eight*. London: Edward Arnold, 1968.

Brown, A.L. 'The Reign of Henry IV.' In *Fifteenth-Century England, 1399–1509: Studies in Politics and Society*. Ed. S.B. Chrimes *et. al*. Manchester: Manchester University Press, 1972, 1–28.

Bumke, Joachim. *The Concept of Knighthood in the Middle Ages*. Trans. W.T.H. and Erika Jackson. New York: AMS Press, 1982.

Caenegem, R.C. Van. *The Birth of the English Common Law*. Cambridge: Cambridge University Press, 1973.

Campbell, J.F.C. 'Honour and the Devil.' In *Honour and Shame: The Values of Mediterranean Society*. Ed. J.G. Peristiany. London: Weidenfeld & Nicolson, 1965, 139–70.

Catto, J. I. 'Sir William Beauchamp: Between Chivalry and Lollardy.' In *The Ideals and Practice of Medieval Knighthood*. Vol. 3. Ed. Christopher Harper-Brill and Ruth Harvey. Woodbridge: Boydell Press, 1990, 39–48.

Clein, Wendy. *Concepts of Chivalry in 'Sir Gawain and the Green Knight'*. Norman, Okla.: Pilgrim Books, 1987.

Colker, Marvin L., ed. 'The Lure of Women, Hunting, Chess and Tennis: A Vision.' *Speculum* 59(1984):103–5.

Davies, R.T. 'The Worshipful Way in Malory.' In *Patterns of Love and Courtesy*. Ed. John Lawlor. London: Edward Arnold, 1966, 157–177.

———. 'Malory's Lancelot and the Noble Way of the World.' *Review of English Studies*. 6(1955):356–64.

Dean, Christopher. *Arthur of England*. Toronto: University of Toronto Press, 1987.

Dessau, Albert. 'The Idea of Treason in the Middle Ages.' In *Lordship and Community in Medieval Europe*. Ed. F.L. Cheyette. New York: Holt, 1968, 192–97.

Dillon, Harold A., Viscount. 'On a MS. Collection of Ordinances of Chivalry of the Fifteenth Century Belonging to Lord Hastings,' *Archaeologia* 57(1900): 29–70.

Donaldson, E. Talbot. 'Malory and the Stanzaic *Le Morte Arthur*.' *Studies in Philology* 47(1950):460–72.

Doob, Penelope. *Nebuchadnezzar's Children:Conventions of Madness in Middle English Literature*. New Haven: Yale University Press, 1975.

DuBoulay, Francis R.H. *An Age of Ambition: English Society in the Late Middle Ages*. London: Nelson, 1970.

Dunham, William H. and Charles T. Wood. 'Right to Rule in England, 1327–1485.' *American Historical Review* 81 (1976):738–61.

Erdmann, Carl. *The Origin of the Idea of Crusade*. Trans. Marshall W. Baldwin and Walter Goffart. Princeton: Princeton University Press, 1977.

Evans, Murray J. 'The Explicits and Narrative Division in the Winchester Ms.: A Critique of Vinaver's Malory.' *Philological Quarterly* 58(1979):263–81.

———. '*Ordinatio* and Narrative Links: the Impact of Malory's Tales as a "hoole book".' In *Studies in Malory*. Ed. James W. Spisak. Kalamazoo: Medieval Institute, Western Michigan University, 1985, 29–52.

Ferguson, Arthur B. *The Indian Summer of English Chivalry: Studies in the Decline and Transformation of Chivalric Idealism*. Durham, N.C.: Duke University Press, 1960.

Field, P.J.C. *Romance and Chronicle: A Study of Malory's Prose Style*. London: Barrie & Jenkins, 1971.

———. 'The Last Years of Sir Thomas Malory.' *Bulletin of the John Rylands University Library of Manchester* 64(1982):433–56.

———. 'Sir Robert Malory, Prior of the Hospital of St. John of Jerusalem in England (1432–1439/40).' *Journal of Ecclesiastical History* 28(1977): 249–64.

———. 'Sir Thomas Malory, M.P.' *Bulletin of the Institute of Historical Research* 47(1974):24–35.

———. 'The Source of Malory's *Tale of Gareth*.' In *Aspects of Malory*. Ed. Toshiyuki Takamiya and Derek Brewer. Cambridge: Brewer, 1981, 57–70.

———. 'Thomas Malory and the Warwick Retinue Roll.' *Midland History* 5 (1979/80):20–30.

———. 'Thomas Malory: the Hutton Documents.' *Medium Aevum* 48(1979):213–39.

———. 'The Winchester Round Table.' *Notes and Queries* 25 (1978):204.

Flew, R. Newton. *The Idea of Perfection in Christian Theology: An Historical Study of the Christian Ideal for the Present Life*. London: Oxford University Press, 1934.

Fries, Maureen. 'Malory's Tristram as Counter-Hero to the *Morte Darthur*.' *Neuphilologische Mitteilungen* 76 (1975):605–13.

———. 'Tragic Pattern in Malory's *Morte Darthur*: Medieval Narrative as Literary Myth.' *The Early Renaissance, Acta* 5 (1978):81–99.

Frye, Northrop. *The Anatomy of Criticism*. Princeton, N.J.: Princeton University Press, 1957.

———. *The Secular Scripture: A Study of the Structure of Romance*. Cambridge, Mass.: Harvard University Press, 1976.

Gardner, Helen. 'Walter Hilton and the Mystical Tradition in England.' *Essays and Studies* 22 (1937):103–27.

Geertz, Clifford. *The Interpretation of Cultures*. New York: Basic Books, 1973.

Ginsberg, Warren. *The Cast of Character: the Representation of Personality in Ancient and Medieval Literature*. Toronto: University of Toronto Press, 1983.

Girard, René. *Violence and the Sacred*. Trans. Patrick Gregory. Baltimore: Johns Hopkins University Press, 1977.

Girouard, Mark. *The Return to Camelot: Chivalry and the English Gentleman*. New Haven: Yale University Press, 1981.

Goodman, J. R. 'Malory and Caxton's Chivalric Series, 1481–85.' In *Studies in Malory*. Ed. James W. Spisak. Kalamazoo: Medieval Institute, Western Michigan University, 1985, 257–74.

Green, Richard Firth. *Poets and Prince-pleasers: Literature and the English Court in the Late Middle Ages*. Toronto: University of Toronto Press, 1980.

Greenblatt, Stephen. *Renaissance Self-Fashioning: From More to Shakespeare*. Chicago: University of Chicago Press, 1980.

Griffith, Richard R. 'The Authorship Question Reconsidered: A Case for Thomas Malory of Papworth St. Agnes, Cambridgeshire.' In *Aspects of Malory*. Ed. Toshiyuki Takamiya and Derek Brewer. Cambridge: Brewer, 1981, 159–77.

———. 'The Political Bias of Malory's *Morte Darthur*.' *Viator* 5(1974):365–86.

Guillemain, Bernard. *The Later Middle Ages*. London: Burns & Oates, 1960.

Gummere, Francis B. 'The Sister's Son in the English and Scottish Popular Ballads.' In *An English Miscellany*. Oxford: Clarendon, 1901:133–49.

Haines, Victor Yelverton. *The Fortunate Fall of Sir Gawain: The Typology of 'Sir Gawain and the Green Knight.'* Washington, D.C.: University Press of America, 1982.

Hindley, Geoffrey. *England in the Age of Caxton*. New York: St. Martin's Press, 1979.

Holbrook, S.E. 'Nymue, the Chief Lady of the Lake in Malory's *Le Morte Darthur*.' *Speculum* 53(1978):761–77.

Howard, Donald R. *The Three Temptations: Medieval Man in Search of the World*. Princeton: Princeton University Press, 1966.

Hughes, Jonathan. *Pastors and Visionaries: Religion and Secular Life in Late Medieval Yorkshire*. Woodbridge: Boydell Press, 1989.

Huizinga, J. *The Waning of the Middle Ages*. London: Arnould, 1924.

Hunt, Lynn, ed. *The New Cultural History*. Berkeley: University of California Press, 1989.

Huppé, Bernard. 'The Concept of the Hero.' In *Concepts of the Hero*. Ed. Norman T. Burns and Christopher J. Reagan. Albany, N.Y.: State University of New York Press, 1975, 1–26.

Hynes-Berry, Mary. 'A Tale "Breffly Drawyne Oute of Freynshe".' In *Aspects of Malory*. Ed. Toshiyuki Takamiya and Derek Brewer. Cambridge: Brewer, 1981, 93–106.

Ihle, Sandra Ness. *Malory's Grail Quest: Invention and Adaptation in Medieval Prose Romance*. Madison: University of Wisconsin Press, 1983.

Iser, Wolfgang. 'The Reading Process: A Phenomenological Approach.' *New Directions in Literary History*. Ed. Ralph Cohen. Baltimore: Johns Hopkins University Press, 1984.

Jauss, Hans Robert. *Toward an Aesthetic of Reception*. Trans. Timothy Bahti. Minneapolis: University of Minnesota Press, 1982.

Jones, Terry. *Chaucer's Knight: The Portrait of a Medieval Mercenary*. London: Eyre Methuen, 1982.

Kato, Tomomi, ed. *A Concordance to the Works of Sir Thomas Malory*. Tokyo: University of Tokyo Press, 1974.

Keen, Maurice H. 'Brotherhood in Arms.' *History*. 47(1962):1–17.

———. 'Chaucer's Knight, the English Aristocracy and the Crusade.' In *English Court Culture in the Later Middle Ages*. Ed. V.J. Scattergood and J.W. Sherborne. New York: St. Martin's Press, 1983, 45–61.

———. *Chivalry*. New Haven, Conn.: Yale University Press, 1984.

———. 'Chivalry, Nobility and the Man-at-arms.' In *War, Literature and Politics in the Late Middle Ages*. Ed. C.T. Allmand. Liverpool: Liverpool University Press, 1976, 32–45.

———. *England in the Later Middle Ages: A Political History*. London: Methuen, 1973.

———. 'Treason Trials Under the Law of Arms.' *Transactions of the Royal Historical Society*. 12 (1962):85–103.

Kelly, Henry A. *Divine Providence in the England of Shakespeare's History Plays*. Cambridge, Mass.: Harvard University Press, 1970.

———. 'English Kings and the Fear of Sorcery.' *Medieval Studies* 39(1977):206–38.

———. *Love and Marriage in the Age of Chaucer*. Ithaca: Cornell University Press, 1975.

———. 'The Non-tragedy of Arthur.' In *Medieval English and Ethical Literature: Essays in Honor of G. H. Russell*. Ed. Gregory Kratzmann and James Simpson. Woodbridge: D. S. Brewer, 1986, 92–114.

Kelly, Robert L. 'Arthur, Galahad and the Scriptural Pattern in Malory.' *American Benedictine Review* 23(1972):9–23.

———. 'Malory's "Tale of Balin" Reconsidered.' *Speculum* 54 (1979):85–99.

———. 'Wounds, Healing and Knighthood in Malory's "Lancelot and Guinevere."' In *Studies in Malory*. Ed. James W. Spisak. Kalamazoo: Medieval Institute, Western Michigan University, 1985, 173–97.

Kelso, Ruth. *Doctrine for the Lady of the Renaissance*. Urbana: University of Illinois Press, 1956.

Kendall, Paul M. *The Yorkist Age: Daily Life During the Wars of the Roses*. New York: Doubleday Anchor, 1962.

Kennedy, Beverly. 'Malory's Lancelot: "Trewest Lover, of a Synful Man."' *Viator* 12 (1981):409–56.

———. 'Northrup Frye's Theory of Genres and Sir Thomas Malory's "hoole book".' In *The Spirit of the Court*. Ed. Glyn S. Burgess and Robert A. Taylor. Cambridge: D. S. Brewer, 1985, 224–34.

———. 'The Re-emergence of Tragedy in Late Medieval England: Sir Thomas Malory's *Morte Darthur*.' *Analecta Husserliana* 18 (1984):363–78.

Kennedy, Edward D. 'The Arthur-Guenevere Relationship in Malory's *Morte Darthur*.' *Studies in the Literary Imagination* 4 (1971):29–40.

———. 'Malory's King Mark and King Arthur.' *Medieval Studies* 37(1975):190–234.

———. 'Malory's Use of Hardyng's *Chronicle*.' *Notes & Queries* n.s. 16 (1969):167–70.

Kennedy, Elspeth. 'King Arthur in the First Part of the Prose *Lancelot*.' In *A Medieval Miscellany* [Presented to Eugene Vinaver]. Ed. F. Whitehead. New York: Barnes & Noble, 1965, 186–95.

———. 'Social and Political Ideas in the French Prose *Lancelot*.' *Medium Aevum* 36(1957):90–106.

Kirk, Elizabeth. ' "Clerkes, Poetes and Historiographs": The *Morte Darthur* and Caxton's "Poetics" of Fiction.' In *Studies in Malory*. Ed. James W. Spisak. Kalamazoo: Medieval Institute, Western Michigan University, 1985, 275–95.

Knight, Stephen. *Arthurian Literature and Society*. N. Y.: St. Martin's Press, 1984.

Knowles, David. *The English Mystical Tradition*. London: Burns & Oates, 1961.

Krieger, Murray. 'The Literary, the Textual, the Social.' In *The Aims of Representation: Subject/Text/History*. Ed. Murray Krieger. N.Y.: Columbia University Press, 1987.

Lambert, Mark. *Malory: Style and Vision in Le Morte Darthur*. New Haven: Yale University Press, 1975.

Lander, J.R. *Conflict and Stability in Fifteenth-Century England*. 3rd. ed. London: Hutchinson, 1977.

———. *Crown and Nobility, 1450–1509*. Montreal: McGill University Press, 1976.

———. *Government and Community: England, 1450–1509*. London: Edward Arnold, 1980.

Leff, Gordon. *The Dissolution of the Medieval Outlook: An Essay on Intellectual and Spiritual Change in the Fourteenth Century*. New York: New York University Press, 1976.

Levine, Joseph M. *Humanism and History: Origins of Modern English Historiography*. Ithaca, N.Y.: Cornell University Press, 1987.

Levy, G. R. *The Sword from the Rock*. London: Faber and Faber, 1953.

Lewis, C.S. 'The English Prose *Morte*.' In *Essays on Malory*. Ed. J.A.W. Bennett. Oxford: Clarendon, 1963, 7–28.

———. [A Review of *Sir Thomas Wyatt and Some Collected Studies* by E.K. Chambers] *Medium Aevum* 3 (1934):237–40.

Life, Page West. *Sir Thomas Malory and the Morte Darthur: a Survey of Scholarship and Annotated Bibliography*. Charlottesville: University Press of Virginia, 1980.

Lukács, George. *Studies in European Realism*. Trans. Edith Bone. London: Hillway Publishing, 1950.

Lumiansky, Robert M. 'Arthur's Final Companions in Malory's *Morte Darthur*.' *Tulane Studies in English* 11(1961):5–19.

———. '"The Tale of Lancelot and Guenevere": Suspense.' In *Malory's Originality*. Baltimore: Johns Hopkins University Press, 1964, 205–32.

McCaffrey, Phillip. 'The Adder of Malory's Battle of Salisbury: Sources, Symbols, and Themes.' *Tennessee Studies in Literature* 22 (1977):17–27.

McCarthy, Terence. *Reading the Morte Darthur*. Woodbridge: D. S. Brewer, 1988.

McCoy, Richard. *The Rites of Knighthood: The Literature and Politics of Elizabethan Chivalry*. Berkeley: University of California Press, 1990.

McFarlane, K.B. 'Bastard Feudalism.' *Bulletin of the Institute of Historical Research* 20 (1945):161–80.

MacRae, Suzanne Haynes. 'A Study of Ideal Kingship in the Middle English Romances.' Diss. University of North Carolina at Chapel Hill, 1972. *DAI* 33(1972–73):4353A.

Mahoney, Dhira. 'The Truest and Holiest Tale: Malory's Transformation of *La Queste del Saint Graal*.' In *Studies in Malory*. Ed. James W. Spisak. Kalamazoo: Medieval Institute, Western Michigan University, 1985, 109–28.

Mann, Jill. 'Knightly Combat in *Le Morte D'Arthur*.' In *The New Pelican Guide to English Literature*. Vol. I, pt. I. Harmondsworth, Eng.: Penguin, 1982, 331–39.

———. '"Taking the Adventure": Malory and the *Suite du Merlin*.' In *Aspects of Malory*. Ed. Toshiyuki Takamiya and Derek Brewer. Cambridge: Brewer, 1981, 71–91.

Matheson, Lister M. 'King Arthur and the Medieval English Chronicles.' In *King Arthur Through the Ages*. Ed. Valerie M. Lagorio and Mildren Leake Day. 2 Vols. N.Y.: Garland, 1990, 1:248–74.

Mathew, Gervase. *The Court of Richard II*. London: Murray, 1968.

Matthews, William. *The Ill-Framed Knight: A Sceptical Inquiry into the Identity of Sir Thomas Malory*. Berkeley, Calif.: University of California Press, 1966.

———. *The Tragedy of Arthur: A Study of the Alliterative 'Morte Arthure'*. Berkeley: University of California Press, 1960.

Medcalf, Stephen, ed. *The Later Middle Ages*. New York: Holmes & Meier, 1981.

Merrill, Robert. *Sir Thomas Malory and the Cultural Crisis of the Late Middle Ages*. N.Y.: Peter Lang, 1987.

Miko, Stephen J. 'Malory and the Chivalric Order.' *Medium Aevum* 24(1966):211–30.

Milosh, Joseph E. *The Scale of Perfection and the English Mystical Tradition*. Madison: University of Wisconsin Press, 1966.

Mitchell, Rosamund. *John Tiptoft, 1427–1470*. London: Longmans, 1938.

Moorman, Charles. *The Book of Kyng Arthur: The Unity of Malory's 'Morte Darthur'*. Lexington: University of Kentucky Press, 1965.

———. 'Internal Chronology in Malory's *Morte Darthur*.' *Journal of English and Germanic Philology* 60(1961):240–57.

———. *Kings & Captains: Variations on a Heroic Theme*. Lexington: University of Kentucky Press, 1971.

Morgan, D.A.L. 'The King's Affinity in the Polity of Yorkist England.' *Transactions of the Royal Historical Society* 23(1973):1–25.

Murray, Alexander. *Reason and Society in the Middle Ages*. Oxford: Clarendon, 1978.

Neilson, George. *Trial by Combat*. Glasgow: Hodge, 1890.

Oberman, H.A. and C.E. Trinkhaus, eds. *The Pursuit of Holiness in Late Medieval and Renaissance Religion*. Leiden: E.J. Brill, 1974.

Olefsky, Ellyn. 'Chronology, Factual Consistency, and the Problem of Unity in Malory.' *Journal of English and Germanic Philology*. 68(1969):57–73.

Orme, Nicholas. *From Childhood to Chivalry: The Education of the English Kings and Aristocracy, 1066–1530*. London: Methuen, 1984.

Owen, Nancy H. and Lewis J. Owen. 'The "Tristram" in the *Morte Darthur*: Structure and Function.' *Tristania* 3.2 (1978):4–21.

Owst, G.R. *Literature and Pulpit in Medieval England*. Cambridge: Cambridge University Press, 1933.

———. *Preaching in Medieval England: An Introduction to Sermon Manuscripts of the Period c. 1350–1450*. Cambridge: Cambridge University Press, 1926.

Painter, Sidney. *French Chivalry: Chivalric Ideals and Practices in Medieval France*. Baltimore: Johns Hopkins University Press, 1940.

Parins, Marylyn J., ed. *Malory: The Critical Heritage*. London: Routledge, 1988.

Parsons, R.G. 'Pelagianism and Semi-Pelagianism.' In *The Encyclopedia of Religion and Ethics*. Ed. James Hastings. Edinburgh, 1917.

Partner, Nancy F. 'Making Up Lost Time: Writing on the Writing of History.' *Speculum* 61(1986):90–115.

Paterson, Linda. 'Knights and the Concept of Knighthood in the Twelfth-Century Occitan Epic.' In *Knighthood in Medieval Literature*. Ed. W.H. Jackson. Woodbridge: Brewer, 1981.

Patterson, Lee. 'Critical Historicism and Medieval Studies.' In *Literary Practice and Social Change in Britain, 1380–1550*. Ed. Lee Patterson. Berkeley: University of California Press, 1990.

———. *Negotiating the Past: The Historical Understanding of Medieval Literature*. Madison: University of Wisconsin Press, 1987.

Pickering, Frederick P. 'Historical Thought and Moral Codes in Medieval Epic.' In *The Epic in Medieval Society: Aesthetic and Moral Values*. Ed. Harold Scholler. Tübingen: Neimeyer, 1977, 1–17.

Pickford, C.E. *L'évolution du roman arthurien en prose vers la fin du Moyen Age* (d'après le manuscrit 112 du Fonds français de la B.N.) Paris: Nizet, 1959.

Pitt-Rivers, Julian. 'Honour and Social Status.' In *Honour and Shame: The Values of Mediterranean Society*. Ed. J.G. Peristiany. London: Weidenfeld & Nicolson, 1965, 21–77.

Pochoda, Elizabeth T. *Arthurian Propaganda: Le Morte Darthur as an Historical Ideal of Life*. Chapel Hill: University of North Carolina Press, 1971.

Pollock, Sir Frederick and Frederic William Maitland. *The History of English Law Before the Time of Edward I*. 2nd ed. 2 vols. 1898. rpt. Cambridge: Cambridge University Press, 1968.

Reeves, Marjorie. *The Influence of Prophecy in the Later Middle Ages: A Study of Joachimism*. Oxford: Clarendon, 1969.

Reiss, Edmund. *Sir Thomas Malory*. New York: Twayne, 1966.

Riddy, Felicity. *Sir Thomas Malory*. Leiden: E. J. Brill, 1987.

Ross, Charles. *Edward IV*. Berkeley: University of California Press, 1974.

Sandoz, Edouard. 'Tourneys in the Arthurian Tradition.' *Speculum* 19(1944):389–420.

Sapir, Edward. 'The Meaning of Religion.' In *Selected Writings of Edward Sapir in Language, Culture and Personality*. Ed. David G. Mandelbaum. Berkeley: University of California Press, 1951, 346–56.

Scattergood, V.J. *Politics and Poetry in the Fifteenth Century*. New York: Barnes & Noble, 1972.

Scofield, Cora L. *The Life and Reign of Edward IV*. 2 vols. London: Longmans, 1923.

Scudder, Vida D. *Le Morte Darthur of Sir Thomas Malory and Its Sources*. London, 1917. rpt. New York: Haskell House, 1965.

Shaw, W.H. *The Knights of England*. 2 vols. 1906. rpt. Baltimore: Genealogical Publishing, 1971.

Signer, Deborah Ann. 'Tristram, Lancelot and Galahad: The Manipulation of Figuralism in Sir Thomas Malory's *Le Morte Darthur*'. Diss. Columbia University, 1979. DAI 40(1979):2657A.

Spisak, James W. 'Malory's "Lost" Source'. In *Studies in Malory*. Ed.James W. Spisak. Kalamazoo: Medieval Institute, Western Michigan University, 1985, 227–29.

Squibb, G.D. *The High Court of Chivalry: A Study of the Civil Law in England*. Oxford: Clarendon, 1959.

Strayer, Joseph R. *On the Medieval Origins of the Modern State*. Princeton: Princeton University Press, 1970.

Stroud, Michael. 'Malory and the Chivalric Ethos: The Hero of *Arthur and the Emperor Lucius*.' *Medieval Studies* 36(1974):331–53.

Thomas, Keith V. *Religion and the Decline of Magic*. Harmondsworth: Penguin, 1971.

Thornton, Ginger. 'The Weakening of the King: Arthur's Disintegration in *The Book of Sir Tristram*.' *Arthurian Yearbook* 1(1991):135–48.

Tillyard, E. W. *The English Epic and Its Background*. N.Y.: Chatto & Windus, 1954.

Tucker P.E. 'Chivalry in the *Morte*'. In *Essays on Malory*. Ed. J.A.W. Bennett. Oxford: Clarendon, 1963, 64–103.

Tuve, Rosemond. *Allegorical Imagery: Some Medieval Books and Their Posterity*. Princeton: Princeton University Press, 1966.

Vale, M. G. A. *War and Chivalry*. London: Duckworth, 1981.

Vinaver, Eugene. 'On Art and Nature: A Letter to C.S. Lewis.' In *Essays on Malory*. Ed. J.A.W. Bennett. Oxford: Clarendon, 1963, 29–40.

Vitz, Evelyn Birge. *Medieval Narrative and Modern Ontology*. N.Y.: New York University Press, 1989.

Walsh, James, ed. *Pre-Reformation English Spirituality*. London: Burns & Oates, 1966.

Weber, Max. *Economy and Society*. Ed. Guenter Roth and Claus Wittich. N.Y.: Bedminster Press, 1968.

Wenzel, Siegfried. 'The Pilgrimage of Life as a Late Medieval Genre.' *Mediaeval Studies* 35 (1973):370–88.

Whitaker, Muriel. *Arthur's Kingdom of Adventure: The World of Malory's Morte Darthur*. Cambridge: D.S. Brewer, 1984.

———. 'Christian Iconography in the Quest of the Holy Grail.' *Mosaic* 12.2(1979):11–19.

White, Hayden. *The Content of the Form: Narrative Discourse and Historical Representation*. Baltimore: Johns Hopkins University Press, 1987.

———. 'The Historical Text as Literary Artefact.' *Clio* 3(1974):277–303. rev. in *The Writing of History: Literary Form and Historical Understanding*. Ed. Robert H. Canary and Henry Kozicki. Madison: University of Wisconsin Press, 1978.

Wilson, Robert H. 'Fate and Choice in Malory's Arthurian Tragedy.' In *Linguistic and Literary Studies in Honor of Archibald A. Hill, IV*. Ed. M. A. Jazayery *et al*. The Hague: Mouton, 1979, 185–90.

———. 'Malory's Naming of Minor Characters.' *Journal of English and Germanic Philology* 42 (1943):364–85.

Winkler, Frances H. 'The Making of King's Knights in England, 1399–1461.' Diss. Yale, 1943. *DA* 29(1965):1185A.

Wright, Thomas L. ' "The Tale of King Arthur": Beginnings and Foreshadowings.' In *Malory's Originality*. Ed. Robert M. Lumiansky. Baltimore: Johns Hopkins University Press, 1964, 9–66.

York, Ernest C. 'Legal Punishment in Malory's *Le Morte Darthur*.' *English Language Notes* 11 (1973):14–21.

Index

ARTHURIAN STUDIES

ISSN 0261–9814